Handbook of Psychotherapy and Religious Diversity

Handbook of Psychotherapy and Religious Diversity

EDITED BY

P. Scott Richards and Allen E. Bergin

AMERICAN PSYCHOLOGICAL ASSOCIATION
WASHINGTON, DC

First printing December 1999
Second printing October 2000

Published by
American Psychological Association
750 First Street, NE
Washington, DC 20002

Copies may be ordered from
APA Order Department
P.O. Box 92984
Washington, DC 20090-2984

In the U.K., Europe, Africa, and the Middle East, copies may be ordered from
American Psychological Association
3 Henrietta Street
Covent Garden, London
WC2E 8LU England

Typeset in Goudy by EPS Group Inc., Easton, MD

Printer: Port City Press, Inc., Baltimore, MD
Cover Designer: Berg Design, Albany, NY
Technical/Production Editors: Rachael Stryker and Jennifer Powers

Library of Congress Cataloging-in-Publication Data

Richards, P. Scott.
    Handbook of psychotherapy and religious diversity / P. Scott Richards and Allen E. Bergin.—1st ed.
      p.   cm.
    Includes bibliographical references and index.
    ISBN 1-557-98624-X (pbk. : alk. paper)
    1. Psychotherapy—Religious aspects—Handbooks, manuals, etc. 2. Psychotherapy patients—Religious life—Handbooks, manuals, etc. I. Bergin, Allen E., 1934– II. Title.

RC489.R46 R527   1999
616.89'14—dc21

                                        99-046210

British Library Cataloguing-in-Publication Data
A CIP record is available from the British Library.

Printed in the United States of America

To H. Newton Malony,
clinical psychologist, Methodist minister, and
international pioneer in the integration of psychology and religion.

CONTENTS

CONTRIBUTORS

Kimberly R. Aay is research coordinator at the National Institute for Healthcare Research in Rockville, MD.

Allen E. Bergin, PhD, is a professor emeritus of psychology at Brigham Young University, where he has also served as director of the Values Institute and director of the PhD program in clinical psychology. He is past-president of the Society for Psychotherapy Research and is coeditor of the classic *Handbook of Psychotherapy and Behavior Change.* He is also coauthor of A *Spiritual Strategy for Counseling and Psychotherapy.* Among his honors are the Award for Distinguished Professional Contributions to Knowledge from the American Psychological Association (APA) in 1989, the William James Award for Psychology of Religion Research from Division 36 (Psychology of Religion) of APA in 1990, and the Society for Psychotherapy Research's Distinguished Career Award in 1998. He is a licensed psychologist and maintains a small consultation practice.

Donelda A. Cook, PhD, is assistant vice president for student development, director of the counseling center, and adjunct faculty in the Pastoral Counseling department at Loyola College in Maryland. She has published several articles and book chapters on multicultural issues in psychology. She is coauthor of *Using Race and Culture in Counseling and Psychotherapy: Theory and Process.*

Richard D. Dobbins, PhD, is an ordained minister with the Assemblies of God, pastor, psychologist, and founder of EMERGE Ministries, Inc., a Christian mental health center in Akron, OH. He is the author of numerous books and articles, including *From This Day Forward, Preparing Couples for Christian Marriage, Your Feelings . . . Friend or Foe,* and *At the Table of the Lord.* He has served on the adjunct faculties at the University of Akron and Central Bible College and holds an honorary Doctor of Humanities degree from Ashland Theological

Seminary. He is a recipient of the American Association of Christian Counselors and the Pentecostal and Charismatic Caregivers Awards.

Natalie J. Dong, MA, is a doctoral candidate in the Graduate School of Psychology, Fuller Theological Seminary, in Pasadena, CA. She is a predoctoral psychology intern at the Los Angeles Veteran Affairs Outpatient Clinic and is involved in research and writing in the integration of faith, health, and culture.

Mark Finn, PhD, is consulting psychologist at North Central Bronx Hospital. He has been contributing to the dialogue between Buddhism and psychotherapy for the past 20 years. He is the coeditor of *Object Relations Theory and Religion.* He maintains private practices in White Plains, New York and New York City.

Zari Hedayat-Diba, PhD, is a private practitioner in Los Angeles. She received her PhD in clinical psychology from the California School of Professional Psychology. She has published extensively on the relationship between Islam and psychology and psychotherapy.

Roger R. Keller, PhD, is the Richard L. Evans Professor of Religious Understanding and professor of church history and doctrine, Brigham Young University, where he teaches courses on the religions of the world. He holds a Bachelor of Music in voice performance from the University of Colorado, a Master of Divinity from Princeton Theological Seminary, and a doctorate degree in biblical studies and hermeneutics from Duke University. He was ordained to the Presbyterian ministry in 1971. He has written a variety of articles and presented a number of academic papers focusing on interfaith issues. He is the coauthor of *Religions of the World: A Latter-day Saint View* as well as other books on interfaith dialogue and the Book of Mormon.

David B. Larson, MD, MSPH, is president of the National Institute for Healthcare Research and adjunct professor, Departments of Psychiatry and Behavioral Sciences at Duke University Medical Center and Northwestern University Medical School. He has published extensively on the relationships of spirituality and religious commitment with mental, physical, and social health.

Robert J. Lovinger, PhD, is former professor of psychology at Central Michigan University in the clinical psychology program (1970–1998). He is also the former director of the Psychological Training and Consultation Center (1979–1995) and a past member of the Board of Directors and treasurer of the Michigan Psychoanalytic Council (1989–1997). Currently, he is serving as president of APA's Division 36 (Psychology of Religion). He is the author of *Working With Religious Issues in Therapy* and *Religion and Counseling.*

Michael A. Mason, PhD, is an anthropologist and exhibit developer at the National Museum of Natural History, Smithsonian Institution. He received his PhD in anthropological folklore and religious studies from Indiana University. His book *Making Santo: Experiencing Afro-Cuban Santeria* is currently in press. He has published in *Journal of American Folklore* and *The Drama Review*. He is currently supported with a grant from the Wenner-Gren Foundation for Anthropological Research.

Michael E. McCullough, PhD, is director of research at the National Institute for Healthcare Research. He investigates the role of forgiveness in health and social relationships, the association of religion and spirituality with physical and mental health, and the influence of religion and spirituality on counseling and psychotherapy.

Lisa Miller, PhD, is assistant professor of psychology and education in the clinical psychology program at Teachers College, Columbia University. Her research in religion, spirituality, and resilience received a 1998 Outstanding Paper in Humility Theology Award from the John Templeton Foundation. She is currently being supported by a W. T. Grant Foundation Faculty Scholars Award. Dr. Miller has a private practice in Manhattan.

Alejandro Murguía is a PhD candidate at the clinical psychology program at the George Washington University and a clinical psychology intern at the University of Miami Mailman Center. He is the recipient of the Thelma Hunt Award and of a National Institute of Child and Health Development (NICHD) Minority Dissertation Fellowship. He is student editor of *Cultural Diversity and Ethnic Minority Psychology*. He has published in *Community Psychologist* and in *Cultural Diversity and Ethnic Minority Psychology*.

Aaron Rabinowitz, PhD, is a faculty member of the psychology department at Bar-Ilan University, Israel. He was the first director of the clinic child psychology graduate program there. Dr. Rabinowitz has published research in a number of areas and is the author of *Judaism and Psychology: Meeting Points*.

Carole A. Rayburn, PhD, M. Div., is a clinical, consulting, and research psychologist in Silver Spring, MD. She is the former president of the APA Division on the Psychology of Religion, the APA Division on Clinical Psychology's section on the clinical psychology of women, the Maryland Psychological Association, the Baltimore Psychological Association, and the Association of Practicing Psychologists of Montgomery and Prince George's Counties (MD). She is a Fellow of APA Divisions 12, 13, 29, 31, 35, and 36. She has published over 80 articles and authored and coauthored 13 inventories on subjects such as spirituality, religiousness, morality, leadership, clergy stress, body image, peacefulness, and life choices. She is coeditor of *A Time to Weep and a Time to Sing*.

P. Scott Richards, PhD, is associate professor in the Department of Counseling Psychology and Special Education at Brigham Young University. He is coauthor of *A Spiritual Strategy for Counseling and Psychotherapy*. Among his honors are the Dissertation of the Year Award in 1990 from Division 5 (Evaluation, Statistics, and Measurement) of APA and the William C. Bier Award from Division 36 (Psychology of Religion) of APA in 1999. He is a licensed psychologist and maintains a private practice at the Center for Change in Orem, Utah.

Jeffrey R. Rubin, PhD, has practiced both psychoanalysis and Buddhist meditation for over 20 years. He has taught psychoanalysis and Buddhist theory and practice at Yeshiva University and Goddard College, and has been a faculty member of the Object Relations Institute, the Postgraduate Center for Mental Health, and the C. G. Jung Foundation in New York City. He is the author of several volumes, including *Psychotherapy and Buddhism: Toward an Integration*; *A Psychoanalysis for Our Time: Exploring the Blindness of the Seeing I*; and the forthcoming *Psychoanalysis and the Good Life: Reflections on Love, Ethics, Creativity, and Spirituality*. He practices psychoanalysis and psychotherapy in Bedford Hills, New York and New York City.

Edward P. Shafranske, PhD, is professor of psychology and Harriet and Charles Luckman Distinguished Teaching Fellow at Pepperdine University. He serves on the faculty of the Southern California Psychoanalytic Institute. He is a Fellow of the APA, former president of APA Division 36, representative to APA Council, and recipient of the William Bier Award and Franz Alexander Essay Prize. He served as an associate editor for the *Encyclopedia of Psychology* and was editor of *Religion and the Clinical Practice of Psychology*.

Anu R. Sharma, PhD, is a research scientist at the Minnesota Institute of Public Health and is a licensed psychologist in private practice in Minneapolis, MN. She has published in *Child Development, Children and Youth Services Review, Developmental Psychology, Journal of Alcohol Studies, Journal of Counseling and Development, Psychological Bulletin,* and *Psychometrika*.

Siang-Yang Tan, PhD, is professor of psychology at the Graduate School of Psychology, Fuller Theological Seminary, in Pasadena, CA. He has authored or coauthored 8 books, including *Lay Counseling, Managing Chronic Pain,* and *Disciplines of the Holy Spirit*. He is associate editor of the *Journal of Psychology and Christianity*, a Fellow of APA, and past-president of Division 36 (Psychology of Religion) of APA. He is also senior pastor of First Evangelical Church, Glendale, CA. He is the recipient of the Distinguished Member Award from the Christian Association for Psychological Studies and the Award for Contributions to Racial and Ethnic Diversity from the National Council of Schools and Programs of Professional Psychology.

Nancy Stiehler Thurston, PhD, is associate professor of psychology at George Fox University in Newburg, OR. Until recently, she was associate professor of psychology at Fuller Theological Seminary, Graduate School of Psychology in Pasadena, CA. She serves on the executive board as secretary of APA Division 36 (Psychology of Religion).

Alex Trujillo, PhD, is a staff member of the counseling and therapy services at the student health center at the University of New Mexico. His professional work is on the areas of mental health and education with numerous Native American tribes in New Mexico, Arizona, Wyoming, Montana, South Dakota, and Idaho. He maintains a private practice.

Wendy L. Ulrich, PhD, is in private practice as a psychologist in Ann Arbor, MI. She received her PhD from the University of Michigan and holds an MBA from the University of California, Los Angeles. She is former president of the Association of Mormon Counselors and Psychotherapists (AMCAP). She has published in *Human Resource Management* and the *AMCAP Journal*.

Andrew J. Weaver, MTh, PhD, is a United Methodist minister and clinical psychologist at Hawaii State Hospital in Kaneohe, Hawaii. He is a member of the clinical faculty, department of psychology, University of Hawaii. He has published several articles and books on the role of clergy in mental care.

Christine Y. Wiley, DMin, is a pastoral psychotherapist and copastor of Covenant Baptist Church in Washington, DC, where she founded the Center for Holistic Ministry. She is a Fellow of the American Association of Pastoral Counselors and has a private practice in Fort Washington, MD. She has published various journal articles and book chapters on pastoral counseling of the African American community.

Tony R. Young, PhD, is a graduate of Fuller Theological Seminary Graduate School of Psychology, is an adjunct professor of psychology at Louisiana Tech University, and is a private practitioner of clinical psychology.

María Cecilia Zea, PhD, is associate professor of psychology at the George Washington University. She is a graduate from the clinical/community psychology program of the University of Maryland at College Park and from Javeriana University in Bogota, Colombia. She is coeditor of *Psychological Interventions and Research With Latino Populations* and has published in the *American Journal of Community Psychology*, *Rehabilitation Psychology*, *Cultural Diversity and Ethnic Minority Psychology*, *Educational and Psychological Measurement*, the *Journal of Culture, Gender and Health*, the *Journal of Social Behavior and Personality*, and the *Journal of Social Psychology*.

PREFACE

When we published our first book, *A Spiritual Strategy for Counseling and Psychotherapy* (Richards & Bergin, 1997), we recognized that there was a need for a clinical compendium to help mental health professionals work more effectively with members of specific spiritual traditions. In *A Spiritual Strategy*, we provided information and suggestions to help therapists adopt an ecumenical therapeutic stance with their clients. We also provided a brief introduction to the beliefs of the major world religions. But we realized that advanced ecumenical therapeutic expertise and denominational expertise require more in-depth understanding of "the religious beliefs, cultures, practices, and clinical issues of members of specific religious denominations" (Richards & Bergin, 1997, p. 341). Because there was not space in our first book to provide such information, we were pleased when Margaret Schlegel and Gary R. VandenBos at APA Books agreed to publish a second book—one that focused on psychotherapy and religious diversity.

There is a great need for mental health professionals to become aware of the religious diversity that exists in the world and to increase their competence in working with clients from diverse traditions. Religious demographic statistics suggest that the majority of people who present for psychotherapy are religious—many of them devoutly so. We are pleased that the American Psychological Association, the American Psychiatric Association, the American Counseling Association, and other professional organizations now include religion as one aspect of diversity that their members are obligated to respect and seek competency in. We hope that this handbook will help mental health professionals better fulfill this obligation.

We have been gratified by the positive responses to our first book and hope that this second one will also prove valuable to practicing professionals, students, and scholars. Our own feelings of appreciation and respect for clients and colleagues from diverse religious backgrounds have deepened as we have read and worked on this project. We believe that we are now better prepared to work more sensitively and effectively with clients whose spiritual beliefs differ from our own. We hope that this will also be your experience as you read it.

ACKNOWLEDGMENTS

We are grateful to Margaret Schlegel, our acquisitions and development editor at the American Psychological Association, who recognized the importance of this volume from the moment we proposed the idea to her. Her support, advice, and encouragement have helped us and the contributing authors to turn our idea into a reality.

We are also grateful to the authors of the chapters who took on the formidable tasks of writing about the beliefs and practices of their religious traditions and offering suggestions for how psychotherapists can work sensitively and effectively with members of these faiths. The contributing authors responded to more than the usual number of reviews in preparing their chapters, and we thank them for their patience and perseverance in doing so. One to three experts in each chapter's religious tradition first reviewed each chapter. Then, we as editors reviewed each chapter. After responding to this feedback, the authors resubmitted their chapters, which were then reviewed by the APA Books development team and two more external reviewers. The authors were then asked to respond to the feedback from the external reviewers, an APA development editor, and some additional feedback from us. Needless to say, we were all tiring of revisions by the time we were done, but the book is much better as a result of this rigorous review process.

We are indebted to a number of consultants who helped in designing the format of the book or who recommended chapter authors to us. Joseph G. Ponterotto, H. Newton Malony, Everett L. Worthington, Jr., and Truman G. Madsen provided extensive helpful suggestions and recommendations. In addition, the following individuals guided our selection decisions: Janet Helms, Stanton L. Jones, Lisa Miller, Robert J. Lovinger, Kalman Kaplan, Reuven Bulka, William R. Miller, Dean L. Jackson, Robert N. Sollod, David B. Larson, and Maurice Friedman.

We wish to thank the reviewers who gave feedback and suggestions to help strengthen the book. Each was a professional who was also a member of, and expert on, the religious tradition he or she reviewed. We thank Spencer J. Palmer, T. D. Bozeman, William Meissner, Archbishop Chrysostomos, Thomas Brecht, Edwin R. DuBose, Ted A. Campbell, Randall L. Sorenson, Mary F. Clark, John K. Vining, Edward E. Decker, Lane Fischer, George T. Harding IV, Gary L. Burlingame, John Berecz, Lilly Dimitrovsky, John Gartner, S. Robert Moradi, William W. Menzies, Albert A. Agresti, Kathleen Ritter, David Klimek, Kathleen Flake, Hossein Ziai, Deep Shikha, James Jones, Deborah G. Haskins, Lilian Comas-Diaz, Rafael M. Diaz, Freda K. Cheung, Alan Y. Oda, and Wilbur Woodis. We also again thank H. Newton Malony, as well as an anonymous reviewer, who read the entire book and provided much in the way of helpful feedback and suggestions for refinement.

We also wish to thank the students in our *Spiritual Values and Methods in Psychotherapy* and *Values, Religion and Mental Health* classes that we have team-taught over the past few years. Their stimulating class presentations on various religions of the world and the implications of these traditions for psychotherapy helped us recognize the need for a handbook on psychotherapy and religious diversity.

Finally, we remain ever grateful to our loving wives, Marcia Richards and Marian Bergin. Without their support, this volume would never have been completed.

I

INTRODUCTION AND OVERVIEW

1

TOWARD RELIGIOUS AND SPIRITUAL COMPETENCY FOR MENTAL HEALTH PROFESSIONALS

P. SCOTT RICHARDS AND ALLEN E. BERGIN

No other human preoccupation challenges psychologists as profoundly as religion. Whether or not they profess to be religious themselves— and many do not—psychologists must take religion into account if they are to understand and help their fellow human beings.
—David M. Wulff

The alienation that has existed between the mental health professions and religion for most of the 20th century is ending. The influence of the naturalistic, antireligious assumptions that once gripped the field have weakened, and there is now a more spiritually open *zeitgeist* or "spirit of the times" (Richards & Bergin, 1997). During the 1990s, many articles on religious and spiritual issues in mental health and psychotherapy were published in mainstream journals. Numerous presentations on these topics were given at conventions of mental health organizations. A sizable number of books on religion and clinical practice were also written. For example, in 1996, the American Psychological Association (APA) published its first book on the topic (Shafranske, 1996). APA followed it with another book on spiritual issues in psychotherapy a year later (Richards & Bergin, 1997) and with another in 1999 (Miller, 1999). Several other important books on religion, psychotherapy, and psychology were published by other mainstream publishers (e.g., Kelly, 1995; Pargament, 1997; Wulff,

1991). Another sign of the "spirit of the times" is that several professional organizations have for the first time explicitly acknowledged in their ethical guidelines that religion is one type of diversity that mental health professionals are obligated to respect (e.g., APA, 1992; American Counseling Association, 1995). In addition, the American Psychiatric Association (1990, 1995) now requires education in spiritual and religious themes during residency training.

With the rise of this more spiritually open *zeitgeist*, and the acknowledgment by professional organizations that competency in religious diversity is an ethical imperative, increasing numbers of mental health professionals are seeking to understand the spiritual orientations of their clients. Many psychotherapists wish to respect, and draw upon, the spiritual resources in their clients' lives and feel a need to increase their competency in religious and spiritual diversity. Unfortunately, it is not easy for mental health professionals to obtain the information and training they need in this domain. Few graduate programs offer training in spiritual diversity, and continuing education opportunities on these topics are limited (Shafranske & Malony, 1996). In addition, until now there have been few, if any, publications by clinicians specifically dedicated to helping psychotherapists gain insight into the spiritual diversity that exists in North America and how they can work sensitively with clients from these diverse traditions.

This handbook addresses this need by providing readers with basic information on the predominant religious traditions in North America that will be useful when they encounter clients whose faith differs from their own. By basic information, we mean not only the religious history, beliefs, and practices of the tradition, but also the commonly held views on such moral issues as marriage and divorce, birth control, abortion, use of alcohol, suicide and euthanasia, and worldviews, including conceptions of a diety, human nature, purpose of life, and life after death. Within the context of the particular faith, chapter authors discuss the therapeutic process, including building relationships with clients from that tradition, assessment and diagnosis, and common clinical issues (e.g., perfectionism, depression, shame, and guilt), and intervention strategies congruent with the faith. How the religious or spiritual tradition may view the mental health profession and psychotherapy is also addressed. Finally, the significance of a tradition's religious beliefs, practices, and culture in providing healing resources in religious and spiritual communities on behalf of clients is discussed. Most of the chapter authors have chosen to provide clinical vignettes to illustrate selected issues, and all chapters in Parts II to VI contain a list of recommended readings so that readers may deepen their understanding of a particular religion or tradition.

A CALL FOR GREATER COMPETENCY IN RELIGIOUS AND SPIRITUAL[1] DIVERSITY

We wish to add our voices to those of other scholars and practitioners who in recent years have urged mental health professionals to acquire greater competency in religious and spiritual aspects of diversity (e.g., Kelly, 1995; Shafranske & Malony, 1996). Why should we seek to do this? There are several compelling reasons.

1. *Religious diversity is a cultural fact, and most mental health professionals will encounter it in their practices.* The religious landscape of North America is breathtaking in its diversity and vibrancy. Members of all of the major world religions and countless smaller ones have found their homes in the United States or Canada. Buddhists, Roman Catholics, Presbyterians, Muslims, Southern Baptists, Hindus, Seventh-day Adventists, Sikhs, Pentecostals, Jews, Episcopalians, Mormons, Evangelicals, Eastern Orthodox, Lutherans, and people from many other traditions coexist and interact with each other on a scale never known before in the human family. Tables 1.1 and 1.2 provide the most current religious demographic statistics available for the world and North America. Table 1.1 shows how the vast majority of people in North America claim affiliation with some Christian denomination. In case one thinks that the large number of Christians in North America indicates that there is much uniformity of religious belief, we point out that the *Yearbook of American and Canadian Churches* (Bedell, 1997) listed over 160 different denominations, most of which are Christian. In the *Encyclopedia of American Religions*, Melton (1996) identified over 20 major religious families in the United States. Within these families, Melton listed over 1,200 Christian groups that differ from each other organizationally and doctrinally. Table 1.2 provides denominational rankings for the largest Christian denominations in the United States and Canada.

In addition to the Christian denominations, there are substantial

---

[1]We use the terms *religious* and *spiritual* frequently in this chapter, as will many of the other authors, and so we wish to offer definitions of them here. We have defined spiritual as "those experiences, beliefs, and phenomena that pertain to the transcendent and existential aspects of life (i.e., God or a Higher Power, the purpose and meaning of life, suffering, good and evil, death, etc.). . . . We view religious as a subset of the spiritual. Religious has to do with theistic beliefs, practices, and feelings that are often, but not always, expressed institutionally and denominationally as well as personally. . . . Religious expressions tend to be denominational, external, cognitive, behavioral, ritualistic, and public. Spiritual experiences tend to be universal, ecumenical, internal, affective, spontaneous, and private. It is possible to be religious without being spiritual and spiritual without being religious" (Richards & Bergin, 1997, p. 13). Spiritual and spirituality suggest a closeness, harmony, or connection with God or the transcendent, whereas a religious practice or experience may not necessarily include this connection. If a religious practice or experience (e.g., saying a prayer, engaging in a ritual, reading a scripture) helps a person feel more closeness and connection with God or transcendent spiritual influences, then that practice or experience is also spiritual in nature. Without it, the practice or experience may be a religious one, but is not a spiritual one. The authors of the chapters in this volume will in most cases be describing both religious denominations, traditions and doctrines, *and* spiritual practices and influences that can be found within these religious denominations and cultures.

TABLE 1.1
Worldwide Adherents of All Religions by Six Continental Areas, Mid-1997

Religious Group	Africa	Asia	Europe	Latin America	North America	Oceania	World	%
Christians	350,892,000	289,784,000	552,183,000	455,183,000	257,129,000	24,117,000	1,929,987,000	33.0
Unaffiliated Christians	30,689,000	10,381,000	21,443,000	2,041,000	5,748,000	4,637,000	104,939,000	1.8
Affiliated Christians	320,203,000	279,403,000	530,740,000	453,841,000	221,381,000	19,480,000	1,825,048,000	31.2
Roman Catholics	117,990,000	111,215,000	286,902,000	442,657,000	73,880,000	7,710,000	1,040,354,000	17.8
Protestants	87,190,000	44,654,000	85,924,000	41,829,000	95,063,000	6,253,000	360,913,000	6.2
Orthodox	32,880,000	15,403,000	166,908,000	620,000	6,698,000	695,000	223,204,000	3.8
Anglicans	20,551,000	641,000	24,338,000	874,000	3,145,000	5,236,000	54,785,000	0.9
Other Christians	68,357,000	125,213,000	5,645,000	40,231,000	47,585,000	826,000	287,857,000	4.9
Non-Christians	407,502,000	3,248,670,000	176,986,000	36,047,000	44,589,000	4,958,000	3,918,752,000	67.0
Atheists	423,000	117,789,000	24,038,000	2,612,000	1,385,000	368,000	146,615,000	2.5
Bahai'is	2,263,000	3,606,000	104,000	880,000	740,000	73,000	7,666,000	0.1
Buddhists	136,000	348,559,000	1,478,000	645,000	2,132,000	191,000	353,141,000	6.0
Chinese Folk Religionists	28,000	362,013,000	216,000	184,000	832,000	61,000	363,334,000	6.2
Confucianists	0	6,078,000	10,000	0	0	24,000	6,112,000	0.1
Ethnic Religionists	90,365,000	138,469,000	1,220,000	1,060,000	331,000	249,000	231,694,000	4.0
Hindus	2,378,000	740,633,000	1,520,000	776,000	1,129,000	361,000	746,797,000	12.8
Jains	65,000	3,946,000	0	0	5,000	0	4,016,000	0.1
Jews	290,000	4,497,000	2,932,000	1,173,000	5,904,000	94,000	14,890,000	0.3

Mandeans	0	40,000	0	0	0	0	40,000	0.0
Muslims	306,606,000	803,605,000	31,347,000	1,632,000	4,066,000	238,000	1,147,494,000	19.6
New Religionists	27,000	97,263,000	122,000	611,000	649,000	27,000	98,699,000	1.7
Nonreligious	4,798,000	597,804,000	113,165,000	15,144,000	26,127,000	3,242,000	760,280,000	13.0
Shintoists	0	2,611,000	0	7,000	54,000	0	2,672,000	0.0
Sikhs	52,000	21,464,000	497,000	0	491,000	14,000	22,518,000	0.4
Spiritists	3,000	2,000	78,000	11,229,000	148,000	7,000	11,467,000	0.2
Zoroastrians	1,000	268,000	0	0	3,000	0	272,000	0.0
Other Religionists	67,000	23,000	259,000	94,000	593,000	9,000	1,045,000	0.0
Total Population	758,394,000	3,538,454,000	729,169,000	491,929,000	301,718,000	29,075,000	5,848,739,000	100.0

Note. This table was adapted from "Religion: World Religious Statistics," by D. B. Barrett and T. M. Johnson, 1998, in *Encyclopedia Britannica*, p. 314. Reprinted with permission of Encyclopedia Britannica, Inc.

Christians: Followers of Jesus Christ affiliated with churches (church members), plus persons professing in censuses or polls though not so affiliated).

Other Christians: This term in the table denotes Catholics (non-Roman), marginal Protestants, crypto-Christians, and adherents of African, Asian, Black, and Latin American indigenous churches.

Atheists: Persons professing atheism, skepticism, disbelief, or irreligion, including antireligious (opposed to all religion).

Buddhists: 56% Mahayana, 38% Theravada (Hinayana), 6% Tantrayana (Lamaism).

Chinese Folk Religionists: Followers of the traditional Chinese religion (local deities, ancestor veneration, Confucian ethics, Taoism, universism, divination, some Buddhist elements).

Ethnic Religionists: Followers of local, tribal, animistic, or shamanistic religions.

Hindus: 70% Vaishnavites, 25% Shaivites, 2% neoHindus and reform Hindus.

Jews: Adherents of Judaism.

Muslims: 83% Sunnies, 16% Shi'ites, 1% other schools.

New Religionists: Followers of Asian 20th-century New Religions, New Religious movements, radical new crisis religions, and non-Christian syncretistic mass religions, all founded since 1800 and most since 1945.

Nonreligious: Persons professing no religion, nonbelievers, agnostics, free thinkers, dereligionized secularists indifferent to all religion.

Other Religionists: Including 70 minor world religions and a large number of spiritist religions, New Age religions, quasi-religions, pseudo religions, parareligions, religious or mystic systems, religious and semireligious brotherhoods of numerous varieties.

Total Population: United Nations medium variant figures for mid-1997.

TABLE 1.2
United States and Canada Christian Denominational Rankings

Denomination	Inclusive membership	Percentage of total reported	Cumulative percentage
United States			
The Roman Catholic Church	60,280,454	38.93	38.93
Southern Baptist Convention	15,663,296	10.12	49.05
The United Methodist Church	8,538,662	5.51	54.56
National Baptist Convention, U.S.A., Inc.	8,200,000	5.30	59.86
The Church of God in Christ	5,499,875	3.55	63.41
Evangelical Lutheran Church in America	5,190,489	3.35	66.76
The Church of Jesus Christ of Latter-day Saints	4,711,500	3.04	69.81
Presbyterian Church (U.S.A.)	3,669,489	2.37	72.17
National Baptist Convention of America	3,500,000	2.26	74.44
African Methodist Episcopal Church	3,500,000	2.26	76.70
The Lutheran Church—Missouri Synod	2,594,555	1.68	78.37
Episcopal Church	2,536,550	1.64	80.01
Progressive National Baptist Convention, Inc.	2,500,000	1.61	81.62
National Missionary Baptist Convention of America	2,500,000	1.61	83.24
Assemblies of God	2,387,982	1.54	84.78
The Orthodox Church in America	2,000,000	1.29	86.07
Churches of Christ	1,655,000	1.07	87.14
American Baptist Churches in the U.S.A.	1,517,400	0.98	88.12
Baptist Bible Fellowship International	1,500,000	0.97	89.09
United Church of Christ	1,472,213	0.95	90.04
African Methodist Episcopal Zion Church	1,230,842	0.79	90.84
Christian Churches and Churches of Christ	1,070,616	0.69	91.53
Pentecostal Assemblies of the World	1,000,000	0.65	92.17
Jehovah's Witnesses	966,243	0.62	92.80
Christian Church (Disciples of Christ)	929,725	0.60	93.40
Seventh-day Adventist Church	790,731	0.51	93.91
Church of God (Cleveland, TN)	753,230	0.49	94.40
Church of the Nazarene	601,900	0.39	94.78
The Salvation Army	453,150	0.29	95.08
Wisconsin Evangelical Lutheran Synod	412,478	0.27	95.34
Canada			
The Roman Catholic Church in Canada	12,498,605	67.90	67.90
The United Church of Canada	1,867,500	10.15	78.05
Orthodox Church in America (Canada Section)	1,000,000	5.43	83.48

Table continues

TABLE 1.2 (*Continued*)

Denomination	Inclusive membership	Percentage of total reported	Cumulative percentage
The Angelican Church of Canada	780,897	4.24	87.72
The Presbyterian Church in Canada	227,814	1.24	88.96
The Pentecostal Assemblies of Canada	218,782	1.19	90.15
Evangelical Lutheran Church in Canada	198,751	1.08	91.23
Canadian Baptist Ministries	130,000	0.71	91.94
The Church of Jesus Christ of Latter-day Saints	130,000	0.71	92.64
Ukrainian Orthodox Church of Canada	120,000	0.65	93.30
Jehovah's Witnesses	112,960	0.61	93.91

Note. Adapted from *Yearbook of American and Canadian Churches*, by K. B. Bedell, 1997, pp. 2, 5. Used with permission of the National Council of Churches of Christ. Note also that non-Christian groups in North America are listed in table 1-1.

numbers of Jews, Muslims, Buddhists, and Hindus, and smaller numbers of people who belong to a variety of other non-Christian traditions in the United States and Canada. Melton (1996) identified over 700 non-Christian groups in the United States, including Eastern, Middle Eastern, Spiritualist, Psychic, New Age, Ancient Wisdom, and Magick groups.

If we examine the religious diversity of North America more closely, we see a rich tapestry of customs, beliefs, doctrines, myths, rituals, music, buildings of worship, clothing, sacred writings, spiritual practices, and healing traditions. From the Tripitaka to the Torah, Satnam to Allah, resurrection to reincarnation, ahimsa to charity, and rabbi to bishop, the diversity in religious beliefs and practices is striking (Smart, 1993, 1994).

Furthermore, as Hoge (1996) pointed out, the diversity of the religious landscape in America is increasing as the result of the effects of higher education, media, world consciousness, individualism, and, most important, immigration. According to Hoge (1996), immigration "will bring unprecedented pluralism and globalization in our religious life" (p. 38). This situation also exists in Canada. Many individuals from various ethnic, racial, and religious groups have immigrated in recent years to North America (Marsella, Bornemann, Ekblad, & Orley, 1994). For example, Buddhists, Hindus, and Muslims have immigrated in increasing numbers, as have members of Latina/Latino spiritual traditions.

In light of demographic statistics that document the prevalence of religious belief and growing religious diversity in America (Hoge, 1996), it seems likely that most psychotherapists will work with clients from a variety of religious traditions during their careers. Shafranske and Malony (1996) argued therefore that "it is incumbent that clinicians develop at least a rudimentary understanding of religion in its institutional expressions" (p. 566). They also argued that religious affiliation and spiritual beliefs "may be a far more potent social glue than the color of one's skin, cultural heritage, or gender.... Religious identification for some may be the thread that unites individuals into a social unit, ... religion must be taken account of as a factor in any appreciation of individual difference and cultural diversity" (p. 564). We agree that training in religious and spiritual diversity is essential for true multicultural competency.

2. *Psychotherapists will enjoy more credibility and trust with religious clients, leaders, and communities if they obtain training and competency in religious and spiritual diversity.* There is evidence that many religious and spiritual people, including religious leaders, have an unfavorable view of the mainstream, secular mental health professions and a distrust of the process of psychotherapy (Richards & Bergin, 1997; Worthington, 1986). This suspicion and distrust may be rooted in an awareness that many psychologists and psychotherapists during the past century have endorsed naturalistic, mechanistic, hedonistic, relativistic, and atheistic values and practices that conflict with those of most traditional religious communities (Bergin, 1980a; Campbell, 1975; Jones, 1994; Richards & Bergin, 1997). In addition, it has not gone unnoticed in religious communities that some prominent leaders of psychology and psychotherapy have been openly critical of religion and religious believers (e.g., Freud, 1927; Ellis, 1971, 1980). Generally speaking, it appears that many members of traditional religious communities perceive mainstream secular psychotherapists as unwilling or incapable of working with them in a religiously sensitive and competent manner.

Several studies have confirmed that devoutly religious persons often express a preference for working with therapists from their own faith, or at least with a religious therapist, because they fear that secular therapists will misunderstand and/or seek to undermine their religious beliefs (Worthington, Kurusu, McCullough, & Sanders, 1996). Furthermore, there is some evidence that religious persons often seek professional therapy as a last resort, after first seeking assistance from family, friends, and their clergy (King, 1978; Sell & Goldsmith, 1988; Veroff, Kulka, & Douvan, 1981). Although we are not aware of any studies on mental health service utilization rates among different religious denominations, we suspect that members of many traditional religious communities, especially more devout members, significantly underutilize such services. This has been shown to be the case with several ethnic minority groups who probably are also religious minorities (Sue, Zane, & Young, 1994). Certainly, the authors of many of the chapters in this book perceive this to be the case for members of their religious traditions. Consider the following case that illustrates one potential consequence of this religiosity gap.

Jack[2]

Jack was a 48-year-old Christian who was affiliated with a conservative denomination. He was married with three children and had been struggling with severe depression for nearly 2 years. When Jack lost his job because of poor performance, he became even more depressed and began contemplating suicide. Despite encouragement from his wife and pastor to ask his physician for an antidepressant, Jack resisted doing so saying, "I just need to have more faith in God's healing power." Jack also rejected suggestions from his wife to seek mental health counseling saying, "Those immoral, anti-God psychotherapists can't be trusted." Unfortunately, his pastor agreed with him. Six weeks after losing his job, Jack committed suicide by shooting himself in the head with his handgun.

A religious person's decision not to seek mental health services can have tragic consequences as illustrated in this case. We will never know whether Jack would have lived had he received counseling and medication, as some patients in treatment do commit suicide, but we can hazard a guess that his odds of surviving his depression might have been better had his pastor had a working relationship with one or more mental health professionals who were overtly involved in or respectful of Jack's religion.

Although most failures to obtain needed mental health services do not have such extreme consequences, it is still extremely unfortunate when people fail to obtain the help they need for their psychological and interpersonal problems. Such people are themselves, of course, ultimately responsible for their decision not to seek professional help. However, if psychotherapists fail to obtain the training and competencies they need to build trust and work more sensitively with members of traditional religious communities, perhaps they ought to share some of the responsibility when people fail to obtain the help they need, or when they terminate therapy prematurely.

Building trust and bridges of mutual respect and understanding with people from diverse religious backgrounds could have many benefits for the mental health professions (Bergin, 1991; Jones, 1994). For psychotherapists, it could lead to increased referrals from religious communities and to more respect from the general public. For the mental health professions as a whole, it could lead to increased credibility, influence, and stature in society. For clients, it could increase the likelihood that they will receive the mental health services they need from "someone who understands their perspective and who does not automatically interpret their beliefs in pathological terms" (Bergin & Jensen, 1990, p. 7).

We think that the first step in building more constructive relationships with members of religious communities is for psychologists and psy-

---

[2]This case vignette and those that follow are based on actual cases, although the names and some of the identifying details (sometimes including religious affiliation) have been changed to protect the anonymity of those described.

chotherapists to obtain training in and a greater appreciation of the religious and spiritual diversity that exists in North America and the world. As professionals gain more understanding of and empathy with religious and spiritual worldviews, they will be in a better position to reach out to members of these communities in mutual respect and trust.[3]

3. *Psychotherapists have an ethical obligation to obtain competency in religious and spiritual diversity.* It is true that many psychotherapists have received training in multicultural counseling, which is a necessary foundation for working effectively with clients from diverse religious and spiritual backgrounds (Richards & Bergin, 1997). However, working sensitively and effectively with religious and spiritually oriented clients often requires more than just general multicultural attitudes and skills. It can require specialized knowledge and training about the religious beliefs and practices of religious traditions and communities, about the spiritual issues and needs of human beings, and about religious and spiritual assessment and intervention techniques. The following case illustrates the potential dangers that exist when therapists lack specialized knowledge about their clients' religious tradition and its teachings.

Susan and Frank

Susan was a 28-year-old, married, Latter-day Saint (LDS) woman with four young children who presented for therapy because she was unhappy in her marriage. After a careful assessment, Susan's non-LDS male psychotherapist concluded that two issues contributing to Susan's marital dissatisfaction were (a) conflict over her sexual relationship with her husband, Frank, and (b) feeling unsupported in her full-time homemaking role. Susan's therapist helped her recognize that when she was not interested in having sex, and Frank reacted to her disinterest by pressuring her to do so, she felt controlled, manipulated, and disrespected. Susan's psychotherapist also empathized with her stressful homemaking role and suggested that Frank needed to give her more support. After inviting Frank to attend a therapy session, and wanting to give Susan more sexual "space," the therapist told Susan and Frank he did not want them to have sexual relations at all during the coming week. Not knowing that masturbation is considered a sin in the LDS

---

[3]We recognize that there is a long history of efforts to collaborate and integrate religious and psychological perspectives and that professional associations (e.g., American Association of Pastoral Counselors, Christian Association for Psychological Studies), graduate training programs in psychology (e.g., at Fuller Theological Seminary, Biola University, Wheaton College), and treatment centers (e.g., Christian Psychopathic Hospital, Bethesda Hospital, Loma Linda University Medical Center, and Pine Rest Christian Medical Center) have been founded for this purpose (Vande Kemp, 1996). Considerable collaboration between mental health professionals and religious leaders and communities also goes on within some mainline religious traditions. Nevertheless, mainstream secular psychological theory, practice, and organizations have been relatively unaffected by these activities, and so the dominant therapy approaches have historically provided an "alien values framework" for many religious people (Bergin & Jensen, 1990, p. 6). An increased commitment to respect for religious diversity from leaders and members of mainstream mental health organizations might help close this religiosity gap (Bergin, 1991; Bergin & Jensen, 1990).

church, the therapist suggested that if Frank found it too difficult to not be sexually active with Susan, he should masturbate. He also encouraged Susan to look for employment so that she wouldn't feel so trapped in her homemaking role, not realizing that Susan and Frank both regarded her homemaking role as a sacred, divinely appointed role. Susan and Frank were offended by the therapist's lack of sensitivity to their religious beliefs and values, and phoned the following day to cancel their next appointment and to terminate therapy.

Such cases, which could be multiplied *ad infinitum*, illustrate a common ethical failure by mental health professionals. Although multicultural specialists have helped mental health professionals to become more aware of differences relating to race, ethnicity, gender, and so on, they have not provided much insight into religious and spiritual diversity. Our informal survey of the leading books on cross-cultural and multicultural counseling and psychotherapy confirmed that most of them rarely mention religious aspects of diversity. Furthermore, although numerous multicultural writers have argued that understanding clients' worldviews and values is crucial for effective multicultural counseling, none of them have provided much information about the nature of religious and spiritual worldviews and values (Richards & Bergin, 1997).

Because of this neglect, many professionals are not adequately prepared to work sensitively and effectively with clients whose worldviews and lifestyles are deeply spiritual. As illustrated in the case about Susan and Frank, we are concerned that ethical violations may occur when therapists who are religiously uninformed, insensitive, or prejudiced "trample on the values" of religious clients and in so doing alienate, offend, and even harm them (Bergin, 1980a, 1980b, 1983; Richards & Bergin, 1997; Worthington, 1986). In light of the empirical finding that "religious beliefs and values . . . are among the best predictors of what people will say or do" (Strommen, 1984, p. 151), it is our hope that psychotherapists will fulfill their ethical obligation to work respectfully and sensitively with religious and spiritually oriented clients by obtaining specialized knowledge and skills in this important aspect of diversity.

4. *Competency in religious diversity may help psychotherapists understand how to access more fully the healing resources in religious communities to assist their clients in coping, healing, and changing.* There is a growing body of evidence that religious and spiritual beliefs, practices, and influences can both prevent problems and help promote coping and healing where problems have occurred (Benson, 1996; Koenig, 1997; Pargament, 1997; Richards & Bergin, 1997). Table 1.3 summarizes some of the empirical findings on religion and mental and physical health that have been reported during the past two decades. In general, people who are religiously and spiritually devout, but not extremists, tend to enjoy better physical health and psychological adjustment, and lower rates of pathological social conduct than

TABLE 1.3
Religiousness, Spirituality, and Mental Health: A Summary of Findings

1. Religiously committed people tend to report greater subjective well-being and life satisfaction.
2. People who engage in religious coping (e.g., praying, reading sacred writings, meditating, seeking support from religious leaders and community) during stressful times tend to adjust better to crises and problems.
3. Intrinsic (devout) religious people tend to experience less anxiety, including less death anxiety. They also tend to be more free of worry and neurotic guilt.
4. Religious commitment is usually associated with less depression. Among elderly people, church attendance is strongly predictive of less depression.
5. People who attend church are less likely to divorce. Studies have also consistently shown a positive relationship between religious participation and marital satisfaction and adjustment.
6. People with high levels of religious involvement are less likely to use or abuse alcohol. There is also extensive evidence that religiously committed people are less likely to use or abuse drugs.
7. Religious denominations that have clear, unambiguous prohibitions against premarital sex have lower rates of premarital sex and teenage pregnancy.
8. Religious commitment, as measured by church attendance, is associated negatively with delinquency.
9. Religiously committed people report fewer suicidal impulses, report more negative attitudes toward suicide, and commit suicide less often than nonreligious people.
10. Religious commitment is associated positively with moral behavior. Devoutly religious people generally adhere to more stringent moral standards, curbing personal desire or gain to promote the welfare of others and of society (e.g., not gambling, drinking, or engaging in premarital or extramarital sex).
11. Intrinsic religious commitment is associated positively with empathy and altruism.
12. Religious commitment is associated positively with better physical health. Religious people have a lower prevalence of a wide range of illnesses, including cancer, cardiovascular disease, and hypertension.
13. As a group, religiously committed people tend to live longer and to respond better once they have been diagnosed with an illness.
14. People's religious beliefs can help them cope better with their illnesses, including a reduced likelihood of severe depression and perceived disability.
15. Religiously committed surgical patients have shown lower rates of postoperative mortality, less depression, and better ambulation status than patients with lower levels of religious commitment.

Note. The information in this table was extracted from "Religious Values and Mental Health," by A. E. Bergin and P. S. Richards, in press. In A. E. Kazdin (Ed.), *Encyclopedia of Psychology.* Reprinted with permission of American Psychological Association and Oxford University Press.

those who are not (Payne, Bergin, Bielema, & Jenkins, 1991; Richards & Bergin, 1997). Studies of the role of spiritual beliefs and influences in healing have also provided evidence that there are spiritual mechanisms of change and healing that scientists are only now beginning to document and understand (Benson, 1996; Richards & Bergin, 1997).

Spiritual views of psychotherapy, along with spiritual assessment and intervention techniques, have been proposed to help therapists understand more fully how they can draw upon the religious and spiritual resources in their clients' lives to assist them in coping and healing. However, an understanding of clients' religious beliefs and backgrounds is an essential foundation or prerequisite for using such resources and interventions. The following two cases illustrate how an understanding of clients' religious beliefs and culture can lead to more positive outcomes in therapy.

Jan

Jan was a 45-year-old, married, devout Evangelical Christian woman who was struggling with depression and full-blown panic attacks. During a panic attack, fearing that she was having a heart attack, Jan's husband, Dave, rushed her to the emergency room of the local hospital. Medical tests confirmed that Jan was not having a heart attack, nor was she in any danger of having one. Jan's physician gave her information about panic attacks, encouraged her to seek the services of a mental health professional, and then released her to go home. Jan and Dave were reluctant to follow her physician's advice because of their fear that psychotherapy might undermine Jan's religious beliefs and values, but after two more panic attacks and another trip to the emergency room, Jan decided to seek help. Jan's pastor referred her to a therapist who was also Evangelical. Once Jan had reassured herself that the therapist would not prescribe any interventions that would "conflict with Biblical teachings," she quickly grew to trust him. Because of their shared religious beliefs, the therapist was able to explore the various ways in which Jan's religious beliefs and lifestyle were intertwined with her psychological issues and symptoms without alarming Jan that he would try to undermine her religious faith. He was also able to tap into resources in Jan's belief system and religious community to help her cope better and work through her issues. For example, the therapist recommended that Jan seek spiritual direction from her pastor regarding some of her doctrinal doubts and concerns that were contributing to her anxiety and panic. He also recommended selected readings in the Bible to help challenge and modify some of Jan's perfectionistic and catastrophic religious understandings. After several months of therapy, Jan's panic attacks subsided and her depression lifted.

Bharati

Bharati was a 23-year-old, single, Hindu college student. He entered psychotherapy reluctantly at the recommendation of his physician because he was experiencing severe test anxiety that was impairing his performance in classes. Therapy with his non-Hindu therapist helped Bharati understand and work through some of the causes of his test anxiety (e.g., irrational beliefs about what it would mean to get a poor grade in a class, high performance expectations from his parents). As his test anxiety problem dissipated, Bharati felt a desire to explore some conflicts he felt between Western dating and marriage practices and his Hindu beliefs. Although somewhat reluctant to discuss his religious beliefs with a non-Hindu therapist, Bharati felt reassured when his therapist demonstrated respect for, interest in, and some understanding of Hindu cultural beliefs and values. As Bharati explored his spiritual concerns, Bharati's therapist listened respectfully and occasionally asked Bharati to elaborate and educate him about Hindu beliefs he was unfamiliar with. On one occasion, Bharati's therapist asked him if he thought it would be helpful for Bharati to discuss his feelings of conflict about dating and marriage with his parents or other respected members of the Hindu community—which Bharati eventually did. After several months, feeling that he had resolved both his test anxiety and his religious concerns, Bharati and his therapist mutually terminated therapy.

These two cases illustrate that when therapists have specific knowledge about the religious background and beliefs of their clients, they often enjoy greater credibility, and it is easier for them to understand how their clients' religious beliefs and culture may be intertwined with the presenting problems and symptoms. It also is easier for them to select spiritual and secular interventions that are in harmony with their clients' spiritual worldview and values.

Increased competency in religious and spiritual diversity will help therapists work more sensitively and effectively with an ecumenical array of clients and will enable them to use spiritual resources more fully in their clients' lives to promote healing and change. As the case with Bharati illustrates, doing so does not require the therapist to be of the same religion as the client or even to be personally religious (Propst, Ostrom, Watkins, Dean, & Mashburn, 1992).

ATTITUDES AND SKILLS OF SPIRITUALLY SENSITIVE AND COMPETENT THERAPISTS

We accept the axiom that "every therapeutic relationship is a cross-cultural experience" (Bergin & Jensen, 1990, p. 3). Thus, the foundations of spiritually sensitive and competent psychotherapy are generally the same as multicultural counseling attitudes and skills. These include attitudes and skills such as

1. an awareness of one's own cultural and racial heritage, values, and biases;
2. a respect for and comfort with cultures, races, and values different from one's own;
3. an understanding of how a client's racial and cultural heritage could affect the clients' worldview and sense of identity;
4. a sensitivity to circumstances that indicate that a client should be referred to a therapist of his or her own race or culture;
5. specific knowledge about one's clients' particular racial or cultural group; and
6. an awareness of one's own helping style and a recognition of how this style could affect clients from different racial or cultural backgrounds (D. W. Sue & Sue, 1990; D. W. Sue et al., 1982). (Richards & Bergin, 1997, p. 119)

Spiritually competent, or what we have called ecumenically effective, therapists must be able to generalize these multicultural attitudes and skills to the religious and spiritual domains. We have defined an *ecumenical therapeutic stance* as "an attitude and approach to therapy that is suitable for clients of diverse religious affiliations and backgrounds" (Richards & Bergin, 1997, p. 118). Table 1.4 summarizes some of the essential attitudes and skills of such an approach. We have suggested that therapists should use an ecumenical therapeutic stance with all clients early in therapy, and over the entire course of therapy with clients whose spiritual beliefs differ significantly from their own.

With members of their own faith, or with members of other faiths whom the therapist deeply understands and enjoys high credibility, therapists may also find it helpful to adopt a *denominational therapeutic stance* (Richards & Bergin, 1997). We defined a denominational therapeutic stance as "an approach to therapy that is tailored for clients who are members of a specific religious denomination" (Richards & Bergin, 1997, p. 121). A denominational therapeutic stance can be potentially more powerful than an ecumenical stance because it allows therapists to respond to the fine nuances of clients' religious beliefs and to use more fully the spiritual resources available in that tradition.

Lovinger (1996) wrote, "Denominations have central qualities that they impart to members, or that attract those who find those qualities important" (p. 328). These qualities include the history, beliefs, worldviews, and values that may be imparted through specific literature, traditions, and practices of the denomination. To tap these qualities, psychotherapists need knowledge of what they are and the functions they serve in their clients' lives.

We have previously made some recommendations about how psycho-

TABLE 1.4
Characteristics of Effective Ecumenical Psychotherapists

1. Effective ecumenical therapists are aware of their own religious and spiritual heritage, worldview assumptions, and values and are sensitive to how their own spiritual issues, values, and biases could affect their work with clients from different religious and spiritual traditions.

2. Effective ecumenical therapists seek to understand, respect, and appreciate religious and spiritual traditions, worldviews, and values that are different from their own.

3. Effective ecumenical therapists are capable of communicating interest, understanding, and respect to clients who have religious and spiritual worldviews, beliefs, and values that are different from the therapist.

4. Effective ecumenical therapists seek to understand how a client's religious and spiritual worldviews and values affect the client's sense of identity, lifestyle, and emotional and interpersonal functioning, but they are sensitive to how their own religious and spiritual values and beliefs could bias their judgment.

5. Effective ecumenical therapists are sensitive to circumstances (e.g., personal biases, value conflicts, lack of knowledge of the client's religious tradition) that could dictate referral of a religious client to a member of his or her own religious tradition.

6. Effective ecumenical therapists have or seek specific knowledge and information about the religious beliefs and traditions of the religious and spiritual clients with whom they work.

7. Effective ecumenical therapists avoid making assumptions about the beliefs and values of religious and spiritual clients on the basis of religious affiliation alone, but they seek to gain an in-depth understanding of each client's unique spiritual worldviews, beliefs, and values.

8. Effective ecumenical therapists understand how to handle sensitively value and belief conflicts that arise during therapy and do so in a manner that preserves the client's autonomy and self-esteem.

9. Effective ecumenical therapists make efforts to establish respectful, trusting relationships with members and leaders in their clients' religious community and seek to draw on these sources of social support to benefit their clients when appropriate.

10. Effective ecumenical therapists seek to understand the religious and spiritual resources in their clients' lives and encourage their clients to use these resources to assist them in their efforts to cope, heal, and change.

11. Effective ecumenical therapists seek to use religious and spiritual interventions that are in harmony with their clients' religious and spiritual beliefs when it appears that such interventions could help their clients to cope, heal, and change.

Note. This table was reprinted from *A Spiritual Strategy for Counseling and Psychotherapy,* by P. S. Richards and A. E. Bergin, 1997. Reprinted with permission of the American Psychological Association. Portions of the ideas in this table were adapted from *Counseling the Culturally Different: Theory and Practice,* by D. W. Sue, & D. Sue, 1990. Adapted with permission of John Wiley & Sons, Inc.

therapists can increase their competency to work with clients from diverse religious and spiritual backgrounds. These recommendations included:

1. reading books on the psychology and sociology of religion;
2. reading current scholarly literature about religion and spirituality in mainstream mental health journals;
3. taking a workshop or class on religion and mental health and spiritual issues in psychotherapy;
4. reading books or taking a class on world religions;
5. acquiring specialized knowledge about religious traditions that they frequently encounter in therapy;
6. seeking supervision or consultation from colleagues when they first work with a client from a particular religious tradition; and
7. seeking supervision or consultation when they first begin using religious and spiritual interventions. (Richards & Bergin, 1997)

The present volume should prove valuable for therapists who wish to increase their ability to work sensitively and effectively in an ecumenical fashion with clients from diverse religious traditions. Although it is beyond the scope of this handbook to address all of the content areas mentioned above, the information provided in the chapters about the beliefs and practices of the various religious traditions, the insights into how religion and spirituality may be intertwined with mental health issues and the process of psychotherapy, and the denominationally specific assessment and treatment recommendations should all be helpful for therapists who are seeking competency in religious diversity.

Although the information in this handbook will not by itself qualify therapists to work in a denominationally specific manner with clients, it can certainly help therapists take the first few steps toward denominational expertise. To obtain true denominational expertise, they must do a more in-depth study of the teachings and history of the religious tradition, immerse themselves in its culture, and develop relationships of respect and trust with members and leaders in the community. In most cases, this occurs naturally when therapists are themselves practicing members of a religious or spiritual tradition. Less frequently, it may occur when therapists work predominantly with members of a faith that is different from their own.

It is also important to acknowledge here that, in addition to the religious diversity that exists in North America, there is also much ethnic and racial diversity that interact or correlate with religious cultures and traditions. As mentioned earlier, many individuals have also recently immigrated to North America (Marsella et al., 1994). Besides facing the challenges of adjusting to a new country and language, immigrants must adjust to a culture that may differ greatly from that of their home country in regards to the dominant religious beliefs and traditions. Many immigrants who were part of the religious and ethnic majority in their home country find themselves to be members of a minority group in North America.

Working with religious clients who are members of racial–ethnic minority groups, or who are recent immigrants, is a challenging multicultural therapeutic task. The information provided in each of the chapters about diversity issues, and particularly the chapters on ethnic spirituality, will assist psychotherapists in this daunting task. Of course, multicultural knowledge and training about other issues specific to various racial–ethnic groups and immigrants is also essential in order to work effectively with such people (Marsella et al., 1994; Ponterotto, Casas, Suzuki, & Alexander, 1995; D. W. Sue & Sue, 1990).

SOME CAVEATS

Some readers may object to our call for psychotherapists to become more religiously informed and sensitive, and disagree with our premise that therapists should tune into the healing potential of traditional religious communities and belief systems. Those who object might do so on the grounds that traditional religious communities and beliefs have done, and continue to do, a great deal of harm in the world (Ellis, 1971, 1986; Meadow, 1982; Shrock, 1984). We acknowledge this reality. We are not endorsing all that happens in religious communities or traditions. As we have said elsewhere,

> we are also deeply pained by the way cultural traditions and categorizations have led to divisions, intolerance, discrimination, coercion, and even warfare. We see such themes justified by ideologies and played out clinically in the social–emotional abuses that occur in relationships and families. To derive hatred and violence from spiritual convictions is high tragedy. (Richards & Bergin, 1997, p. 4)

Yet despite such realities, we do not think that it is necessary to throw out all of the good with the bad, for it is also true that religious and spiritual beliefs and communities contain much that is healing and therapeutic. We endorse, in religious communities and traditions, only that which is healthy and beneficial for all of the human family. We encourage all helping professionals to join with us in attempting to discern and use that which is positive in religious communities to promote the welfare of humankind.

We encourage readers to approach each chapter in this book with an attitude of open-mindedness and tolerance. When we read about traditions that differ from our own, it is sometimes easy to be critical and perhaps to wonder, "How could anyone believe this?" Perhaps, it is helpful to remember that others may also think this about our own beliefs—what makes total sense to us may seem like complete foolishness to others.

All worldviews, including naturalistic and atheistic ones, require that we make certain nonempirical assumptions about the nature of reality and the universe. When we try to understand a culture or religion from the "outside," we often do not understand the history, shared assumptions, and contextual understandings that make the worldview coherent and believable to "insiders." It is essential to immerse ourselves in a culture and worldview in order to understand it and appreciate it fully. As we do, it becomes easier to understand why intelligent, good people throughout the world can differ so much in the spiritual beliefs and traditions that they find appealing, believable, and helpful.

As you read the chapters in this book, we hope you make a sincere effort to understand those who differ from you. As you do, you may find common ground that helps you empathize with and appreciate them more fully. Despite religious differences that have often been a source of conflict and tragedy in the world, there are fundamental commonalties among spiritual worldviews and moral values that can potentially unite people of faith in promoting healing and growth (Smart, 1993). It is our hope that this handbook will make at least a small contribution to that end.

PLAN OF THE BOOK

Professor Roger R. Keller, an expert in world religions, wrote Chapter 2. It provides an introduction to the religious diversity that exists in the world and particularly in North America. Dr. Keller briefly mentions where each religion originated, its current global demographics, and some historical perspectives regarding its spread and diversification in North America. He also provides an introduction to some of the more distinctive beliefs of the major world religions, including Christianity, Judaism, Islam, Hinduism, and Buddhism. We think readers will find that this chapter provides a helpful overview of the breathtaking array of beliefs and practices that exist in North American culture.

Parts II to VI of the book include a broad range of chapters about many religious and spiritual traditions. These chapters were written by an outstanding and distinguished group of mental health professionals who are members of the religion they wrote about. In each of these chapters, the authors have sought to help readers understand their religion and its members better by providing a brief description of its history, distinctive beliefs and practices, and major types of diversity.

The authors have also provided readers with insights and guidelines to help psychotherapists understand better how they can work sensitively with people from their faith. The authors discuss their religion's view of the mental health professions and psychotherapy and offer guidelines and suggestions for how therapists can build trust and credibility with clients from that community. They also discuss assessment and diagnostic issues, offer treatment and intervention suggestions, and provide case examples to illustrate some key principles in working with clients from their tradition. A list of suggested readings is also provided at the conclusion of these chapters.

Because so little research relevant to mental health issues and psychotherapy has been done with members of most of the religions in this handbook, many of the authors were forced to rely heavily on their own clinical experience as they wrote their chapters. A lack of research on minority groups has plagued the mental health professions (Ponterotto et al., 1995; S. Sue et al., 1994), and in the area of religion the situation is no better. We hope that the chapters in this book will help stimulate more research on people from diverse religious traditions so that scholars and clinicians in the future will have more data on which to base their work. In the meantime, we think the chapter authors have done an admirable job of offering guidelines and suggestions based on clinical experience and the limited research that is currently available.

Part VII is a brief afterword in which we, as the editors, discuss themes, similarities, and differences that are present in the book. We also discuss the relation of mainstream professional psychotherapy to traditional religious communities and offer suggestions for building bridges between these domains. We also offer a few recommendations regarding research, training, and practice.

In a relatively short book such as this one, it was a difficult task to decide what religions to include or exclude. As we have already acknowledged, there is such great religious diversity in the world and in North America that it was impossible to include all of them. We therefore decided to include those whose members or adherents are, on the average, most likely to be seen by psychotherapists in North America. A major consideration in making this judgment was membership statistics (see the membership demographics in Tables 1.1 and 1.2 of this chapter). On the average, therapists are most likely to see clients who belong to the larger groups.

If we were to use this criterion alone, however, we would have ended up with a book devoted almost exclusively to mainstream Christian denominations. Religious "minority" groups and some important non-Christian groups in America would have been excluded. This we did not wish to do, and so we have also included chapters on important movements that fall outside of the mainstream Roman Catholic and Protestant Christian traditions (i.e., Eastern Orthodox, Latter-day Saints, Seventh-day Adventists, etc.), a number of the most prominent non-Christian groups (i.e.,

Judaism, Islam, Hinduism, Buddhism), and four chapters on racial–ethnic religious communities.

Another pragmatic consideration in deciding which religions to include was the availability of authors to write about them. Some traditions were excluded because we were unable to find an author who was qualified to write the chapter. We hope that, in future editions of this handbook, we will be able to include additional religious and spiritual traditions. Although we acknowledge the impossibility of doing justice to the great diversity that exists, we hope that we have at least provided a sample that will be useful to practicing psychotherapists, academicians, and graduate students in the mental health professions.

REFERENCES

American Counseling Association. (1995). *Code of ethics and standards of practice.* Alexandria, VA: Author.

American Psychiatric Association. (1990). Guidelines regarding possible conflict between psychiatrists' religious commitments and psychiatric practice. *American Journal of Psychiatry, 147,* 542.

American Psychiatric Association. (1995). American Psychiatric Association practice guidelines for psychiatric evaluation of adults. *American Journal of Psychiatry Supplement, 152*(11), 64–80.

American Psychological Association. (1992). Ethical principles of psychologists and code of conduct. *American Psychologist, 47,* 1597–1611.

Barrett, D. B., & Johnson, T. M. (1998). Religion: World religious statistics. In *Encyclopedia Britannica book of the year* (p. 314). Chicago: Encyclopedia Britannica, Inc.

Bedell, K. B. (1997). *Yearbook of American and Canadian churches.* Nashville, TN: Abingdon Press.

Benson, H. (1996). *Timeless healing: The power and biology of belief.* New York: Scribner.

Bergin, A. E. (1980a). Psychotherapy and religious values. *Journal of Consulting and Clinical Psychology, 48,* 75–105.

Bergin, E. (1980b). Religious and humanistic values: A reply to Ellis and Walls. *Journal of Consulting and Clinical Psychology, 48,* 642–645.

Bergin, A. E. (1983). Religiosity and mental health: A critical reevaluation and meta-analysis. *Professional Psychology: Research and Practice, 14,* 170–184.

Bergin, A. E. (1991). Values and religious issues in psychotherapy and mental health. *American Psychologist, 46,* 394–403.

Bergin, A. E., & Jensen, J. P. (1990). Religiosity of psychotherapists: A national survey. *Psychotherapy, 27,* 3–7.

Bergin, A. E., & Richards, P. S. (in press). Religious values and mental health. In

A. E. Kazdin (Ed.), *Encyclopedia of psychology.* Washington, DC and New York: American Psychological Association and Oxford University Press.

Campbell, D. T. (1975). On the conflicts between biological and social evolution and between psychology and moral tradition. *American Psychologist*, 1103–1126.

Ellis, A. (1971). *The case against religion: A psychotherapist's view.* New York: Institute for Rational Living.

Ellis, A. (1980). Psychotherapy and atheistic values: A response to A. E. Bergin's "Psychotherapy and religious values." *Journal of Consulting and Clinical Psychology, 48,* 635–639.

Ellis, A. (1986). Fanaticism that may lead to a nuclear holocaust: The contributions of scientific counseling and psychotherapy. *Journal of Counseling and Development, 65,* 146–151.

Freud, S. (1927). *The future of an illusion.* Garden City, NY: Doubleday.

Hoge, D. R. (1996). Religion in America: The demographics of belief and affiliation. In E. P. Shafranske (Ed.), *Religion and the clinical practice of psychology* (pp. 21–41). Washington, DC: American Psychological Association.

Jones, S. L. (1994). A constructive relationship for religion with the science and profession of psychology: Perhaps the boldest model yet. *American Psychologist, 49,* 184–199.

Kelly, E. W. (1994). The role of religion and spirituality in counselor education: A national survey. *Counselor Education and Supervision, 33,* 227–236.

Kelly, E. W. (1995). *Religion and spirituality in counseling and psychotherapy.* Alexandria, VA: American Counseling Association.

King, R. R., Jr. (1978). Evangelical Christians and professional counseling: A conflict of values? *Journal of Psychology and Theology, 6,* 226–281.

Koenig, H. G. (1997). *Is religion good for your health? The effects of religion on physical and mental health.* New York: Haworth Press.

Lovinger, R. J. (1996). Considering the religious dimension in assessment and treatment. In E. P. Shafranske (Ed.), *Religion and the clinical practice of psychology* (pp. 327–363). Washington, DC: American Psychological Association.

Marsella, A. J., Bornemann, T., Ekblad, S., & Orley, J. (1994). *Amidst peril and pain: The mental health and well-being of the world's refugees.* Washington, DC: American Psychological Association.

Meadow, M. J. (1982). True womanhood and women's victimization. *Counseling and Values, 26,* 93–101.

Melton, J. G. (1996). *Encyclopedia of American religions.* Detroit, MI: Gale Research.

Miller, W. R. (1999). *Integrating spirituality into treatment: Resources for practitioners.* Washington, DC: American Psychological Association.

Pargament, K. I. (1997). *The psychology of religion and coping: Theory, research, practice.* New York: Guilford Press.

Payne, I. R., Bergin, A. E., Bielema, K. A., & Jenkins, P. H. (1991). Review of religion and mental health: Prevention and the enhancement of psychosocial functioning. *Prevention in Human Services, 9,* 11–40.

Ponterotto, J. G., Casas, J. P., Suzuki, L. A., & Alexander, C. M. (1995). *Handbook of multicultural counseling.* Newbury Park, CA: Sage.

Propst, L. R., Ostrom, R., Watkins, P., Dean, T., & Mashburn, D. (1992). Comparative efficacy of religious and nonreligious cognitive–behavioral therapy for the treatment of clinical depression in religious individuals. *Journal of Consulting and Clinical Psychology, 60,* 94–103.

Richards, P. S., & Bergin, A. E. (1997). *A spiritual strategy for counseling and psychotherapy.* Washington, DC: American Psychological Association.

Sell, K. L., & Goldsmith, W. M. (1988). Concerns about professional counseling: An exploration of five factors and the role of Christian orthodoxy. *Journal of Psychology and Christianity, 7,* 5–21.

Shafranske, E. P. (Ed.). (1996). *Religion and the clinical practice of psychology.* Washington, DC: American Psychological Association.

Shafranske, E. P., & Malony, H. N. (1990). Clinical psychologists' religious and spiritual orientations and their practice of psychotherapy. *Psychotherapy, 27,* 72–78.

Shafranske, E. P., & Malony, H. N. (1996). Religion and the clinical practice of psychology: A case for inclusion. In E. P. Shafranske (Ed.), *Religion and the clinical practice of psychology* (pp. 561–586). Washington, DC: American Psychological Association.

Shrock, D. A. (1984). Suppression of women by religion. *Counseling and Values, 29,* 49–58.

Smart, N. (1993). *Religions of Asia.* Englewood Cliffs, NJ: Prentice Hall.

Smart, N. (1994). *Religions of the West.* Englewood Cliffs, NJ: Prentice Hall.

Strommen, M. P. (1984). Psychology's blind spot: A religious faith. *Counseling and Values, 28,* 150–161.

Sue, D. W., Bergnier, J. E., Duran, A., Feinberg, L., Pedersen, P., Smith, E., & Vasquez-Nuttall, E. (1982). Position paper: Cross-cultural counseling competencies. *The Counseling Psychologist, 10,* 45–52.

Sue, D. W., & Sue, D. (1990). *Counseling the culturally different: Theory and practice* (2nd ed.). New York: Wiley.

Sue, S., Zane, N., & Young, K. (1994). Research on psychotherapy with culturally diverse populations. In A. E. Bergin & S. L. Garfield (Eds.), *Handbook of psychotherapy and behavior change.* New York: Wiley.

Tan, S. Y. (1993, January). *Training in professional psychology: Diversity includes religion.* Paper presented at the National Council of Schools of Professional Psychology Midwinter Conference on "Clinical Training in Professional Psychology," La Jolla, CA.

Vande Kemp, H. (1996). Historical perspective: Religion and clinical psychology in America. In E. P. Shafranske (Ed.), *Religion and the clinical practice of psychology* (pp. 71–112). Washington, DC: American Psychological Association.

Veroff, J., Kulka, R. A., & Douvan, E. (1981). *Mental health in America*. New York: Basic Books.

Worthington, E. L., Jr. (1986). Religious counseling: A review of published empirical research. *Journal of Counseling and Development, 64,* 421–431.

Worthington, E. L., Jr., Kurusu, T. A., McCullough, M. E., & Sanders, S. J. (1996). Empirical research on religion and psychotherapeutic processes and outcomes: A ten-year review and research prospectus. *Psychological Bulletin, 119,* 448–487.

Wulff, D. M. (1991). *Psychology of religion: Classic and contemporary views.* New York: Wiley.

2

RELIGIOUS DIVERSITY IN NORTH AMERICA

ROGER R. KELLER

In interfaith dialogue, if you want to know about someone else's faith, (1) ask them; (2) compare your best with their best; and (3) leave room for holy envy.

— Krister Stendahl

This chapter provides an introduction to the major religions of the world, their distribution globally and in North America, and the basic tenets which they hold. Most persons whom therapists encounter in North America will be of Christian origin and, therefore, a large portion of this chapter will deal with various major Christian denominations, citing the unique elements that might be helpful in a counseling setting. However, the North American religious landscape is clearly pluralistic. Hence, it is not sufficient to assume that all clients will be Christians. Therapists will be seeing practicing Jews, Hindus, Muslims, Buddhists, Sikhs, and members of a variety of other spiritual traditions, including those influenced by African, Asian, Latino/Latina, and Native American worldviews. Although it is impossible to discuss all of the spiritual traditions that therapists might encounter, this chapter and those that follow will provide therapists with a sampling of the great religious and spiritual diversity that exists in North America. It is hoped that familiarity with the basic ideas and practices of these faiths and traditions will be helpful to therapists as they seek to assist people live healthier, fuller lives.

27

RELIGIOUS DISTRIBUTION AROUND THE WORLD

The largest religious group in the world is Christianity with a total world membership of approximately 1,929,987,000 or 33.0% of the world population (Barrett & Johnson, 1998).[1] Membership is distributed over the world fairly evenly with the largest number of Christians in Europe, followed by Latin America, Africa, Asia, North America, and Oceania. Of these, 53.9% are Roman Catholic, whereas 18.7% are Protestant, 11.6% are Eastern Orthodox, 2.8% are Anglican (Church of England), and 14.9% are of other Christian traditions. All groups are well represented in North America.

Islam is the second largest religion in the world. It claims 1,147,494,000 adherents or 19.6% of the world population. Over 800 million of these are found in Asia, whereas over 300 million are in Africa. Approximately 31 million live in Europe and an additional 4.06 million live in North America. Islam is a growing religion worldwide and is experiencing significant growth in North America.

Other religious traditions of interest in the North American context are Judaism, Hinduism, Buddhism, and Sikhism. Jews are found scattered across the world in most countries. However, the largest Jewish populations are found in Asia with approximately 4.5 million (most of whom now live in Israel), in North America with 5.9 million, and in Europe with 2.9 million. Hinduism has a world population of 746,797,000, most of whom live in Asia, and the vast majority of these are found in India. There are, however, approximately 1,129,000 Hindus in North America, with most living in large metropolitan areas in Canada and the United States. Similarly, there are over 2 million Buddhists in North America, even though their world population is only 353,141,000—a relatively small number when compared with Christianity, Islam, or Hinduism. In addition, there are almost half a million Sikhs in North America out of a world population of 22.5 million. Clearly, the search for a better life has drawn people with their different religions to North American shores.

Finally, there are 146,615,000 Atheists worldwide. When this figure is added to the 760,280,000 persons identified as nonreligious, the portion of the world population with no strong religious roots is 15.5%. By far the largest number of those claiming nonbelief or little interest in religion are in Asia, with North America having 1.38 million Atheists and 26.1 million nonreligious persons. This is only 9.1% of the North American population, and a sign that at least in North America most people will bring some religious commitments to therapy.

---

[1]Unless otherwise specified, all future statistical information will be drawn from this source.

THE NORTH AMERICAN RELIGIOUS EXPERIENCE

Religiosity in the United States and Canada has taken different courses. In Canada, religious life has been much more closely tied to the state and its institutions than has been the case in the United States. In the latter, there has been distinct aversion to church–state relationships, despite relatively brief periods of established (state-supported) religion in colonies such as Massachusetts and Virginia. Generally, there has been a religious marketplace in the United States, whereas in Canada, the religious scene has been less diverse. Bibby (1993) showed that formal religious activity has declined markedly in all parts of Canada in the last three decades, although this does not necessarily mean that Canadians are not concerned about ultimate questions. They are, but institutional religion does not seem to be meeting those needs. Even so, most Canadians have strong memories of denominational ties and will be found in churches at least for rites of passage.

In contrast, the United States has a vibrant institutional religious life among Christians, as well as among persons of other faiths (see Noll, 1992; Finke & Stark, 1992). Indicative of this is the large array of religious groups in the United States. For example, J. Gordon Melton (1996c) identified 1,299 Christian groups, 218 spiritualist, psychic, and New Age groups, 100 Ancient Wisdom groups, 125 Magick groups, 104 Middle Eastern groups, 274 Eastern groups, and 15 unclassified religious groups, for a total of 2,135 identifiable religious groups in the United States.

The above totals suggest that among clients for therapy, those in the United States are likely to be directly active in a religious organization, whereas those in Canada, if not active, will still have memories of religious ties and will probably claim them.[2] With this in mind, we will explore the origin of the various religious traditions in North America.

WESTERN TRADITIONS

Christianity

History in North America

Christianity is composed of various family relationships, and a brief summary of these relationships may be useful. Catholicism can be divided between Eastern Orthodoxy and Roman Catholicism, the two having separated in 1054 C.E. (the traditional date). The Reformation period gave rise to other schisms. The first was the establishment of Lutheran churches,

---

[2]For a developed treatment of these themes, see Noll, 1992; Finke and Stark, 1992; and Bibby, 1993.

first in Germany, which broke off from the Roman Catholic tradition in the early 16th century. Also, separating itself from the Roman Catholics was the Anglican Church, or the Church of England. In both Lutheran and Anglican traditions, ties with Roman Catholicism are still evident, especially in worship practice. Additional reactions to the Anglican Church were the Puritan and Separatist movements, which gave rise to the Congregational Church in the United States, as well as the Methodist and Baptist movements. Another strong stream of Protestant thought in the 16th century arose in Geneva, Switzerland, under the guidance of John Calvin. Again, it was a reaction to Roman Catholicism, but it took a different direction than did the Lutherans, placing greater authority in the hands of laity. This stream of faith gave rise to the Reformed tradition which is manifest denominationally by the Presbyterian and various Reformed churches. Beyond these major streams are the less hierarchical traditions which reacted to perceived weaknesses in these "mainline" churches. Thus, we see the rise of Mormonism, Jehovah's Witnesses, Pentecostals, Seventh-day Adventists, Christian Science, and so on.

Of those who are religiously affiliated in the United States, approximately 94.4% are Christians, with Catholics (Roman Catholic and Orthodox) constituting 37.8% of the religiously affiliated and Protestants constituting 56.6% of the religious total. The remaining 5.5% of religiously affiliated people are composed of Jews, Muslims, Buddhists, and persons of other religions (Wright, 1997). The religiously affiliated represent 62.2% of the population (Wright, 1997).

In Canada according to 1991 census figures, 45.2% of the population is Roman Catholic, with 35.8% being Protestant; 12.4% said they had no religious affiliation; and 6.6% were of non-Christian traditions. Clearly, there are similarities between the two North American sister countries. The dominant difference is reflected in the levels of religious activity, as noted above.

Christianity arrived in the United States and Canada in much the same way. It was brought by explorers, merchants, and settlers. In the United States, Roman Catholicism came primarily with the Spanish, and the Franciscans were particularly important in spreading the faith among Native American peoples in the southwestern United States beginning in the late 1500s. Their practices were often paternalistic, however, leading to revolts among the native peoples. The exception to the Spanish infusion of Catholicism in what is now U.S. territory is found in the colony of Maryland, which was established in 1634 by George Calvert and his son, Cecil, for the express purpose of providing a refuge for English Catholics. Roman Catholicism came to Canada with the French who founded Quebec in 1608, and the Jesuits, who seemed to be better prepared to address cultural issues among Native American converts than were the Franciscans, spearheaded missionary work in areas explored by the French.

The first Protestants to stay in the American colonies were Anglicans (members of the Church of England) who arrived in Jamestown, Virginia, in 1607. Even though the colony was founded for commercial reasons, Anglican priests arrived to serve the colony. Prior to the Revolutionary War, Anglicanism was strong from Maryland to Georgia and was often the established (government-supported) faith. Congregationalism dominated the northeastern colonies, beginning with the Separatists who settled Plymouth in 1620, and the Puritans who established the Massachusetts Bay Colony in 1630. Other denominations began to arrive in colonial areas, some to have religious freedom (at least for themselves) and others to seek new beginnings and opportunities. Thus, the Dutch Reformed Church arrived when the Dutch founded New Amsterdam (today's New York City) in 1629. William Penn created in 1682 an island of religious tolerance in Pennsylvania for Quakers, as well as for all other faiths that might want to settle there. Thus, German Lutherans, Mennonites, and others found their way to Pennsylvania. Another colony with high religious tolerance was Rhode Island, founded in 1643 as a haven for persons fleeing the intolerant colony of Massachusetts. It was in Providence, soon to be part of the colony of Rhode Island, that Roger Williams established in 1639 the first Baptist church in the new world. Presbyterianism was brought to the colonies by Scottish settlers, especially in the 1740s, who were seeking inexpensive land. By the Revolutionary War, most of the major denominations of today had a foothold in what was to become the United States.

The revolutionary period in the 13 colonies also affected the nature of Christianity in Canada. During the 17th century, France was dominant in Canada. However, the British grew interested in this northern land. By the beginning of the 18th century, Britain was gaining the upper hand. With the French had come Catholicism, and with the British came Anglicanism. In 1763, the Treaty of Paris made Canada officially British and, for a brief time, there was an attempt to limit Catholicism. However, in 1774, the Act of Quebec guaranteed a significant degree of religious tolerance to Catholics (Melton, 1996f). By this time also, most of the major denominations had made their way into Canada, with a number of Protestant traditions moving to the Maritime provinces. With the defeat of the British in the American colonies, many Anglicans fled to Canada, since during the war they had remained loyal to England. By the end of the 18th century, a dominant difference between church life in the United States and Canada was that the latter still had strong ties across the Atlantic, whereas the former did not.

The 19th century saw the spread of the various Christian denominations across both countries. Because of their willingness to evangelize on the frontier, Methodists and Baptists grew dramatically in this period. Catholics also grew immensely through immigration with large numbers of Irish reaching American shores before the Civil War and Catholics from other parts of Europe coming after the war. Thus, at the beginning of the 20th century, Roman Catholics were the largest denomination in the United States, followed by the Baptists and Methodists.

In Canada in the 19th century, expansion to the west was also taking place, but at the same time, there was a loosening of the ties between the government and the Anglican Church. In 1853, all clergy land reserves which had provided income for the church were secularized. With the completion of the transcontinental railroad in 1885, Canada was bound together, and this allowed for growth in the west in both population and religion. The Catholic Church was the first to exploit the western possibilities, followed later by the Anglican Church. Gradually, other denominations also moved westward (Melton, 1996f).

The 20th century has been traumatic for churches in both countries. Science and new techniques of biblical criticism challenged long-accepted theories about the origin of human beings, the age of the earth, and the infallibility of the scriptures. Some denominations accepted the new directions and sought ways to bring the Bible and science together. Others clung tenaciously to traditional views. The issues split denominations, and those tensions are still in evidence between fundamentalist groups and the mainline Protestant denominations, the latter usually including Episcopalians, Presbyterians, Methodists, Lutherans, Congregationalists, United Church of Christ, and Disciples of Christ.

One of the most important movements in both countries was the ecumenical movement, which sought cooperation or even union among the various denominations. In the United States, union occurred between denominations of the same family which had often separated at the time of the Civil War (e.g., the Presbyterians). Others, like the Lutherans, brought groups together that had originally had differing national roots. Thus, an atmosphere of cooperation (ecumenism) has been created among the mainline denominations in the United States, but more conservative Christians often see ecumenism as being defined by the lowest common denominator among traditions, thus eliminating the evangelistic thrust of the Christian gospel.

Similar interest was expressed in ecumenical relationships in Canada, but they went farther than in the United States. In 1925, the Methodist, Congregationalist, and Presbyterian churches merged to form the United Church of Canada, the third largest denomination in Canada behind the Catholics and the Anglicans (Melton, 1996f).

In both Canada and the United States, Blacks have played a significant role in the various denominations. In Canada, Blacks may be found in virtually every denominational body, and the same is true in the United States. However, in the United States, sizable Black denominations have also been created. This was in part a product of slavery. In the early history of the country, some Christians questioned whether Blacks were human and whether they had souls. If not, then it was unnecessary to teach them the Christian gospel. However, others felt that both the Blacks and Native Americans should be taught. Among Blacks, this led initially to participation in White churches, with the Blacks seated in the balcony or in the back. Eventually, Blacks began to teach Blacks and to establish churches of their own. The church became the one arena in which Blacks could exercise leadership without White interference. Thus, independent Black denominations began to appear, the dominant ones being the African Methodist Episcopal Church (1814) and the African Methodist Episcopal Zion Church (1820). Black congregations of Baptists and Presbyterians also formed. Today, there are strong Black Christian congregations that hold their destinies in their own hands and are not dependent upon White participation.

Finally, the Pentecostal movement appeared in the United States at the beginning of the 20th century. From these beginnings, it has become an international movement and is found in Canada, as well as in many other countries. The focus of the movement is on the gifts of the Spirit, the most visible being "speaking in tongues," an unintelligible prayer language, seen as the sign of a person's reception of the Holy Spirit. Although there are various accounts of the gift of tongues in both European and American Christianity, the actual beginning of the movement is normally traced to the Reverend Charles Parham who, with his students at Bethel Bible College in Topeka, Kansas, received in 1901 the gift of tongues after seeking it. In Houston, Texas, William J. Seymour was convinced by Parham's teaching and preaching and the mantle of leadership was passed on to him. Seymour moved to California where, in 1906, a group formed in a rented building on Azusa Street in Los Angeles. They began to receive the gift of tongues (Melton, 1996e). From these beginnings, the Pentecostal movement has grown significantly. There are 10,281,559 Pentecostals in the United States (Wright, 1997) and 436,435 in Canada (*Canadian Almanac Directory*, 1997). The largest Pentecostal denominations in the United States are the Church of God in Christ (a Black denomination) and the Assemblies of God (Wright, 1997). In Canada, the largest is the Pentecostal Assemblies of Canada.

As can be seen, the Christian religious tapestry of the United States and Canada is varied. Both have strong histories of Christian influence, and most persons will have Christian backgrounds and feel some affinity for a Christian communion. However, they may or may not be actively involved regularly in a Christian congregation. This is especially true for Canadians.

Catholicism

Catholicism includes two denominational groups: Roman Catholicism and Eastern Orthodoxy. Theologically, they are very similar, agreeing, for example, on the traditional Trinitarian formula that the Godhead is composed of three simultaneously coexistent beings who are of one essence. Thus, differences need to be examined more in terms of structure and practice than in theology.

Roman Catholicism

Roman Catholicism is a connectional denomination in which there is a strong, worldwide, apostolic hierarchical structure. It begins with the Pope, the Bishop of Rome, who is God's vice-regent on earth. He, along with the bishops and priests of the Church, is the one charged with giving direction to the faithful on issues of faith and morals. However, some Catholics in both the United States and Canada do not accept papal guidance as authoritative. For them, his is only one voice among many, especially on issues related to sexuality. Thus, there are sometimes rifts between Rome and some Catholics in the pew.

Perhaps a stronger influence in the life of Roman Catholics are the sacraments of the church. Roman Catholicism has always been a sacramental faith, meaning that God is encountered in the seven sacraments of the church: baptism, confirmation, eucharist, penance and reconciliation, anointing, holy orders, and marriage. These cover the entire life cycle and serve as rites of passage (Melton, 1996f). For example, baptism forgives original sin and welcomes children into the world and the church, and confirmation admits them to full membership in the church and to adult responsibilities. The two sacraments in which Roman Catholics may regularly participate are penance and reconciliation and the eucharist. Penance and reconciliation is a sacrament of spiritual healing, for through the process of self-examination, confession, and penance, persons can become reintegrated with God and themselves. Eucharist is also a regular means through which persons can encounter God, for as they take the bread and wine, which they believe have actually become the body and blood of Christ during consecration by the priest, they are cleansed from sins and given new life in Christ. It is through these sacraments that the spiritual tenor of the Christian life can be maintained.

The sacraments of marriage and holy orders are designed to lead people to serve others, for they are termed "sacraments at the service of communion" (Catechism of the Catholic Church, 1995). Whether people are serving through the building of family relationships and the attendant responsibilities within the community, or whether they are serving through the priesthood or the religious life, they are all moving beyond themselves and meeting the needs of others. This can only create mental and spiritual health in people, both among those who serve and those who are served. The final sacrament, anointing, is a sacrament of healing, both physically and spiritually. When people are seriously ill, they may be anointed with oil, and this act is accompanied by prayers which seek divine intervention or solace. At the moment of death, anointing is also used to bring persons into a state of grace as they leave this world. Thus, life's joys, sorrows, and transitions are marked by the sacraments of the church.

The final goal for Roman Catholics is heaven: the place of God's dwelling where they may receive the beatific vision, the vision of God. To enter this realm, one needs to be holy, not just forgiven. Thus, there is purgatory, a place in which final cleansing from sins can occur, thus bringing a person to holiness. For those who die outside the state of grace, the end is hell or eternal suffering. Through the Roman Catholic faith and practice, time and eternity, the past, present, and future, are all encompassed and given meaning.

Eastern Orthodox

Eastern Orthodoxy is similar to Roman Catholicism in its theology (because it accepts the first seven councils), its sense of apostolic succession, and its sacraments. The dominant difference is that rather than being fully united, the Eastern Orthodox communion is managed within national boundaries (Melton, 1996f). The structure is episcopal, meaning that bishops manage the church, but there are independent Patriarchs or Bishops over national churches. Thus, there are the Russian Orthodox Church, the Greek Orthodox Church, the Bulgarian Orthodox Church, and so on. Unity among the national churches is found in the Patriarch of Istanbul (formerly Constantinople), who is an equal among equals, but who is given a position of primacy. He cannot interfere, however, in the management of another patriarchate.

Another distinction, which is more sensed than articulated perhaps, is that there is less focus on doctrine than in the west and more on spirituality. The true center of Orthodoxy is worship, and around the worship liturgy, a wonderful musical tradition has grown. In addition, icons play a special role. These two dimensional representations of Christ or events in his life, as well as other scriptural events, are designed to draw worshipers spiritually into the sacred events themselves. They are almost sacraments for through the icon, one encounters God or participates once again in his work among human beings. They are a powerful means of bringing people face to face with things spiritual.

In summary, Roman Catholicism and Eastern Orthodoxy, through their sacraments and their worship, both provide means for self-examination, for life transitions, and for finding wholeness in life.

Mainline Protestantism

Episcopalians, Lutherans, Presbyterians, Methodists, Congregationalists, the United Church of Christ, and Disciples of Christ are usually considered to be *mainline*. What this means is that they are well integrated into the fabric of national life and reflect the social norms of the society. They share a common belief in the two sacraments of baptism and eucharist, the centrality of the preached word accompanying the sacraments, a strong sense of social responsibility, a pastoral response to human needs, and a hope for ultimate salvation in the presence of God. They differ in the way worship is organized and in the way the churches are structured. Only some will be examined specifically because of the general similarities they share with others.

Episcopalians

Episcopalian religious beliefs often work themselves out in a strong sense of involvement in the communities in which the people live. Although the church has clear doctrinal norms stated in the Thirty-Nine Articles, these seem to be less important to the average Episcopalian than does social involvement from a Christian perspective. Worship services may vary in format. A high or liturgically formal Episcopal church service will essentially be the Mass, and the culminating event is the eucharist, although there is a greater stress on the preached word than one would find in a Roman Catholic Mass. In the high tradition, the priest's fundamental role is to provide the sacraments to the people. In contrast, however, some Episcopal churches have a much less structured service and can be quite evangelical in their worship. Here, the preached word and a personal relation with Christ become central, even when the eucharist is provided. Episcopalians believe in original sin and in the necessity of grace through Jesus Christ for salvation.

Lutherans

At one time, there were as many as 150 different Lutheran groups in the United States, the result of national groupings attempting to remain independent. However, in this century, Lutherans have tended to reduce these groups through mergers, such that today the largest Lutheran groups in the United States are the Evangelical Lutheran Church with 5.2 million members and the Missouri Synod Lutheran Church with 2.6 million. The Lutheran Church in Canada has 79,844 members, but the estimated number of Lutherans in the country is 636,205 (*Canadian Almanac Directory*,

1997). Like the Episcopal Church, there can be a range of styles present in Lutheranism, but the essential elements theologically are always present: Christ is met in the preached word and the sacraments; persons are justified in Christ through faith alone; and the Bible is the sole rule of faith.

Worship services may be very formal, following the basic structure of the Mass, but with the preached word being central. Although there are only the two sacraments of eucharist and baptism for Lutherans, the preached word is the place where Lutherans encounter the Word of God —Jesus Christ—most consistently. Preaching is an "almost sacrament."

Lutherans are strongly middle class, but are not necessarily rooted simply in the cities. Many came to farm, and thus large concentrations are found in the Midwest of the United States and the plains of Canada. The people tend to be conservative religiously, holding to the basic doctrines of virgin birth, divinity of Christ, the substitutionary atonement, and the power of God to work in human lives today.

Presbyterians

Historically, there has always been a strong emphasis on an educated clergy, and thus the more educated persons of communities tended to gravitate to the Presbyterian Church. The name of the church is derived from the Greek word for elder—*presbuteros*—and defines the form of government present in the church. Presbyterians believe in rule by groups of persons and are generally wary of placing too much power in the hands of any one individual. They possess a representative form of government in which there is numerical equality between clergy and laity in all judicatories above the local level.

Theologically, Presbyterians stress God's divine control in all things. God approaches humans, which in turn elicits a response from human beings. This understanding of God's approach to humanity arises from a belief in original sin, which makes it impossible for persons to want to turn to God, before God has sought them out and enabled them through the Holy Spirit to respond to his initiative. The clearest manifestation of this tendency is seen in the doctrine of predestination. However, most Presbyterians today would draw back from this doctrine with its implied determinism. Still, God definitely remains in control.

Worship services may vary, but they would normally find a middle ground between very structured and unstructured. The preached word is a central event, but equally important is the congregational response to the preached word, which should empower people to live creatively in a broken world. The eucharist or Lord's Supper is normally served only six times a year, so that it does not become "common." Presbyterians tend to be moderate to liberal in their theological and political views. Many feel it important for the church to speak out on social issues, and there are struggles over whether gays and lesbians should be ordained ruling or teaching elders and whether marriage is the only appropriate arena for sexual relations. Episcopalians are wrestling with similar issues.

Methodists

Methodists are the second largest Protestant group in the United States, but in Canada, they were absorbed into the United Church. They experienced remarkable growth in the 19th century because of their emphasis on frontier evangelism through circuit riders. In the 20th century, Methodists have become very much a part of mainstream America.

Methodists have always been deeply involved in moral issues. Strong antislavery and temperance movements found helping hands among Methodists. Whereas Presbyterians may have tended to be thinkers, Methodists have always been doers. That trend continues as they seek to bring their Christian vision to bear on a wide variety of issues. Like Presbyterians and Episcopalians, they too struggle with the issues of the day, particularly those dealing with sexual mores.

Upstart Protestants

Roger Finke and Rodney Stark (1992) used the term "upstart sects" for non-Mainline traditions that stand in high tension with the cultural environment. Their basic thesis is that, as a group of religious people becomes absorbed into the values of their culture, their market share of the religiously inclined begins to diminish. People are no longer challenged. They can find little in the church that they could not find in society. Finke and Stark showed clearly from a statistical standpoint that this is precisely what has happened to the mainline denominations in the 20th century. Episcopalians, Presbyterians, and Methodists have all declined in their market shares between 1940 and 1985. The Methodists lost 48%; the Presbyterians, 49%; and the Episcopalians, 38%. In contrast over the same period of time, the Southern Baptists gained 32%; the Assemblies of God, 371%; the Church of the Nazarene, 42%, and the Church of God (Cleveland, Tennessee), 260% (Finke & Stark, 1992). The conclusion is that churches have to demand something of the faithful, otherwise they fall away.

> Humans want their religion to be sufficiently potent, vivid, and compelling so that it can offer them rewards of great magnitude. People seek a religion that is capable of miracles and that imparts order and sanity to the human condition. The religious organizations that maximize these aspects of religion, however, also demand the highest price in terms of what the individual must do to qualify for these rewards. ... There comes a point ... when a religious body has become so

worldly that its rewards are few and lacking in plausibility. . . . [Thus] the mainline bodies are always headed for the sideline. (Finke & Stark, 1992, p. 275)

We will now examine some of those denominations that have experienced significant growth in recent years at the expense of the mainline traditions.

Evangelicals

The word *evangelical* comes from the Greek word *euangelion* meaning "good news." Thus, the characteristics that define evangelicals are

1. a profound desire to preach the life-changing message of Jesus Christ—the good news—to all who will listen;
2. a deep personal relationship with Christ;
3. a joyous attitude in the worship of God;
4. a Bible-centered faith; and
5. the belief that changed individuals will change a sick society.

Representative of the evangelical community are the Southern Baptists and other conservative Baptist congregations, the Churches of Christ, the Evangelical Free Church, and numerous independent congregations.

As the word *evangelical* suggests, the Christian message is good news to a dying and sinful world. People need to be changed and, consequently, Evangelicals actively seek to bring people into their churches. The worship services are usually not highly structured. There may be a good deal of singing to invite the Spirit into the worship service. Prayers are spontaneous rather than written. Lay involvement is the norm. A sermon is central, usually by a pastor, although laypersons can also preach. Worship services will often end with an altar call in which persons who wish to commit their lives to Jesus Christ are invited to come forward and make a public profession of their faith. Billy Graham crusades utilize this latter practice.

Congregations are usually independent, meaning that there is no hierarchical structure with authority above the congregational level. Even in the Southern Baptist Convention, local churches belong only by their choice, and they can withdraw at any time. The only things over which the Convention has any authority are denominational seminaries, and we see today the struggle between moderate and conservative forces over these. However, the individual churches do as they see fit, calling their own ministers, ordaining them if necessary, establishing budgets, and owning property.

Theologically, evangelical churches are conservative. They generally see themselves as correctives to mainline denominations which have lost the emphasis on the proclamation of the gospel. Evangelicals believe in the virgin birth, Christ's full divinity and full humanity, salvation by grace, the authority of the Bible, the literal resurrection from the dead, and the return of Christ in glory. Although there is scepticism about scientific conclusions and modern means of biblical criticism, evangelicals are not totally opposed to thoughtful participation in these fields.

There is another group, however, within the evangelical tradition known as Fundamentalists. These are persons who do have significant problems with both modern biblical criticism and science, the two together constituting "modernism." In response to modernism, Fundamentalists believe that there are certain "fundamentals" to the faith that cannot be compromised. These are "the inspiration and infallibility of the Bible, the deity of Christ (including his virgin birth), substitutionary atonement of Christ's death, the literal resurrection of Christ from the dead, and the literal return of Christ in the Second Advent" (Melton, 1996d, p. 108). The touchstone for many fundamentalists, which would set them apart from some evangelicals, would be their belief in the verbal inerrancy of the Bible on all issues.

Pentecostals

Pentecostals are characterized by a "conscious" search for the gifts of the Spirit, especially for the gift of tongues, which is seen as a special sign of the gift of the Holy Ghost. In addition, they believe in the other gifts of the Spirit that Paul lists in I Corinthians 12. Theologically, they are conservative and may range from Evangelicals who interact with modernism to Fundamentalists who stand at odds with modernism. Furthermore, they may be found among persons of the mainline traditions. In the 1960s and thereafter, there was a movement to rediscover the Spirit in Christian living, and many mainline members participated in "charismatic" groups which sought the gifts of the Spirit. They were Pentecostals, but they never left the Catholic, Methodist, Episcopalian, or Presbyterian churches. Many persons in the mainline churches were uneasy about the charismatic movement, but most major denominations have found ways of accommodating it. The largest Pentecostal denomination in the United States is the Assemblies of God, but there are other Pentecostal denominations and many independent congregations.

Denominations With American Roots

The three most visible denominations in this category are The Church of Jesus Christ of Latter-day Saints, Jehovah's Witnesses, and the Seventh-day Adventist Church. All arose in an atmosphere that believed Christ's second coming was near, and a sense of the nearness of Christ's return is still present in each. Each believes in 1,000 years of peace (the millennium) ruled by God or Christ. Seventh-day Adventists are theologically in line with traditional Christianity, especially on doctrines such as the Trinity and creation out of nothing. Their special uniqueness lies in their belief that the Sabbath should be celebrated on the seventh day of the week (i.e., from sundown Friday until sundown Saturday). They also do not use alcohol or tobacco.

The Church of Jesus Christ of Latter-day Saints (Mormons) and Jehovah's Witnesses do not always agree with traditional Protestant theology. Both deny the doctrine of the Trinity, Latter-day Saints believing that there are three members of the Godhead—Father, Son, and Holy Ghost—but that they are not of one essence. Jehovah's Witnesses believe that there is one God—Jehovah—and that Jesus Christ was his first creation. The Holy Spirit is not a personage but is rather the influence of Jehovah. Latter-day Saints are very involved in the world and its political organizations as individuals. Jehovah's Witnesses are not, holding that worldly institutions and rituals are a product of the devil's work or of humanity's degeneration. Whatever their origin, they are not of God.

Latter-day Saints believe that God continues to speak to his people through living prophets, and thus a Prophet, Seer, and Revelator always stands at the head of the church as God's mouthpiece in the present day. Latter-day Saints also possess additional volumes of scripture beyond the Bible, such as the *Book of Mormon*, the *Doctrine and Covenants*, and the *Pearl of Great Price*. Beyond this, they believe in the substitutionary atonement of Jesus Christ, the presence of the gifts of the Spirit, an authoritative priesthood, and a Word of Wisdom which prohibits the use of alcohol, tobacco, tea, and coffee. In addition, Mormons have temples in which saving work is done for the dead, and thus they are deeply involved in genealogical work and discovering information about their ancestors. For Latter-day Saints, the family is an eternal unit, and thus the central unit, of all life and practice.

Judaism

History in North America

The history of Judaism in the United States and Canada has been quite different in the two countries. Twenty-three Sephardic Jews first arrived in the American colonies in 1654, settling in New Amsterdam. Other Jews arrived in Newport, Rhode Island, in 1677. The first synagogue was built in 1728 in New York City. Jews also settled in South Carolina in 1697 and in Georgia in 1733. In 1768, Gershom Mendes Seixas (1745–1826) became the first American-born cantor of the synagogue in New York. When it appeared that New York would be taken by the British in 1776, Seixas led the congregation to safety in Stratford, Connecticut. Four years later, he led them to Philadelphia where, in 1782, they built a synagogue. In 1789, Seixas was one of the 13 religious leaders who participated in George Washington's inauguration (Eck, 1997d).

Judaism in America is marked by three major groupings. The most conservative are the Orthodox Jews, and they were the first Jews to arrive in the colonies. In the 1800s, however, two other forms of Judaism appeared: Reform and Conservative. The first Reform Jews from Germany began to appear in Charleston, South Carolina, in 1824 (Eck, 1997d). Later in the century, as new immigrants began to arrive, Conservative Judaism arose as a mediating influence between the Orthodox and Reform views (Melton, 1996a). Essentially, most Jews fall somewhere on a spectrum between tradition and modernity, and as we examine the beliefs of Jews later, we will highlight some of the differences in these traditions. Today, Jews are found in most areas of the United States, with large concentrations in the northeast. There are over 5 million Jews in the United States (Barrett & Johnson, 1998), 50% of those practicing their religion being Conservative, with 25% being Orthodox and 25% being Reform. Jews have an importance in the North American scene far beyond their numbers. They have heavily influenced education, science, music, and business.

In Canada, Jews were initially excluded by French law. The first Jews arrived in Halifax in 1749, but left shortly thereafter. By 1825, there were less than 100 Jews in Canada. However, in 1832, Jews were granted equal rights as British subjects. Jews were among the first settlers in the western provinces. A synagogue appeared in Victoria, British Columbia, in the 1860s. Near the end of the century, a wave of Jewish immigrants arrived, followed by another wave after World War II. In contrast with the United States, most Jews in Canada are Orthodox, although there is a growing Conservative presence (Melton, 1996f). Today, there are 318,070 Jews in Canada (*Canadian Almanac Directory*, 1997).

Beliefs

Judaism is a monotheistic faith very much centered around the family and around God's history with his people. From the weekly Sabbath to the Passover, the home is the center for celebrations, and most of the holidays are oriented toward events in which Jews believe that God has involved himself in human life and history. The focus of Jewish life is to live in such a way that God is always remembered. Thus, an ethical life is essential. Part of those ethics may include keeping a kosher diet, which excludes certain foods or prohibits the mixing of certain foods. As one observes these restrictions, God's rule is constantly kept in view. The place in which the Jewish life is learned is the home.

Jews have great diversity. Most live on a continuum between the poles of *tradition* and *modernity*. A few, however, live outside this continuum, choosing to deal with one or the other of the poles exclusively. Those Jews who deal only with tradition are normally called Ultra-Orthodox. To this group belong those who have tended to freeze time, and who try to deal with tradition only. Many of them dress in the black clothing of 17th-century eastern Europe and may be classified as Mitnagdim (those who emphasize practice of the law) or the Hasidim (those who emphasize a mystical relationship with God through a mediator known as the Rebbe). Despite the apparent differences, their practices are essentially the same. Both prefer to live in isolation from the modern world.

On the other end of the spectrum are those Jews who have become assimilated into the national fabric, and who do not want to be identified as Jews. They are Canadians or Americans, and the religious life has become essentially meaningless to them. They deal only with the modern world. Most Jews, however, fall between these poles. Those who still try to keep all the commandments while living in the modern world are Modern Orthodox Jews. Those who see some commandments as time bound and thus not binding in the modern world, but still try to keep most commandments, are Conservative Jews. These will normally continue to keep the kosher laws and will observe the prayers and holidays. They will, however, drive to synagogue, and men and women will sit together for worship. Women may be counted in the minyan (10 adults required for prayer) and, in 1980, the Rabbinical Assembly of Conservative Judaism approved the ordination of women (Trepp, 1982). Lastly, those Jews who see much of tradition as no longer applying to today's world are known as Reform Jews. Kosher laws are often not observed, with the probable exception of not eating pork. Women have been ordained as rabbis since 1972. Services are mostly in the language of the people.

Binding the three major divisions of Judaism together are the major festivals. Unquestionably, the most important event in the Jewish liturgical cycle is the Sabbath. All that is required to celebrate it is a family or others gathered around a table with two loaves of bread, if available, and a cup of wine. Remembered are God's activities in the creation of the universe and his creative activity in bringing Israel into existence.

The cycle of annual festivals begins with Rosh Hashanah (New Year), when God enters his throne room to judge his people. There is a 10-day grace period, however, between Rosh Hashanah and Yom Kippur (the Day of Atonement) during which Jews examine their lives over the past year and seek forgiveness from God and their neighbors for acts done against them. Services in the synagogues stress the ability of human beings to repent. Yom Kippur is a day of fasting and prayer, by the end of which God's judgments for the coming year have been made. There is an emphasis in the synagogue services on God's goodness and mercy.

Five days after Yom Kippur is Succoth, or the Festival of Booths. It recalls God's goodness in leading the children of Israel through the wilderness. The last major festival is Passover, commemorating Israel's deliverance from Egypt. All of the above festivals center on the family and do not need a synagogue or a rabbi to celebrate them. Each reminds the Jewish people of who they are, giving unity and identity to them in the midst of a changing world.

Finally, all Jews are bound together by the written Torah—the first five books of what Jews call the Tanak and Christians call the Old Testament. The accounts of God's historical activities on behalf of Israel are found here, as are the laws by which the people of God should live. Here also, however, is the root of disunity among the branches of Judaism, for there is disagreement about what is essential in the law and what is not. The recent trend has been for the Reform Jews to become more conservative and for the Conservative Jews to move closer to their Orthodox brothers and sisters.

Islam

History in North America

Islam is a rapidly growing religion in the United States. The first Muslims arrived in the colonies as slaves in the 17th century, but they had no hope of practicing their religion. Most simply became absorbed into the Christian community. One of the first Muslims to leave his mark on the United States was a slave, Yarrow Mamout, who was freed in Washington, DC, in 1807. He remained in the country, becoming an early shareholder in the Columbia Bank. Another Muslim, Hajji Ali, who was nicknamed "Hi Jolly," came in 1856 to assist the United States Army develop camels for use by the cavalry in the southwest deserts. As with many of the eastern faiths, Islam received attention at the Parliament of the World's Religions in Chicago in 1893, when Mohammed Alexander Russell Webb, one of the first American converts to Islam, gave lectures on the faith (Eck, 1997c).

From that time, Islam has grown slowly but steadily in the United States. The first Muslim prayers of record occurred in Ross, North Dakota, among some Arab immigrants in 1900. A barometer of the spread of Islam can be seen in the construction of mosques. Albanian Muslims built mosques in Biddeford, Maine (1915), and Waterbury, Connecticut (1919). Other mosques appeared in Ross, North Dakota (1920), Brooklyn, New York (1922), Highland Park, Michigan (1923), Michigan City, Indiana (1925), Pittsburgh, Pennsylvania (1930), Cedar Rapids, Iowa (1934), Sacramento, California (1947), New York City, (1955, to serve the African American Muslim community), Detroit, Michigan (1963, the first Shi'ite mosque), and Quincy, Massachusetts (1964). Today, mosques continue to rise against the American horizon in all parts of the country. Other indications of the assimilation of Islam into American culture have been the rise of The Nation of Islam among African Americans (1933), the recognition of the right of persons in the military to identify themselves as Muslims (1952), President Eisenhower's dedication of the Islamic Center in Washington, DC (1957), and the offering of a Muslim prayer at the opening of the U.S. House of Representatives (1991; Eck, 1997c). In addition, Muslims now have active duty chaplains in the military. Thus, Islam is making a growing contribution to the American scene. There are approximately 4 million Muslims in the United States (Barrett & Johnson, 1998), and that number is steadily growing. The Muslim population is also growing in Canada, with the largest groups being in the major cities like Toronto and Montreal. To date, there are 253,260 Muslims in Canada (*Canadian Almanac Directory*, 1997).

Beliefs

Islam is a highly ethical faith which focuses on one God who gives commands by which human beings should live. Its simplicity and high moral standards have made it attractive to people ever since its inception. It is probably the fastest growing religion in the world today. It is clearly growing in the United States and Canada both through immigration of Muslims from other countries as well as through conversions to the faith. For many, institutional Christianity has not met their spiritual needs or their needs for clear standards in life. Islam does this as well as cutting across racial barriers. Many Blacks in the United States, who have been excluded by White Christianity, have found a refuge in Islam.

Islam focuses on what are called the Five Pillars, the defining principles for all Muslims. The first of these is the confession of faith (Shahada): "There is no God but Allah, and Muhammad is his messenger." Contained in this is the strong affirmation that there is only one God (Allah, which means "the God") who is self-existent, omnipotent, and omnipresent. Anything apart from God is created by him out of nothing. He communicates through prophets, angels, and the Qur'an, which is the incarnate Word of God, equivalent to Jesus Christ's place in Christianity. The person who delivered this book was Muhammad, God's messenger, and the Qur'an is his great miracle. Both Christianity and Judaism point beyond themselves to their fulfillment in Islam, according to Muslims. For example, Muhammad is the comforter of whom Jesus spoke in John 14:16; 15:26; and 16:7 (The Presidency of Islamic Researches, 1405 H/1969). The ultimate goal for the Muslim is to dwell as a resurrected being in the presence of Allah.

Prayer (Salat) is the second pillar. Muslims pray five times a day, but the prayers are more acts of praise than what the traditional Christian thinks of as prayer. However, the concept of personal prayer is very much a part of Islam, but it is called Du'a. Salat occurs just before sunrise, midday, mid-afternoon, sundown, and after dark. Before each of these times, a call to prayer is given, inviting people to come to God. These regular times of prayer have a wonderful way of reminding the worshipers who they are before God. Men are generally seen in the mosques, although women may go, but women will normally be found at the back or in an area separated from the men. Usually, though, women pray at home with the children, teaching them this central principle of the faith.

Almsgiving (Zakat) is the third pillar. This is a tax of differing amounts on various possessions which is dedicated to the poor and to the upkeep of the mosque. In addition, persons are expected to give to the poor in other ways (e.g., giving to beggars after Friday prayers). Essentially, Zakat is the community welfare program which sees that no one is without the essentials of life.

The fourth pillar is the fast during the month of Ramadan (Al Sawm), the month in which the angel Gabriel first appeared to the prophet Muhammad. Ramadan is much like Lent for Christians. It is a period of introspection and self-examination in which the spiritual aspects of life should be emphasized over the physical. Muslims fast for each of the 30 days during the daylight hours. This means that they are to have no food, drink, or sexual contact. After sundown, however, the fast may be broken, and extended families join together for meals. In addition, the poor are included.

The final pillar is the pilgrimage to Mecca (Hajj) which occurs in the last calendar month of the Islamic year. Since the Islamic calendar is lunar, it is not possible to locate either Ramadan or the Hajj on a western calendar. They move back through the year over time. The Hajj is a once in a lifetime requirement for all Muslims who are physically able to do it and who do not have to go into debt to accomplish it. In the experience of the Hajj, Muslims learn that their faith cuts across all racial and national barriers. Identity comes from participation in the community, and the pilgrimage is a life-changing religious experience for most. During the Hajj, they have stood before God and sought forgiveness and new life.

Native American Religions

The religions of the first Americans have been very diverse and very old in both the United States and Canada. They date back thousands of years. For a time, after the coming of migrants from the Old World, the native religions declined, but there seems to be a resurgence of them among the young both on and off the reservations. Native Americans may be found in most segments of society, but many still reside on reservations.

The word *diverse* would be a good description of Native American religions. There is no one binding element, but there are some common threads. Most believe in a supreme deity or force, but there may also be many other deities who are close to human kind. Usually, there are initiation ceremonies, and an almost universal symbol has been that of the pipe. The use of the latter binds people together. There are rituals which usually mark life passages—birth, adulthood, marriage, and death—as well as healing ceremonies. There is often a closeness to the land and the animals, with the distinction between human beings and the natural world being blurred. As with Islam or Judaism, there is a strong sense that identity comes from participation in the group, not from some innate identity in the individual. The Shaman or Medicine Man has filled the role of the psychotherapist, for it is he who deals with the world that is not accessible to the average person (Native American Religions, 1993).

EASTERN TRADITIONS

Hinduism

History in North America

There are reported to be approximately 910,000 Hindus in the United States and 157,010 in Canada (*Canadian Almanac Directory*, 1997). In the United States, Hindu influence was felt first through trade and literature before there was an actual Hindu presence in the country. Trade with India began in the 1780s and writers, such as Emerson and Thoreau, were influenced by such Hindu classics as the *Rig Veda* and the *Upanishads*. In 1851, however, a small group of Hindus marched with the East India Society in Salem, Massachusetts, in the Fourth of July parade. Hindu teachings were presented at the World's Parliament of Religion in 1893. Following the Parliament, Swami Vivekananda toured the United States and gave talks in Madison, Wisconsin; Minneapolis, Minnesota; Des Moines, Iowa; Detroit, Michigan; and Memphis, Tennessee. In 1894, the first Vedanta Society was founded in New York, with another established in San Francisco in 1899. Other Hindu teachers followed Vivekananda's example and taught in the United States. In 1906, the first major Hindu temple was built in San Francisco by the Vedanta Society. Hindu migration, as well as Asian migration as a whole, was brought to a halt by the Asian Exclusion Act of 1917, but this did not stop teachers such as Paramahansa Yogananda from touring and teaching. Yogananda founded the International Headquarters of the Self-Realization Fellowship in Los Angeles in 1925. The organization has attracted many Americans (Eck, 1997b).

The Immigration Act of 1965 lifted restrictions against Asian immigration and placed the Asian quotas on a par with those from other parts of the world. Thus, immigration from India grew, with many of the immigrants being well educated and affluent. With these people came the desire for temples, and Hindu temples now dot the United States in places like Pittsburgh, Pennsylvania; Flushing, Queens, New York; Troy, Michigan; Albany, New York; Houston, Texas; Calabasas, California; Chicago; Boston; and Middletown, Connecticut. Most of these were built between 1975 and 1979. Many others have been built since then. The most visible and well-known Hindu movement is that of the International Society for Krishna Consciousness, known to most Americans as the Hare Krishna movement. In a word, Hinduism is taking its place among the religions of America, and although the largest populations may still be on the West Coast, their presence is being felt all across the country (Eck, 1997b).

In Canada, Asian religions generally arrived first in British Columbia on the West Coast and then moved eastward. Most adherents of Asian religions in Canada reside in British Columbia or Ontario (Menendez, 1996).

Beliefs

The Hindu umbrella is exceptionally broad. It is possible to be a polytheist, a monotheist, or a nontheist and still be a Hindu. Thus, no simple explanation of Hinduism is possible. At best, we can look at the common principles that bind all forms together. All Hindus believe in reincarnation and the law of Karma. Karma is the law of cause and effect, but the effects of people's actions may not become manifest until a future life. Thus, persons are what they have created themselves to be. The Karma from all of their past lives, traveling on a transmigrating soul, dictates the content of their current lifetime. Until Karma is eliminated, persons will return on the rounds of rebirth.

There have been three historic ways in which persons may break the rounds. The first is the way of works. Persons simply live out to the best of their abilities the lot in life that they have created for themselves. They abide by their caste laws. Traditionally, this was the way of the lower castes, for the higher way—the way of knowledge—was only for those who had a spiritual propensity to gain release from the wheel of rebirth. These higher spiritual beings were the priests. The way of knowledge included studies of the idea that the universe is Brahman and that no person exists as a separate individual apart from Brahman. To believe otherwise is illusion. The illusion is broken through the enlightenment experience derived from meditation. When persons come to the existential realization that their individuality is illusory, they are assured of release. Both the way of knowledge and the way of works were "self-help" ways. Neither involved gods who could assist in a person's release.

The problem involved in the first two ways is that release appears to take forever. There is no immediate hope of release. Thus, the third way —the way of devotion—developed. Here, gods do help, particularly the gods Shiva and Vishnu with their female consorts and, in the case of Vishnu, his incarnations. By devotion to one of these deities, persons may gain assistance in finding release from the round of rebirths, thus providing much more immediate hope of achieving the ultimate goal. Virtually all Hindus practice some form of devotion, although they may tie it to living caste laws or a meditative and renunciant life. For most Hindus, release means immersion and loss of identity in the impersonal Brahman. This is Nirvana and is deliverance from the pains of illusion and unreality.

Buddhism

History in North America

Buddhism arrived in the United States with the Chinese who came to work on the railroads and in the mines. The first Buddhist temple was constructed in San Francisco's Chinatown in 1852, and by 1875, there were eight more temples. In 1882, the Chinese Exclusion Act was passed which banned any Chinese migration for 10 years. This diminished somewhat the spread of Buddhism. However, the World's Parliament of Religion served as a vehicle for making Americans aware of Buddhism, and one American, Charles T. Strauss of New York, became the first person on American soil to become a member of the Buddhist order (Eck, 1997a).

Japanese Buddhism entered the United States initially through Hawaii where the first Buddhist temple of the Jodo Shinshu lineage was built in 1889. By 1898, this devotional form of Buddhism had arrived in San Francisco and temples were built in Sacramento (1899), Fresno (1900), Seattle (1901), Oakland (1901), San Jose (1902), Portland (1903), and Stockton (1906). In 1944, the Jodo Shinshu Buddhists incorporated as the Buddhist Churches of America, and today have 60 temples and approximately 19,000 members (Eck, 1997a).

The form of Buddhism most attractive to Americans is Zen. The first Zen mission to Hawaii was established in 1913 to serve Japanese, and then moved on to Los Angeles in 1927 to serve Japanese and others attracted to Zen meditation. In 1961, the San Francisco Zen Center was established with other centers springing up around the country. In 1969, the first Tibetan Buddhist center was established in Berkeley, California, and other ethnic centers have been established as Koreans, Thais, Vietnamese, Laotians, Cambodians, and Burmese have migrated to the United States, especially in the years following the war in Southeast Asia. With them have come temples and centers in various parts of the United States, for example, Leeds, New York; North Hollywood, California; Boulder, Colorado; Germantown, Maryland; Woodstock, New York; Silver Spring, Maryland; Catlett, Virginia; Houston, Texas; Bolivia, North Carolina; Tacoma, Wasington; and Dade County, Florida (Eck, 1997a). As with Hinduism,

Buddhism is making inroads into the American religious scene. The Zen Buddhist form has proved particularly attractive to Americans, and there is growing interest in Tibetan Buddhism. There are today approximately 2 million Buddhists in the United States (Barrett & Johnson, 1998).

In Canada, the distribution of Buddhists is much like that of Hinduism. The Chinese came first to work and arrived on Canada's west coast. From there, they moved to other areas, most notably Ontario. There are approximately 163,415 Buddhists in Canada (*Canadian Almanac Directory*, 1997).

Beliefs

Because Buddhism arose out of Hinduism, Buddhists accept the concepts of Karma and reincarnation. They differ, however, in their understanding of the nature of the human being. Whereas in Hinduism there is a soul which transmigrates or moves from one life to the next, in Buddhism, there is no soul. Instead, a person is composed of five Skandhas— body, perceptions, feelings, reasoning, and the unconscious—which disintegrate at death. Thus, the Buddha's assertion that all things are transitory, including the constituent elements of human beings, is affirmed. However, at the time of one's next reincarnation, five new Skandhas are drawn together and "stamped" by one's Karma, thereby bringing the same person into existence once again, since Karma is absolutely individual.

The essence of the Buddha's enlightenment is captured in what is known as the Four Noble Truths. These state that life is suffering, that suffering is caused by desire, that suffering will cease when desire ceases, and that desire will cease by following the Eightfold Path. The Eightfold Path consists of elements dealing with correct understanding, morals, and concentration. In Theravada Buddhism, the form of Buddhism found in south Asia, release from the rounds of rebirth is achieved through progressive mastery of the steps on the Eightfold Path. Understanding and morals can be accomplished in the context of daily life, and these involve proper speech and sexual mores, nonviolence, no stealing, and an appropriate means of livelihood that does not involve injury to others. However, concentration, which contains the last three steps, can be accomplished only by withdrawing into a monastic way of life. As with the ways of works and knowledge in Hinduism, there are no gods to assist in the quest for release. Theravada Buddhism is nontheistic, and its goal is to gain Nirvana and "go beyond" the rounds of rebirth.

There are two other forms of Buddhism, however, that have many helping beings. The first is Mahayana Buddhism, which is found throughout Southeast and East Asia. Accessible to the practitioner through worship is assistance from heavenly enlightened beings, the most prominent of these being Amitabha or Amida, who is Lord of the Western Land, a heavenly paradise. The goal of the worshipper of Amida is to gain his presence through faith in him in order that the person may turn back from Nirvana and help others attain release from the wheel of rebirth also. This path is one of eternal help to others, and it is this form of Buddhism that has come to the United States and Canada with many Japanese Buddhists. Salvation in Amida's presence is attained through faith, and one's life should reflect what Amida would expect of those who worship him.

The second form is Vajrayana or Tibetan Buddhism, which is an extension of the Mahayana tradition. This form has been quite attractive in recent years in the United States. Like Mahayana, it has many Buddhas and Buddha figures who can assist practitioners off the round of rebirths. Added to Mahayana practices are the use of mantras (repeated mystical syllables or phrases), mudras (mystical hand positions), and sadhanas (visualizations) during meditation (Layman, 1976). Central to Tibetan practice is the presence of a teacher who passes on the esoteric knowledge of the tradition to students. Best known of Tibetan Buddhists is the Dalai Lama, the repeated incarnation of a heavenly Buddha figure known as Avalokitesvara.

Another form of Japanese Buddhism which is very popular in North America is the meditative tradition known as Zen. Although the devotional form is practiced primarily by Japanese, the Zen tradition has attracted practitioners all over the world. The goal is to seek enlightenment through the quieting of the mind, and the vehicle is sitting meditation (Zazen). Enlightenment is the realization that there are no distinctions between things and people, but all things are part of a great stream of life. There is no individuation, but rather all things are interrelated and integrated.

Sikhism

History in North America

The first Sikhs arrived in the United States in 1903. They came to work on the railroads, in lumber mills, and on bridges and tunnels. In 1907, approximately 500 lumberjacks in Bellingham, Washington, attacked about 250 Sikh mill workers, throwing their belongings into the streets and stealing valuables. Unfortunately, the press sympathized with the attackers. Because of the resistance experienced in the northwest, Sikh immigration between 1910 and 1920 shifted to California, where Sikhs, who were traditionally farmers, began to settle in the San Joachin and Imperial Valleys. In 1912, the first Gurdwara or Sikh temple was established in Stockton, California. Two laws hit the Sikh community very hard. The first was the Alien Land Law which prevented persons not eligible for U.S. citizenship from owning or leasing land. This was devastating, for many Sikhs were making their living from the land, either through leases or ownership. The second law was the Immigration Act of 1917, which prohibited any further immigration from India which was in a barred zone. In 1938, the India League of America was founded which fought for the restoration of Sikh rights to American citizenship. The Immigration Quota Bill of 1946 relieved the situation somewhat by allowing citizenship to Sikhs and an annual quota of 100 immigrants. By 1956, a Sikh, Dalip Singh Saund, had been elected to congress from California. As already noted, the 1965 Immigration Act opened the doors to Asian immigration, especially to those who had skills needed in the United States. Under this act, many Sikhs entered the country, but they were from professional classes, and thus distinctly different from those who had arrived early in the century. From these beginnings, Sikhs have now spread across the country. There are now approximately 350,000 Sikhs in the United States (Barrett & Johnson, 1998). The highest concentration is still in California, but large numbers now live in the New York/New Jersey area.

Sikh immigration to Canada began at about the same time it did in the United States with Sikhs hoping to find jobs. Their first point of contact was Vancouver. However, jobs were not available and opposition to the Sikhs existed in Canada as it did in the United States. In 1908, Canada closed the door to Sikh immigration (Singh, 1994). Thus, until 1947, little occurred in the Canadian Sikh community. Those few Sikhs living in the country adjusted to the Canadian lifestyle (Singh, 1994). In 1951, Canada modified its immigration policy toward Indians generally and established quotas for immigration. Sikhs took advantage of this and, as in the United States, it was the more professionally trained Sikhs who arrived. The climate in Canada had changed, and the racial discriminations that earlier Sikhs encountered had essentially vanished (Singh, 1994). Today, the largest Sikh concentrations are in Vancouver and in Toronto, with smaller concentrations in Montreal, Edmonton, Calgary, Regina, Saskatoon, and Winnipeg. According to Narindar Singh (1994), there are 300,000 Sikhs in Canada, but the Canadian Almanac Directory (1997) identifies only 147,440.

Beliefs

Like Buddhism, Sikhism is a product of India. Thus, it too includes the concepts of Karma and reincarnation, but it has a very "this worldly" orientation. For the Sikhs, reincarnation is a warning that persons may become less than they were created to be and that they should not prolong their time in the round of rebirths longer than necessary. The goal is to become one in this life with the one God, known as True Name. Hence, there is a mystical dimension to Sikhism. Every person contains a spark of the divine, and that spark should seek reintegration with God. The barrier to oneness with God is ego, which must be laid aside to discover our divine natures. If persons attain oneness with God in this life, that oneness will continue after death. Nirvana for Sikhs means to become absorbed into the very being of God.

Religion is for the purpose of making life better in this world. Ritual is not the essence of religion, although the Sikhs do have some rituals. Instead, service to humankind is the way to God. This is coupled with keeping company with spiritually minded persons and with meditation focused on God.

Sikhs who have reached a spiritual maturity and who seek to live religiously dedicated lives may be initiated into the Khalsa. The tenth Sikh Guru, Gobind Singh, established this group of Saint/Soldiers to defend the rights of all oppressed peoples, not of just Sikhs. He initiated, through a baptismal ritual, five men who had shown their willingness to die for the faith. He then gave them five marks which would set them apart from all other peoples. Men and women are equal and receive the same marks which are known as the five Ks. They are the Kesh (long uncut hair and beard), the Kanga (a comb that holds the hair in place), the Kachh (a pair of short under drawers), the Kara (a steel bracelet), and the Kirpan (a short dagger). Men and women both assume names as a sign of their membership in the Khalsa that become part of their birth names (i.e., men add Singh [lion] and women add Kaur [princess]).

The equality of men and women, the centrality of families, and the strength of faith exhibited by many Sikhs are impressive. Some Sikhs move away from the faith elements when they come to North America, but many more continue their traditions.

CONCLUSIONS

The United States and Canada are religiously diverse cultures. There have always been closer ties between the Canadian Christian churches and the government than there has been in the United States. Both countries are predominantly Christian, with Roman Catholicism being the largest religious group in both. However, more persons in the United States are involved in organized religious activities, such as weekly worship. Non-Christian religions are present in sizable numbers in both countries, and their patterns of activity parallel those of their Christian neighbors. Therapists, especially those in the larger cities of both countries, will undoubtedly find themselves confronted with non-Christian clients.

Similarities across religions can best be identified when east and west are separated from each other. As has been shown, commonalities among western traditions are that they are monotheistic, believe in a gracious God who gives commands by which life is regulated, believe God is personal and can be accessed through prayer, and believe that persons can live with this God in a life after death.

The Indian-based religions, by contrast, believe that Karma explains differences among people, that there is reincarnation, and that there may or may not be gods who can assist persons gain Nirvana. The concept of an afterlife is quite varied, being for some the extinction of individuality and for others the belief that individuality may be maintained in a place like the Western Land. In summary, the American religious scene is a tapestry of different ideas and cultures, all seeking to find meaning in human life.

REFERENCES

Barrett, D. B., & Johnson, T. M. (1998). Religion: World religious statistics. In *Encyclopedia Britannica book of the year*. Chicago: Encyclopedia Britannica, Inc.

Bibby, R. W. (1993). *Unknown gods: The ongoing story of religion in Canada*. Toronto, Canada: Stoddart.

Canadian almanac directory, 1997. (1997). Toronto, Canada: Copp Clark Professional.

Catechism of the Catholic Church. (1995). New York: Doubleday.

Eck, D. L. (Ed.). (1997a). Buddhism: U.S. timeline [CD-ROM]. In *On common ground: World religions in America*. New York: Columbia University Press.

Eck, D. L. (Ed.). (1997b). Hinduism: U.S. timeline [CD-ROM]. In *On common ground: World religions in America*. New York: Columbia University Press.

Eck, D. L. (Ed.). (1997c). Islam: U.S. timeline [CD-ROM]. In *On common ground: World religions in America*. New York: Columbia University Press.

Eck, D. L. (Ed.). (1997d). Judaism: U.S. timeline [CD-ROM]. In *On common ground: World religions in America*. New York: Columbia University Press.

Finke, R., & Stark, R. (1992). *The churching of America, 1776–1990: Winners and losers in our religious economy*. New Brunswick, NJ: Rutgers University Press.

Layman, E. M. (1976). *Buddhism in America*. Chicago: Nelson-Hall.

Melton, J. G. (1996a). The development of American religion: An interpretive view. In *Encyclopedia of American religions*. Detroit, MI: Gale Research.

Melton, J. G. (1996b). Eastern liturgical family. In *Encyclopedia of American religions*. Detroit, MI: Gale Research.

Melton, J. G. (1996c). *Encyclopedia of American religions*. Detroit, MI: Gale Research.

Melton, J. G. (1996d). Independent fundamentalist family. In *Encyclopedia of American religions*. Detroit, MI: Gale Research.

Melton, J. G. (1996e). Pentecostal family. In *Encyclopedia of American religions*. Detroit, MI: Gale Research.

Melton, J. G. (1996f). Religion in Canada: An historical survey, 1500 to the present. In *Encyclopedia of American religions*. Detroit, MI: Gale Research.

Melton, J. G. (1996g). Western liturgical family. In *Encyclopedia of American religions*. Detroit, MI: Gale Research.

Menendez, A. J. (1996). *Church and state in Canada*. Amherst, NY: Prometheus Books.

Native American religions. (1993). In R. C. Bush (Ed.), *The religious world: Communities of faith* (3rd ed.). New York: Macmillan.

Noll, M. A. (1992). *A history of Christianity in the United States and Canada*. Grand Rapids, MI: William B. Eerdmans.

The Presidency of Islamic Researches, IFTA, Call and Guidance. (1969). *The Holy Qur'an: English translation of the meanings and commentary*. The Custodian of the Two holy Mosques, King Fahd Complex for the printing of the Holy Quraan, 61:6, fn. 5438. (Original work published 1405 H)

Singh, N. (1994). *Canadian Sikhs: History, religion, and culture of Sikhs in North America*. Ottawa, Canada: Canadian Sikhs' Study Institute.

Trepp, L. (1982). *Judaism: Development and life* (3rd ed.). Belmont, CA: Wadsworth.

Wright, J. W. (Ed.). (1997). *The universal almanac, 1997*. Kansas City: Andrews & McMeel.

II

CHRISTIANITY

3

PSYCHOTHERAPY WITH ROMAN CATHOLICS

EDWARD P. SHAFRANSKE

A new spirit is alive in American Catholicism, and the 21st century belongs to it. The challenge of the future still remains the timeless question that people have wrestled with for 200 years: how the new generation of Catholics solves this riddle will determine the shape that American Catholicism will take in the years ahead.

—Jay P. Dolan

An examination of the religious landscape of America suggests a nation that is unparalleled in its diversity of spiritual expression and religious preference, affiliation, and practice (Hoge, 1996; Kosmin & Lachman, 1993). Roman Catholicism, which is the largest denomination in the United States, reflects a diverse membership (Bedell, 1996; Davidson et al., 1997; Roof & McKinney, 1987; Wright, 1994). It is a challenge to develop an inclusive understanding of the dimension of faith as practiced by the lives of over 60,000,000 Catholic Americans (Bedell, 1996). However, this wide variance is faced every day by clinicians when assessing the role of religious belief, affiliation, and practice in the lives of individual clients and particularly in understanding the influence of faith on the processes and outcomes of psychological treatment. Psychologists are nevertheless ethically compelled to develop an appreciation of the religious dimension as a feature of diversity (American Psychological Association, 1992). This chapter provides a context through which such an appreciation of the role of religion in the lives of Roman Catholic clients may be obtained. This will not be accomplished through the provision of a stereotype of a typical Catholic for it is a myth to consider the Catholic population to be homogeneous or to assert that there are distinctive characteristics that are universally held. This chapter provides multiple avenues to consider in developing an understanding of the influence of religion.

AMERICAN CATHOLICISM: A HISTORICAL OVERVIEW

An inspection of Catholicism in America reveals the complex interrelationships among culture, ethnicity, and religiosity. An appreciation of Catholicism's history in America and of the functions that the Church has provided furnishes a backdrop upon which to understand contemporary trends and tensions. It is important to keep in mind that American Catholicism does not exist as a separate institution; rather, it participates in the Universal Church. Catholicism, in both Roman Catholicism and in the Orthodox Church, finds its origins in the earliest expression of Christianity founded by Jesus Christ (see chapter 2). With the Edict of Milan in 313, Catholicism was accepted within the Roman Empire and became the "universal religion of the Mediterranean" (Weaver, 1988, p. 154). Its contribution to the social, religious, moral, and political fabric of Western civilization is unquestioned. Roman Catholicism shaped the consciousness of countless generations and established a canon of fundamental beliefs that it sustains to this day.

The Roman Catholic Church in America, grounded in the theological understanding of its inclusion in the mystical body of Christ and existing within a larger international and transgenerational institutional setting, influences and is influenced by the universal Church. A comprehensive discussion of the history of American Catholicism is beyond the scope of this chapter and will be necessarily limited. Three areas will be examined: the parish and the immigrant church, the parish and Catholic identity, and Vatican II and the reshaping of Catholicism.

The Parish and the Immigrant Church

Catholicism has and continues to serve a vital role in acculturation as "the immigrant Church" (Dolan, 1992, pp. 127–157). Coming to a new land, facing prejudice in a Protestant country, unfamiliar with the language and the customs, these immigrant groups migrated to both urban centers and rural locales. The parish became the focal point of the neighborhood, and religion served as the crucial bridge between the old and new worlds of experience. Religious observances and devotions offered in the parish expressed the distinctive sacramental life of Catholicism and provided a means of solidifying the immigrant parish.

During the hundred-year period commencing in 1820, over 33.6 million immigrants landed on the shores of America. Dolan (1992, p. 135) reported that "six groups—the Irish, Germans, Polish, Italians, French Canadians, and Mexicans—were the largest Catholic communities in the United States [and], [u]sing the 1916 religious census as an indicator, accounted for at least 75% of the American Catholic population." In many locales, national parishes were established to serve the needs of specific ethnic groups. "By organizing their own national parishes, immigrant Catholics hoped to hear sermons in their mother tongue, practice the devotions and customs of the old country, and raise their children in the faith of their fathers and mothers" (Dolan, 1992, p. 162). As the catalyzing force of the community, the parish served many of the needs of the neighborhood and belonged to its people. The laity were actively involved in the organization and governance of the parish and preserved a high degree of autonomy in managing its religious, social, and economic affairs. The immigrant parish served as a way station in the early phase of the process of acculturation. As individual immigrants became better assimilated into American life, developed proficiency in English, and gained in economic status, they would look beyond the immigrant neighborhood and national parish. The parish, whether defined primarily by territory or ethnicity, continued to provide stability and identity within the neighborhood and offered recent immigrants a solid footing to begin the process of assimilation.

The importance of the Catholic parish during this period cannot be overstated. We may conjecture that religion provided a buffer against the psychological stress that immigration posed and was essential in "the conservation of significance" (Pargament, 1997), which is crucial to coping. Within this context, a parochialism was established in which the tenets and practices of the faithful and affiliation to the Church were fostered and maintained even as the model of the national parish waned in the early 1920s (following a freeze on the establishment of new national churches imposed by Canon Law) and parishes reflected greater ethnic and, at times, social and economic diversity (Linkh, 1975, p. 108).

The Parish and Catholic Identity

The parish occupied a central position as Catholics continued the process of assimilation and faced both overt and subtle discrimination and oppression. Although spirituality was the primary focus of the parish, a number of psychosocial functions were provided, including many forms of assistance, education, and the creation of a sustaining economic and social community. In light of the multiple functions that the Catholic parish uniquely fulfills, priest–sociologist Andrew Greeley (1990) concluded that "the American neighborhood parish is one of the most ingenious communities that human skill has ever created" (p. 154).

The spiritual and sacramental life was supported through parish missions, and the publication of prayer books and devotional guides in the

19th century sustained the uniqueness of Catholicism within Protestant America. Sunday observance and reception of the sacraments expressed the faith of the Catholic community. Although serving a host of the congregation's need, spiritual life was the focus of the parish and remains so to this day.

The influence of the clergy in American Roman Catholicism was gradually bolstered within the 19th century as a clerical model superseded a congregational model in parish life. The authority of the clergy was readily accepted within the Irish Catholic community from which the majority of American bishops was drawn (Linkh, 1975) and paralleled a move toward increased centralization of authority in Rome. This was punctuated in 1870 at the First Vatican Council when the doctrine of the infallibility of the Pope was proclaimed. Anti-Catholic prejudice, in addition to class stratification, contributed to the perpetuation of a parochial culture in which American Catholics married other Catholics, as well as established youth groups and fraternal organizations, professional societies, magazines, and other publications. Following the Third Plenary Council of Baltimore in 1884, the hierarchy of the American Church sought uniformity in organization, belief, practice, and governance (Williams, 1988).

Sacramental life and religious tradition were sustained within the parish through parochial education. The building of secondary schools and Catholic colleges was in response, in part, to anti-Catholic sentiment and was one remedy to the problems that Catholics faced because of prejudice and exclusion. The development of Catholic institutions of higher education extended the sectarian socialization process into early adult years and fostered the maintenance of a "Catholic identity." In addition, the development of the Catholic educational system advanced the cause of standardization, reinforced views of faith and morals, and maintained the separation between Catholics and non-Catholics. American Catholicism, born out of its immigrant roots, provided a unified worldview and established a pattern of segregation in which Catholicism became a defining feature of personal identity.

With increased educational opportunities and advances in socioeconomic status, Catholics in post–World War II America entered into each strata of society. The election of John F. Kennedy as President of the United States symbolically marked what some viewed as the progress of Catholics to participate more fully in the mainstream of American culture. The Catholic American family and milieu were changing as well. They were becoming smaller, which contributed in part to fewer religious vocations. The reduction in vocations changed the demographics of personnel within Catholic education as well as initiated what would become significant changes in the staffing and roles within parishes. More important, the 1960s brought a decisive event in the history of Roman Catholicism—the convening of the Second Vatican Council—which to this day continues to reshape Catholicism throughout the world.

Vatican II and the Reshaping of Catholicism

Vatican II (1962–1965) was convened by Pope John XXIII in the spirit of *aggiornamento*, or bringing the church up to date. It inaugurated a radical reexamination of all areas of the life of the Universal Church. Within its 16 documents, the synod reshaped the fundamental orientation of the Church in the world, promoting greater ecumenism, collegiality within the structure of the Church, and increased participation of the laity in the leadership of the Church. A number of liturgical changes were instituted that struck at the heart of the sacramental life of the Church. The Latin (Tridentine) Mass at which the priest faced the altar was changed; the Eucharist was now offered in the vernacular of the congregation and the priest faced the people. A number of liturgical innovations were introduced within each of the sacraments, including, for example, the form in which the Sacrament of Penance was offered. Confession, which had been conducted with ritual piety and within the anonymous confines of a confessional box, was modified to allow the penitent to face the priest confessor directly, at the discretion of the penitent. Although there was no change in the essential spiritual elements, the new form of the sacrament conveyed and involved a different kind of relationship between the church and the penitent, between the priest and the parishioner. Indeed, as Dolan (1992, p. 425) observed, "The Second Vatican Council ushered in a new era for Roman Catholics. The age of Tridentine Catholicism had come to an end, and a new Catholicism came to life . . . [Vatican II] changed the way Catholics prayed. . . . Gone was the juridical, institutional image of the church, and in its place was a more biblical understanding first captured in the concept of the mystical body of Christ and developed further by the notion of the church as the people of God." Ecumenism and the declaration of religious freedom, as well as the evidence of change in the church, contributed to a newfound belief in personal religious and moral authority and the politics of dissent.

For Americans, these changes in the universal Church paralleled and contributed to the challenges of the civil rights movement and to what was a decade of questioning and protest of institutional and governmental authority coalescing around the Vietnam War. Many leaders within the Catholic Church contributed to the debates concerning the war and advocated civil rights and social justice. Within this period, ecclesiastical authority was questioned and, seemingly, a division was cleaved between pre-Vatican II structures, beliefs, and authority and an emerging post-Vatican II church. These changes were not universally applauded: For some, Vatican II set the stage for confusion and disaffection among some

Catholics. James Hitchcock (as cited in Gleason, 1987, p. 154) observed that virtually all Catholics had experienced "a weakening of belief—a loss of certitude, a diminution of joy and serenity, an unaccustomed cynicism and vague spiritual malaise, an embarrassment about expressing beliefs." For others, these were welcome changes in which their faith was reinvigorated and brought a renewal within the Catholic community. The effects of Vatican II reverberate throughout the Church today and will reach into every aspect of American Catholicism in the new millennium.

This brief examination of the history of American Catholicism leads to the observation of three distinct threads that weave the character of the contemporary church. The first concerns immigration; the second, the development and maintenance of Catholic identity within America; and the third, the ongoing application of Vatican II. In the first instance, America is experiencing a second wave of immigration, primarily from Mexico and secondarily from Asia. The church plays a similar role to that found in history in providing a touchstone of continuity with the past as well as a bridge to the future. The role of immigration is significant in light of its impact on the growth in the Church (Hoge, 1996) and its effect on the life of many parishes. To illustrate, Hispanics are among one of the fastest-growing segments of the population because of immigration (Moore, 1992, p. 6). They make up a significant demographic group in a number of major cities, for example, 40% of Los Angeles's 1990 population was Latino (p. 12). Through population forecasting, it is clear that the Hispanic population will significantly impact the character of American Catholicism, and the Church will face significant challenges in serving both immigrant and established populations.

The second aspect concerns the uniqueness of Catholicism within Christian religious traditions. Perhaps more than any other Christian denomination, the Catholic Church places as much emphasis on being Catholic as it does on being Christian. The ability of the parish to provide many functions, from the sacramental to the psychosocial, and to provide a foundation for Catholic identity is a significant present and future challenge. The third strand concerns the tension that exists for some Catholics in participating in the life of the Church which includes elements of both pre- and post-Vatican II and must accommodate the spiritual needs and traditions of an increasingly diverse community of the faithful.

TENETS, PRACTICES, AND MORAL PRESCRIPTIONS AND PROSCRIPTIONS

Roman Catholicism is distinctive among Christian religions in its Petrine ministry, which reflects the succession from St. Peter through the pope as Bishop of Rome. Roman Catholicism in America is in union with the pope and the Universal Church. The teaching authority of the Church may initially appear to be situated hierarchically; however, closer inspection suggests that this view is limited and inaccurate. The teaching authority belongs to the whole Church; although in a more restricted sense, authority for official teaching comes through recognized scholarly competence or by office, as in the case of the pope and other bishops (cf. McBrien, 1994, pp. 65–66). In considering the tenets, practices, and moral perspective within Catholicism, it is important to acknowledge the dialogue within the Church that embodies its teaching mission.[1]

The locus of Catholic faith is the belief that the Word of God is made flesh, and that Jesus becomes 'the sacrament of the encounter with God'—the material reality through which one meets the invisible God. As one approaches God through Christ, one approaches Christ through the Church, which becomes, by extension, the sacrament of the encounter with Christ: participation in divine life (grace) is mediated to Catholics by Christ and by the Church" (Weaver, 1988, p. 154). The Church claims its essential role in the faithful's relationship with God and through participation in the sacramental life of the Church forms the foundation of that relationship. For Catholics, participation in the Church takes on heightened significance.

Following the Protestant reformation, the Church clarified matters of faith and defined Catholic dogma at the Council of Trent (1545–1563). The authority of the Church was further sustained when Vatican I (1869–1870) located increased authority in the papacy and proclaimed the doctrine of papal infallibility. The authority of the entire ecclesiastical structure was bolstered through this event and reaffirmed in America at the Third Baltimore Council in 1884 (Dolan, 1992, pp. 222–223). These distinctive features of Catholicism—sacramental life as the primary means to relate to God and the authority of the church in matters of faith—established the irreducible relationship between the faithful and its church. Unlike some Protestant traditions in which "one's personal relationship with Jesus Christ" takes precedence at times over institutional affiliation, Catholicism provides a context in which a seamless bond between the relationship with God and participation in life of the church is established.

Vatican II (1962–1965) sought renewal of the Church and, like previous councils, established the official articulation of the tenets of Roman Catholicism. Vatican II maintained the authority of the pope and the bishops, however, emphasized that this authority was exercised as a service to the church and in the spirit of collegiality. Following Vatican II, a *Cate-*

---

[1] A wide range of commentary exists in the Roman Catholic community concerning matters of faith and morality. Presentation of this theological discourse is beyond the scope of this chapter. Discussion has been limited to a brief presentation of selected aspects of teachings drawn directly from the *Catechism of the Catholic Church* and does not include presentation of the wider theological and pastoral discourse.

chism of the Catholic Church (1994) was produced to answer the need for a compendium or a reference text of Catholic dogma. This need had been previously met in America by the *Baltimore Catechism* (McGuire, 1961). Unlike previously published catechisms, which used a simple question-and-answer format, such as, "Who made us? God made us," the new catechism is intended for the universal church and provides a scriptural and theological commentary regarding each tenet of faith.

Tenets

A comprehensive presentation and exegesis of the tenets of Catholic faith is beyond the scope of this discussion. What is presented reflects official teachings culled from the *Catechism*. This approach provides an initial and limited orientation to Catholic teachings. Scholarship, tradition, and ongoing dialogue and individual discernment of fundamental beliefs inform the faith of Catholics. Clinicians should be aware that a diversity of perspectives exist within the Catholic community.

Fundamental to Catholicism is the view that the person is created in God's image and is called to know and love him. It is through "openness to truth and beauty, his sense of moral goodness, his freedom and the voice of his conscience, with his longings for the infinite and for happiness, [that] man questions himself about God's existence. In all this he discerns signs of his spiritual soul . . . 'the seed of eternity we bear in ourselves, irreducible to the merely material' . . . [which] has its origin only in God. . . . [I]n different ways, man can come to know that there exists a reality which is the first cause and final end of all things, a reality 'that everyone calls 'God'" (*Catechism*, 1994, p. 15). Knowledge of God can be known by reason and is revealed by God's deeds and words (Sacred Scripture), and through the living transmission of tradition, accomplished in the Holy Spirit through the church preserved in the continuous line of succession. This conveys the integral relationship among God, Jesus Christ, Sacred Scripture, and the life of the Holy Spirit within the Church. For Catholics, each aspect is integral to their relationship to God; this both reflects the nature of God as Trinity, three persons in one God as Father, Son, and Holy Spirit, and emphasizes the importance of the Church. Catholics identify participation in the life of the Church as integral to their relationship with God. This is crucial in understanding the gravity that conflict with the church holds for Catholics when questioning fundamental beliefs, determining personal morality, and affiliating with the church.

The corpus of Catholic dogma is found in the Apostles' Creed, which constitutes "the oldest Roman catechism" (*Catechism*, 1994, p. 53), and the Nicene Creed, which draws from the first two ecumenical councils. Exhibit 3.1 presents the Credo, which provides the structure for the Catechism.

The majority of these tenets is shared with other Christian traditions; however, there are unique features to the interpretation of these beliefs

EXHIBIT 3.1
The Credo

The Apostles' Creed	The Nicene Creed

I believe in God,
  the Father almighty,
  creator of heaven and earth.
	We believe in one God,
	  the Father, the Almighty,
	  Maker of heaven and earth,
	  of all that is, seen and unseen.

I believe in Jesus Christ,
  His only Son, our Lord.
	We believe in one Lord,
	    Jesus Christ,
	    the only Son of God
	    eternally begotten of the Father
	    God from God, Light from Light,
	    true God from true God,
	    begotten, not made, one in
	    Being with the Father.
	    Through him all things were made.
	    For us men and for our salvation.
	    he came down from heaven:

He was conceived by the
  power of the Holy Spirit
    and born of the Virgin Mary.
	By the power of the Holy Spirit
	  he was born of the Virgin Mary,
	  and became man.

He suffered under Pontius Pilate,
  Was crucified, died, and was
  Buried.
He descended into hell.
	For our sake he was crucified
	  under Pontius Pilate;
	  he suffered, died, and was buried.

On the third day, he rose again.	On the third day he rose again in fulfillment of the Scriptures;

He ascended into heaven
  and is seated at the right
  hand of the Father.
  He will come again to judge
  the living and the dead.
	he ascended into heaven
	  and is seated at the right
	  hand of the Father.
	  He will come again in glory
	  To judge the living and the dead,
	  and his kingdom will have no end.

I believe in the Holy Spirit
  the holy catholic Church,
  the communion of saints,
  the forgiveness of sins,
  the resurrection of the body,
  and the life everlasting.
  Amen.
	We believe in the Holy Spirit,
	  the Lord, the giver of life,
	  who proceeds from the
	  Father and the Son.
	  With the Father and the Son
	  he is worshipped and glorified.
	  He has spoken through the
	  Prophets.
	  We believe in one holy
	  catholic and apostolic Church.
	  We acknowledge one
	  baptism for the forgiveness of sins.
	We look for the resurrection
	  of the dead,
	  and the life of the world to
	  come. Amen.

within Catholicism. The following examples illustrate both the crises of faith and potential sources of values and strength that may emerge as Catholics consider their tenets of faith within a pluralistic culture. The first concerns faith in one God. There is no provision for holding multiple constructions of the sacred—all manifestations are conceived within one God; furthermore, one is called to trust God in every circumstance. It is not uncommon for persons to experience a crisis in faith and anxiety when first exposed to the diversity of religious expression. Adolescents, as well as adults, may seek consultation when they address challenges to a once secure and unitary worldview. Furthermore, Catholics may be uneasy in seeking psychological treatment to deal with conflict or loss in light of the faith perspective that it is sufficient to trust in God's providence. Seeking professional consultation may appear to express doubt in God or a lapse in faith.

The incarnation of Jesus Christ constitutes the fundamental perspective in Catholic faith, and the resurrection of Jesus is a pivotal belief, which Catholics hold sacred. Roman Catholicism believes that "the Father's power 'raised up' Christ his Son and by doing so perfectly introduced his Son's humanity, including his body, into the Trinity. Jesus is conclusively revealed as 'Son of God in power according to the Spirit of holiness by his Resurrection from the dead'" (Catechism, 1994, p. 169). The power of this belief cannot be underestimated in its role in shaping a consciousness of salvation and internalizing a model of emancipation from suffering and death by hope through resurrection. The suffering and death of Christ, including His suffering at Gethsemane, for many Catholics provide a meaningful context for enduring moments of suffering and doubt and constructing meaning based on the promise of salvation.

Catholicism holds special reverence for Mary as seen in the widely recited "Hail Mary." The belief that the Holy Spirit conceived Jesus and that Mary remained chaste promotes a unique piety and some suggest an important view of female sexuality. Mary days, and other Marian devotions, such as those to Our Lady of Guadeloupe within the Mexican culture, express the unique place that Mary holds within the Catholic tradition. Prayers and intercessions to Mary as well as identification with her suffering and example (and that of saints) have provided many Catholics with sustenance during times of distress.

Practices

Religious practices include sacraments, prayer, and devotions. Catholicism is a sacramental religion and holds that encounters with God occur through the Eucharist and other sacramental actions in which the divine presence is available through concrete, visible, historical events or things (cf. Weaver, 1988, pp. 153–154). The Eucharist is the defining experience in Catholicism in which Jesus Christ is present under the appearances of bread and wine when consecrated by a validly ordained priest. Sacraments provide unique experiences of God's presence and blessing upon the recipient and mark significant events (e.g., baptism, marriage, etc.) in the life of the Catholic within the Christian community. Affiliation with and participation in the sacramental life of the Church weighs significantly in the spirituality of most devout Catholics.

Prayer is deemed an essential aspect in the spiritual life. Prayer may be offered in community or may be private and individual; it may take a specific form or may be a spontaneous expression. Forms of prayer include blessing and adoration, petition, intercession, thanksgiving, and praise. Prayer may take a devotional form as it does when one prays the rosary. It may include universally known prayers that convey a theological understanding as well as devotion and are commonly taught in religious education, such as the "Our Father." The Spiritual Exercises of St. Ignatius, ascetical discipline, and meditation practices involve religious aspects that reflect the mystical or contemplative traditions within Catholicism.

Devotions are forms of prayer and expressions of piety that often evolve out of distinct ethnic and cultural milieus. Devotions are sanctioned and supported by the local church and reflect significant ties to the cultural heritage of the past. For example, Hispanic devotional piety includes features of *religiosidad popular* and emphasizes "the simple faith of Latin American people—a people's Catholicism as opposed to the more formally structured hierarchical Catholicism" (Romero, 1991, p. 16). Embedded in these traditions one finds a rich cultural history, often expressing themes of salvation within circumstances of adversity. Devotions, such as those to Our Lady of Guadeloupe, memorialize particular moments of faith in the life of the community and sustain a continuity of the indigenous faith tradition. Traditions such as the Quinceanera in Hispanic culture, which acknowledges a young woman's capacity for motherhood, celebrates a developmental milestone through a blending of religious and secular rituals (Romero, 1991, pp. 71–82). Catholicism, in contrast with some Christian religions, places considerable emphasis on sacramental and devotional participation. The importance of participation within the parish community and affiliation with the institutional church may be understood in light of this feature of faith.

Moral Prescriptions and Proscriptions

Catholic moral teaching includes the authority of the church through its *magisterium*, the divinely empowered teaching authority of the church, and the "right to the exercise of freedom, especially in moral and religious matters [as] an inalienable requirement of the dignity of the human person" (*Catechism*, 1994, p. 431). "Human acts, that is, acts that are freely chosen in consequence of a judgment of conscience, can be morally evaluated ... the morality of human acts depends on: the object chosen, the end in view or the intention, and the circumstances of the action" (*Catechism*, 1994, p. 433). Conscience includes the perception of the principles of morality, their application in the given circumstances, and final judgment about the acts committed. Conscience requires *interiority*, the ability to be present to oneself. Ultimately, moral conscience is conceived as:

> Deep within his conscience man discovers a law which he has not laid upon himself but which he must obey. Its voice, ever calling him to love and to do what is good and to avoid evil, sounds in his heart at the right moment. . . . For man has in his heart a law inscribed by God. . . . His conscience is man's secret core and his sanctuary. There he is alone with God whose voice echoes in his depths. (*Catechism*, 1994, p. 438)

These excerpts illustrate the emphasis that is placed on personal freedom and responsibility. Scrupulosity and blind obedience, absent free will, do not, in the eyes of the Church, express maturity in moral character. Considering Catholic moral teaching, it is important to note the *aspirational* tenor in which prescriptions and proscriptions are offered. Persons are *called* to live a moral life. The reality of Original Sin draws into reference the human situation in which the capacity to decide in favor of salvation may be weak and yet every person is offered grace and salvation through Jesus Christ (McBrien, 1994, pp. 184–199).

The moral teachings of the church are based on the proscriptions of the Ten Commandments, the prescriptions expressed in the Beatitudes, and an understanding of natural law. In addition, the church has asserted explicit moral positions on issues of sexual and reproductive ethics as well as promulgated social teachings that concern the morality of social, economic, and political conditions. In the first regard, the church holds that premarital sex, artificial birth control, abortion, and homosexual activity are ethically wrong. The full expression of sexuality is found within the sacrament of marriage, as a holy union, and as such sexual relations outside of marriage are considered sinful. The church's position on sexual ethics is based on natural law and is derived historically from St. Augustine, who anchored sexuality to procreation, and St. Thomas Aquinas, who allowed for pleasure governed by reason. These positions strongly influenced attitudes toward sexuality in general and established prescriptions concerning masturbation and sexual behavior outside of marriage. Homosexuality as a feature of the self or sexual orientation is not inherently sinful; however, homosexual acts are considered to be "intrinsically disordered" and "[h]omosexual persons [like heterosexual persons] are called to chastity" (*Catechism*, 1994, p. 566). This position is not without its critics within the Catholic theological community who contend that "homosexuals have the same rights to love, intimacy, and relationships as heterosexuals" (cited in Fox, 1995, p. 143).

Marriage is sanctified as a holy union that is joined under conditions of freedom and not impeded by any natural or ecclesiastical law. Civil divorce is not sufficient to allow Catholics to marry again; however, the Church grants annulments in circumstances in which the condition of freedom was not in effect when the marriage was blessed. A tribunal, sometimes referred to as the Marriage Tribunal within a diocese, hears evidence under Canon Law of the circumstances of the marital commitment. Once a rarity in the Church, annulments are now granted more frequently; however, the circumstances under which they are granted remain stringent. Persons suffering from mental illness or impaired by alcoholism are examples in which the sufficient conditions to enter into the sacrament were not met and situations in which an annulment would most likely be granted (Young & Griffith, 1991). Ethics concerning procreation are established on principles derived from natural law. Artificial means of birth control as well as fertilization techniques that "entail the dissociation of husband and wife," such as, heterologous artificial insemination, are considered gravely immoral. "Techniques involving only the married couple (homologous artificial insemination and fertilization) are perhaps less reprehensible, yet remain morally unacceptable" (Catechism, 1994, p. 571). Abortion constitutes a grave offense that results in excommunication and is contrary to Roman Catholicism's unwavering position that "From the first moment of his existence [i.e., moment of conception], a human being must be recognized as having the rights of a person—among which is the inviolable right of every innocent being to life" (Catechism, 1994, p. 547). These are issues which may be of clinical significance for couples experiencing marital conflicts in which personal beliefs and morality are concerned.

Church teaching prescribes temperance rather than abstinence regarding the use of alcohol, tobacco, and medicine and considers the use of illegal drugs a grave offense. Any form of direct euthanasia is considered morally unacceptable, as is suicide. "Discontinuing medical procedures that are burdensome, dangerous, extraordinary, or disproportionate to the expected outcome can be legitimate; it is the refusal of 'over-zealous' treatment" (Catechism, 1994, p. 549). Encyclicals and pastoral letters authored over the last century have called for the equitable distribution of economic resources, social justice, access to political power, and the pursuit of peace (Davidson et al., 1997, pp. 48–49). Ultimately, moral decision making resides within the integrity of the person, informed by the church and under the condition of openness to the voice of God.

DEMOGRAPHICS OF FAITH, BELIEF, AND PRACTICE

Roman Catholicism is the largest religious denomination in the United States. As in the past, its population is increasing largely because of immigration; the largest contingent of immigrants is Hispanic, residing mostly in the Southwest. Beyond the sheer number of Catholics in America, there are important trends in the faith and practices within the church. Hoge (1996, pp. 36–37) concluded "[a] substantial proportion of laity does not agree with the Church's unchanging positions on the ordination of women, divorce, premarital sex, and birth control." Studies by D'Antonio, Davidson, Hoge, and Wallace (1996) and Davidson et al. (1997) found a clear demarcation among pre-Vatican II, Vatican II, and post-Vatican II Catholics (see also Greeley, 1990, and Gallup & Castelli, 1987). The oldest cohort was born before 1940, the middle generation between 1940 and 1960, and the younger generation after 1960. The era of the 1960s, which included Vatican II, appears to be the locus of a sea change of religious and moral sentiment. These cohorts also differed in socioeconomic status: Pre-Vatican II Catholics were first- or second-generation immigrants, were less educated, and were still in the formative stage of assimilation; the second cohort was upwardly mobile, enjoyed the opportunities of higher education, and attained full membership into the mainstream of American culture; and the third cohort was raised with full assimilation with marginal ties to the ethos of the pre-Vatican II generation.

Survey and interview data consistently find that pre-Vatican II parishioners locate their faith with the institutional church; participation in the church, its beliefs, and sacramental life constitutes their relationship with God. This religious orientation diminishes in the later cohorts. Davidson et al. (1997) found "a linear trend away from conventional religious sensibilities, with the youngest Catholics being least inclined to maintain traditional faith and morals. This trend is especially apparent with regard to traditional beliefs and practices, the sexual and reproductive norms, and recent ideas. On each of these three indices, we see a general decline in acceptance of church teachings and traditional Catholic practices" (p. 137). The often seen incongruence in faith and morals between generations may predispose Catholics to familial conflict as well as to alienation from the institutional church.

However, Davidson et al.'s (1997) study identified a core set of beliefs that are transgenerationally held, suggesting a corpus of faith within the Catholic community. These "pan-Vatican II" beliefs reflect the faith statements articulated in the Creed presented in Exhibit 3.1 and include ideas such as the Incarnation and the Resurrection. The survey literature suggests a core set of beliefs that are points of commonality within the Catholic community as well as widening diversity, particularly in matters of morality and forms of identification and participation in the Church. This later trend suggests a decline in institutional allegiance and may reflect the consequence of assimilation into the mainstream of American culture and exposure to the multiplicity of faith perspectives. Increasing plurality within the Catholic community is likely to result in further erosion in institutional authority or a countertrend may occur in which the faith is sustained.

THE ORGANIZATION OF THE CHURCH

A diocese, led by a bishop who is appointed by the Pope, is organized into neighborhood parishes. Cardinals are members of the College of Cardinals that bears the responsibility of selecting the Pope. Priests are ordained following seminary training and serve within a specific diocese or are members of a religious order, such as Society of Jesus (Jesuits), Franciscans, and Benedictines. Religious orders were established according to specific charisms (gifts of the Holy Spirit) and fulfill particular apostolic works within the church; some are within the monastic, contemplative tradition (e.g., Trappists) and others perform missionary work (e.g., Maryknoll). Diocesan priests serve within parishes and sustain the spiritual life in the local community. In addition to priests, religious orders often include brothers who take vows and are involved in specialized ministries but do not perform all of the sacramental functions of a priest (such as hearing confession). Women take vows as religious, known as sisters or nuns, within specific congregations (e.g., Sisters of Charity, Maryknoll). Each religious order has a distinctive spiritual life and ministry. In recent times, the permanent deaconate has been reestablished in which married and single men are ordained as deacons and serve a number of ministries within a parish. Deacons may serve the church full time or may perform these responsibilities while being employed in a secular occupation.

Diocesan priests typically live within a rectory serving a specific parish. Historically, a pastor, who was assisted by one to two associate pastors, lead the parishes. Pastors serve a number of years and at times are granted life appointments. Associates are assigned for a few years depending on the guidelines of the diocese. Parish administration ranges from very hierarchical in which the pastor dictates all matters of parish and rectory life to shared ministry in which a consensual leadership model determines roles and responsibilities. Priests, brothers, and sisters in religious orders live in a community. Community residences in the past were large; however, with declining vocations and specialization within ministry, communities may be as small as 2–3 religious living together, often in secular housing.

Vatican II placed particular emphasis on the church as the people of God. In keeping with this perspective, the laity took on new significance as members of the universal Church and local faith community. Parish councils have been established in which administrative leadership includes the laity as well as the clergy. In addition, the role of the laity has expanded to include the distribution of the Eucharist and performing many of the catechetical functions within the parish. The role of women in the church is for many a source of conflict. The limitations placed on ministry and leadership within the church along gender lines maintain an inequality that many consider sexist and offensive. In a recent study of conservative and liberal Catholic women, 79% reported dissatisfaction with women's roles in the institutional church, and 62.1% were personally dissatisfied as women in the institutional church (Schwarz, 1998). This is a significant issue as approximately two-thirds of parishioners are women, and survey data find an increasing number of young women (post-Vatican II cohort) are inclined to disagree with church teachings, especially on issues such as the ordination of women (Davidson et al., 1997, pp. 141–154). Feminist theologians call for the use of inclusive and nonsexist language, ordination of women priests, and greater opportunities for leadership and equity at all levels of the church (Donovan, 1997; Pieper, 1997). The modern parish is experiencing significant changes that affect all members of the faith community. These changes reverberate throughout the institution and for some Catholics shake the structural foundation of their religious involvement.

IMPLICATIONS FOR COUNSELING AND PSYCHOTHERAPY

Understanding the role of personal spirituality and religious affiliation complements assessments in other areas of psychological functioning that are crucial to diagnosis and treatment. Spiritual resources may play a significant role in psychological coping and may be explicitly integrated into treatment. The influence of religious faith and affiliation is highly variable among individuals within a given denomination. The face of American Catholicism reflects significant diversity. Among those who identify themselves as Catholics are persons who believe in the core tenets yet rarely participate in the sacramental life of the church nor incorporate a spiritual perspective as well as those who are highly devout in their religious practice and for whom their faith directly influences daily life. Church members vary in terms of conservatism and liberalism in their response to ethical and social teachings and, as the survey research has shown, Catholics frequently hold to the core of Catholic teachings while rejecting specific positions (Davidson et al., 1997, p. 51). Religious orientation may be primarily extrinsic or intrinsic and shapes to varying degrees personal meaning, moral behavior, and motivation and serves as a source of coping as well. An appreciation of the nuances of individual personal faith taken within the backdrop of larger denominational influences provides a clinician with a perspective to understand better the role of religious belief, affiliation, and practice in a client's life.

Psychotherapy inevitably involves an examination of motivation, which includes implicit and explicit moral decision making. In working with Catholics, it is useful to keep in mind the emphasis placed on interiority and personal freedom as well as the responsibility to be receptive to God's voice in discernment and to the moral teaching of the church. Examination of behavior may lead to psychological and spiritual tension as multiple motivations and moral values come into conflict. Clients may approach such decision making in an "all or nothing" fashion, with errant preconceptions about the teachings of the church and authority. The clinician may be looked upon to serve as the moral compass to resolve this conflict. Understanding the rudiments of the church's approach to morality may provide a foundation to assist clients in the process of decision making rather than failing the client by providing an answer.

Establishing the Therapeutic Relationship

Establishing therapeutic relationships in which the religious dimension is taken into account requires sensitivity and the awareness that clients consciously integrate to varying degrees a religious or spiritual outlook in their lives. The role of religion should neither be ignored nor overstated on the basis of reported affiliation and salience. Rapport is enhanced through expressing interest in the faith perspective of the client, appreciating a client's religious and spiritual perspective both in terms of its inherent values and in terms of its impact on psychological functioning, respecting the value-based nature of psychological treatment, and developing a familiarity with the client's religion and, where appropriate, local religious leaders.

Religion and psychology offer perspectives on the nature of the human condition and provide commentaries on human values as well as encourage distinct moral prescriptions and proscriptions. Psychotherapy, in its practice, is not a value-neutral exchange but rather is a "value-laden enterprise" (Bergin, Payne, & Richards, 1996, p. 297). Perry London (1964) observed that psychotherapists served the role of secular priests and would be increasingly called upon to "fill a moral vacuum" (p. 171; see also Frankl, 1963, 1965; and May, 1961, on the ontological dimension in psychotherapy). Catholic laity, as well as the clergy, may harbor concern about a secular process, which they intuitively understand may challenge or potentially contradict their religious orientations. They may seek clinicians whose faith perspective is consonant with their own. Establishing relationships with clergy and encouraging dialogue on the interface of religion and psychology promote rapport and provide clients a background of assurance that a clinician is mindful and respectful of their faith commitment.

Clinicians ensure ethical practice in maintaining awareness of the implicit moral statements that are embedded in their interventions and counsel. Treatment that explicitly examines matters of faith and morals requires the psychotherapist to be especially mindful of ethics and the potential for undue influence based on personal beliefs and moral standards. Tan (1996) suggested that informed consent to treatment be obtained whenever explicit integration of religion in clinical practice occurs, and Richards and Bergin (1997) cautioned psychotherapists "to be aware of and to avoid displacing, usurping or undermining the authority and credibility of their clients' religious leaders" (p. 148). Understanding the confluence of the values and religious worldviews of the client and the clinician provides an orientation to examine the influence of the religiosity in the mental health of the client, as a clinically useful variable in assessment and as a potential resource in psychological treatment.

Diagnostic Assessment

Understanding the denominational context provides an initial means of assessing personal religious experience as a feature of mental status. A thoughtful assessment of religion's role takes place over time; initial inquiry during a formal intake should include past and present religious experience and affiliation, taking a religious history that includes an overview of religious training and a review of the sacraments received, salience of church teaching and authority, use of religious resources during periods of difficulty, and an assessment of the image of God. Asking clients to describe God or their relationship with God in daily life is more useful than inquiring about beliefs. Simply including inquiry concerning religiosity signifies to the client that this is a domain that is considered important within treatment.

Holding beliefs and performing rituals that are outside of normative religious experience may be suggestive of psychological disorder. For example, within Catholicism, the belief of the intercession of Mary or saints on one's behalf, offering devotions, or looking to church authority for a code of behavior is in keeping with the tradition of the Church. Lighting votive candles and offering ritual prayers for the resolution of personal conflicts and suffering is in keeping with this tradition. Although such beliefs and practices suggest direct communication with Mary and the saints, reports of visions and direct verbal dialogue are not commonplace. Prayers are answered through changing life circumstances or by the provision of reassurance and trust in divine providence. Belief in the devil, Satan, or demonic forces is in keeping with Catholic beliefs; however, apparitions of the devil or hearing voices or directives by the demonic are outside of the tradition. Glossolalia or "speaking in tongues" is normative within the charismatic movement in Catholicism; however, its appearance outside of that subgroup is highly unusual. Perfectionism and obsessive compliance with religious observance are beyond the expectations for devotion and warrant close examination of the psychological function of the ritual behaviors. Scrupulous piety and absence of commonplace emotional reactions and motivations under the guise of holiness may suggest the use of religious ideals to maintain an unhealthy psychological equilibrium. Catholics who do not report moments of aggression, disappointment, doubt, frustration, sexual desire nor demonstrate agency in their daily lives in the name of piety or in following God's will are misunderstanding the

Gospel message and may be using religious conceptions to mask psychological conflicts involving affects, drives, and autonomy.

Assessing the normative status of a given belief or behavior requires an understanding not only of the denominational context but also of the distinctive features of the family of origin as well as ethnic and racial features within the parish. Beliefs and practices within the immigrant church often include rituals from the former country, which serve as a cultural bridge to identity. The psychological significance of such devotions should include an appreciation of the ethnic and cultural as well as spiritual functions.

Clinical Issues

Catholics are similar to others in terms of the psychological challenges faced in life as well as dispositions to psychiatric illness. However, there are psychological issues and life events that take on particular meaning within the setting of Catholicism. These include authority, sexual ethics, interreligious marriage, divorce, abortion, suicide, genetic engineering, and euthanasia as examples.

Authority

As discussed above, a dialogue is required between the Church's authority and teaching in matters of faith and morals and individual conscience. Conflicts or tension may result from this process of discernment. The emphasis on being faithful to God through the church places considerable responsibility on Catholics to be mindful of personal decision making within the context of church teaching and their personal relationship with God. This takes on increased significance as relationship with God is reliant upon the sacramental life of the church, and therefore conflicts between the individual and the Church pose grave consequences. Catholics are often placed in the crossfire among the institution's prescriptions, secular cultural mores, and individual desires. For example, the church considers premarital sexual relations immoral, yet popular culture, expressed in part through its media, hardly portrays such an ethic, nor may the virtue of such an injunction be apparent in the throes of passion. In this circumstance and in many others, the individual is called to moral discernment and personal responsibility. Conflict may occur as the individual wrestles with arriving at a moral position. Such conflicts are matters of integrity and, although not instances of mental illness, may cause emotional distress. Persons may seek psychotherapy to assist in the process of values clarification. Clinicians are helpful in identifying and clarifying the authentic challenge in reconciling differing perspectives and supporting the process of discernment. This does not involve speaking from a position of moral authority but rather encouraging mature consideration of the issues. Sometimes it is useful for clients to seek clarification of church teaching through consultation with a priest or other religious leader.

Psychological conflict exists in instances where ethical decision making is impeded by immature attachments to images of God and to the church that were fashioned out of identifications and beliefs formed solely in childhood. Inhibition in response to fear or behaviors enacted with accompanying anxiety and subsequent guilt and depression foreclose mature decision making and predispose the person to psychological difficulties. Patterns of acting out with attempts at undoing establish maladaptive and regressive responses. This psychological sequalae is the consequence of the failure to apply ethical decision making and is related to dependence on prereflective religious and familial internalizations. Reliance upon a righteous, authoritarian religious stance may constitute conflicts in appropriate individuation. Clients may seek to do right not out of conviction but out of a desire to maintain a childlike dependency with the church as the good parent and themselves as good children (Ritter & O'Neill, 1996). Psychological intervention is useful in forwarding processes of individuation and reducing reflexive, unthinking responses to psychological conflict. Treatments that aim at increasing psychological freedom by working through immature attachments and neurotic compromises do so not to encourage acting out but rather to enable the patient to engage in mature decision making and personal responsibility.

Sexual Ethics

In light of survey research, it is clear that there is a disparity between the moral position of the church and the attitudes and behaviors of many Catholics concerning premarital sexual behavior, contraception, and homosexuality. Psychological intervention may be sought with regard to these conflicts with authority and conscience and may result in emotional distress as discussed above. It is also likely that conflict will occur not only within the individual but also between the individual and his or her family and religious community. Differences demonstrated in the age cohort studies lead to the prediction of considerable intrafamilial conflict particularly between pre-Vatican II and post-Vatican II Catholics. Psychological intervention may be aimed at establishing an environment for discussion and establishing conditions for autonomy. For example, a devout Catholic mother discovers that her college-age daughter is using birth control pills and a confrontation ensues regarding sexual ethics. The clinical issues involve a disparity in ethics, freedom and autonomy, separation and individuation, and the ability of the family to effectively respond to interpersonal conflicts.

Interreligious Marriage

In keeping with the church position of one true God and the authority of the Catholic Church, conflicts may occur in interreligious couples. Although interreligious marriages are acknowledged and blessed by the church, tensions may emerge as issues involving the religious education of children and the full participation in the sacramental life of the Church become relevant issues. The blending of differing religious traditions and support for each spouse's faith orientation often poses challenges to a marriage. The importance of participation in Catholicism is often misunderstood by spouses of other Christian faiths who may not fully appreciate the importance that is placed on the sacramental nature of the church and the real presence of God in the sacraments. Premarital counseling should always include an assessment and practical discussion of potential conflicts related to faith commitment and its expression.

Divorce

In Catholicism, a valid marriage is indissoluble and requires inviolable fidelity. Civil divorce does not permit subsequent marriage in the church. Yet, many thousands of Catholics divorce and remarry each year and Catholic lay persons increasingly believe that remarriage following divorce is morally acceptable (D'Antonio et al., 1996). Church teaching results in significant pressure to remain in a marriage and exacts sanctions for leaving a marriage with the intent to remarry in the future. Catholics therefore take the issue of separation and divorce very seriously. This is particularly the case in the pre-Vatican II cohort. Clinicians may be struck by marriages that remain intact despite significant dysfunction and at times emotional and physical abuse. Understanding these religious pressures may assist in clarifying the basis for the intent in remaining married. Clinicians should also be aware of the conditions under which a marriage may be annulled and the procedures for filing such a claim. An annulment decrees that the sacrament of marriage is invalid. The local diocesan Tribunal may be consulted for further information about Canon Law and the juridical procedures.

Abortion, Suicide, Genetic Engineering, and Euthanasia

These issues conjoin as they concern the church's unwavering position on the sanctity of life from conception to death. Abortion poses serious consequences for the Catholic woman and couple as the fetus possesses unalienable rights to life and willful termination constitutes a grave offense resulting in excommunication from the church (*Catechism*, 1994, p. 548). The clinician is not in the position to render judgment on the ethical and canonical matter of abortion; however, it is important to understand the particular gravity of this act within Catholicism. In light of church teaching, women who have had abortions may experience a painful isolation from and condemnation from the church and may seek the means for forgiveness and institutional reconciliation and may work through personal responses to the abortion. Suicide is also a grave offense. Family members and significant others may experience particular concern regarding the spiritual status of the deceased as well as ambivalence regarding what interventions might have been taken. The church offers that "We should not despair of the eternal salvation of persons who have taken their own lives. By ways known to him alone, God can provide the opportunity for salutary repentance" (*Catechism*, 1994, p. 550).

With the continuing breakthroughs in medical practice, Catholics are faced with decisions unforeseen decades ago. Increasingly, decisions will need to be made regarding genetic screening and *in utero* procedures that involve risk to the unborn person as well as the possibility of engineering genetic features. At the other end of the life span, decisions are required regarding life-sustaining procedures, quality of life, and euthanasia. Again, the sanctity of life is the preeminent principle that guides moral decision making within the church.

Psychological Treatment

Psychological treatment of Catholics is not distinct from that of others; however, there are certain clinical features that illustrate the interface of religion and psychology within clinical practice. These include the influence of religious experience on the therapeutic process, distinctions among theological beliefs and internalized God representations, countertransference, use of religious resources, and consultation with Catholic clergy and religious.

The Influence of Religious Experience on the Therapeutic Process

It is useful to consider that the provision and conduct of psychotherapy is not extant from many therapeutic (and at times countertherapeutic) experiences that Catholics encounter within the church. In its theology, eschatology, salvation history, sacramental life, and pastoral care, the church offers models for the resolution of psychological conflict, establishes a basis for hope, and issues explicit moral prescriptions and proscriptions. Catholics coming into psychological treatment bring these experiences to the consulting room. The following examples drawn from Christology and the sacramental life of the church illustrate how beliefs and experiences may influence the formation and process of psychological treatment.

Suffering, Death, and Resurrection

Central to Christianity is its depiction of suffering as meaningful and leading to the promise of the resurrection. This establishes a deeply held motif of faith in transformation and meaning. Accounts within the mystical tradition of the "dark night of the soul" and examples of doubt, betrayal, anger, and forgiveness in the New Testament often contribute to a person's coping with suffering and conflict. Catholics facing significant difficulties and tragic losses are at times bolstered by the belief that suffering has meaning, that there is a purpose in what at the moment appears only as misfortune and may find comfort in an identification with Christ's suffering and resurrection. For these individuals, there is a conservation of significance, which encourages coping and resolution (Pargament, 1997). In such a context, psychological treatment benefits from an underlying optimism and willingness to endure difficulty for an ultimately greater good.

For many clients, suffering is tied to personal failing and sin. Hardship is attributed to be the consequence of moral failure and is exacted as a form of punishment. Within this moralistic construction, patients may relentlessly attack themselves and spiral into a deepening depression filled with guilt and self-condemnation. Resistance to interventions aimed at restoring an orientation to reality and offering hope may take on a masochistic cast in which reality is denied and an obsessive focus on imperfection ensues. Examination of the genesis of these psychodynamics as well as exploration of religious beliefs provides an initial therapeutic aim. At times, clients may benefit from consultation with a priest, religious, or spiritual director to clarify misunderstandings concerning the occurrence of human suffering. Clients who perpetuate suffering, perform ritual self-injury, or refuse to provide care for themselves are clearly outside of the tradition. Such behaviors suggest psychopathology.

Finally, a significant loss of faith occurs for some when adversity and pain are experienced as utterly meaningless. In such circumstances, suffering, initially located in a singular life event, undermines the client's core beliefs about the self and the human condition. A loss of ontological significance occurs which threatens the integrity of the self and may lead to a precarious hold onto life. Treatment in these dire circumstances is directed to assist in a transformation of significance that will provide resources for coping and resolution (Pargament, 1997). Trauma, which results in the collapse of all sense of meaning, is diagnostically significant in assessing suicide risk. As religious belief and affiliation have been shown to be a buffer to suicide (Gartner, 1996), a dramatic loss of faith, in my clinical experience, is one indicator of increased risk. A perilous course of treatment must be undertaken in which meaning is gradually restored under the threat of anomie and despair. In these circumstances, previously held beliefs and assurances do not offer succor but rather may intensify processes of disintegration. Referral to church leaders may result in an intensification of despair should the minister fail to appreciate the depth of the loss of faith.

Confession

The Sacrament of Penance or what is commonly referred to as confession critically shapes early ritual experiences of reconciliation and forgiveness. Inherent within the sacrament is a psychological process in which personal failing is acknowledged; sins are confessed to another (i.e., the priest); penance or an action to bring about reconciliation is given; sins are forgiven and absolution obtained with the admonition to sin no more. In the depictions of clients, there is a wide variance in the experiences and effects of these sacramental and pastoral engagements. For some, the experience is filled with shame, reinforcing scrupulosity, anxiety, and sole reliance on external authority for guidance and judgment; for others, confession has been a pastoral experience of intimate understanding, which encouraged acceptance and the fortitude to improve oneself. The correspondence between confession and psychotherapy is obvious although certainly neither the relationship nor the experience is literally the same. Catholics may expect, consciously or unconsciously, a reenactment of the confessional process within the course of therapy. Clients may hold the belief that the psychotherapist is the final arbiter of good and evil, can produce experiences of forgiveness, expect penance and harsh judgment, and will tell them how to live their lives and admonish them to sin no more. Clinicians may better understand the underlying psychodynamics and transference manifestations in taking into account and exploring the influence of early confessional experiences and modes of forgiveness within the client's family. Misattunement may occur should the clinician not understand the unconscious expectations of some Catholic clients for a reenactment of an internal working model of reconciliation. Resolution does not consist in enacting this unconscious role but rather in elucidating the dynamics and providing a context for the patient to work through new modes of resolution.

Theological Beliefs and Internalized God Representations

Psychoanalytic theory and clinical case studies suggest a distinction between theological beliefs and internalized unconscious God representations (Meissner, 1984; Rizzuto, 1979, 1996). Religious beliefs are for the most part conscious ideas, which are learned through formal and familial religious training. God representations, on the other hand, are predominantly unconscious mental schema culled from internalizations of object relations and influenced by fantasy, memory, and ongoing compromise formation. Theological beliefs and God representations belong to two different classes of mental phenomena. Theology and religious beliefs are primarily artifacts of a secondary process, and God representations reflect mentation involving both primary and secondary levels of thought.

The distinction between religious beliefs and God representations may become most apparent within psychotherapy. Clinicians may observe that there are discrepancies between "what patients believe" and "the God that they appear to experience." Patients may state a belief in "a loving and forgiving God" and yet cower in fear of committing any transgression, appear scrupulous in their behavior, and may be plagued by debilitating guilt and depression. Clinically, it is important to explore this discrepancy and to examine and interpret the origins of these representations. Through treatment, a greater convergence in God concept and representation often parallels improvement in anxiety and depression.

Religious language, including beliefs and representations of God, also provides a form to communicate aspects of transference and intrapsychic conflict. As such, clinicians should pay close attention to veiled communication about the therapeutic relationship and internal conflicts. A client who repeatedly refers to longing for a God who perfectly understands and can wash away all suffering may be commenting on both idealized wishes and disappointments within the treatment relationship as well as point to misattunement in life. Religious narrative provides a structure to contain and to express the most intimate aspects of self-experience and to formulate ineffable mental contents. Religious leitmotifs in a given culture provide an avenue into the deep structure of the psychic life. The clinical process is enriched through understanding religious material from multiple theoretical perspectives. An appreciation for the multiple meanings that are expressed in religious language do not allow for a simplistic, reductionistic reading of such ideation as solely reflecting psychological features of transference or object relations nor a naive understanding that religious ideations have no psychological or clinical relevance.

Countertransference

Countertransference refers to the entire range of responses engendered in the psychotherapist, and intersubjectivity emphasizes the active participation of the clinician in the construction of meaning within treatment. The clinician's personal values and subjective experiences inevitably influence the therapeutic enterprise. Various manifestations of countertransference have been discussed in the psychological literature; however, few, if any, comment on countertransference presented in a religious or spiritual form. Bergin and his collaborators (Bergin, 1991; Bergin, Payne, & Richards, 1996; Richards & Bergin, 1997) have articulated the importance of recognizing the implicit values orientation within treatment. Clinicians need be mindful of the influence of their own perspective in apprehending their clients' worldview as well as in their therapeutic interventions, particularly those couched within the guise of neutrality. In subtle forms, the clinician may endeavor to influence the client's basic beliefs as differences in perspective are encountered. The point is not that one should or can eliminate personality; however, clinicians should be mindful of the "irreducibility of [the psychotherapist's] subjectivity" (Renik, 1993) and potential for inappropriate influence. The ethical conduct of clinical practice is supported through an ongoing self-assessment of the theoretical and empirical basis for all clinical interventions.

Religious Resources

The explicit integration of religious and spiritual resources within psychological treatment should be conducted with utmost respect for the client, with clinical acumen and supervised experience, and, in keeping with Tan (1996), with informed consent. Use of such resources should be considered only after clearly establishing that such resources have been of consistent benefit to the patient within the course of his or her life. This assessment must take into account the denominational setting and the unique personal experiences of the patient. In general, Catholics, because of the spiritual traditions within Catholicism, may derive particular benefit from individual, personal prayer and devotion, forms of interior meditation and contemplation, and participation in the sacramental life of the community. The use of religious cognitive therapy and religious imagery, as discussed by Propst (1988), may offer additional resources. The use of literal interpretations of Scripture or specific healing prayers and rites common in Protestant Evangelical denominations are unfamiliar to most Catholics and therefore inappropriate. The introduction of any intervention, including those of a religious and spiritual nature, requires clinical justification and assessment. Clinicians should be clear about their intent, timing, professional competence in the use of such interventions, complementarity with the treatment model, countertransference, likely reception by the client, potential iatrogenic effects, alternative interventions, and mode of assessing efficacy. Systematic clinical research is required to empirically establish the effects of the use of religious resources on the process and outcome of treatment with the general population as well as with specific religious subgroups.

Consultation With Clergy and Religious

The development of an understanding of Catholicism is crucial in treating Roman Catholic clients. Such understanding can be obtained through reading and course work in comparative religions and can most usefully be initiated through consultation with a member of the clergy within the local community. Such consultation promotes a common dialogue between mental health professionals and church leaders and provides an important resource for considering the worldview of Catholics and the possibilities for the integration of religious resources.

Clergy and religious seek professional consultation both to strengthen their skills in pastoral counseling and psychological intervention and to obtain treatment. The first instance can bring about a fruitful discourse on psychological approaches to a broad range of clinical topics. As clergy are often the first contact that a distressed person makes, professional consultation on managing psychiatric emergencies and identifying conditions for referral is often appreciated.

Priests and religious often seek psychotherapy not only for maladies similar to that of the general population (i.e., anxiety, depression) but also concerning unique vocational challenges (e.g., conflicts concerning obedience, celibacy, intimacy). In addition, the decline in vocations has increased the already considerable demands upon priests, brothers, and sisters. There were 47% fewer ordained men between 1980 and 1984 compared with between 1966 and 1970 and by 2000, one-third of priests in some dioceses will retire (Fox, 1995, p. 173). The declining number of vocations, together with changes in parish and community life, produces significant psychological and physical stress and taxes the spiritual resources and commitments of many.

In treating clergy and religious, one must be particularly mindful of providing and ensuring an environment of privacy. Furthermore, matters concerning limits of confidentiality, particularly in terms of payment through diocesan self-indemnity insurance plans or in circumstances in which mandated treatment has been contracted or in which mandated reporting of abuse to civil authorities is likely, should be clearly stated and informed consent obtained. Clinicians should be mindful that although religious and spiritual issues may be included within treatment, the primary focus should concern mental health. The provision of spiritual counseling is outside the sphere of competence of most clinicians, and appropriate referral to a spiritual director is recommended. A client's penchant for bringing theological discussion into treatment may also serve to deflect awareness and inquiry away from psychological difficulties and to avoid the development of a psychotherapeutic process.

RELIGION AND THE CLINICAL PRACTICE OF PSYCHOLOGY

This chapter has provided an overview to Roman Catholicism and introduced a clinical perspective that values the role of spiritual and religious orientation, affiliation, and practice in the psychological life of the individual. This discussion aimed to identify issues to be considered in psychological assessment, treatment formulation, and clinical practice.

Rather than supplying a set of stereotypes, this essay presented general features of Catholic history, beliefs, practices, and culture as starting points for inquiry. Central to this approach is the belief that understanding best occurs through a sophisticated inquiry into the psychological life of the *individual*. Spiritual and religious orientation, which forms the bedrock of attributions about the self and the world, is a uniquely individual construction and can never be captured by simply knowing a person's denominational affiliation. Appreciation of religion and spirituality as clinical variables is supported through ethical practice, developing theory, conducting empirical research, and through teaching and supervision (Shafranske & Malony, 1996). It is the intent of this chapter, as well, to encourage dialogue within the mental health community and to encourage multidisciplinary collaboration as these variables are examined as clinically relevant features of diversity.

SUGGESTED READINGS

Brown, R. E. (1981). *Critical meaning of the Bible*. Mahwah, NJ: Paulist Press.

Brown, R. E. (1990). *Responses to 101 questions on the Bible*. Mahwah, NJ: Paulist Press.

Brown, R. E. (1994). *An introduction to New Testament Christology*. Mahwah, NJ: Paulist Press.

Dolan, J. P. (1992). *The American Catholic experience*. Notre Dame, IN: University of Notre Dame Press.

Donovan, D. (1997). *Distinctively Catholic: An exploration of Catholic identity*. Mahwah, NJ: Paulist Press.

McBrien, R. P. (1994). *Catholicism: New edition*. San Francisco: HarperSan Francisco.

REFERENCES

American Psychological Association. (1992). Ethical principles of psychologists and code of conduct. *American Psychologist, 47,* 1597–1611.

Bedell, K. B. (Ed.). (1996). *Yearbook of American and Canadian churches, 1996.* Nashville, TN: Abingdon Press.

Bergin, A. E. (1991). Values and religious issues in psychotherapy and mental health. *American Psychologist, 46,* 394–403.

Bergin, A. E., Payne, I. R., & Richards, P. S. (1996). Values in psychotherapy. In E. P. Shafranske (Ed.), *Religion and the clinical practice of psychology* (pp. 297–325). Washington, DC: American Psychological Association.

Catechism of the Catholic Church (English Translation). (1994). Mahwah, NJ: Paulist Press.

D'Antonio, W. V., Davidson, J. D., Hoge, D. R., & Wallace, R. A. (1996). *Laity: American and Catholic—transforming the church.* Kansas City, MO: Sheed & Ward.

Davidson, J. D., Williams, A. S., Lamanna, R. A., Stenftenagel, J., Weigert, K. M., Whalen, W. J., & Wittberg, P. (1997). *The search for common ground: What unites and divides Catholic Americans.* Huntington, IN: Our Sunday Visitor, Inc.

Dolan, J. P. (1985). *The American Catholic experience: A history from Colonial Times to the present.* Garden City, NY: Doubleday.

Dolan, J. P. (1992). *The American Catholic experience.* Notre Dame, IN: University of Notre Dame Press.

Dolan, J. P., & Deck, A. F. (Eds.). *Hispanic Catholic culture in the U.S.: Issues and concerns.* Notre Dame, IN: University of Notre Dame Press.

Donovan, D. (1997). *Distinctively Catholic: An exploration of Catholic identity.* Mahwah, NJ: Paulist Press.

Fox, T. (1995). *Sexuality and Catholicism.* New York: George Braziller.

Frankl, V. E. (1963). *Man's search for meaning.* Boston: Beacon Press.

Frankl, V. E. (1965). *The doctor and the soul: From psychotherapy to logotherapy* (2nd ed., R. Winston & C. Winston, Trans.). New York: Knopf.

Gallup, Jr., G. & Castelli, J. (1987). *The American Catholic people: Their beliefs, practices, and values.* Garden City, NY: Doubleday.

Gartner, J. (1996). Religious commitment, mental health, and prosocial behavior: A review of the empirical literature. In E. P. Shafranske (Ed.), *Religion and the clinical practice of psychology* (pp. 187–214). Washington, DC: American Psychological Association.

Gleason, P. (1987). *Keeping the faith: American Catholicism past and present.* Notre Dame, IN: University of Notre Dame Press.

Greeley, A. M. (1990). *The Catholic myth: The behavior and beliefs of American Catholics.* New York: Scribner's.

Hoge, D. R. (1996). Religion in America: The demographics of belief and affiliation. In E. Shafranske (Ed.), *Religion and the clinical practice of psychology* (pp. 21–41). Washington, DC: American Psychological Association.

Kosmin, B. A., & Lachman, S. P. (1993). *One nation under God.* New York: Crown Trade Paperbacks.

Linkh, R. M. (1975). *American Catholicism and European immigrants (1900–1924).* Staten Island, NY: The Center for Migration Studies.

London, P. (1964). *The mode and morals of psychotherapy.* New York: Holt, Rinehart & Winston.

May, R. (1961). *Existential psychology.* New York: Random House.

McGuire, M. A. (1961). *Baltimore catechism, No. 1* (Rev. ed.). New York: Benzinger Brothers.

Meissner, W. W. (1984). *Psychoanalysis and religious experience.* New Haven, CT: Yale University Press.

Moore, J. (1992). The social fabric of the Hispanic community since 1965. In

J. P. Dolan & A. F. Deck (Eds.), *Hispanic Catholic culture in the U.S.: Issues and concerns* (pp. 6–49). Notre Dame, IN: University of Notre Dame Press.

Pargament, K. I. (1997). *The psychology of religion and coping*. New York: Guilford Press.

Pieper, J. (1997). *The Catholic woman*. Chicago: Contemporary Books.

Propst, R. (1988). *Psychotherapy in a religious framework. Spirituality in the emotional healing process*. New York: Human Sciences Press.

Renik, O. (1993). Analytic interaction: Conceptualizing technique in light of the analyst's irreducible subjectivity. *Psychoanalytic Quarterly, 62*, 553–571.

Richards, P. S., & Bergin, A. E. (1997). *A spiritual strategy for counseling and psychotherapy*. Washington, DC: American Psychological Association.

Ritter, K., & O'Neill, C. (1996). *Righteous religion: Unmasking the illusions of fundamentalism and authoritarian Catholicism*. New York: Haworth Press.

Rizzuto, A. M. (1979). *The birth of the living God*. Chicago: University of Chicago Press.

Rizzuto, A. M. (1996). Psychoanalytic treatment and the religious person. In E. Shafranske (Ed.), *Religion and the clinical practice of psychology* (pp. 409–431). Washington, DC: American Psychological Association.

Roof, W. C., & McKinney, W. (1987). *American mainline religion*. New Brunswick, NJ: Rutgers University Press.

Romero, C. G. (1991). *Hispanic devotional piety*. Maryknoll, NY: Orbis Books.

Schwarz, K. A. (1998, August). *In the wake of patriarchy: Roman Catholic women's psychological development*. Paper presented at the meeting of the American Psychological Association, San Francisco.

Shafranske, E. P., & Malony, H. N. (1996). Religion and the practice of psychology: A case for inclusion. In E. P. Shafranske (Ed.), *Religion and the practice of psychology* (pp. 561–586). Washington DC: American Psychological Association.

Tan, S. Y. (1996). Religion in clinical practice: Implicit and explicit integration. In E. Shafranske (Ed.), *Religion and the clinical practice of psychology* (pp. 365–387). Washington, DC: American Psychological Association.

Weaver, M. J. (1988). The Roman Catholic heritage. In C. H. Lippy & P. W. Williams (Eds.), *Encyclopedia of the American religious experience* (pp. 153–170). New York: Scribner's.

Williams, P. W. (1988). Catholicism since World War I. In C. H. Lippy & P. W. Williams (Eds.), *Encyclopedia of the American religious experience* (pp. 375–390). New York: Scribner's.

Wright, J. W. (1994). *The universal almanac, 1994*. Kansas City: Andrews & McMeel.

Young, J. L., & Griffith, E. E. (1991). Understanding due discretion of judgment in Catholic marriage courts. *Bulletin of the American Academy of Psychiatry and the Law, 19*, 109–118.

4

PSYCHOTHERAPY WITH EASTERN ORTHODOX CHRISTIANS

TONY R. YOUNG

Christianity is more than a theory about the universe, more than teachings written down on paper; it is the path along which we journey—in the deepest and richest sense, *the way of life.*
—Bishop Kallistos Ware

Orthodox Christians trace their beginnings to the disciples of Jesus Christ and to the Church, the *ekklesia*, established on the Day of Pentecost as told in the New Testament in the *Acts of the Apostles*. This history makes its way through the death of the Apostles; the persecutions by the Roman Empire; the legitimization and installation of Christian faith as the religion of the realm, under the rule of St. Constantine; the establishment of the canon of the New Testament; the hermits and ascetic monks known as the Desert Fathers; the several heresies or doctrinal distortions that led to the Seven Ecumenical Councils of the Church, in which was established, among others, the doctrine of the Trinity and the Nicene Creed; the conversion of Russia to Christianity in 988; the Great Schism in 1054; the Crusades; the fall of Constantinople in 1453; the occupation and persecutions at the hands of the Turks in the Middle East and Eastern Europe; the Communist persecutions in Russia and in the Soviet Republics in recent memory; and the present day. The Orthodox Church lives in vivid recollection of the past. In it, the past lives.

For the first 1,000 years, the Christian Church existed in virtual unity, albeit subject to many heresies which arose during the first 700 years of the Church's life. The Church had weathered the storms of gnosticism, Arianism, monophysitism, Nestorianism, iconoclasm, and other heresies by the early to mid 800s only to split in 1054 into the Eastern Orthodox and Roman Catholic churches. This schism had its roots in both political and theological differences that are linked. Politically, the Pope of what is now the Roman Catholic Church was one of the five patriarchs or bishops, and they held the chief positions of power politically. The other four were from Constantinople (New Rome, now Istanbul, Turkey), Jerusalem, Antioch, and Alexandria (Egypt). Rome enjoyed the first place of honor because of its importance as the capital of the empire, and the eastern bishops saw the Pope as the first among equals.

During the 900s, the bishop of Rome added to the Nicene Creed, the central doctrinal statement of faith, a phrase, *filioque*, meaning in Latin, "from the son." This changed a sentence of the Creed that read, "and in the Holy Spirit, the Lord, the giver of life, Who proceeds from the Father" to "Who proceeds from the Father and the Son." To the eastern bishops, this changed the Trinitarian structure by subjugating the Holy Spirit to the Son, a point with which they strongly disagreed.

Politically, the eastern bishops also felt that it was unacceptable that such a change be made without an ecumenical council of all bishops, which had been the practice and pattern to that point with regard to all major issues of faith. This change in the Creed, both in its content and in the process by which it was made, led to the schism between the bishop of Rome, the Pope, and the other bishops that continues to this day. By the accounts of historians, the fault line had been widening for centuries before this time, with the western church and the Roman bishops themselves viewing the bishop of Rome as more powerful in the structure of the church than the eastern bishops. But the schism (called the Great Schism to differentiate it from the later schism of the Protestant churches) was unequivocal in 1054, with the mutual anathemas issued by the eastern bishops and the bishop of Rome. It produced what are now known as the Roman Catholic Church with the bishop of Rome, the Pope, and the Eastern Orthodox Church, with bishops representing the several national self-headed churches. In considering the Eastern Orthodox Church in America, it is important to keep in mind that originally it was united with the Roman Church and shares many of its beliefs, sacraments, and rituals.

ORTHODOX CHURCHES IN AMERICA

Orthodox Christianity is the faith of about 250–350 million people worldwide. Estimates, obviously, vary. There are Orthodox Christians in every country of the world. Orthodoxy is the predominant faith in much of central and eastern Europe, Russia, and Greece and is the predominant

Christian faith in the Middle East and northern Africa. Recently, it has been the fastest growing faith in sub-Saharan Africa.

More than 4.5 million Americans are Orthodox Christians, among whom are nearly 2 million who attend Greek Orthodox churches. Other American Orthodox churches or jurisdictions include Antiochian, Russian, Serbian, and several others. The practice of Eastern Orthodox churches has been to grant jurisdiction, in a newly evangelized geographical area or country, to the national church body that begins the missionary work in that area.

Following this pattern, the Russian Orthodox Church assumed jurisdiction on the North American continent because of its beginnings with missionaries from Russia who landed on Kodiak Island, Alaska, in 1794, and who evangelized the Aleut peoples. Churches were established there which remain to this day. With the fall of the Russian Czar, who was a protector of the Russian church, and the rise of the Soviet state with its severe antireligious stance, the Russian Orthodox Patriarch was unable to hold jurisdiction in America, and this led to jurisdictional proliferation and some confusion. There are now about 15 different jurisdictions in this country, principally from the various ethnic and national churches from the Old World. This situation of overlapping administrations and ethnic jurisdictions is in direct contradiction to church canons and is viewed as irregular by all Orthodox Churches (Stokoe, 1995). The Orthodox faithful in America look forward to the day when there is truly one Orthodox church in America.

Despite the jurisdictional differences, there is often little to distinguish one church from another except perhaps the primary language used in the liturgy and the style of music. A person familiar with the Divine Liturgy, the central service of the church, from one jurisdiction would be able to participate meaningfully in the liturgy of any church of another jurisdiction.

To the western outsider, the Orthodox Church would appear to be very conservative and traditional, with the liturgy having remained virtually unchanged for 1,500 years and with little to mark a theological change through the years. Recently, sharp disagreement has arisen among the more traditionally minded Orthodox (the Holy Synod of the Russian Orthodox Church Abroad and the American Exarchate of the True [Old Calendar] Orthodox Church of Greece) and virtually the rest of the American jurisdictions about the place and the effects of modernism or of westernizing in the churches. A central issue in this dispute, one that is symbolic, has to do with the acceptance and use by most American churches of the new calendar, the Gregorian calendar (which was imposed on the Roman Catholic Church by Pope Gregory in the 16th century), rather than the Julian calendar (which was in effect at the time the Orthodox Church was established in 33 A.D.). The resolution of the conflict remains to be seen. Difficult words have passed among Orthodox faithful.

Orthodox peoples did not come to American shores in any substantial numbers until the 1850s. The first Orthodox church in the contiguous states was established in New Orleans in 1864—Holy Trinity. Immigrants from Greece, Russia, Eastern Europe, and the Middle East brought with them their Orthodox faith. Conversion to Orthodoxy, in America, has increased in recent years.

It may be important to note with Ware (1991) that Christians of the East have a very different past from that of Christians of the West, Roman Catholics and Protestants alike. The Eastern Christian background has no Middle Ages, no Reformation and Counterreformation, no Inquisition, and no Renaissance. Christians of the East and West start with different questions.

Central Beliefs

The Orthodox Church holds the Nicene Creed, a product of ecumenical councils in Nicaea in the year 325 and in Constantinople in 381, as its central doctrinal statement. The Creed occupies a central place in its recitation during many worship services of the Church, but most prominently in the Divine Liturgy, the central Eucharistic service of the Church (Exhibit 4.1).

For Orthodox, the Creed provides the theological boundary for the Church. Although diverse in many less important, less central doctrines,

EXHIBIT 4.1
The Nicene Creed

I believe in one God, the Father, the Almighty, the Creator of heaven and earth and of all things visible and invisible.

And in one Lord, Jesus Christ, the only begotten Son of God, begotten of the Father before all ages: Light of Light, true God of true God, begotten not created, of one essence with the Father through Whom all things were made.

For us and for our salvation, He came down from heaven and was incarnate by the Holy Spirit and the Virgin Mary and became man.

He was crucified for us under Pontius Pilate, suffered, and was buried.

On the third day, He rose according to the Scriptures. He ascended into heaven and is seated at the right hand of the Father.

He will come again in glory to judge the living and the dead. His kingdom will have no end.

And in the Holy Spirit, the Lord, the Giver of Life, Who proceeds from the Father, Who together with the Father and the Son is worshiped and glorified, Who spoke through the prophets.

In one, holy, catholic, and apostolic church.

I acknowledge one baptism for the remission of sins.

I expect the resurrection of the dead and the life of the age to come. Amen.

---

all Orthodox hold to the Creed. Other important theological ideas of the Church are also worth mentioning.

Orthodox Distinctives

Although something may be lost in describing Orthodoxy in comparison with other Christian churches, because Orthodoxy is among the least known of Christian faiths in North America, definition by way of distinctiveness might be a good approach.

For Orthodox, God is always the Ultimate Mystery. The Fathers always point to the absolute unknowability of God. Many said that the God who would be comprehended was not God. At the same time, He is nearer to us than we are to ourselves (Ware, 1998). Orthodox theologians seldom have felt the need to explain further.

Dionysius the Areopagite (Luibheid, 1987) in his treatise *The Divine Names* lists and enumerates all the names of God used in Scripture and cautions us not to hold tightly as symbols the divinely given names, for all offer, at best, only a partial understanding of God. In his short work *The Mystical Theology* (in Luibheid, 1987, p. 141), he writes:

> There is no speaking of It (God), nor name nor knowledge of It. Darkness and light, error and truth—It is none of these.

For Orthodox, the essence of the Creed is that God Himself is revealed in Jesus Christ and that human beings are redeemed by the Son. As Orthodox through the years have loved to quote, "God became man that man might become God" (St. Athanasius, 1975). Most of the words of the Creed have to do with the Son, Jesus Christ. Orthodox insist that Jesus was fully God and fully man. The early heresies were largely ways of mistakenly attempting to reduce this tension. Even the last of the great heresies, iconoclasm, resolved in the last of seven Ecumenical Councils, focused on the denial of the incarnation of God in Jesus Christ. The Orthodox faithful reasoned that it was good to depict God as Jesus Christ visually because He had taken the form of a human.

Orthodox hold God to be the Creator as stated in the first line of the Creed. They also believe that He is in and throughout all of His creation. Also, and paradoxically, all things are within Him, and He is beyond and above all things. The theological term that seems to fit best this notion of God's relationship to creation is *panentheism* (see Ware, 1996). (This is not to be confused with pantheism, which suggests that creation itself is God.)

Orthodox hold very tightly to the notion of God being the Trinity, that is, one in essence but three in persons. God, the Father, is seen as the source of both the Son and the Holy Spirit. The Son is seen as the Redeemer Who became a human being, and the Holy Spirit is the person of the Trinity Who continues or completes the work of the Son, proceeding from the Father. Orthodox say little else beyond this formulation and feel little need to explain this mystery further.

Humans are believed to be essentially good by the Orthodox. Holding to the Genesis account, it is asserted that all things made by God are "very good." With the rebellion of Adam and Eve, death entered the world. Orthodox understand the fall of humanity as the loss of the likeness of God. The image of God, in which humans were made by God, is never lost in any human. One Church Father has said that at the core of the core, the heart of the heart of every person, there is that which is eternally, inalterably divine. The work of humanity consists of uncovering the image of God and developing the likeness of God in themselves.

In Orthodoxy, the fundamental witness to Christian Tradition is considered to be Holy Scripture. Orthodox rely heavily on the liturgical texts of the Church and on the divinely inspired Fathers of the Church and their interpretation of Scripture and Tradition. The Fathers of the Church are considered to have known better than we the meaning of Scripture, both because of their nearness in time to the events of Scripture and to their having led lives of perfection and having gained a full understanding of the Christian gospel. The books of the Old Testament and New Testament are believed to be inspired Scripture, as are several "deutero-canonical" books.

Many of the Sundays of the Church's liturgical year are named for the gospel passage read on that day. For example, as I write this on a Sunday morning, I am aware that today is the Sunday of the Samaritan Woman. The Gospel reading on this day tells of the interaction between Jesus and the Samaritan woman at the well of Sychar, in which He offers to her living water and tells her about her own life, then she goes to the village and tells her friends.

Orthodox do not see Scripture as standing alone in authority. The Orthodox view is that the Scripture comes from the Church, not vice versa, because the canon of Scripture came to exist, as we know it today, only in the 4th century. The Church wrote and formed the New Testament. The Church believes Herself alone to be rightly able to interpret Scripture (Whiteford, 1997). Orthodox do not view Scripture as inerrant but as a reliable guide to the knowledge of God and His plan for humanity. The Orthodox Church holds Herself to be infallible and incapable of error. Orthodox do not trust the strength of words to fully convey ideas about God. The belief that God is ultimately mysterious and not containable with words weighs against the Church trusting fully any formulation of words.

Orthodox hold the entire church—all the bishops, all the priests, and all the people—Herself to be infallible. The Ecumenical Patriarch, the Patriarch of Constantinople, is sometimes mistakenly spoken of as the Orthodox pope. He is perceived to have a primacy of honor or to be the "first among equals."

Father Michael Azkoul (1994) has written of other, less obvious, distinctives. He points first to the role of human reason in faith. The Orthodox Church makes little or no effort to reconcile faith and reason. Orthodoxy accepts support from the sciences but feels no need to justify Herself to the findings of science. Orthodoxy recognizes external changes in the expression of Her faith but does not endorse the view that the teachings of Jesus Christ have changed from time to time. She holds that the faith delivered to the Apostles of Jesus is now as it was in the 1st century.

The writings of the Church Fathers also are held to be authoritative. Often, modern-day Orthodox quote the writings of these persons who wrote 1,500 years or more ago. The writers are deemed to be Fathers of the Church, sometimes after hundreds of years, by the consensus of the entire Church.

Another distinctive feature of Orthodoxy pertains to its understanding of the process of salvation for human beings. The Orthodox soteriology is oriented around the incarnation, the coming in the flesh, and the resurrection of Jesus Christ. Other Christian faiths hold to a more legal or propitiational view. The legal view is that Jesus, by His dying, paid the debt of sin owed by all humans to satisfy the justice of God. For Orthodox, by His coming in the flesh and His victory over death in His resurrection, Jesus Christ provided a way for humans to defeat death. This salvation is accomplished by a synergy of the gift of God's grace and man's effort. Orthodox do not speak of having been saved but of being in the process of being saved. Salvation is never spoken of in the past tense with regard to living human beings. (See Bishop Kallistos Ware's book, *How We Are Saved* [1996], for a fuller presentation of these ideas.)

Worship for Orthodox is a distinctive feature and is central to the Church's ethos. Orthodox services have changed little for hundreds of years. The Church sees Herself first as a worshipping community. Orthodox people worship together in prayers and hymns, most of which are sung or chanted. Incense is used at several points of the Divine Liturgy. Orthodox hold that the way in which people worship is nearer to their true faith than what they believe or think about God. The word *Orthodox* itself means "right worship" and "right belief." When the Prince of Kiev, Vladimir, sent his emissaries to investigate the religions of the world in the 980s, they went to various countries to observe the faiths of the world. Reaching Constantinople and attending the Divine Liturgy at *Agia Sophia*, the Church of Holy Wisdom, they wrote to Prince Vladimir:

> We knew not whether we were in heaven or on earth, for surely there
> is no such splendor or beauty anywhere upon the earth. We cannot
> describe it to you: only this we know, that God dwells there among

men, and that their service surpasses the worship of all other places, for we cannot forget that beauty. (Ware, 1991)

The full liturgical cycle of the Church is accomplished only in monasteries. Monastery churches spend 6–8 hours in worship daily. The structure is elaborate and moves in cycles of hours, days, seasons, and years. The Church year is centered on *Pascha*, or Easter, which is both a Sunday in the spring and a season of the Church year. The rest of the year revolves around it. It is said that the full cycle of worship in the Orthodox Church repeats itself only once in over 500 years.

For Orthodox people, the church is the *ekklesia*, or the gathering of persons called out, who believe in the living God as revealed in Jesus. The Church is governed by the Holy Spirit for it is viewed as a community of persons who are in the process of being purified and reformed through its mysteries or sacraments and communion with God (Constantelos, 1982). The Orthodox Church sees itself to be in direct lineage to the Church instituted by the Holy Spirit on the day of Pentecost. The Mysteries of the Church are services and rites in which gifts of God are given to man. The Mysteries transmit a supernatural grace by physical means. The chief of the mysteries is the Eucharist or, as the Orthodox say, the Body and Blood of Christ. Orthodox have always asserted that the Eucharist was the very Body and the very Blood of Jesus, not merely symbolic, but a sacrament that actually delivers the grace of God. Other sacraments of the Church include baptism, chrismation (similar to confirmation, the believer being anointed with a special holy oil, the chrism), repentance or confession, holy orders, marriage, and the anointing of the sick. All of the mysteries are personal. God's grace is given to every Christian individually.

Life in The Church

Orthodox are accepted into the church by way of baptism and chrismation. Orthodox see the Christian way of life as one of continuous effort and spiritual growth in moral perfection. The goal of life in the Church and of life itself for the Orthodox is to achieve *theosis* or divinization, that is, becoming by grace what God is in His nature. This idea is found in the Sermon on the Mount by Jesus Christ in Matthew 5:48, "Be perfect as your Heavenly Father is perfect." The Church has taught that it is a hospital for sinners who seek spiritual health. She offers her cure in full to all. For Orthodox, repentance, or *metanoia*, is the way to keep from allowing sin to become a permanent state of being and is a change of mind—a turning about of one's mind and behavior. The Church sees Herself as composed of persons who are continually repenting.

For Orthodox, repentance is not only continuous internally but finds an externalization in confession to a priest. The Orthodox Church sees itself as having the authority to accept repentance and to forgive. Confession is practiced in the Orthodox Church, and the church's representative, the priest, is not the source of forgiveness, but the instrument of forgiveness.

Contemporary Social/Moral Issues in the Church

Generally, the Orthodox Church maintains a very conservative or traditional moral system. Orthodox believe that a life of holiness is required to please God. The moral standards are high; however, in practice a great deal of flexibility is found. The interpretation and implementation of rules may be strict or lenient, depending on the situation. Human weakness is recognized.

The Orthodox Church holds marriage to be sacramental. By this is meant that marriage is an event through which God imparts His grace to two people. Orthodox consider marriage to be sacred. For Orthodox, the outcomes or goals of marriage include procreation and the comfort to individuals who link themselves together to work out their own salvation. One of the canons of the Church forbids divorce and remarriage. However, through the *economia* (accommodation of the rules according to circumstances or needs and the frailty of humanity) of the Church, divorces are granted on several grounds including abandonment, incompatibility, and abusiveness by one partner to the other. A person who is divorced is asked to go through a time of repentance and reflection by the Church before being admitted to a full communion status with the Church again. Generally, a person may be divorced three times, despite the canonical rule to the contrary.

Birth control has been a controversial topic in the Orthodox Church. Birth control has been condemned by Church canons, but it is not a matter of dogma. It appears that in America most Orthodox of child-bearing age practice some form of birth control. Generally, the decision about birth control is left to the married couple itself. Several bishops and even the Ecumenical Patriarch have suggested that this was a matter to be decided between husband and wife, rather than to involve their priest.

The Church, though rather lenient with regard to divorce and birth control, is without question against abortion. Respect for life underlies the Church's response to abortion. Orthodox believe that even when the mother's life is in danger, consideration must be given to the two lives involved.

Eastern Orthodoxy holds that the practice of homosexuality is sin, as is any sexual relationship between persons who are not married to each other. There has been no flexibility on this issue throughout the Church's history. However, it should be clearly pointed out that the Church does not see homosexual acts as different from any other habitual sin which humans find themselves engaged in. Homosexuality and its practice are not relegated to a special category of sinfulness.

Spiritual *Praxis* in Orthodoxy

In many ways, Orthodoxy is long on explanations of *praxis* or spiritual practice and short on systematic formulations of doctrine. Much more emphasis is put on the process of *theosis* or divinization through spiritual or ascetic practice than on systematic or dogmatic theological exposition.

There are many intertwining ways of speaking about spiritual development in the Orthodox Church. One is *theosis*. Another is transforming or overcoming the passions. Another classical formulation relates the image of God in humans, which is never lost or changed, and the likeness of God which for most of us is either very dim and weak, if apparent at all. Orthodox are asked to become more like God to increase the likeness of God on the basis of the image of God in each one of us.

Fasting is part of the Orthodox *askesis* or spiritual training and is central to faithful practice. Fasting generally means abstaining from certain kinds of foods as well as limiting the quantity of food taken. Foods avoided during fasting periods include animal products (meat, cheese, and eggs), fish, wine (or alcohol), and oil (specifically, olive oil). Nearly half of the days of the year are fasting days. For Orthodox, fasting is not so much about giving something up but about remembering God and combating the passions (Father Pangratios, 1992). Asceticism today usually connotes strictness and denying oneself. *Askesis* originally had to do with the training that athletes undertake to succeed in their struggles. This approaches the Orthodox view of fasting.

Another distinctive feature of Orthodox spirituality has to do with the centrality of a spiritual father, or *staretz*, in the Russian tradition. Orthodox do not set out on the spiritual path with any seriousness without a spiritual father. This is a cause for concern now in America because of the lack of spiritual fathers.

It is the Orthodox tradition to offer daily, morning and evening prayers, and prayers at meals. These tend not to be spontaneous, but to be taken from the prayers of the Fathers. Orthodox faithful are urged to adopt a rule of prayer that they strive to fulfill. One Orthodox view of prayer sees human beings as being shaped by the prayers they say rather by stressing the need for any spontaneity on the part of the faithful.

St. Seraphim of Sarov was quoted by one of his spiritual children, N. Motovilov, in a conversation that took place between them in the early 1800s:

> Prayer, fasting, vigil, and all other Christian practices, however good they may be in themselves, do not constitute the aim of our Christian life, although they serve as an indispensable means for reaching this

end. The true aim of our Christian life consists in the increasing acquisition of the Holy Spirit of God. As for fasts and vigils and prayer and almsgiving and every good deed done for Christ's sake, they are only means of acquiring the Holy Spirit of God. (*Little Russian Philokalia*, 1996)

Many Orthodox pursue knowledge of God or the process of *theosis* by way of the Jesus Prayer, sometimes called the Prayer of the Heart. In many ways the *Philokalia*, a collection of the writings of the Fathers, is a manual for those following this path. Perhaps the best known writing about the Jesus Prayer is the Russian book, *The Way of the Pilgrim* (French, 1991). This little book is the story of a Russian pilgrim or wanderer who is struck by a sermon on St. Paul's injunction to Christians in Thessalonica to "pray without ceasing." The pilgrim searches for a spiritual father who will teach him how to pray without ceasing and ultimately finds one. The book itself is a chronicle of his use and practice of the Jesus Prayer. The prayer has several forms, but perhaps the most popular is "Lord Jesus Christ, Son of God, have mercy on me, a sinner." The Fathers of the Church write that this prayer, when said in a continuous fashion, will find its way from the lips and the mind to the hearts and it is there where it will pray itself to produce a constant communion with God. Many of the Fathers also say that the prayer itself contains the entire Gospel.

Faithful Orthodox are offered communion at every Divine Liturgy. The Divine Liturgy may be offered on most days of the year, but in most parishes, only on Sundays and on major feast days. The Orthodox priests in some churches require that a communicant avail himself or herself of confession before receiving communion. Others require only that confession be done yearly. Also, to prepare to receive communion, a worshiper is asked to abstain from eating from midnight until communion is received. Communion is offered only to Orthodox persons and only to those in good standing with the Church. As communion is considered to be the Body and Blood of the Lord, receiving communion is taken with utmost seriousness. The Church remembers the words of St. Paul, "For this reason, many of you are sick. You have taken the Body and the Blood in an unworthy manner" (I Corinthians 11:27–30).

IMPLICATIONS FOR COUNSELING AND PSYCHOTHERAPY

Relationship Issues and Suggestions

Eastern Orthodox people in the United States and Canada can be distinguished according to whether they are first- or later-generation immigrants. First-generation immigrants bringing to a new country the faith of their upbringing will, of course, bring their culture as well. These persons will not likely seek therapy, as they would probably view getting therapy as bringing shame on themselves and their families. They will be less likely to self-disclose and, in some cases, language barriers may be present. A therapist would do well to be careful and to take things slowly for these reasons. The language of feelings of the immigrant may not be shared by the therapist. In general, immigrants to the United States have done what they could do to appear American, and this is evident most profoundly in their children and grandchildren. When second- and third-generation immigrants from Orthodox countries are treated in therapy, they will share more common ideas and patterns of thought with the typical therapist. This pattern is much the same as would be seen in immigrants from any traditional country, such as India or Iran. Many of the Orthodox immigrants came to the United States before the pervasive influence of modern or Western ideas took hold in their home countries.

Orthodox converts tend to be relatively devout given that they have made changes in their lives to become Orthodox. Paradoxically, most converts are trying to understand and convert to more Eastern ways of thinking and many cradle Orthodox are trying to think in more Western ways.

Assessment and Diagnostic Issues and Approaches

Assessing the level of involvement of patients in the Orthodox faith might begin with finding out the frequency with which they participate in the liturgical life of the Church, such as how often they attend services and how often they receive communion. Second, the extent to which they follow a rule of prayer would be important, such as whether they say their prayers and what prayers they routinely use. Third, whether they regularly avail themselves of the Mystery of Confession would be important. Next, whether they practice the Jesus Prayer. And last, whether they have a relationship with a spiritual father or guide.

ORTHODOX PERSPECTIVES ON HEALING AND SPIRITUAL DEVELOPMENT

Many of the spiritual practices and beliefs of Eastern Orthodoxy can have a positive emotional or psychological effect. This is despite the fact that they are not designed for psychological health, but for spiritual health. Perhaps the two most important of these practices are the Mystery of Confession and the practice of the Jesus Prayer. The benefits of confession are well known, even having made its way into the common phrase, "Confession is good for the soul." The Jesus Prayer, in addition to focusing the mind and heart on God and moving the person toward living minute-by-minute in the consciousness of His presence, tends to have a calming effect.

It leads a person to better awareness of the self and its passions and to self-knowledge.

Two recent writers have done extensive work in the psychology of the Fathers of the Orthodox faith which relates either to the psychology of spiritual development in Orthodoxy or to Orthodox practice as therapy. These two are Archbishop Chrysostomos of Etna, California, and Archimandrite Hierotheos Vlachos.

From the collection of the sayings and lives of these Fathers, titled *Evergetinos* (Langes, 1977), Archbishop Chrysostomos, who holds a PhD in personality psychology from Princeton University, has found that four themes or elements touch on each aspect of the process of transformation known as *theosis* or divinization. The four themes are elaborated in the four books titled *Humility* (Chrysostomos et al., 1983), *Obedience* (Chrysostomos et al., 1985), *Repentance* (Chrysostomos, 1986), and *Love* (Chrysostomos & Thornton, 1988). Together these four books form the series, *Themes in Orthodox Patristic Psychology*. He has also outlined his work in an article published in the journal, *Pastoral Psychology* (1989). As Archbishop Chrysostomos points out, *theosis*—becoming by grace what God is by nature—is the fundamental goal of Christianity for the Fathers. As he points out (1989), humans never become God but become an icon of God by virtue of participation in the divine energies of God.

Humility is found in recognizing and acknowledging the great gulf that separates us in our fallenness from God and His divine potential in us. Humility is seeing ourselves as we truly are. Obedience involves aligning our will with the will of God as it has been known within the Church, her saints, and spiritual guides. Humility and obedience lead to repentance, the changing of the mind—*metanoia*. It is in effect a turning away from our fallen selves with the distortions and self-gratifications of sin and the return to our true nature, the authentic purity of the image of God in us. Love for God and for our fellow human beings is the pinnacle of development. A person who has repented and begun the process of cleansing the mind by freeing it from the passions is able to love other people unconditionally, to put other people's needs ahead of one's own, or to see another person's needs as more important than one's own. The person also comes to love God with his or her whole mind, soul, and body, as commanded by Jesus Christ. In an explanation contrary to most Western understandings of the types of love, Archbishop Chrysostomos points out that for Eastern Fathers *eros* is the form of love that is most appropriate between human beings and God, that is, persons are to seek God with all their strength and desire only Him. Obviously, the term *eros* in our fallen world has taken on quite a different connotation.

Archimandrite Hierotheos, a priest and psychotherapist, has, in several written works, systematized the ideas of the Church Fathers on the therapeutic aspects, goals, and activities represented by the Orthodox spiritual tradition (Vlachos, 1993, 1994a, 1994b). He sees the principal therapeutic goal of Orthodoxy as the healing of the *nous*, meaning the highest faculty in human beings, through which God is known when purified and healed. *Nous* is distinct from reason, feeling, and conceptual knowledge. Though sometimes translated as intellect, it is distinct from what we normally consider intelligence. *Nous* is seen as the highest part of the soul, the psyche, the eye of the soul. Cleansed, the *nous* is capable of immediate experience of God as opposed to experience of mere ideas or notions about God. Other ways of speaking of this state would include becoming Christ-like and becoming pure in heart (Matthew 5:8, Romans 12:2, and II Corinthians 5:17).

Using the metaphor of the Church as hospital, the pathology of humans is the passions. By passions, the Fathers refer to that which darkens the soul or *nous*, and these are seen as perversions of what is natural and good in the powers and potentials of the soul of human beings. Some Fathers see the passions as intrinsically evil, whereas others see the passions as originally placed in humankind by God, therefore good but distorted by sin. According to Archimandrite Hierotheos (1994b), several passions are noted by the Fathers as being central or as leading to all the rest: Self-love, love of glory, spiritual ignorance, forgetfulness (of God), laziness, and love of possessions are seen as leading to a long list of the ills and sins of the soul.

Cure of the passions and of their transformation is the penultimate goal of Orthodox faith. The ultimate goal is communion with God and vision of God. Motivation to heal the passions may include being released from the pain of the passions, but is, at its best, about love and desire for God.

PSYCHOLOGICAL INTERVENTIONS CONGRUENT WITH ORTHODOXY

Virtually any psychological intervention would be all right to use with the majority of Orthodox persons. Outlining the treatment plan with a client would avert most conflicts in this regard. A therapist would do well to consider carefully interventions that are intended to influence a client's religious views, as would be the case in dealing with clients of any tradition. A conference with the client's parish priest, of course with the person's permission, would also help any therapist to plan better and more effective interventions.

SPIRITUAL INTERVENTIONS INDICATED (OR NOT)

Most Orthodox will not respond well to spiritual interventions in psychotherapy or counseling. They will likely see the area of spiritual guidance or development as the domain of their priest. Certainly, before using a behavioral prescription or suggestion for a spiritual practice as a part of therapy, the therapist would best discuss the specific intervention fully with the client and perhaps with the client's priest. Many, if not most, Orthodox clients will have spoken with their priest about their psychological problems before making an appointment with a therapist. In most cases, the priest will have already made his suggestions to the client. The suggestions will have covered both the psychological and spiritual aspects of the situation.

WORKING WITH RELIGIOUS LEADERS

Generally, it is safe to assume that Orthodox clergy are open and willing to work with psychotherapists. Many clergy have training in psychotherapy, and several are clinical psychologists. However, Orthodox priests may be more possessive than their counterparts in the Western churches, that is, they may feel more responsibility for members of their flock than other pastors. As most of the churches are small, the parishioners are likely well known to the priest along with their families. This need not hinder the therapist and will not, if the priest has confidence in the therapist, and if a level of contact and understanding, appropriate for the specific case, is maintained with the priest.

SUGGESTED READINGS

Ware, K. (1993). *The Orthodox church*. London: Penguin Books.

Ware, K. (1998). *The Orthodox way*. Crestwood, NY: St. Vladimir's Seminary Press.

On-line sources of information include The Orthodox Christian Information Center, *http://www.orthodoxinfo.com*; The Greek Orthodox Archdiocese home page, *http://www.goarch.org*; and The Orthodox Church in America page, http://www.oca.org.

REFERENCES

Athanasius, St. (1975). *On the incarnation of our Lord*. Crestwood, NY: St. Vladimir's Seminary Press.

Azkoul, Father M. (1994). What are the differences between Orthodoxy and Roman Catholicism? *The Orthodox Witness*, 27–28.

Chrysostomos, Bp. (1986). *Repentence*. Etna, CA: Center for Traditionalist Orthodox Studies.

Chrysostomos, Bp. (1989). Towards a spiritual psychology: A synthesis of the Desert Fathers. *Pastoral Psychology, 37,* 255–273.

Chrysostomos, Bp., & Thornton, J. (1988). *Love*. Brookline, MA: Hellenic College Press.

Chrysostomos, Bp., Williams, T. M., & Williams, P., Sr. (1983). *Humility*. Etna, CA: Center for Traditionalist Orthodox Studies.

Chrysostomos, Bp., Young, A., & Derugin, V. (1985). *Obedience*. Brookline, MA: Holy Cross Orthodox Press.

Constantelos, D. J. (1982). *Understanding the Greek Orthodox Church: Its faith, history, and practice*. New York: Seabury Press.

French, R. M. (1991). *The way of a pilgrim: And the pilgrim continues his way*. San Francisco: Harper.

Langes, M. (Ed.). (1977). *Evergetinos*. Athens, Greece: Monastery of the Transfiguration.

The Little Russian Philokalia: Volume 1. St. Seraphim of Sarov. (1996). Platina, CA: St. Herman of Alaska Brotherhood.

Luibheid, C. (1987). *Pseudo-Dionysius: The complete works*. New York: Paulist Press.

Pangratios, Father. (1992). "Fasting." In *Chronicle of Christ of the Hills Monastery*. Blanco, TX: Christ of the Hills Monastery

Palmer, G. E. H., Sherrard, P., & Ware, K. (Trans.). (1990). *Philokalia, I–IV*. London: Faber & Faber.

Stokoe, M., with Kishkovsky, L. (1995). *Orthodox Christians in North America: 1794–1994*. Wayne, NJ: Orthodox Christian Publishing Center.

Vlachos, Archmandrite Hierotheos. (1993). *The illness and cure of the soul in the Orthodox Tradition* (Effie Mavromichali, Trans.). Levadia, Greece: Birth of the Theotokos Monastery.

Vlachos, Archimandrite Hierotheos. (1994a). *Orthodox psychotherapy: The science of the Fathers* (Esther Williams, Trans.). Levadia, Greece: Birth of the Theotokis Monastery.

Vlachos, Archimandrite Hierotheos. (1994b). *Orthodox spirituality: A brief introduction* (Effie Mavromichali, Trans.). Levadia, Greece: Birth of the Theotokos Monastery.

Ware, Bishop Kallistos. (1991). *The Orthodox Church*. London: Penguin Books.

Ware, Bishop Kallistos. (1996). *How we are saved*. Minneapolis, MN: Light and Life Publishing Co.

Ware, Bishop Kallistos. (1998). *The Orthodox way*. Crestwood, NY: St. Vladimir's Seminary Press.

Whiteford, J. (1997). *Sola Scriptura*. Ben Lomond, CA: Conciliar Press.

5

PSYCHOTHERAPY WITH MAINLINE PROTESTANTS: LUTHERAN, PRESBYTERIAN, EPISCOPAL/ ANGLICAN, AND METHODIST

MICHAEL E. McCULLOUGH, ANDREW J. WEAVER, DAVID B. LARSON, AND KIMBERLY R. AAY

Where, then is boasting? It is excluded. On what principal? On that of observing the law? No, but on that of faith. For we maintain that a man is justified by faith apart from observing the law.
—Romans 3:27–28, NIV

The Protestant traditions to be covered in this chapter—Lutheran, Presbyterian, Episcopal/Anglican, and Methodist—constitute approximately 18% of the U.S. population. According to the National Survey of Religious Identification (NSRI), the largest survey of American religion in history, approximately 8%, 5.2%, 2.8%, and 1.7% of Americans identify themselves as Methodist, Lutheran, Presbyterian, and Episcopal, respectively (see Kosmin & Lachman, 1993, for a detailed description of the NSRI). Scholars of religion usually lump these traditions together as "Mainline Protestants" (Kosmin & Lachman, 1993; Lovinger, 1996). This grouping is somewhat unfortunate because these four groups are diverse in origin, history, and particular beliefs and practices. Indeed, to summarize the distinctives of these four traditions—and their effects on counseling and psychotherapy—in one chapter almost necessitates imprecision and overgeneralization. For example, the Lutheran tradition incorporates three sizable churches (Evangelical Lutheran Church in America, Lutheran Church—Missouri Synod, and Wisconsin Evangelical Lutheran Synod); the Presbyterian tradition comprises two large churches (Presbyterian Church—U.S.A. and the Presbyterian Church of America) and several smaller ones; the Methodist tradition comprises several churches as well. There is also now a modest Episcopal break-away group (Table 5.1).

To complicate matters even further, other denominations could (and probably should) be classified as Mainline Protestant as well. These include the Congregationalist Church (now part of the United Church of Christ), Disciples of Christ, American Baptists, and the Reformed Churches that came out of the Dutch Reformed Church (such as the Reformed Church of America and the Christian Reformed Church). These other mainline Protestant churches together comprise several million adult members nationally (see Kosmin & Lachman, 1993).

The term *mainline* refers to the fact that these denominations have traditionally been at the center of American culture: They were (with the Puritans and Congregationalists) the faiths held by the majority of Americans through the early period of the American republic (Kosmin & Lachman, 1993). Because of their traditional comfort with American culture, persons from these denominations tend to be more at home in the secular world than do persons from other Christian traditions (e.g., Fundamentalists and Evangelicals). Their comfort with secular American culture is almost certainly because members of the mainline Protestant churches helped, in large part, to create secular American culture.

Moreover, fewer than 20% of the nation's Presbyterians, Episcopalians, and Methodists would need to be distributed to other states for the denominations' state-level distributions to match the geographical distribution of all other American religions combined. Substantially more Lutherans would need to be redistributed to other states to achieve the same effect because they are highly concentrated in the Midwest (Kosmin & Lachman, 1993). (This geographic "similarity index" helps to identify the degree to which a particular denomination is geographically isolated from the others.)

Given the central place of these Protestant traditions in the history of the United States and their relative geographical integration into American society, it is safe to say that Mainline Protestants interact with mainstream American culture from within rather than from without (Kosmin & Lachman, 1993).

DESCRIPTION OF THE RELIGIOUS TRADITIONS

Despite their diversity, the denominations covered in this chapter are linked by several common factors:

TABLE 5.1
Major Subgroups Within Each of the Four Major Mainline Protestant Denominations

Lutheran	Presbyterian	Episcopal	Methodist
Evangelical Lutheran Church in America	Presbyterian Church (U.S.A.)	(Protestant) Episcopal Church in the U.S.A.	United Methodist Church
Lutheran Church—Missouri Synod	Presbyterian Church of America (PCA)	Anglican Church of North America	African Methodist Episcopal Church
Wisconsin Evangelical Lutheran Synod	Evangelical Presbyterian Church (EPC)		African Methodist Episcopal Zion Church
	Orthodox Presbyterian Church		Christian Methodist Episcopal Church

1. their derivation (at least initially) from Europe's Protestant Reformation;
2. the influence of the 20th-century Protestant liberalism on all four traditions; and
3. their continued adherence to basic beliefs of the Protestant worldview.

Origins and Historical Perspectives

Three of the four denominations discussed in this chapter (Lutheran, Presbyterian, and Episcopal) find their roots in the Protestant Reformation of Europe, which took place at the beginning of the 16th century (Chadwick, 1986). In the Western and Central Europe of the 1500s, there was great agitation for religious change, but not much agreement about *what* specifically in the Church needed to be changed. Clearly, the bureaucracy of the Church had swelled in its inefficiency. The Pope was seen by some as having too much power. Church offices could be bought. Laws were exceedingly lenient toward church officials. People with money were able to buy almost anything religious (including sacraments, blessings, prayers for the remission of pain in purgatory, and even positions in the church bureaucracy). Indeed, by the beginning of the 16th century, the sale of "indulgences" was an important way for the church to raise revenue. Most common people thought that the ties of the Church to state governments dissipated the Church's spiritual functions. However, when people of the early 1500s spoke of reformation, they usually referred to administrative changes, not to basic changes in the authority structure of the Church (Chadwick, 1986).

Two unique factors at the advent of the 16th century facilitated the Reformation. First, unlike in previous years, secular government was gaining efficiency and wealth at the same time that Church government was losing them. Indeed, secular governments became aware that to gain power and sovereignty, the power of the Church over matters of the state had to be limited. Thus, reformers looked to the secular government to provide power for reforming the Church (Chadwick, 1986). Second, a rise in literacy and changes in academics gave lay persons new opportunities for learning, opened scholarly debate of theological issues to all persons, and promoted a general disdain for narrow philosophical principles that stifled intellectual inquiry into theological matters. The books of Erasmus, who criticized the stifling intellectual traditions of religious scholarship, were best sellers of the time.

Lutheran

The founder of Lutheranism was a German priest named Martin Luther. A Roman Catholic monk himself, Luther came to believe that salvation came not through acts of asceticism, good works, the purchase of indulgences, or other forms of human efforts. Luther's central turning point was a growing despair in his own inability to live a perfect, sinless life (Chadwick, 1986). From this despair, Luther came to realize and began to preach that salvation came by the grace of God through faith alone (Harris-Abbott, 1996). This was a significant departure from Catholic doctrine, which taught that salvation was the product of faith and works (i.e., one acquired saving faith only after one had done all in one's power to acquire it).

Another principle equally important to Luther's thought was his conviction that the Bible (i.e., Hebrew and Christian scriptures) was the final source of authority for religious doctrine. This conviction stood in contrast with the Roman Catholic belief that the Bible *and* church tradition formed a single, unbroken source of authority for faith and doctrine. Luther's proposed changes in religious doctrine came during the advent of the printing press. Luther capitalized on this new technology by making a simple, German translation of the New Testament affordable and readily available. This was an important strategy for decentralizing religious power and authority away from a select few because it allowed each person to use the teachings of scripture to guide his or her own life.

Luther presented his theological ideas publicly for the first time in 1517, when he nailed his famous "95 Theses" to the door of the church in Wittenberg, Germany. Although the 95 Theses contained no mention of the doctrine of justification by faith, Luther felt that the theses—indictments of the Church's practice of selling indulgences—sprang from his conviction of God's grace. The 95 Theses and Luther's theology in general resonated with the common people.

In 1530, the Holy Roman Emperor and the German princes who supported Luther presented the Augsburg Confession (written by Melanchthon, an associate of Luther) at an Imperial Diet. This confession became the most important statement of the fundamental beliefs of Lutheranism. Luther considered himself a Roman Catholic and had no intention of starting a new religious faith. Nevertheless, following a period of political upheaval, Lutheranism spread through many German and Scandanavian states as princes and cities adopted Lutheran reforms.

Emigration from Western Europe brought Lutherans from many Western European nations into the United States by 1850. Because the spread of Lutheranism across Europe was so successful, there were as many as 150 groups of American Lutherans in 1850 (Harris-Abbott, 1996). Since then, these groups have united and merged into 9 discernible groups called Synods (Harris-Abbott, 1996). Nearly 50% of the nation's Lutherans live in the upper Midwest (Kosmin & Lachman, 1993).

Presbyterian

The Presbyterian Church (and other Reformed churches, such as the Dutch Reformed Church) also traces its roots back to the 16th century. The main promoters of Reformed theology were Ulrich Zwingli and John Calvin. Calvin was a French theologian and lawyer who spent the better part of his professional life in Switzerland.

The works of Erasmus and other Catholic humanists fueled the reformation movement in Switzerland, just as they had in Germany. However, Calvin was active almost a generation after Luther. Although they had the same desire to restore the Church to its earliest form (as described by the Apostle Paul in the New Testament), Zwingli and Calvin had greater suspicion of the corruptions of the past than did Luther, and they quickly did away with many of the outward appearances of the Catholic Church. Luther's reformation was guided by the principle that "anything not expressly forbidden in scripture is permissible"; Zwingli and Calvin's reformation was guided by the principle that "anything not expressly condoned in scripture is not permissible" (Chadwick, 1986).

Calvin's greatest strengths were his systematic mind and his deep desire for order. His *Institutes of the Christian Religion*—originally published in 1536—was the theological treatise that organized Calvin's theology around his conviction that God had complete control over all events that occurred in the world (Chadwick, 1986). The most important corollary of this conviction is the *doctrine of predestination* (Harris-Abbott, in press). The doctrine of predestination teaches that although all people are justly condemned to hell because of their inheritance of original sinfulness, God chooses some to whom he gives faith, which allows them to be saved. Although Christian theologians from Augustine to Aquinas to Luther had believed in predestination, Calvin made predestination—and the conviction of God's complete control over the entire world—a major point for religious devotion and practice (and he also added to the doctrine of predestination the proposition that God also chooses who will be damned to eternal punishment). Today's Presbyterian and Reformed churches formally acknowledge the teaching of predestination, but the Presbyterian Church (U.S.A.) has added a critical note to its *Book of Confessions* indicating that the mystery of predestination must be held in tension with the belief that God intends the salvation of all persons.

Calvin turned his love for order in religious life to the functioning of the city of Geneva itself. As a lawyer, he revised the city code, developed a plan for the city's security, and even developed a more efficient mode for garbage collection (Chadwick, 1986). Also, he occupied himself with ensuring that the citizens of Geneva lived moral, upstanding lives that were consonant with the teachings of the New Testament. He also established a college for the education of Protestant theologians and pastors. All of

Calvin's activities were motivated by his desire to bring the ethos of the New Testament church to life in Geneva. His relentlessness won him few friends. If the common people of Germany loved their Martin Luther, the people of Geneva respected and feared their John Calvin. Nevertheless, the discipline that Calvin's theological system inspired helped to spread Calvinism across Europe.

Reformed churches are still prominent in Switzerland, the Netherlands, Scotland, Korea, Lebanon, and parts of Africa (Harris-Abbott, in press). The largest Reformed church in the United States is the Presbyterian Church (U.S.A.), which was formed in 1983 through the merger of two groups of Presbyterians who had split during the Civil War (Harris-Abbott, in press). The growth of Presbyterianism in the United States was linked to Scottish and Scottish–Irish immigration (Kosmin & Lachman, 1993). In 1780, the Presbyterian Church was the second largest church in the United States (Kosmin & Lachman, 1993). In nearly every state today, Presbyterians represent 2–4% of the total population, with slightly higher representations in the Western and Eastern states (Kosmin & Lachman, 1993).

Episcopal/Anglican

Although the Lutheran and Calvinist reformations were primarily motivated by religious conviction, the Reformation in England was motivated at first by the desire for political change (Chadwick, 1986). King Henry's disappointing marriage to Catherine of Aragon failed to yield a male heir to the throne, so Henry turned to Rome for dissolution of the marriage. The Roman Church would not honor his request, so Henry summoned the Parliament to draft several bills to reform the Church in England—including a ruling that the Pope did not possess divine authority (Chadwick, 1986; DuBose, 1996). Following the ruling against papal authority, Henry successfully argued that the Pope had erred in ruling that the King's marriage to Catherine was legitimate.

After the separation of the English Church from continental Catholicism, English officials under Thomas Cromwell dismantled most vestiges of Roman religious authority in England. By 1540, most of the monasteries were closed, their property reverting to the crown. Many ex-monks became clergy, and retired nuns were given marriage dowries to promote their reintegration into secular society. Much of the money gained from dissolution of the monasteries, however, became revenue for the state. The primary interest of Henry and his followers was in conserving the Catholic ideal that religious authority was centralized. The difference was that Henry wanted religious authority for himself.

Following Henry's death in 1547, the door was opened for true Protestant reformation in England. Henry's successor, Edward VI, allowed for church liturgy to be adapted into a more characteristically Protestant form. Services were no longer conducted in Latin, and the prayer book was rewritten to make it useful to all people. Backlash against the Protestant church occurred during the reign of Queen Mary, who attempted to restore papal authority in England. Mary's efforts galvanized many of the common people, making "the Catholics more Roman and the Protestants more reformed" (Chadwick, 1986, p. 131).

Queen Elizabeth I, the daughter of Henry VIII and Anne Boleyn, is the central figure responsible for securing the long-term success of the Anglican tradition in England. In 1558, England was divided between Catholicism and Protestantism (approximately two thirds of English citizens were still Catholic). Moreover, most of England's allies were applying pressure for England to remain Catholic, even though Elizabeth herself was no doubt Protestant and felt pressure to oblige the religious changes that Protestant leaders in England were demanding. Elizabeth's success came from the fact that she was able to find a *via media*, or middle-road position between Catholicism and Calvinism. She retained for the Anglican Church many elements of Catholicism, including a celibate clergy and a more or less traditional Catholic doctrine about the Eucharist or Holy Communion, yet she still maintained that the Pope had no authority over the church in England and that legitimate religious authority in England remained with the Monarchy. Through an act of Parliament, England was officially declared Protestant in 1559. To this day, many Anglicans still identify themselves closely with Catholicism.

The Protestant Episcopal Church in the United States is the American branch of the Church of England or Anglican Church. In 1780, the Anglican/Episcopal church was the fourth largest in the United States, although many Anglicans' ties to England during the Revolution forced them to immigrate to Canada. Those Anglicans who remained in the colonies during the revolution were regarded with some suspicion, and the Anglican Church in America nearly became inoperative (J. W. Wright, 1994). Today, the Episcopal Church is strongest in the northeastern United States. By and large, it identifies itself with Protestantism, although a wing of the Episcopal Church continues to emphasize the Church's Catholic heritage. A recent division of the Protestant Episcopal Church over (a) a revised prayer book and (b) the ordination of women led to the formation of the Anglican Church of North America.

Methodist

The Methodist tradition dates back to the 1720s when John Wesley, an Oxford don and priest in the Church of England, organized a group of Oxford undergraduates committed to living a life of personal devotion and service to others, patterned after the teachings of the early Church (Outler,

1964). Like Luther, Wesley never intended to found a new church. Methodism was an evangelical movement formed to bring renewal within the Church of England (Harper, 1983).

Influenced by the early church fathers and mothers of the Eastern and Western traditions, as well as by devotional writers like William Law, Jeremy Taylor, and Thomas à Kempis, Wesley began a lifelong pursuit of what he called "holy living" or "holiness." Holy living consisted of religious devotion, intense study of scripture, and works of charity that included assisting the poor, the sick, and the imprisoned. "Methodist" was one of the several derogatory names, including "Bible Moths," that Oxford students gave to Wesley and his "holy club." The term Methodist stuck (Outler, 1964).

In 1735, John Wesley went to Georgia with James Oglethorpe to work as a chaplain to the English colonists and a missionary to the Native Americans. The mission was largely a failure—the natives of Georgia were uninterested in hearing about Wesley's stiff Anglican form of Christianity. Perhaps the most important consequence of his time in Georgia was Wesley's acquaintance with a group of German Moravians who impressed him with their joyful devotion and deep faith (M. Schmidt, 1960).

Upon returning to England, Wesley had a crisis of faith. He had gone to Georgia confident in himself and his views, but returned to Britain humbled by his failures in the New World. His soul searching brought him to a deeper spirituality and a new inner assurance of his faith. After this crisis, rarely did Wesley question his calling during the next five decades. He showed an inner trust and reliance on God that moved him from a somewhat priggish Oxford don to the pastoral leader of a genuinely evangelical revival (Outler, 1994).

From the itinerant preacher George Whitefield, Wesley learned the art of outdoor preaching. Though the idea of preaching outside the walls of a church was unheard of, Wesley received an incredibly warm response from ordinary people (especially the poor) when he led services outdoors. Outdoor preaching remained an important vehicle of evangelism for the next 50 years of Methodist revival. Wesley devoted the rest of his life to proclaiming the simple gospel message of faith, heartfelt conversion, devotional practice, and charity as the keys to "holy living."

For 50 years, Wesley preached and organized the Methodist people into small support groups, called classes, throughout England, Scotland, Ireland, and Wales. The sermons of John Wesley and the 50 volumes in his *Christian Library* represent a staggering accomplishment. The *Christian Library* was developed primarily to educate the Methodist people and preachers. It included titles such as *Compendium of Logic*, *History of England*, *Dictionary and Compendium of Natural Philosophy*, as well as grammars in English, Latin, French, Greek, and Hebrew. In his sermons and other writings, Wesley developed a distinct theological linkage between *sola fide* (justification by faith alone) and holy living that had no precedent in Protestantism (Outler, 1994).

In the United States, Methodism separated from the Church of England in 1784 when Church of England priests were no longer available in the New Republic to minister to the Methodists. One of the first acts of the Methodist Church was to call for the abolition of slavery. Earlier, Wesley had declared the slave trade to be "that execrable villainy which is the scandal of religion, of England, and of the human nature" (Whaling, 1981). Although Methodists later compromised somewhat with regard to slavery, the Methodist faith is personal first and social always, and the two are never to be separated.

Today, worldwide there are about 70 million Methodists and the greatest growth is in Africa (Whaling, 1981). The largest of the Methodist churches is the United Methodist Church. It is the most geographically diverse Protestant church in the United States with a congregation in 94% of American counties—a percentage equaled only by the Roman Catholics (Bradley, Green, Jones, Lynn, & McNeil, 1990).

Basic Beliefs and Practices

Each mainline Protestant Church has its own unique history and development that shape the thinking and behavior of its followers. However, all four of the Protestant traditions reviewed in the present chapter and the smaller related groups have several features that unite them. First, they emphasize the Bible (i.e., the Hebrew Old Testament and the Greek New Testament) as a primary source of authority for faith and doctrine. Despite the special place that Scripture holds as a source of authority about faith and doctrine, all four traditions also value church tradition, common sense, and conscience in making decisions about life and how it should be lived.

It should be noted that the four mainline Protestant traditions are also distinct from one another in this domain. For example, Episcopalians value tradition in a distinctive way (identifying rather closely, in some Episcopal churches, with the Catholic understanding of religious authority). Also, Methodists affirm the importance of religious experience as a means of knowing God's will in a way that is distinct from Lutherans, Presbyterians, and Episcopalians. In addition to the value placed on Scripture, all four traditions adhere to a belief that salvation comes through faith, rather than through good works. However, this statement also needs to be qualified because the term "salvation through faith" means different things within the four mainline Protestant traditions. Faith, in this context, may be understood as a pietistic experience (a traditionally Methodist understanding), as an objective reliance on Divine grace (a typically Lutheran understanding), or as trust in God through the Church and sacraments (a typically Anglican understanding).

Finally, 20th-century Protestant liberalism played a major role in shaping all four mainline traditions into what they are today. As many diverse scientific and intellectual efforts (including evolutionary theory, psychoanalytic understandings of human nature, and the promise of a behavioral technology that could improve quality of life) coalesced in the first few decades of the 20th century, the mainline Protestant churches found ways to accommodate to the changes in worldview that these intellectual and scientific developments ushered in. By contrast, many American religious traditions reacted to these intellectual developments by becoming more sectlike, isolated, and fundamentalist (Hunter, 1985). One benefit of this accommodation process was that mainline Protestants continued to contribute to mainstream American culture. As a result, all four traditions developed the following qualities:

1. an optimistic estimate of human nature;
2. more latitude in questioning scripture and church tradition;
3. an eschewal of Biblical literalism;
4. more openness to scientific discovery, as well as to medical and psychological therapies; and
5. less stress on the distinctive traditions of the denominations themselves.

The net impact of Protestant liberalism on the psychological thinking of people from mainline Protestant traditions can be easily noticed by perusing the work of devotional writers such as Harry Emerson Fosdick and Norman Vincent Peale (Vitz, 1994).

Positions on Important Social and Moral Issues

It is usually dangerous to imply that any group of people has uniform set of beliefs, values, or attitudes toward social, moral, or political issues. Reflective of the political diversity that exists within these denominations, a variety of positions on social, moral, and political issues may be found within the mainline churches. However, it is possible to get a sense of where the denominations officially stand on a variety of issues by examining official church documents. The editors of the series, *Religious Beliefs and Health Care Decisions* at the Park Ridge Center for the Study of Health, Faith, and Ethics developed their summaries of the mainline churches' stances on a variety of social, moral, and health care issues by examining official church documents. Where possible, the official church documents were quoted verbatim. We borrow liberally from this edited series in the sections that follow.

Marriage, Divorce, and Remarriage

All four traditions reviewed here have high views of marriage. Unlike Catholicism, they do not view marriage as a sacrament, but rather, as a blessing from God or even a vocation (DuBose, 1995; Garrett, 1996; Gillespie, 1996). Marriage is expected to be a lifelong commitment that God uses to conduct important work on earth (e.g., raising healthy children); divorce was traditionally considered to be wrong (Harris-Abbott, 1996, in press).

Moralization about divorce changed dramatically in all four denominations following the massive cultural changes of the 1960s and 1970s. As mainline Protestants divorced more frequently and formed single-parent families, all four churches' traditions became more tolerant of divorce, single-parent households, and remarriage (Garrett, 1996). Thus, those within the Presbyterian Church—U.S.A. [PC (USA)] tend (along with Episcopalians) to be wary of prescribing child-centered heterosexual marriage as the normative family unit (Garrett, 1996). For the PC (USA), the focus has shifted from dictating normative family forms to helping families of all forms to function better (Garrett, 1996). In the Episcopal Church, remarriage after divorce is welcomed (Gillespie, 1996). In the Methodist Church, the emphasis has moved from dictating morality regarding divorce to helping people who have been through divorce to find comfort and healing (J. M. Schmidt & Murphy-Geiss, 1996).

Sexuality

All four mainline denominations view sexuality as the highest form of human intimacy. Sexuality has been traditionally reserved for marriage and is typically discouraged outside of marriage. In their discussions of sexuality through the first half of the 20th century, the Lutheran, Presbyterian, and Methodist denominations took moral stands against homosexuality (Harris-Abbott, 1996, in press; DuBose, 1995), whereas the Episcopal church tended to be somewhat silent regarding homosexuality (Gillespie, 1996).

The 1960s and 1970s were a turning point for all four denominations with regard to their policies and beliefs on sexuality. From the 1970s through to the present, homosexuality—indeed, issues related to sexuality in general—have been of major concern. In contrast with the first half of the 20th century, however, the theological emphasis seems to be clearly on mutual understanding, tolerance, and acceptance rather than on prescriptions about normative sexual orientations. Nonetheless, the issue of how to respond to homosexuality continues to be hotly debated by church members and clergy in all four traditions. At least in the United Methodist Church and the Presbyterian Churches, homosexuality (and all sexual activity outside of committed, heterosexual marriage) continues to be officially viewed as incompatible with scriptural teachings, even though minority voices within both denominations are at work to change this traditional position. All four mainline denominations acknowledge that sexual activity does occur outside of committed, heterosexual marriage even though marriage continues to be viewed as the only legitimate vehicle through which sexual love can be an expression of God's love (DuBose, 1996; Gillespie, 1996). Promiscuity of all types is viewed typically as destructive and sinful (Gillespie, 1996).

Contraception

All four churches accept the use of contraception (DuBose, 1995, 1996; Harris-Abbott, 1996, in press). Their tolerance of contraception is usually related to the view that sexuality is intended for the enjoyment of both partners as well as a means of procreation. The use of contraception is also viewed as a responsible way to limit reproduction in a world where the population is increasing rapidly (DuBose, 1995, 1996; J. M. Schmidt & Murphy-Geiss, 1996). Knowledge about contraception should be made available to all sexually active persons (Harris-Abbott, 1996). Contraception should not be viewed as a vehicle for guaranteeing childlessness, however, because having children is understood to be one of the creative tasks of marriage (DuBose, 1995).

Abortion

Abortion is generally discouraged except in cases in which the mother's life is in danger, the child was conceived during involuntary sexual intercourse, or the fetus has extreme abnormalities (DuBose, 1995, 1996; Harris-Abbott, 1996, in press). The conservative Lutheran Church—Missouri Synod views abortion as permissible only when it is an inevitable byproduct of medical procedures designed to save the life of a mother (Harris-Abbott, 1996). The position of the United Methodist Church is similar.

Both major Presbyterian churches in the United States and the Episcopal Church have indicated that abortion can be morally justifiable (DuBose, 1996; Harris-Abbott, in press), though typically only for extreme situations (DuBose, 1996). However, abortion has been a contentious issue for Presbyterians, especially in the PC (USA), whose leadership tends to be more liberal and pro-choice than the majority of its members (Harris-Abbott, in press). Currently, the PC (USA) endorses a statement indicating that abortion ought to be a last resort (Harris-Abbott, in press). Episcopalians are urged to examine their conscience in prayer and to seek the guidance of the Christian community prior to making a decision to abort (DuBose, 1996). They oppose legislation that would make medically safe abortions unavailable (DuBose, 1996).

Physician-Assisted Suicide

Both liberal and conservative Lutheran traditions are opposed to physician-assisted suicide (Harris-Abbott, 1996). The Presbyterian, Episcopal, and Methodist churches distinguish between active and passive euthanasia, making more room for the withdrawal of life support and the foregoing of heroic measures than they do for active euthanasia. This more liberal stance toward passive euthanasia (or the foregoing of life-sustaining treatment) emerges from their recognition that although life is valuable, it is also finite (Dubose, 1996; Harris-Abbott, in press). Thus, a life filled with irreversible pain and suffering that cannot sustain itself should not necessarily be sustained simply because the means exist for doing so. Provided that the intention is to relieve pain and not to kill, the Episcopal and Methodist churches condone the relief of pain and suffering, even if palliative measures might possibly lead to the death of the patient (DuBose, 1995, 1996).

Alcohol and Drug Use

Characteristic of their generally protective attitudes toward human life, Lutherans, Presbyterians, and Episcopalians discourage improper and excessive use of alcohol, tobacco, and other drugs because of their deleterious effects on individual and collective health and well-being (Harris-Abbott, 1996, in press). Moderate use of alcohol in low-risk situations is tolerated and not prohibited (DuBose, 1996; Harris-Abbott, in press). Methodists take a harder line against even moderate alcohol use (DuBose, 1995).

IMPLICATIONS FOR COUNSELING AND PSYCHOTHERAPY

Relationship Issues and Suggestions

In discussing psychotherapy and counseling with people from mainline traditions, Lovinger (1996) has suggested that such clients reflect what is typical of American clients in general. However, as noted before, there are beliefs and practices that distinguish among the four traditions and among subgroups that exist *within* each of the four traditions. Nevertheless, it is probably safe to assume that most professional counselors and psychotherapists will see a substantial proportion of people from mainline Protestant traditions in their caseloads.

View of the Mental Health Professions

Partly because of their inheritance from 20th-century Protestant liberalism, members of these four Protestant denominations have positive views of the mental health professions and tend to view physical health, mental health, and spiritual health as distinct but interrelated (DuBose, 1995; Harris-Abbott, 1996; Malony, 1998). Official documents of the Lutheran and Episcopal churches call for people to be more responsive to the concerns of people who have mental disorders (Harris-Abbott, 1996; DuBose, 1996). They also call for local Lutheran and Episcopal churches to ensure that the needs of individuals or families dealing with mental illness are being met within the Church (DuBose, 1996; Harris-Abbott, 1996). Official documents from the Presbyterian and Methodist churches suggest that these denominations are open to the biological and medical understandings of mental illness (Harris-Abbott, 1996; DuBose, 1995).

Lay persons are encouraged to learn about mental illness so that church policies regarding the proper assessment, treatment, and referral of people with mental health needs can be based on up-to-date scientific information (Harris-Abbott, in press). The development of lay counseling programs within local churches is welcomed, as is training in mental health care for clergy (DuBose, 1996). Using psychotropic medications to treat psychiatric symptoms is also generally condoned (Harris-Abbott, in press).

In spite of their openness to mental health providers, data suggest that "Protestants" (an obviously imprecise group of Christians that include Mainline Protestants, as well as many others) find their way into mental health research samples with less frequency than one would expect on the basis of their representation among the national population (Larson et al., 1989). Larson and colleagues conducted a meta-analytic review of data from 15 mental health studies that reported the distributions of religious affiliations (using only the crude categories of Protestant, Catholic, Jewish, and Other/None) in the sample. They found that despite the fact that the national population is approximately 62% Protestant, in the seven studies that sampled people from the community, only 50% identified themselves as Protestant; in the eight studies that sampled people from inpatient or outpatient psychiatric settings, only 32% of the individuls identified themselves as Protestants.

These figures suggest that Lutherans, Presbyterians, Episcopalians, and Methodists might be less likely to find their way into inpatient or outpatient psychiatric settings. It should be noted, however, that it is not clear to what extent these results apply to Protestants from mainline traditions because mainline Protestants were combined with Protestants from non-mainline traditions. Also, these findings could be the result of biased sampling techniques (because Protestants are underrepresented in community-based surveys of mental health as well as in clinical samples), but it might also suggest that Protestants have some hesitation about seeking formal treatment for their mental health needs (because their underrepresentation appears to be even more severe in clinical samples). However, direct data on denominational differences in mental health services use are scant.

Concerns That Members May Have About Therapy and Therapists

Like many persons, people from mainline Protestant denominations are likely to experience some discomfort regarding psychotherapy. However, given Mainline Protestants' typically high degree of educational attainment and comfort with the worldview of Protestant liberalism, their hesitation about psychotherapy is likely to be much less than it might be among people from other Christian traditions.

Some Protestants are probably informed enough to understand that psychotherapy is not a value-free enterprise, and that psychotherapies do take value stances (e.g., regarding optimal human functioning, pathology, and what people must do to become healthy). Some potential clients from mainline Protestant traditions might fear that counselors will encourage them to weaken their ties and commitments to marriage, family, or religious tradition to achieve psychological health. To the extent that Christian clients (including mainline Protestants) believe that their therapists might attribute their psychological difficulties to their religion or spirituality, they also are likely to anticipate negative outcomes of counseling and psychotherapy (Keating & Fretz, 1990). Other prospective clients might be concerned that they will be encouraged to do something unethical or immoral to achieve psychological well-being.

Suggestions for Building Trust and Credibility

Most of the widely used strategies for building trust and credibility with all patients would apply to Mainline Protestants. With appropriate tact and timing, some clients from mainline traditions would probably respond positively to the assessment of their religious or spiritual issues during an intake interview. To the extent that such an informal screening reveals religious or spiritual issues to be salient, more formal assessment interviews or instruments (see below) might be used to gather more detailed spiritual information in a respectful and structured way.

Psychologically sophisticated clients who have concerns about the value base of psychotherapy might also benefit from some explicit disclosure of the therapists' stances regarding religion and spirituality. Such pretherapy might include disclosure of the therapists' opinions regarding:

1. whether religion and spirituality are causally related to mental health and illness;
2. the appropriateness of addressing (in appropriate proportions) religious and spiritual concerns in the context of counseling and psychotherapy;
3. the therapists' comfort with addressing religious/spiritual concerns; and
4. how the therapists' religious/spiritual beliefs (or lack thereof) influence the process of counseling and psychotherapy.

Such information could be presented in the form of brochures, videotapes, audiotapes, or compact discs (Worthington, Kurusu, McCullough, & Sandage, 1996). However, most clients—including Mainline Protestant clients—do not want to focus exclusively (or even primarily) on religious or spiritual issues (Wyatt & Johnson, 1990; see also Malony, 1998). Thus, too much pretherapy information related to the counselor or psychotherapists' views on religion may also interfere with the building of trust and credibility (Worthington et al., 1996).

Multicultural Considerations

All four major mainline Protestant denominations have some ethnic diversity. Black Americans are represented among Episcopalian and Methodist churches in proportions that are approximately representative to their national presence (and the African Methodist Episcopal, African Methodist Episcopal Zion, and Christian Methodist Episcopal churches are historically African American). Black Americans are considerably underrepresented in Presbyterian and Lutheran denominations. Hispanic Americans are vastly underrepresented in all four traditions. Asians are present in Presbyterian and Episcopal denominations in approximately representative proportions but are vastly underrepresented in Lutheran and Methodist churches (Kosmin & Lachman, 1993). Mainline Protestants from more geographically isolated mainline traditions, such as the Lutheran Church and the smaller Christian Reformed Church (a Protestant denomination that grew out of the Dutch Reformed Church), have more uniform ethnic/cultural identities. Although it should be expected that such strong ethnic identities will shape the religious worldviews of people from such backgrounds, no scholars of counseling and psychotherapy to date have discussed these interactions in any formal way.

Assessment and Diagnostic Issues and Approaches

Because Mainline Protestants represent, more or less, the historic center of American religion and culture, they tend to be similar to what one would expect of American clients in general. Indeed, this has been one of the main points of this chapter. Thus, one should expect that clients from Mainline Protestant backgrounds will have more or less typical psychosocial problems.

Perhaps the most salient tasks in assessing clients from Mainline Protestant traditions is (a) assessing their religious and spiritual functioning, (b) assessing how their religious and spiritual functioning might influence their psychosocial functioning, and (c) assessing how their religious and spiritual functioning might influence counseling and psychotherapy. A good religious or spiritual assessment for people from Mainline Protestant denominations is likely to follow the same guidelines as those given by Richards and Bergin (1997).

Unfortunately, although measures of religious and spiritual involvement abound (Gorsuch, 1984), we know of no program of research devoted to creating measures of religious or spiritual functioning with meaningful norms, cutoff scores, or standard errors (Richards & Bergin, 1997). Without such benchmarks, it is not clear whether the existing measures of religious and spiritual involvement have a scientifically valid clinical application.

In the absence of such scientific data justifying the clinical use of the existing measures of religious and spiritual involvement, counselors and psychotherapists must gain information about clients' religious and spiritual functioning in a more informal way. Structured assessment instruments might be used to pinpoint aspects of clients' religiousness and spirituality that could be strengths (or causes for concern). Therapists can use such information in an ideographic manner to inform treatment planning (see Richards & Bergin, 1997).

Healing Potential of the Traditions' Beliefs and Practices

In principle, Mainline Protestant belief places great emphasis on the power of God's grace and forgiveness. Salvation, according to Protestant theology, originates with God, not with human works. As such, one would expect people from Mainline Protestant traditions to place an emphasis on grace and forgiveness as potential solutions to many of life's difficulties. Thus, Mainline Protestants are likely to view discussions of grace and forgiveness favorably in the context of counseling and psychotherapy. In general, religious Americans have more favorable views of forgiveness than do the less religious (for review, see McCullough & Worthington, in press). Thus, Mainline Protestants might be prone to grant forgiveness when they suffer damage by other people and more prone to seek forgiveness when they have damaged others (McCullough, Sandage, & Worthington, 1997; McCullough, Worthington, & Rachal, 1997). Given recent studies suggesting that interventions designed to promote forgiveness might have important clinical benefits (e.g., Al-Mabuk, Enright, & Cardis, 1995; Coyle & Enright, 1997; Freedman & Enright, 1996; Hebl & Enright, 1993), interventions designed to help clients grant forgiveness, seek forgiveness, and feel forgiven should be given serious consideration in clinical practice with Mainline Protestants.

Another important resource for healing that currently exists in the mainline denominations is church-based counseling. Pastoral care centers are hosted by many local churches and frequently provide counseling, consultation, and education to people within the local churches. The Samaritan Counseling Centers, for example, began in the Presbyterian Church in 1972. By 1996, this national pastoral counseling corporation provided over 400,000 billable hours of counseling (Laurie, 1997). Because local churches and benefactors often subsidize the operations of such pastoral counseling agencies, services are frequently provided at reduced fees, and their overhead rates are often remarkably low (Laurie, 1997). Counselors and psychotherapists should recognize the popularity and availability of church-based counseling among the mainline churches and forge relationships with local centers that provide such services.

Mainline Protestant traditions are also using lay counseling with increasing frequency (e.g., Wilcox, 1997). It is unknown how many thousands of hours of counseling are provided by trained lay counselors, but this number is likely to be high. Available evidence suggests that Christian lay counseling can be effective in reducing psychological symptoms, at least among moderately distressed clients (Toh & Tan, 1997).

Psychological Interventions Congruent or Incongruent With the Tradition

There are few standard psychological interventions that would be perceived as being particularly incongruent with Mainline Protestant traditions. Research demonstrates that when clients' religious beliefs appear to be interfering with psychological functioning, challenges to those religious beliefs will be tolerated only if the clients' overall religious value framework is supported simultaneously (see McCullough, Worthington, Maxey, & Rachal, 1997, for review). Thus, interventions that are intended to influence clients' religious beliefs and values should be executed with caution.

Spiritual Interventions That Are Likely to Be Indicated (or Contraindicated)

In keeping with Richards and Bergin's (1997) recommendations, spiritual interventions are probably not warranted in counseling and psychotherapy with Mainline Protestants unless an initial assessment reveals that the client is interested in integrating religious or spiritual issues into his or her treatment. Although we know of no data that are germane to the topic, we believe that some of the spiritual interventions proposed by Richards and Bergin (1997, pp. 234–235) are likely to be perceived more positively by Mainline Protestants than are others. References to scripture, in-session prayer, referral for blessing, blessing by therapist, encouraging client confession, and scripture memorization would not be perceived as favorably as would spiritual interventions such as spiritual self-disclosure, encouraging forgiveness, use of religious community, encouraging private prayer, religious journal writing, spiritual meditation, and religious bibliotherapy. Above all, counselors should remember to *ask* their clients about which of their religious traditions might be useful to include in counseling and psychotherapy because such information is much more valuable than guesswork.

Pastors from Mainline Protestant denominations are likely to be fairly open to working with mental health professionals. Each of these denominations has formal statements recognizing the importance of mental health as an example of overall health, and each appears to recognize the importance of mental health professionals for preventing and ameliorating mental health problems. Many pastors have clinical caseloads that rival many clinical and counseling psychologists' caseloads (Worthington et al., 1996). Among clergy, counseling caseload is correlated with higher education (Wright, 1984). Clergy in all four mainline denominations are more likely to have large, active caseloads than clergy from other denominations. Moreover, many religious leaders in the Mainline Protestant denominations have received formal graduate training in one or more of the mental health professions. Thus, it is likely that counselors and psychotherapists would find it relatively easy to work with mainline Protestant religious leaders. It is unfortunate that so little attention has been given in the psychological literature on how psychologists might productively collaborate with clergy (Weaver, Sanford, et al., 1997). It is clear that clergy desire and need more collaboration with mental health specialists in several areas (Weaver, Koenig, & Larson, 1997; Weaver, Koenig, & Ochberg, 1996).

CASE STUDY: "MARGO"

Margo is a 35-year-old woman who was recently beaten and robbed at gunpoint in a grocery store parking lot. She now exhibits several signs of posttraumatic stress disorder (PTSD), including nightmares of the assault and fears about going shopping. She relived the horrific experience over and over again in her mind. Margo's United Methodist pastor referred her to the clinical psychologist Dr. Lopez. The pastor told Dr. Lopez that Margo and her husband had become members of the church 5 years earlier. She is a very active and supportive church member who is bright, articulate, and deeply spiritual. Margo had been raised in a harsh, fundamentalist church, and she had found the United Methodist Church to be a more inviting environment. Margo's pastor assured her that she was not going "crazy" and that other church members had found Dr. Lopez helpful.

Margo's pastor drove Margo to her first session for support. Margo was a well-dressed, dignified person, somewhat anxious about going to the session. She explained that her pastor had recommended that she seek help. Margo said that her anxiety about therapy was related to an experience she had shortly after the assault. Through her health maintenance organization, she had been referred to a mental health specialist who spent 20 minutes with her and gave her a prescription for tranquilizers. He reassured her that she would get over her problems soon. When she said that her faith and prayer life were important factors in her coping, he snickered. When she asked why, he replied that he believed that religion is magical thinking, and that she needed to face reality. That experience had made her suspicious of therapists.

Dr. Lopez explained that she was a practicing Roman Catholic, and she understood that faith has been shown to be a positive resource for healing, especially when people have been through traumatic experiences. She told Margo that research studies show that people often use religion to cope effectively with highly stressful situations. Dr. Lopez said that by offering the social support of community, nurturing nonpunitive religion can provide a means of addressing a traumatic experience that enhances well-being, lowers distress, and may facilitate faster and more effective recovery (Pargament, 1997).

Dr. Lopez reassured her that it was normal to feel fearful and anxious after the sort of trauma she had gone through. Dr. Lopez explained that PTSD symptoms are an expected reaction to life-threatening experiences, and that psychological trauma is not a sign of being "emotionally weak" or "crazy." Many people exposed to this type of assault find their ordinary coping processes overwhelmed. The "shock effect" of psychologically distressing events (such as assault and physical injury) is outside the range of normal human experience, frequently eliciting intense fear, helplessness, loss of control, and fear of annihilation. She noted that Margo showed a key sign of PTSD: repeated, intrusive thoughts of the experience in the form of nightmares. Dr. Lopez suggested it would be good to meet three times a week for a few weeks while Margo was working through the crisis period.

Like most psychologists who treat PTSD, Dr. Lopez began by providing an opportunity for Margo to feel safe in confronting the traumatic event and understanding its connection with her symptoms. The overall treatment strategy was to help Margo to understand and integrate the traumatic experience into the ongoing context of her life. Experienced psychologists concentrate on the present in the aftermath of trauma by exploring the immediate effects. Victims of violence need to rebuild self-esteem and their sense of control, as well as to develop a renewed sense of personal dignity. A knowledgeable practitioner will assess and support positive coping skills, including nonpunitive religious expression. Dr. Lopez facilitated the natural grieving process and assisted Margo in formulating concrete, realistic plans to restart her life. Dr. Lopez helped to reframe the trauma experience by affirming Margo's belief that a loving God helps us through painful situations and uses those experiences to help us understand ourselves and God more deeply.

Couples therapy was also useful in this case. This approach used the primary support of Margo's spouse to assist in coping with, integrating, and healing the traumatic experience. Dr. Lopez recognized that a psychological trauma affects family members as well as survivors (Figley, 1989). Couples therapy worked well because Margo and her husband were solution oriented rather than blame oriented, had open communication, valued commitment, shared common values, and expressed affection. Medications were used early in the therapy in conjunction with psychotherapy to decrease anxiety, agitation, and depression, to promote sleep, and to reduce nightmares.

After several months of therapy, Margo decided to start a church-sponsored interfaith, self-help group for survivors of trauma. Margo, like many survivors of violence, believed that helping others was a way in which she could make meaning out of her suffering (Herman, 1992). Over the next several years, the self-help group educated the church on violence in the community. Led by Margo, the congregation became involved in advocating for school-based violence prevention programs to encourage nonviolent conflict resolution and reduce aggressive behavior in young people (Cotten et al., 1994).

SUGGESTED READINGS

Chadwick, O. (1986). *The reformation*. New York: Viking Penguin.

Lutheran

Harris-Abbott, D. (1996). *The Lutheran tradition: Religious beliefs and health care decisions*. Chicago: Park Ridge Center for the Study of Faith, Health, and Ethics.

Presbyterian

Harris-Abbott, D. (in press). *The Presbyterian tradition: Religious beliefs and health care decisions*. Chicago: Park Ridge Center for the Study of Faith, Health, and Ethics.

Lingle, W. E. (1995). *Presbyterians, their history and beliefs*. Lexington, KY: John Knox Press.

Episcopal

Clark, K., & Steen, C. (1997). *Marking sense of the Episcopal Church*. Atlanta: Morehouse.

DuBose, E. R. (1996). *The Episcopal tradition: Religious beliefs and health care decisions*. Chicago: Park Ridge Center for the Study of Faith, Health, and Ethics.

Methodist

DuBose, E. R. (1995). *The United Methodist tradition: Religious beliefs and health care decisions*. Chicago: Park Ridge Center for the Study of Faith, Health, and Ethics.

Outler, A. C. (1994). *Theology in the Wesleyan spirit*. Nashville, TN: Abingdon.

REFERENCES

Al-Mabuk, R., Enright R. D., & Cardis, P. (1995). Forgiveness education with parentally love deprived college students. *Journal of Moral Education, 24,* 427–444.

Bradley, M. B., Green, N. M., Jones, D. E., Lynn, M., & McNeil, L. (1990). *Churches and church membership in the United States, 1990.* Atlanta: Glenmary Research Center.

Chadwick, O. (1986). *The Reformation.* New York: Viking Penguin.

Clark, K., & Steen, C. (1997). *Making sense of the Episcopal Church.* Atlanta: Morehouse.

Cotten, N. U., Resnick, J., Brown, D. C., Martin, S. L., McCarraher, D. R., & Woods, J. (1994). Aggression and fighting behavior among African-American adolescents: Individual and family factors. *American Journal of Public Health, 84,* 618–622.

Coyle, C. T., & Enright R. D. (1997). Forgiveness intervention with post-abortion men. *Journal of Consulting and Clinical Psychology, 65,* 1042–1046.

DuBose, E. R. (1995). *The United Methodist tradition: Religious beliefs and health care decisions.* Chicago: Park Ridge Center for the Study of Faith, Health, and Ethics.

DuBose, E. R. (1996). *The Episcopal tradition: Religious beliefs and health care decisions.* Chicago: Park Ridge Center for the Study of Faith, Health, and Ethics.

Freedman, S. R., & Enright, R. D. (1996, August). Forgiveness as an intervention goal with incest survivors. *Journal of Consulting and Clinical Psychology, 64,* 983–992.

Figley, C. R. (1989). *Helping the traumatized family.* San Francisco: Jossey-Bass.

Garrett, W. R. (1996). Presbyterian: Home life as Christian vocation in the reformed tradition. In P. D. Airhart & M. L. Bendroth (Eds.), *Faith traditions and the family* (pp. 114–125). Louisville, KY: Westminster John Knox.

Gillespie, J. B. (1996). Episcopal: Family as the nursery of church and society. In P. D. Airhart & M. L. Bendroth (Eds.), *Faith traditions and the family* (pp. 143–156). Louisville, KY: Westminster John Knox.

Gorsuch, R. L. (1984). Measurement: The boon and bane of investigating religion. *American Psychologist, 39,* 228–236.

Harper, S. (1983). *John Wesley's message for today.* Grand Rapids, MI: Zondervan Press.

Harris-Abbott, D. (1996). *The Lutheran tradition: Religious beliefs and health care decisions.* Chicago: Park Ridge Center for the Study of Faith, Health, and Ethics.

Harris-Abbott, D. (in press). *The Presbyterian tradition: Religious beliefs and health care decisions.* Chicago: Park Ridge Center for the Study of Faith, Health, and Ethics.

Hebl, J. H., & Enright, R. D. (1993). Forgiveness as a psychotherapeutic goal with elderly females. *Psychotherapy, 30,* 658–667.

Herman, J. L. (1992). *Trauma and recovery.* New York: Basic Books.

Hunter, J. D. (1985). Conservative Protestantism. In P. E. Hammond (Ed.), *The sacred in a secular age* (pp. 150–166). Berkeley: University of California Press.

Keating, A. M., & Fretz, B. R. (1990). Christians' anticipation about counselors in response to counselor descriptions. *Journal of Counseling Psychology, 37,* 293–296.

Kosmin, B. A., & Lachman, S. P. (1993). *One nation under God: Religion in contemporary American society.* New York: Harmony Books.

Larson, D. B., Donahue, M. J., Lyons, J. S., Benson, P. L., Pattison, M., Worthington, E. L., Jr., & Blazer, D. G. (1989). Religious affiliations in mental health research samples as compared with national samples. *Journal of Nervous and Mental Disease, 177,* 109–111.

Laurie, J. R. (1997). Samaritan counseling centers extend congregational ministry. *Journal of Psychology and Christianity, 16,* 108–114.

Lingle, W. E. (1995). *Presbyterians: Their history and beliefs.* Lexington, KY: John Knox Press.

Lovinger, R. J. (1996). Considering the religious dimension in assessment and treatment. In E. P. Shafranske (Ed.), *Religion and the clinical practice of psychology* (pp. 327–363). Washington, DC: American Psychological Association.

Malony, H. N. (1998). Religion and mental health from the Protestant perspective. In H. G. Koenig (Ed.), *Handbook of religion and mental health* (pp. 203–210). San Diego: Academic Press.

McCullough, M. E., Sandage, S. J., & Worthington, E. L., Jr. (1997). *To forgive is human.* Downer's Grove, IL: InterVarsity Press.

McCullough, M. E., & Worthington, E. L., Jr. (in press). Religion and the forgiving personality. *Journal of Personality.*

McCullough, M. E., Worthington, E. L., Jr., Maxey, J., & Rachal, K. C. (1997). Gender in the context of supportive and challenging religious interventions. *Journal of Counseling Psychology, 44,* 80–88.

McCullough, M. E., Worthington, E. L., Jr., & Rachal, K. C. (1997). Interpersonal forgiving in close relationships. *Journal of Personality and Social Psychology, 72,* 321–336.

Outler, A. C. (1964). *John Wesley.* New York: Oxford University Press.

Outler, A. C. (1994). *Theology in the Wesleyan spirit.* Nashville, KY: Abingdon.

Pargament, K. I. (1997). *The psychology of religion and coping: Theory, research, practice.* New York: Guilford Press.

Richards, P. S., & Bergin, A. E. (1997). *A spiritual strategy for counseling and psychotherapy.* Washington, DC: American Psychological Association.

Schmidt, J. M., & Murphy-Geiss, G. E. (1996). Methodist: 'Tis grace will lead us home. In P. D. Airhart & M. L. Bendroth (Eds.), *Faith traditions and the family* (pp. 85–99). Louisville, KY: Westminster John Knox.

Schmidt, M. (1960). *John Wesley: A theological biography.* Nashville, TN: Abingdon.

Toh, Y. M., & Tan, S. Y. (1997). The effectiveness of church-based lay counselors: A controlled outcome study. *Journal of Psychology and Christianity, 16,* 260–267.

Vitz, P. C. (1994). *Psychology as religion.* Grand Rapids, MI: Eerdmans.

Weaver, A. J., Koenig, H. G., & Larson, D. B. (1997). Marriage and family therapy and the clergy. *Journal of Marital & Family Therapy, 23,* 13–25.

Weaver, A. J., Koenig, H. G., & Ochberg, F. M. (1996). Posttraumatic stress, mental health professionals, and the clergy: A need for collaboration, training, and research. *Journal of Traumatic Stress, 9,* 861–870.

Weaver, A. J., Sanford, J. A., Kline, A. E., Lucas, L. A., Larson, D. B., & Koenig, H. G. (1997). What do psychologists know about working with the clergy? An analysis of eight APA journals: 1991–1994. *Professional Psychology, 28,* 471–474.

Whaling, F. (1981). *John and Charles Wesley.* New York: Paulist Press.

Wilcox, G. (1997). A model for training lay persons in counseling skills: The Barnabas ministry. *Journal of Psychology and Christianity, 16,* 121–125.

Worthington, E. L., Jr., Kurusu, T. A., McCullough, M. E., & Sandage, S. J. (1996). Empirical research on religion and psychotherapeutic processes and outcomes: A 10-year review and research prospectus. *Psychological Bulletin, 119,* 448–487.

Wright, J. W. (Ed.). (1994). *The universal almanac: 1994.* Kansas City and New York: Andrews & McMeel.

Wright, P. G. (1984). The counseling activities and referral practices of Canadian clergy in British Columbia. *Journal of Psychology and Theology, 12,* 294–304.

Wyatt, S. C., & Johnson, R. W. (1990). The influence of counselors' religious values on clients' perceptions of the counselor. *Journal of Psychology and Theology, 18,* 158–165.

6

PSYCHOTHERAPY WITH EVANGELICAL AND FUNDAMENTALIST PROTESTANTS

NANCY STIEHLER THURSTON

For God so loved the world that he gave his one and only Son, that whoever believes in him shall not perish but have eternal life.
—John 3:16

EVANGELICAL AND FUNDAMENTALIST PROTESTANT CHURCHES: A BRIEF DESCRIPTION

The recent rise of the Evangelical Christian movement in the United States suggests that it is no longer a marginal religious movement. During the past 30 years, Evangelicals (including its more conservative subset of Fundamentalist Protestants) have grown from 51 million to 77 million members nationwide. Concurrently, membership in such traditional Christian denominations as Presbyterian, Methodist, Episcopal, and Congregational has steadily declined at a rate of 20% to 40% (Rourke, 1998).

A result of these shifting demographics is that Evangelical Christians now comprise a potentially substantial market for psychologists, but one that they have traditionally been undertrained to serve. This chapter will provide information that is designed to equip psychologists with tools for providing clinical services to this population.

Origins and Historical Perspectives

The earliest roots of Evangelical and Fundamentalist Protestant Churches are found in the New Testament Christian community, where apostles like Paul urged people to convert their lives to Jesus Christ's lordship (Fackre, 1990). Centuries later, Evangelicalism and Fundamentalism began as a loosely confederated movement that emerged from 19th-century revivalism. By 1889, Evangelical Protestantism was the dominant religious ideology in America (note that at that time, there was no distinction between Evangelicalism and Fundamentalism in the Protestant Church; the evangelical ideology referred to here embraced fundamentalist doctrines). Between the 1890s and 1930s, however, Evangelicalism collapsed under the influence of Darwinism, science, and German higher criticism. As a result, religious leaders attempted to tone down Biblical doctrines that appeared counter to such scientifically progressive notions as evolution. During that generation, Fundamentalism (as separate from Evangelicalism) began to rise as "the response of traditionalist evangelicals who declared war on these modernizing trends" (Marsden, 1987, p. 4).

The rise of Fundamentalism as a separate ideology from Evangelicalism was fueled by a set of books called *The Fundamentals*, which the Bible Institute of Los Angeles published in 1909. Its purpose was to unite Christians squarely on the fundamental Biblical doctrines (e.g., God's creation of the world in 7 days, the virgin birth of Christ) and to erect barriers to the inroads of liberalism (Rice, 1975). The name *Fundamentalist* was first coined at this time to describe persons who adhered to the principles found in *The Fundamentals*. In 1925, the Scopes Monkey Trials represented a major public attempt to win mainstream America back to its traditionalist evangelical (fundamentalist) roots. When the verdict came, which validated evolution, Fundamentalists were devastated, and their humiliated withdrawal likely fed their subsequent separatist stance (Dobson, 1990).

In 1941, Fundamentalist Protestants across America confederated to form the American Council of Christian Churches. A year later, the National Association of Evangelicals was also founded in the "hope for a fundamentalist comeback" (Marsden, 1997, p. 5). It is curious that as late as 1947, there was still no clear distinction between Evangelicals and Fundamentalists; they were still a relatively united force in denouncing modernism and in calling Christians back to the "fundamentals" of their faith. However, the 1950s brought a definitive schism between these two groups. In 1957, Harold Ockenga popularized the ideology of the "new Evangelicalism," which represented a definitive break from traditionalist Evangelical fundamentalism. Both the neo-Evangelical and Fundamentalist groups passionately held onto the need to witness the Gospel and convert unbelievers to the Christian faith. However, with equal passion, they disagreed on how to do this. The neo-Evangelicals decided that they could best witness the Gospel by remaining within mainstream culture. The Fundamentalists, on the other hand, saw themselves as a "holy remnant" whose duty it was to keep themselves separate and unstained by mainstream culture (Lindsell, 1976).

It was the rise of the television into most American households by the late 1950s that enabled neo-Evangelicalism to catapult itself firmly into mainstream American culture, through the enormously popular televised Billy Graham crusades. During such televised crusades, Billy Graham expressed his support of Martin Luther King, Jr.'s ministry of racial reconciliation. This offended the "White-only" Fundamentalist groups who championed segregation as part of God's plan (Ulstein, 1995). As a result, Fundamentalists deepened their resolve to split off from the Evangelical platform. Furthermore, during the social upheaval of the late 1960s and early 1970s (e.g., the hippie movement, student revolution, and Viet Nam War protests), Billy Graham led Evangelicals in responding with a spirit of accommodation. Fundamentalists, on the other hand, denounced the social upheaval and demanded separation from it (Dobson, 1990). By the 1970s, Evangelicalism became further integrated into mainstream American culture with self-professed Evangelical U.S. President Jimmy Carter.

Today, considerable overlap remains between these two movements. It may be useful to conceive of Protestant Evangelicalism as containing a continuum of faith and practice that goes from very conservative to moderately conservative, with Fundamentalist Evangelicals on the very conservative end. For the purposes of this chapter, these Fundamentalist Evangelicals will be referred to as Fundamentalists, and the moderately conservative Evangelicals as Evangelicals.

Overview of Evangelical and Fundamentalist Denominations

Both Evangelical and Fundamentalist denominations in the United States are largely comprised of churches in the Anabaptist tradition. By far the largest of these is the fundamentalist Southern Baptist Convention, with 16 million members nationwide (heavily represented in the southern Bible belt states). The National Baptist Convention of the U.S.A., Inc. (the oldest Black Baptist denomination) has 5.5 million members. A membership of 2.5 million is found in the National Baptist Convention of America (unincorporated). The evangelical American Baptist churches currently have 1.5 million members nationwide.

Beliefs common to all Baptists include the idea that the rite of baptism should be given only to believers who are old enough to choose salvation independently (usually beginning at age 6 or 7). Unlike most other Protestant denominations, the Baptists usually baptize their believers by total immersion in water. Also common to all Baptists is the value of vesting church authority within each particular congregation. This has resulted in a number of independent Baptist congregations (both Evangelical and Fundamentalist), some with large memberships (Ban, 1990).

Some other evangelical denominations in the United States currently include Evangelical Presbyterian churches and the Evangelical Covenant Church, as well as evangelical branches of Quakers, Mennonites, and Congregationalists. Also included are the Churches of Christ (3.7 million members), Church of the Nazarene (500,000 members), and Christian Missionary Alliance (250,000 members). The latter two emerged out of the Holiness Church movement (late 1800s), in which believers were urged to attain purity of lifestyle and attitudes. Pentecostal churches also emerged out of this movement. Today, many of the Pentecostal churches in the United States are Evangelical or Fundamentalist in faith and practice. However, Protestant Fundamentalists generally draw an emphatic distinction between themselves and Pentecostals, rejecting the latter's manifestations of the "gifts of the Spirit" such as prophesyzing and speaking in tongues (Wright, 1994). For a more in-depth discussion of Pentecostalism, please refer to Chapter 7 of this book, which is devoted to Pentecostal denominations.

A growing number of Evangelical and Fundamentalist Christians do not consider themselves to be affiliated with any particular denomination. Instead, they have joined the ranks of nondenominational megachurches which favor conservative values, but which avoid elaborate doctrines. In the past 30 years, the number of these megachurches in the United States has risen from 10 to nearly 400, with as many as 20,000 members in a single church (Rourke, 1998). Many of these churches are psychologically minded and offer a variety of self-help groups to their members.

Beliefs and Practices of Evangelicals and Fundamentalists

Beliefs

Evangelicals and Fundamentalists hold in common many beliefs, including the virgin birth of Jesus Christ, which made him both fully divine and fully human. They also assert that people need to repent for their sins, and that in doing so they become saved through Christ's atoning death on the cross. They view Jesus as the "Lamb of God" who sacrificed his life to pay for their sins; hence, the term "saved by the blood of the Lamb" is frequently used. Converts who repent are believed to die (metaphorically) to their old self, thus giving rise to the expression "born again Christians." Because they believe that Jesus was resurrected from the dead and now lives in the hearts of believers, they emphasize the need to cultivate a personal relationship with Jesus. They view the Bible as "God's Word," which serves as a rule of both belief and practice (Wright, 1994).

Evangelicals draw their very name from their emphasis on the "great commission" of Christ to evangelize all nations by preaching the gospel and witnessing to others. They (including Fundamentalists) approach the need to evangelize the world with grave urgency because of their belief that Christ will return to earth one day unannounced, and that he will judge all living and dead people. They believe that on that Last Judgment Day, all unbelievers will be separated from God's presence eternally (i.e., they will be condemned to Hell), whereas all of the faithful believers will live forever with God in eternal joy in heaven.

Practices

Along with these common beliefs, Evangelicals and Fundamentalists share various practices in common. Among the foremost of these is regular participation in local churches, with heavy emphasis on supporting its missionaries. Members are urged to tithe (10%) their income to support church ministries.

A second practice involves embracing a strong Protestant work ethic, driven ultimately by Christ's Great Commission to evangelize the world. As Hubbard (1979), a prominent spokesperson for Evangelicals observed, "As Evangelicals, we believe men and women are lost without Jesus Christ; we believe that terrible judgement awaits all who reject Jesus as Lord and Savior. There is, therefore, an urgency about the way we go about our work. We resent unnecessary distractions; we resist unbiblical diversions" (p. 2).

The biggest difference between Evangelicals and Fundamentalists in praxis involves their degree of engagement with secular culture (Marsden, 1991). Unlike Fundamentalists, Evangelicals desire to reform and redeem the world from within its institutions and structures. Thus, they emphasize the value of obtaining a quality education, as well as maintaining one's "witness" in the workplace (e.g., by obeying rules, respecting authority, forgiving offending coworkers, working diligently).

Unlike Evangelicals, Fundamentalists maintain a praxis of separatism. This principle of behavior is reflected in the way in which they strive for personal holiness, as they refrain from drinking, dancing, smoking, swearing, and gambling. This "separates" them from "the world." Their commitment to personal purity is also seen in their strict dress code for believers. For instance, in the more strict Fundamentalist groups (e.g., Apostolic churches), women are forbidden to wear slacks, tight fitting clothes, flashy jewelry, make-up, miniskirts, shorts, or bikinis; women should not dress like men or like prostitutes. Modest apparel is the standard, as is long hair. Men, on the other hand, are forbidden to have long hair, and they are to refrain from wearing scruffy looking jeans or tight pants.

The Fundamentalist practice of purity also extends to admonitions not to associate with unbelievers (it is noteworthy that even non-Fundamentalist Christians are included here as unbelievers). As Rice (1975), a prominent Fundamentalist leader, exhorted his Fundamentalist flock,

> We are not to receive them in fellowship as Christians, not support them as prophets, not receive them in our churches for membership, not receive them as teachers in our colleges or seminaries, not promote their ministries or their institutions. And since marriage is also a spiritual institution, we are commanded not to yoke up with unbelievers in marriage. (p. 23)

The home schooling movement of the 1990s currently holds wide appeal in Fundamentalist circles, as a way to keep children unstained by the carnal influences of the public school system. For instance, James Dobson, the leader of the nationally syndicated radio show *Focus on the Family*, has been a strong proponent of the home schooling movement for his conservative Protestant constituents.

In summary, there is no such thing as a nominal Fundamentalist. Their lifestyle requires that their lives almost totally revolve around the Church. For example, they may attend church services from three to five times per week, all their social activities will be church related, and all the children growing up in the Church will only be allowed to date and marry one another.

Evangelical and Fundamentalist Positions on Social and Moral Issues

Evangelicals and Fundamentalists generally unite in opposing homosexuality, extramarital sex, abortion, divorce (except resulting from spouse's infidelity), remarriage (except if the divorce was due to spouse's infidelity), alcohol use, and other drug use (Marsden, 1987). What tends to set Fundamentalists apart from Evangelicals is their extreme (at times even militant) stance against these issues. For example, some Fundamentalists have protested abortion by setting up picket lines at abortion clinics. Also, some Fundamentalist churches punish the disobedience of the social stance listed above by excommunicating and shunning the erring believer.

Additionally, Fundamentalists emphasize stricter adherence to hierarchical authority structures than do other Evangelicals. For instance, Fundamentalists assert that wives are to submit to their husbands. By contrast, Evangelicals tend to view marriage as a partnership of equals. Fundamentalists also stress that church members are to submit to the authority of the pastor and elders. Additionally, many of them believe that parents have a duty to discipline rebellious children with corporal punishment (Ammerman, 1988). For Fundamentalists, church authority (as well as church-sanctioned authority, such as husbands) is not to be questioned or criticized.

IMPLICATIONS FOR COUNSELING AND PSYCHOTHERAPY

Therapeutic Relationship Issues and Suggestions

View of Mental Health Professions and Therapy

Evangelicals and Fundamentalists differ substantially in their views of the mental health professions, as well as in their therapy usage tendencies. Evangelicals, for instance, generally embrace the mental health field. Even sermons in these churches are often quite psychologically minded. These church members often first seek out the pastor for counseling. Then, if they are referred for therapy, they usually prefer to see a therapist whose religious beliefs are congruent with their beliefs. It is curious that such congruence matters more to most of these religious clients than does preference in treatment modality (e.g., behavioral vs. psychoanalytic; Dougherty & Worthington, 1983).

In contrast with Evangelicals, Fundamentalists are generally more suspicious of the mental health field. They are far more likely to seek out only their pastor or a church elder for counseling (Dobson, 1990). Indeed, some Fundamentalist church leaders admonish their flock to avoid counseling with anyone other than themselves.

Concerns That Church Members May Have About Therapy

Members of Fundamentalist churches tend to avoid secular therapists (and therapy in general) because of various concerns (a number of which they share with many Evangelicals). One such concern is that the therapist may resemble a pastor with whom they had a negative experience (Lovinger, 1984). A second, a more prevailing fear is that therapy will erode one's core beliefs (such as the authority of the Bible). A third fear is that entering therapy will make them "look bad," thus embarassing one's self, family, and church (i.e., resulting from admitting that one has problems that were unable to be solved within one's marriage or family or church). Yet another concern is whether the therapist is "saved." If the client believes that the therapist is unsaved, there may be awkward attempts by the client to evangelize the therapist.

Rayburn (1985) documented additional fears that her theologically conservative Protestant patients experienced. These included the fear that they might never be whole again, fear that the therapist would misunderstand and criticize their religious beliefs, fear that the therapist would encourage them to renounce their religious convictions in favor of more worldly ones, fear that receiving psychotherapy implies a decrease of faith in God, and fear of accessing the darker sides of their natures.

Suggestions for Building Trust and Credibility

Given these fears and concerns that Fundamentalist (and some Evangelical) persons may have about seeking psychotherapy, it is helpful for therapists to know how to build up trust and credibility with them, particularly in the initial phase of treatment. One suggestion for doing so is to work within the client's idioms. The objective here is to enter the client's world and meta-communicate that you are connected to their frame of reference. For example, asking a conservative Protestant client during an intake, "Tell me about when you were saved," generally has the same positive effect that it would to ask a Viet Nam veteran, "Where were you during the Tet Offensive," or to ask an older Catholic person how she reacted to Vatican II.

Along with working within the patient's idioms, it is imperative for the therapist to listen to the patient sensitively and nonjudgmentally. "Religious patients more than any other kind of patients are apt to experience their problems as felt punishment for some sin and to sense varying degrees of guilt for the misdeed" (Rayburn, 1985, p. 38). The caveat to therapists here is not to minimize or rationalize to the patient, but instead to validate their affect, especially in the initial phase of therapy.

One danger to watch out for, however, involves situations in which patients are very critical of their pastors or churches in the initial sessions of therapy (keeping in mind that the hierarchical authority structure usually does not permit criticism). This presents a dilemma for the therapist, who can easily become triangulated in this conflict. What seems to help the patient the most is having the therapist validate his or her feelings of disappointment, anger, disillusionment, and so on. The caution here is about joining with the patient's affect with too much gusto. Even though the patient is conflicted about his or her feelings toward the pastor or church, there may well be a split off part of the patient that is still intensely loyal to the pastor, despite the hurt that he or she feels. It might be more useful to explore and validate the patient's feelings of ambivalence, rather than to focus on the rightness or wrongness of the church leaders.

For therapists who wish to gain credibility with their religious patients, they might consider joining one of the professional societies that promote the interface of religion and psychotherapy. These societies include the American Association of Christian Counselors, the Christian Association for Psychological Studies, the Society for the Scientific Study of Religion, or the Psychology of Religion Division (No. 36) of the American Psychological Association. "Focus on the Family," headed by James Dobson, manages an extensive, nationwide referral network for conservative Christian therapists. Networking with local pastors is another way of gaining credibility with this population. For instance, some psychologists offer free consultation or educational workshops to pastors as a means of networking. A referral from one's pastor is likely to instill trust and credibility in a therapist for many conservative Protestant persons who seek counseling.

Diversity Considerations

Along with building trust and credibility, therapists would do well to consider diversity issues that pertain to this population. The first of these involves the interaction between gender and religious beliefs. For instance, a male therapist working with a female Fundamentalist patient will likely draw strong transference around authority issues. This might take the form of either unquestioning obedience to the male therapist or outright rebellion, or sabotage, or passive–aggressive behavior. In any case, the "authority figure" issue should be addressed, and roles clarified (more than once). Even if a male therapist does not present himself as authoritative, the female patient is conditioned to see him as such.

A second diversity issue among conservative Protestants involves a recent rise in non-Caucasian membership. For example, the Southern Baptist Convention's 16 million members currently includes 3 million persons who are Asian or Latino. This represents a 50% growth of these two ethnic groups among Southern Baptists in recent years (Rourke, 1998). Thus, therapists who work with this population are advised to obtain training in multicultural issues as well.

A third diversity issue involves the range of beliefs and practices ascribed by various subcultures within conservative Protestantism (as described more fully elsewhere in this chapter). For example, I encountered such diversity during job screening interviews that I once conducted with two members of the same Evangelical denomination. The first interviewee described himself as "creative," adding that when he created something, he felt the pleasure that God must have felt in creating him. This belief seemed to bring him a deep, sustaining sense of contentment and well-being. The second interviewee, however, took offense at this belief, arguing adamantly that to be creative is to be unbiblical. He explained that the Bible is God's Word—period. He added that any attempt on our part to be "creative" represents an ungodly embellishment on God's command that we obey His Word. Thus, clinicians who work with conservative Protestants would do well to inquire about the substance and meaning of their patients' belief systems, instead of assuming that they will all be similar.

Assessment and Diagnostic Issues and Approaches

Before describing some of the psychological problems that therapists may observe in some Evangelical and Fundamentalist Protestant clients, I wish to emphasize that not all Evangelical and Fundamentalist persons struggle with such problems. Quite to the contrary, it seems to be far more the case that members of these religious groups tend to be wholesome, productive, well-balanced people who have an added clarity and purpose to life that their faith provides. Nevertheless, some members of these churches evidence toxic aspects of their faith, and I hope that the information below is helpful to therapists who observe such psycho-spiritual issues during therapy.

Common Psycho-Spiritual Issues Seen in Evangelical Clients

In his psychotherapy work with Evangelical Christians, Sloat (1990) identified a syndrome of behaviors, attitudes, beliefs, and feelings that emerged from dysfunctional family backgrounds of many of these clients. Noting the similar dynamics of these patients' families to those of recovering alcoholics, he modified the term "adult children of alcoholics" to name this syndrome "adult children of Evangelicals" (ACE). Sloat stressed that not all Evangelical Christians evidence this syndrome. For those that do, however, he explained that

> The persons who have grown up in a dysfunctional Christian environment have not only many of the same emotional complications as their non-Christian counterparts, they also have theological distortions and fears to sort out. Unfortunately, many people have been taught—in the name of God—not to question or challenge what they have learned, which is an added complication in the already difficult process of working towards wholeness. (Sloat, 1990, p. 17)

According to Sloat, ACE persons are subtly admonished with toxic messages similar to those found in alcoholic family systems: don't talk, don't trust, don't feel, and don't want. "Don't talk about inconsistencies in one's parents or church" is one such insidious admonitions. Unfortunately, this dysfunction results in dishonesty, inhibition of personal growth, interference with communication, and difficulty with intimacy. He asserts that the subtle message, "Don't trust your reasoning ability or your competence" results in self-doubt, which cripples one's ability to evaluate situations, make decisions, and act autonomously. Sloat finds that the insidious message, "Don't feel pain, anger toward God, sexual feelings, or self-worth" interferes with emotional integration and results in low self-esteem. He contends that the subtle admonition, "Don't want your basic needs met or want things for yourself" stunts personal growth toward autonomy (Sloat, 1990).

According to Sloat, ACEs tend to react to toxic Christian rules by assuming one of several roles. The *rebel* defies these rules outright, resulting in disapproval by parents and church. The *surface pleaser* pays lip service to parents and church, but then sneaks off to break the rules. Note that this type of person tends to experience little guilt for such infractions, and that emotions tend to remain compartmentalized and unintegrated. The *struggler* tries to please parents and church but suffers dissonance internally. This kind of person is vulnerable to feelings of anxiety or depression, because of violating one's true feelings to reduce inner conflict. The *obedient* person wholeheartedly embraces the rules. This person does not suffer from internal dissonance, but this comes at a cost of splitting oneself off from negative feelings. Unfortunately, this results in a poor ability to tolerate negative feelings in others and produces attitudes that tend to be dogmatic, legalistic, and separatist (Sloat, 1990).

In contrast with these dysfunctional roles, if or when ACEs can take the risk to learn healthy self-assertion in the context of a healthy therapy relationship, this skill may be transferred back to one's family and church system. Then, it is possible to integrate the positive aspects of the faith and the fellowship while avoiding the toxic aspects. In rare instances, the church system may be so dysfunctional that a healthy person may have no place in it at all, and a "divorce" may be necessary to maintain health.

In their book, *Twelve "Christian" Beliefs That Can Drive You Crazy: Relief From False Assumptions,* Cloud and Townsend (1994) identified a set of toxic "Christian" beliefs that sound similar to those described by Sloat. These include, "It is selfish to have my needs met"; "If I'm spiritual enough, I will have no pain or sinfulness"; and "If I have God, I don't need people" (p. 8). Cloud and Townsend offer both psychologically and spiritually based interventions for each of these 12 false assumptions.

Common Psycho-Spiritual Issues Seen in Fundamentalist Clients

Although there is considerable overlap between Evangelicals and Fundamentalists in the clinical issues that they tend to intertwine with faith issues, there seem to be some issues more endemic to Fundamentalist Protestants in particular. Richard Yao (1987) identified a set of attitudes embedded in some conservative religious institutions that he termed a "fundamentalist mindset." He described it as "authoritarian, intolerant and compulsive about control; an absolutist all-or-nothing, either-or, us against them, 'I've got the truth and you don't' mindset. One which does not see the grays in life. One which seeks to impose itself on others" (p. 4). Yao pointed out that this mindset transcends religious denominations. However, because Protestant Fundamentalist churches tend to be closed systems, they are more apt to evidence this mindset.

Kirkpatrick (1987) applied Rokeach's (1954) model of the closed system to make a convincing case that Fundamentalist churches that insist on unquestioning obedience to church authority require total involvement as well as separation from the "world"—and thus suffer from the pitfalls of any closed system. Perhaps the most devastating of these pitfalls for parishioners come when the strain of obeying any one aspect of church authority becomes too great, precipitating the entire system to cave in on the person like a house of cards (resulting in a sweeping, trauma-laced rejection of one's entire Christian faith). Yao (1987) contended that such occurrences are highly enough scripted to form a syndrome, which he termed *shattered faith syndrome*. Symptoms of this syndrome, according to Yao, include addictive withdrawal from a totalistic church system, along with chronic fear, depression, isolation, aversion to authority, inadequate social skills, distrust of others, and a persistent fear of divine damnation.

Rothbaum (1988) quoted a member of such a totalistic, closed-system religious community who grew disillusioned and left: "I thought I'd known what was going to happen for the rest of my life. I'd thought I was going to grow old and die there. Suddenly my social identity was no longer there. My family ties were no longer there. My career and job functioning were no longer there. All the things upon which I had built a life were no longer there" (p. 205). Rothbaum added that breaking away from such a religious group may literally feel life endangering, with threats of eternal damnation, and at times treated by the group "as if you were dead." The therapist's job is to help the client adjust to the culture shock of emigrating to an entire new world and realize how very drastic a change it can be.

For those clients who evidence symptoms of the shattered faith syndrome, it is helpful to make the first line of intervention be to help clients solve their issues within the folds of their church (M. F. Clark, personal communication, June 1997). For example, this might involve helping a woman with dependency issues to individuate gradually, without necessarily having to withdraw her membership from the church (i.e., that one does not always need to throw the baby out with the bathwater).

However, some of these clients may have already made a choice to leave their church. For such clients, Rothbaum (1988) suggested a series of psychological interventions, including helping clients develop coping skills, form relationships outside of the church, and deal with suppressed emotions, and teaching them about the expected phases of transition out of the church.

Religious and Spiritual Assessment Measures That May Be Useful

Just as Evangelicals tend to be more open to psychotherapy than are Fundamentalists, they also tend to be more open to psychological and religious assessments. Duncombe (1990) cautioned mental health professionals that Fundamentalists who claim a strict separatist stance will tend to assert that religious and psychological concepts are not interchangeable; therefore, "psychological testing is seen as of no value and often misleading" (p. 517).

For those Fundamentalist and Evangelical clients wishing to assess aspects of their psycho-spiritual functioning, however, a number of excellent measures are available. For a comprehensive survey of such measures, *Measures of Religiosity* (Hill & Hood, 1999) is a valuable resource. It contains over 100 measures, along with descriptions, psychometric data, and applications for each measure. Among the assessments featured in this volume is the Nelson–Malony Religious Status Interview. This measure of religious maturity is scaled along the following eight dimensions: "awareness of God, acceptance of God's grace and steadfast love, being repentant and responsible, knowing God's leadership and direction, involvement in organized religion, experiencing fellowship, being ethical, and affirming openness in faith" (Malony, 1985, p. 30).

Another measure surveyed in this volume is the Spiritual Themes and Religious Responses Test (Saur & Saur, 1990). This is a projective measure along the lines of the Thematic Apperception Test (TAT), in which the client is asked to make up a prayer or story in response to a series of pictures depicting people in various religious settings (such as taking communion in church). It is an excellent resource for psychologists whose theoretical orientation is contemporarily psychoanalytic. Lovinger (1984) suggests that religious material such as the dynamics of one's relationship with God can be analyzed for resistances, transferences, and so on just as any other aspects of the patients' lives that they discuss in therapy. In the same spirit, results of the above two assessments may be useful in uncovering the religious patients' spiritual as well as psychological functioning.

Treatment Issues and Approaches

The Healing Potential of the Traditions' Beliefs and Practices

Having discussed some of the psychological pitfalls associated at times with Evangelical and Fundamentalist Protestantism, it is important to stress several points. First, the above described disorders pertain likely only to a small fraction of persons from these religious traditions. For the most part, members of these religious groups likely find that their faith (as well as their church membership) enhances their mental health. Some of these benefits are obvious: social support by one's congregation in times of stress, the anchoring of ultimate meaning in times of life transition, and the physical health benefits of living with purity of lifestyle (this is particularly true for separatist fundamentalists who abstain from smoking, alcohol, and so on). Lovinger (1984) observed, "What is less obvious is that there are many avenues for satisfaction of emotional needs in intense, expressive religious activities, for gratification of dependency and intimacy needs in the close circle of the church 'family', and for opportunities to discharge aggressive impulses in combating disapproved-of activities in the larger society" (p. 151).

For Fundamentalist churches in particular, the tendency to form tightly knit communities provides much in the way of social support for their members. An experience I had that illustrates this point occurred several years ago while I was visiting a Fundamentalist church. While I chatted with the pastor in the narthex after the service, several parishioners came up to speak with the pastor. They needed to ask him how to assist a homeless person whom one of them had befriended. Their goal was not only to have the homeless person "get saved" but also to integrate him into "the fold." The pastor responded swiftly and decisively, pointing one by one to these parishioners as he said something like, "Okay, you invite the guy to live at your house for the next few months, until he gets on his feet. And you—go find him a job with [name of another church member]. And you—have him come to prayer meeting with you on Wednesday." Members of such churches find considerable support and security as part of "the fold," particularly in times of personal upheaval.

In a chapter such as this, which has discussed various pathological ways in which conservative Protestant faith may interface with mental health, it is important that one not minimize the profoundly positive aspects of such faith. I witnessed another vivid example of the healing power of faith during a recent interview I had with a conservative Protestant seminary student. When telling her life's story, she mentioned that her father had died of cancer on the day before her wedding. She added that God had been gracious to her family by allowing him to die at that time. Her father was in intolerable pain, and the wedding would have been eclipsed by the family's anguish at knowing that he was suffering. Instead, by dying, he was now part of the "great cloud of witnesses" (Hebrews 12:1, *New International Version Study Bible*) and could be lovingly present at the wedding, in a more intimate way than he could have if he had still been alive. The student's face seemed sad and yet radiant as she recounted this to me, and I experienced in her the "peace that transcends all understanding" (Philippians 4:7, *New International Version Study Bible*) regarding an incident that many other people would have experienced as traumatizing. I wondered at first if the student might be using her religion defensively at that moment (i.e., reaction formation or denial). Instead, she seemed to have integrated her deep sorrow at losing her father with her faith-inspired comfort that he was now, in death, experiencing both eternal bliss and an eternal connection with her in spirit. In other words, her faith enabled her to evidence an impressive degree of constancy during a difficult life event.

Psychological Interventions Congruent or Incongruent With These Traditions

Jones and Butman (1991) have written an excellent book that analyzes the major approaches to psychotherapy within the context of its degree of fit with Evangelical Protestant beliefs. Their findings include the following:

On the one hand, many Christians have uncritically accepted Rogerian person-centered therapy (chapter 10) because its techniques of counseling superficially resemble one understanding of agape love, thus missing the deeper system of thought of Rogers which is radically incommensurate with the faith. On the other hand, the offensive atheism and hedonism of Albert Ellis, the founder of Rational Emotive Therapy (RET; chapter 12), have led many Christians to an overly quick dismissal of the theory, thus causing them to miss some of the areas of compatibility between RET and Christianity in the understanding of the place of rationality in human emotional life. (p. 35)

Jones and Butman (1991) concluded that many mainstream theories and approaches of psychotherapy may be helpful with Evangelical Protestants so long as they are framed in ways that are consistent with Evangelicals' religious beliefs and values.

Spiritual Interventions

Forgiveness

Perhaps the most powerful (and yet the most often misused) spiritual intervention used by therapists with Evangelical and Fundamentalist Christians is that of forgiveness. When done properly, it results in tremendous feelings of freedom, reclaimed personal power, and integrity for the client, as well as in significant spiritual and psychological growth. However, too often, these clients are exhorted by their church to forgive others in a way that denies the extent of their injury, and which both forecloses and short-circuits vital steps in the process, which leads to powerlessness and a lack of internal integration in the client. It is more useful for the therapist to encourage the client to experience and express the full extent of his or her injury. Only when the client reaches a place where the client feels more powerful than the offender will it be possible for him or her to forgive that person, while retaining a healthy sense of self. Only then can the client build empathy for the offender (this might involve having the client remember instances in which the client offended someone else and was forgiven by that person). McCullough (1995) used these principles of forgiveness in constructing a psychoeducational group intervention curriculum on forgiveness, which clinicians may well find helpful (McCullough & Worthington, 1995; McCullough, Sandage, & Worthington, 1997).

Image of God

For clients who feel disappointed or angry with God, it is contraindicated for therapists to read Bible passages to clients that exhort them to trust in God. I know of an Evangelical pastor, for example, who has had disastrous results in pastoral counseling when he has done this. Such an intervention risks invalidating (and threatening) clients, and may intensify their feelings of distress, and lead them to distance themselves from the counselor.

Instead, I recommended that therapists give their clients a safe, permissive environment to explore their disappointment and anger at God. The therapist may suggest to such clients that "God already knows what you are feeling. He will not get angry with you for telling him how upset you are feeling at him." Such clients need the therapist to help them fully experience and express the extent of their feelings of anger or disappointment at God. Lovinger (1984) suggests that material like this could be interpreted in the light of the client's resistances and transferences, much the same as any other material in the session would be handled. For such clients, the therapist might also consider referring them to Philip Yancey's book, *Disappointment With God* (1988). A book like this may help them to feel validated, and not alone in their experience.

Perfectionism

Other clients from these religious traditions tend to struggle with perfectionism, particularly as they consider Jesus' admonition, "Be perfect, therefore, as your heavenly Father is perfect" (Matthew 5:48, *New International Version Study Bible*). Rayburn (1985) notes that perfectionism in conservative Christian churches can lead to depression and even suicidal ideation. She encourages her clients to develop a more realistic conception of perfection. She goes so far as to point out the underlying narcissism in such perfectionistic strivings.

A spiritual intervention for perfectionism might involve pointing out a number of Bible characters who messed up badly and, then, reflecting on how these were some of the people most deeply loved by God. For example, King David in the Old Testament had a man murdered so he could marry the man's widow, Bathsheba, with whom he was having a sexual affair. Despite David's sins, in which he broke several of the Ten Commandments, "Thou shalt not commit murder," "Thou shalt not commit adultery," "Thou shalt not covet anything that is thy neighbor's," God still blessed him with a wise, wonderful son named Solomon. Moreover, God chose to have his son Jesus descend through David's and Bathsheba's lineage, even despite his sin. Another relevant Bible character is the apostle Peter, who denied three times that he knew Jesus, on the very night before Jesus was crucified. Despite Peter's faithlessness, Jesus later built his entire church on Peter's leadership and gave Peter the very keys of heaven.

The Protestant Work Ethic

Related to perfectionism is a tendency for conservative Christians to disown one's limits and to distort one's thinking into believing that no amount of work or service for God's kingdom is enough to satisfy God. This is a toxic, extreme version of the Protestant work ethic. Note that clients who evidence this might be holding onto Bible verses such as, "I can do everything through him [Christ] who gives me strength" (Philippians 4:13, *New International Version Study Bible*). A useful spiritual intervention here is to reflect with the client on the limits that Jesus faced. At the time of His crucifixion, there were countless poor, sick, and needy people that he had not helped. However, on the night before his crucifixion, he prayed to God, "I have brought you glory on earth by completing the work you gave me to do" (John 17:4, *New International Version Study Bible*). In other words, if Jesus could glorify God by working within his limits, presumably so can the rest of God's people.

Prayer

Unlike liberal or mainstream Protestant clients, conservative Protestant clients may expect that their therapist will pray with them during sessions (Malony, 1998; Tan, 1990). Evangelical Christian psychologists generally agree that if a therapist and client do pray together, it should be at the initiative of the client. For many such clients, prayer in session yields deeply restorative benefits. However, the present author cautions that this practice can set up clouded interpersonal boundaries, and that it is rife for the therapist and/or the client to communicate indirectly with each other by this venue in a way that is not therapeutic. For example, if a client's prayer contains transference issues, this should be processed in the session.

Submission

For a female client whose presenting problem involves abuse by her spouse, it is contraindicated for the therapist (as well as the woman's pastor) to exhort her to submit to her husband (Fortune, 1987). Note that this is particularly an issue in those Fundamentalist churches that stress submission of wives to husbands. Clark (1985, p. 43) observed such a contraindicated intervention: "A minister advised a battered wife to return home and bear her cross." It is important, however, not to contradict the pastor or what the client has been taught that the Bible says. Rather, the therapist can add perspective, for example, that submission is meant to be a voluntary and loving response to a loving husband (as evidenced in the Biblical passage of Ephesians 5:25–31).

Rigidity Problems

For religious clients whose issues involve rigidity of their personality structure, Stovich (1985) advises using a spiritual intervention that he termed *multidimensionality*. He states,

Perhaps the greatest trap to fall into when working with clients who use a lot of religious language is to begin to argue with the oftentimes rigid, absolute judgementalism these clients exhibit. This is especially true of clients with a Fundamentalist background or who are dealing with obsession, compulsion, and guilt. However, a useful therapeutic goal is to assist the client into a position wherein two or more types of religious images are coexisting. At times this can break through the rigid holding pattern and pave the way for more movement. (p. 121)

Suggestions for Working With the Religious Leaders and Religious Community

Psychologists who want to network with the Evangelical and Fundamentalist Christian communities in their areas may do so in a variety of ways. First, they can offer to lead Sunday School programs or church retreats on psycho-spiritual issues. Next, they can offer pastors consultation on tough pastoral counseling cases (for example, those counselees who evidence personality disorders). Also, a psychologist can "help the pastor develop an in-depth program of premarital counseling—one that realistically approaches subjects such as anger, conflict, and violence" (Strom, 1986, p. 117), to help to prevent domestic violence. Strom also suggests that psychologists would do well to encourage pastors to take workshops on such problems as domestic violence and substance abuse, and for these pastors to tell their congregations that they are enrolling in such workshops. It helps hurting parishioners to feel more permission to step forward, and to trust that both the pastor and the psychologist are competent and involved.

Process and Ethical Guidelines for Implementing Spiritual Interventions

The ethical guidelines of the American Psychological Association suggest several principles that apply to the psychological treatment of religious clients. First, therapists need to be cognizant of the limits of their training, particularly when considering implementing spiritual interventions. Second, if a prospective client is a member of the same church as the therapist, the therapist needs to provide the client with several referrals to other therapists and to refrain from taking on this client into one's own caseload. This may be more difficult to do in small towns. The Christian Association for Psychological Studies has composed ethical guidelines for dual-role problems between a therapist and church members. Because the Fundamentalist churches prefer in-house, same-faith referrals, the dual-role issues could be important for the therapist and client to resolve.

Case Study[1]

"Nora," a 32-year-old woman, sought me out because she wanted a Christian therapist. Her presenting problem was that she was in a marriage that felt psychologically intolerable to her. She reasoned that, according to the Bible, there were only two ways that she could get out of this marriage: either through divorce (only on grounds of spouse's infidelity) or through death (i.e., "till death do us part"). Since her husband gave no indication of being sexually unfaithful to her, she concluded that the only way out of the marriage was death—for her, this meant suicide. She had florid suicidal ideation and had made several half-hearted suicide attempts a few weeks before beginning therapy with me. The clearly psycho-spiritual nature of this case should be noted from the outset. It was this woman's interpretation of the Bible, at least in part, that was threatening her very life.

Nora and her husband were members of a Fundamentalist Protestant church. She and her husband went for marital counseling with church elders. They were told that the answer to their strife was that Nora had to submit herself more to her husband, and they offered Bible verses to back up this admonition. Nora was also told by the pastor and elders that if she were to divorce her husband, the church would excommunicate her. This would involve the pastor asking Nora to come up in front of the entire congregation and to have the pastor declare to the congregation her sin of leaving her husband. Then she would have to walk out of the church, never to return. From then on, church members would be instructed to shun Nora (i.e., to treat her as if she did not exist). The prospect of excommunication was extremely stressful to Nora, and it fed into her sense of feeling trapped, with suicide as her only way out. Because her church was a closed system, to leave it would mean leaving nearly her entire support system and to leave it in an intensely shaming manner. Moreover, she was terrified at the prospect that God might never forgive her if she left her husband, and she wondered whether God would punish her with eternity in Hell.

An example of how miserable Nora felt in her marriage involved finances. Her husband insisted on controlling their finances, including retaining custody of their checkbook. She often did not have a check to pay for her weekly sessions with me, because (according to her) she would put the checkbook in her purse, and then he would take it out and keep it. This became an issue between her and me, but I tried to deal with it therapeutically, reflecting on the obvious stress that her marital strife over money was causing her. She recounted how, in church, her husband would often put far more of their savings in the offering plate than she felt that

[1]This is a hypothetical case that resembles a synthesis of cases that I have treated in psychotherapy.

they could afford. When she objected to it, he would confront her with not being submissive enough to him.

I tried psychological as well as spiritual interventions with Nora. I think that she was so hungry for support and validation that a little went a long way with her. It took 18 months of weekly therapy sessions, however, to work through her dysthymia and some of the deeper internal conflicts that were driving it.

After a year or so of working together, we uncovered an unconscious torch that she had been carrying over a former boyfriend. It seemed to be draining off a lot of the erotic energy that might have otherwise been funneled into her marriage. We finally arrived at the connection that she was replaying her longings to be close to her father and his rejection of her. This brought a wellspring of tears and deep, aching waves of grief over a number of sessions.

It was only after this that she was able to take ownership of several previously disowned things: (a) her fantasies of having an affair with her former boyfriend, (b) the fact that nobody had forced her to marry her husband, and (c) a deeply repressed memory of having had an abortion years ago (while she was an unwed teenager), and the tremendous guilt and shame that she was carrying over it (exacerbated by her church's militant stance against abortion). This was a pivotal time in her therapy, particularly as she came to see that she was not initially a victim in her marriage; she had freely chosen to marry this man. Once she came to this realization, she decided that she could also take ownership to leave her husband, which she then, in fact, did. This was a tough moment for me in terms of countertransference, because of my own deep Christian convictions of the sanctity of marriage. However, as her therapist, I felt that it was my job to provide her with a safe place to take an honest look at her life and, then, to own her decisions.

Rather than face excommunication from her church over leaving her husband, Nora made a simultaneous decision to leave her church as well. She tried to avoid joining a new church that might also shun her over her divorce. She eventually joined another, less Fundamentalist Protestant church. However, she spoke longingly of the close-knit, "Bible-believing" church that she had left, feeling that the new church was flaccid and diluted in the passion to obey God. Nora had to compromise the theology and benefits of her close, Fundamentalist church for a place that could offer her emotional and psychological safety.

Overall, as her therapist, I had tried to offer Nora permission to feel negative feelings, to question me, and to want more from her life. This was obviously quite different from what her church elders had offered her. I believe that when she terminated therapy, Nora was significantly more healthy psychologically than when she had been at the time of intake. On the one hand, a casualty of that process was her marriage—which might not have been a casualty if she had listened to her church elders. On the other hand, a casualty of listening to her church elders would quite possibly have been her suicide.

Conclusion

The religious subcultures of Evangelical and Fundamentalist church members contain many psychological strengths, along with some potential psycho-spiritual risks. Sensitivity on the clinician's part to these psycho-spiritual nuances will hopefully enhance the healing potential of therapy for clients from these traditions.

SUGGESTED READINGS

Barker, K. L., & Kohlenberger, J., III (Eds.). (1994). *New international version Bible commentary: Vol. 1. Old Testament.* Grand Rapids, MI: Zondervan.

Barker, K. L., & Kohlenberger, J., III (Eds.). (1994). *New international version Bible commentary: Vol. 2. New Testament.* Grand Rapids, MI: Zondervan.

Bedell, K. B. (Ed.). (1997). *Yearbook of American and Canadian churches, 1997.* Nashville, TN: Abingdon Press.

Brown, S. S., Fitzmyer, S. J., & Murphy, R. E. (Eds.). (1990). *The new Jerome biblical commentary.* Englewood Cliffs, NJ: Prentice Hall.

Elwell, W. A. (Ed.). (1991). *The concise Evangelical dictionary of theology.* Grand Rapids, MI: Baker Book House.

New international version study Bible. (1985). Grand Rapids, MI: Zondervan.

REFERENCES

Ammerman, N. T. (1987). *Bible believers: Fundamentalists in the modern world.* New Brunswick, NJ: Rutgers University Press.

Ban, J. D. (1990). Baptist education. In I. V. Cully & K. B. Cully (Eds.), *Encyclopedia of religious education* (pp. 53–55). San Francisco: Harper & Row.

Bible Institute of Los Angeles. (1909). *The fundamentals.* Los Angeles: Author.

Clark, M. F. (1985). *Hiding, hurting, healing: Restoration for today's woman.* Grand Rapids, MI: Zondervan.

Cloud, H., & Townsend, J. (1994). *Twelve "Christian" beliefs that can drive you crazy.* Grand Rapids, MI: Zondervan.

Dobson, E. G. (1990). Fundamentalism. In I. V. Cully & K. B. Cully (Eds.), *Encyclopedia of religious education* (pp. 263–265). San Francisco: Harper & Row.

Dougherty, S. G., & Worthington, E. L. (1983). Preferences of conservative and moderate Christians for four Christian counselors' treatment plans. *Journal of Psychology & Theology, 10*, 346–354.

Duncombe, D. C. (1990). Psychological testing. In I. V. Cully & K. B. Cully (Eds.), *Encyclopedia of religious education* (pp. 516–517). San Francisco: Harper & Row.

Fackre, G. (1990). Evangelicalism. In I. V. Cully & K. B. Cully (Eds.), *Encyclopedia of religious education* (pp. 236–238). San Francisco: Harper & Row.

Fortune, M. M. (1987). *Keeping the faith: Questions and answers for the abused woman*. San Francisco: Harper-Collins.

Hill, P. C., & Hood, R. W. (Eds.). (1999). *Measures of religiosity*. Birmingham, AL: Religious Education Press.

Hubbard, D. A. (1979). *What we believe and teach* [Brochure]. Pasadena, CA: Fuller Theological Seminary.

Jones, S. L., & Butman, R. E. (1991). *Modern psychotherapies: A comprehensive Christian appraisal*. Downers Grove, IL: InterVarsity Press.

Kirkpatrick, L. (1987, August–September). *Fundamentalists anonymous: Perspectives from social psychology and the empirical psychology of religion*. Paper presented at the 95th Annual Convention of the American Psychological Association, New York, N.Y.

Lindsell, H. (1976). *The battle for the Bible*. Grand Rapids, MI: Zondervan.

Lovinger, R. J. (1984). *Working with religious issues in therapy*. New York: Jason Aronson.

Malony, H. N. (1985). Assessing religious maturity. In E. M. Stern (Ed.), *Psychotherapy and the religiously committed patient* (pp. 25–33). New York: Haworth Press.

Malony, H. N. (1998). Religion and mental health from the Protestant perspective. In W. Koenig, (Ed.), *Handbook of religion and mental health* (pp. 203–210). New York: Academic Press.

Marsden, G. M. (1987). *Reforming fundamentalism: Fuller Seminary and the new Evangelism*. Grand Rapids, MI: William B. Eerdmans.

Marsden, G. M. (1991). *Understanding Fundamentalism and Evangelicalism*. Grand Rapids, MI: William B. Eerdmans.

Marsden, G. M. (1997). "It's way okay": Evangelicalism 50 years later. In *Theology, news, and notes*. Pasadena, CA: Fuller Theological Seminary.

McCullough, M. E. (1995). *Forgiveness as altruism: A social–psychological theory of interpersonal forgiveness and tests of its validity*. Unpublished doctoral dissertation, Virginia Commonwealth University.

McCullough, M. E., & Worthington, E. L. (1995). Promoting forgiveness: A comparison of two brief psychoeducational group interventions with a wait-list control. *Counseling and Values, 40*, 55–68.

McCullough, M. E., Sandage, S. J., & Worthington, E. L. (1997). *To forgive is human*. Downers Grove, IL: InterVarsity Press.

New international version Bible (1985). Grand Rapids, MI: Zondervan.

Rayburn, C. A. (1985). The religious patient's initial encounter with psychotherapy. In E. M. Stern (Ed.), *Psychotherapy and the religiously committed patient* (pp. 47–53). New York: Haworth Press.

Rice, R. R. (1975). *I am a Fundamentalist*. Murfreesboo, TN: Sword of the Lord.

Rokeach, M. (1954). *The open and closed mind*. New York: Basic Books.

Rothbaum, S. (1988). Between two worlds: Issues of separation and identity after leaving a religious community. In D. G. Bromley (Ed.), *Falling from the faith: Causes and consequences of religious apostasy* (pp. 205–228). Beverly Hills, CA: Sage.

Rourke, M. (1998, June 21). *The Los Angeles Times*, pp. A1, A24–A25.

Saur, M., & Saur, W. (1990). *Spiritual Themes and Religious Responses Test*. Unpublished manuscript.

Sloat, D. (1990). *Growing up holy and wholly: Understanding and hope for adult children of Evangelicals*. Brentwood, NJ: Wolgemugh & Hyatt.

Stovich, R. J. (1985). Metaphor and therapy: Theory, technique, and practice of the use of religious imagery in therapy. In E. M. Stern (Ed.), *Psychotherapy and the religiously committed patient* (pp. 117–127). New York: Haworth Press.

Strom, K. M. (1986). *In the name of submission: A painful look at wife battering*. Portland, OR: Multnomah Press.

Tan, S. Y. (1990). Explicit integration in Christian counseling. *Christian Journal of Psychology and Counseling, 5*(2), 7–13.

Ulstein, S. (1995). *Growing up Fundamentalist: Journeys in legalism and grace*. Downers Grove, IL: InterVarsity Press.

Wright, J. W. (Ed.). (1994). *The universal almanac*. New York: Andrews & McMeel.

Yancey, P. (1988). *Disappointment with God*. Grand Rapids, MI: Zondervan.

Yao, R. (1987, August–September). *Addiction and the Fundamentalist experience*. Paper presented at the 95th annual convention of the American Psychological Association, New York, NY.

7

PSYCHOTHERAPY WITH PENTECOSTAL PROTESTANTS

RICHARD D. DOBBINS

From the words of Jesus as He spoke in the synagogue at Nazareth, quoting from the Book of Isaiah in the Old Testament of the Holy Bible: "The Spirit of the Lord is upon me, because he hath . . . sent me to heal the brokenhearted . . . to set at liberty them that are bruised."

—Holy Bible, Luke 4:18

ORIGINS AND HISTORICAL PERSPECTIVE

To understand more fully the belief system of Pentecostals and its implications for therapy, one must know something of the religious heritage from which these people come. The Pentecostal movement began around the turn of the 20th century, almost in concert with the emergence of Fundamentalism. Both groups rose largely in protest against what they believed were the "manmade creeds" and "cold worship styles" of Mainline Protestant churches (Cox, 1995).

One byproduct of an economic upturn in American history after the Civil War had been a virtual "academic explosion" (Noll, 1994, p. 112), funded primarily by wealthy new entrepreneurs and state governments rather than by the Christian communities that had previously funded colleges. New universities were founded to meet the needs of the donors, and established schools like Yale and Princeton became universities as graduate and professional programs were added (Noll, 1994). As Christianity lost

---

All Bible quotations and references are from the King James translation of the Holy Bible, unless otherwise noted.

All names in the case history examples have been changed.

ground in the universities, many Mainline Protestant denominations sought to hold at least some of their cultural ground by revising their theology to make it more acceptable to the new intellectuals who were taking the church's place in the academic world.

The new and enlarged schools, meanwhile, engaged administration and faculty who exhibited little concern for religious education or the Christian outlook on life (Noll, 1994). They were profit-driven businessmen who wanted a good return for their businesses in exchange for their contributions to the schools.

> The new universities took a German model of education to replace the older British standard. Not character, but research, not the handing on of tradition but the search for intellectual innovation became the watchword. . . . Thus it was that industrialists and bankers replaced clergymen as [college] trustees, and laymen replaced ministers as college presidents. (Noll, 1994, p. 111–112)

The new breed of university presidents, trustees, and instructors were more interested in science than in morality; more interested in a good return on their investment than in furthering Christian educational ideals that had been prevalent in American colleges and seminaries alike. In return for these investments, the new colleges and universities turned out students who were well trained in techniques that would further fuel economic and industrial growth, while offering no criticisms of their new benefactors. In many colleges, attempts to continue any kind of religious education were either abandoned or "greatly modified, under the felt need to align religion with the certainties of modern thought" (Noll, 1994, p. 114). The new theology confused and frustrated many long-time church members among Mainline denominations.

The Fundamentalist movement in America came about in response to this and other changes in Americans' way of life during this rapidly changing era. In all fairness to Fundamentalists of the early 20th century, it must be said that they worked very hard to defend Christian ideals and convictions, thus protecting them from being swept away in the rapid social changes.

> At a time when naturalism threatened religion, when relativism assaulted social morality, when intellectual fashions were turning the Bible into a book of merely antiquarian interest, fundamentalists said what needed to be said about the supernatural character of religion, the objectivity of Christian morality, and the timeless validity of Scripture. (Noll, 1994, p. 115)

An unfortunate byproduct of early Fundamentalism, however, was a general distrust of almost all intellectual activity among conservative Evangelical Christians, including the Pentecostal groups that would soon emerge and largely separate from the Fundamentalist movement.

At the time when Fundamentalism and its offspring, Pentecostalism, came into being, not only secular and liberal arts colleges but also American seminaries of Mainline denominations were being influenced more and more by the "higher criticism" of such German theologians as Friedrich Schleiermacher, sometimes called the "father of Modernism," and his followers Albrecht Ritschl and Adolph Harnack (Menzies, 1971). These and other theologians were attacking the infallibility of Scripture and seeking to "demythologize" the Bible to make it more palatable to 20th-century believers. The experiential theology of Pentecostals was developed to counter this typically rationalist Enlightenment theology (Poloma, 1989).

Building largely on Wesley's writings and 19th-century Restorationism (a belief that the church today should contend for and experience the same Christianity that is described in the Book of Acts), Pentecostals have sought to extend this theology into the 20th century (Poloma, 1989). They insist that it is God's will to restore the beliefs and practices of the First Century Church.[1]

In pursuit of this belief, Pentecostals preach and teach what they describe as a "full Gospel message." This message embraces the New Testament Church's belief that Jesus forgives and saves from sin those who believe in Him (Holy Bible, John 1:12; John 3:16–17; 1 John 1:7–9); He heals the sick in response to prayer (Holy Bible, Matthew 10: 1, 7–8; James 5: 14–16); He baptizes believers in the Holy Spirit (Holy Bible, Luke 24: 49; Acts 1:4, 5, 7–8); and He is literally, physically coming again to reign over this earth as King of Kings and Lord of Lords (Holy Bible, Revelation 19:11–20:4). They believe Jesus is mankind's only Savior and God's love gift to a world that is lost and eternally damned without Him (Holy Bible, Mark 16:15; John 3:16–18, 36).[2]

Pentecostals believe that prayer for the sick and miracles of healing should be as prominent in the Church today as they were in the 1st century. Healing is to come to the sick through prayer and the laying on of hands or through anointing with oil and prayer (Holy Bible, James 5:14–16). Pentecostals differ from most Evangelicals in that they believe those miraculous signs and wonders that were characteristic of the First Century Church—including healings—should once again be a normal part of the Church's life (Lawrence, 1989, cited in Blumhofer, 1989).

Pentecostals owe their name and their uniqueness among Evangelicals to their insistence that when Jesus baptizes believers in the Holy Spirit today, they will have the same kind of experience common to believers in the First Century Church on the Day of Pentecost (Holy Bible, Acts 2:43;

---

[1]Pentecostals, as used in this chapter, refers to typical Classical Pentecostal beliefs. The author does not presume to speak for all Pentecostals. Generalizations are made with the understanding that there will be exceptions to them.
[2]The frequent use of scripture in this chapter reflects the core position that the Holy Bible holds in the worldview of Pentecostals.

4:29, 30; 5:12; 8:13; 14:3). *Pentecost* refers to an event that occurred 50 days after the crucifixion of Christ, on a traditional Jewish day of feasting and pilgrimage occurring 7 weeks after Passover. John the Baptist, who referred to it as a baptism in the Holy Spirit, predicted this experience (*Holy Bible*, Matthew 3:11; Acts 2:1–4).

Remembering that this experience is a *baptism* helps one to better understand it. There are three components to every baptismal experience:

1. The Celebrant (the one who does the baptizing).
2. The Communicant (the person who is baptized).
3. The Element involved in the baptismal experience (the means by which the transformation implied in the word *baptism* is accomplished).

For example, when a person is baptized in water as a public expression of faith in Jesus Christ, the Celebrant is the minister who performs the baptism. The Communicant is the person being baptized. The Element is the water in the baptismal font or immersion tank.

In a person's Christian conversion experience, the Holy Spirit is the Celebrant. The believer is the Communicant. The Body of Christ is the Element into which the believer is baptized. This experience places the believer "in Christ" and makes him/her "a new creature."

When one is Spirit Baptized, Jesus is the Celebrant. The believer is the Communicant. The Holy Spirit is the Element. Pentecostals insist that just as First Century believers spoke in "other tongues" when they received this experience, so will those believers who receive this experience today.

WHO ARE THE PENTECOSTALS?

Included in my use of the term *Pentecostals* are three distinct groups:

1. Classical Pentecostals: These are the denominational groups that were formed in the first two decades of the 20th century (Burgess, McGee, & Alexander, 1988).

2. Charismatics: These are Protestants in traditional Mainline denominations and Catholics who embrace the Pentecostal experience (commonly known as Charismatic Renewal) while choosing to remain in their traditional churches. Originating in the 1940s and 1950s, the movement is generally dated from occurrences in two Episcopalian congregations in California in 1959–1960 (Burgess, McGee, & Alexander, 1988).

3. Independent Charismatics: These are other Pentecostals (many of whom have come from Classical Pentecostalism and the Charismatic Renewal movement) represented by independent churches not affiliated with any parent organization. Since the late 1970s, there has been "an explosion

of nondenominational charismatic assemblies," according to one researcher, who concludes that "complete classification is virtually impossible" for this group. He further indicates that most such groups "acquire affiliations with some network or association of charismatic assemblies and/or pastors" (Burgess, McGee, & Alexander, 1988, p. 141), but they generally have no denominational ties.

The roots of Classical Pentecostalism may be traced back to several significant spiritual events transpiring from the 18th century to the early part of the 20th century. Among these were the following:

1. *The Wesleyan Revival.* John Wesley, as the founder of the Methodist Church, is seen by many historians and theologians as one of the most influential—if controversial—leaders of the Protestant faith since Martin Luther.

Probably few figures in church history have generated more diverse judgments about their positioning among the Christian traditions than Wesley. At different times, he has been blamed, praised, championed, or claimed as one of their own by various branches of Protestant Christendom.

Wesley taught that *subsequent to conversion*, the Christian should have a definite experience of sanctification. He made a distinction between ordinary Christians and those who had been "sanctified" or baptized with the Holy Spirit. This experience, most often referred to as a "second definite work of grace" or "second blessing" (Moriarty, 1992), created a spirit of elitism among believers. Although Wesley reintroduced the role of experience in the Christian life, he also placed great importance on subjecting experience to the discipline of Scripture.

2. *The Holiness Movement.* By the early 1830s, American Methodism was neglecting Wesley's teaching on holiness. In the late 1830s, at Oberlin College in Ohio, Charles Finney and Asa Mahan sought to reawaken the Methodist Church with their message of Christian perfectionism.

In 1870, Mahan convinced popular preacher and publisher Phoebe Palmer to publish his *Baptism of the Holy Ghost*, a book that referred to the believer's sanctification in terms of the Holy Spirit Baptism. Palmer felt the book was too controversial and was hesitant to accept it for some time. The book had an immediate impact on the Holiness movement in America, Britain, Germany, The Netherlands, and numerous mission fields around the world.

Mahan's reference to the experience of sanctification as the "Baptism of the Holy Spirit" (Bassett & Greathouse, 1985) and believers' experiences following publication of this work eventually helped bring division between the Holiness movement and the later Pentecostal movement. The Pentecostals insisted that speaking in other tongues was the initial physical evidence that a believer had received the baptism of the Holy Spirit. Those involved in the Holiness movement believed this teaching to be in error and denounced it as heresy.

3. *The Keswick Conference.* In the late 1870s at the parish of Keswick in northern England, an interdenominational Bible Convention developed around a common hunger for a deeper, more profoundly devoted Christian life. Unlike the Wesleyan branch of the Holiness movement, the Keswick meetings did not focus on perfectionism and eradication of sin. Instead, they addressed the need for what they called a "higher" or "more spiritually aware" life and an "enduement of power"—a divine gift of power with which one could live that higher life and bear witness to the unconverted of Christ's power to forgive their sin. Thus, their desires and supplications were more often for empowerment for Christian service than for the cleansing of sin from their lives. Teaching centered on the time of Christ's return to earth, faith healing, and the gifts of the Spirit, which had been promised to believers in New Testament times (Synan, 1975).

4. *The Welsh Revival.* In 1903–1904, a revival broke out in a church at New Quay on Cardigan Bay in Wales (Hollenweger, 1988). This revival also left its mark on the Pentecostal movement. Believers were challenged to obey the Holy Spirit's leading through spontaneous and fervent worship, repeated singing of choruses, and unstructured services which sometimes lasted for several hours. The revival was eschatological (end times) in its focus and was believed to be in fulfillment of (*Holy Bible*) Joel 2:28, "And it shall come to pass in the last days, that I will pour out my Spirit upon all flesh" (Blumhofer, 1989).

5. *The Azuza Street Revival.* African American evangelist William Seymour led a virtual 24-hour-a-day revival meeting in Los Angeles, California, from 1906 to 1909. This 3-year revival is credited with launching the worldwide Pentecostal movement which would "encircle the globe and become a 'third force' in Christendom." The Azuza Street revival was marked by unusually powerful and life-changing spiritual experiences among participants (Synan, 1975, pp. 2, 29, 52).

In the early years, most Pentecostal/Charismatic clergy considered formal education a hindrance to the Holy Spirit's anointing upon their ministry. Fervent preachers often felt they could not afford the time to be educated for their task: Time was too precious to waste years in seminary or even a 2-year Bible college, when so many souls were waiting for this glorious new message.

When viewed within the context of these historical roots, one can more easily understand why Pentecostals place more emphasis on spiritual experience than any other branch of Christianity. This has always made them vulnerable to strong, erratic personalities and emotional extremes (Moriarty, 1992). Historian Michael Moriarty considers Pentecostalism to have been "theologically thin" (Moriarty, 1992) through much of its history, neglecting many great doctrines of the Bible while overemphasizing uniquely Pentecostal beliefs. This kind of history has taught Classical Pentecostals the wisdom of subjecting spiritual experience to the discipline of Scripture.

The one distinguishing characteristic that Classical Pentecostal, Charismatic, and Independent Pentecostal believers have in common is their belief in *glossolalia*, or speaking in tongues. The word *glossolalia* comes from two Greek words: *glossa* (the tongue) and *lalein* (to talk). The definition given for *glossolalia* in *Webster's Third New International Dictionary* is "ecstatic speech that is usually unintelligible to hearers." The *Random House Dictionary* (unabridged) defines *glossolalia* as "a prayer characterized chiefly by incomprehensible speech."

The practice of speaking in tongues was common among Christians during the first century. *Speaking in tongues* is mentioned especially as accompanying evidence to being "filled with the Spirit" (*Holy Bible*, Acts 2:4; 10:44–48; 19:1–6). Most of the 14th chapter of (*Holy Bible*) 1 Corinthians is devoted to instruction on the regulation of speaking in tongues during a public worship service so that it enhances, rather than detracts from, the experience of those present.

GEOGRAPHIC HIGHLIGHTS AND DEMOGRAPHICS

According to David Barrett, a respected church statistician, over 400 million people in the world embrace some form of Pentecostalism. The Pentecostal–Charismatic movement is, he says, largely an "urban phenomenon," which is "proliferating most rapidly today in the gigantic megacities of the third world such as São Paulo, Seoul, and Lusaka [Zambia]" (Cox, 1995, pp. 14, 15).

Pentecostalism accounts for one in every four Christians. It is "the largest non-Catholic group" of Christians in the world, "increasing more rapidly than either militant Islam or the Christian Fundamentalist sects, with which it is sometimes confused" (Cox, 1995, pp. 14, 15). When Fundamentalism initially surfaced in the more conservative Protestant churches in the 1920s, adherents were expected to abstain from all use of alcohol, tobacco, or drugs. They were not permitted to engage in such "worldly" forms of entertainment as dancing, movies, or visiting the neighborhood pool hall. Such activities as bowling, mixed swimming (swimming with members of the opposite sex), theater, movies, or (more recently) television are still forbidden by many Fundamentalist groups. Makeup, short hairstyles, slacks, shorts, sleeveless clothing, and most jewelry items are also forbidden to women by some Fundamentalist groups.

Although they encompass a number of denominations, all Fundamentalists share a belief in the Bible as an inerrant document inspired by God and as the "final and complete authority for faith and practice" in one's life (Burgess, McGee, & Alexander, 1988, p. 324). Fundamentalists adhere to a rigid and dogmatic interpretation of Scripture. They insist that their views are the "right" ones and look upon those who differ from them with great suspicion.

Fundamentalism gained great notoriety in the 1925 Scopes Monkey Trial, when Tennessee public school teacher John T. Scopes was put on trial for teaching the theory of evolution. Following that trial, Fundamentalists were generally described as "anti-intellectuals who stood in the way of social and academic progress" (Burgess, McGee, & Alexander, 1988, p. 324).

Fundamentalism had waned somewhat by the end of World War II, and it never regained its previous level of popularity. However, together with the Evangelical Protestant churches, which are its "more respectable form" (Burgess, McGee, & Alexander, 1988, p. 324), it comprises a large segment of Protestant Christendom today.

Some theologians believe that Pentecostalism's separation from Fundamentalism was decidedly for the good. "The breaks with Fundamentalism in 1928 and 1943 turned out to be a blessing that freed the rising Pentecostals from the dead cultural and theological baggage of a discredited movement and opened the way for unparalleled influence and growth [of Pentecostalism] in the last half of the 20th century" (Burgess, McGee, & Alexander, 1988, p. 327).

MAJOR SUBTRADITIONS OR DENOMINATIONS

Anyone attempting to understand people from Pentecostal Protestant churches needs to develop an appreciation for the heterogeneous backgrounds from which they come.

The Wesleyan–Holiness Pentecostal Groups

These groups are characterized by a belief in three distinct experiences in the development of one's Christian faith. They are:

1. Salvation, which occurs when one accepts Christ as Savior,
2. Sanctification, which occurs when the sin principle in one's life is broken, and
3. The Baptism in the Holy Spirit, which occurs as one is initially empowered to witness for Christ.

Remembering that the Pentecostal experience is a "baptism" helps clarify what Pentecostals believe happens when one is baptized in the Holy Spirit. Just as the Holy Spirit baptizes the believer into the Body of

Christ (the worldwide community of born-again believers) at the point of conversion or being "born again," Pentecostals believe that Jesus baptizes the believer in the Holy Spirit. Classical Pentecostals believe this experience is accompanied by *glossolalia*. Subsequent to this Holy Spirit baptism experience, the believer is more spiritually sensitive to the operation of the "gifts of the Spirit" referred to in 1 Corinthians chapters 12–14.

Among the largest of the Classical Pentecostal groups from the Wesleyan tradition are the Church of God in Christ, a predominantly African American group numbering several million and comprising one of the largest Pentecostal constituencies in the world (Burgess, McGee, & Alexander, 1988); the Church of God with headquarters in Cleveland, Tennessee; and the Pentecostal Holiness Church.

Because many groups may have similar names, identifying the headquarters city is useful in distinguishing a group's identity. For example, the Church of God headquartered in Anderson, Indiana, is a non-Pentecostal group which the public often confuses with the Church of God headquartered in Cleveland, Tennessee (a Pentecostal group), because of the similarity of their names.

The Non-Wesleyan Pentecostal Groups

The non-Wesleyan Pentecostal groups are characterized by a belief in two, not three, distinct experiences in the development of one's Christian faith: Salvation (when one accepts Christ as Savior) and the Baptism in the Holy Spirit (when one is empowered to witness for Christ).

The General Council of the Assemblies of God, with over 30 million adherents worldwide, is the largest of these Pentecostal groups. The International Church of the Foursquare Gospel, the Open Bible Standard Churches, and The United Pentecostal Church are also prominent among this group of Pentecostals.

The origin of this last group (The United Pentecostal Church) may be traced to 1913 when their early founders rejected the Trinitarian formula for baptism found in (*Holy Bible*) Matthew 28:19, 20 and insisted that believers be baptized in the name of "Jesus only" (*Holy Bible*, Acts 2:38). Their contention was that if believers baptized by the Trinitarian formula were not baptized again in the name of "Jesus only," their salvation was in question. This brought dissension and division to the young Pentecostal movement. Originally known as "Oneness" or "Jesus Only," believers in the United Pentecostal Church embrace a Unitarian view of God, seeing Him as totally revealed in Jesus Christ (Menzies, 1971).

The Charismatic Renewal

In the 1950s and 1960s, large numbers of people from traditional Christian churches—both Catholic and Protestant—began to develop an interest in the Holy Spirit and Spirit Baptism. Four factors seem to have converged in the launching of the Charismatic movement: (a) the Van Nuys revival, (b) the "Full Gospel Business Men," (c) the influence of David J. Du Plessis, and (d) Roman Catholic Pentecostalism (Hollenweger, 1988).

Many of the people from these traditional Christian churches who received a Pentecostal experience chose to stay in their own churches. Both Catholic and Protestant parishes often chose to provide structure for people from the Charismatic Renewal so that the faith and energy of these believers could be preserved within their own traditions. Others were more wary of this way of expressing one's faith.

Today, traditional churches are less likely than in the past to ask people to leave simply because they believe in speaking in tongues and in divine healing. Consequently, thousands of Spirit-baptized people have retained their traditional church identity and, by doing so, are trusting God to use them in the revitalization of their church.

The Classical Pentecostals and the Charismatic Renewal believers share many common characteristics (Burgess, McGee, & Alexander, 1988): Jesus is the central focus of their worship; they spend much of their worship time in informal singing and praising; there is a deep love for the Scriptures among them; they believe that God presently speaks to the individual believer as well as to the entire church; there is a strong emphasis on evangelism; they share a heightened awareness of evil; there is a longing for the return of Christ among them; and they believe in and pray for manifestations of spiritual power both in themselves personally and in their worship services. They also believe in and practice the spiritual gifts that Paul refers to in his epistles (*Holy Bible*, 1 Corinthians, chapters 12–14).

In addition to Classical Pentecostal groups and the body of Charismatic Renewal believers remaining in traditional churches, there are also a growing number of Independent Charismatics. Since the 1970s, many traditional Pentecostals and Charismatics have grown dissatisfied in their local churches. Subsequently, they have left their former churches and formed often large, independent, Charismatic churches (Burgess, McGee, & Alexander, 1988), which are frequently located in easily accessed facilities.

Most of these churches have grown up around the teaching–preaching ministry of a dynamic and gifted pastor who is relatively autonomous in the way he governs the church. Often, church boards are appointed by and serve at the pleasure of this pastor, who is generally accountable to no governing body beyond the local congregation. In a few instances, the property is held in the pastor's name.

The theology of such a church is largely determined by the pastor and, thus, varies from church to church. Pastors of Independent Charismatic churches often tend to embrace one of two popular teachings rejected by both the Classical Pentecostals and those Charismatic believers who have chosen to remain in traditional churches. The first of these is some form of the "Word of Faith" teaching, sometimes referred to as the "health-wealth" gospel, which asserts that (a) if one's faith is strong enough, one will always be healed of any illness one may experience; and, (b) if one gives generously (more than a tithe, which would be 10%) and "believes" for it, God will richly reward him or her with material wealth (Cox, 1995).

Many Independent Charismatic churches also embrace some form of the second referenced teaching, "Dominion Theology," which is an extension of Puritanism and teaches that before Christ can return, the Church must take dominion (or control) over all nations of the world (Cox, 1995).

POSITIONS ON THEOLOGICAL AND SOCIAL ISSUES

Theologically, Classical Pentecostals and Independent Charismatics are conservative Evangelicals. The Assemblies of God Statement of Faith, as printed in an abbreviated form in denominational publications (*Pentecostal Evangel*, 1999), states:

WE BELIEVE . . .

- The Bible is the inspired and only infallible and authoritative written Word of God.
- There is one God, eternally existent in three persons: God the Father, God the Son, and God the Holy Ghost.
- In the deity of our Lord Jesus Christ, in His virgin birth, in His sinless life, in His miracles, in His vicarious and atoning death, in His bodily resurrection, in His ascension to the right hand of the Father, in His personal future return to this earth in power and glory to rule a thousand years.
- In the blessed hope—the rapture of the Church at Christ's coming.
- The only means of being cleansed from sin is through repentance and faith in the precious blood of Christ.
- Regeneration by the Holy Spirit is absolutely essential for personal salvation.
- In water baptism by immersion.
- The redemptive work of Christ on the cross provides healing of the human body in answer to believing prayer.

- The baptism in the Holy Spirit, according to (*Holy Bible*) Acts 2:4, is given to believers who ask for it.
- In the sanctifying power of the Holy Spirit by whose indwelling the Christian is enabled to live a holy life.
- In the resurrection of both the saved and the lost, the one to everlasting life and the other to everlasting damnation.

The foregoing statement should be similar in content to most statements of belief for Classical Pentecostal and Independent Charismatic groups. Those involved in the Charismatic Renewal will hold to the theological views of their respective traditions.

Classical Pentecostals and Independent Charismatics share many beliefs in common. Among these are the infallibility of Scripture and its legitimate rule over their faith and conduct (*Holy Bible*, 2 Timothy 3:16–17); the deity of Jesus and His virgin birth (*Holy Bible*, Matthew 1:18–25; Luke 1:26–38); the reality of Satan, the fall of Adam, the sinful nature of the human race, and their need for a sinless Savior (*Holy Bible*, Luke 22:31–32; Romans 5:6–21; 1 Peter 5:8); the good news of the Gospel, that Christ has atoned for the sins of the world, so that anyone who accepts Him as Savior receives forgiveness of their sins and the gift of eternal life (*Holy Bible*, Luke 4:18; 1 John 5:9–13); the freedom of man's will to accept or reject the initiatives of God's grace (*Holy Bible*, Philippians 2:12–13; Titus 2:11–14; Revelation 3:20); the power of prayer as a means of forming Christ's character in the believer, interceding for divine intervention in the well-being of others, or petitioning God for one's own needs (*Holy Bible*, Matthew 6:5–34; Romans 8:26–28; 1 John 5:14–15); the survival of the spirit and soul; the resurrection of the body (*Holy Bible*, 1 Corinthians 15; 2 Corinthians 5:1–9); the accountability and ultimate judgment of all human beings: believers for their works and unbelievers for their sins (*Holy Bible*, 1 Corinthians 3:10–15; 2 Corinthians 5:10; Revelation 20:11–15); and the final judgment of Satan and all those spirit beings allied with him (*Holy Bible*, Revelation 20:7–10).

Classical Pentecostals are generally urged to vote in civic elections, but tend not to be involved formally in political activism. Independent Charismatics who embrace Dominion Theology are more likely to be zealously involved in the political process (Cox, 1995). However, both groups are in agreement on most popular social issues.

Pentecostals and Independent Charismatics generally agree on sexual issues. They see sexuality as a sacred gift from God and sexual intercourse as an experience to be celebrated only in marriage. In marriage, sexual expression between a husband and wife serves three functions: (a) a unitive function—a divine means for making two people become one (*Holy Bible*, Genesis 1:27–28); (b) a reproductive function—a divine means for making two people become three . . . or more (*Holy Bible*, Genesis 1:27–28); and

(c) a recreational function for the married couple (*Holy Bible*, 1 Corinthians 7:3–5).

Homosexuality is seen by Pentecostals as unnatural and contrary to Scripture (*Holy Bible*, Genesis 13–19; Romans 1:20–32). This leaves homosexuals with two options if they wish to remain in good standing in a Pentecostal church and, more importantly, in a personal relationship with God. They may (a) seek deliverance from homosexuality and become heterosexual or (b) remain celibate.

Most Pentecostals and Charismatics view birth control as a matter of private conscience for couples wanting to limit the number of children in their family. Pentecostals are opposed to using it as a means to encourage sexual intercourse among the unmarried. Abortion is heatedly opposed, but some would permit it in ectopic pregnancies or other situations in which there is a clear threat to a mother's life.

There are differing opinions about divorce and remarriage among Pentecostal groups. In some groups, if the divorce occurred before a person accepted Christ, adherents are entitled to participate in the church in any way consistent with their gifts—including the ministry. In other groups, if the divorce occurred before a person accepted Christ or was the result of sexual infidelity or physical abuse, the person is allowed to participate in the life of the local congregation. However, these people are restricted from the office of deacon and from the ministry. In a few groups, divorced people are permitted to be members but not allowed to hold any elected office.

Pentecostals hold varying beliefs about remarriage following divorce. In some groups, if a divorced person is being remarried, the pastor will be permitted to perform the ceremony so long as the divorce occurred before the person accepted Christ as his or her Savior. In other groups, the pastor would be permitted to perform the remarriage ceremony only if the person's first marriage ended as a result of his or her mate's marital infidelity or physical abuse. In a few groups, the pastor is forbidden to perform a wedding ceremony for any remarrying couple.

Child care and corporal punishment are treated consistently among Pentecostals. All Pentecostal groups oppose any treatment of children that could be classified as physical, sexual, or emotional abuse. However, non-abusive corporal punishment of young children is accepted among Pentecostals.

Pentecostals are intolerant of substance abuse. All Pentecostal and Charismatic groups are opposed to drunkenness and drug abuse in any form. Classical Pentecostals take a stand of total abstinence from alcohol. Some of the Charismatic Renewal believers and some Independent Charismatic churches take a position of temperance toward the use of alcohol.

IMPLICATIONS FOR COUNSELING AND PSYCHOTHERAPY

Traditionally, Pentecostals have embraced the historic antipathy between religion and psychology or psychiatry. Leaders have often been suspicious of the behavioral sciences and opposed to any kind of counseling or therapy that is not strictly Biblical. Since the exposé of televangelists in the 1980s, there has been some softening of this attitude. This is evidenced by a growing number of Pentecostal professional counselors and the formation of such associations as the Fellowship of Pentecostal/Charismatic Caregivers. However, opposition to therapy is still typical of Pentecostals in general.

For most Pentecostals, even the act of sitting in the office of a mental health professional generates guilt-provoking questions: Why haven't I been able to trust God for this problem or condition? Why don't I have the faith to rise above this? As a Spirit-baptized Christian, what kind of a testimony am I to this therapist, when I can't manage my own life? What will this therapist think of my faith? Will my faith be respected or come under attack?

A large measure of the Pentecostal believer's guilt and fear comes from both the erroneous teaching (mentioned earlier) which was so common in earlier years and the doctrinal emphasis on their responsibility to live a life that is holy and pleasing to God. Thus, they often reason that if they are "living for God," He can and will keep bad things from happening to them. Of course, this kind of magical thinking is contrary to Scripture. The entire Book of Job in the Old Testament chronicles the trials of Job, a man declared by God himself to be "my servant . . . a perfect and an upright man" (Holy Bible, Job 1:8). Jesus reminds believers that God sends rain "on the just and on the unjust," and that the storms of life come to both the "wise man" (a believer) who builds his house on "a rock" and the "foolish man" (or unbeliever) who builds his house on an unstable foundation—"the sand" (Holy Bible, Matthew 7:24–27).

Forgetting these passages of Scripture and many others with similar messages, some Pentecostals mistakenly believe that bad things are happening to them because they are somehow displeasing God in their lifestyle. This mindset is often accompanied by the belief that if they could just get back into a right relationship with God, all of their problems would vanish.

Neutralizing this kind of guilt and any accompanying suspicion of mental health care should be among the earliest issues in building a healthy therapeutic alliance with Pentecostals. The following are some suggestions for doing this.

The client should be reassured that the spiritual resources of his or her faith will be used in therapy. If the therapist is a Christian, either Pentecostal or non-Pentecostal, it will be helpful and reassuring to share this information with the client. The appropriate use of Scripture and prayer as meaningful parts of the therapeutic process will also go a long way toward relieving the client's initial distrust of therapy. A therapist of other than the Christian faith may reassure Christian clients by acknowledging the importance attributed to each client's faith. Any effort to assure clients that their faith will be respected will go far in disarming their suspicions and enhancing the therapeutic alliance.

If the Pentecostal client is of a different gender or ethnic group than the therapist, additional challenges arise. Here are some suggestions for neutralizing these concerns. It often helps to acknowledge that although one cannot know what it is like to be of a different gender or ethnic group, the therapist will try to be sensitive to these differences in perspective. The client should be given permission to call to the therapist's attention any issues of gender or ethnicity that appear to have been overlooked. If the client should question the therapist's sensitivity to his or her uniqueness, it is important for the therapist to avoid being defensive and to ask for the client's help in arriving at a better understanding.

Religious and Spiritual Assessment Measures

When collecting information about the Pentecostal client's personal history, exploring the role and importance of the client's faith will prove helpful in defining the extent of theological overlays in their issues. The therapist should inquire into such things as the denomination in which the clients were raised, the role religion played in their upbringing, how frequently they attend church (an objective indicator of how central or peripheral the church is in their life), how they pictured God in their mind as a child, the three things they would most like God to do for them, the three greatest sins they believe a person can commit, and the three most "Christian" things a person can do.

A sentence completion test that includes some theological stems should prove helpful. Here are some suggested stems: God is —, I feel guilty —, Church people —, The Bible —, My pastor —, Satan is —, Prayer —, and so on. Using the responses to these stems as a projective device can provide valuable insight as to the growth-stimulating or -crippling nature of the client's religious beliefs.

Common Clinical Issues Among Pentecostals

There are several common clinical issues that may be observed with Pentecostals. First, there is the client's image of God. Many Pentecostal clients will suffer from an overly harsh and punitive image of God that leaves them feeling guilty, angry, and anxious much of the time.

Most will be unaware that this image of God stems from how they saw their parents when they were growing up. That is, if they saw their parents as difficult to please, they will tend to see God's approval as difficult (if not impossible) for them to achieve. If they saw their parents as more punitive than rewarding, then that is the way they will tend to see God. The basis of their view of God is formed *not from the way He is presented in Scripture*, but from *the introjection and projection of their early views of their parents*. However, they are usually unaware of any correlation between the way in which they perceive God and the way in which they perceived their parents as a child.

Serious Pentecostal believers are more concerned about what God thinks of them than they are about what people think of them. So, sooner or later, external approbation proves inadequate as a source of affirmation for these believers. Unless there is a Biblical correction of the way in which they see God, issues of guilt and self-condemnation will continue to weigh heavily on their mental processes.

One way of helping Pentecostal clients correct a distorted image of God is to remind them of the price Scripture says He was willing to pay for the redemption of the human race. This reflects His loving nature toward both believers and unbelievers (*Holy Bible*, John 3:16–17; Romans 5:8–10; 1 Peter 1:18–19). Refer them to passages of Scripture that picture how simple it is to please God (*Holy Bible*, Matthew 10:42; 11:28–30; 25:34–40). Helping them to first define God as being separate from their parents and then to see Him as One who loves them and is easy to please will help bring about the necessary change in their intrapsychic structure to provide them with a gentler and less severe superego.

Second, the self-image of many Pentecostal clients will need attention in treatment. Because the Pentecostal accepts Scripture as the infallible rule of faith and conduct, the use of Scripture in addressing the need for altering one's self-image should meet with less resistance than other approaches. Reminding the Pentecostal of Scripture passages that refer to believers in very complimentary terms should be helpful. The New Testament says that believers are "heirs of God and joint-heirs with Christ," "members" of the Lord's body, and "a royal priesthood" (*Holy Bible*, Romans 8:17; Ephesians 5:30; 1 Peter 2:9).

Like many other Protestants, Pentecostals tend to suffer from a body image defined by celibate Gnostic theologians who taught that the body was evil; only the soul was good (Brown, 1990). Protestant Christianity's theology is heavily influenced by this part of Catholic theology that still awaits reformation. As a rule, Christian men have learned to feel good about their bodies; however, many Christian women still suffer from a very poor body image that leaves them fearful of their sexual impulses and feeling guilty for their normal sexual desires. Some parents inadvertently compound this problem for their daughters by the overzealous methods they use to teach premarital chastity. Since it is girls, and not boys, who become pregnant, sex and the body are likely to be presented in negative terms more to girls than to boys. Scripture makes it clear that the human body is a good gift from God; so is human sexuality, so long as its expression is confined to marriage (*Holy Bible*, Genesis 1:27–28, 31: 2:21–25; 1 Corinthians 7:3–5). One's personhood is expressed through the body. Scripture describes the body as the temple of the Holy Spirit (*Holy Bible*, 1 Corinthians 6:19–20). Giving Scriptural permission to feel good about one's body and the celebration of one's sexuality in marriage can be very liberating for Pentecostals seeking help in these areas.

Third, Pentecostals are as susceptible to depression as the general population. However, some aspects of the Pentecostal belief system decrease their willingness and ability to reach out for help when they are depressed. Their belief in divine healing tends to make them feel that they are somehow failing to exercise their faith when they need assistance in dealing with depression. Medication for depression is strongly stigmatized for many. Pentecostal believers generally will submit to medical assistance with problems of the thyroid, pancreas, heart, or other physical organs. However, they probably will find it very difficult to accept medical assistance in managing their mental and emotional processes in connection with depression.

Taking away the stigma associated with depression and the need for medication in managing it will be very helpful to Pentecostals. There are many Biblical examples of depression which can be useful in destigmatizing this illness (*Holy Bible*, 1 Kings 19:4; Job 3; Psalm 55; Jonah 4:3–8).

Fourth, Pentecostals are likely to bring guilt issues into therapy: things they have done for which they cannot forgive themselves, or things other people have done to them for which they have difficulty forgiving them.

In the first instance, it may help to inquire whether they believe God has forgiven them for what they have done. If they do not feel forgiven, the therapist may direct them to appropriate Scriptures (*Holy Bible*, Ephesians 4:32; Hebrews 8:12, 10:17; 1 John 1:7–9; 1 John 2:1–2). A good Bible concordance (generally available through the public library's reference department) will help the client discover other passages of Scripture related to God's forgiveness. This could be a "homework" assignment for those who would appear to benefit from it.

Often, even though they feel forgiven by God, Pentecostal believers have difficulty forgiving themselves. When this is the case, it may help to raise questions such as: "Is your conscience more difficult to satisfy than the holy nature of God? Are you implying that although the sacrifice of Christ was adequate to satisfy the holy nature of God, your own conscience requires more than this?" Raising questions like these often enables the person to see the inconsistency of feeling forgiven by God but condemned by one's self. Responding to this inconsistency often results in the realization that if God—by His grace—has forgiven them, they ought to be able to forgive themselves.

Some believers are reluctant to forgive others who have harmed them. This often stems from both their outrage at being wronged and the fear of being hurt in this way again. By separating the issues of forgiveness and the reinvestment of trust, the therapist can minimize a client's resistance to forgiveness. Once the person understands that forgiving those who have harmed them does not mean they must immediately trust those people again, much of the resistance to forgiveness is broken. Usually, the remaining reluctance can be managed by reminding the believer that other people's wrongs against us could never hurt us as much as our sinful behaviors hurt Jesus. This gives clinical meaning to, "Forgive us our trespasses as we forgive those who trespass against us" (*Holy Bible*, Matthew 6:12).

In working with issues of forgiveness, it is helpful to explain forgiveness as (a) *an act of the person's will, empowered by God* (*Holy Bible*, Philippians 4:13), in which one determines to forgive another person for something he or she has done; (b) *a process* which occurs over a period of time as trust is regained by appropriate behaviors; and (c) finally, arriving at *a state of forgiveness* where the unpleasant memories are relegated to their proper place in one's personal history—no longer a painful current event.

Fifth, Pentecostals will present with fairly predictable sexual issues. They are much like those found among Evangelicals in general. Pentecostal men typically experience problems with guilt over masturbation, pornography, and adultery. Women have difficulty with sexual repression and inhibition. Often, these problems are related either to unhealthy attitudes in their families of origin or to sexual molestation in the client's childhood or adolescence. Occasionally, Pentecostal women will present with problems stemming from their own adultery; however, adultery is much more common among the men.

Sixth, Pentecostals will present with anger management problems. These generally fall in three distinct areas: Some are angry with God either for allowing certain things to happen or for not intervening when prayer is offered during personal crises. Others are angry with themselves for the consequences of unwise decisions they made or for wise decisions they entertained but failed to make; still others are angry toward those whom they believe have wronged them in one way or another.

The Wesleyan Pentecostals will have difficulty dealing with any component of anger in their depression. Perhaps anger is the most difficult emotion for all Christians to deal with, but it is particularly onerous for Wesleyans since they believe that the experience of sanctification totally delivers the believer from anger. The denial of anger in this population can be a major roadblock to their therapy. However, Scripture allows for healthy expressions of believers' anger (*Holy Bible*, Ephesians 4:26). Sometimes it helps to remind them that even Jesus experienced anger and expressed it. The clinician may be more successful with this treatment population by using euphemisms for anger such as frustration, irritation, being upset, and so on.

An approach to anger management I have used successfully with many Pentecostals is outlined in a simple A-B-C-D formula:

A—Accept anger as a normal emotion in life. Even Jesus experienced and expressed anger (*Holy Bible*, Mark 3:5).

B—Become aware of the early physical evidence your body provides to indicate that you are becoming angry (tension in neck and shoulders, shortness of breath, visceral rumblings).

C—Control your urges to act or speak in ways that further complicate the provoking situation. The earlier you detect the onset of anger, the more likely you are to control it successfully.

D—Direct the energy generated by your anger into creative, recreative, or nondestructive activities. Sublimation is recognized as a healthy way of dealing with anger.

As in other populations, divorce and remarriage bring anger and confusion into the lives of many Pentecostals. In addition to the usual problems connected with these issues, the contradiction between belief and practice presents a burdensome therapeutic challenge for Pentecostals.

Pentecostals generally believe that divorce and remarriage are permitted only when there is a history of adultery, physical abuse, or sexual abuse. Some Pentecostal groups do not permit divorced and remarried people to enter the clergy and, as lay members, may limit their participation on church boards.

Therefore, when divorce is in the history of a Pentecostal, the therapist will need to determine whether the person has dealt successfully with the emotional issues surrounding it. When there is guilt, the therapist may suggest that even though divorce is frowned upon by the church, it is not unpardonable. Helping the person experience forgiveness from God and enabling the person to forgive himself or herself become important therapeutic tasks. Remind them that God hates divorce (*Holy Bible*, Malachi 2:15, 16) because of the pain it causes in people's lives, but He does not hate divorced people. This is seen in His compassionate approach to the woman at the well in Samaria (*Holy Bible*, John 4: 3–30).

When there is frustration over restricted participation in the governing or teaching positions in the church, the person should be encouraged to consult with the pastor. If this does not resolve the frustration, then the person will need to weigh the benefits of belonging to that particular church against the benefits of going to another Pentecostal church where restrictions may be less severe.

Treatment Issues and Approaches

Here are some Pentecostal beliefs and practices that bring resources for healing and recovery. First, the Bible is seen as the infallible rule of faith and conduct. Appropriate passages of Scripture can be extremely effective in correcting false beliefs, encouraging the client, and defining contradictions between the client's stated beliefs and practices.

Second, Pentecostals believe that God intervenes in the affairs of life on behalf of His children, and there is nothing impossible to Him. This is a legitimate source of hope for clients. However, care must be taken to assure that the client's expectations are realistic. Often, their pain and sorrow in life come from hasty and impulsive decisions made without giving due consideration to the long-term consequences of those decisions. It is unrealistic to plant poor seeds—make unwise decisions—and expect a rich and abundant crop. Disillusioned, they decide God is ignoring them rather than accepting personal responsibility for living with the consequences of unwise decisions.

The story of Moses, familiar to followers of Islam and Judaism as well as of Christianity, offers an excellent object lesson for believers struggling with the inability to accept their responsibility for poor decisions in the past and realistic expectations for the future. Moses made both wise and unwise decisions during his lifetime. He (and those around him) lived with the results of those decisions—good and bad.

For example, his good decisions included choosing to be identified with his own people rather than be called the son of Pharaoh's daughter. He chose the option that was in his long-term best interests. He chose "rather to suffer affliction with the people of God, than to enjoy the pleasures of sin [by his people's definition] for a season; Esteeming the reproach of [living for] Christ [to be] greater riches than the treasures in Egypt" (*Holy Bible*, Hebrews 11:24–26). The decision Moses made at this point in his life altered his identity and changed his future forever. His poor decisions included murdering the Egyptian overseer, smashing the two tablets of stone which contained the Ten Commandments, and striking the rock with his staff to bring water from it instead of simply speaking to it, as God had commanded him to do. Murdering the Egyptian forced Moses to flee from Egypt. Striking the rock instead of speaking to it led to him being forbidden by God to enter the Promised Land during his lifetime— after spending 40 years en route!

God has given to each believer the same freedom that He gave Moses: the freedom to alter his or her personal future, for better or for worse. Many believers have a magical or superstitious approach to their faith, believing that many choices in life are more or less beyond their control. However, Scripture makes it clear that there are four forces involved in the life choices that one makes. Two are supernatural forces: sin and eternal life (*Holy Bible*, 2 Corinthians 10:4–6; Ephesians 6:12); the other two are natural forces: human will and chance.

The first supernatural force to be considered is the concept of *sin*. This may be acceptably defined for most Pentecostals as, "An invisible power, *emanating from the person of Satan*. It impacts on the mind to stimulate the brain to think in terms of urges, fantasies, and ideas that detract from and destroy one's divine potential" (Dobbins, 1991). Many believers tend to think of sin as specific behaviors; the foregoing definition targets the source of those behaviors.

The second supernatural force to be addressed here is the concept of *eternal life*, which may be defined as, "An invisible power *emanating from Christ*, to which the unregenerate (non-believers) are insensitive. It impacts on the mind of the regenerated (the believer) to stimulate the brain to think in terms of urges, fantasies, and ideas which enhance and develop one's divine potential" (Dobbins, 1991). Believers tend to think of eternal life as that time beyond their earthly death when they will go to be with God in heaven for eternity. The foregoing definition addresses the function of eternal life in the believer's decision-making process during his or her time on earth.

A third force involved in each person's life choices is one's own will. Again, Scripture is replete with admonitions to believers to make the right choice. Many Pentecostal believers are hesitant to take responsibility for their choices. However, Scripture clearly shows that (a) the supernatural forces of both sin and eternal life present each person with choices; and (b) human will combined with one of these two supernatural forces determines each person's course of action in any given circumstance. One of the believer's tasks in life is to learn how to discern the source of his or her thoughts so that those stimulated by eternal life may be chosen, and those stimulated by sin may be rejected (*Holy Bible*, Hebrews 4:12–16).

This will be a new way of looking at personal responsibility for some Pentecostals; however, it is consistent with Pentecostal beliefs. Such an approach to personal responsibility should help these believers understand that they are responsible for their choices and that, although God forgives them for unwise decisions and sins of the past, He does not automatically cancel the consequences (*Holy Bible*, Galations 6:7–8). Their expectations and hopes need to be tempered with reality as they work toward improvement, keeping in mind that God does at times break through natural processes and perform a miraculous physical or emotional healing.

A fourth factor affecting the life of the believer is chance (*Holy Bible*, Ecclesiastes 9:11). This is a world in which accidents and chance events may deal severe and undeserved blows. Pentecostals should be reassured that God promises never to abandon them in their time of trouble; instead, He will support and encourage them through such times (*Holy Bible*, Psalm 23; Psalm 139:1–10; Isaiah 43:1–5).

A third very powerful Pentecostal belief is that the power of prayer is unlimited. Prayer can be used as a source of endurance and encouragement. It can also be used in venting pain and anger. In prayerful meditation, the client can discover new and less traumatic ways to view painful experiences. Prayer can also be the source of guidance and direction for important decisions in one's life. Again, requests made to God in prayer must be tempered with reality.

Fourth, Pentecostals believe the natural healing processes are enhanced through divine intervention. God may at times override natural processes to bring about instantaneous or greatly accelerated "divine healing" for a believer's physical or emotional need. Such a belief reinforces the hope of recovery.

At times, the Pentecostal may suffer from ambivalence toward God when God does not respond to prayers for healing. This may involve an illness from which the counselee is suffering, an illness from which a friend or loved one is suffering, or an illness from which a friend or loved one has died.

This confusion comes from the Pentecostal's belief in divine healing. For those who are able to relegate to God the wisdom to determine how His gifts of healing are distributed, the fact that some believers are healed and others are not poses no problem. However, for those who believe that if God heals some who pray for a healing, then He must heal all who pray for healing, real difficulties arise when that healing is not forthcoming. Help for these people may best be found by consulting their pastor. The counselor may choose to refer such counselees for pastoral counseling to deal with these questions.

Fifth, the Pentecostal's practice of Holy Spirit-inspired *glossolalia* provides relief from times of extreme tension and anxiety. It also provides Pentecostal believers a way in which to pray "with the Spirit" (1 Corinthians 14:15) and commit to God's care those overwhelming concerns that are difficult or impossible to articulate in a known language.

The therapist should remember that some psychological interventions may be incongruent with the Pentecostal tradition. Any suggestion that the Bible is not infallible, the miracles of Scripture are not literal, or that other events referred to in the Bible are not historically real will severely damage or destroy therapeutic rapport with Pentecostals. In my own practice, I have elected to subject all psychological intervention methods to the discipline of Scripture. Interventions that are obviously supported by Scripture—or are at least not contradictory to Scriptural principles—are more likely to be acceptable to Pentecostal believers.

Pentecostals will be more comfortable if the therapist can couch therapeutic intervention strategies in Biblical terms. For example, if dream analysis is going to be used, introducing it by referring to the prominent role of dreams throughout Scripture will make it more palatable to Pentecostals. Remind them of the significance of dreams in such Bible stories as Gideon's victory over Midian (*Holy Bible*, Judges 7:13–15). Also, an angel spoke to Joseph in a dream to reassure him of Mary's innocence before the birth of Christ (*Holy Bible*, Matthew 1:20–21). Joseph was warned in a dream to take Mary and the infant Jesus and flee to Egypt

(*Holy Bible*, Matthew 2:13). Paul's invitation to minister in Macedonia came in a dream (*Holy Bible*, Acts 16:9).

Spiritual Interventions That May Be Indicated or Contraindicated

Some Pentecostals, as previously mentioned, take an obviously magical or superstitious view of life. They are so experiential in their faith that they are unable to make even minor decisions in life until they "hear from God." They tend to overspiritualize their approach to life and are at the mercy of those who would take advantage of their external locus of control.

These people should be helped to develop the rational side of their faith. They need help in applying their faith in God and His Word to the problem-solving, decision-making responsibilities of life. Helping them use the resources of their faith in strengthening their ego function will enable them to operate from an internal locus of control, leaving them much less at the mercy of skillful manipulators. In helping Pentecostals who suffer from an overpowering superego function, the therapist will find it helpful to confront the superego with appropriate passages of Scripture (*Holy Bible*, Hebrews 10:17; 1 John 1:7–9).

In enabling sexually inhibited people to celebrate healthy sexuality in marriage, the therapist may want to both suggest appropriate Scriptures (*Holy Bible*, Song of Solomon; 1 Corinthians 7:3–5) and ask that they read one or more books written by Christian physicians or Christian sex therapists. Three reliable books in this category are *The Gift of Sex* (Penner & Penner, 1981), *Restoring the Pleasure* (Penner & Penner, 1993), and *Intended for Pleasure* (3rd ed.; Wheat & Wheat, 1997). Mentioning that these authors are Christians who thus take a Biblical approach to this sensitive subject will help Pentecostals find the materials more acceptable.

I have found the following techniques to be acceptable and highly effective with Pentecostal clients. The first is useful for dealing with trauma; the second is very compatible with a cognitive–behavioral approach for dealing with compulsive–addictive behavior.

Intervention by Means of "Praying Through"

Instead of referring to changing the way one looks at a traumatic experience as *cognitive restructuring* or *reframing*, therapists may suggest the client "pray through" this painful past episode until God helps him or her to see it in healing and liberating ways. "Praying through" a problem is a familiar expression to Pentecostals, although most would not be able to delineate the steps involved in accomplishing this task. Dynamic therapists are familiar with the process of "working through" insights gained in therapy. "Praying through" is similar in its goals—gaining new and less painful ways of looking at painful past relationships and experiences, while reinforcing the new thoughts and feelings by repetitious reflection.

The process of praying through consists of four steps. First, the believer is encouraged to talk honestly with God about what is hurting him or her. Some believers are reluctant to boldly pour out their feelings to God, especially if He is the object of their feelings. The believer should be reminded that God loves His followers and will not express anger toward them when they deposit their pain in Him. Getting these clients to read the imprecatory Psalms (those in which David asked God to curse his enemies) can also be helpful. Examples are found in Psalms 55–60.

It is helpful to have the client write an extended therapeutic letter (not to be mailed) to the people responsible for the pain—or a letter to God—in which the painful feelings are expressed. Each installment should be dated and read to God in prayer, much like Hezekiah read Sennacherib's letter to God (*Holy Bible*, 2 Kings 19:14–19).

The second step in praying through is to relate emotionally to the content of the letter. During this step, the believer is encouraged to weep or otherwise express himself or herself and pray intensely so that the underlying emotions may be discharged, in readiness for a less painful way of interpreting the events and relationships referred to in the letter.

The third step is to meditate, asking God for help in finding a different and less disturbing way of interpreting the events and relationships referred to in the letter. Just as God gave Joseph a less painful way of looking at his brothers' hate and betrayal (*Holy Bible*, Genesis 50:20), so the client should be encouraged to believe God will provide a less painful way of viewing the events and relationships that have brought so much pain.

The fourth step is to spend time thanking and praising God for the new way of looking at the old hurt and mentally rehearsing the new interpretation. This step is important in consolidating therapeutic gain.

This four-step process is to be repeated until there is nothing more to write. At that time, the client should be encouraged to put closure on the matters rehearsed in the letter by defining a creative way of destroying the letter, such as burning or burying it. This will lessen the likelihood of further rumination and increase the possibility of permanent closure on the issues prayed through.

Intervention by Means of "Putting Off the Old Man; Putting On the New Man"

A Pentecostal will probably be resistant to the behavior modification terms generally used to help clients extinguish a compulsive or addictive behavior. Such a believer will also be very likely to be frustrated by the inability to rid himself or herself of a "sinful nature" as evidenced by what are considered to be worldly desires, addictions, or other behaviors. However, this person will almost certainly be open to the process of behavior modification when it is couched in the Biblical definition of how to "put off the old man" and "put on the new man." Two functions are extremely important in this process.

Defining "triggering mechanisms" for the behavior being targeted for change is an important step in putting off the old behavior. Defining "substitute behaviors" is also important. These are behaviors that the person can initiate in response to triggering mechanisms, to help avoid acting out the undesirable behaviors. New behaviors are reinforced over time, as the person is able to respond to triggering mechanisms with the new, less destructive behavior. Through this process, the new behavior gradually replaces the old behavior. The client's sense of well-being and self-worth improves with each success as, little by little, the "old man" is left behind or "put off," and the "new man" becomes a reliable tool in managing his or her life. Clients should be reminded periodically that this is not a one-time-only act of the will; it is a process that is completed over a period of time, and their freedom from the destructive behavior will be worth the time and effort.

The following model and instructions illustrate how to present this idea to a Pentecostal believer who is struggling to overcome compulsive or addictive behaviors (Figure 7.1).

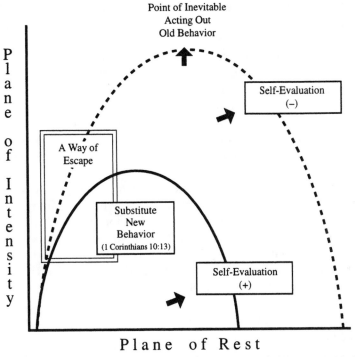

Figure 7.1. Putting Off the Old Man/Putting On the New Man. Ephesians 4: 22–24; 1 Corinthians 10:13.

A Model: Putting Off the Old Man; Putting On the New Man

The Plane of Rest represents the time during which you are free from temptation (see Figure 7.1). The Plane of Intensity represents the degree of your temptation's intensity. The Window of Control represents the time between when you become aware of your temptation and the point of inevitable acting out or losing control of your behavior. It represents that period of time during which you are still able to apply your chosen "way of escape," as mentioned in (*Holy Bible*) 1 Corinthians 10:13, thus avoiding acting out your temptation.

When you can implement some substitute behavior or find the way that God has provided for you to escape, the intensity of your temptation will diminish until you are again at the Plane of Rest. To help you learn how to "put off the old man" and "put on the new," you need to develop two skills with God's help.

1. *Define the "triggering mechanisms" that start escalating the Plane of Intensity toward acting out your temptation and avoid them whenever possible.* These may be places, moods, certain people, and so on. Ask God to help you discover what triggers your temptation. If being alone with nothing to do too much of the time is responsible, structure more activity into your life. Perhaps a certain part of town, a particular store, or a particular person triggers these thoughts. Avoid these places and people (*Holy Bible*, 1 Corinthians 6:18; 1 Thessalonians 5:22).

2. *Develop substitute behaviors.* Find some activity that will remove you mentally, emotionally, physically, and spiritually from the temptation; find your "way of escape" referred to in 1 Corinthians 10:13.

Remember that temptation thrives on secrecy. Share the secret with your therapist. Confess your problem to a close, trusted friend, perhaps to your spouse. This kind of confession will help to break its hold. Ask them to pray with you (*Holy Bible*, Galatians 6:2; James 5:16).

Resist the urge to avoid sharing your need for fear of being embarrassed: "If they knew what I know about me —." Humbling yourself and sharing your need is much more likely to help you break out of this bondage than trying to do it alone.

Be patient with yourself. Realize that you did not get this way overnight, and you will probably not overcome this problem immediately. Be honest with God if or when you act out. Ask for His help in overcoming this behavior and remember that as long as you sincerely want to break this bondage, He will forgive you every time you ask. Each time you are helped to escape temptation by substituting that "new behavior" and you are able to return to that "Plane of Rest," thank God for His divine help.

Process and Ethical Guidelines for Implementing Spiritual Interventions:
Two Brief Case Histories

Mental health professionals working in a public agency will have prescribed policy guidelines to determine their approach to therapy. Those in group practice may have the opportunity to help shape their organization's ethical policy and guidelines. Therapists in private practice will need to be transparent about the therapeutic approach to be taken.

Because the therapist is serving the client in the counseling process, the client's wishes should be respected in determining the therapeutic role of any spiritual intervention. For example, a woman named Catherine was suffering from a postpartum psychosis. Her symptoms were rooted in her strong delusion that she had somehow committed "the unpardonable sin" (Holy Bible, Matthew 12:31–32; Hebrews 10:26–29; 1 John 5:16). To escape her pain, she had already made one suicide attempt by the time she and her husband sought help from a secular therapist. When the therapist discovered the nature of her delusion, he immediately concluded she was involved in some "crazy religion" and advised her husband to get her out of it. This was so offensive to Catherine and her husband that they refused to accept any help from this therapist.

A more sensitive approach to Catherine's faith would have contributed to the kind of therapeutic relationship that she and her husband needed. It would have commended her for her faithfulness to her religious beliefs and reassured her that a person who had committed "the unpardonable sin"—which even theologians cannot identify with any certainty —would not be found trying to live a life pleasing to God. Such an approach also would have left them with a positive, rather than negative, attitude toward psychology and psychotherapy.

On the other hand, a couple named Frank and Ethel went to a Christian mental health agency for help with their troubled marriage and were disappointed when the therapist made no reference to Scripture. Neither did the therapist pray for the couple. They were so disappointed that they called the director of the agency and lodged a major complaint.

It is important for the therapist to determine the spiritual expectations of the client early in the relationship. If the therapist cannot reasonably meet these expectations, he or she should discuss this with the client in the early stages of the therapeutic relationship.

Suggestions for Working With Religious Leaders and the Religious Community

Even though Pentecostal clergy generally participate in both communitywide local ministerial associations and in their own ministerial meetings, many still work within narrowly defined boundaries. Calling a prominent Pentecostal pastor and setting up a breakfast appointment often results in being invited to the ministerial meetings he or she attends. Making oneself available to speak on mental health topics to Pentecostal ministerial groups and local congregations can help Pentecostal pastors feel comfortable in referring members and adherents for counseling or therapy.

A therapist's willingness to approach clergy with respect for their profession and an obvious desire to learn how he or she can be of help to the clergy will undoubtedly foster a better professional relationship. This kind of interdisciplinary approach in turn offers parishioners a much wider array of help with emotional problems.

CONCLUSIONS AND FUTURE DIRECTIONS

That a patient's spiritual concerns can now be addressed and that the resources of the patient's faith can be accessed in the therapeutic process is a welcome and long-overdue change in the behavioral science world. However, much remains to be done.

The religious community can be helped to overcome its suspicion of the behavioral sciences by being made aware of this new approach to therapy. Therapists should be encouraged to seize the initiative in building a bridge of understanding with pastors, priests, rabbis, and other religious leaders in their communities. A growing body of research affirms the therapeutic benefits of this rapprochement between the behavioral sciences and the Church. As this relationship continues to develop, it will become an obvious win–win situation. Practitioners in the behavioral sciences will learn more about the impact of religious faith on a person's mental health, and the religious community will discover the benefits of the kind of mental health care that integrates a person's faith with the healing process.

The resulting information should lead to improved mental health care for adherents. Religious education programs can be developed to meet expanded areas of need. New information can also be used to take a more disciplined look at the clergy selection process. More productive ministerial rehabilitation programs can also result from this kind of study and research.

SUGGESTED READINGS

Blumhofer, E. L. (1989). *The Assemblies of God: A chapter in the story of American Pentecostalism, Vol. 2.* Springfield, MO: Gospel Publishing House.

Christenson, L. (Ed.). (1987). *Welcome, Holy Spirit: A study of charismatic renewal in the Church.* Minneapolis, MN: Augsburg Publishing House.

Cox, H. (1973). *The seduction of the spirit: The use and misuse of people's religion.* New York: Simon & Schuster.

Dayton, D. W. (1987). *Theological roots of Pentecostalism.* Grand Rapids, MI: Francis Asbury Press (Div. of Zondervan Publishing House).

McMahan, O. (1997). *Scriptural counseling: A God-centered approach.* Cleveland, TN: Pathway Press.

Poloma, M. (1982). *The Charismatic movement: Is there a new Pentecost?* Boston: Twayne Publishers (Div. of G. K. Hall & Company).

Purkiser, W. T. (1983). *Exploring Christian holiness: Vol. 1. The biblical foundations.* Kansas City, MO: Beacon Hill Press of Kansas City.

Spitler, R. P. (Ed.). (1976). *Perspectives on the new Pentecostalism.* Grand Rapids, MI: Baker Book House.

Vining, J. K. (1997). *The Spirit of the Lord is upon me: Essential papers on Spirit-filled caregiving.* East Rockaway, NY: Cummings & Hathaway.

Womack, D. A. (1968). *Wellsprings of the Pentecostal movement.* Springfield, MO: Gospel Publishing House.

REFERENCES

Bassett, P. M., & Greathouse, W. M. (1985). *Exploring Christian holiness: Vol. 2. The historical development.* Kansas City, MO: Beacon Hill Press.

Blumhofer, E. L. (1989). *The Assemblies of God: A chapter in the story of American Pentecostalism, Vol. 1.* Springfield, MO: Gospel Publishing House.

Brown, P. (1990). *The body and society: Men, women, and sexual renunciation in early Christianity.* New York: Columbia University Press.

Burgess, S. M., McGee, G. B., & Alexander, P. H. (Eds.). (1988). *Dictionary of Pentecostal and Charismatic movements.* Grand Rapids, MI: Zondervan Publishing House.

Cox, H. (1995). *Fire from heaven: The rise of Pentecostal spirituality and the reshaping of religion in the twenty-first century.* Reading, MA: Addison-Wesley.

Dobbins, R. D. (1991). Putting off the old man; putting on the new man (model). In *God's man in today's world* (Video series). Akron, OH: EMERGE Ministries.

Dobbins, R. D. (1993). *Your feelings . . . friend or foe?* Akron, OH: Totally Alive Publications.

Hollenweger, W. J. (1988). *The Pentecostals.* Peabody, MA: Hendrickson Publishers.

Menzies, W. W. (1971). *Anointed to serve: The story of the Assemblies of God.* Springfield, MO: Gospel Publishing House.

Moriarty, M. G. (1992). *The new Charismatics: A concerned voice responds to dangerous new trends.* Grand Rapids, MI: Zondervan Publishing House.

Noll, M. A. (1994). *The scandal of the evangelical mind.* Grand Rapids, MI: William B. Eerdmans Publishing Co.

Penner, C. L., & Penner, J. J. (1981). *The gift of sex.* Dallas, TX: Word Publishing.

Penner, C. L., & Penner, J. J. (1993). *Restoring the pleasure.* Dallas, TX: Word Publishing.

Poloma, M. M. (1989). *The Assemblies of God at the crossroads: Charisma and institutional dilemmas*. Knoxville: The University of Tennessee Press.

Synan, V. (Ed.). (1975). *Aspects of Pentecostal–Charismatic origins*. Plainfield, NJ: Logos International.

Wheat, E., & Wheat, G. (1997). *Intended for pleasure* (3rd ed.). Ada, MI: Fleming H. Revell (Div. of Baker Book House).

8

PSYCHOTHERAPY WITH LATTER-DAY SAINTS

WENDY L. ULRICH, P. SCOTT RICHARDS, AND ALLEN E. BERGIN

I saw a pillar of light exactly over my head, above the brightness of the sun, which descended gradually until it fell upon me. . . . When the light rested upon me I saw two personages, whose brightness and glory defy all description, standing above me in the air. One of them spake unto me, calling me by name and said, pointing to the other—This is My Beloved Son. Hear Him!

—Joseph Smith, Jr.

Members of the Church of Jesus Christ of Latter-day Saints[1] who seek mental health services are similar in mental, emotional, and social characteristics to those in other mainstream religious organizations, such as Evangelical Protestants, Conservative Jews, and conventional Roman Catholics (Bergin, Payne, Jenkins, & Cornwall, 1994). In addition, Latter-day Saints are unique in that they believe in an original combination of Jewish and Christian traditions, melded with modern prophetic inspiration. This perspective is not easy to comprehend or appreciate by outsiders, but it is deeply meaningful and powerfully motivating to committed church members. Most Latter-day Saints are conversant with LDS church history and doctrine and actively draw on it in solving problems and creating

---

[1]The Church of Jesus Christ of Latter-day Saints is often referred to for convenience as the Mormon or Latter-day Saint (LDS) Church. Members tend to prefer the latter name because the term Mormon was first used by the Church's enemies in a derogatory way, and because this name fails to acknowledge the centrality of Jesus Christ in LDS theology. Thus, many church members prefer to call themselves Latter-day Saints. However, people are usually not offended by the term Mormon, in part because Mormon is the name of one of the greatest prophets in the *Book of Mormon*, but they still consider it a sign of respect when non-LDS people do not use it as a label. For such reasons, we use the terms Latter-day Saints, Saints, and LDS church in this chapter.

personal identity. For such reasons, the content of this chapter may prove valuable to mental health professionals who work with persons from this tradition. We will focus here on more active and devout Latter-day Saints, because it is for them that awareness of and sensitivity to their religious beliefs will prove to be most clinically fruitful.

HISTORICAL AND DOCTRINAL BACKGROUND AND OVERVIEW

The Latter-day Saint tradition begins with remarkable events that stretch many people's boundaries of belief, but to church members they are consistent with events in Biblical times and are a sign of God's will in these latter-day times. Joseph Smith, a 14-year-old farm boy living in up-state New York in 1820, was unable to determine which of the many Christian churches was right. After reading in the *Holy Bible,* "If any of you lack wisdom, let him ask of God, that giveth to all men liberally, and upbraideth not; and it shall be given him" (James 1:5), Joseph Smith decided that he must "either remain in darkness and confusion, or else . . . do as James directs" (LDS, 1981c, p. 48). After retiring to some nearby woods to pray, Joseph Smith was astonished to see a pillar of brilliant light descend from the heavens and two glorious Personages appear to him. One of them called him by name and introduced the other, saying, "This is My Beloved Son. Hear Him" (LDS, 1981b, p. 49). Barely able to speak, young Smith presented his dilemma and was told not to join any of the existing churches for God had a special work for him to do. Believed only by his family, Smith spoke little of his vision to others for some time (LDS, 1981b).

Three years later, in September 1823, Joseph Smith was visited by another heavenly messenger who proclaimed himself to be the last pro-phetic author of a collection of ancient scriptural texts inscribed on metal plates and buried in a nearby hillside. Later, Smith obtained these plates and translated them through divine guidance. He was allowed to show them to a few select individuals, who described them as having "the ap-pearance of fine gold . . . [with] engravings thereon, all of which has the appearance of ancient work" (LDS, 1981a, Testimony of the eight wit-nesses, Introduction to the *Book of Mormon*).

The resulting translation, the *Book of Mormon: Another Testament of Jesus Christ* (LDS, 1981a), which Latter-day Saints accept as scripture along with the *Holy Bible,* was first published in 1830, when Joseph Smith was 24 years old. Since then, millions of copies have been published in many languages. The *Book of Mormon* tells of two Israelite families in Jerusalem in approximately 600 B.C. Warned by God to flee the city, which was soon to be destroyed, the families eventually sailed to a new "promised land."

Settling in an area probably around Mesoamerica (Sorenson, 1985), they flourished and divided into two competing civilizations. The *Book of Mormon* describes their spiritual history over a 1,000-year period. In the climactic scenes, the resurrected Jesus descended from heaven to visit the most righteous among this group, calling them the "other sheep" of whom He spoke to His disciples in Jerusalem (John 10:16). He taught them His gospel, healed and blessed them, and established His church among them. The book ends in 421 A.D. as one civilization completely destroyed the other, and the Christian religion was lost from among them.

The Church of Jesus Christ of Latter-day Saints was officially organized by Joseph Smith and a small group of believers in 1830, the same year in which the *Book of Mormon* was published. The title of the Church is significant in every particular: It purports to be a latter-day restoration of the original church established by Jesus Christ among the *Saints*, as His followers were called in the ancient world. Priesthood authority to establish and operate the Church was also restored to Joseph Smith and others. Over the ensuing 15 years, Joseph Smith continued to receive inspiration concerning church organization, the teachings of Jesus Christ, and the covenants between God and His people, all in preparation for the second coming of Christ at some unknown future time. Additional canonized texts record some of these revelations.

Growth and Persecution

Persecuted for their claims of heavenly visitations and golden plates, the growing body of Latter-day Saints soon left New York to establish communities in and around Kirtland, Ohio, and then Independence, Missouri, on the very edges of the American frontier. An active missionary program drew members from the United States and northern Europe to this "new world Zion." As converts arrived *en masse* in their utopian settlements, local frontiersmen often saw them as a political, economic, and religious threat. Latter-day Saints tended to be northerners or "foreigners" who voted similarly, bought from one another, befriended the Native Americans, and eschewed slavery—not popular characteristics on the rough edges of frontier America. The Latter-day Saints formed a strong group identity as they banded together against hostility and persecution.

Mob violence soon drove them from Missouri to settle Nauvoo, Illinois, which the Saints turned into the largest city in the state within a few years. Women played an active, independent role in this community, forming the Female Relief Society of Nauvoo as a self-governing charitable organization within the Church. With Joseph Smith as both mayor and church president, once again the political presence and religious peculiarities of some 15,000 Latter-day Saints threatened their neighbors. In addition, defectors from the faith revealed the fact that some Saints were practicing Old Testament-style polygamy as part of the "restoration of all things." In 1844, Joseph Smith and several other church leaders were jailed in Carthage, Illinois. The jail was stormed by a mob who murdered Joseph Smith and his brother, Hyrum, and wounded others.

Utah Migration

Joseph Smith was not the first martyr to the cause he founded, nor would he be the last. In less than 3 years, ongoing persecution became so intense that the Saints were forced to begin evacuating Nauvoo in the dead of a bitter winter (February 1846). Under a new leader, Brigham Young, the first pioneer company traveled on foot or by covered wagon to the isolated desert and Rocky Mountain valleys of what became the Utah territory, arriving in July 1847. During the years 1847 to 1869, about 70,000 Latter-day Saints followed, about 5,000 of them dying during or soon after the journey (Black, 1998). Hoping their new territory would be so inhospitable and remote that no one else would want it, the Saints established settlements throughout the west, centering in Salt Lake City. Expansive missionary efforts continued to attract converts who were actively encouraged to "gather to Zion" in Utah. LDS culture and the identity of many devout Latter-day Saints in North America continues to be strongly influenced by this legacy of persecution, self-sacrifice, and independence.

The Latter-day Saint Tradition Today

Latter-day Saints' political solidarity and continuing practice of polygamy prolonged the process of obtaining statehood for Utah until the practice was officially discontinued in 1890 after the U.S. Supreme Court upheld congressional antipolygamy laws. Once viewed as a very liberal or even radical religious group, since the turn of the century, the LDS Church has taken on an increasingly conservative image in the United States. Latter-day Saints tend to support traditional family values and conservative causes. With missionaries taking the faith to every nation where they are allowed, more of the Church's 10 million current members now live outside of the United States than in it (LDS, 1998). On the basis of a statistical and social model of church growth from 1830 to the present, sociologist Rodney Stark (1984, 1996) has projected that the LDS faith may have over 250 million members by the year 2080.

Major Sources of Diversity Within the Culture

Reorganized Church

When the Saints left Nauvoo for Utah, a substantial minority stayed behind, including Joseph Smith's widow, Emma. Fifteen years later, members of this group called on her son, Joseph Smith III, to assume leadership of the Reorganized Church of Jesus Christ of Latter-day Saints. Headquartered today in Independence, Missouri, Reorganized Latter-day Saints believe in the *Book of Mormon* and in Joseph Smith, but reject some of the beliefs and practices of Utah Saints. About 250,000 members strong, the Reorganized Church is ecumenical in theology and mainstream Protestant in practice. Whereas other break-off groups from the LDS tradition have proliferated, their adherents are generally few.

Conservatives and Liberals

Within the Utah-based Church, unofficial divisions occur between more liberal and more conservative factions. The general leadership of the Church censures both when they lean too far from mainstream teachings. Revisionist intellectuals, radical feminists, extremist conservative groups, and advocates of polygamy have been chastised or even excommunicated by church leaders. Nevertheless, so long as they do not publicly promote teachings that conflict with core official church doctrines, members with a wide range of sociopolitical beliefs are accepted. They are also encouraged to exercise their individual consciences as they face moral and ethical choices.

Gender

At the local level, all LDS church units function under lay leadership which includes both men and women, but certain leadership positions are restricted to ordained priesthood holders, always men. The family is regarded as the most important stewardship of both women and men, and marriage is advocated as the ideal status for all. Husbands and fathers are expected to be deeply involved in family life and to provide leadership and financial support via a role characterized by service, respect, and equality. Wives and mothers are considered to be equal partners in all family decision making and to have somewhat greater responsibility for home life and child nurturing.

Women are encouraged to become educated and plan for careers but to avoid working outside the home while they have young children. Women who choose full-time homemaking receive official and cultural support, but may still feel the pull of the Church's emphasis on developing talents and education. Women who choose less traditional paths find ample role models of accomplished women in church history, but may feel guilty not giving more time to their families. Church leaders encourage women to make their choices prayerfully, with attention to individual circumstances. Some LDS women would like to see priesthood ordination opened to them; most call for women to develop uniquely feminine forms of spirituality and leadership. Both men and women contribute time to church service in a wide variety of teaching and leadership roles.

Race and Culture

Race and culture are increasingly important issues in the global Church as growth has accelerated throughout Third World countries and among diverse groups in North America (Heaton, 1998). Because of a now-abandoned church policy that men of African descent could not be ordained to the priesthood, many non-LDS people once perceived the Church and its members as racist. When this policy was changed in 1978, most Latter-day Saints welcomed it. Since 1978, the number of converts in African countries and among African Americans has dramatically increased. In addition, because of missionary success in Central and South America, the second largest percentage of members are of Latin American descent. Most Latter-day Saints today welcome people from racial and ethnic minority groups into the Church as valued and fully equal "brothers and sisters."

Such demographic and institutional changes have also prompted efforts to separate the "mountain west" LDS subculture from the essential core principles of the gospel of Jesus Christ. The Church actively supports efforts to preserve the cultures of many nations, including Polynesians and Native Americans who, it teaches, descend from *Book of Mormon* peoples. In the United States, groups of members speaking a particular foreign language may be voluntarily organized to meet independently in their own congregations. For example, there are more than 200 Spanish-speaking church units in California. Inner-city congregations are growing in numbers and leadership, but in more homogeneous suburban congregations, people of minority races and cultures can at times still feel less valued.

Basic Beliefs and Practices

Latter-day Saints consider themselves Christians. They believe in God, the Eternal Father, and in His son, Jesus Christ, and in the Holy Spirit (LDS, 1981c). They believe that they are literally children of God with divine potential (Romans 8:16–17). They believe that through the atonement of Jesus Christ all of humanity may be saved by obedience to His teachings, "for we know that it is by grace that we are saved, after all we can do" (II Nephi 25:23; LDS, 1981a, pp. 99–100). This philosophy blends both faith and works as being essential to salvation. LDS people also believe that the Holy Bible is the word of God "as far as it is translated correctly" (LDS, 1981c, pp. 60–61). They also believe that the Book of Mormon and other latter-day scriptures are the word of God. Following, we elaborate further on additional important LDS beliefs and practices.

Continuing Revelation and Personal Inspiration

The Church is founded on a claim of divine authority and continuing revelation to leaders and members. Church members and nonmembers studying with the missionaries are encouraged to obtain a personal spiritual confirmation of the truthfulness of the *Book of Mormon* and other church teachings through personal study and sincere prayer. Like Joseph Smith, LDS people believe that they may ask God for wisdom and expect inspired direction concerning immediate and long-term life choices or extra help in coping with problems that may seem intractable. This may come as a feeling, an insight, a voice in the mind, or some other spiritual communication. This feeling of closeness to God is normative and can be useful in therapeutic healing if it is not interpreted by the therapist as being irrational (except in those cases in which the content clearly meets diagnostic criteria of maladaptiveness).

The Plan of Salvation

According to LDS theology, before the mortal experience, all men and women lived with God the Father as His spirit children (Romans 8: 16–17). God proposed a plan whereby His children could come to earth, gain a physical body, and exercise their will so as to learn by experience to discern and choose good from evil. Jesus Christ is central to this plan. He is the Son of God in the flesh and a member of the Godhead. He lived a perfect life, atoned for all the sins of humanity and, after His death on the cross, was resurrected with a body of flesh and bone. Because of His resurrection, all humankind will be resurrected. Through His atonement and on condition of personal repentance and desire to follow Christ, any person may return to live with God and continue to progress eternally after death.

When death separates the spirit from the body, the spirit goes for a time to the "spirit world," a separate dimension of learning and repentance. People will be judged on the basis of their desires, intentions, actions, and choices in this life and in the spirit world, including their willingness to accept Jesus Christ as their Savior and follow His teachings. After this judgment, each soul will attain one of three heavenly kingdoms with varying degrees of blessedness and opportunity. To enjoy the most exalted of these three kingdoms, one must accept Jesus as the Savior, repent of one's sins, obey God's commandments, and receive the ordinances of His Church, either personally or vicariously. Little children who die before they are old enough to be accountable for their choices automatically go to this kingdom.

Church Organization

Latter-day Saints believe that God and Jesus Christ direct the affairs of the Church through revelation to their appointed leaders. *The First Pres-*

idency, consisting of the church president (prophet) and two counselors, a *Quorum of Twelve Apostles*, and several *Quorums of Seventy* (assistants to the prophet and apostles) preside over the worldwide Church. These priesthood leaders are collectively referred to as the General Authorities of the Church. In addition, female General Presidencies preside over the adult women's Relief Society, Young Women's program, and Primary Organization for children.

At the local level, all males in good standing are ordained to the priesthood beginning with initial offices at age 12. An unpaid lay ministry of both male and female volunteers operates the local church congregations. These are organized geographically with a deliberate effort to include people from a variety of socioeconomic backgrounds. Local congregations are called *wards* or, if they are small, *branches*. They are led by either a *bishop* or a *branch president*—a priesthood holder chosen from the local congregation to serve without pay in this part-time position for approximately 5 years. Seven to 12 wards and branches form a *stake*,[2] presided over by a *stake president*, also a lay priesthood position. In 1999, there were about 25,000 wards and branches and about 2,600 stakes. Nearly every active member serves in a "calling" and is involved to some degree in helping the ward or branch function as a mutually beneficial spiritual and social community.

Sacred Ordinances and Life Transitions

There are a number of religious practices or ordinances that Latter-day Saints regard as especially sacred and essential for one's spiritual growth and salvation. These include blessings for infants; baptism and confirmation; partaking of the Sacrament; and temple endowments, marriages, and "sealings" for the living and the dead. These ordinances are associated with and are symbolic of essential life transitions (e.g., birth, adulthood, marriage, death) and spiritual covenants (e.g., conversion, repentance, forgiveness), and as a result, have deep emotional and spiritual significance for devout Latter-day Saints.

Within a month or two after birth, infants are presented to God before the ward congregation during a Sacrament (communion) meeting by a circle of priesthood holders where one of them (usually the father) gives the baby a name and a blessing. The blessing is regarded as an inspired prayer on behalf of the child and is often a source of comfort for the parents and loved ones.

Ordinarily, at age 8, children are baptized as full members of the church. Baptisms may be performed by a father or other priesthood holder and involve ritually immersing the candidate in water as a symbol of spir-

---

[2]*Stake* is an Old Testament term referring to the stakes of Zion, a metaphor derived from the stakes that held up the curtains of Israel's Tabernacle in the wilderness (Isaiah 54:2).

itual rebirth and of one's covenant to follow Jesus Christ. When adult converts join the Church, they are also baptized by immersion. The ordinance of baptism is followed by the ordinance of "laying on of hands for the gift of the Holy Ghost," known as *confirmation*.

Each Sunday, Latter-day Saints gather in their ward community for a 3-hour period of church meetings at a local chapel. Besides Sunday School and other meetings for all age groups, 1 hour of the services is devoted to a Sacrament meeting, the most sacred session of the day. During this meeting, the sacrament of bread and water, commemorating the Last Supper of Jesus and His apostles, is ritually blessed and reverently distributed to the members of the Church by young priesthood holders. In an atmosphere of quiet meditation, members silently pray, seek forgiveness as needed, and recommit themselves to God and Jesus Christ.

Some ordinances are only performed in temples, the most sacred edifices constructed by the LDS church. More than 60 temples currently operate worldwide and another 60 are currently in planning or under construction in various parts of the world. Once a temple is dedicated, only members in good standing who adhere to the moral standards of the Church may enter. Temple ordinances are considered essential for all people who wish to receive the fullness of God's blessings after this life.

According to LDS theology, when LDS couples are united in temple marriages, if they remain true and faithful to each other and to God, their marriage and relationships with their children will endure for "time and eternity." Temple marriage ceremonies are performed in small sealing rooms with only close family and friends present. Temple marriages are solemnized or *sealed* for "time and for all eternity," rather than until death. Couples previously married outside of the temple may also be sealed.

Because all people will not have the opportunity for temple ordinances during mortality, once LDS people receive these ordinances for themselves, they may return to the temple to perform the ordinances by proxy for those who have died, and who have been taught the gospel in the spirit world after death (I Peter 4:6). These proxy ordinances may be accepted or rejected by those in the spirit world. Baptism and confirmation for the dead are also performed vicariously in the temples (see I Corinthians 15:29). Members do genealogical research to identify deceased family members or others for whom they perform these ordinances. Latter-day Saints consider temple ordinances sacred and only discuss them in general terms outside of the temple. Members go to the temples to meditate, find spiritual direction or renewal, and recommit themselves to God's service.

Lifestyle Practices

Latter-day Saints are encouraged to adhere to the moral standards of the Bible, modern scripture, and the teachings of living prophets. Active church members donate 10% of their income to support church programs, buildings, and schools. Members fast (abstain from food and water) one day each month, contributing the money saved to care for the poor and needy. Self-reliance is emphasized, and families are encouraged to store a year's supply of food, clothing, and fuel in case of personal financial problems or community disasters. Alcohol, tobacco, tea, and coffee are prohibited. Latter-day Saints are encouraged to avoid shopping and recreation on Sunday and to focus on church attendance and spiritually uplifting family activities. Sexual abstinence is espoused before marriage, and sexual fidelity after.

To enhance personal spirituality, members read scriptures, keep journals, fast, attend church services, and pray individually and in their families. Service to others is considered essential to the spiritual life, and ample opportunities for service are provided through church callings and humanitarian service projects that are designed to assist those in need in the local community and throughout the world. Religious and recreational opportunities are also provided in weekly Young Men and Young Women meetings for adolescents. Many youth also attend a daily scripture study class with peers.

At the age of 19, all young men are asked to serve 2-year missions for the church, usually in a foreign country. Young women may also serve at age 21 if they desire, serving for 18 months. Retired adults may also serve proselyting, humanitarian service, temple, welfare, educational, or family history missions throughout the world. Nearly 60,000 missionaries are currently serving at their own or their family's expense in more than 160 nations and territories. Missionaries have significant exposure to other cultures and lifestyles, deepen their scriptural knowledge, and gain maturity, leadership skill, independence, and self-discipline.

Families are encouraged to hold a weekly "Family Home Evening" during which family members come together to teach one another gospel principles, discuss family problems and goals, and enjoy recreational activities. Keeping personal journals and family histories, holding family reunions, doing genealogical research, and enjoying family traditions are formally encouraged as ways to involve people in their extended families.

Social and Moral Issues

The Church's position on many of today's social issues stems from the importance of the family as the central unit of church and society, now and in eternity. Sex outside of a legal, heterosexual marriage is viewed as sinful. The Church teaches that God's standard for church members is chastity before marriage and fidelity afterward. Those attracted sexually to people of their own gender and single heterosexuals must all abide by this rule which is rooted in the principle that sexual relations are sacred.

Church leaders express love and concern for those who may experience homosexual thoughts and feelings, but affirm that all are responsible for controlling their sexual behavior. Pornography or anything salacious is considered to be evil. Masturbation is also viewed as sinful, though it is not considered as serious as fornication, adultery, or homosexual behavior. Spiritual and, if necessary, professional counseling may be encouraged to help people keep their sexual behavior in harmony with the Church's teachings.

Abortion is opposed and may be considered only in cases of rape, incest, or potential harm to the mother's life or health. Even then, personal prayer and consultation with spiritual leaders are expected before a decision is made. Domestic violence or abuse of any kind is strongly censured and may be grounds for church discipline, including excommunication. Although divorce is strongly discouraged, it is accepted, especially in cases of abuse, adultery, or other severe violations of the marriage covenant. Children are prized, and their welfare is paramount.

Those who violate God's laws are to be treated with compassion and helped to change. However, those who persist in violating church moral standards concerning sexual conduct, abortion, abuse, and so on are subject to church counsel and, if unrepentant, may be censured by church leaders or, in severe cases, severed from church membership.

IMPLICATIONS FOR COUNSELING AND PSYCHOTHERAPY

Relationship Issues

Although historically some LDS leaders and many lay members have viewed the mental health professions and psychotherapy with distrust because of their potential to undermine morality and self-reliance, modern attitudes are generally more positive. A church-owned mental health agency, LDS Family Services, employs professional therapists who provide clinical services, adoption counseling, and other assistance to members. LDS church leaders often provide financial support to help needy members pay for counseling and psychotherapy. Church leaders often refer members to LDS Family Services or other mental health professionals whom they are confident will respect LDS values and beliefs.

An LDS mental health organization, the Association of Mormon Counselors and Psychotherapists (AMCAP), was founded in 1976. It is not officially affiliated with or sponsored by the Church but enjoys considerable unofficial approval by church leaders. It publishes a journal (AMCAP Journal) and newsletter, holds semiannual conventions, and has approximately 800 members.

When LDS people seek therapy, they generally prefer to work with professionals from their own faith, believing that LDS therapists will better understand and respect their religious values and beliefs. Latter-day Saints, like other conservative Christians (e.g.,Worthington, 1986), also often fear that secular counselors will prescribe counseling interventions that conflict with their values or will misunderstand or pathologize their religious beliefs. Because of such concerns, building trust with LDS clients may be an added therapeutic challenge for non-LDS therapists. Even when LDS clients agree to work with a non-LDS therapist, they may refuse to discuss certain issues and concerns, particularly religious and spiritual ones, with the therapist. A minority of LDS clients prefer to work with non-LDS therapists out of concern that LDS therapists might harshly judge them (e.g., about violations of the Church's moral teachings) or just give them "more of the same" advice already received from church leaders.

Diagnostic and Assessment Methods and Issues

Therapists can use their regular diagnostic methods with LDS clients, including clinical interviewing and standardized assessment measures. It is recommended that psychotherapists assess their clients' religious background and current spiritual orientation (Richards & Bergin, 1997), paying attention to the role that religion plays in their lives. To what degree does the client's religion seem to be a positive influence as a source of support, strength, and meaning? To what degree does it seem to be a negative influence: a source of conflict, guilt, shame, or avoidance?

Richards and Bergin (1997) suggest a variety of assessment questions and describe several dimensions of religiousness that may be important to assess for LDS (and other) clients, including religious problem-solving style, orthodoxy, spiritual identity, God image, and value–lifestyle congruence. Their book also includes copies of several religious measures that could be useful in assessing the degree of commitment and maturity of clients' religious orientation.

There is currently no evidence that LDS people, in general, have higher or lower rates of any of the *Diagnostic and Statistical Manual* or DSM mental disorders (Bergin et al., 1994). However, there is some evidence that devout Latter-day Saints have lower rates of divorce, delinquency, suicide, alcohol and drug abuse, and greater marital adjustment and feelings of life satisfaction and well-being, compared with less devout Latter-day Saints and the general population (Bergin et al., 1994; Judd, 1999). Despite these positive trends, Latter-day Saints do, of course, struggle with many of the same psychological and interpersonal issues and concerns as other people.

In our clinical work with LDS clients, we have found a number of psychological and interpersonal issues that may be especially likely to get intertwined with religious beliefs and values—namely, perfectionism and shame, abuses of authority, sexual guilt and inhibition, denial of anger and conflict, gender role conflict, divorce and singlehood, and social pressure and conformity (see Koltko, 1990). Latter-day Saints do not necessarily struggle with these issues more often than others, but when they do, their concerns often have religious overtones. To help LDS clients cope, heal, and change, it is often necessary to address the religious aspects of these problems.

Perfectionism and Shame

Latter-day Saints believe that one of the purposes of mortal life is to actualize one's spiritual and intellectual potential. The Biblical words of Jesus: "Be ye therefore perfect, even as your Father which is in heaven is perfect" (Matthew 5:48) motivate members to work actively at improving themselves intellectually, socially, and spiritually and to avoid behaviors (e.g., substance abuse) which could impair their growth. They can be hard-working clients if they view counseling as an opportunity to facilitate personal progress.

On the other hand, sometimes this belief operates in a dysfunctional way by reinforcing perfectionistic tendencies (Koltko, 1990). Some Latter-day Saints seem to believe not only that should they become perfect, but that they should be so now. Instead of accepting their inevitable imperfections, they conclude that they are bad, worthless, and eternally flawed because they continue to struggle. Perfectionistic tendencies in most clients, LDS or not, often mask deep-seated feelings of shame, low self-esteem, worthlessness, and deficiency originating in shaming and abusive experiences in childhood. Church teachings about repentance, sin, or even the qualities of good parents may motivate and encourage members with more positive self-esteem, but trigger feelings of inadequacy and depression in members with perfectionistic tendencies and low self-esteem (Richards, Smith, & Davis, 1989).

Latter-day Saints who struggle with perfectionism and shame may have considerable difficulty knowing when they have done enough. More conservative Saints in particular are apt to presume that all problems can be solved by increasing one's devotion to the minutia of the moral code, and that their problems must therefore reflect some moral failure or inherent spiritual deficit. Self-righteousness may prevail in members not psychologically strong enough to accept their weaknesses, or deflation may prevail in members overwhelmed by what seems to be an unending list of religious expectations.

Church doctrine does not support the belief that perfection is possible in this life. General Authorities' writings advise members that whereas excellence is good, perfectionism is not. In LDS theology, Jesus Christ is the only perfect being to live on the earth, and all must rely on his atonement for salvation from sin. Although non-LDS therapists will probably gain little ground by directly confronting LDS clients' doctrinal understandings, they may find it helpful to be aware of church teachings and refer clients to LDS colleagues or church leaders for clarification if necessary. Exploring painful early childhood experiences is often valuable with clients who have deep-seated feelings of shame and inadequacy. It can also be beneficial to refer to the LDS doctrine that we are all children of God with divine potential, and that the Lord beckons us to receive His forgiveness.

Abuses of Authority

LDS scriptural teachings abjure *unrighteous dominion*, characterized by pride, ambition, hypocrisy, control, and dominating behavior of all kinds, while promoting persuasion, long-suffering, gentleness, meekness, love, and kindness as the markers of true spiritual authority (*Doctrine and Covenants*, 121:37–46; LDS, 1981c, pp. 242–243). These teachings provide critical caveats in a religion which places great emphasis on parents' or church leaders' authority to act in God's name and church members' duty to listen to their counsel. Most church leaders and parents strive to avoid unrighteous dominion, but abuses of power sometimes occur, confusing and challenging the faith of followers.

Occasionally spouses, parents, or leaders will use their authority or presumed revelations as an excuse to be controlling and domineering. Highly controlling parents may have particular difficulty with individuating teenagers. In a religion that places such emphasis on the family, rebellious children can feel like a mark of shame and failure to worried parents. Although General Authorities make concerted efforts to denounce abuse of any kind, an abused wife with an uninformed local male priesthood leader may feel that she is not being heard and supported. Adult children may also be irrationally loyal to parents whose shortcomings psychotherapists encourage them to consider.

In the clinical situation, we at times find it necessary and helpful to confront LDS clients who are abusing their authority with the fact that such behavior is condemned in the scriptures and by church leaders. We help such clients examine the consequences of such behavior on their relationships and the well-being of their loved ones. We teach family members who are being controlled or abused to be more assertive, and we help them understand that church leaders do not expect them to submit to unrighteous dominion or abuse of any kind. Clients may meet with their church leaders about such problems to reinforce that the Church does not condone abuse. Likewise, church leaders do not expect anyone to stay in a destructive relationship, and as therapists we report abuse to both church authorities and the appropriate legal authorities.

Sexual Guilt and Inhibition

The LDS sexual standard of chastity before marriage and fidelity afterwards is strict compared with normative standards in mainstream American society. If adhered to, the Church's sexual code helps adherents avoid unwanted pregnancy, sexually transmitted diseases, and the anxiety associated with such problems. People enter marriage free of sexual baggage and jealousies from premarital relationships. Sex can have added sacred and emotional dimensions as a special experience reserved for the expression of love for one's spouse. Sexual jealousies and affairs are also less likely to be a source of marital conflict.

If active and devout church members violate their sexual code, however, anxiety, shame, and guilt or defensiveness are likely to be intense because of the strong religious and cultural prohibitions against such behavior. Adolescents may also experience intense guilt when they violate the Church's sexual standards. If married Latter-day Saints have an affair, they not only face a hurt, angry spouse, but disciplinary action from the church. Latter-day Saints may experience guilt even over sexual fantasies, because in Christian theology even "lusting in your heart" is considered to be sinful (Matthew 5:27–28). LDS people who experience homosexual tendencies must decide between whether to continue in the Church (which requires them to abstain from homosexual behavior) or to adopt the gay lifestyle and risk losing their church membership. In societies that presume regular sexual activity among single adults, chastity can be a challenging standard.

When LDS clients express concerns about sexuality in the clinical setting, a therapist can

1. ascertain their beliefs about sexual standards,
2. give them accurate information about normal human sexuality, and
3. assess both to understand to what extent their sexual behavior is congruent with their own moral beliefs and how they feel about discrepancies.

Most devout Latter-day Saints will be deeply concerned about violations of the Church's sexual standards, and a therapist can help them explore their feelings and goals. A therapist may ask clients about their beliefs about forgiveness and grace and how these can be accessed, and may then support clients who wish to speak of transgressions to their bishop or branch president. If clients are abnormally inhibited about sex, a therapist can explore the sources of such inhibitions and ask about church teachings or personal beliefs regarding the acceptability and role of committed marital sexuality.

Therapists can assist LDS clients who are struggling with homosexuality by helping them clarify their moral values and goals. Many LDS clients struggling with homosexual tendencies do not value the gay lifestyle and request help in minimizing and overcoming these tendencies. Therapists should respect clients' right to seek such assistance. Sexual reorientation therapy is available through LDS Family Services and from some LDS therapists in private practice.

Non-LDS therapists need to be especially careful not to disregard church sexual standards or prescribe interventions that conflict with church teachings about sexuality (e.g., prescribing interventions that use pornography, masturbation, sexual experimentation outside of marriage, or homosexual activity) as this is a sure way to lose credibility with devout LDS clients. By carefully working within LDS clients' belief systems and consulting with LDS colleagues or church leaders if there is a concern that church teachings about sexuality have been misunderstood or distorted, non-LDS therapists can undoubtedly help many LDS clients resolve sexual concerns and problems.

Denial of Anger and Conflict

Latter-day Saints are generally taught from an early age to treat others with kindness and love and to treat authority figures with honor and respect. Whereas such teachings encourage cooperation and obedience and reduce aggressive and antisocial behavior, they can act as a two-edged sword if Latter-day Saints become reluctant to challenge authorities or stand up for themselves when they are being mistreated or abused. Although there are a variety of views in the Church about the role and expression of emotions, such as resentment and anger, LDS people sometimes conclude that anger is a negative emotion to be avoided at all costs.

Some LDS clients who have been abused by parents, spouses, or others are reluctant to admit that these people made mistakes and even more reluctant to admit anger toward them. When offended by other people, particularly their church leaders, they may be very reluctant to blame other people, faulting themselves instead. Some Saints choose passive–aggressive styles because they are unwilling to admit that they are angry.

In the clinical situation, we attempt to help LDS clients to distinguish between simply experiencing emotions, such as anger and resentment, and how they choose to express such emotions. Communicating that emotions are friendly in the sense that they give us valuable information about ourselves and the situations we are in may help clients distinguish feeling anger or resentment from venting feelings inappropriately. Discussing ways of assertively but appropriately expressing anger, hurt, and resentment without attacking or harming others may help.

Gender Role Conflict and Sexism

The LDS Church's emphasis on the importance of the family and nurturing of children by both men and women does much to promote healthy families and children. However, many LDS women experience role conflict as they struggle to reconcile church teachings about gender roles with individual goals and modern societal norms. Men may also struggle with role conflict as they try to balance expectations for job success with responsibilities to family and church.

In addition, although much in LDS theology and culture encourages equality, mutual devotion, and respect between the sexes, the LDS Church's priesthood system and view that there are divinely prescribed gender roles exacerbates the possibility that some LDS couples will struggle with issues of sexism. An LDS woman who is a full-time homemaker with a sexist husband will often feel powerless, neglected by her husband, overburdened with child rearing and household work, and isolated from adult contact.

Therapists working with LDS clients who are struggling with gender role concerns or sexism can encourage couples to explore what they believe would be healthy and acceptable role divisions in light of personal beliefs and church teachings. It may help non-LDS therapists to know that although the Church does prescribe certain divisions in limited aspects of gender roles, considerable flexibility in male and female roles is acceptable. When women are burned out in a full-time homemaking role or stressed by role conflicts, or when men are overwhelmed by multiple and competing expectations, therapists can validate how challenging these roles are and help the couple understand the value of time to pursue individual interests and marital closeness.

It may also be helpful for therapists to know that church leaders have vigorously condemned the imposition of role divisions (or anything else) by coercion or force or by using role divisions as a means for gratifying men's needs at the expense of women or children. In LDS theology, husbands and wives are considered to be equal partners and are meant to cooperate together in mutual love and respect. Therapists can challenge sexist attitudes and behavior without questioning their LDS clients' belief in divinely appointed gender roles. Church leaders can also help correct sexist behaviors, particularly if a husband is using his priesthood authority or church responsibilities as a means to neglect or abuse his wife and children.

Divorce and Singlehood

The LDS belief that marital and familial relationships can endure for eternity, and the many church resources devoted to helping families, do much to promote strong families. However, the downside of this emphasis is that members who experience severe family conflict or who get divorced can feel a powerful sense of spiritual failure. In addition, because traditional, two-parent, heterosexual marriage and family life are the normative ideal for Latter-day Saints, couples who divorce can feel alienated from their religious community, along with all of their other social and emotional challenges (Mattson & Scharman, 1994; Scharman, 1994). For some LDS people, divorce provokes a serious emotional and spiritual crisis (Mattson & Scharman, 1994). Although members who never marry, or who become single through the death of their spouse, do not face the stigma associated with divorce, they also may feel marginalized. As awareness of the challenges faced by divorced and single members has grown, church leaders have made efforts to help them feel more valued and accepted.

Therapists who work with divorced or single Latter-day Saints may find such issues at the forefront. Exploring feelings of alienation or stigmatization about being single in a "married" church may be helpful. Some clients may struggle spiritually and question whether they want to remain involved in the Church. Therapists can provide a safe, nonjudgmental climate in which clients can explore their spiritual doubts and concerns.

Non-LDS therapists need to be especially careful not to criticize the Church or suggest leaving it, for this might undermine their credibility. It may also create alienation from the very social structure that could provide support and healing. Many LDS single people are deeply committed to the Church and their spiritual beliefs, but need help coming to grips with cultural biases favoring marriage. Non-LDS therapists may find it helpful to consult with LDS colleagues or church leaders about such clients. Church leaders are often able to help single LDS clients gain more social support and integration in the LDS community.

Social Conformity and Pressure

As described earlier, the Church is organized to offer a great deal of social support to its members, which can be a great resource and strength to them. On the other hand, some members at times perceive that the close-knit LDS community intrudes on their privacy. Inactive members may experience pressure from other members to conform to the Church's moral teachings and return to church activity. Even devout members may feel pressure to give more of their time and money to the Church than they are capable of giving. Church activities and contact may be so frequent that some members may feel overwhelmed and perceive that their lives are completely dominated by the religious community. The church ethic of being "anxiously engaged in a good cause" may contribute to excessive busyness, stress, and burnout (Barlow & Bergin, 1998; Koltko, 1990), particularly among those with perfectionistic tendencies.

LDS scripture asserts that all things should be done "in wisdom and order; for it is not requisite that a man should run faster than he has strength" (Mosiah 4:27; LDS, 1981a, p. 157). Helping clients learn how to set limits on how many activities they get involved in, even church activities, will validate their need for time for their own recreation and renewal. LDS clients who are seriously overwhelmed might be encouraged to talk to their bishop or branch president about the possibility of being released from a demanding church calling. General Authorities have instructed local church leaders to be sensitive to such situations and to encourage members to attend to primary responsibilities of family and personal health and well-being. We have found that almost without exception, local church leaders are responsive and appreciative of our feedback if one of their members is struggling in this manner. Non-LDS therapists who have built some trust and credibility in the LDS community should also find their input about such matters appreciated.

Treatment Issues and Approaches

Psychological Interventions Incongruent With LDS Culture

So long as therapists avoid interventions that conflict with LDS clients' religious and moral beliefs, a wide range of standard therapeutic approaches and interventions may be suitable for them. Interventions and theories that may not be acceptable to devout LDS clients include

1. sex therapies involving sex outside of marriage or masturbation techniques,
2. some marathon group therapies involving high levels of self-disclosure or emotional venting (this does not include 12-step programs or standard group therapies),
3. feminist therapies that devalue the role of motherhood and homemaking,
4. gay affirmative therapies, and
5. variants of rational emotive therapy calling for swearing or denouncing of authority figures.

Some LDS clients may also be uncomfortable with long-term analytic approaches because of the Church's emphasis on agency, self-reliance, and goal-oriented action (Koltko, 1990).

The Healing Potential of the LDS Community and Theology

Practical and financial assistance. When personal emergencies arise, LDS people may receive food and other basic supplies from a bishop's storehouse, help with job search skills and placements, low-cost short-term counseling, and adoption services. Ongoing social events for youth and adults, literacy programs, homemaking skill classes, and regular visits from home teachers (males) and visiting teachers (females) provide much help to families and individuals. Even nonpracticing members have access to these benefits. Just as important perhaps, members help provide these services to others in turn. These resources provide a holding environment in which basic needs are met in crisis situations or as people learn new skills to change dysfunctional patterns.

Religious practices. The emphasis on caring for the body through exercise, healthy eating, and avoidance of harmful substances promotes physical self-care and health. The patterns of church attendance provide structure to a person's week, ensuring social contact and moral teaching. Church teachings about paying tithing, staying out of debt, and storing food for emergencies help both rich and poor members toward financial responsibility and self-reliance. Other spiritual practices such as temple rituals, scriptural readings and metaphors, meditative prayer, fasting, journaling, church attendance and worship, and healing blessings assist individuals on journeys of emotional and spiritual healing and growth (Richards & Bergin, 1997; Ulrich, 1995).

Family relationships and social support. Where past family patterns have been dysfunctional, family history work, genealogy, and temple services may provide symbols for renewal, forgiveness, and change. Interactions with other church members provide new models for healthy interaction. Young families and those who geographically relocate generally find an instant support group in the typical ward. As adolescents begin to individuate, a circle of caring adults in the larger ward family surrounds them—role models with similar values but differing skills and perspectives than the parents. Many individuals who might not find it otherwise receive the benefit of family support as the extended ward family gives singles, single parents, and adults without children at home many opportunities to give and receive care. Such social support helps prevent psychosocial problems and facilitates remediation and recovery when problems do occur (Pargament, 1997).

Empowering theology. LDS theology empowers members to believe in their divine worth, expect divine care and guidance, and actively choose their life's course. LDS doctrine teaches that human beings are literally spirit children of God and that, after this life, virtually everyone will be resurrected to one of the three kingdoms of wonderful opportunity. This teaching underscores the fundamental LDS belief that every soul is worth perpetuating for eternity and worthy of love and help. LDS teachings empower individuals to seek spiritual truth, guidance, and forgiveness from a loving Heavenly Father and a merciful Savior in full confidence of receiving them. There is ample reinforcement in LDS theology and culture for personal initiative and responsibility, as well as humble reliance on God and on the help of others in developing and fulfilling one's potential. Such beliefs appear to bode well for health and healing (Benson, 1996).

Spiritual Interventions for LDS Clients

A variety of spiritual interventions may be helpful with LDS clients, including prayer, discussing scriptures or spiritual concepts, spiritual imagery, encouraging forgiveness, referral to church leaders, spiritual journaling, and spiritual bibliotherapy (Richards & Potts, 1995). It may be appropriate for non-LDS therapists to use some of these interventions depending on their own beliefs and comfort with using spiritual interventions. It is beyond the scope of this chapter to describe spiritual interventions in detail or how to apply them appropriately during therapy, but this has been done in other publications (e.g., Richards & Bergin, 1997; Richards & Potts, 1995; Shafranske, 1996; Ulrich, 1992, 1995).

Working With Religious Leaders and the Religious Community

To work effectively with the LDS community and draw upon its many potential resources, therapists need to obtain some familiarity with it and develop trusting relationships with LDS leaders and helping professionals. Bishops, branch presidents, and stake presidents are often very helpful when clients need

1. blessings of comfort, inspiration, and healing,
2. doctrinal clarification,
3. financial and employment assistance,
4. social support and fellowship,
5. confession and help with the repentance process, and
6. adoption services.

Bishops and branch presidents can also provide valuable assessment information by giving therapists insight into how clients function outside of therapy. Therapists need to ascertain in each case how helpful a given leader can be and obtain written permission before contacting religious leaders on the clients' behalf (Richards & Bergin, 1997).

CASE VIGNETTE

JoAnne was a young LDS woman who was referred by her LDS bishop for treatment because of discouragement and moderately severe depression, including occasional suicidal ideation. JoAnne had been married 7 years to her husband, Bill, and they had three children (ages 5, 3, and 1). JoAnne was a full-time homemaker, and Bill was a full-time student who also worked part time. Bill also served in a demanding church calling in their local ward one or two evenings a week and most of the day on Sundays. JoAnne felt isolated, starved for adult contact, and burned out from being at home with her children so much. The couple's sexual relationship had also deteriorated in recent months, with Bill complaining that JoAnne was never interested in sex. JoAnne replied that she was "always too tired." Several of their "fights" had become heated and ended when JoAnne, in tears, would angrily state, "Maybe I should just leave!"

Psychotherapy focused on helping JoAnne explore and express her feelings of being "stuck" and "burned out" in her full-time homemaking role and her anger at Bill for not providing more support. This was difficult for her at first because of her belief that "this is what I am supposed to be doing." Whenever JoAnne experienced anger or unhappiness, she felt guilty and inadequate because of her irrational belief that only unworthy LDS women feel frustrated about being a homemaker. The therapist challenged this belief by suggesting that perhaps many wonderful, good LDS women find being a full-time homemaker an extremely challenging task. The therapist validated just how difficult it must be for JoAnne to be isolated at home with only her children most of the time, receive so little support from Bill, and have little time to pursue her own interests and talents.

At this point, the therapist asked JoAnne if they could involve Bill in therapy. JoAnne resisted at first, not wanting to "overburden Bill even more." Finally, she agreed, acknowledging that if she did not do something to improve her situation, her depression and anger would continue. Bill readily agreed to come to therapy, wanting to understand better why JoAnne was having problems. It was immediately obvious that Bill had minimized in his mind how difficult it was for JoAnne to be a full-time homemaker, but as JoAnne shared her feelings and the therapist validated and affirmed that many women struggle in this way, Bill gained more empathy for her. Feeling a responsibility to provide more support, he asked JoAnne what she would like him to do. Although it was difficult to get past her maladaptive belief that good LDS women do not ask anything for themselves, JoAnne eventually told Bill she needed more time for herself. She also told him she wanted to pursue her interest and talent in art again by enrolling in an evening art class in the community.

The next few sessions focused on discussions about how Bill and JoAnne could arrange to provide JoAnne more support at home. In addition to discussing this issue in therapy, the therapist suggested that Bill and JoAnne each prayerfully consider this alone and together outside of therapy. This ultimately led to explorations of Bill's perfectionistic tendencies and his difficulty setting appropriate limits at school, work, and church. Bill acknowledged his underlying feelings of inadequacy and his need to do everything perfectly to prove that he was okay. As these insights came, Bill realized that his "hyperactivity" was counterproductive and not a solution to his feelings of inadequacy. He recognized that these feelings originated in parental neglect and shaming and that there were more direct and helpful ways to heal and cope.

As Bill worked on these issues, he also gained the emotional strength to set some healthy limits. He dropped a class at school, cut back some hours at work, and visited with his bishop about being released from his heavy church responsibilities so that he could devote more time to his family. The bishop also called JoAnne to a position in the women's Relief Society organization to give her opportunities for more adult companionship with "sisters" in her ward. Several months after beginning therapy, JoAnne reported feeling much better, enjoying her children and homemaking role again, and feeling enthusiasm about her developing art talents. Bill was less stressed, more emotionally and spiritually available to JoAnne and their children, and feeling better about himself. JoAnne and Bill reported that "things were good again" emotionally, sexually, and spiritually, as the barriers to good communication, mutual valuing, and physical communion had gradually dissolved.

CONCLUSIONS AND FUTURE DIRECTIONS

If the LDS Church continues to grow at projected rates, more Latter-day Saints will inevitably show up in the client pools of non-LDS therapists. Increasingly, those clients will be converts, facing the particular challenges of joining a new social group and subculture and a new religion. It is our hope that the information we have provided in this chapter will help mental health professionals work more effectively and sensitively with LDS clients. The LDS tradition has much healing potential, and we hope that helping professionals will use the Church's resources more widely on behalf of their clients.

SUGGESTED READINGS

Arrington, L. J., & Bitton, D. (1979). *The Mormon experience*. New York: Vintage/Random House.

Duke, J. T. (Ed.). (1998). *Latter-day Saint social life: Social research on the LDS church and its members*. Provo, UT: Religious Studies Center, Brigham Young University.

Ludlow, D. H. (Ed.). (1992). *Encyclopedia of Mormonism* (5 vols). New York: Macmillan.

Millet, R. L. (1998). *The Mormon faith: A new look at Christianity*. Salt Lake City, UT: Shadow Mountain.

Reynolds, N. B. (Ed.). (1997). *Book of Mormon authorship revisited: The evidence for ancient origins*. Provo, UT: Foundation for Ancient Research and Mormon Studies.

Shipps, J. (1985). *Mormonism: The story of a new religious tradition*. Urbana: University of Illinois Press.

The Church of Jesus Christ of Latter-day Saints (LDS). (1981). *The Book of Mormon: Another testament of Jesus Christ*. Salt Lake City, UT: Author.

REFERENCES

Barlow, S. H., & Bergin, A. E. (1998). Religion and mental health from the Mormon perspective. In H. Koenig (Ed.), *Handbook of religion and mental health* (pp. 225–243). New York: Academic Press.

Benson, H. (1996). *Timeless healing: The power and biology of belief*. New York: Scribner.

Bergin, A. E., Payne, I. R., Jenkins, P., & Cornwall, M. (1994). Religion and mental health: Mormons and other groups. In M. Cornwall, T. Heaton, & L. Young (Eds.), *Contemporary Mormonism: Social science perspectives* (pp. 138–158). Chicago: University of Illinois Press.

Black, S. E. (1998). I have a question: Do we know how many Latter-day Saints died between 1846 and 1869 in the migration to the Salt Lake Valley? *Ensign, 28*(7), 40–44.

Heaton, T. B. (1998). Vital statistics. In T. J. Duke (Ed.), *Latter-day Saint social life: Social research on the LDS Church and its members* (pp. 105–132). Provo, UT: Religious Studies Center, Brigham Young University.

Judd, D. K. (1999). *Religion, mental health and the Latter-day Saints*. Provo, UT: Religious Studies Center, Brigham Young University.

Koltko, M. E. (1990). How religious beliefs affect psychotherapy: The example of Mormonism. *Psychotherapy, 27*, 132–141.

Mattson, R., & Scharman, J. S. (1994). Divorce in Mormon women: A qualitative study. *AMCAP Journal, 20*, 39–60.

Pargament, K. I. (1997). *The psychology of religion and coping: Theory, research, practice*. New York: Guilford Press.

Richards, P. S., & Bergin, A. E. (1997). *A spiritual strategy for counseling and psychotherapy*. Washington, DC: American Psychological Association.

Richards, P. S., & Potts, R. W. (1995). Using spiritual interventions in psychotherapy: Practices, successes, failures, and ethical concerns of Mormon psychotherapists. *Professional Psychology: Research and Practice, 26*, 163–170.

Richards, P. S., Smith, S. A., & Davis, L. F. (1989). Healthy and unhealthy forms of religiousness manifested by psychotherapy clients: An empirical investigation. *Journal of Research in Personality, 23*, 506–524.

Scharman, J. S. (1994). Relationship issues in LDS blended families. *AMCAP Journal, 20*, 15–38.

Shafranske, E. P. (1996). *Religion and the clinical practice of psychology,* Washington, DC: American Psychological Association.

Sorenson, J. L. (1985). *An ancient American setting for the Book of Mormon.* Salt Lake City, UT: Deseret Book and Foundation for Ancient Research and Mormon Studies.

Stark, R. (1984). The rise of a new world faith. *Review of Religious Research, 26,* 18–27.

Stark, R. (1996). So far, so good: A brief assessment of Mormon membership projections. *Review of Religious Research, 38,* 175–178.

The Church of Jesus Christ of Latter-day Saints (LDS). (1981a). *The Book of Mormon: Another testament of Jesus Christ.* Salt Lake City, UT: Author.

The Church of Jesus Christ of Latter-day Saints (LDS). (1981b). *The pearl of great price.* Salt Lake City, UT: Author.

The Church of Jesus Christ of Latter-day Saints (LDS). (1981c). *The Doctrine and Covenants.* Salt Lake City, UT: Author.

The Church of Jesus Christ of Latter-day Saints (LDS). (1998). Church membership reaches 10 million. *Ensign, 28*(1), 74.

Ulrich, W. L. (1992). The temple, psychotherapy, and the traditions of the fathers. *AMCAP Journal, 18,* 53–74.

Ulrich, W. L. (1995). Rites of healing. *AMCAP Journal, 21,* 19–37.

Worthington, E. L., Jr. (1986). Religious counseling: A review of published empirical research. *Journal of Counseling and Development, 64,* 421–431.

9

PSYCHOTHERAPY WITH SEVENTH-DAY ADVENTISTS

CAROLE A. RAYBURN

The world, though fallen, is not all sorrow and misery. In nature itself are messages of hope and comfort. There are flowers upon the thistles, and the thorns are covered with roses.

—Ellen G. White

The Seventh-day Adventist Church dates from the Millerite movement of the mid-1800s. Conservative on most matters of morality and ethics, it is one of the few Christian denominations to have begun in North America. Also, it is one of the few denominations to have a woman as one of its founders. With its belief in the Protestant tradition, Seventh-day Adventism has conservative standards and practices concerning dress, dietary habits, abstinence from sex outside marriage, smoking and drinking alcohol, and in selection of certain types of entertainment.

The 1998 *Yearbook* published by the General Conference of Seventh-day Adventists notes that the worldwide membership of the Church is 9,470,718 people and 4,682 churches. With 865,187 members in North America, the largest concentration of Seventh-day Adventists (SDAs) is in California, Nevada, Utah, Arizona, and Hawaii. The second largest concentration is in Tennessee, Mississippi, Alabama, Georgia, and Florida, and the third largest in the District of Columbia, Virginia, Maryland, Pennsylvania, New Jersey, Delaware, and Ohio. A smaller number of SDAs reside in New York, Connecticut, Rhode Island, Maine, and Bermuda (General Conference of Seventh-day Adventists, 1998).

The world conference of Seventh-day Adventists, the General Conference, is in Silver Spring, Maryland. The General Conference president meets with and advises church leaders from the 12 divisions of the Church (such as the North American Division), unions (made up of conferences or fields within a larger territory), and local conferences (comprised of churches within various cities). Traditionally, the Church governance has been male-dominated and male-controlled (C. S. Rochester, personal communication, June 26, 1998).

The SDA Church has an extensive educational system consisting of hundreds of elementary and secondary schools, as well as many colleges and universities throughout the world. There are 10 colleges and universities in the United States. The extensive hospital system, better known outside of North America, includes every facet of health care. Loma Linda University Medical Center, in California, has gained worldwide prominence in medical research and treatment. Andrews University, in Berrien Springs, Michigan, boasts the major theological seminary for SDAs.

BELIEFS AND TRADITIONS

Millerism and Its Influence

William Miller, a Protestant preacher of the mid-1800s, taught that Christ would soon be returning in regal glory to claim those who believed in him and take them to their heavenly abode for 1,000 years. This was to occur on a specific day and year. Members of the Millerite group sold all of their earthly possessions in preparation for their relocation to heaven. The 1,000-year period described in the Book of Revelation involves the battle between Jesus and Satan, the defeat of Satan and thus of evil, the destruction of the world, and its purification and rehabilitation by the faithful.

Because the end of the world predicted by William Miller did not come about, the Millerites had to do much prayerful rethinking. They decided that the specific date predicted by Miller was actually the time that Jesus as Priest of the heavenly temple entered the temple to go over the Book of Life. Ellen G. White, then a member of the Methodist Church, began prophesying and writing prolifically to elucidate scriptural writings. SDAs regard such a corpus of literature not as new scripture but as commentary on scripture (though some non-SDA writers have misinterpreted this position). Ellen G. White is regarded by most SDAs not only as a founding pioneer of the SDA Church but as a prophet of Seventh-day Adventism.

Seventh-day Sabbath Observance

The Millerites ultimately became known as Adventists because they anticipated that Christ would soon come again. However, it was not until another Methodist woman, Rachel Oakes Preston, became interested in the seventh-day sabbath that emphasis on sabbath observance on the seventh day was brought into the Adventist Church. Preston became a Seventh-day Baptist, and she finally was successful in convincing Adventists of the importance of observing the sabbath on the seventh day rather than on the first day of the week. (First-day Adventists, also influenced by Miller, worship on Sunday.) Thus, the denomination became known as Seventh-day Adventism: anticipation of the advent of Christ and worship on the seventh day being the two most prominent distinctions for SDAs.

The sabbath is set aside for worship activities from sundown Friday to sundown Saturday. During this time, there is a prohibition against working and against "buying and selling" (exchanging money or bartering other goods); church members also refrain from "doing one's own pleasure" (which has been interpreted in a variety of ways). Medical work, however, is an exception, because this may involve life and death issues or at least very urgent health concerns. David Reile (1997) noted that what is considered to be acceptable for sabbath observance varies significantly from one individual to another and may seem inconsistent or contradictory within the belief system of one individual.

Gift of the Spirit of Prophecy

Seventh-day Adventists believe in the gift of prophecy in post-biblical times, as described in scripture, particularly as this is associated with the last days of earth before the Second Coming of Christ. Ellen G. White is considered to have been such a prophet, as her visions about religious and spiritual matters provided guidance to the newly formed Adventist Church. Many believers have taken these visions and White's writings as being truth for the latter days of the church of Christ.

State of the Dead

SDAs believe that the dead know nothing but are in a state of "sleep" until they are awakened at the Second Coming of Christ. The righteous dead will be resurrected to immortality; the unrighteous dead will return to life temporarily with the same diseases and corruption that they had at the time of the first death. These unrighteous will die a second death and be completely destroyed after the battle between good and evil.

Baptism by Immersion

SDAs dedicate infants in a church ceremony by a blessing and laying on of hands. Generally, only adolescents and adults are baptized, however. This symbolic going down to a watery grave with Christ and rising with the victorious Lord are carried out by immersion in a baptistry or a body of water. Pouring and sprinkling cannot substitute for immersion.

Tithing

Many SDAs give the Church one tenth of their earnings before they deduct anything for their expenses. This money is considered to be God's money. There has been a dispute by some ethnic minority SDAs because proportionately they give more money to the Church than ethnic majority members, but they get less back when the Church redistributes the funds. Tithing is given in addition to contributions to be used in the local church.

Healthful Living and Modest Dress

Abstaining from alcohol and other drugs and not smoking, maintaining a kosher or even a vegetarian diet, getting adequate sleep and rest, and exercising regularly are espoused by the Church for keeping the body—the temple of God—pure, holy, and healthy. Modesty in dress is also taught, because use of jewelry (often including wedding rings) and very elaborate clothing is held to be worldly, wasteful, and ungodly. The wearing of cosmetics is also frowned upon by very conservative SDAs. Bringing attention to oneself is not viewed as good or wise. However, these restrictions are gradually declining; using cosmetics tastefully and wearing wedding bands (especially by non-North American SDAs) are more widely acceptable now, as is wearing pins and some semiprecious stones. These differences reflect generational and geographical variations. For instance, the West Coast and the East Coast of the United States may differ in the ways in which SDAs live their faith. Reile (1997) has observed that some younger and new SDAs *may* accept moderate drinking. Case (1996a), in a very large study of SDAs, commented that there is a trend of increased wine usage by younger Adventist adults: SDAs over 65 years of age have a ratio of 1 in 20 who used wine, whereas those 18–29 years of age have a ratio of 1 in 4 who have used wine.

Prohibition Against Dancing

Any type of dancing, even square dancing, is viewed by many SDAs as unacceptable and sinful, especially among older and non-North American SDAs. This prohibition is based on the belief that improper sexual intimacy for a couple and even married couples may occur while they engage in dancing. Although less of a concern among younger SDAs, for older members (over 60 years of age) and for those in conservative regions, the belief may still be strong. In the Value-Genesis Study of the SDAs, Dudley (1992) reported that 58% of the SDA youths in Grades 6–12 disagreed with the Church standard on dancing.

Avoidance of Movies, Theaters, Nightclubs, and Circuses

This is the belief that any form of entertainment might distract individuals from the strictly spiritual pursuits of Bible study and church activities. Although this belief is still held by many conservative SDAs, it is beginning to lessen among the more liberal and younger members. SDAs have performances of plays such as *The Diary of Anne Frank* in their schools and Barbra Streisand movies such as *What's Up, Doc?* at Andrews University, the university that houses the only full seminary in Seventh-day Adventism. In Berrien Springs, Michigan, the home of the seminary, more liberal SDA teachers and professors, the university bookstores, and film programs often lean more toward liberal thinking. However, Takoma Park, Maryland, former home of the General Conference and local conference, has far more conservative members in general. Nonetheless, the main SDA bookstore in Takoma Park now sells items of jewelry, such as religious pins and refrigerator magnets of angels. Initially, conservatives frowned upon anything that would present a vaudeville or circus thrill, tempting the saints of God from their first love: reflecting the love and spirit of Jesus Christ to other believers and to the world.

Case (1996c) found that, although the SDA Church maintains its official stance against movies, most SDAs watch movies regularly in theaters and in their homes and that they may even go to movies more often than do their secular counterparts. He suggested that values related to central SDA theological issues may be believed and well-kept, whereas those reflecting more popular culture tend to be less maintained. Dudley (1992) found that 64% of SDA youths disagreed with the Church standard on attending movies in theaters. Furthermore, 55% of these youths disagreed with the Church about listening to rock music.

Avoidance of Premarital Sexual Intimacy

Although not necessarily observed by all SDAs, strict sexual abstinance before marriage is observed by conservative members. Indeed, not only sexual intimacy but excessive masturbation (any masturbation for conservative members), pornography, and obsessions about sexual activities might be deemed sinful and unacceptable. Knott (1996) reported that youths in SDA schools are far less likely to be involved in sexual practices.

Dudley (1992) found that two thirds of SDA students in Grades 6–12 agreed with their Church's standards on sexual morality, but 18% (almost one fifth) disagreed on this, and 14% was not sure; SDA youth, surrounded by the cultural sexual revolution, may be turning away from the SDA traditional ideal of sexual purity. Corea (1996), studying the nonvirgin status of SDA youth, reported an increase in sexual activity with increasing age and, among those who indicated that they were not virgins, there was a higher percentage in the SDA group than in "mainstream Protestant churches" of those who had been sexually intimate before marriage.

Ordinance of Humility (Foot Washing)

The Ordinance of Humility or Foot Washing was mentioned in the Old Testament as a rite of hospitality and in the New Testament as an ordinance done just before the feast of Passover. Jesus washed the feet of the disciples and instructed them to wash each other's feet. A woman is described in all four Gospels as washing Jesus' feet. SDAs believe that this ordinance teaches people to come into a holy union with one another and to help and bless one another. It is not intended as anything degrading, but rather it is a demonstration of kindness and tenderness toward one another.

Ellen G. White spoke of the biblical example of women washing male believers' feet, but not of brethren washing women's feet (White, 1882). In practice, however, pairs of same-gender individuals wash each other's feet before the service of the Lord's Supper. In the more conservative SDA churches, even husbands and wives may not wash each other's feet. The justification given for this segregation is that it would be immodest for women to take off their stockings in front of men or for men to have to kneel before a woman's skirt or undergarments (Rayburn, 1993).

The Trinity

The Trinity is a basic belief of the SDA Church. There is one God, a unity of three coeternal persons of the Godhead: "God the Father, Son, and Holy Spirit." For a fuller overview of this and other SDA beliefs, please refer to the "Fundamental Beliefs of Seventh-day Adventists" (General Conference, 1998).

Unity in the Body of Christ and the Role of Women

One of the fundamental beliefs of SDA is the unity in the body of Christ: The Church is one body with many members, a new creation transcending distinctions of culture, gender, ethnic identity, nationality, education, and socioeconomic level. All people are equal in Christ; SDAs are to serve and to be served without reservation or partiality.

There is a growing concern and displeasure among some SDAs, particularly some women, who do not believe that the traditional role of women in the SDA Church reflects such unity in the body of Christ. This is especially painful to some SDA women in light of the vital roles that women such as Ellen G. White and Rachel Oakes Preston played in the development of the Seventh-day Adventist Church. Furthermore, women such as Charlotte Elizabeth Poor and Harriet Livermore were of crucial importance to the Millerite and Adventist movements, writing significant religious literature. Some SDAs do not think that women of more current times have been given responsibilities and leadership positions commensurate with those of men. During the Millerite movement, women were more concerned about religious issues on average than were men, and women played important roles in public and in private (Rayburn, 1997b).

Today, educational pursuits are encouraged for all SDAs, and many roles outside the ecclesiastical structure are open to women. Nonetheless, women are denied full participation within the governance of the Church itself. In fact, for the most part, women who have limited ministerial roles are not even called minister or pastor but rather *associates in pastoral care*. They do not have the professional status of clergy, nor do they receive the salary and other clerical job opportunities that male clergy do. The effect of such limitations for preaching, administering, and performing the sacred roles in the Church is sweeping. Girls and women have no adequate female ecclesiastic role models at the highest level of participation. Men as well as women may need to choose between their dreams of equality and shared roles in the Church and the reality of a church with male dominance and control (Rayburn, Natale, & Linzer, 1982).

The importance of the role of girls and women is one to which both SDAs themselves and therapists who work with SDAs should not take lightly nor dismiss as tangential to the SDA faith experience as it is lived in everyday existence. Adventist writers such as Gillespie (1996) and Dudley (1992) have shown laudable sensitivity to this grave concern. They are concerned that denying women an ordained ministerial role may lead to a schism and to people leaving the SDA Church. Speaking of values concerning women and social justice, Dudley sees the role of women in ministry as one of the most widely debated current issues in the SDA Church. Young people are as badly split on this issue as their parents and church leaders, with 54% somewhat or strongly favoring having women ordained as local church elders, 47% favoring having women pastors, and 42% favoring having women ordained as pastors in the SDA Church governance (not just limited to the local church). No gender differences were reported by Dudley. Furthermore, loving and serving other people was weakly related to favoring women in ministry.

THE SDA POSITION ON IMPORTANT SOCIAL
AND MORAL ISSUES

Divorce and Remarriage

The SDA position is that divorce is not part of God's plan. However, the Church recognizes that in the current day, with its problems of disobedience toward God and disrespect for self, others, and God, divorce will occur. The most accepted reason to allow divorce is adultery. In practice, one person is usually considered to be primarily responsible for the dissolution of the marriage, with the other seen as being relatively innocent. Both the divine and civil aspects of divorce are recognized by the Church.

Remarriage is also not looked upon as God's plan. Marriage is not dissolved except for infidelity, adultery, and fornication (including a homosexual partner). The estate of marriage has both divine and civil aspects. According to the church discipline, individuals have no right to remarry if the "innocent" party is living, unmarried, and chaste. Should the noninnocent person remarry before the innocent partner, the noninnocent individual would most likely be disfellowshipped by the Church.

Birth Control

The SDA Church supports birth control through the methods of abstinence, protective devices, and birth control pills. Abortion is not an approved method of birth control.

Abortion

Seventh-day Adventists believe that all life is sacred. Abortion for gender selection, birth control, or convenience is not condoned. Nonetheless, in cases of rape, incest, or danger to the health of the woman, abortion can be condoned. Thus, there is a limited, conservative position on prochoice, but a predominant position held by the Church authorities supports probirth or prolife. This position of probirth, however, is not unilaterally supported by all SDA women and men.

Homosexuality

The official position of the denomination on homosexuality is that the behavior and lifestyle are not condoned, but the homosexual person is to be loved and accepted. This acceptance is encouraged with the goal of changing the gay men and lesbians, however. There is a serious question of whether a person is allowed to be SDA and gay. This is not a position held by all SDAs, however.

Corporal Punishment

In disciplining children, the SDA position accepts spanking a child within reason: A very mild application of the biblical injunction, "Spare the rod, spoil the child." Certainly, no abusive situation would be acceptable (C. S. Rochester, personal communication, June 26, 1998).

While attending seminary for a Master of Divinity degree, I was called upon to give counsel on a matter involving a minister who was also attending the seminary. The minister disciplined his children harshly by beating them when they disobeyed him. He was warned by church and seminary authorities to discontinue such behavior. He excused himself, saying that he was from the West Indies, and that this form of discipline was a cultural matter. Nonetheless, he was instructed that such behavior would not be permitted in North America. Church leaders required him to accept counseling and to stop this maltreatment of his family. He appeared to comply with this requirement, and counseling was also arranged for the children and their mother.

IMPLICATIONS AND GUIDELINES FOR COUNSELING AND PSYCHOTHERAPY

Ellen G. White's Guidelines to Mental and Spiritual Health

Ellen G. White, a founder and the recognized prophet of the Seventh-day Adventist Church, addressed matters of character, mind, and personality in many of her writings. These writings were much later put in a compilation, *Mind, Character, and Personality: Guidelines to Mental and Spiritual Health* (White, 1977). Some older and many conservative SDAs may be influenced by White's early comments on Satan's being able to work through the sciences, including psychology, phrenology, and mesmerism—psychology, to influence the mind. Her fear was that mind control could be used to delude unsuspecting Christians. White's primary message here was that only through complete dependence upon Christ might people escape the snare of deception and evil. She warned others that, in the last days, Satan would work unceasingly to bring fanaticism among even SDAs and thus to bring extreme criticism and harsh treatment from the world on SDAs. Her remedy for dealing with the fanatical mind, with its unreasoning zeal, dazed self-importance, excessive pride, and combative ways, was to rely on Christ only and not on one's own strength, not enter into controversy with the fanatic but to affirm everything about God with "It is written" and "Thus saith the Lord" (White, 1915). To White, mind control was a form of fanaticism. On the other hand, a healthy normal mind involved neither cold orthodoxy nor careless liberalism (White, 1977).

White urged that people control their impulses and emotions or, at least, control their will; this strength comes only from God. Feelings are often deceiving. At times, the Lord may disturb the mind with feelings of unrest or loneliness to teach dependence on God and turn people's attention to eternal realities. She warned of the danger of becoming self-absorbed in self-study or emotions, but taking problems to God and occasionally to a pastor–counselor was urged.

Guilt or a sense of sinfulness put clamps on a truly happy life. Repentance, confession of sins, and true humiliation in asking God's forgiveness for the sin, along with true forsaking of the sin, is needed to get the person back on the path to a sanctified and productive life. Worry kills and brings on unrest and anxiety. She urged that worries be taken to God and that people take each day at a time ("Sufficient unto the day is the evil thereof," Matthew 6:34). "Let us not make ourselves miserable over tomorrow's burdens" was White's strong recommendation (White, 1902). Faith dispels anxiety (White, 1905).

Seeing the connection between mind and body functions, White (1891) wrote, "Those who are sick in body are nearly always sick in soul, and when the soul is sick, the body is made sick." In counsel that would agree with much modern feminist therapy, White wrote in 1900 (White, 1977) that counselors can help those who have erred by telling them of the counselor's experiences to show how others gave the erring person courage and hope by expressions of patience, kindness, and helpfulness. She instructed people not to talk of negative feelings lest they discourage both themselves and others (White, 1905). Although this might initially be viewed as a form of denial of one's feelings, it is more a power of positive thinking, à la Norman Vincent Peale. In her most widely read book, *Steps to Christ*, White wrote in 1892, "Jesus did not suppress one word of truth, but he uttered it always in love."

White (1880) wrote in a patriarchal structure of her times that a counselor be a *man* of sound judgment and undeviating principle, a person of moral influence who knows how to deal with minds, who possesses wisdom, culture, affection, and intelligence. Gentleness and unbending integrity in a counselor are needed to contend with prejudice, bigotry, and error of every form and description. A kindly approach without reproach is needed, with no blame or condemnation in coming close to a troubled person's side to help him or her. Yet, in counsel to a minister (White, 1889a, 1977), she cautioned that private counseling on private matters concerning either families or individuals can become a snare for both the pastor and those counseled because people might turn in their dependence on another person and not on God. In 1915, she wrote that the work of the pastor–counselor is more important than that of the physician in dealing with sin-sick souls: Eternal life is more valuable than temporal existence.

Counselor–Client Relationship

Counselors and psychotherapists who are SDA themselves or who see SDA clients and patients have often reported being distrusted by older and more conservative SDAs concerning psychology, psychotherapy, and psychiatry. These individuals may experience difficulty in perceiving that anyone can be both a psychologist and a believer or a therapist and a Christian. Barbara Suddarth (personal communication, November 2, 1997), a fifth-generation SDA and a counseling psychologist, found such distrust curious in an organization that places much importance on health care but seems to overlook mental health, at least for more conservative members. Some may fear that psychotherapy will involve mind control, brainwashing, or hypnosis. Some more conservative SDAs may suspect psychotherapists and counselors who were not trained in SDA graduate schools or who are not "Christian counselors" (which would imply a specialty in Christian counseling). Because some SDAs may be very critical of themselves and of others, they usually respond well to a psychotherapeutic approach that is nonjudgmental.

Reile (1997) pointed out that SDAs are similar in many ways to "mainstream" conservative Christians: Usually fervent believers in prayer, they may fear that seeking mental health remedies would suggest that they doubt God's power to overcome problems and show their lack of faith and good prayer life. As with all religious clients, therapists must support the client's belief system at least initially and not challenge or label it (e.g., magical thinking). Because new clients may think that psychology and psychotherapy involve Freudian "obsession with sexuality," hypnotizing people to do something against their will, and invasion into the more private facets of their lives, they need to hear from the therapist at the outset what type of therapy will be practiced and what results might be anticipated. Therapists need to recognize that there are many individual differences among SDAs and that SDA beliefs different from their own do not usually indicate bizarre or unhealthy conditions (R. Proctor, personal communication, September 2, 1997).

Assessment and Diagnostic Issues

SDAs may be very selective as to which assessment tool they will tolerate. For instance, they may not react well to the Minnesota Multiphasic Personality Inventory if they interpret it as being unsympathetic toward religious persons. The same may be true of the Thematic Apperception Test. The therapist may be able to use these instruments with more liberal SDAs, however. The more projective tools, such as the House–Tree–Person, Human Figure Drawings, Draw-A-Person-in-the-Rain, Kinetic Family Drawing, Self-Image Drawing, Sentence Completion, and Rorschach Inkblot Test may be seen as being safer by most SDA patients and clients. Also, they might be assessed with the Faith Maturity Scale (Benson, Donahue, & Erickson, 1993) and with other religiousness and spirituality measures, such as the Inventory on Religiousness (Rayburn, 1997a) and the Inventory on Spirituality (Rayburn & Richmond, 1997).

John Berecz (1998), a clinical psychologist in both private practice and academia, sees working with SDA clients as a unique experience in multiculturalism. He has found differences among SDAs to be as great as differences between Adventists and United Methodists. Berecz views California Adventists as being rather wry and stereotypical liberals and intellectuals who believe in the full equality of women, favor the ordination of women to the gospel ministry, and consider sexuality to be part of human functioning in both the procreational and recreational senses. Furthermore, California SDAs are generally more trusting of psychology and psychotherapy than SDAs from other regions of the United States. At the opposite pole, Berecz described Third World Adventists as insisting on the patriarchal view of the male person as the biblically ordained priest of the home, with the wife created to be subservient and to function as a helper to her husband; these SDAs think that sexuality is a very private matter, primarily for procreation. They do not think that women should ever function as ordained ministers or have equal rights.

Frederick Kosinski, Jr. (personal communication, January 3, 1998), a counseling psychologist in private practice and academia, notes that half of his clients are SDAs, ex-SDAs, or have been part of the SDA community. Having worked in several states in North America, he has observed that rather conservative SDAs in western Nebraska nonetheless ate beef and drank bitter black coffee. At an SDA college in Lincoln, Nebraska, however, the SDAs were more liberal. Michigan SDAs were more conservative than California SDAs but more liberal than SDAs in Nebraska, Maryland, or the District of Columbia. SDAs living around large Adventist institutions may be more conservative than those who work for those institutions and less conservative than SDAs living in small communities. SDAs seem to exist on a continuum, with most being centrist or moderate. It is important for therapists to determine what kind of Adventist an individual is, what the person believes, and how these beliefs affect and shape the individual's personality.

COMMON CLINICAL ISSUES

Perfectionism

SDAs who believe that they can and should attain perfection on this earth during their lifetime are often quite critical of themselves and others and suspicious of the motives of others. They spend much time in avoiding blame, limit themselves to restricted areas of enjoyment in interpersonal relationships, and rarely allow others a broad range of enjoyment. F. Kosinski, Jr. (personal communication, January 3, 1998) reported that the theological perfectionism of SDA clients seems to contribute to their anxiety or depression. He encourages these clients to look at the compassionate side of God. Lovinger (1990), admitting that he had not worked with any Adventist clients, thought that they might be vulnerable to anxiety about making errors and giving in to evil temptations from which they cannot escape. Berecz (1998) noted that SDAs might get caught in a web of perfectionism and scrupulosity connected more to their upbringing and religious subculture than to any real behavioral misdeeds.

B. Suddarth (personal communication, November 2, 1997) remarked that some SDAs, like other religious people, have a highly developed and often rigid superego, with a splitting off or total denial of the *id* or pleasure principle. There are many shoulds, oughts, and musts in SDA clients, often with a failure to understand from where these strictures come. Although it will probably promote anxiety, these clients may need to question and explore these attitudes for the sake of their emotional growth. Authority issues are important because conservative SDAs tend to assign respect to hierarchy and authority figures. Therapists and their clients should explore what authority means to the client, stressing an open and questioning orientation. When clients insist that something is true because the pastor said so, the therapist may find it helpful to get clients to trust their own thinking and feeling more, to become more self-sufficient, and to develop a healthier skepticism toward "total authority." To develop themselves as independent individuals who formulate their own values, clients need to be helped to gradually separate the cultural aspects of Adventism from their own religious beliefs. Additionally, individuation may be furthered by helping clients see past surface cultural meanings to understand deeper, underlying connections and symbolism. For example, a client might be encouraged to think more deeply about what is expressed by wearing jewelry or colorful clothing instead of automatically ascribing such behavior as being evil or sinful.

Sexuality

Some SDAs, including some SDA pastors, are not comfortable with their bodies, their own sexuality, or touching others, with the possible exception of a handshake. Resolving their sexual attitudes through counseling or therapy sessions would be most beneficial for such individuals.

Berecz (1998) believes that many SDAs might suffer from *unintegrated sexuality*, or compartmentalizing their sexual functioning into a secret, never discussed corner of the psyche. Repressing sexuality as advocated in the writings of Ellen G. White often leads to compulsive sexuality, sexual dissociation, sexual acting out, and other unhealthy sexual attitudes. Berecz noted that, with couples, such repressed sexuality may take the form of one partner being uninterested in sex while the other is overly interested or of the couple compulsively using sexual frequency as a measure of self-esteem or the status of the marital relationship. Modern updating on sexuality has not occurred for many SDAs. With growing numbers of Third World SDAs entering North America, a trend toward more conservatism on human sexuality is evident.

Suggesting that SDAs may have more guilt about masturbation than average individuals do, Berecz (1998) connects such attitudes and feelings to the influence of the writings of Ellen White on these SDAs. Whereas some persons may view masturbation as a "loser" position if it is the only means an individual depends on for sexual gratification, SDAs may rigidly follow the counsel of White and view the matter through Victorian eyes that see it as a secret vice, self-abuse, or self-murder, as well as a cause of physical or mental distress.

Projection and Anger

B. Suddarth (personal communication, November 2, 1997) recognized that many SDAs project *id* impulses onto a family member. In these instances, clients must normalize desires, wishes, and emotions as healthy dimensions of human activity rather than as sinfulness if they are to incorporate previously split-off parts of themselves into a holistic identity. Therapists need to proceed slowly to make such admissions less threatening. If the client thinks anger is an unacceptable emotion, the therapist should avoid saying that the client is enraged and instead comment that there is a *part* of the client that feels angry. Clients can often deal with this gradual admission more easily.

Fear of Dependency

Adventists may fear becoming overly dependent on therapists and counselors and ending up so emotionally distraught that they regret ever being in treatment. Such dependency might signal to SDAs that they have taken their eyes from their first love, God. Of course, they realize that they have not yet attained such a position of closeness to the divine, but they strive hard to reach this plane of faith and belief. Ellen G. White warned SDAs against allowing others to control any person's mind, as with hypnosis. Her warning has contributed to SDAs' excessive concern about becoming helplessly dependent on their counselors or therapists. Therapists need to reassure clients that the treatment will not undermine their emotional freedom or their religious beliefs (even if neurotic). Therapists and counselors should work within the clients' belief system and help them to function more effectively on their own. Ironically, SDAs who are most fearful of losing their independence in therapy are sometimes the ones most likely to become dependent on the clergy and to view this form of dependence as reverence for God's anointed representatives (Berecz, 1998).

Guilt and Shame

Many SDA clients may accumulate a lot of guilt and shame, not differentiating between the good guilt, which people feel after real wrong doing, and shame, which is the feeling of overall badness that is not actually rooted in real misbehavior. Therapy allows clients to examine why they sense guilt and to discern whether such a feeling is connected with misdeeds or results from seeking perfection to an unhealthy extreme.

Depression

Some SDAs become frustrated, angry, and even depressed when the ideals of the Church do not match the practice of the Church. Then they become angry with themselves for even experiencing any anger. They often need to be reminded that even Jesus Christ experienced anger and depression—or at least deep sadness. A serious and obvious source of depression for many SDA women and some men is the nonacceptance of women for ordination to the full gospel ministry. Some women have left the SDA Church, whereas others remain halfheartedly in the pews. Furthermore, for the growing number of religious feminists in the SDA Church and for those who belong to groups that favor ordaining women as full gospel ministers (there have been at least three such groups), there has been a tremendous inner struggle, anger, and depression in striving to be true to one's womanhood and one's denominational ties (Rayburn, Natale, & Linzer, 1982).

F. Kosinski, Jr. (personal communication, January 3, 1998) indicated that he had worked with ex-SDA clients who saw themselves as having been victimized by the Church and its restrictions. He encouraged such clients to find their own spiritual way and to give up the role of victim.

SDA women, however, often remain faithful to sabbath observance and are unwilling to join a church that observes Sunday as its day of worship. For these women, little in therapy can alleviate the pain of their intense struggle within the religious community and within themselves. They must deal continually with the problems of gender discrimination within sanctuary walls. Therapy might provide these women an opportunity to sort more fully through the religious, spiritual, and feminist values in their lives, however.

Another source of depression is illustrated by a case described by Ferris (1983). A married couple had been committed Christians, health conscious, careful in selecting their diet and in using vitamin supplements, and conscientious in exercising and in following the healthiest lifestyle possible. When they learned that the husband had a terminal malignancy, they were unable to accept this in light of their careful lifestyle. As the wife watched her husband grow weaker, she and he constantly voiced their regrets: "What if I had only...?" They felt helpless, followed by anger toward the diagnostician, the institution, themselves, and even God. The couple experienced frustration and guilt in having failed to deal as Christians with their own mortality.

To reduce the anxiety and depression level of such clients, the therapist needs to help them rephrase the basic question of "Have I made all of the right choices?" Reality must be faced in working through all of the concomitant feelings in the stress of the problem, remaining open to God, self, and others. Psychic and spiritual energy need to be focused upon lessening devastating pessimism, replacing this with healing optimism. This couple had an unspoken but strongly felt hope that healthy living would bring a reward of near immortality. They had assumed that if they followed divine plans for healthy living, illness and death would bypass them indefinitely. There was, then, a kind of bargaining of right living for immortality. Through therapeutic intervention, couples like this can be helped to see that their careful lifestyle might have warded off diseases more effectively than an unhealthy one, but it could not guarantee against all physical problems and weaknesses. Therapists who are nonjudgmental, warm, and caring can help such a couple to accept the reality of the husband's mortality and help the wife to anticipate her reunion with her husband at the resurrection.

Clergy depression and burnout are important matters to work with in counseling and psychotherapy. The few women who work as ministers are actually called *associates in pastoral care*. Furthermore, when Dudley and Cummings (1982) studied SDA pastoral morale, they found that a substantial minority of male ministers desired to be relieved of administrative minutiae of the Church, to have more meaningful continuing education to develop their abilities and talents, and to have a more equal relationship as pastors with conference administrators. Related to pastoral morale was the pastor–spouse relationship. The women associates in pastoral care often are depressed because they are rarely given pastoral responsibilities or authority but usually are assigned jobs that the male clergy do not want to have. They are understandably resentful, although they may express their feelings in more passive than assertive ways.

Clergy in general have trouble setting priorities and saying "no" to the requests of others. But when there is little time for themselves or for their families, they become frustrated, anxious, angry, and depressed. In counseling or therapy, they can learn to deal more effectively with their frustration and anger. Admitting that they have a problem is a first step. They may need to overcome their tendency toward perfectionism to set priorities, to refuse to respond to all or most requests when time and energy are limited, and to make sure that they get enough rest and relaxation. A need to see themselves as superclergy on a clerical pedestal is an unhealthy position that must be resolved in treatment. The health consciousness of SDAs proves to be helpful because they tend to refrain from drinking and smoking, and to have strict kosher or vegetarian diets. These health measures have been shown to lower stress levels in general.

Forgiveness

Berecz (1998) found the concept of forgiveness useful in treating even very conservative SDAs. Because forgiveness reflects the expectation that weak humans make mistakes, SDAs can be reminded that forgiveness involves reframing mistakes as feedback and proceeding with one's life. The SDA culture of shame and guilt stresses right living, right doing, and right attitudes. When members of this culture fail in achieving the degree of perfection that they expect of themselves and that they perceive to be expected of them by their Church and other believers, they become depressed. For many SDAs, tolerance for ambiguity is low.

TREATMENT AND INTERVENTION ISSUES

For SDAs suspicious of psychology and psychotherapy, the tendency toward perfectionism, the patriarchal attitudes toward women, and the critical outlook in general may hinder optimal psychotherapeutic processes. Potential healing properties, on the other hand, for this religious culture may be the genuine motivations to seek goodness and truth, to be healthy, to be close to God, to help other struggling beings, to be more acceptable in the eyes of God, and to prepare themselves for better living and better service to others. These motivations and values will facilitate the process of therapy.

Relaxation training for SDAs can be very helpful, as can Rogerian

Therapy, Transactional Analysis, cognitive behavioral therapy (emphasizing thinking and feeling elements with equal importance), and any other modalities that focus on the realistic and the logical with both feeling and thinking components. Thus, a psychotherapeutic approach that appeals to the client's reasoning abilities and does not prematurely get into possibly threatening emotional areas would be best in working with SDAs. With very conservative SDAs, Freudian psychoanalysis might be less acceptable and less appropriate because of the perceptions of these SDAs that psychoanalysis dwells on sexual subject matter and has less than accepting attitudes toward organized religion; hypnosis might also be linked with Freudian psychoanalysis in their thinking.

Reile (1997) offered some further guidance in providing psychological services to SDA institutions, organizations, and individuals: Because SDAs observe sabbath from sundown Friday to sundown Saturday, no business meetings or appointments should be scheduled at that time. Facilities and treatments in the medical and related fields, including psychology, are exceptions to this guideline as these are deemed necessary services to life, even on the sabbath. A general rule is to schedule only emergency vital sessions of therapy on the sabbath.

As with other denominations, SDAs usually prefer to deal with "one of their own" whenever possible. If this is not possible, they at least want to work with a therapist or counselor who understands and appreciates their value system. Networking, especially in large SDA communities that are usually very insular, is quite important.

Psychological services may be viewed with suspicion outside the medical community, especially, by very conservative SDAs. Therapists need to explain their credentials, therapeutic orientation, and therapy goals very clearly, and they should avoid references or terms that might be misinterpreted. Child, marriage, and family counseling, as well as individual counseling and therapy, are fairly acceptable among SDAs.

A therapist should consider dressing modestly when meeting with SDA clients for the first time, not smoking during sessions, and making sure that there is no smoke odor in the room. Often perfectionistic and sensitive to criticism, often feeling more guilty about not having achieved perfectionism, SDAs benefit most from working with a very nonjudgmental, accepting therapist whose tolerance extends to being criticized by the client.

CASE EXAMPLE

Matthew, a 38-year-old convert to the Seventh-day Adventist faith, a former Southern Baptist, had married Lilly, a 35-year-old fourth-generation SDA. Their three children were ages 5, 7, and 13. Matthew had diabetes, serious allergies, and asthma. Both he and Lilly were depressed. They were living on the West Coast of the United States until Matthew was laid off when his company was downsized. He reported that he was a good worker. Lilly worked in a day-care center, but this was not enough to support their family. After looking for work for almost a year, they reluctantly went on welfare.

At this point, Lilly decided that they were going to live with her mother and unmarried sister (age 32) temporarily. Lilly's mother, Rose, and her sister, Jean, wanted to have Lilly home with them in Tennessee, but they did not want Matthew to stay with them. They had always opposed his marriage to Lilly. Lilly's family was much more well-to-do than was Matthew's family. This financial advantage and the fact that they were fourth-generation SDAs and Matthew was just a convert led Lilly's family to be less than accepting of him. Nonetheless, Lilly and Matthew and their three children moved in with Rose and Jean. However, the agreed upon division of labor was not carried out to the satisfaction of Rose and Jean, who had lived together since the death of Rose's husband 10 years earlier. They were used to an orderly, quiet, immaculate home. Rose gave Lilly a job in her nursing home, but she found only odd jobs there for Matthew. With his medical and emotional traumas, Matthew was fatigued much of the time and rarely went out of the house when he did not have some job to do. Rose and Jean accused Matthew of being lazy and complained that the children made messes around the house.

The fact that Matthew was of the same faith and followed the same religious traditions as Lilly and her family was one significant strength for Matthew's and Lilly's relationship. In addition, Lilly and Matthew had several years of college training. However, they were suffering from unresolved anger, guilt, perfectionistic goals, blame avoidance, and depression. Lilly felt intense anger at her mother's demeaning attitudes toward Matthew, but she denied her own anger toward Matthew and secretly thought that he could do better. Though Lilly sympathized with his physical and emotional problems, she blamed him for having such difficulties at all and for not being more healthy and perfect. Lilly was getting criticism from Rose and Jean: They criticized her appearance and objected to her allowing Matthew to just sit or lie around the house. They pressured her and Matthew to do the major part of the cleaning and cooking. Lilly reminded them that the husband is the priest or head of the home, as she had been taught as a child by her mother. Changing her earlier view, mother Rose now argued that woman and man share the responsibilities for the home and that they control life together.

During therapy, I first asked Matthew and Lilly to focus on commonly held goals for their family and for individual members of their family. The goal of the family was to move to their own apartment or house as soon as possible. A reasonable timetable for achieving this was agreed upon. I also encouraged Matthew and Lilly to look for temporary and permanent jobs in Tennessee and elsewhere. Finally, I agreed to work on helping them to overcome patterns of negative thinking about themselves and others.

As therapy progressed, it became clear that Matthew and Lilly were experiencing much guilt and shame for having to depend so much on others during this period of their lives. Their children shared these feelings, along with anger and frustration that things were not better for them. Many "shoulds" needed to be worked through:

- A good Christian should be charitable all of the time and especially to other family members.
- A daughter should be listening more to her mother than to anyone else.
- A mother and sister should be more supportive and less critical of their own family members.
- Everyone should know how hard one is trying to do better.
- Everyone should show more love and respect for others.
- Everyone should know what others think and feel.
- People who practice healthful living should enjoy a perfectly healthy body, mind, and spirit.
- God should allow those who are following the divine plan of living to enjoy a happier and more rewarding life.

Both Transactional Analysis and cognitive–behavioral therapy (logical reasoning and feeling) were helpful in working with Lilly and Matthew. Helping them to examine their irrational thinking was beneficial; for example, it may be desirable for everyone at all times to show more love and respect to all others, but this might not be happening in reality. Those who practice healthful living may ward off diseases and other problems for a period of time, but they may still be susceptible to illnesses no matter how hard they are trying to fight the good fight. No guilt or shame is implied by having an illness; it is harmful to flog oneself for not being perfect. Practicing more "love thyself" as well as loving others in the spiritual sense is vital to good health.

Matthew revealed that he had been so depressed, he failed to take his medication regularly or in the recommended dosages. As therapy progressed and he worked through his depression, he went back on his medication. Then, he became less fatigued and more motivated to work around the house and to look for work more appropriate to his training. Therapy with the family—Matthew, Lilly, Rose, Jean, and the children—looking at the realities of having several physical problems as did Matthew and bringing about better understanding and empathy for Matthew was one major outcome. Matthew was encouraged to take better care of his health (including taking his medicines and maintaining a proper diet) and not allowing depression and anxiety to imprison him into a box of self-pity.

Matthew and Lilly realized that the two families could not live indefinitely in the same house. They looked for job opportunities even outside Tennessee. Matthew negotiated with Rose and Jean for his family to remain living with them for 6 months until they could establish themselves elsewhere. In therapy, he worked on being less passive, especially with strong women with whom he was particularly intimidated, and developing more self-esteem. Within 3 months, he heard of a job in a neighboring state that would be available 1 month later. He interviewed for the job and was hired. Although it was not just what he wanted, the job provided training opportunities to secure the desired type of position. Lilly too found suitable employment. They found a modest apartment. Most important, there was more respect that each of these persons gained toward other family members as well as toward themselves. All of them seemed to have gained a lot by being in therapy.

HEALING PRACTICES AND BELIEFS

SDAs have an active prayer life and find comfort in worship services in general. Rituals or ordinances, such as foot washing, the Eucharist, laying on of hands, and anointing with oil, are seen as healing practices and social supports of the ecclesiastical community for SDAs. Reading Scripture and inspired works of Ellen G. White and other inspirational religious and spiritual writers is also viewed as healing for many problems.

CONCLUSIONS AND RESEARCH RECOMMENDATIONS

Further research on SDAs would promote insight into how to work more effectively with SDA clients. The following are some of the issues that might be studied further for more effective therapy and counseling with SDAs:

1. Gathering and analyzing data on perfectionism and authoritarian tendencies in SDAs, especially with regard to gender, ethnic, and age differences.

2. SDA attitudes about sexuality might be examined in light of the embodiment of religious experience (Rayburn, 1995) and the interface of theology and biology (Rayburn & Richmond, 1998). Although the Valuegenesis studies (Case, 1996b; Dudley, 1992) have made a good start, a large part of the adult population, especially single persons, was not included to any real extent.

3. Because clergy in most denominations experience stress that is related to difficulties in setting priorities, wanting to please everyone, desiring to maintain a saintly image, and other such issues, an assessment of

such stress before doing therapy with clergy would be helpful. The Religious Occupations and Stress Questionnaire (Rayburn, Richmond, & Birk, 1997) could be used for this.

4. The SDA population has many individuals who strive to attain and maintain very high moral standards or values. Having a measure of comparison between the generally held moral values and those situationally held by the person (as might be measured by the State-Trait Morality Inventory by Rayburn, Birk, & Richmond, 1996) would be helpful in conducting therapy or counseling with SDAs.

SDAs are similar to mainstream Christians in many ways. However, as demonstrated throughout this chapter, in some very important ways, SDAs are rather unique or at least different from other Christian believers. Knowing these similarities and differences will allow the therapist to work more effectively with Seventh-day Adventist women, men, and children. In working with Adventists, it is necessary to take into account geographical and subcultural differences and the fact that subtle changes take place over time, that is, even the most homogeneous denomination or group experiences a fluidity of movement over time. Thus, as with many other group observations, greater within-group differences are sometimes more evidenced than between-group differences. It is hoped that this chapter will help to ease the transition of therapists into a new and challenging culture in the world of religion and spirituality and to lend to the enjoyment and success of the dialogue between client and therapist.

SUGGESTED READINGS

Brunt, J. (1993). *Good news for troubled times.* Hagerstown, MD: Review & Herald.

Damsteegt, P. (1988). *Seventh-day Adventists believe.* . . . Hagerstown, MD: Review & Herald.

Knight, G. R. (1999). *A brief history of Seventh-day Adventists.* Hagerstown, MD: Review & Herald.

REFERENCES

Benson, P. L., Donahue, M. J., & Erickson, J. A. (1993). The Faith Maturity Scale: Conceptualization, measurement, and empirical validation. *Research in the Social Scientific Study of Religion, 5,* 1–26.

Berecz, J. (1998). *Beyond shame and pain: Forgiving yourself and others.* Lima, OH: CSS Publishing.

Case, S. (1996a). Basic considerations. In S. Case (Ed.), *Valuegenesis: Shall we dance?* (pp. 40–55). Riverside, CA: La Sierra University Press.

Case, S. (1996b). Thinking about jewelry In S. Case (Ed.), *Valuegenesis: Shall we dance?* (pp. 178–183). Riverside, CA: La Sierra University Press.

Case, S. (1996c). Thinking about movies. In S. Case (Ed.), *Valuegenesis: Shall we dance?* (pp. 331–337). Riverside, CA: La Sierra University Press.

Corea, V. (1996). The purity challenge. In S. Case (Ed.), *Valuegenesis: Shall we dance?* (pp. 172–176). Riverside, CA: La Sierra University Press.

Dudley, R. L. (1992). *Valuegenesis: Faith in the balance.* Riverside, CA: La Sierra University Press.

Dudley, R. L., & Cummings, D., Jr. (1982). Factors related to pastoral morale in the Seventh-day Adventist Church. *Review of Religious Research, 24,* 127–137.

Ferris, R. H. (1983). Pastoring the family of the institutionalized. In E. Hartbauer (Ed.), *Pastoral care of the handicapped,* (pp. 45–66). Berrien Springs, MI: Andrews University Press.

General Conference of Seventh-day Adventists. (1998). *Yearbook.* Silver Spring, MD: Author.

Gillespie, V. B. (1996). The butcher, baker, and candlestick maker. In S. Case (Ed.), *Valuegenesis: Shall we dance?* (pp. 225–236). Riverside, CA: La Sierra University Press.

Knott, B. (1996). Shall we dance? In S. Case (Ed.), *Valuegenesis: Shall we dance?* (pp. 65–78). Riverside, CA: La Sierra University Press.

Lovinger, R. J. (1990). *Religion and counseling: The psychological impact of religious belief.* New York: Continuum.

Rayburn, C. A. (1993). Ritual as acceptance/empowerment and rejection/disenfranchisement. In L. A. Northrup (Ed.), *Women and religious ritual* (pp. 87–101). Washington, DC: Pastoral Press.

Rayburn, C. A. (1995). The body in religious experience. In R. W. Hood, Jr. (Ed.), *Handbook of religious experience* (pp. 476–494). Birmingham, AL: Religious Education Press.

Rayburn, C. A. (1997a). *Inventory on Religiousness.* Washington, DC: U.S. Copyright Office.

Rayburn, C. A. (1997b). Women heralds of "The Advent Near." *Adventist Hentage, 17*(2), 11–21.

Rayburn, C. A., Birk, J., & Richmond, L. J. (1996). *State-Trait Morality Inventory.* Washington, DC: U.S. Copyright Office.

Rayburn, C. A., Natale, S. M., & Linzer, J. (1982). Feminism and religion: What price holding membership in both camps? *Counseling and Values, 26,* 154–164.

Rayburn, C. A., & Richmond, L. J. (1997). *Inventory on Spirituality.* Washington, DC: U.S. Copyright Office.

Rayburn, C. A., & Richmond, L. J. (1998). "Theobiology": Attempting to understand God and ourselves. *Journal of Religion and Health, 37,* 345–356.

Rayburn, C. A., Richmond, L. J., & Birk, J. (1997). *Religious Occupations and Stress Questionnaire*. Washington, DC: U.S. Copyright Office.

Reile, D. H. (1997). *Working with Seventh-day Adventist clients*. Silver Spring, MD: Unpublished paper.

White, E. G. (1880). *Testimonies for the church*. Mountain View, CA: Pacific Press.

White, E. G. (1882). *Early writings*. Washington, DC: Review & Herald.

White, E. G. (1889a). *Letter 7*. Silver Spring, MD: White Estate, General Conference of Seventh-day Adventists.

White, E. G. (1889b). *Review & Herald, 66*(1), 1.

White, E. G. (1891). *Review & Herald*. 68(20), 305.

White, E. G. (1892). *Steps to Christ*. Battle Creek, MI: Review & Herald.

White, E. G. (1900). *Manuscript 62*. Silver Spring, MD: White Estates, General Conference of Seventh-day Adventists.

White, E. G. (1902). The trial of your faith. *Signs of the Times, 28*(45), 707.

White, E. G. (1905). *Ministry of healing*. Mountain View, CA: Pacific Press.

White, E. G. (1915). *Gospel workers*. Washington, DC: Review & Herald.

White, E. G. (1977). *Mind, character, and personality: Guidelines to mental and spiritual health, 1–2*. Nashville, TN: Southern Publishing Association.

III

JUDAISM

10

PSYCHOTHERAPY WITH ORTHODOX JEWS

AARON RABINOWITZ

A person lives with himself for seventy years, nevertheless he doesn't really know and understand himself.

The gulf separating one's knowledge from one's actions is as wide as that separating the actions and knowledge of two separate people.

—Rabbi Israel Lipkin-Salanter

ORIGINS AND DESCRIPTION

Jews are acutely aware of their roots; this awareness is an important component of their character. Abraham and Sarah, Isaac and Rebecca, Jacob, Rachel, and Leah are not perceived as living in the distant past. Their presence is palpably felt and they are mentioned in every major prayer. God's commandment to Abraham to leave his father's land and travel to an unknown destination is not a dry historical fact; it signifies the beginning of Jewish history. The binding of Isaac as preparation for his sacrifice, the *Akeida*, occupies a central position in the collective Jewish consciousness. It is constantly referred to in prayer and served as a model to follow countless times in their long tragic history. The descent into Egypt of the patriarch Jacob, the enslavement of the Israelites by the Egyptians is the key to the forging of the national spirit, the evolvement of a tribal community to that of a nation. The miracles wrought by Moses and his brother Aaron leading to their redemption from slavery are understood as proof of God's omnipotence. Many *mitzvot* (commandments) of the To-

The author wishes to acknowledge the *Journal of Jewish Communal Service* for its permission to use material published in the journal.

237

rah are accompanied by the exhortation to view them as remembrance of those miracles and the redemption, as are the principal holidays, Passover, Sukkot, and Shavuot.

The most glorious moment in Jewish history is the revelation at Mt. Sinai, a unique religious experience in that it is communal, not individual. The two tablets containing the Ten Commandments and the Torah with its 613 mitzvot (commandments) are the symbol and essence of the Jewish spirit and character. The frailty of the human condition is exemplified by the sin of the adoration of the golden calf. This grave offense estranged them from God and has repercussions to this day (Exodus 32: 34).

Joshua, Moses' disciple, led them into the promised land, a conquest accompanied by miracles. The era following the conquest and colonization is identified as that of the "judges" culminating with Samuel who at first crowned Saul and, when he erred, crowned David. David occupies a special niche in Jewish history. He, the warrior, is the author of many psalms that express his complete devotion to the Almighty and that are an integral part of the Hebrew Bible. He was promised by God that the throne would be occupied by his descendants. Indeed, Jewish belief is that the awaited Messiah will be a scion of the house of David. Solomon, David's son, renowned for his wisdom, erected the temple on the mountain chosen by God upon which Isaac was bound, the *Akeida*. This was the golden age of Israel in that it was marked by enhanced spirituality. This, however, was marred by the split between the tribes of Judah and Benjamin on the one hand and the remaining 10 tribes, which came about upon Solomon's death. It is a matter of belief that the remaining tribes will in the future be reunited with the others to form a united nation once more.

The kingdom of Israel was vanquished by the Assyrians in 721 BC, and its people were exiled. The other kingdom, Judah, lasted longer until it was conquered in 587 BC by the Babylonians, who razed the temple that had stood for 410 years. This exile lasted 70 years, after which the state was reestablished and a second temple built, which lasted for 420 years until its destruction by the Romans. Both temples were destroyed on the same day, the ninth day of the month of Av, *Tisha B'av*, the saddest day of the Jewish calendar year, which is marked by fasting.

The era of the Second Temple witnessed the passing of the era of prophecy, which began with the Patriarchs and the emergence of scholars who interpreted Scripture following the rules laid down by previous generations. This body of laws (Halakhah) and homiletic sayings is the oral law. It is a cardinal belief of orthodox Judaism that Moses received both the written and oral Torah at Sinai. At first, the oral law was not permitted to be written, the intent being that Torah is to be an integral part of the person. However, circumstances dictated that it be written and codified in the Mishna and Talmud.

It is interesting that the rise of oral law scholarship in approximately the 5th century BC coincided with the termination of prophecy and the flowering of Greek culture. This resulted in the clash between traditional and Hellenistic Jews during the era of the Second Temple. The holiday of Hanukah was decreed by the sages to celebrate the victory of the Hasmoneans over the Hellenistic armies that sought to subjugate Judah and force upon them the worship of Hellenistic deities and the adoption of Hellenistic culture. In this context, Hanukah is viewed as a victory of traditional Torah values over Greek culture.

Study of the Mishna and Talmud, the task of deducing from them the law to be followed—the Halakhah—is an ongoing task. The Jews who were exiled by the Romans immersed themselves in study. The aura of intellectuality which earned for Jews the appellation "people of the Book" stems from the intensive efforts invested in Talmud study. The Rambam, Maimonides, codified Halakhah in his monumental *Mishna Torah* in the 12th century. The final and authoritative codification of the laws operative in the Diaspora, the *Shulhan Aruch*—the set table—was completed in the 16th century.

The Middle Ages

The early Middle Ages found the Jews dispersed in Europe, North Africa, and the Middle East. This led to the emergence of two traditions: (a) the Sephardic tradition, followed by the Jews of Spain, Portugal, North Africa, and the Middle East; and (b) the Ashkenazic tradition of France, Germany, England, Poland, and other European countries. This evolved because scholars of different countries at times differed in their interpretation of the Talmud and rendered differing Halakhic decisions. These divergent opinions are recorded in the Shulhan Aruch, the authoritative code of laws. These differences are minor and have not led to a schism. A distinguishing feature between members of the two traditions is that Ashkenazic Jews spoke among themselves in Yiddish, which is based on German; whereas Sephardic Jews conversed in Ladino, an offshoot of Spanish. American Jewry is mostly of Ashkenazic origin, although the first Jews to arrive in the Americas were Sephardic.

The Middle Ages witnessed the emergence of Jewish philosophy and Kabbalah, loosely identified as Jewish mysticism. This laid the framework leading to a systematic formulation of Jewish theology which articulated and defined Jewish belief. Biblical and prophetic Judaism was not presented as systematic theological principles. It was a system of laws, behavior, and moral precepts. The theological philosophical basis was not, prior to the Middle Ages, viewed as an essential component although, of course, it is the foundation of the religion. The most famous philosophical work is the *Guide to the Perplexed*, authored by the Rambam, Maimonides, who, in addition to being a major Halakhic authority, was also the leading physician of his era and a most distinguished philosopher who is quoted by St. Thomas Aquinas.

Kabbalistic scholars trace the origins of Kabbalah to ancient esoteric writings and to hints contained in Rabbinic Talmudic writings. The study and development of Kabbalah reached its zenith in the teachings of the Ari, Rabbi Isaac Luria of Sefad in the Galilee in the 16th century. It deals with basic theological issues such as the meaning of transcendence and immanence as well as revealing deeper meanings in the performance of the mitzvot. Kabbalah has had a profound influence on Jewry. In particular, its influence was pronounced on Hasidism, the movement founded by Rabbi Israel Baal Shem Tov (the good name) in the early 18th century. This movement rapidly gained adherents, Hasidim, and came to be embraced by millions of Jews in Eastern Europe. The movement poured new life and meaning into Judaism, rejuvenating religious behavior. It succeeded in this task without abrogating or altering the Halakhic framework of the mitzvot. Hasidism emphasized joy and prayer, forming communities gathered around a master, Rebbi. Often, the Rebbi founded a dynasty, many of which are still extant. Each school has its unique qualities as, for example, Habad (Lubavitch), which has established Habad houses on many American college campuses. Some Hasidim are identified by their clothing, long black coats, and other special garments and headgear worn on the Sabbath.

The Modern Era

The modern era wrought profound changes in European Jewry and to a lesser extent in the Sephardic community. Some abandoned their roots, becoming completely assimilated in the gentile community. Others saw fit in the late 18th and 19th centuries to found reform Judaism. This movement reformulated Judaism to conform to the then prevalent theories relating to the human condition, deleting the supernatural and negating the revelatory aspects of religion. At its inception, it substituted Sunday instead of Saturday as the Sabbath holiday. It has since reversed itself and follows the traditional Jewish calendar. The granting of civil rights to the Jews led to their participation in all aspects of culture and political life. The drive to achieve intellectual excellence nurtured for ages in the field of Talmudic study was for some transferred to scientific and humanistic studies. The changing political scene led to the formation of the Zionist movement, culminating in the establishment of the State of Israel in 1948. This and the Holocaust are the two events of the 20th century having the greatest impact on contemporary Jewish history.

Jewish presence in the Americas stems from the time of their discovery and settlement. The immigration of Jews to the United States was in waves, the greatest beginning in the late 19th century and overlapping into the early 20th century, when pogroms in Eastern Europe initiated mass immigration to the United States. Many were traditional Orthodox Jews who, however, in the main were not able to instill their religious values in their children. The freedom of opportunity, the education in the public schools which stressed the concept of the melting pot, effectively prevented the incorporation by the children of their parents' values, which were perceived as being old fashioned, backward European values. Many of the parents as well abandoned their way of life, some because of harsh financial realities. The work week consisted of 6 days, including Saturday, which is the Jewish Sabbath to be observed as a day of rest. Nonobservance of the Sabbath invariably led to discarding the other mitzvot as well.

The American experience spawned another religious movement, conservative Judaism. Many were dissatisfied with the solution provided by reform Judaism and yet were intimidated by orthodoxy's stringent requirements. Conservative Judaism's intent was to fashion a framework for religion more congenial to tradition and yet not hampered by what it considered orthodoxy's rigidity. Orthodox Jews are emotionally closer to conservative Jewry than to reform but are equally critical of both on ideological grounds. The orthodox position is that the Torah and its mitzvot are God's will and commandments and are therefore immutable and cannot be compromised.

Relations among the movements are strained, particularly between Orthodoxy and the other movements. A number of issues have contributed to the tension. Foremost is the controversy as regards the criterion for being Jewish. The traditional measure is that the mother's religious affiliation is the sole deciding factor. This principle had in the past been accepted by both reform and conservative Judaism, that is to say, they had not questioned the validity of this criterion. Recently, however, reform Judaism has accepted as Jewish, children born to a Jewish father even if the mother is not Jewish, a position adopted by some conservative clergymen as well. Another issue is the question of conversion. Judaism discourages conversion, wishing to be certain that the potential convert is motivated solely by inner convictions. It asks that the person fully accept the "yoke of Torah and its mitzvot." This is not required by the conservative and reform movements.

Despite these differences, the tension does not necessarily extend to relations between individuals. This is so because, although Judaism is a religion in the classical sense in that a set of religious beliefs and behavior binds people together in a religious community, it is also a community in another sense—a people bound together by common ancestry and a long shared history. This fact binds Jews to one another in spite of different religious ideologies. The basis, however, is a religious one. Therefore, individuals who come to share Judaism's religious convictions can join the community. The most famous example is Ruth, King David's ancestor.

Basic Beliefs

In addition to the Ten Commandments heard by all Israel, Moses was instructed in the Torah (Five Books of Moses) and was told to teach it to all. Moses is called Moshe Rabainu, our teacher. The Five Books of Moses, prophetic texts, and later works such as the Psalms believed to have been written by major figures, among them David and Solomon, constitute the Old Testament.

Orthodox Judaism's distinguishing feature is its commitment to Halakhah. The theological and philosophical premises were defined and formulated at a comparatively late date in its history, from approximately 900 AD by Saadia Gaon and others. The overriding influence of Halakhah has often been cited as being responsible for what some view, usually in a derogatory sense, as the overly legalistic face of Judaism. This criticism has been refuted by the eminent Christian theologian, Niebuhr (1963).

The basic theological beliefs accepted by Jewry were formulated by Maimonides on the basis of the teachings of the sages and their interpretation of Scripture. These stress that God is the sole creator of the universe and is intimately involved in the lives of humans. He is not corporeal, and His essence is unknowable. The truthfulness of the prophets, the uniqueness of Moses' prophecy, and the eternal nature of Torah are cardinal principles. God knows what humans do and think and will reward or punish them accordingly. Belief in the coming of a Messiah and the eventual reawakening of the deceased are also considered to be basic.

Non-Jews are required to observe seven mitzvot and thereby be granted eternal life. The mitzvot are general broad principles that cover numerous additional details. These include the prohibition of idol worship, murder, thievery, incestuous relationships, eating the flesh of live animals, and the positive commandment to establish courts of justice. Jews are bidden to observe 613 commandments. In this sense, they perceive themselves as a chosen people who shoulder additional responsibilities. It is expected of them, by dint of serving God, to remind and to rekindle in others the realization that there is a Creator to whom we all owe allegiance.

The mitzvot may be classified as (a) those that define our relationship with God and (b) those regulating relationships with fellow humans. The two tablets of the Ten Commandments are perceived as demonstrating this division and asserting that they are of equal importance. Men observe more mitzvot than women as, for example, donning tefillin (phylacteries) during the morning weekday prayer. *Phylacteries* are leather boxes containing Biblical verses. One is worn on the head, and the other is attached to an arm by leather thongs. Although the Torah does not specify why, it is commonly accepted that the reason for this is that a woman's time is limited because of her child-bearing and child-rearing responsibilities. Rabbi Samson R. Hirsch, a prominent rabbi of the late 19th century, reasoned that women are more inclined to spirituality. This is why, he explains, observance of even a lesser amount of mitzvot is sufficient to enable them to realize their spiritual potential. Prayers are recited three times a day, preferably in a synagogue having a quorum of 10. Women are required to pray, although they do not usually attend synagogue (shul) during weekdays. On the Sabbath and holidays, those who can usually do.

The Biblical holidays are Rosh Hashanah (New Year) and Yom Kippur (Day of Atonement). These days are set aside for soul searching and repentance and are days of judgment. Three other Biblical holidays are festive days commemorating aspects of the deliverance from bondage in Egypt. They are celebrated by performing specific mitzvot, for example, eating matzah (unleavened bread), having the seder ceremony on Pessah (Passover), and sitting in the *sukkah*, a hut not having a permanent roof, during the Sukkot holiday.

It is an interesting comment on Jewish character and Judaism's perception of spirituality that Torah study is the most important mitzvah. Although it is a cognitive task, it is perceived as cleaving unto God. Slander is the converse of Torah study and, as such, is considered to be a heinous transgression, the underlying concept being that speech, the unique human quality, is to be sanctified. Charity occupies a central place in the hierarchy of mitzvot. Charity and its twin mitzvah, deeds of loving kindness, are considered to be one of the three pillars upon which the world rests, the other two being Torah study and worship (Pirkei Avot, *Sayings of the Fathers*, Chapter 1, Mishna 2). It is not uncommon for orthodox Jews to tithe their income for charity.

Observing the mitzvot properly requires no small measure of knowledge. This is why Jews have always established educational systems, from grade school through yeshivot, institutions dedicated to intensive Talmud study. Orthodox Jewry is proud of the hundreds of day and high schools established by its communities in the United States.

Judaism's Position on Pressing Social and Moral Issues

The Jewish perception of sex is positive (Meiselman, 1978; Rosenheim, 1980). Marriage is a mitzvah, as is having children, and it is permissible to enjoy sexual relations provided certain rules are followed. This includes abstention for a period of approximately 12 days from the onset of menstruation, after which the woman is required to immerse herself in a ritual bath (mikveh). The concept of holiness that implies that one should strive to minimize physical enjoyment is important, but it is recognized that wide individual differences exist and that only the most spiritually inclined abstain from what may be considered superfluous physical enjoyment, even though they marry, beget children, and partake of the Sabbath and holiday feasts. Premarital sex is considered to be sinful. Homosexuality, male and female, is forbidden. Male homosexuality, involving as it does spilling seed, is considered to be a much graver offense. Binding homosexuals in marriage is considered an abomination.

Divorce is permissible, but not lightly considered. Both parties can sue for divorce in Beth Din, the court of law, but the power of divorce is vested in the male; divorce is not a court function. The husband divorces the wife by giving her the *get*, the divorce document. In bygone times, the Beth Din, if it considered the woman's claim valid, forced the husband to divorce his wife, by physical coercion if necessary. In our era, this is a sore point, in some instances causing hardships and problems. In Israel, the court can jail a recalcitrant husband, a course of action not possible in the United States. The German rabbis of the early 11th century decreed that henceforth the husband cannot divorce his wife against her will, which he had been able to do until then. In addition, they outlawed polygamy for European Jewry. Polygamy continued to be practiced until the modern era by Sephardic and Yemenite Jews who lived in Moslem countries. Divorced people are permitted and encouraged to remarry.

Birth control is generally not permissible. When there are pressing medical reasons, and emotional well-being is considered to be a valid medical reason, certain methods may be used. Halakhically, the rhythm method and the pill are more acceptable than other methods. Using the male condom is the least acceptable. Abortion is a grave sin, except during the first 40 days of pregnancy when it may be sanctioned by an orthodox rabbi. Thereafter, only if the pregnancy poses a serious threat to the mother will it be permitted. In such a situation, the mother's life is paramount and supersedes consideration of the fetus.

The Torah sanctions corporal punishment. However, the Talmud (Tractate Makot, p. 7, side A) teaches that the supreme court of law, the *Sanhedrin*, which is empowered to inflict the death penalty, should do so very sparingly. The use of alcohol is permissible; wine plays an important role in many ceremonies. On the other hand, the sages pointed to the righteous Noah as an example of the dangers of indulging in wine drinking. Illegal drug use is considered reprehensible; harming oneself is no less sinful than harming others. This is also the reason why suicide is forbidden. Contemporary Halakhic authorities have voiced their strong displeasure with smoking.

The Midrash (Kohelet Rabbah, chapter 7) relates that when the Almighty created Adam, He showed him all the trees in the garden of Eden. He then told him to cherish them and warned him not to harm them and destroy the world which was created for his use and benefit. This is a clear indication of the importance attached to environmental issues.

IMPLICATIONS FOR COUNSELING AND PSYCHOTHERAPY: THE JEWISH PERCEPTION OF ILLNESS AND HEALING

The Torah refers to God healing and preventing sickness (Exodus 15: 26; 23: 25) and to His blessing people with good health and fruitfulness (Leviticus 26: 9; Deuteronomy 28: 11). There is, however, only one mention of the physician practicing medicine. The verse refers to a quarrel in which a person is injured and treated by a physician (Exodus 21: 19). Nahmanides (Ramban), the medieval scholar whose commentary on Torah is second only to that of Rashi, explains (Leviticus 26: 11) God's promise to Israel that He will reside among them to mean that they will not require a physician's services. According to him, in the era of prophecy, a righteous person when ill would turn to the prophet to ascertain the spiritual cause of the illness. In spite of this, the Torah permits the physician to minister to the patient's needs and entitles him or her to payment. The physician should not refrain from doing so on the pretext that illness is God's punishment. When prophecy ceased, it was considered a mitzvah to seek a physician's help.

Religious Issues Relating to Psychotherapy

Seeking assistance for emotional problems is a bit more problematic than turning to physicians to cure a physical ailment. My experience indicates that orthodox Jews do not hesitate to seek a psychiatrist's help. They see no problem with medicine taking to alleviate symptoms. Psychotherapy, however, is for some problematic because it is perceived as denoting a value system not always congruent with theirs. The reluctance to turn to therapy is more pronounced for the dynamic psychotherapies and almost nonexistent for the behavioral approaches. There are a number of reasons for this attitude. The dynamic therapies are identified with the early Freudian version which is perceived as stressing the sexual factor to the exclusion of all other factors. Higgins (1959) discusses this perception of Freudian therapy which he sees as being raised by all religious people. In addition, it is perceived as advocating a libertarian attitude and promoting the pursuit of personal satisfaction rather than of responsibilities. Menninger (1973) traces the disappearance of the concept of sin in part to the rise of psychoanalysis and to the attitude it represented. There are, however, different opinions and some take kindly to dynamic therapy. The importance attached to the unconscious by both Judaism and dynamic psychology (Rabinowitz, 1989) and the method of analytic reasoning common to both (Jennings & Jennings, 1993) appeals to many orthodox Jews. It is axiomatic that the most important factor determining the efficacy of therapy in relation to this issue is whether the therapist respects the client's beliefs and customs.

The importance of modesty in the relation between the sexes has important repercussions. For some, especially for Hasidic Jews, a therapist of the same sex as the client is called for. This, however, is not an ironclad rule, and some deeply orthodox Jews do not regard this as being overly important.

Diagnostic and Assessment Issues: Presenting Problems

Orthodox Jewry was presented as a monolithic entity; this is correct insofar as basic beliefs and important customs are concerned. However, as has been noted above, there are certain divisions, and these are relevant to therapeutic concerns. Hasidic Jews, and to these may be added Yeshiva (Talmudic seminaries) students who elect to continue intensive Talmud study after marriage, constitute a slightly different population than modern orthodox Jews. The former are concentrated in the cities, for example, New York, Baltimore, Los Angeles, Chicago, Cleveland, Toronto, and so on, whereas the latter are in other areas of the country as well.

The presenting problems of the two groups are in the main similar; indeed, they are not much different from those of the general population. In general, the modern orthodox Jew, if concerned with a religious issue causing psychological disturbance, experiences anxiety because of the realization that he or she may indeed be deficient in his or her level of observance. The therapist should help them clarify for themselves their ideals and aspirations in light of their background, knowledge, and, if married, their spouse's expectations. The other type of orthodox Jew can experience anxiety because of a feeling of being below par as to religious observance. In this instance, the therapist should be aware that this feeling may be unrealistic, stemming from inflated expectations of themselves. The therapist may then have to concentrate on the patient learning to accept himself or herself.

A short list of some of the more common problems is provided below. At this point, it should be noted that the patient–client may consciously or unconsciously inject religious considerations or nuances, beclouding the issue at times. Spero (1986) summarizes two views of the issue: One holds that when "psychopathology is evident within an individual's overall religious commitment, such commitment may and sometimes must be sacrificed in the interest of securing mental health." He takes issue with the generality of this position. Another view, also extreme in his opinion, is "that religious acts retain their 'religiosity' . . . no matter what disruptive elements pervade the individual's life" (p. 34). Spero analyzes and discusses when a religious act is authentic, quoting the Talmud which, for example, denounces the "pious fool" who refuses to rescue a drowning woman lest he defile himself.

Allport's distinction between intrinsic and extrinsic religion seems relevant. Persons whose religious sentiments stem from deeply held convictions reflecting genuine involvement with religious concerns will probably be more amenable to realizing if and when their behavior is religiously authentic or is a neurotic manifestation. Allport's intrinsic–extrinsic scale does not seem to be useful for Orthodox Jews. Some of its questions do not tap fundamental characteristics of orthodox versus nonorthodox Judaism. Perhaps other measures noted by Richards and Bergin (1997) may be more useful. There is a scale which, although it does not explicitly measure this factor, is useful for clinicians who wish to assess the measure of religious observance (Vane & Hatch, 1997).

Marital Discord and Sexuality

A proper understanding of this necessitates knowledge of the laws pertaining to the relation of intimacy and menstruation. This has been noted in the section on Judaism's position on social and moral issues. Observance of these laws can cause sexual tension, at times accompanied by the wife's feelings that during that period she is considered less worthy. The positive side of abstinence is that it refreshes and renews the love and sexual attraction between the couple. This psychological effect has been noted by the sages (*Talmud*, Nidah, p. 31, side B). In instances of infertility because of the woman ovulating during the period when the menstrual laws prohibit relations, a competent orthodox rabbi should be consulted.

Fertel and Feuer (1981) have written a useful article, "Treating Marital and Sexual Problems in the Orthodox Jewish Community." The authors are a husband-and-wife team, orthodox Jews, a physician and nurse who are certified sex therapists and educators. They describe the technique they use, but perhaps more importantly, they discuss the broader issues such as diverse reactions by husbands and wives to the secular world, and the impact that this may have on sexual and marital problems. They also relate to latent homosexual feelings among males who attend all-male schools forming close relationships with their study partners, and the possible effect that this may have on marital and sexual relations.

Homosexuality and, to a much greater extent, perceived attention to other males pose a problem. Guilt feelings are pronounced because, as noted above, homosexuality is a grave offense. Spero (1986) maintains that this does not preclude professional attention of empathy and sensitivity when treating the homosexual, a position held by this writer and other orthodox clinicians. Male masturbation is not permissible, and its practice by adolescent males is a frequent cause for turning to therapy.

Intermarriage

The problem of intermarriage of Jews with members of other faiths is not common among orthodox Jews. However, the issue arises in those instances in which an individual wrestles with this upon being attracted to a person of another faith. Experience indicates that this may transpire in an individual who is not deeply committed. It is a basic therapeutic rule that it is unethical for the therapist to decide what is best for the client. The therapist, however, can and should point out the difficulties faced by couples who intermarry. Gleckman and Streicher (1990) reviewed the literature and suggested that religiously intermarried couples, one being Jewish, are at a much higher risk for anomie than comparable intermarried couples. The difficulties which may be encountered refer not only to the problem of different beliefs, but to a host of other issues including different customs, family orientation, schooling for children, and so on. This is an instance when the therapist can discuss with the client the feasibility of meeting with the community orthodox rabbi.

Identity Crisis

This in itself is not usually a presenting factor, but it does infuse other areas as, for example, the issue of intermarriage. When such a marriage is subjected to stress, as are most marriages, the identity issue is likely to surface. Questions such as, "Who am I? What do I represent in terms of values and traditions?" are asked. The issue of identity crisis is probably more prevalent today than in the past, when the American ideal was the melting pot, and many were eager to shed their roots. In the contemporary atmosphere, recognizing ethnicity and the wish or need to return to or, at least, recognize one's roots, are greater than in the past. Excellent psychological source material containing insights relevant to orthodox Jews (as well as to other Jews) are Kurt Lewin's (1948) essays (chapters 9–12 are enlightening; chapter 11 "Bringing Up the Jewish Child" is particularly useful).

The question of identity has significance for Holocaust survivors. Sanua (1992) quotes a study which found that survivors of the Holocaust who were conscious of their ethnic identity and cultural heritage were, in many ways, less vulnerable to severe psychic trauma. Sanua (1992) discusses the long-term effects of the Holocaust on children and grandchildren, as well as on the survivors themselves. In his review, Sanua also discusses alcoholism, drugs, and suicide in the Jewish community, citing some studies specific to orthodox Jews.

Terminal Illness and Death

Therapists see clients who are confronted with issues of death and the problems arising from such a confrontation. Judaism's attitude toward death is presented in two articles, by rabbis Soloveitchik (1974) and Feldman (1974). Rabbi Soloveitchik was a foremost Halakhic authority as well as the leading Jewish orthodox philosopher of our era. Chapter 1 in the volume containing the essays listed above, as well as other chapters in that volume, may also prove useful. They discuss the need to transcend death and to view it and the laws of mourning as a profound religious experience.

Treatment: General Issues

The question of which therapeutic approach is best suited for orthodox Jews is no different than that raised when applied to the general population. The therapist's respect for the religious values and beliefs is the essential ingredient for a successful therapeutic encounter; if, however, the therapist is convinced that the patient's piety indicates an emotional problem and believes that only a materialistic conception of the world is valid, the therapist should not accept orthodox Jewish patients. Ostow (1959) writes

> Every person whom the psychiatrist encounters has some attitude toward his religion, whether it is belief, disbelief, or merely a reluctance to commit himself; moreover he may be militant, casual, or indifferent about his attitude. In my opinion, none of these attitudes can be assumed necessarily to indicate neuroses. Militant piety is not a more certain sign of illness than is militant atheism, nor is casualness always a manifestation of a purely rational approach. (p. 1,790)

This leads us to the sensitive issue of the justifiability of offering treatment to a client if the therapy may undermine the client's religious beliefs. Consistent with Spero's (1980) views, I think therapists are obligated to explore every possible way to ensure that therapy be undertaken without upsetting the patient's beliefs. The theoretical basis for this position is that psychotherapy and religion serve different purposes and address different needs. Just as it is not expected that religious counseling usurp therapy when it is called for, in like fashion, it is correct to maintain that therapy not be used to undermine religious belief. For religious people, therapy, including modern therapeutic approaches attuned to concerns bordering on the spiritual, is not a substitute for religion.

This should not be interpreted to mean that religious behavior is not to be scrutinized, evaluated, and analyzed. It is a truism that religious clients may use their beliefs to justify avoiding discussing important issues. Some have voiced their displeasure about discussing their parents by invoking the commandment to respect parents. They can be told that competent Halakhic authorities have ruled that such discussions are permissible on the grounds that it is not meant to be disrespectful and that it is necessary to help the patient. It is the therapists' duty to help their clients recognize their use of defenses to skirt the issues. This will help them attain emotional well-being and hopefully strengthen authentic religious sentiments and belief. Orthodox Jews accept scientific frameworks, provided that they are not opposed to basic Torah teachings. It is axiomatic that God granted wisdom to people (Midrash Aicha, B., 17); therefore, scientific and scholarly findings are legitimate.

Therapy and Clergy Collaboration and Boundaries

There are rabbis and religious clients who feel that therapeutic alliances are subject to review by religious authorities. Discussion of this issue is clarified if a division is made between two situations: (a) when the therapist is knowledgeable in Halakhah, and (b) when he or she is not. Spero (1986) criticizes this position, targeting specifically the situation in which the therapist is knowledgeable; his position is not clear as regards the second situation. He writes, "Once a therapeutic alliance is entered into, the therapist can no longer allow his authority to be challenged or manipulated by encouraging the patient to maintain the surveillance of third parties" (p. 204). Greenberg (1984), Robinson (1986), and others felt that collaboration of clergy and psychiatrists is helpful. They did not relate to a situation in which the therapist is knowledgeable in Jewish law. This writer feels that in that situation as well, it would be presumptuous on the part of the therapist, even of one knowledgeable in Halakhah, to expect patients to regard him or her on a par with the teachers or eminent rabbis with whom the patients consult. In addition, barring the rabbi from the process is likely to be perceived by patients as interfering with their value systems.

The involvement of religious authorities in the therapy should be discussed at the onset of therapy, and guidelines should be drawn. The patient should be permitted and, if the situation warrants, be encouraged to consult with a rabbi. However, it should be made clear to both patient and rabbi that, barring unusual circumstances, no attempt should be made by the rabbi to influence therapy. The following vignette is an example of a situation in which guidelines were not specific and, consequently, the therapy encountered difficulties.

> A 24-year-old *baal-teshuva*, one who changed his previous nonreligious life to an orthodox orientation, married his wife on the advice and cajoling of his rather young rabbi-teacher. The marriage was foundering, and the couple entered therapy. The rabbi insisted upon playing an active role during therapy in advising the couple: at times, he sided with the husband and at other times, with the wife. The therapist was not comfortable with the rabbi's intervention but did not feel that the best interests of therapy called for him to object at that point. He sensed that his objection would result in the termination of therapy. The situation changed when the rabbi attempted to influence the therapist's handling of the sessions and when he offered advice to the couple that the therapist had strongly cautioned against. The therapist

became frustrated, which was sensed by the husband and interpreted as hostility directed toward him. This was correct; the therapist felt anger toward the client for not being able to leave his teacher whom, at this point, the therapist did not respect.

The referral source has an important effect on the patient's motivation and expectations from therapy. Patients referred by a rabbi may not be motivated to seek help as understood in the therapeutic sense; rather, their seeking help is seen as the fulfillment of a religious obligation to heed rabbinic advice. It is, therefore, incumbent upon the therapist to explore with patients their motivation in seeking therapeutic help.

Even when both the therapist and the client are orthodox, difficulties may arise in the relationship. Apolito (1970) suggested that analysts often encounter difficulty when treating patients with religious conflicts because their own conflicts in this area are unresolved. In addition, different levels of religiosity may be perceived as a barrier. If the therapist's level of observance is greater than that of the clients, the client may feel that the therapist looks askance at him or her. Conversely, if the client is more observant, the therapist may suspect the client of denigrating the therapist and the therapy.

Referral to marital therapy by a rabbi may be predicated upon the supposition that the therapist's primary function is to heal the rift and bring the couple to greater harmony. This is so because of the importance attributed in Judaism to consolidating marital harmony. It is therefore advisable that the therapist explain the difference between rabbinical intervention in marital discord which, in most instances, is geared toward healing the rift, and the therapeutic intervention which is primarily to deal with the pain, to empathize with the clients, and to foster better communication. My technique is to state that, although my hierarchy of values places a high premium on marital harmony, my primary function is to facilitate communication and empathic understanding of one another. I make it clear that this approach is not to be construed as denigrating the rabbinical approach, which is to minimize differences and appeal to ethical values, and that the therapeutic approach addresses different needs. I further point out that, although therapy usually leads to greater mutual understanding and in many cases reconciliation, this is not the only possible sequence of events. Greater self-awareness and understanding of one's spouse may cause the couple to feel that they are not meant for one another. This is understood and accepted because Judaism recognizes the validity and legitimacy of divorce. It does, however, teach that divorce is not to be taken lightly. The sages taught (Talmud, Gittin 90, side B) that the dissolution of a first marriage causes the altar to shed tears.

Religious and Spiritual Interventions

Exploring and Challenging Unrealistic Religious Expectations

Some schools in the orthodox circle teach the young female student that the ideal spouse is a scholar who will devote his life to Torah study. This generates a climate wherein piety and scholarship are the qualities looked for in a prospective husband. The bride may believe that her groom is a future leading Torah luminary. This expectation is potentially problematic and may result in disappointment, frustration, and anger. The situation is aggravated when the woman's continued employment is necessary to provide the family with basic necessities. The wife may feel that, whereas she is doing all she can—pushing herself to the utmost—her husband is not fulfilling her expectations. The therapy must include a thorough discussion of her expectations and a realistic appraisal of her perception of the ideals she was taught in school. The character, personality, aspirations, anxieties, and difficulties faced by her husband must also be discussed in full. This is necessary so that the wife gain a truer picture of her husband and not the idealized one imprinted upon her. The following example illustrates a conflict of idealized expectations with reality.

> A wife complained that her husband looked at other women. In addition to feeling slighted, she voiced her opinion that her husband was not spiritually inclined and that she felt cheated. She expected to be married to a completely spiritual individual and on the contrary, he, her husband, was gross and materialistic. Therapy, following the guidelines presented above, paved the way for a less distorted, more valid perception of her husband and her expectations of him. She began to realize that her husband, although a scholar, was human and subject to natural desires.

Citing and Discussing Religious Writings

Interspersed in this chapter are concepts and insights based on the teachings of the sages and later Jewish scholars. These can and have been used by therapists to elucidate a point or clarify a position in direct fashion, in addition to serving as useful background material to understand the patient better. Nadler (1983) used this technique. Spero (1986) also cited Talmudic sayings and other religious sources to make a point in therapy (see, for example, Spero, 1986, p. 197). Some additional examples of how I sometimes discuss and cite religious sources to help clients reexamine religious understandings that seem distorted and dysfunctional are described later.

Religious people live with the concept of the evil inclination (Yetzer Hara). This may bring them to view themselves as unworthy. This, of course, has important dynamic implications. The spiritual connotations may be no less important. A useful technique is to develop the theme that the evil in us is not the whole, the entire person. I have (Rabinowitz, 1994) analyzed the Jewish perception of human nature. The evil inclination, notwithstanding its power and influence, is not the totality of the person. The "I," the person in the natural state, is good because of the enveloping embrace of the divine soul (neshama). The Creator, however, has endowed the evil inclination with the power necessary to ensure that the person will always be confronted with situations in which freedom of choice is equally balanced. Viewed thusly, the Jewish conception of human nature is a sophisticated one. Man and woman are basically good. However, because reward and punishment, which is a cardinal principle, can be justified only if there is complete freedom of choice, it must then follow that the evil inclination be granted the power needed to balance the person's natural tendency to goodness. I further develop this idea by invoking the concept taught by the Hasidic master, Rabbi Shneur Zalman of Lodi, in his classic *Tanya*, chapter 9. He teaches that there are two souls (neshamot): an earthly one and a spiritual one that are in eternal conflict. It follows that the evil we may have or do is not the entire "I." This concept can serve to help the client see himself or herself as a basically worthy person.

The second example relates to the mistaken assumption by some that Halakhah recognizes only a whole or nothing attitude. Operationally, this means that the patient feels that he or she must be completely pure; nothing less is acceptable. This is a false assumption.

> A 30-year-old man was in therapy because of homosexual practices. He was not a confirmed homosexual, but did form liaisons for mutual masturbation, stopping short of intercourse. Slow but certain progress was made in therapy, but the therapist discerned the patient's dissatisfaction. The therapist's comments prompted a discussion that revealed that the patient did not regard his progress as meaningful because his homosexual practices were not completely eradicated. The patient regarded himself as a confirmed sinner because of his mistaken perception that Halakhah did not consider him a penitent unless he completely stamped out his behavior. The therapist pointed out the patient's error, asserting that progress in the proper direction, as codified in Halakhah, is considered invaluable and edifying and confers upon the person the status of a baal-teshuva (penitent). The therapist was aware that dynamic forces were at play. Nevertheless, becoming aware of the requirements of Halakhah was a positive contribution.

Penitents, those who choose to henceforth lead a relgious life, are frequently overly critical of themselves. In a sense, this is to be expected, entailing as it does a complete change of lifestyle. Their previous behavior, which is now seen as wrong and sinful, causes them great consternation. This usually disappears; if it does not, it should be perceived as an emotional problem and treated as such, meaning that the emotional issues present prior to the change of lifestyle have to be analyzed. At times, however, they tend to focus on relatively unimportant customs, wrongly perceiving them as essential. This leads to overstressing certain behaviors, even to the point where this can interfere with healthy personal and interpersonal functioning. My experience has been that this behavior subsides the more knowledgeable the person becomes.

I have found that emphasizing the importance that joy occupies in Judaic thought is helpful. This is so when the client's depression stems from a distorted perception of what God expects of him or her. This is not a panacea and cannot be expected to alleviate clinical depression. I refer the client to the verse (Deuteronomy 28: 47) wherein God chides us for not serving Him with joy. I then quote Hasidic masters who developed this theme. Rabbi Ahron of Karlin (1760/1981) taught that sadness is the basis of negative character traits and is the evil inclination's method of preventing the person from serving God. He traced its roots to arrogance, the person feeling that he or she should have reached a higher spiritual level because of perceived sterling character traits. This is arrogant and pompous, stemming from the person's belief that he or she is entitled to "more" in both the materialistic and spiritual spheres. There is no question but that one should aspire to greater spiritual levels and not be satisfied with what is attained. This leads to *merirut*, literally sorrow tinged with bitterness, not sadness. One can, he claims, distinguish easily between the two emotions or feelings. If the person becomes listless, wishing to sleep, and cannot stand himself or others and is slowly filled with anger, that is symptomatic of sadness. If, however, the feeling leads to renewed study or prayer, it has healthy roots. It is as if the person is saying, all is not over, I can become closer to the Almighty, I am alive and can rectify the situation, and immediately sets about doing so.

The presentation of these concepts and insights by the therapist is a form of spiritual intervention that can be practiced even by therapists who do not share the basic beliefs of the patient. The therapist can also discuss with the client his or her involvement with the community. Judaism is a communal religion in that its adherents share a long history and in the sense that many of its obligations are community oriented. A person who attends synagogue three times a day for prayer is involved with other members. This obligation, however, is mandatory when feasible, only for males. Women are not obligated to pray with others and can do so at home. There are, however, many communal activities for women which combine religious obligations and social activities.

The problem of male masturbation can be treated by adhering to the following principles:

(a) The therapist must accept the fact that male masturbation is considered sinful.

(b) This is not due to medical consideration, therefore, although modern medical opinion holds that it is not detrimental to health, nevertheless it is considered to be a transgression.

(c) Therapy can and should explore why the patient deems this particular transgression to be so grave that it brings him to therapy in contrast with, for example, slander, which is no less grave and yet in all probability is not as reprehensible to him. This approach can reveal the patient's conception of sex and its implications. The therapist should emphasize that in spite of its gravity, one can do penance. Rabbinical sources attest to the fact that Torah study and Sabbath observance are powerful antidotes. This argument and the other insights mentioned have to be worked through in true therapeutic fashion.

(d) Without minimizing the severity of the transgression, the therapist can also point out that it is much more difficult to refrain from masturbation in the modern era, which is characterized by open sex, immodest provocative dress, and mass media that openly flaunts different sexual standards from those in bygone times.

(e) The therapist can enter into a discussion of the sadness caused by the guilt feelings using the concepts presented above—the importance of joy and the nonconstructive aspects of sadness that can only serve to wean the adolescent away from spirituality.

(f) The patient may quote rabbinic sources that masturbation is damaging to one's health.

This is a sensitive issue and should be referred to a competent rabbi. The basic point is that, although rabbinic authority is accepted without question, this is so only in relation to Jewish law, Jewish philosophy, and ethics, but not necessarily when their writings relate to medicine.

These insights and case examples can serve to sensitize the therapist to issues in therapy with religious Jewish patients. The basic therapeutic principles are the same as those used in other therapeutic encounters (Rizzuto, 1996). It seems to be a safe prediction that in the future, orthodox Jewish therapists will glean additional insights from the rich store of wisdom contained in the Talmud, Midrash, and ethical writings (see Paley, 1993). This will be useful for clinicians working with patients, although it should be emphasized, mainly as an adjunct to therapy and not as a replacement of therapy. These guidelines and insights can be of assistance to therapists, Jewish or otherwise, religious or not. The most important factor governing relations among therapist, client, and religious leaders is the respect and sensitivity shown by the therapist to the client's beliefs and lifestyle. If this is evident, orthodox Jewish clients will feel comfortable with a non-Jewish therapist. Indeed this may be preferred by some clients. They would rather undergo therapy with a sensitive non-Jewish therapist than with a nonreligous Jewish therapist whose comments may reflect a secular viewpoint.

SUGGESTED READINGS

The following may prove useful when working with orthodox Jewish patients, either as background material or for clinical work. Material may be found in studies published in the *Journal of Psychology and Judaism*, and as proceedings of the Association of Orthodox Jewish Scientists in special publications and in their scholarly newsletter, *Intercom*. They are located at 1577 Coney Island Avenue, Brooklyn, New York 11230. Mention should also be made of A. J. Twerski, who is a rabbi and a psychiatrist. He is considered an expert on substance abuse. His publications are available at most Hebrew bookstores. Jewish religious and scholarly works are also published by and available from Art Scroll–Mesorah Heritage Foundation, 4401 2nd Avenue, Brooklyn, New York 11232. These include translations and commentaries on the Jewish Bible, Talmud, and prayer books.

Bulka, R. P. (1987). *The Jewish pleasure principle.* New York: Human Sciences Press.

Rabinowitz, A. (in press). *Judaism and psychology: Meeting points.* New York: Jason Aronson.

Spero, M. H. (1980). *Judaism and psychology: Halakhic perspectives.* New York: Ktav Publishing House, Yeshiva University Press.

Spero, M. H. (1985). *Psychotherapy of the religious patient.* Springfield, IL: Charles C Thomas.

REFERENCES

Ahron of Karlin (1981). *Beit Karlin Stolin.* Tel-Aviv. (Original work published 1760)

Apolito, A. (1970). Psychoanalysis and religion. *American Journal of Psychoanalysis, 30,* 115–123.

Feldman, E. (1974). Death as estrangement. In J. Reimer (Ed.), *Jewish reflections on death* (pp. 84–94). New York: Schocken Books.

Fertel, N. S., & Feuer, E. G. (1981). Treating marital and sexual problems in the orthodox Jewish community. *Journal of Psychology and Judaism, 5*(2), 85–94.

Gleckman, A., & Streicher, P. (1990). The potential for difficulty with Jewish intermarriage: Interventions and implications for the mental health counsellor. *Journal of Mental Health Counselling, 12,* 480–494.

Greenberg, D. (1984). Are religious compulsions religious or compulsive? A phenomenological study. *American Journal of Psychotherapy, 38,* 524–532.

Higgins, J. W. (1959). Religion: Contributions from related fields. In S. Arieti (Ed.), *American handbook of psychiatry* (Vol. 2, pp. 1783–1788). New York: Basic Books.

Jennings, J., & Jennings, J. P. (1993). I know the method: The unseen midrashic origins of Freud's psychoanalysis. *Journal of Psychology and Judaism, 17*(1), 51–75.

Lewin, K. (1948). *Resolving social conflicts.* New York: Harper & Row.

Meiselman, M. (1978). *Jewish women in Jewish law.* New York: Ktav Publishing House, Yeshiva University Press.

Menninger, K. (1973). *Whatever became of sin?* New York: Hawthorn Books.

Nadler, S. (1983). Torah-based family therapy. In C. S. Naiman & P. Kahn (Eds.), *Proceedings of the Associations of Orthodox Jewish Scientists* (Vol. 7, pp. 51–70). New York: Sepher-Hermon Press.

Niebuhr, H. R. (1963). *The responsible self.* New York: Harper & Row.

Ostow, M. (1959). Religion: Contributions from related fields. In S. Arieti (Ed.), *American handbook of psychiatry* (Vol. 2, pp. 1789–1801). New York: Basic Books.

Paley, M. G. (1993). Psychoanalytic teachings of the Talmud. *American Journal of Psychoanalysis, 53*(3), 247–253.

Rabinowitz, A. (1989). The unconscious: Its relation to the Judaism–psychology dialogue. *Journal of Psychology and Judaism, 13,* 149–162.

Rabinowitz, A. (1994). Human nature: Thanatos revisited. *Journal of Psychology and Judaism, 18,* 219–229.

Richards, P. S., & Bergin, A. E. (1997). *A spiritual strategy for counseling and psychotherapy.* Washington, DC: American Psychological Association.

Rizzuto, A. M. (1996). Psychoanalytic treatment and the religious person. In E. P. Shafranske (Ed.), *Religion and the clinical practice of psychology* (pp. 409–431). Washington, DC: American Psychological Association.

Robinson, L. H. (1986). Therapist–clergy collaboration. In L. H. Robinson (Ed.), *Psychiatry and religion: Overlapping concerns* (pp. 21–31). Washington, DC: American Psychiatric Press.

Rosenheim, E. (1980). Sexuality in Judaism. *Journal of Psychology and Judaism, 4,* 249–260.

Sanua, V. D. (1992). Mental illness and other forms of psychiatric deviance among contemporary Jewry. *Transcultural Psychiatric Research Review, 29,* 197–233.

Soloveitchik, J. B. (1974). The Halakhah of the first day. In J. Reimer (Ed.), *Jewish reflections on death* (pp. 76–83). New York: Schocken Books.

Spero, M. H. (1980). The contemporary penitent personality: Diagnosis, treatment, and ethical considerations with a particular type of religious patient. *Journal of Psychology and Judaism, 4,* 133–184.

Spero, M. H. (1986). *Handbook of psychotherapy and Jewish ethics.* Jerusalem: Feldheim.

Vane, J., & Hatch, M. (1997). Family environment as a function of religious observance in American Jews. *Journal of Psychology and Judaism, 21,* 121–134.

11

PSYCHOTHERAPY WITH CONSERVATIVE AND REFORM JEWS

LISA MILLER AND ROBERT J. LOVINGER

You shall love the Lord your G-d with all your mind, with all your strength, with all your being. Set these words which I command you this day, upon your heart. Teach them faithfully to your children; speak of them in your home and on your way, when you lie down and when you rise up.

—Central Conference of American Rabbis

THE PEOPLE OF THE BOOK: A BRIEF HISTORY OF CONSERVATIVE AND REFORM JUDAISM

Jewish history, as may be true of many histories, is compounded with fact, emphases, and interpretation. The history presented in this chapter is our interpretation and emphases on Jewish history, for the purpose of clarifying Conservative and Reform Judaism primarily as it is exists in the United States. It can usefully be read with the history in chapter 10, which, with its somewhat different emphases and interpretation, expands the reader's grasp of how it was that so small a tribal group came to have so large an impact on human history and society.

The Revolution of the Word

Jewish origins are not lost in the mists of a Golden Age nor are they part of an endless cycle. Jewish history begins after the Flood, when 10 generations of God's silence is suddenly broken with the startling command to Abram, "Go forth from your native land and from your father's house to the land that I will show you" (Sarna, 1989, p. 88). Well after the creation of the world, the curtain is lifted on the encounters between God and the people who became the House of Jacob and later, part of the history of Islam and Christianity. Jewish history begins with a most unlikely man, afraid of local kings but politely demanding that the judges of the world act justly. Absences characterize this narrative. There is no patricidal god murdering his father as in Greek legend, no masturbating god as in Egyptian legend. There is only one God whose spoken word quietly brings the universe into existence.

The Destruction of the Temple and the Creation of a Portable Judaism

Thus we have the roots of a narrative based on God's inscrutable selection of a flawed human being, a passionate concern for justice, and the promise of a land contingent upon an agreement between two parties and the good behavior of one of the parties. Out of the repetitive collisions between God and the people who came to bear His name, out of their struggles, frustrations, and demands came a text known as the *Torah*, often translated as Law but also meaning path, teaching, or way. *Torah* (the Pentateuch or Five Books of Moses) was their constitution.[1] This community came to choose a king, despite the prophet Samuel's warning not to replace God with an earthly ruler. With the defeat of Saul in battle, David was chosen, whose son centralized the worship of the people in one city and one place (the Temple in Jerusalem).

The death of Solomon split the kingdom into a civil war: Israel in the north and Judea in the south. Israel vanished into the Assyrian maw, whereas Judea was later swallowed, but not digested, by Babylonia. With many Judeans now by the waters of Babylon, their Temple in ruins, their God vanquished, they ingeniously created a portable religion (Dimont, 1962). Prayer replaced sacrifice, and study replaced the rituals that could only be enacted in the now desolate Temple.

Torah, Talmud, Community, and Temple

The detailed commandments of Torah were insufficient as life grew more complex, so an oral law (*Talmud*) emerged to interpret the written law (*Torah*). The Persian conquest of the Babylonian empire allowed the Judeans to return to their homeland, but their restoration of the Temple did not end this new form of religious expression. The Second Temple was

---

[1] For Jews, the Bible is composed of *Torah* (the five books of Moses), *Neviim* (the Prophets), and *Ketuvim* (miscellaneous writings such as Esther, Ruth, Lamentations). The initials form an acronym of TNK or *Tanakh*, a common Jewish reference to the Bible. Old and New Testament are not Jewish terms, nor is the organization and composition of the *Tanakh* identical with the Old Testament.

destroyed in the great Jewish rebellion against Rome in the year 70 CE[2] and a new and wider dispersion (Diaspora) began. Nevertheless, the communities that arose after the fall of the First Temple were strengthened by academies devoted to the study of both Torah and Talmud. They trained generations of teachers, counselors, scholars, and judges known as rabbis who went forth to disperse Jewish communities to provide the glue to bring them under one code of law and a coherent body of ritual, legal, ethical practice. These were the roots of modern Judaism. The tradition of priestly and Levitical descent continued, but priests no longer mediated between the people and God. The rabbi was a judge, lawyer, ritual expert and was learned in Torah and Talmud, but was not a minister and did not preach. Traditionally, they had other occupations because the Talmud forbade payment for being a rabbi. *In My Father's Court* by Isaac Bashevis Singer (1966) gives a clear view of the role of the rabbi in Europe as it changed in the 19th century.

IN THE DIASPORA

Dispersion and Adherence

Torah and Talmud are much more than religious law. There is civil and criminal law, a justice system, public education, marital law, parables, and so on. There was no essential distinction among the various domains. Despite the loss of civic, emotional, and religious life based on the land of Israel, the people never lost their yearning to return to their homeland (*Eretz Yisrael*).[3]

The Two Great Branches—Sephard and Ashkenaz

Jews branched out as far away as China and India, but the great twin trunks were sited in Europe. The *Sephardim* (a Spanish Hebraicized form) achieved a brilliant cultural life in Spain, whereas the *Ashkenazim* settled first in Germany. The most famous of the many Sephardic scholars was Rabbi Moses Ben Maimon, physician to the court of Saladin. Known as Maimonides or the Rambam (an acronym of his name), his profound commentaries and writings had a lasting influence on Jewish thought and were known to Christian theologians.

The high cultural achievements in Spanish society came to an abrupt end for Jews with the stark choice offered by King Ferdinand: conversion

---

[2]CE refers to the Common Era, whereas BCE refers to Before the Common Era. This is more neutral compared with the more common BC and AD.

[3]A number of common Hebrew words are transliterated into English to provide the therapist with a basic glossary of terms likely to be encountered.

or exile. Some accepted conversion, some converted insincerely, but many chose to leave. Jewish life continued for many of the exiles around the Mediterranean in Muslim countries where, although not accorded equal rights, Jews were nonetheless protected under Muhammad's laws as People of the Book. Life was often better in Muslim countries than it was for their compatriots in Christendom.

Jews in Northern Europe and England suffered numerous travails, expulsions, and migrations, partly from persecutions during the Crusades. Many migrated to Poland and Russia where life was peaceful. Eventually, persecutions increased and impacted Jewish communal existence. Nevertheless, a lustrous scholarly culture grew in such places as Vilna, Lithuania.

ONE JEWISH PEOPLE, MANY VOICES

Hasidic, Orthodox, Reform, Conservative, and Others

Hasidic, Orthodox, Reform, and Conservative are modern labels. The Orthodox (or modern Orthodox) arose from Rabbinic Judaism, the survivor of the many forms competing around the time of Jesus. It reached an efflorescence in 17th-century Eastern Europe in spite of local atrocities such as periodic pogroms. However, Jewish life was unprepared for the widespread slaughters instigated by the Cossack leader Bogdan Chmielnitzki. Angered at the oppression of Cossack peasants by Polish nobles, he struck at Jews, some of whom served as tax collectors and stewards of Polish estates. It is estimated that in the decade from 1648 to 1658, at least 700 communities were destroyed, 100,000 Jews perished, and Jewish life was devastated (Martin, 1974). Although Jewish life recovered slowly, it was left with an arid formalism in scholarship and worship.

The tradition of scholarship was revived after the Chmielnitzki slaughters, but Jewish life sank under the burdens of increased taxation, the decline of the Polish state, and emotional deprivations brought on by a sterile religious life. In the early part of the 18th century, change came from Israel ben Eliezer. He was not an exceptional scholar but enjoyed contact with the natural world and was an extraordinary teacher of children. Known as a healer, he brought a radically different approach to God. He was called the Baal Shem Tov (master of the Good Name) and taught that God could not be worshiped in sadness, but that joyfulness was essential. In addition, humility or modesty, and enthusiasm or fervor were required (Martin, 1974). The name that was applied to this movement was *Hasid* (pious).

Although the Baal Shem Tov left no writings, he did leave disciples (*tzaddikim* or righteous) who spread his teachings. This had a powerful, revivifying impact on ordinary Jews. The disciples of the Baal Shem Tov were powerful teachers who were regarded not just as interpreters of the law but as mediators between the people and God. Even more deviant was the development of inherited dynasties among their followers. Although there was little initial opposition, as the movement spread, those scholars and people not engaged by the Hasidic movement were outraged; conflict was inevitable. Some did the unthinkable; they complained to the civil authorities about the Hasidim (the followers of the Baal Shem Tov and his disciples), which further alienated many Jews.

The horrors of the Chmielnitzki massacres and later the pogroms sent waves of refugees toward the West where many settled in Germany and France. Eastern European Jews were not as influenced by the Renaissance and Enlightenment as were Western European Jews. The Jewish understanding of finance and trade[4] may have motivated some non-Jews to allow Jews to go outside the ghetto (Martin, 1974). Also, the humanism that suffused the Age of Reason led some non-Jewish thinkers to argue for easing the lot of Jews in Western Europe. Such opportunities collided with the complex, detailed, pervasive observances of Jewish life.

After the French Revolution, the National Assembly was formed as a legislative body that proclaimed the principle of religious freedom, but enfranchisement also impacted the tight coherence of Jewish communal life. Napoleon's effort to deal with Jews in the French Empire led to some retreat from the principles of the National Assembly, but much less than the wholesale withdrawal seen elsewhere after Napoleon's final defeat. The retreat was temporary and by the end of the 19th century, Jews in Western Europe had largely achieved civil rights. Reform Judaism, beginning in Germany in the early part of the 19th century, developed to take advantage of these opportunities. Reform held to the ethical essence of Judaism, but largely deleted the detailed ritual observances that were integral to Jewish life. Soon a reaction in Germany to these radical changes led to a partial return to traditional practices and education, known as the Conservative movement.

As more and more Jews in Western Europe took the opportunity to enter into and even assimilate into the cultural, economic, and political life of their countries, anti-Semitism intensified. Even conversion to Christianity, long held out as the entrée into European culture, often failed to provide full acceptance while cutting off converts from their people (Ettinger, 1976). Radical politics such as socialism became attractive, and some Jews joined in the general unrest in midcentury that led to the Revolution of 1848. Its suppression increased emigration to the United States. The Dreyfus affair in the mid-1890s was a crucial event. Alfred Dreyfus, a French General Staff officer, was accused of espionage after a cursory, biased investigation. Although it became known that another officer was respon-

---

[4]Because Jews operated from a single legal code based in Torah and Talmud, a Jewish merchant from Cologne knew what to expect when dealing with a Jewish merchant in Venice.

sible, forged evidence led to a conviction that was reversed only after an intense political uproar. Theodore Herzl, a well-assimilated Jew and Paris correspondent for a major Viennese newspaper, was shocked by the intense anti-Semitic reaction in France. His proposal of the creation of a Jewish State electrified the emerging program to reclaim Palestine and gave it an enduring impetus (Ettinger, 1976).

Jews Come to the United States

Jews first arrived in the New World in 1654, but their numbers were relatively small until the failure of the Revolution of 1848 and the Russian pogroms of the 1880s spurred emigration to the United States. Although anti-Semitism existed here too, it did not take on the established, institutional character that it had in Europe. Nevertheless, the anti-immigration movement of the early part of this century promoted legislation to restrict the arrival of undesirable elements from southern and eastern Europe, which included Jews among others.

Jewish life in America was less difficult, and because many Jews were from Europe, they brought a thriving Yiddish culture (theater, newspapers, books, and films) with them. The Yiddish language is based on 14th-century German with a mixture of some Hebrew elements and local languages. Yiddish culture might be characterized by sardonic humor, music, an enjoyment of legitimate pleasure, and a propensity for study, debate, and argument. In Europe, it was a thriving but largely self-enclosed society. The opportunities in the United States of the wider society facilitated assimilation as Jews moved into professions that were either closed or severely restricted in many European countries. They became craftsmen, police officers, labor leaders, and teachers; their children became physicians, lawyers, politicians, and college professors. Yiddish culture all but disappeared.

Jewish culture in the United States also was strongly impacted by the grave atrocities in Germany during the Nazi regime and then the development of Israel. The terrible pall of Nazism united Christian anti-Semitism with technology to nearly eradicate European Jewry. Most nations were "unable" to do anything, which may have fostered among American Jews a sense of distrust and isolation from non-Jews. In that a sense of oppression is woven historically into the Jewish identity, the Holocaust engraved this notion upon the identity of contemporary Jews. Yet, that out of the Holocaust came the state of Israel for American Jews echoed of fierce Jewish freedom fighters from ancient history. That Jews could fight in this century and win against overwhelming odds began a reversal in the Jewish self-image that was extremely important, especially to the older generation. The contemporary Jewish identity—enlivened and empowered by the formation of Israel—involves a commitment to justice and liberation from oppression through strength.

In the United States, some Jews felt that Reform Judaism went too far in deleting the Hebrew language from worship and discarding ritual. Conservative Judaism in the United States developed in reaction to Reform, as it had in Germany. Jews who came to the United States earlier in the 19th century were usually from Western Europe and favored a Reform practice. Conservative Judaism tended to attract those Eastern European Jews who were neither Orthodox nor socialist. For all this diversity, Jewish culture heavily influenced the wider American culture in language, literature, medicine, music, food,[5] the sciences, and the media. Some non-Jews assume that Jews comprise a sizable portion of the population but they are only 2% or 3%, about 5 million people. Their impact is much out of proportion to their numbers.[6]

Most American Jews are Ashkenaz, but some are Sephardic. There are differences in the vernacular,[7] Hebrew pronunciation, liturgy, music, traditional dress, culinary styles, and acceptable holiday foods, such as for Passover.[8] Depending on how assimilated to American life a Jewish patient is, the background factors of Ashkenazi and Sephardics may be of importance. Also, there may be differences within these two broad streams; for example, a Jew of Lithuanian extraction (a Litvak) may look down on a Jew from Galicia (a Galitzianer) in terms of intellectuality or refinement.

A devout Catholic patient once asked whether Jews believed in God. She may have heard that it is not *necessary* to believe in God to be a Jew. To not believe in God for a Christian may mean that one is not a Christian; however, among Jews, this is not the case. Many Jews have a strong identification as ethnic Jews but do not observe any of the religious aspects, although if pressed, these may see themselves as being within the Reform sector. Not infrequently, one finds confusion and even ignorance about traditions, holidays, history, and Tanakh. We have noticed that when Jewish students are interviewed about the holidays for the campus paper, their accounts can be sadly muddled.

ESSENTIAL LESSONS IN JUDAISM

Live in the Here and Now

Spinoza's characterization of Jews as a God-intoxicated people is correct but can mislead the unwary. Jews tend to be reticent in talking about

---

[5]The Campus Crusade for Christ Bagel Sale occurs without awareness of the irony.
[6]About one in seven of Nobel laureates is Jewish or of Jewish background.
[7]The common language of European Jews is Yiddish, derived from 14th-century High German; whereas for Mediterranean Jews, it is Ladino, a variant of Spanish.
[8]In the Temple, a lamb or kid would be sacrificed at Passover and eaten in a communion meal with God. European custom forbade lamb or kid in memory of the destruction of the Temple, but Mediterranean Jews allowed it. No leavening was allowed for the week of Passover, but European Jews prohibited rice (for example), whereas Mediterranean Jews allowed it.

God. Judaism emphasizes this life, and the reward of a good life is having lived it. Although it is believed that this life is not the end, what comes after is not speculated on. The Torah, which details the covenant between the Israelites and God, makes no mention of an afterlife; that is a much later development. Even the common toast, a central song in the film *Fiddler on the Roof*, is *l'chayim*, to life. This emphasis is not a form of hedonism. Legitimate satisfactions are God's gift and are to be enjoyed. Asceticism in a Jewish patient is a notable anomaly.

Attempting to Understand God

Many denominations begin religious instruction through teaching a creed and by defining God so a child can understand. This is not consistent with the Jewish understanding of God. Thus, although many characteristics of God are described in prayers (e.g., merciful, compassionate, forgiving, and so on), the essential view is that God is described by what God is *not*, as any positive characterization is a limit placed on the infinite. Thus the dictum that "anything that can be created is not God" summarizes the Jewish view of Jesus as being great teacher but not divine.

The Evil Impulse

The Jewish understanding of evil is that people are capable of evil (the evil impulse) since "the devisings of man's mind are evil from his youth" (Gen. 8:21, Sarna, 1989, p. 59) but not from birth. Thus, people can choose to resist evil motives and are responsible for their behavior.

There Is No Devil to Blame

Satan (*satahn*) first appears as a common noun, not a person, in the stories about David. An adversary (*satahn*) induced David to conduct a census (1 Chron. 21) which caused him a lot of political trouble. Later, in the Book of Job, Satan takes on a somewhat more distinctive character but is never an entity independent of God. In translating the Old Testament into Greek, demon (*daimon*) and accuser (*diabolos*) became connected with Satan as a more definite personage. To some degree, Satan or devil has been used by Jews when it was a popular concept in the surrounding culture, but it did not flourish in a Jewish environment.

Sin, Repentance, and Forgiveness

Nearly all the words for sin (*chet*) in Tanakh derive from archery, meaning to miss the mark (i.e., error). Two other words refer to transgression (*pesha*) and iniquity (*avon*) and appear infrequently. This is inconsistent with the modern understanding of sin as being deliberate; but even if sin is unintended, corrective action is needed. In ancient times, this meant a sacrifice to atone (literally cover) for one's error before God. Changing direction, often translated as repentance, first appears in God's actions early in Genesis. Later Israelite society is exhorted to turn or to change course. This expanded to include repentance over injuries done to other people. God is understood to accept repentance (turning away) from errors (sins) related to God and to forgive them. Injuries to others are not forgiven by God; reparation must be made to the injured party. Thus, murder may be regretted but is not forgiven because the injured party is not alive to grant forgiveness. This is extensively and poignantly discussed in *The Sunflower* (Wiesenthal, 1997).

Justice, Mercy, and Charity

The issue of justice appears early in Genesis with Abel's murder and God's punishment of Cain, but is imposed from above. The desire for justice also appears in Genesis when Abraham, told of God's plan to destroy Sodom and Gomorrah, challenges God to act justly for the innocent who might be there. But also Abraham's challenge asks for mercy for the guilty who are spared for the sake of the innocent. Favoring either the rich (because one is afraid) or the poor (out of compassion) is prohibited, but only "Justice, justice shall you pursue" (Deut., 16:20; Sarna, 1989, p. 161). Thus, the tension between justice and mercy is unresolved.

Charity is not the gracious and benevolent granting of help to the less fortunate. In Jewish thought, the word translated as charity comes from a root meaning righteous or justice. Charity, then, is the right of the recipient as a matter of justice, an obligation upon the giver, that may not be done in a way to humiliate or embarrass the recipient.

The Obligation to Enjoy

The narrative in Genesis explicitly describes God's creations as good —every day except Monday when God did not say it was good. The value of Monday has not increased in recent historic times. Certain things in the Garden of Eden were forbidden to humans, but God's creations are good. The duty to enjoy lawful pleasures is based on this and suffuses Jewish life.

The Messiah

Originally, a messiah (*meshiach*) was a human leader, anointed by God, and anointment is still found in coronation rites. As life became harder for Jews, the hope for a divinely appointed leader to rescue the Jews intensified and occasionally some individuals have claimed to be the Messiah, followed by intense disappointment in their followers. The dominant concept expects that the Messiah will appear when the world has been made ready to begin the messianic age, that is, it has been perfected through universal peace, justice, and plenty. In other words, not any time soon.

Holidays and Festivals

The holidays include the Sabbath, three festivals, the New Year, and the Day of Atonement. Some minor holidays developed later and, one, Hanukkah, coming near Christmas has been emphasized because many parents needed to "meet the competition" with their children. The Sabbath (*Shabbat* or *Shabbos*) is the first and in ways the most important holiday. A day of complete rest, it was a great humane invention and applied equally to men, women, children, foreigners, and animals. There is a Jewish saying that "as much as Jews have preserved the Sabbath, the Sabbath has preserved the Jews." For many Jews, it is a time for rejuvenation.

That which the Sabbath breeds is antithetical to depression: The celebration of the Sabbath emphasizes appreciation of and the opportunity to partake of life. Even the 7 days of intense mourning after a death (*Shiva*) are interrupted for the Sabbath. In contrast with the busy week, the day of rest is designed to evoke an appreciation of God's world.[9] The communal nature of the Sabbath allows for the fortifying of relationships on the basis of joyous terms. It is considered meritorious (a *mitzvah*)[10] to have sex with your spouse on the Sabbath.

The three harvest festivals are Passover (*Pesach*), Feast of Weeks or Pentecost (*Shavuot*), and Booths (*Sukkot* or *Sukkos*). Passover is in the Spring and celebrates the Exodus. Fifty days later, the Israelites received the Ten Commandments before Mt. Sinai. In the Fall, the late harvest festival of Booths recalls the sojourn in the wilderness. Also in the Fall is the New Year (*Rosh Hashonah*) and the Day of Atonement (*Yom Kippur*).

Responsibility

The view Jews have of themselves is complex. The Hebrews were not selected by God because they were better but because of a mission. The

---

[9]Some more traditional Jews will write God as "G-d," omitting the vowel. This is an extension of a basic characteristic of written Hebrew which has no written vowels. Vowel markings were eventually added at a time when Hebrew was not a living language. Since God's name was never pronounced except by the High Priest in the Temple during Yom Kippur, the practice arose of not using vowel markings whenever God's name was spelled in the text. An alternative developed by which the wrong vowels were used, which led to a transliteration of the name YHVH as Jehovah. What is known is that this was not how the name was pronounced.
[10]Mitzvah translates as commandment but commonly refers to a good deed.

chosen people understood themselves to be a people who also chose God, which led to a personal relationship in which God's demands were countered with Jewish expectations. This is perhaps most poignantly exemplified in the Book of Jonah by the account of a group of rabbis in a concentration camp who convened a Jewish court (*bet din*) and tried God for the unrelieved horrors then being endured. Being chosen for a prophetic mission did not make Jews better than others—it made their life harder.

SOCIAL AND MORAL ISSUES

There is considerable consistency between Reform and Conservative Jews, as compared with Orthodox Jews, in beliefs about social and moral issues. Were an overarching difference to exist between the beliefs embraced by Reform and Conservative Judiasm versus Orthodox Judaism, it might be that beliefs among the former perhaps reflect more readily those of the contemporaneous surrounding culture. The relatively integrated Reform or Conservative Jew may interpret Jewish law at a symbolic level rather than at the literal level, allowing for greater latitude in the formulation of the law and personal choice in its acceptance.

Sexuality

Superficially, the laws on prohibited sexual relationships in the Torah may seem hostile to sexuality, but this is not correct. Lawful sexuality is regarded as a gift and a joy. Embedded in the marriage contract is the man's promise of sex to his wife; the wife does not promise reciprocally nor may she be forced by her husband to have sex. Premarital sex is highly discouraged among Orthodox Jews; among Conservative and Reform Jews in the United States, it is largely a matter of personal choice. Incest and adultery are forbidden. Divorce is simple, easy, but less frequent. Only men may issue a divorce; however, a wife may sue in rabbinic court to compel a man to issue a divorce on many grounds, and Israeli courts enforce such rabbinic decrees. Homosexuality in men is prohibited, but the law is silent with regard to homosexuality in women. Both males and females are prohibited from engaging in sex with animals. It has been suggested that the prohibition of male homosexuality arose from the sexual–religious practices of the Canaanites.

Children, Parents, and Families

Children are very important in Jewish families and are often indulged. Boys have traditionally occupied a special place, partly because of certain ritual obligations; but for Conservative and Reform Jews, the *Bar Mitzvah*, which shows that the boy has reached religious maturity, is paralleled by the *Bat Mitzvah* for girls. Injunctions to "spare the rod" in Proverbs were probably a reaction to the overindulgence of children, clearly not a warrant for child abuse. Child sacrifice, so common in the Mediterranean world, was loathsome. Torah did not allow a Jewish man to execute his children as could Roman and Greek family heads. The offending child had to be brought before a court.

Children are expected to study, learn, and follow certain behavior patterns. Thus it is common for the child to hear "Jews don't . . . " as in "Jews don't get drunk," a powerful restraint on alcohol abuse. Although fathers are the leaders nominally, women typically run the family and if they are less idealized than in American culture, they have more power. The Jewish mother, fabled in song, story, and humor, is no joke. On Friday night, at the start of the Sabbath dinner, a traditional Jewish man would recite Proverbs 31:1–10, which begins with "A woman of valor . . . "

Traditional male and female roles over the past 30 years have shifted or perhaps merged. The scholarly ideal holds for young women and men. Increasingly, both fathers and mothers hold central roles in familial functioning.

Abortion and Birth Control

Child murder or child sacrifice is strictly prohibited in Judaism, but abortion to preserve the life or health of the mother is permissible. The Hebrew word for the fetus is derived from pursuer, recognizing the danger that the fetus poses for the mother's life. Abortion for frivolous purposes is not acceptable, but this may not be interpreted with rigor. An Orthodox Jew would most likely consult a rabbi on the struggle over whether to have an abortion; a Conservative or a Reform Jew would be more likely to accept abortion for an individually determined range of reasons.

Routine birth control is acceptable among Conservative and Reform Jews. Among Orthodox Jews, by contrast, birth control is acceptable only for specific reasons to include preservation of the life, physical health, or mental health of a woman.

Medical Treatment and Euthanasia

Medical care has an ancient and honorable history. Ascetic reliance on divine healing without seeking human help is incompatible with the Jewish view of the world. Related to this is the rabbinic dictum that to preserve life, it is permissible to break all the commandments (613 in all) except the three that forbid murder, idolatry, or adultery.

Alcohol and Drugs

Alcohol, in moderation, is a gift from God and features in many rituals and holidays. Drunkenness is not acceptable. In Israel, the sole alcohol treatment unit has empty beds. As Jews become more assimilated, alcohol is an increasing problem. Drugs are new, so Jewish law does not have a tradition to fall back on. If drugs mistreat the body, they are not acceptable. An ancient dictum states, "The law of the land is the law," so civil law on drugs is to be obeyed.

Dietary Laws

Jewish dietary laws are explicit but not explained and are often given a modern gloss to make them seem rational. Animals that have a cloven hoof and chew their cud are kosher (fit). The rabbit and pig are specifically prohibited because they have one characteristic but not the other. The animal must be slaughtered, free of blemishes (internal lesions), and the blood drained thoroughly. Fish with fins and scales are acceptable; shellfish are not. Acceptable fowl are listed, but none is a predator. Dairy and meat may not be eaten together, which includes fowl but not fish. The modern gloss is appealing: Pigs carry trichinosis, lesions indicate disease, shellfish are affected by pollution, predatory birds carry disease, draining blood is good because it is an excellent bacterial medium in a hot climate, and meat and dairy contain high cholesterol.

All this is plausible and attractive to modern Jews, but there is no evidence that this was the intent although before meat was marked USDA Grade A, kosher meat was as safe as it got. It is likely that these practices were, in part, a revulsion against Canaanite practices and that which was kosher was that which fit the category. Thus, meat came from herding animals, a nomad could work, fishness was fins and scales (Douglas, 1966), and if their herds were not predators, neither should their birds be. Eating a slaughtered animal meant taking a life given by God so such a meal was a communion with God. Only an unblemished animal was fit for sacrifice. To a lesser degree, there should be no blemishes internally even for ordinary meals.

The dietary mandates and prohibitions are observed by Reform and Conservative Jews to greater or lesser degrees. Some Conservative Jews are indistinguishable from Orthodox Jews, whereas some Reform Jews pay no attention to the dietary laws at all. Typically, there are varying degrees of observance.

The Holocaust

For some years after the end of World War II, relatively little was written about the Holocaust. Few survivors would talk about it even to their families, although there are data to suggest intergenerational effects. As the Holocaust gained more attention, the trickle of literature swelled into a stream and, finally, a flood. The return of neo-Nazi groups, the rise of skinheads, and the reappearance of a variety of hate literature has drawn attention. Later genocidal and ethnic brutalities have expanded the range beyond just Jews. What it means may well bear upon the nature and meaning of evil. There are experts who specialize in the treatment of Holocaust survivors and their children (sometimes referred to as the "second generation"). Although a wide range of coping strategies exist among survivors, there are important common issues that are likely to arise in treatment.

Anti-Semitism

Because of the history of the Jews over the past 2,000 years, Jews are alert to anti-Semitism as it is expressed in their own time as a continuation of this history. If times have changed more than this vigilance among Jews, it is because that many Jews know that this too has happened before.

Older Jews may actually have directly confronted anti-Semitism as a social hurdle, whether in attempting to purchase a house or in looking for a job. The younger generation, however, is less likely to have observed anti-Semitism detract from their personal or professional opportunities. In that a sensitivity and vigilance for anti-Semitism has become part of Jewish–American culture, the younger generation nonetheless remains primed to react to any trace of discrimination.

IMPLICATIONS FOR COUNSELING AND PSYCHOTHERAPY

We have highlighted a few elements of interpersonal style and attitudes toward treatment frequently found among Jews. As may be the case within any religious denomination, creed either directly informs individual psyche or indirectly informs it through culture. In this section, we point out ways in which Judaism and Jew history, either directly or as mediated by culture, shape some prevalent attitudes among Jews that can be relevant to treatment.

Debate

As an action-oriented religion, Judaism emphasizes knowing what should be done and doing it. Although the Torah provides many, relatively detailed behavioral prescriptions, these still do not cover all contingencies. But, there are also directions in the Torah to take the words to heart (i.e., the ancient concept of the mind) which supports studying in order to learn what to do. Because very few of the commandments are explained, Jews understand that their task is to interpret the Torah. To accomplish this requires study and debate. *Arguing With God* (Laytner, 1990) begins in Genesis, so unsurprisingly study, debate, and argument are Jewish indoor sports. Although argument can, at times, express oppositionalism in therapy, it has cultural roots. The old joke that if you have three Jews in a room, you get four opinions has a reality.

The tradition of debate, perhaps transformed into a cultural tendency to argue one's opinion, may enter into the psychotherapist–client relationship. Such a communication pattern is readily regarded as a sign of resistance, ambivalence, or confrontation were it not a customary style of communication and method of intellectual exploration among Jews. As in the case of any communication style, however, debate can be marshaled as the spokesperson for a defense.

Occasionally, in treatment debate may be conducted on both sides by the patient. Self-debate of this sort vividly resembles a conflict in that it involves competing sides and pulls the patient away from a sense of presence in the room. For some Jews, self-debate is a well-honed skill and not simply conflict, so it is worth exploring in an open-ended manner. For instance, self-debate was explored at the level of process with a patient named Martin.

Martin, was a 23-year-old graduate student who, at the time of treatment, would take substantial session time to weigh both sides of even the most trivial decisions. When we explored how he might be regarding my presence in the room during these protracted self-debates, he explained that he took my listening to be a sign of interest. As a child, Martin had come home from school each day and promptly reported to his mother the events of his day. His mother would listen and challenge him on various points. As he grew older, Martin would argue both sides of a point while she listened. Martin's interpretation of my listening perhaps illustrates a general principle that communication style reveals assumptions about the relationship in the room. That Martin had felt loved through debate per se was perhaps specifically Jewish.

Prayer as a Healing Practice

The development of prayer as a substitute for sacrifice after the destruction of the First Temple made Judaism portable (Dimont, 1962), but Jewish prayer serves to provide not only communion with God, expression of gratitude, and petitionary functions but also a form of self-instruction. The word in Hebrew for prayer (*pallel*) means to pray, to judge, or to examine. In the conjugation used, it can mean self-examination, compatible with a dynamic psychotherapy.

In Judaism, the usual worship service follows a structured pattern in the prayer book and although concentration or focus (*kavanah*) and emotional investment are considered essential, prayers are aimed at reminding Jews of their covenantal relationship with God, understanding what God wants and how one should live. Prayer and study can, in a sense, be equated. However, there are times when, in the course of a synagogue service, a public prayer for someone's medical recovery would be made.

Jewish prayer, usually sung or chanted, is learned very early in childhood. It is therefore not surprising that the familiar words and melody of traditional prayer can evoke a profound set of emotional and spiritual memories among adults. If prayer harkens in the psyche to a time prior to illness, it may exert an uplifting or organizing effect on the patient's psyche. In its content, Jewish prayer may exert this effect through engendering an appreciation for the elements of life: nature, sustenance, protection, and family. Counting one's blessings is essential to traditional prayer; 19 blessings are specifically stated during a central portion of the regular weekday service. Finally, prayer is typically a communal activity, requiring a minimum of 10 adults as a quorum (*minyan*) to link Jews with their ancestors as people in prayer throughout time. This is perhaps illustrated in the story of an elderly Jewish man who says to his friend, "When you *daven* (pray), you recite so rapidly, but when I see you study Talmud, you speak so slowly." The friend replies, "When I *daven*, I am talking to God, but when I study, God is talking to me."

For some Jews, particularly for Orthodox Jews, it may seem inappropriate to conduct traditional Jewish prayers in session because Jewish law stipulates specific occasions and settings in which many traditional prayers are to be said. There is likely to be great benefit to a treatment, however, in drawing upon the client's experiences associated with traditional prayer. When introduced into the treatment process, the client's experience associated with prayer can illuminate the greater spiritual Truth underneath a treatment issue. For example, the sense of renewal associated with the traditional prayers of Yom Kippur may uproot entrenched guilt or anger and inspire interpersonal forgiveness. Unresolved grief may become less intransigent if the client recalls the spiritual comfort and sense of purpose evoked through the Mourners Kaddish. Wedded to traditional prayers are psychospiritual experiences that can broaden the material in session beyond that produced by the habitual working of the ego, often prompting fresh insight and clarity.

Although the conduct of a traditional prayer in session would be unusual for some Jews, other Jews (particularly more Reform Jews) may benefit from prayers spoken from the heart, if not in traditional language. A prayer for guidance or a prayer for deepened love toward family or God may reorient the psyche along the axis of truth, creating emotional strength, greater moral regard, and vision.

Some less observant Jews may feel estranged from prayer or doubtful about the existence of a spiritual force, perhaps as part of an estrangement from Judaism associated with its social–political history. For such a client, a shared prayer or even an exploration of prayer may prompt a spiritual reawakening. In that religious observance and comfort with prayer are often transmitted through family, a spiritual reawakening may generate insight into the suffering and gifts of familial history as well as acceptance.

Community

The role of the Jewish community in healing, as well as in celebration of joy, is a central method of sustenance in Judaism. The Mourners Prayer said for a deceased relative is recited in unison, often as the entire prayer community stands together. Throughout the conduct of a prayer service in Reform or Conservative Judaism, specific prayers are to be recited as a community, never alone. Before a Torah service can begin, at least 10 adult Jews must be present.

Rituals surrounding the full spectrum of life events often are conducted before the entire Jewish community. A baby usually receives a Hebrew name before the entire congregation. Members of the Jewish community, whether or not close personal friends, visit the family following the death of a fellow member of the community, as that family "sits Shiva." Bar Mitzvah and Bat Mitzvah concern entrance as an adult into the Jewish community; marriage is a contract before the community. Following the most sacred prayer service of all, weekly Sabbath, the entire community breaks bread together. In a practical, every day sense, a Reform or Jewish community often will have a youth group and social events to spawn personal friendships.

Psychotherapy may benefit from an appreciation of the role of community in coping and healing. A Jewish community rallies in support, celebration, or mourning around any given member. Picking and choosing to show interest or offer assistance on the basis of personal taste in companionship is inconsistent with the very nature of the Jewish community. One interpretation of the often recited refrain of thanks to "God of Abraham, Isaac, and Jacob" (each of the three men having varying capability) is that Jews are joined together simply for being Jews. In the concise words of one contemporary rabbi, "Our community is not exclusively comprised of 'best-hits' Jews—it is every Jew." A Jewish community is predicated on global acceptance and support of all members.

Ritual

For Reform or Conservative Jews, who often are integrated into the surrounding contemporaneous culture, Jewish ritual can serve as the primary vehicle for the transmission of Jewish values and beliefs. "More than Jews have kept Shabbat, Shabbat has kept the Jews" is one example of the power of observance of ritual in maintaining faith. Jewish rituals, like many religious rituals, induct observers into the history and spiritual knowledge held in the religion. Often returning to this place of knowledge can be quite healing for a patient who through painful life events or depression has become estranged.

June, a 38-year-old depressed woman on an inpatient unit had intense feelings of guilt and unworthiness. Her stay on the inpatient unit happened to overlap with Yom Kippur, such that she participated in a service that included the ritualized collective recitation of prayer, admission of sin, and request for forgiveness. Following the service, June noted that although each year she had participated in Yom Kippur, this year in her condition, she had a fresh insight. She explained, "I always knew that I could ask for forgiveness, this year it dawned on me that I could be forgiven." June's insight, derived through the spiritual experience of Yom Kippur, was then integrated with help from her therapist in ongoing psychotherapy.

A Jewish Science

Jews are typically familiar with and comfortable with therapy whether or not they have personally been in treatment. That Freud was a Jew and worried that psychoanalysis would be dismissed in the anti-Semitic climate of some areas of Europe as a Jewish science, perhaps even raises a question of how the very process of psychotherapy may reflect Jewish cultural and religious traditions and values (Bakan, 1958). Elements of Jewish law and its study may have informed psychoanalysis. For instance, Jewish law acknowledges and allows for the full range of human motives (provided that we engage in right action), much as psychoanalysis is predicated on the existence of both constructive drives (Eros) and destructive drives (Thanatos). Study of Jewish law involves exploration of the meaning and motive in the narrative of the Torah to include interpretation of symbol, much in the manner by which dreams, daydreams, and perceptions are interpreted through psychoanalysis. Jewish scholars attempt to near the truth through a collaborative analysis, a process that parallels elements of the working relationship in psychoanalysis. The analyst, as a presumed learned person, is granted the authority to make interpretation of psychic narrative, much as a rabbi derives authority and offers counsel through interpretation of Jewish law.

The broad epistemological similarities between study of Talmud and psychoanalysis may contribute to a particular comfort with psychoanalysis among Jews. At the very least, there may be a Jewish sensibility embedded in the assumptions underlying psychoanalysis which allows Jews to feel at home in the process of psychoanalysis. A study conducted during the initial popularization of psychoanalysis in the 1950s found 83% of Jewish psychiatrists to be psychoanalytically oriented, whereas 88% of non-Jewish psychiatrists were found to be biologically oriented (Hollingshead & Redlich, 1958). During the subsequent heyday of psychoanalysis, there was a particular tendency for Jewish psychotherapists to be psychoanalytically oriented (Lewis, 1978) and for Jews to be highly represented among patients seeking psychoanalysis. Data ascertained from 30 analysts from the East Coast in the mid to late 1960s showed that 40% of their patients were Jewish, 33% were Protestant, 13% were Catholic, and 12% were without religious affiliation (Weintraub & Aaronson, 1968). As these findings suggest, coming to therapy is generally not stigmatized among Jews. It may even be viewed by some Jews as being a routine approach to resolving personal distress or to deriving meaning. Among Jews who feel estranged from Judaism, the insights derived through psychoanalysis may provide meaning or even inform a worldview. In the face of the current move away from psychoanalytically oriented treatments, there remains a high rate of Jews seeking psychotherapy (Larson & Larson, 1994), perhaps reflecting a comfort with the fundamental elements of psychotherapy (such as healing through relationship or interpretation of the narratives in the living).

Non-Jewish Therapists

Non-Jewish society in the abstract is likely to be regarded with some degree of wariness by the older generation of Jews or perhaps by Orthodox Jews, but most Reform and Conservative Jews have extensive, warm relationships with Gentiles. Overt anti-Semitism is at nearly historic lows in the United States, but there are incidents of synagogue vandalism or violence, and one may hear phrases like "to Jew someone down." If a client has experienced anti-Semitism directly, then a therapist might explore the issue with considerable gentleness, as in the case of any trauma or experience of discrimination. Absent specific experience of anti-Semitism, a patient's difficulty with trust is likely to stem from other issues.

There is a shared language and set of sensibilities that tend to create an instant ease between Jews. A non-Jewish therapist may find that Jewish patients consider it essential to explain certain cultural aspects of their lives and how Judaism was expressed in their family of origin. Direct questioning of even mistaken perceptions of Judaism by a non-Jew can pose a bump in the road unless an alliance has been established. But once the therapist is seen to appreciate the significance of Judaism in the patient's life, the patient is likely to feel significantly more understood.

Belief and Action

Judaism emphasizes right action (orthopraxis). Good actions are imperative, whereas good beliefs (orthodoxy) are not. Action will bring justice, not a passive reliance on divine intervention. Turning to action in times of discomfort and tribulation is therefore stylistically familiar for many Jews.

The notion that action resolves difficulty may lead to several assumptions worthy of being examined in treatment, the most prominent perhaps being that of responsibility and guilt. In the face of misfortune, Jewish patients may be particularly likely to insist that somehow they might have reversed the course of misfortune. A haunting sense of responsibility for the suffering of others is religiously and culturally innate to many Jews.

TREATMENT ISSUES

Religious beliefs alone do not present as problem areas in therapy. Rather, the therapist seeks to decipher how the client's individual issues have picked up, often to the point of distortion, a creed or religiously informed culture. We do not mean to claim that the following treatment issues are expressions of Judaism. Rather, we highlight specific expressions of how Judaism and elements of Jewish culture are sometimes appropriated by the conflicts, defenses, and misunderstandings of specific individuals. In other words, the normative stuff of psychotherapy must present within some cultural and religious context (even if it is secular materialism). We wish to show how typical treatment issues might discolor otherwise auspicious Jewish beliefs and practices.

Changing Jewish Identity

Following immigration to the United States, many Jews had a strong sense of being a Jew, at least culturally if not religiously. This was reinforced by the treatment they received. Now that many Jews have assimilated into American culture, the centrality of Jewish identity considerably varies, and for some, it is not what it used to be. Some self-identified Jews have been to synagogue less than a dozen times, have never lit Sabbath candles in their home, nor learned any Hebrew. Others, after an aversive Jewish upbringing, have consciously separated themselves.

Among nonreligious Jews, there is a lingering sense of being Jewish that is perhaps based upon a sense of family identity, heritage, or tribe. The obvious history of oppression for many is woven into this sense of tribal membership. What results is a sense of belonging to a tribe that had been oppressed. Such an identity is difficult to maintain, however, in that being an oppressed tribal member has become more difficult to confirm in the United States. This collective change in Jewish identity may affect old and young people differentially. Young Jews may see an identity based on oppression and a thorough Jewish education to be something of a paradox or perhaps even puzzling. Older Jews may view this shift in Jewish identity as something of a loss and perhaps a surprise, for it was once taken for granted among Jews that a certain base of Jewish knowledge would naturally be passed through the generations.

Idiosyncrasy or Tradition

Whatever one's position on the ultimate question of the source(s) (human, divine, or a mixture) of various scriptures important to different traditions, once past the point of origin, human influences appear. Because all religions contain the record of human experience, they are complex and show real or apparent inconsistencies. Individual adherents select what to emphasize and to underplay, and it is at this juncture that individual or group motives come into play. Thus when some religious practice, belief, or sentiment is emphasized, it may express the significance either to the group or to the individual. The therapist may want to make this distinction to evaluate whether this is an idiosyncrasy or a tradition. For instance, a non-Jewish therapist working with a troubled Jewish youngster recounted, as evidence of psychotic thinking, that the child reported putting a spread on bread and other foods composed of animal fat. He told this to a knowledgeable Jewish colleague but further inquiry disclosed that the animal fat was rendered chicken fat. The colleague laughed and said this was *schmaltz*, a common European practice, since butter as a spread could not be combined with meat in the same meal.

For a Conservative Jew close to the Orthodox end of the spectrum, a strong concern about giving to charity, to the point of substantially reducing available income for the genuine family needs, may be unusual but perhaps within the range of group practice. For a Reform Jew close to the liberal end of the spectrum, this would likely be idiosyncratic. Because Judaism is a highly detailed, articulated religion, it is impossible in this space to detail the various possibilities, so consultation with a rabbi or a person knowledgeable in that segment of the tradition is likely to be necessary. If the client is a woman and the issue has to do with some culinary, household, or feminine practice, consulting a male rabbi may not be one's first choice.

Rates of Depression and Substance Abuse

Epidemiological findings suggest that, among Jews, rates of depression are slightly higher, whereas rates of substance use and abuse are somewhat lower than among Catholics or Protestants (Yeung & Greenwald, 1992). Despite a century-old perception among psychotherapists consistent with these epidemiological findings (Charcot, 1889), to date there exists no conclusive evidence explaining the difference in rates of psychiatric disorder. It may be that among Jews a tendency toward an enmeshed family structure or possibly a culturally based internalizing style of dealing with stress contributes to the elevated rates of depression. Although it is comparably difficult to speculate on the cause of low rates of alcoholism, it may be that Jewish law protects against externalizing behavior through ritual that binds painful emotion. The emphasis in Jewish law that prayer and ritual be conducted as a community may also serve to protect against substance abuse.

Paranoia

Belief that hostility lives outside of the self is not without valid historical precedent among Jews. As such, paranoia among Jews might be viewed as being reality based. Particularly among elder Jews, the echo of the Holocaust continues to inspire a fear and distrust of non-Jews, as well as a vigilance with regard to the use and abuse of power. Insofar as anti-Semitism has waned and the Holocaust is less immediate for younger Jews, paranoia might be viewed as an element of personality or a habit of thought handed down through generations, if not selected for by the hand of injustice. Another possibility is that extreme paranoia, cloaked in the language of tradition, is a thinly veiled primitive defense.

Intellectual Identification

There is a tradition of prestige in Judaism associated with learning Torah and Talmud, which culturally has been expressed as status and appeals through knowledge and intelligence. Traditionally reserved for men, this prowess was passed from father to son or teacher to student. A son might borrow his father's style of reasoning or quote bits of rabbinic wisdom. Masculinity was intertwined with learnedness.

Daughters have more recently become official intellectual keepers, raising the interesting question of how learnedness presents in Jewish women. The role of the father in female development can sometimes be traced through the threads of intellectualism. In this sense, father-identified Jewish daughters may resemble the once canonical firstborn Jewish son. In that intellectualism can serve as a bridge for connection between Jewish children and their fathers, it may be fruitful in treatment to consider what is revealed about primary childhood relationships through the role of intellectualism in psychological functioning.

Feeling Responsible

Emphasis upon the intergenerational family often accentuates feelings of responsibility and commitment among children, parents, and grandparents. In a Jewish client seeking psychotherapy, responsibility may present as guilt, not because the client has been remiss in familial duties but rather because of enmeshment among generations or excessive reliance on one generation by another.

Josh, a businessman his 30s, reported a family situation that was in some ways typical of this phenomenon. Over 15 years prior to his seeking therapy, Josh's parents had divorced. Both his father, a successful real-estate developer, and his mother, an independent business woman, had gone on to remarry. As is often the case in adult children of divorce, Josh felt somehow responsible to look after his mother. Perhaps less typical, his mother expected—in fact overtly requested—excessive and unnecessary financial assistance from her son. Despite her income being considerably greater than his, Josh had recently laid the down payment on a new home for his mother. Josh explained this responsibility by his role as a good Jewish son. That this arrangement did not reflect the duty of a Jewish son occurred to Josh only after considerable exploration of his own feelings of anger about the relationship. His culturally based view of familial commitment had been distorted into a misguided sense of duty by a maternal sense of entitlement and mother–son enmeshment.

Intermarriage

Because Jews have always been few in number compared with the larger societies they lived in, marriage outside the group threatened group survival. Such marriages are attractive for various dynamic reasons (Lovinger, 1984). In Europe where prejudice against Jews was more severe and pervasive, such marriages often presaged the loss of a community member, if not outright conversion. In the United States, the situation is more complex. The Jewish spouse might drift away, convert, convert the non-Jewish spouse, or both may remain within their respective traditions, or neither tradition will be maintained.

Against the backdrop of a 4,000-year-old legacy, some Jews feel that intermarriage is an act of killing off a faith guarded, cherished, and a source of sacrifice by ancestors. Parents of adult children can feel very guilty and responsible for not having more thoroughly educated their children about Judaism or observed the traditions. Where a Jewish client has little or no reaction, or thinks intermarriage is a desirable event, the therapist may want to be alert to specific deficiencies in the early parent–child relationship.

Not infrequently, the non-Jewish spouse will convert, to keep peace in the family, or for dynamic reasons related to the family of origin, or because the person is attracted to Judaism. Strictly speaking, such conversions are technically invalid because one may not convert for any gain, even though this is the most frequent motive. Genuine conversion to Judaism may be more readily likened to immigrating than to rearranging the intellectual furniture. Rabbinic law requires that the conversion never be mentioned after the first time the convert is "called to the Torah" during a worship service, but this is not always observed and occasionally, in anger, a reminder of conversion may used as a criticism. Only Orthodox conversions are recognized in Israel, so for Conservative or Reform purposes, the convert with such concerns may find it useful to undergo an Orthodox conversion process. The Orthodox conversion is relatively protracted and rigorous as it involves study with a mentor for nearly a year followed by an examination on Jewish law and exploration of the motives for conversion before a Rabbinic Law Court.

The weave between family identity and Jewish identity becomes intricate around the issues of intermarriage. The case of David is not an atypical illustration of the complex dynamic, family, and religious issues in intermarriage.

David is a 28-year-old Jewish man who came to psychotherapy in considerable distress over the impact upon his family of his recent engagement to Claire, a non-Jew. David was raised in a close-knit Midwestern Jewish family. As an adolescent, his mother persistently urged him to date only Jews saying, "Once you are in love, it is difficult to cut it off." David had largely ignored his mother's advice, having only one relationship with a Jewish woman throughout his dating years.

David and Claire had dated exclusively for 2 years while both were students in law school. Throughout the courtship David's mother had expressed strong sentiment against Claire and had been uncommonly reserved on the rare occasions that David had brought Claire home. David reported several telephone conversations with his grandmother in which she implored him not to marry as it would "absolutely break her heart." Reportedly, within 24 hours of David's announcement of engagement, his grandmother had a stroke and his mother stopped speaking to him.

David's work in treatment involved basic separation–individuation work along with a long neglected assessment of religious identity. In treatment, David came to believe that he had been attracted to Claire for being different from his mother, including the ways in which his mother was a "prototypical Jewish mother." Ironically, only once he had announced the engagement did David start attending synagogue. David also noted that his ambivalence about Judaism had started after his mother had committed what he saw as an injustice against him in high school. Falling out of Judaism—at the emotional level—was associated with suppressed pain and disillusionment toward his mother. In starting to explore the role of Judaism in his life, David regained an authentic sense of his own experience sitting in synagogue.

Family Dynamics

Religion is usually transmitted through family, so there is an inextricable weave among religious belief, culturally informed family dynamics, and issues of personal development. Passage through potentially universal stages of development presents in patients through religiously based, culturally specific ways.

A principal responsibility of Jewish parents is teaching the ways of God's Torah to their children. Numerous reminders to parents of this essential responsibility are embedded in the standard worship service, the observances around Passover, Hanukkah, and memorial prayers for the dead (*Kaddish*), among others. It is this religious imperative that binds the generations together through teaching, observance, and prayer. In light of this religious imperative it is a considerable loss that, despite strong emotional ties among generations, young adult American Jews sometimes look to their grandparents with a sense of awe, cultural distance, and, at times, even nostalgia. For some less observant families, over the past three generations of Jewish–American life, religious practice has been stripped from the principles of cultural Judaism.

A close-knit family is perhaps the strongest virtue of Judaic culture, highly exemplified by the current generation of grandparents, and perhaps prized but less observed by young adults. A sense of out-group status is more pronounced among the current generation of grandparents than among young adults. A sense of trust and intimacy with non-Jews is therefore far more prominent among the younger generation.

The Jewish value of family has a downside, which, under the pressure of individual psychodynamics, can present in treatment as diffuse familial boundaries. In the case of an attentive parent, a diffuse boundary can lead to enmeshment; whereas in the case of a self-involved parent, a diffuse boundary can lead to guilt, rage, and idealization of the parent by the child. Two cases are presented to illustrate issues associated with diffuse family boundaries that may arise among relatively healthy young adults during the period of adult separation–individuation.

Enmeshment

Robert was a 26-year-old graduate student who had been referred to the student counseling center by a neurologist for psychological assessment. Despite several full work ups, the neurologist had found no basis for Robert's persistent and intrusive headaches that he described as a squeezing phenomenon. After several weeks in treatment, it became clear to Robert that his headaches intensified following telephone calls from his mother. Upon further exploration, Robert identified more precisely that the headaches were associated with specifically those calls in which his mother expressed her desire to relocate from the West Coast to his East Coast city so that she might be closer to him.

The boundary between Robert and his mother was clearly quite thin. Yet, much to Robert's distress, he was not desirous of asserting limits with his mother nor of expressing dissatisfaction with her plans. To the contrary, he expressed feeling great guilt about his parent's divorce of 10 years, and he wished that his mother might find a "nice Jewish man so that [he] would be off the hook."

While clearly the germaine dynamic issue could be found in a son of any religious faith, the Jewish norm of a strong mother–son relationship delineated the experience driving Robert to treatment.

The Idealized Parent

An idealized parent can be observed in the treatment of a person of any denomination and usually serves as a hallmark of childhood conflict. This idealization, often associated with an emotionally unavailable parent, may be cast in cultural and religious ideals of fatherhood, motherhood, or the parent–child relationship. The case of Suzy illustrates an idealization of fatherhood and a parent–child relationship expressed through Jewish ideals.

Suzy, a graduate student in English, came to the clinic for treatment of depression resulting from complicated grief over a break-up with a boyfriend. As she described her pain, Suzy chose her words with extreme care, noting that her father (a professor of literature) had taught her the value of expression. Suzy explained that her father, a brilliant scholar, had taught her a talent for, and love of, scholarship—such that she now sought to become an academic. She noted with some pride that she had also inherited a facial tic from her father (as he suffered from Tourette's disease).

In light of her intense admiration of her father, after several sessions I was surprised to learn that Suzy saw him for only a couple of days each year. During this time, Suzy started to scratch the surface of her idealization of her father. In the following session she seemed compelled by an awareness that her former boyfriend had actually belittled her scholarship and often ignored her attempts to share literary insights. Eventually, Suzy drew a comparison between the neglect she experienced from her exboyfriend and the neglect perpetrated by her father. As her idealization of her father gradually relaxed, so too did her grip on the former boyfriend.

SUMMARY

With some 4,000 years of exciting, turbulent, and tragic history, Judaism is a complex, even daunting culture overlaid by a transcendent purpose inconsistently glimpsed by its adherents. Because no standard creedal statement was ever laid down and because debate is valued and minority opinions preserved, the intellectual effort to grasp its essences often produces bafflement. The overlay of religious creed, culture, and history that is expressed with great individual variability among contemporary American Jews suggests the need to ask each client about his or her own sense of Jewish identity and personal Jewish history. Enormous variation also exists in how a client's clinical issues may seize on otherwise life-affirming Jewish beliefs, values, and cultural norms. Consulting knowledgeable people (and not only rabbis) can also help. Therefore, asking the patient to explain an issue is more likely to be an occasion for intellectualization than for resistance. We list a few useful sources in the reference section. We conclude with an ancient story of the sage Hillel who was approached by a pagan who asked Hillel to tell him what was the essence of Judaism, while he stood on one foot. Hillel replied "What is hateful to you, do not do to others. All the rest is commentary. Now go and study."

SUGGESTED READINGS

Central Conference of American Rabbis. (1975). *Gates of prayer: The new union prayer book*. New York: Author.

Dimont, M. I. (1962). *Jews, God, and history*. New York: Simon & Schuster.

Kushner, H. S. (1989). *When children ask about G-d*. New York: Schocken Books.

REFERENCES

Bakan, D. (1958). *Sigmund Freud and the Jewish mystical tradition*. Princeton, NJ: Van Nostrand.

Charcot, J. M. (1889). Tuesday lessons at the Salpetriere. *Medical Progress, 2*, 11–12.

Dimont, M. I. (1962). *Jews, God, and history*. New York: Simon & Schuster.

Douglas, M. (1966). *Purity and danger: An analysis of concepts of pollution and taboo*. New York: Praeger.

Ettinger, S. (1976). *A history of the Jewish people*. Cambridge, MA: Harvard University Press.

Hollingshead, A. B., & Redlich, F. C. (1958). *Social class and mental illness: A community study*. New York: Wiley.

Larson, D. B., & Larson, S. S. (1994). *The forgotten factor in physical and mental health: What does the research show?* (An independent study seminar). Rockville, MD: National Institute for Healthcare Research.

Laytner, A. (1990). *Arguing with God: A Jewish tradition*. Northvale, NJ: Aronson.

Lewis, A. (1978). Psychiatry and the Jewish tradition. *Psychological Medicine, 8,* 9–19.

Lovinger, R. J. (1984). *Working with religious issues in therapy.* New York: Aronson.

Martin, B. (1974). *A history of Judaism* (Vol. 2). New York: Basic Books

Sarna, N. M. (1989). *The JPS Torah commentary, Torah.* Philadelphia: Jewish Publication Society.

Singer, I. B. (1966). *In my father's court.* New York: Farrar, Straus, & Giroux.

Weintraub, W., & Aronson, H. (1968). A survey of patients in classical psychoanalysis: Some vital statistics. *Journal of Nervous and Mental Disease, 146,* 98–102.

Wiesenthal, S. (1997). *The sunflower: On the possibilities and limits of forgiveness.* New York: Schocken Books.

Yeung, P. P., & Greenwald, S. S. (1992). Jewish Americans and mental health: Results of the NIMH Epidemiologic Catchment Area Study. *Social Psychiatry & Psychiatric Epidemiology, 27,* 292–297.

IV

ISLAM

12

PSYCHOTHERAPY WITH MUSLIMS

ZARI HEDAYAT-DIBA

> And to God is the journeying.
>
> —Koran (3:28)

Islam has been the fastest growing religion in America during the last two decades and is predicted to become the second largest religion in North America (after Christianity) by the first decade of the millennium (Haddad & Lummis, 1987). Currently, there are an estimated 6 million Muslims in the United States, of which 12.4% are Arab, 42% are African American, 24.4% are Asian, and 21% are "other" (Power, 1998). Yet, most Americans continue to think of Islam as a foreign religion and view Muslims as some "other" from a faraway land, typically an Arab, probably a fanatic, and at worst a terrorist! This is not too surprising given that most people's exposure to Islam in the last two decades has been tainted by the media's depiction of Muslims as warriors, suicide bombers, hostage takers, and flag burners. A study regarding Americans' ratings of various religious groups showed that "only 23 percent of people interviewed had a good impression of Islam . . . the most serious charges made against Muslims is that they are fanatics and that this fanaticism breeds terrorism" (Wormser, 1994, p. 4).

As Islam is now in America, there is a need for psychotherapists to broaden their views and deepen their understanding of what Islam means and how it may be changing with the new generation of Muslims, especially those being raised in this country. As pointed out in *Newsweek* (Power,

1998), "The children of the prosperous Muslim immigrants of the 60s and 70s are coming of age, and with them arrives a new culture that is a blend of Muslim and American Institution" (p. 35).

The present chapter will offer a psychologically informed introduction to Islam's history, traditions, and rituals as well as to the Muslim community at large. The hope is that such information may give the mental health professional a wide-angle lens through which to view a Muslim client. Because the Muslim immigrants are quite varied culturally and ethnically, clinicians who come into contact with them will need to inform themselves further about the national–political–economical–educational background of each individual and abstain from any temptation to generalize only on the basis of their religion.

HISTORICAL BACKGROUND

Islam originated in the heart of nomadic and tribal Arabia, whose people were heretofore polytheistic, worshipping pagan gods. The word *Islam* means to surrender or to submit, implying commitment and obedience of one's whole self to the will of God. A Muslim recognizes that there is only one God, that Muhammad is his last Prophet, and that the Koran the last holy book revealed to humankind.

Muhammad was born in the commercial town of Mecca in 570 AD. His early childhood was fraught by loss as both his parents died when Muhammad was young. He was raised by an uncle. In his 20s, he worked for a wealthy widow named Khadija, 15 years his senior, who offered herself to him in marriage. Muhammad, who was 25 at the time, accepted and did not remarry until after Khadija died when he was 50. Together they had seven children, four boys and three girls. The boys all died, but the girls all survived. It is noteworthy that having lost his mother early on, Muhammad would subsequently marry an older woman who both supported his convictions and protected him from his enemies. In fact, she was the first to become Muslim after Muhammad's call. Thus, the first Muslim was a woman. This along with the survival of their daughters seems to be a testimony—and maybe symbolic—of women's strength in early Islam. This fact makes it that much more puzzling that the role and value of women in Islam were subsequently diminished and still remain largely so.

Muhammad received God's message through the Archangel Gabriel. Molla (1989) described the calling:

Muhammad tells us: I had fallen asleep in the cave of Hira, when the Angel Gabriel appeared to me. He was waving a long silk cloth embroiled with writings. "Read," he told me. "I am not of those who read"[1] I answered. He seized me at once and crushed my limbs and mouth in the silk cloth with such force that I could no longer breathe and believed I was dying. Then, when I released myself, He repeated: "Read!". "I am not of those who read" I answered again. He crushed me once more, and I felt a last breath escaping from my chest. Finally he released me and for the third time repeated "Read!". "What should I read?" I asked in despair. He then told me: "Read in the name of your Lord Who created; Who created man from congealed blood. Read, for your Lord is most generous Who taught the Word to him who did not know it." I repeated these words; he disappeared. Then I woke up with the impression that an entire book had been carved in my heart. (pp. 13–14)

Thus began the revelation of what would become the Koran, the Holy Scripture of Islam, which continued to be revealed in an episodic manner over the next 20 years. It is the essential core of Islam and the source of doctrine, law, knowledge, and spiritual experiences of Muslims across the globe. The book rather than the Prophet symbolizes the manifestation of the divine existence, and Muslims accept all verses of its content as it has existed unmodified since its inception. As the word of God, the Koran cannot be used for ritual purposes in any language other than its own, Arabic. Muslims recite it only in Arabic regardless of their local language.[2]

GEOGRAPHICAL AND DEMOGRAPHIC HIGHLIGHTS

Islam embraces close to 900 million people of all races and cultures across nations. There is a misconception about Muslims being Arabs. This is perhaps because Islam originated in Arabia. An Arab is, by definition, one who speaks Arabic. Not all of the Middle-Eastern countries are Arab. Iran, Pakistan, and Turkey are largely Muslim but have their own native language. As Lippman (1990) explained:

The three biggest Muslim nations are Indonesia, with about 160 million Muslims; Pakistan, with 100 million; and Bangladesh with 90 million. The list of countries of which the population is more than half Muslim includes Mali, Afghanistan, Malaysia, Albania, and of course, Iran—none of them Arab. (pp. ix–x)

According to Wormser (1994), "emigration from the Middle East to America began in 1869 when a group of Muslims from Yemen arrived soon after the completion of the Suez Canal in Egypt. In 1875, both Christian and Muslim immigrants came to the United States from Syria, Lebanon,

---

[1]Muhammad was illiterate.
[2]The Koran consists of 114 *surah* or chapters, each composed of *ayah* or verses. The numbers in the parentheses, following a quotation from the Koran, indicate the chapter and the verse number, respectively.

Jordan, and Palestine. Muslims were also emigrating from Poland, Russia, Albania, and Yugoslavia" (pp. 12–13). The presence of Islam amongst African Americans can be traced back to their Muslim origins in Africa at the time of their arrival to America as slaves (McCloud, 1995, p. 1).

MAJOR SUBTRADITIONS

The commonly known subtraditions of Islam in the United States are that of Sunnism, Shi'ism, Sufism, and African American Muslim. A brief summary of each is presented below.

Sunnism

After the passing of the Prophet in 632 AD, there were disputes over who should be his successor as the central religious authority. Those who accepted the *Caliph* as successor of Muhammad are Sunnis. The Caliph was a designated religious leader, who would continue the Prophet's traditions as recorded in the *Sunnas;*[3] 80% of Muslims in the world and 70% of those in America are Sunni (GhaneaBassiri, 1997). They are the orthodox Muslims.

Shi'ism

This subtradition comprises only about 10% of the Muslim population with the countries with the largest number being Iran and Iraq. Shi'is are partisans of Ali, who was the Prophet's cousin and son-in-law (he had married Muhammad's daughter, Fatima). He was also the first, after Khadija, to convert to Islam and follow Muhammad. Shi'is contend that Ali, as a descendant and close follower of the Prophet, should have been his successor. Ali was eventually elected as the fourth Caliph. Some Shi'is believe in the succession of 12 *imams*, or religious leaders, the last of whom is present but hidden and will remain the "permanent imam until the end of time" (Glasse, 1989, p. 367).

Sufism

Sufism is a branch of Shi'ism. Sufis are often considered to be the mystics of Islam. They are more spiritually inclined and more esoteric as well. There are Sufi groups and organizations with very devout and active

---

[3]The *Sunnas* are the recorded words and actions of the Prophet. It includes all that he approved, disapproved, allowed, or took issue with. Next to the Koran, the Sunnas are the most important books to which Muslims turn when in need of guidance. The collection of Sunnas are referred to as the *Hadith.*

members, operating in the United States. They meet on a weekly basis in private homes. The group has a leader, one who is idealized as a master and teacher. Their activities are very much group oriented and have been described to function in ways similar to group psychotherapy. Sufis have attracted Westerners in a similar manner as the Buddhists. Of the branches of Islam, the Sufis are the ones who most actively seek to convert non-Muslims.

African Americans

Islam was originally brought to America in the early 17th century when slaves were uprooted from Africa. It is estimated that about 20% of those brought here were Muslim (Wormser, 1994). They were forced to give up their religion, just as they had to give up any type of freedom. But in the late 1900s and early 20th century, as African Americans sought to reclaim their identity, their interest in Islam was revived. There are sub-traditions among them too, the main one being the Nation of Islam led by Louis Farakhan.

According to Wormser (1994), "in 1930, as the Great Depression caused tremendous suffering . . . a peddler arrived in Detroit. . . . He called himself Fard Muhammad. Fard Muhammad said he was born in Mecca of an Arab father and a European mother and had come to America on a mission" (p. 74). His mission was to bring freedom and justice to African Americans in the United States. He believed the latter had been separated from their true identity and he "advocated a separate Black nation where African Americans could govern themselves. . . . Today, it is known as the Nation of Islam" (p. 74). Malcolm X was perhaps the most popular spokes-person for the Nation of Islam during the 12 years that he belonged to it. Today, Louis Farakhan leads the Nation of Islam.

Although there are numerous Shi'ii, Sunni, Sufi, and African American institutions and organizations operating in America, as a minority, the Muslims' sense of "sameness" is greater than that of their "differentness," providing them with a sense of community, which in turn is an essential source of solace and support.

THE FIVE PILLARS OF ISLAM

The Shahada, or Profession of Faith

The Shahada, is probably the most significant saying of the Koran: *La ilaha ill Allah, Muhamadan rasul Allah*—There is no God but God, and Muhammad is His apostle. To convert to Islam, one only needs to recite these words. The word Shahada comes from the verb *shahida* which means to witness or to testify. It is the Muslim's confession of faith; the first and most important of the five pillars of Islam, in that it affirms that above all there is only one God and that his apostle is Muhammad.

Ritual Prayer

Islam requires five prayers daily at dawn, noon, midafternoon, sunset, and evening. The prayers are to be preceded by a ritual cleansing that symbolizes a state of purity. The prayers can take place anywhere: at home, at the office, at school, outside, or inside; it may be done alone or in group, so long as the person faces in the direction of Mecca. The Friday prayer is special (comparable to Sunday for Christians and to Saturday for Jews, although in Islam Friday is not considered a day of rest) in that people are called to prayer by a *muezzin* (one who makes the call to prayer) who recites the Koran loudly from the minaret. The Friday prayer is preferably —but not necessarily—performed in group and in a Mosque. In the case of group prayer, one man must serve as *imam*, or leader, by standing in front of the others. As explained by Denny (1985), "any Muslim of moral life and sincere faith may serve as *imam* so long as that person is familiar with the procedure. This position is not a clerical one; there is no ordained clergy in Islam" (p. 108). Women are allowed in Friday prayers, but need to be in a separate room. However, they cannot serve as *imam* or religious leader.

Zakat, or Alms Giving

Alms giving is an institutionalized form of charity. Muslims are asked to give 2.5% of their income to the poor. Although some countries have mandated it as a tax, alms giving is generally voluntary. According to GhaneaBassiri (1997), it is "obligatory only to those who at the year's end have certain specified savings or assets. Hence, those who do not have this form of wealth need not pay zakat" (p. 62). In sharing their comfort with the less fortunate ones, the giver demonstrates an inner state of gratitude and generosity. Gratitude holds an almost sacred value in Islam; the Koran continually reminds its people that they should be grateful for all they have: health, wealth, happiness, and everything in between.

Fasting

For the entire month of Ramadan, commemorating when the Koran was first revealed, Muslims are to abstain from drinking, eating, smoking, or having sexual relations during the time between sunup and sundown. The elderly, physically or mentally ill people, and travelers are exempt. Children from age 7 are encouraged to participate. The Ramadan is a joyous month. Eating an early breakfast in family before sunup or breaking the fast after sunset is a festive event. Indeed, the end of the month is celebrated by the *Eid fitr*, one of the two main Islamic holidays.

Pilgrimage

Muslims are to perform a pilgrimage to Mecca at least once in their lifetime. They must be at least 16 years old, physically healthy, and wealthy enough to be able to pay for their expenses as well as to provide for their dependents while gone.

During their stay in Mecca, the male pilgrims all wear a white garb symbolizing equality, purity, and unity among them, whereas women wear a variety of clothes usually of their home region, thus symbolizing "the diverse and creative character of Islam as a global community" (Denny, 1985, p. 118). The rite of pilgrimage, which brings together millions of Muslims each year, thus represents a unique opportunity for a worldwide community of believers to stand united and equal in testimony of their faith.

BASIC DOCTRINES OF ISLAMIC FAITH

As mentioned earlier, the Shahadah is the closest thing to a creed in Islam; but in addition, there are some doctrines of importance that collectively represent the meaning of "faith." One who says the Shahadah is a Muslim. One who follows the doctrines listed below is one who has faith.

Faith

Faith (*iman*) means "acknowledgment of God, his Messengers, his Books, his Angels, and the Last Day" (Haddad & Lummis, 1987, p. 17). Whereas Islam means "surrender" and the Shahadah means "testimony," faith means abiding by this surrender and testimony, living it.

Beliefs in Angels

Angels are believed to exist and to be important helpers of God. Denny (1985) explained:

> Although most of the great angels are good creatures of God, one is evil. That is Satan, who was cast out of heaven after he refused God's command to bow down to Adam. . . . The angels, which have no sex, are made of light, whereas humans are created from clay. . . . In addition to the angels are the supernatural beings, created of fire, known as *jinn* . . . the invisible beings that possess poets, filling them with

special awareness and power in speech. One who is possessed by a *jinni* is rendered *majnun*, meaning insane. (p. 93)

So, people who suffer from "insanity" (florid psychosis) are viewed as not quite human and not quite angel but are associated with the supernatural. In Denny's words, "they are feared by humans, for they are associated with the spooky and uncanny dimensions of life" (p. 93). This is to suggest that mental illness is regarded with some respect and fear of God.

Prophets and Scriptures

Muhammad is believed to be the last but certainly not the only Prophet. Twenty-five Prophets including Adam, Abraham, Jesus, and Moses are mentioned in the Koran. All Prophets are believed to have received their revelations directly from God, and Scriptures are considered to be only God's work.

Last Judgment

According to Denny (1985), the doctrine of the final judgment is closely connected to that of the one about faith in that the judgment is a test of faith. The persons who have stood by their religious convictions will be rewarded by finding eternal paradise, and those who have betrayed their faith will suffer the fires of hell. The day of judgment is described as the end of the world as we know it, that is, the natural order of things is turned upside down, much like a massive earthquake and volcanic eruption.

Predestination

The belief in predestination has been a controversial one because it is not clearly stated in the Koran; one can find statements that lead to belief in predestination as well as others that contradict it. According to Haddad and Lummis (1987), in the growing body of literature produced by 20th-century Muslim thinkers, man is seen as a responsible agent of God placed on earth to care for it. This is based on an interpretation of the Koran (2:30) in which God designated "the first man, Adam, to be his vicegerent on earth. . . . Humans have the responsibility to choose and implement a moral and righteous life in obedience to God's commandment" (Yusuf Ali, 1983, p. 1771). Nonetheless, it would seem that historically, the idea of things being predestined was deeply anchored in the Muslim psyche, at times obviously so and at others operating silently, unconsciously.

Life After Death

There is a strong emphasis on the Hereafter in Islam. Indeed, the Koran affirms over and over again, that compared with the life to come, the present life on earth is hardly worthwhile because it is transitory. The Hereafter, though, promises an eternal life in paradise to those who have believed. Muslims are encouraged to sacrifice worldly (materialistic) desires and strive for purity so that they may be rewarded in the next life.

SOCIAL, MORAL, AND LEGAL DUTIES

Family Life

Marriage

Muslims are encouraged to marry and have children as early as possible. Their marriages are usually arranged and represent the "uniting of *families* as much as of individual" (Denny, 1985, p. 301). The couple may know each other prior to marriage but cannot be together unaccompanied. There is no dating or courtship as in the Western tradition, nor is love seen as a prerequisite for marriage. As Denny (1985) explained, "romantic love is regarded as a feeble basis for something as important as marriage. The Muslim view is that love should grow out of marriage but that at the outset, commitment, honor, mutual respect, and friendliness are most important" (p. 301). Both parties have duties to fulfill: The man must provide for his family, and the wife must attend to the home and children, although in rural areas, she also works out in the field. In recent times, Muslim women do work outside the home, especially in America, and that has become increasingly well tolerated by both parties. In Haddad and Lummis (1987) study, 73% of the respondents agreed that "a wife should work outside the home if she wishes" (p. 108). There were a lot more ambivalent feelings when the question was one of necessity—because in Islam a man is expected to provide for his wife and family; not being able to do so is injurious to his honor. If the wife has any money or property of her own, she is allowed to hold on to it. She needs not relinquish or share any material possession.

Traditionally, men are allowed to have four wives, but *only* if they are able to love and treat all their wives justly and equally. The Koran said: "If you fear that you cannot maintain equality among them (your wives) then marry only one" (4:3). A little later in the same chapter (4:128), the Koran says that a man will never be able to maintain fairness between women, however much he may wish to be equal and just. Therefore, one could interpret the Koran as not forbidding polygamy but discouraging it.

Initially, polygamy served the function of protecting women who may otherwise have been without a spouse, unattended and unable to provide for themselves. Today, this practice is still legal in some Muslim countries but is rarely practiced. It is illegal in the United States.

Men are allowed to marry outside their religion because in Islam, the children inherit the father's religion. But it is preferable to marry within the religion. American-born Muslim women find most of the Islamic marriage laws unjust and are now marrying outside their faith.

Birth Control and Abortion

The issue of contraception has been a controversial one in Islam because different interpretations exist of what Muhammad may have said about it. One version has it that the Prophet condoned *coitus interruptus* —which was the pre-Islamic mode of contraception. After the Prophet, most Muslim jurists and theologians "have permitted contraception and even abortion within the first four months of pregnancy before the fetus is 'infused with life'" (Rahman, 1987, p. 114). Historically, abortion has been forbidden, especially after the fetus starts to move and is therefore considered to be infused with life, except perhaps if the mother's life is at risk or in cases of rape or incest (Haddad & Lummis, 1987). For those living in Western countries, the issue has become a very personal and individual one, with contraception being widely used and abortion being considered sometimes.

Divorce and Child Custody

Separation of the spouses is not forbidden by the Koran, but it is discouraged. The families on both sides should do all they can to facilitate reconciliation. Religious leaders should be brought in to mediate between the couple. Islam does recognize that divorce is sometimes inevitable, therefore, it is allowed. Contrary to popular belief by non-Muslims, women do have a legal right to divorce their husband, just as men do, although it is much easier for men.

Traditionally, in Muslim countries, the children of a divorced couple would stay with their father, unless agreed otherwise by him. In America, however, the mother more often gains custody of the children.

Child-Rearing Practices

Historically, the birth of a boy has been cause for celebration, whereas the birth of a girl has been cause for shame and embarrassment. A woman who could not bear boys was considered to be incompetent.

Babies are usually swaddled for 6 to 9 months and breast-fed on demand for at least 1 year. A boy may be nursed up to 3 years, whereas a girl is weaned at 1 year. Boys are circumcised. The time of circumcision varies from country to country. It could be as early as 7 days after birth or as late as 12 years of age to mark puberty. It is done without anesthesia, in public, and with joyous festivity. Historically, girls were sometimes circumcised at birth, in private without celebration. According to Denny (1985), "female circumcision is not an essentially Islamic practice; it is more a pattern of culture in those regions where it is practiced" (p. 300).

Generally speaking, the Muslim child is raised with a high degree of gratification and indulgence, with little structure or boundary until the ages of 3 or 4. This indulgent attitude is present in toilet training as well, it "tends to start early, to be erratic, is accomplished late, and is generally lax by Western standards" (Racy, 1977, p. 285).

The father is the disciplinarian, whereas the mother is the nurturer. Corporal punishment is used, especially with the boys, to instill respect and obedience. Being like one's father or mother—that is, being an extension of them—is praised and valued in a way that autonomy and initiative are not.

Care of the Elderly

Islamic upbringing advocates respect for the elderly. The adult children are expected to take care of their aging parents. There are no nursing homes in Muslim countries. In a study by Haddad and Lummis (1987), American Muslims were asked, "If it is too difficult or expensive to care for elderly parents at home, should a good nursing care facility be found?" (p. 88). Almost half the respondents disagreed, yet slightly less than a fourth agreed, and slightly more than a fourth had mixed feelings. Muslims feel that going outside the extended family or immediate community to have their needs met is shameful, and much care is taken to avoid such embarrassment.

Death and Mourning

Typically, Muslims are private people, keeping their emotions well hidden from outsiders. There are two exceptions to this rule: child birth and funerals, for both of which Muslims display an excessively passionate expression of grief, anguish, or pain.

When a person dies, the body is to be washed and buried as soon as possible, no later than 24 hours if possible. The person who does the final ablution should be reciting appropriate prayers. Scented water and perfumes that do not contain alcohol are permitted, but embalming is not. The deceased is then wrapped in a white cotton cloth and buried with or without a coffin. In America, the above is often performed at a Mosque, or the coffin is taken to the Mosque prior to burial. The Mosque's designated leader or *imam* recites the appropriate Koranic prayers during the funeral, while friends and family express their grief freely, wailing for the dead.

Community Life and Duties

Muslims are a highly group-minded and socially affiliative people. They value family and close friends above all else. They are generous, hospitable, and loyal to a fault. In America, the mosque has become central to an Islamic lifestyle.

IMPLICATIONS FOR PSYCHOTHERAPY

Islam's View of Health and Medicine

Medicine is not a new entity to Muslims. One thousand years ago, the renowned philosopher–scientist–physician Avicina (980–1037 AD) wrote a famous manuscript, *Canon of Medicine*. Therein, he described numerous medical conditions including what could be interpreted today as affective disorders (Bazzoui, 1970). Avicina showed great sensitivity and intuition for the mind–body connection, believing that the mind had a dominating power over the body. To Muslims, the mind–body–spirit connection forms a unit, which, when disturbed, results in a lack of harmony between the inner and outer self.

With the advent of modern medicine, Muslims have come to respect and rely on medical help. That respect is a double-edged sword: On the one hand, the patient endows the doctor with such unquestioned authority that he remains totally passive in the patient's own treatment; on the other, expectation for rapid cures can lead to disappointment and to a return to folk medicine. As explained by Kulwicki (1996), "Arab American clients often expect doctors to make medical decisions without the need for the collection of a medical history and without consultation with the patient. In cases in which patients are asked to participate in decision making about their medical regimen, they may lose trust in the medical experts and discontinue treatment" (p. 201).

Islam imparts a sense of personal responsibility regarding one's health, which is a gift of God that needs to be preserved with outmost respect. However, Muslims also generally have a tendency to resign themselves to God's care and thus may neglect or deny symptoms for a long time.

Mental ailments such as depression and psychotic illnesses cause even greater passivity in that it is often believed to be a result of loss of faith in God. As Kulwicki (1996) explained, "Madness is, perhaps, the illness most feared by Muslims. Since humans are considered the highest form of life because of their possession of a rational faculty, loss of reason is the most serious illness that can befall them. The only cure . . . is for victims to reaffirm their belief in God. This can be done directly or through the assistance of a religious intermediary or folk healer" (p. 195).

Difficulties in Establishing a Therapeutic Relationship

Although there are some exceptions based on level of education and degree of acculturation, it can be safely assumed that most Muslims' view of the mental health field is negative, and consequently utilization of mental health services is unusual or rare. There is not much distinction made between psychiatrists, psychologists, or other professionals in the mental health field. All are viewed suspiciously as researchers or doctors who discard religious values and fail to see them as a true source of solace and healing. Within such a context, it is difficult to establish trust. There is no notion that the therapist–patient relationship could involve a sincere emotional connection that involves mutuality, let alone the idea that such a relationship has a central therapeutic and healing value.

Paradoxical to this lack of trust, the Muslim who seeks therapy will generally assign a great deal of authority to the therapist and conform to what is advised or prescribed—at least on the surface—because to disagree is equated with confronting, which is considered to be rude. The mental health provider can expect the Muslim patient to remain passive during the assessment interview and the therapeutic process in general. The patient might wait for the questions to be asked, will not complain much about emotional distress, but might do so for physical ailments. Because their psychological symptoms are experienced and interpreted physically rather than emotionally, they frequently expect to be cured of symptoms without having to bare their soul, much as one does when visiting a physician. Therefore, it is important that the clinician stay close to the here-and-now and to invest time in understanding what the symptoms mean to the patient.

In other cases, it is the family who intervenes on behalf of the "identified patient," although they, too, lack in trust while they expect much. The family's involvement often makes the therapist's work more difficult. For example, they might try to control the interview by answering the questions directed at the patient while withholding information that may be perceived as embarrassing. The family members' involvement can easily be experienced as arrogant or verging on insult when they act as authorities on matters that pertain to the therapist's area of expertise. This problem can best be managed by the therapist's willingness to tolerate the enmeshment so characteristic of Muslim families, by educating himself or herself regarding Islamic family values so that he or she can, in turn, sensitively educate the family about the necessary requirement for a workable therapeutic relationship. For example, considering the patriarchal nature of these families, the therapist should address fathers first (or older brothers if father is absent) as the head of family and "should not attempt to change cultural power hierarchies or role patterns since this will alienate the family" (Jalali, 1982, p. 398).

The family unit is sacred in Islam, and Muslims are raised to depend on it as a continual source of support. Extended family members are highly valued as well. They are expected to be involved and are consulted in times of crisis. When a family member is sick, the restoration of health is of concern to all other members. As pointed out by Meleis and La Fever (1984), although Muslims "value privacy and guard it vehemently . . . their personal privacy within the family is virtually non-existent. . . . Decisions regarding health care are made by the family group and are not the responsibility of the individual" (p. 76).

The clinician working with a Muslim individual will by necessity come into contact with the family and needs to consider that a Muslim family's overinvolvement, overprotection, blatant codependency, and enmeshment are perhaps appropriate in a culture where any less involvement would be considered neglect, if not abandonment.

The therapist should reconsider what would constitute intrusion on therapy or on the privacy of the patient based on the latter's expectations and not on the American standards. In a clinic or hospital setting in particular, the family may have difficulty with limited visiting hours, which may have to be extended, especially for those from Arab nations. Arabs' notion of time is different, more fluid, not as structured or determined. As a rule, they are not bound by time. In the Arabic language, there are no clear distinctions between various forms of past and future. As Patai (1973) explained, "it is almost as if the past were one huge undifferentiated entity, within which time distinctions are immaterial and hence not noticed and which, almost imperceptibly, merges into the present and continues into the future" (p. 70). Psychologically speaking, this can be viewed as advantageous in that it fosters flexibility in one's adaptation to life circumstances, with an ability for prompt readiness when facing the unforeseen. It is a disadvantage, however, when living in cultures that require a time-sensitive attitude. Thus making and keeping appointments at fixed times or starting and ending sessions promptly might be a source of difficulty. The therapist will do well to establish clearly, early on, what the rules are regarding appointment time, lateness, and missed sessions. This will be part of the therapist's role as an educator about the process of psychotherapy.

If the cultural gap is too large, as for example when there is a language barrier, involving a cultural consultant might be imperative, especially if working in a hospital or clinic setting, where the family is often involved in the treatment. A cultural consultant could function as mediator between the parent and the institution in which the family member is being treated.

Understanding Stereotypes

An essential part of the counselor's self-education when working with the Islamic religion is to understand commonly held stereotypes and prejudices regarding the American culture. Equally important is the therapist's willingness to reflect about one's own stereotypic views of Islam.

Muslims' Views of Americans and How They Feel Perceived by Them

American Muslims born or raised in the United States are well acculturated and do not feel much ambivalence regarding their non-Muslim peers. New immigrants, however, are predictably ambivalent: Although they place considerable judgment on the American lifestyle, they also carry an idealized image of the freedom and possibilities available in the host country. A study by GhaneaBassiri (1997) showed that the immigrant Muslims' view of Americans was derived largely from the media rather than from personal experience and that at least half of the respondents stated that "the popular culture and values of the United States have caused them to become more religious" (p. 46). This was true among African American Muslims as well. On the other hand, those who felt positively about the United States, and sought to defend it, stated that "the freedom and democracy found in the United States are more in compliance with Islamic values than any social or governmental structure found in the so-called Islamic countries" (pp. 46–47).

Taking into consideration the family and community values of Islam along with clearly delineated gender roles, it is easy to imagine how a Westernized lifestyle, in which separation–individuation from family is highly valued, in which the individual is more important than the group, and in which sexualization is well tolerated, would be viewed with great ambivalence if not outright dismay by people with an Islamic upbringing. A conservative Muslim will view the American lifestyle as being morally corrupt at best and sinful at worst and will feel a religious obligation to protect kin from it. The children of such a Muslim will most likely suffer from this clash in worldviews. They will inevitably be conflicted by the inner experience of having to either betray the parents in the service of assimilation in the majority culture or betray themselves and their growth in the service of protecting the parents who live in terror of losing their child to a Western society.

According to GhaneaBassiri (1997), although most Muslims in America agreed that their fellow Americans hold a negative view of Islam, they rarely felt directly victimized by prejudice or discrimination. One of the reasons for this is that religious beliefs are not displayed in public unless one is observing the Islamic dress code. The women who choose to do so experience far greater negative responses.

Assessment and Treatment

Religious and Spiritual Assessment

To most Muslims living in their home countries, Islam is a way of life, its five pillars being the structure around which all else is organized. In some of those countries, such as Saudi Arabia and Iran, there is no separation of religion and state. The very constitution is based on Islamic law. However, in America, living a strict Islamic lifestyle, following all its practices, is nearly impossible (e.g., integrating five daily prayers in a work schedule). A study by Haddad and Lummis (1987) on Islamic values in the United States suggested that Muslims of varying levels of religious devoutness in America felt a necessity to reform some of the traditional praxis of Islam to be able to be both Muslim and American.

Therefore, the question arises as to how to assess the orthodoxy and devoutness of a Muslim in America. One way to do so might be to ask the clients what it means to them to be Muslim here. Most likely there will be three category of answers:

1. Detachment and denial of Islam as being meaningful to the individual. Such a person might say, "Oh! I'm not religious at all. Islam has no bearing on me." But if you pay attention, you may in time, detect words such as *inshallah* or *mashallah* in their vocabulary, with an undercurrent religious meaning of which the individual is unconscious.

2. Acknowledgment that the religion carries some meaning and has had an impact on the individual's development. These Muslims would not appear to be devout on the basis of their behavior or lifestyle. The mental health provider may never guess the patient's religious sentiments if he or she does not actively ask and pursue the question. Such a person might say, "Yes, Islam is important to me. I feel God is with me at all times, but I get to pray only when I can, and when I do, it feels really good."

3. Explicit communication of Islam as being the central organizing principle around which the person's life is structured. But even then, the question needs to be pursued as to what that means in their current life context.

On the basis of Haddad and Lummis's (1987) study, I believe that the following characteristics may be the most reliable indicators of orthodoxy and devoutness among Muslim Americans:

- Client's country of origin, with Pakistanis being more likely to be more devout.
- Client's length of stay in United States: The longer the stay, the more moderate the client will be.
- Whether clients consider themselves observant of Islam and, if so, whether they follow the five pillars: praying five times daily, paying the zakat, fasting during the month of Ramadan,

and hoping to do a pilgrimage during their lifetime. Doing the above, even if once in a while, would indicate a significant Islamic identity.

- Whether clients live close to a Mosque and attend religious or social services.
- Whether clients drink alcoholic beverages. If yes, how they feel about it—that is, guilty, ashamed, conflicted, or fine? (I would not ask about halal food because it is simply too difficult to eat halal in a non-Muslim country.)
- Whether clients believe women should wear the Islamic dress code, with a yes suggesting strict adherence to the faith. Note that a woman who comes to a counseling session with her head covered might not want to uncover herself or might agree do so only with the permission of a male family member.

Common Clinical Issues

Depression and Somatization

Depression and somatization are so intertwined in the Islamic culture that it is almost impossible to separate them in two distinct categories as is done in the *Diagnostic and Statistical Manual of Mental Disorders* (4th ed.; American Psychiatric Association, 1994). Indeed, as cross-cultural studies of depression have so far indicated:

> The *experience* and *expression* of depression varies across ethnocultural boundaries. Reviewers concur that feelings of guilt, self-deprecation, suicidal ideas, and feelings of despair are often rare or absent among non-European populations, whereas somatic and quasi-somatic symptoms, including disturbances of sleep, appetite, energy, body sensation, and motor functioning are more common. (Marsella, Sartorius, Jablensky, & Fenton, 1985, p. 306; italics added)

The expression of conflict, whether internal or external, and the expression of negative feelings are not well accepted in Islamic culture. The anxious self-absorption that often accompanies a depressed mood is negatively viewed as "thinking too much"; it is seen as narcissistic self-preoccupation. Physical symptoms, however, are accepted as legitimate, morally acceptable expressions of pain. Even the way the language is used lends itself to a confusion of psyche and soma, as depressive symptoms are depicted in physical imagery, especially involving the chest and abdomen.

The literature on affective and somatic disorders in Islamic countries seems to indicate a curious lack of mood symptom for both depressed and manic or hypomanic patients. That is, when the patient is asked if he or she feels sad or elated, the patient generally answers, "No" or perhaps "I don't know." Similarly, a lack of cognitive symptoms has been noted, especially those associated with guilt and loss of self-esteem. So, whereas a patient may feel incapacitated by psychomotor retardation, extreme fatigue, and other physical symptoms, he or she will not interpret these as mood related, the way a Westerner more typically would.

Suicide is practically nonexistent among Muslims in traditional Islamic countries. But the more Westernized Muslims, notably those in transition, are susceptible to suicidal feelings and ideations. In fact, those who do attempt suicide or suffer from self-deprecating feelings tend to be raised in more urban and westernized settings. Whereas Western society is guilt inducing and guilt oriented, Islamic cultures—especially those from the Middle East—are shame inducing. Shame is a more archaic feeling than guilt, and it is more dependent on the community; because to be shamed is to be uncovered and exposed. Shame is public, whereas guilt is more internal (Rosalyn Benitez, personal communication, September 28, 1998).

Patients who have somatized their emotional symptoms, especially the women, are usually passive dependent on the mental health professional. They will seek a cure, usually of a medicinal kind, and will be reluctant to discuss their personal concerns or difficulties. Behind this resistance lies a fear of embarrassment and of shaming the family. As Racy (1980) discovered while working with Muslim women in Saudi Arabia, "much effort is required to break through the barriers of somatization and passivity in order to get any specific picture of that particular patient's life; . . . when such effort is successful, one frequently is able to discover . . . feelings of loneliness on separation from parents and siblings . . . fatigue from prolonged child-rearing, and conflicts with in-laws" (p. 214). He suggested one may take advantage of the patient's passivity as well as the authority placed in the therapist to engage the patient in her own treatment, as in having her keep a diary, or perform certain tasks, or assign an exercise regimen.

Family Problems

The family values of Muslims, along with the idealization of the family as the central source of social organization, inevitably leads to psychological conflict when living in a Western country where psychological health and maturity rests on the young adult's ability to separate and establish his or her own individuality apart from the family. The family problems that a mental health provider may encounter are either of a marital nature or a parent–child issue. A study by Aswad and Gray (1996) at a community mental health center for Arab Americans in southeast Dearborn, Michigan, revealed that marital problems were mostly women's problems, that is, a wife whose unemployed husband cannot pay the bills yet will not let her work (50%); immigration problems (30%), such as husbands bringing a second wife from abroad or marrying another woman for a green card; spouse abuse (7%); and problems relating to children, especially discipline issues (38%).

Because the culture requires a woman to be virgin at the time of marriage, adolescent girls are prone to a great deal of conflict, guilt, and trouble over the issue of dating and sex. Indeed, as reported by Aswad and Gray (1996), the threat of suicide in their sample was coming primarily from adolescent girls. They also noted that "the majority of cases reported were of difficulties between mother and daughter (43%), mother and son (36%), father and son (17%), and father and daughter (4%). . . . Mothers are held responsible for their children behavior, and their daughters reputation are a major concern to the family name" (p. 232). In thinking of the above percentages, one needs to keep in mind that 80% of those seeking help were women; should more men reach out for counseling, we might find different figures.

Psychosis

Clinical cases of schizophrenia in Muslim Americans have been reported in the literature, especially of the paranoid type, with challenging treatment issues regarding their hospitalization and treatment. When Muslims with schizophrenia need to be hospitalized, conventional therapeutic stances may need to be modified to facilitate a more personal and supportive relationship between patient and staff. It may be helpful to use "a consultant who translates for the staff the symbolic meanings of behavior and action, and clarifies cultural properties, can be invaluable to treatment planning, and a key factor in staff acceptance of the patient" (Meleis & La Fever, 1984, p. 85). For example, most Middle Easterners are hypervigilant regarding matters of "ingestion and elimination" (p. 85) and consequently, may refuse medication or medical treatment that would lead to constipation or other abdominal discomfort. In the case reported by Meleis and La Fever (1984), "proper nutrition and elimination, and conditions for restful sleep were promptly established" as an important aspect of the psychiatric treatment plan (p. 85).

Assessing Suicide

Because suicide is considered to be criminal and punishable by death in Islam, few actually feel suicidal, but when they do, they may not divulge it easily. While working in Saudi Arabia as a psychiatrist, Dubovsky (1983) discovered that "if asked directly if they are having thoughts of killing themselves, most depressed patients reply that they are good Muslims and would never entertain such thoughts. If, however, potentially suicidal patients are asked if they wish that God would let them die, they usually will reply in the affirmative" (p. 1457).

Risk of suicide seems to be associated with strong feelings of guilt and worthlessness and also correlated with the degree of Westernization. Thus, all of the above need to be considered and assessed in detail.

Family Therapy

As previously mentioned, when family problems occur among Muslims, the tendency is to bring in a third party to settle the dispute as in with a marital conflict or to talk to the child when the conflict revolves around a parent–child issue; but because a lot of Muslim immigrants do not have their extended family available to them, they may need to turn to professionals for help.

Most styles of family therapies do focus on communication patterns and levels of individuation versus enmeshment. Generally, separation is viewed as healthy, and autonomy is valued in the American culture; whereas family cohesion, togetherness, and interdependency are what is most valued in Islam. As pointed out by Daneshpour (1998), "The Muslim heritage is based on shared loyalty and strong kinship bonds . . . thus, one's self-image, esteem, excellence, security, and identity are evaluated on the basis of their relationships with family" (p. 361). It would be more commonplace for a Muslim family to be distressed over their children's lack of connectedness with the family unit, rather than with that child's difficulty in separating. Closeness, dependency, and loyalty are valued as healthy and necessary for one's emotional development.

In assessing communication skills or planning interventions along those lines, the non-Muslim counselor needs to know that direct, open, and assertive communication is not appreciated or even allowed in Islamic culture. Whereas Americans place great value on explicit forms of expression, "Muslims, like other non-Muslim Easterners, are not encouraged to make their desires explicit to others. Instead, they are expected to be highly sensitive to what other people have in their minds despite the minimal use of verbal interaction" (Daneshpour, 1998, p. 362). Therefore, the therapist may feel some unconscious pressure in having to *know* what the family members feel or think without them having to overly express it. If that is the case, the therapist should verbalize the fact that he or she does not know what the family member needs or wants and should invite a more direct explanation. Some acknowledgement about the fact that such demand may seem unusual to them might be helpful. Furthermore, in family therapy, the counselor is often taught to help clients learn to express their feelings and needs directly. With Muslim clients, direct confrontations or even direct communications should not be encouraged because that can be viewed as being selfish and insulting to the group as a whole. As pointed out by Daneshpour (1998), what would be more consonant with the Muslim family needs "would be focusing on each person's sensitivity to others' expectations and wishes and being respectful to others' feelings and messages" (p. 363). For example, seeing members of a couple individually to get a clear picture of the marital situation rather than seeing them together from the beginning may help. A wife may not be willing to criticize her husband in front of him, or a man may find it difficult to express his feelings openly in front of his wife. Individual sessions also help "confirm the communication style, which avoids direct confrontation. It would be particularly useful when trying to engage unmotivated fathers who are reluctant to come to a conjoint session" (p. 365). The father could be asked to come in as a way of "helping" the therapist understand the situation. This may help alleviate any sense of shame involved on the part of the father or the family, for having to reach out for help outside of their community.

Finally, as suggested by Daneshpour (1998), the use of genograms can be very helpful in working with Muslims, not only for understanding the family, but also for conveying the therapist's appreciation for transgenerational family patterns. Also, because most Muslims value education, interventions that emphasize education and advancement of the children in a family as a goal are welcomed by Muslim families.

Working With the Religious Community: The Mosque as a Source of Support

In America, the mosque has become a central source of social and psychological support. In Islam, there are no holy places comparable with the church in Christianity or the temple in Judaism. The mosque of Islam is a holy place that facilitates religious rites but is not a requirement for the performance of any of them. It is purely a matter of choice. As Denny (1985) explained, "the word mosque comes from the Arabic Masjid, which simply means 'place of prostration' and in no way implies that there must be a building for the purpose" (p. 108).

In America, the mosque has taken on a new significance. Whereas in their home countries Muslims may have not placed any importance on living near a mosque or on visiting a mosque weekly, here it has become a major source of support and of social activities for them. As pointed out by Haddad and Lummis (1987), there are some 600 mosques and Islamic centers operating in the United States. For the older generation, it is a place to bring their children and educate them about Islam; for the younger generations, it is a place to safely explore or practice their religion without being under the scrutiny of their non-Muslim peers.

The clinician working with a Muslim patient would want to know about the mosques or Islamic institutions in the community as well as the services they provide, so that he or she can be informed about the resources available in that geographic area.

Case Example

Mr. A. was a single, 31-year-old Muslim man from Lebanon, who had lived in the United States for 11 years. He sought therapy at a community clinic because of feelings of depression. About 6 months earlier, he was laid off from a job at an aerospace company where he had worked for 2 years. On the one hand, he was angry with his employer and colleagues because he perceived them as being unfair and prejudiced; on the other hand, he was depressed and felt that he had lost his confidence as well as his ambitions. He had a hard time waking up in the morning, felt idle, and was unable to make decisions.

The second presenting problem was in finding an appropriate relationship. When Mr. A. was in his 20s, he was confident and flirtatious with women, but that was prior to his becoming a devout Muslim. In the past 2 years and especially since all the painful experiences at work, he had become a "real" Muslim. He now fluctuated between being painfully shy with women or reverting to a "sinful" flirtatiousness. He could not find a happy medium. He wanted to be married and start a family. He once explained that "in the Koran, it says that marriage for a man is the other half of religion. It completes it, because without being married, the devil is ubiquitous and temptation is everywhere. However, the woman one marries must have faith too." He is currently actively seeking to find a suitable wife through the Muslim community.

Prior to seeing me, Mr. A. had started therapy with another counselor who was leaving the clinic. Mr. A. was thus transferred to me. It was an interesting coincidence that I was a Muslim therapist. I did not know anything about him except for his first name, which I immediately recognized as either Arab or Persian. The first time we met, I reached out to shake his hand, but he declined. I did not know what to make of it. Once in the consulting room, he apologized and explained that he is a Muslim and as such is not allowed to touch women. I expressed my understanding and shared that I was Muslim too. He was both surprised and relieved to hear that. He did not feel he could talk about Islam to the prior therapist for fear it would lead to judgment. He referred to Islam as the best thing that ever happened to him. For the first time in his life, he felt that he belonged to a community. He goes to the mosque every night to do his "duties." The Koran was a source of guidance and ideals, which he quoted in our sessions. For example, in speaking of his conflicts, he would say, "Muslims are to be tested by the devil. The devil tries to distract us by presenting us with 'good' things. The devil makes us love life and forget about God. In this life, we pay the price for what we will gain later. I will gain something from life after life. God says 'I created you to worship me. Take your share of life within the limits of God and his teachings.' Once you taste the fruit of faith your perspective changes. What I seek is johar, meaning the inner beauty, because a Muslim is the mirror of another Muslim."

Some of these comments I thought were indicative of how he felt about our relationship. I believe he aspired to mirror the johar of a faithful Muslim to me, especially as he struggled between wanting to share and demonstrate his Muslim values versus his intrinsic prereligious proclivities to flirt with women and seek material goods. In some of our interactions, he would take on the role of teacher–educator–religious mentor and in some others, he would be playful and as he put it "flirtatious." I felt part of my role was to welcome both aspects of him in the hope that that would neutralize some of the split.

Although he would ask personal questions that pertained to my religiosity, he luckily did not insist on answers. I knew the answers would be disappointing to him and felt protective in that I knew he needed to be able to maintain a view of us as being "alike," because he was in desperate need of someone he could trust who could understand him—which I could. I tried not to interpret any of his religious statements or assertions. Instead, if something struck me as psychologically defensive or otherwise "off," I would say, "I don't really understand, and I would like to, can you say more about that?" In this way, he did not have to take a defensive stance. Instead he could elaborate on his thoughts, which generally led to some new insights.

I felt that Mr. A. was confused about our relationship and his feelings toward me. His longings for an attachment figure was stirred up and perhaps intensified by the fact that I was a female therapist. He enjoyed talking to me and trusted me to the degree that we shared a religion in common, but a part of him felt that he needed to fight these longings as they felt potentially dangerous. Ending therapy and trying to get married was more congruent with his views of life. Mr. A.'s therapy ended within 3 months.

CONCLUSION AND RECOMMENDATIONS

A cultural gap is a given when a non-Muslim mental health provider comes into contact with a Muslim patient. Therefore, the therapist's first task is that of educating him- or herself about the religious, cultural, and national background of the client. Before formulating a treatment plan, the therapist should take a detailed history of information such as length of time outside the country of origin, reasons for and conditions under which emigration occurred, level of social and family support available, and degree of religious affiliation.

American Muslims face the very difficult task of having to adjust to a new and very different culture in America, while attempting to maintain a link to their religious heritage. To live in the present and hope for the future while remaining loyal to something that stems from the past is challenging. American Muslims are having to be bicultural, yet the two cultures often appear to be mutually exclusive. Some live one culture (Islam) at home and the other (American) outside the home. Others try to integrate the two.

Our psychological theories may not be sufficiently culturally attuned to facilitate the development of "biculturism." In fact, as pointed out by Triandis (1996), "almost all the theories and data of contemporary psychology come from Western populations (e.g., Europeans, North Americans, Australians, etc.). Yet about 70% of humans live in non-Western cultures. If psychology is to become a universal discipline it will need both theories and data from the majority of humans" (p. 407).

As previously mentioned, Muslims, like Christians and Jews, are very diverse even among themselves because they come from many different parts of the world, and each nationality may have its own ease or difficulties adjusting to a Western culture. Therefore, the mental health professional cannot generalize only on the basis of religion. Perhaps, the most help one can provide is to facilitate the Muslim patient's need to honor his or her heritage, while giving himself or herself permission to live a "reformed" lifestyle.

Traditional Islam as it had originally been imported by the first immigrants is in transition; all we know is that the identity of the new generation of American Muslims is "in process" and in due time will emerge with its own distinct characteristics. In the meantime, we must attempt to understand with tolerance the differences between East and West so that we may facilitate the necessary changes in either culture that may help bridge the gap between them. More research is necessary to inquire about the developing identity of American Muslims, to identify what their needs are, and to determine their mental health characteristics.

SUGGESTED READINGS

Aswad, B., & Bilge, B. (Eds.). (1996). *Family and gender among American Muslims.* Philadelphia: Temple University Press.

Brown, C., & Itzkowitz, N. (Eds.). (1977). *Psychological dimensions of Near Eastern studies.* Princeton, NJ: Darwin Press.

Daneshpour, M. (1998). Muslims, family and family therapy. *Journal of Marital and Family Therapy, 24,* 355–390.

Denny, F. (1985). *An introduction to Islam.* New York: Mcmillian.

Haddad, Y., & Lummis, A. (1987). *Islamic values in the United States: A comparative study.* New York: Oxford University Press.

Hedayat-Diba, Z. (1999). The self-object functions of the Koran. *International Journal for the Psychology of Religion, 7,* 211–236.

Lippman, T. (1990). *Understanding Islam: An introduction to the Muslim world.* New York: New American Library.

Nasr, S. H. (1966). *Ideals and realities of Islam.* London: Allen & Unwin.

REFERENCES

American Psychiatric Association. (1994). *Diagnostic and statistical manual of mental disorder* (4th ed.). Washington, DC: Author.

Aswad, B., & Gray, N. (1996). Challenges to the Arab-American family and ACCESS (Arab Community Center for Economic and Social Services). In B. Aswad & B. Bilge (Eds.), *Family and gender among American Muslims.* Philadelphia: Temple University Press.

Bazzoui, W. (1970). Affective disorders in Iraq. *British Journal of Psychiatry, 117,* 195–203.

Daneshpour, M. (1998). Muslims families in family therapy. *Journal of Marital and Family Therapy, 24,* 355–390.

Denny, F. (1985). *An introduction to Islam.* New York: Macmillian.

Dubovsky, S. (1983). Psychiatry in Saudi Arabia. *American Journal of Psychiatry, 140,* 1455–1459.

GhaneaBassiri, K. (1997). *Competing visions of Islam in the United States.* Westport, CT: Greenwood Press.

Glasse, C. (1989). *The concise encyclopedia of Islam.* San Francisco: Harper & Row.

Graham, W. (1985). Qu'ran as spoken word: An Islamic contribution to the understanding of scripture. In W. Graham (Ed.), *Approaches to Islam in religious studies* (pp. 23–41). Tucson: University of Arizona Press.

Haddad, Y., & Lummis, A. (1987). *Islamic values in the United States: A comparative study.* London: Oxford University Press.

Jalali, B. (1982). Iranian Families. In M. McGoldrick, J. Pearce, & J. Giordano (Eds.), *Ethnicity and family therapy* (pp. 288–309). New York: Guilford Press.

Kulwicki, A. (1996). Health issues among Arab Muslim families. In B. Aswad & B. Bilge (Eds.), *Family and gender among American Muslims* (pp. 187–207). Philadelphia: Temple University Press.

Lippman, T. (1990). *Understanding Islam: An introduction to the Muslim world.* New York: New American Library.

Marsella, A., Sartorius, N., Jablensky, A., & Fenton, F. (1985). Cross-cultural studies of depressive disorders: An overview. In A. Kleinman & B. Good (Eds.), *Culture and depression: Studies in the anthropology and cross-cultural psychiatry of affect and disorder* (pp. 299–324). Berkeley: University of California Press.

Meleis, A., & La Fever, C. (1984). The Arab American and psychiatric care. *Perspectives in Psychiatric Care, 12*(2), 72–86.

Molla, C. F. (1989). *L'Islam c'est quoi?* Geneva: Labor et Fides.

Patai, R. (1973). *The Arab mind.* New York: Scribners.

Power, C. (1998, March 16). The new Islam. *Newsweek Magazine*, 35–37.

Racy, J. (1977). Psychiatry in the Arab East. In C. Brown & N. Itzkowitz (Eds.), *Psychological dimensions of Near-Eastern studies* (pp. 279–329). Princeton, NJ: Darwin Press.

Racy, J. (1980). Somatization in Saudi women: A therapeutic challenge. *British Journal of Psychiatry, 137*, 212–216.

Rahman, F. (1987). *Health and medicine in the Islamic tradition*. New York: Crossroad.

Triandis, H. (1996). The psychological measurement of cultural syndromes. *American Psychologist, 51*, 407–415.

Wormser, R. (1994). *American Islam: Growing up Muslim in America*. New York: Walker Publishing Inc.

Yusuf Ali. (1983). *The Holy Qu'ran: Translation and commentary*. Brentwood, MD: Amana Corp.

V
EASTERN TRADITIONS

13

PSYCHOTHERAPY WITH BUDDHISTS

MARK FINN AND JEFFREY B. RUBIN

What is the way of the Buddha? It is the study of the self. What is the study of the self? It is to forget oneself. To forget oneself is to be enlightened by everything in the world.

— Zen Master Dogen

HISTORICAL BACKGROUND AND OVERVIEW

Siddhartha Gautama, the Buddha, was born around 536 BC in a small province in northern India on the border of present day Nepal. His title —the Buddha—became his message. The Sanskrit root *Budh* connotes both to wake up and to know. *Buddha* means the "Awakened One" or the "Enlightened One." Although the vast majority of humans lived as if they were emotionally asleep, that is, unable to escape from stifling patterns and unending suffering, Buddha roused himself from psychological slumber. Buddhism is the ethical psychology based on his discoveries.

Legend has it that before he was born, his father, Suddhodana, the head of the Shakya clan and ruler of the principality of Kapilavastu, received a disturbing prophecy about his future son. A choice between two diametrically opposed destinies lay before the rajah's heir: He might become a great sovereign or a famous ascetic. Fearing the latter, Gautama's father attempted to prevent him, at all costs, from witnessing misery or unhappiness. Gautama lived amidst great luxury and was shielded from exposure to sickness, old age, and death. In his 20s, he disobeyed his father's injunctions and left the sheltered palace compound. In the streets of Kapilavastu, he encountered four sights: an old man, a corpse, a sick man, and a holy mendicant, known in Buddhism as the four signs, which fundamentally transformed the direction of his life. He was bewildered and horrified by the realization that old age, sickness, and death were the common fate of humankind. Before returning to the palace, he saw a peaceful wandering ascetic. In the serenity of this recluse, Gautama sensed the only response to his growing disillusionment.

After witnessing these three disturbing signs of human suffering and mortality, he returned to the splendor of his home. He fell asleep. When he awoke, his attendants, who usually entertained him with dance and song, were asleep. As he observed their "bodies wet with trickling phlegm and spittle, some grinding their teeth, and muttering and talking in their sleep" (Warren, 1977, p. 61), he was filled with aversion. His home "began to seem like a cemetery filled with dead bodies and impaled and left to rot" (p. 61). He felt that "life in the home is cramped and dirty, while the life gone forth into homelessness is wide open" (quoted in Carrithers, 1983, p. 21). He said out loud to himself, "How oppressive and stifling is it all .... It behooves me to go forth on the Great Retirement this very day" (Warren, 1977, p. 61). Once he had perceived the inevitability of illness, bodily pain, and mortality, he could not return to the normal pleasures of worldly pursuits. He said, "Why, since I am myself subject to birth, aging, disease, death, sorrow and defilement, do I seek after what is also subject to these things. Suppose being myself subject to these things, seeing danger in them, I were to seek the unborn, undiseased, deathless, sorrowless, undefiled, supreme surcease of bondage, the extinction of all these troubles" (Carrithers, 1983, p. 21). Because he felt that life was inevitably painful and enslaving, renouncing worldly life seemed, in his view, the only way to escape human bondage. His encounter with old age, sickness, and death was so troubling that he decided to forsake his life of ease, leave his home, his wife, and his children that very evening and become a spiritual seeker.

His quest lasted 6 years and exposed him to a variety of spiritual teachings and practices. It is said that his journey occurred in three phases. First, he studied yoga and philosophy with two Hindu masters propounding ascetic and sensualistic practices. But he did not find what he sought, neither pursuing self-mortification nor self-indulgence released him from suffering. Recognizing that neither method extinguished the flame of desire or led to the liberation he sought, he devoted the final phase of his search to religious contemplation and meditation.

He decided to explore a more moderate path involving intensive self-scrutiny in the hopes of "destroying passions net" (Warren, 1977, p. 76). One evening, he sat under a papal tree in a lotus position in northern India, south of the town now known as Patna, vowing that he would not move until he solved the vexing problems that besieged him. After 6 days, it is said that his eyes opened on the rising morning star and he experienced a profound clarification of his searching, an understanding of the riddle of human existence, a freedom from crippling psychological illusions, and a vision of the path to eradicating human suffering and attaining freedom.

His self-investigations led to what he termed an "exalted calm" and a "blissful self-emancipation." He said:

> Through birth and rebirth's endless round,
> Seeking in vain, I hastened on,
> To find who framed this edifice
> What misery! Birth incessantly!
> O builder! I've discovered thee!
> This fabric thou shalt ne'er rebuild!
> The rafters all are broken now,
> And pointed roof demolished lies!
> This mind has demolition reached,
> And seen the last of all desire. (Warren, 1977, p. 82)

After this experience, he eventually returned to the quotidian world and became a religious teacher. He taught that suffering pervades human existence and is caused by one's attachment and clinging to an illusory belief in the notion that there is an independent, abiding self. He claimed that there is no self and that there is no inner director in control. Psychic reality, in his view, is created by what we think is not by a self or an external world, "The mental natures are the result of what we have thought, are chieftained by our thoughts, are made up of our thoughts" (Buddha, 1950, p. 58).

Through purity of thought and deed, he maintained that it is possible to escape the tormenting cycle of rebirth with its unending suffering and inevitable death. Unwholesome thinking usually leads to unwholesome actions, which create negative consequences such as creating another life and body and causing one to be reborn, "To be born here and die here, and die here and be born elsewhere, to be born there and die there, to die there and be born elsewhere . . . this is the round of existence. . . . He that still has the corruptions is born into another existence; he that no longer has the corruptions is not born into another existence." Awareness, Buddha maintained, is the path to the *deathless*: "Vigilance is the abode of eternal life, thoughtlessness is the abode of death. Those who are vigilant (who are given to reflection) do not die" (Buddha, 1950, p. 66).

BUDDHIST TENETS IN HISTORICAL CONTEXT

Buddha's teachings can best be understood against the background of the Hinduism out of which they arose. Buddhism was an Indian Protestantism in the original sense of witnessing (testis) for (pro) and in the more recent connotation of protesting against something else. Buddhism began as a revolt against six aspects of Hinduism: authority and tradition, ritual, speculation, grace, mystery, and a personal God. Buddha felt each had gotten out of hand (e.g., Smith, 1986).

Slavish adherence to authority and tradition had justified and perpetuated the privilege and dominance of the ruling Brahman class. Spiritless performance of rituals and preoccupation with metaphysical questions had become a sterile substitute for authentic religious experience. Concepts of divine sovereignty and grace had promoted passivity rather than spirituality. Religious mystery had degenerated into religious mystification.

Onto this sterile religious stage, Buddha emerged and forged a religion devoid of each of these six elements. His attack on authority and tradition was unequivocal, "Do not accept what you hear by report, do not accept tradition, do not accept a statement because it is found in our books, nor because it is in accord with your beliefs, nor because it is the saying of your teacher. . . . Be a lamp unto yourselves" (Burtt, 1955, pp. 49–50).

Ritual and speculation fared no better. Buddha advocated a religion without ritual. In fact, "Belief in the Efficacy of Rites and Ceremonies" is one of the ten fetters or obstacles to spiritual practice in classical Buddhism. Buddha was not uninterested in metaphysical questions—he had given them close attention—but he felt that "greed for views" on such questions tended "not toward edification" (Burtt, 1955, p. 15), detracting from the crucial concerns of reducing human misery. There is some evidence that when abstract inquiries were put to him, he remained silent or directed the interrogator toward the more important subject of how best to lead one's life.

Buddha's concerns were pragmatic and therapeutic. His primary focus was psychological and ethical. He was more interested in alleviating human suffering than in satisfying human curiosity about the origin of the universe or the nature of divinity. For Buddha, neither God's grace nor divine intervention could aid in this endeavor. He condemned all forms of supernatural divination and soothsaying. The fatalism and passivity that God's sovereignty and grace often fostered was replaced by an encouragement to intense personal effort. He took pains to emphasize to his followers that none of them was to look upon him as a Divine Savior, that he only pointed out the path to freedom, and that they had to "work out their salvation with diligence" (Burtt, 1955, p. 49).

BASIC BELIEFS

Buddha's central teaching was the four Noble Truths. This doctrine delineates the symptom, diagnosis, prognosis, and treatment plan for addressing human suffering. The first Noble Truth presents the salient characteristic of human life, *Dukkha*, a Sanskrit word for awryness, unsatisfactoriness, and suffering. It refers to an "axle which is off-center with respect to its wheel" and to a "bone which has slipped out of its socket" (Smith, 1986, p. 150). Life, according to Buddha, is dislocated, out of joint, and full of suffering.

According to Buddha there are three types of suffering. There is the ordinary suffering of old age, sickness, and death. Then there is the suffering caused by change. Change—personal, relational, environmental, occupational—can be unsettling. The next type of suffering parts company from Western psychological understandings. Buddha maintains that all conditioned states of mind inevitably lead to suffering. By becoming attached to what changes, humans, according to Buddhism, sow the seeds of their own suffering.

The second Noble Truth presents the cause of suffering: desire, attachment, and craving. There are three types of desire: desire for sense gratification, existence or nonexistence, and the clinging to self.

A brief synopsis of the Buddhist model of the mind helps place the second Noble Truth in perspective. Mind, according to Buddhism, is composed of two elements:

1. Consciousness of one or more of the five senses—seeing, hearing, tasting, touching, smelling—plus thinking (which in Buddhism is considered to be a sixth sense).
2. A reaction of attachment, aversion, or impartiality to whichever of the six facets of experience one is aware of.

Reading this paragraph, for example, there is aversion, affection, or neutrality toward the thoughts that are arising. In this impersonal theory of mind, every instant of seeing, hearing, tasting, touching, smelling, or thinking is responded to with pleasure, unpleasure, or neutrality, but without anyone having those experiences.

Suffering, according to the Buddhist account, derives from our difficulty in acknowledging a fundamental aspect of life, that everything is impermanent and transitory. Suffering arises when we resist the flow of life and cling to things, events, people, and ideas as permanent. The doctrine of impermanence also includes the notion that there is no single self which is the subject of our changing experience.

The third Noble Truth is that suffering can be eradicated. It is possible, according to Buddhism, to extricate oneself from psychological imprisonment and to reach a state of complete awakening or liberation, called *Nirvana*, which means "to blow out" or "to extinguish." What is extinguished is personal desire. In this state, grasping and suffering have disappeared and the oneness of all life is evident. There is no equivalent in the history of Western psychology. *Health* in Western psychology, whether Maslow's self-actualization or psychoanalysis' fully analyzed patient, is an arrested state of development according to Buddhism.

The fourth Noble Truth provides the map of how to experience enlightenment, the Noble Eightfold Path: right understanding or accurate awareness into the reality of life; right thought or aspiration; right speech, speaking truthfully and compassionately; right action, abstaining from killing, lying, stealing, adultery, and misuse of intoxicants; right livelihood, engaging in occupations that promote, rather than harm life; right effort or the balanced effort to be aware; right mindfulness, seeing things as they are; and right concentration or meditative attentiveness.

The Theravadin ideal of spiritual development was nirvana or complete awakening and liberation. The *Arahant*, or one worthy of praise for conquering the enemies of awareness and wisdom, that is, greed, hatred, and delusion, attained this state and was believed to have escaped from reincarnation.

BUDDHISM AFTER THE BUDDHA

None of Buddha's teachings were recorded during his lifetime. In the first few centuries after his death, several Great Councils were held by the leading members of the Buddhist order at which time the entire Buddhist teachings were recited aloud and interpretative disputes were addressed.

During the rainy season after Buddha's death, it is said that 500 of his leading disciples convened the First Great Council. Ananda, Buddha's attendant, repeated all of the sutras or sermons and discourses; Upali recited the *Vinaya*, the 250 rules of morality and discipline; and Mahakashyapa presented the *Abhidharma*, the higher philosophical and psychological teachings.

MAJOR SOURCES OF DIVERSITY

Buddhism, like psychotherapy, developed partisan schools and schisms. A complete presentation of all the forms of Buddhism is beyond the scope of this chapter. See Prebish and Tanaka (1998) for a comprehensive picture of American Buddhist culture and history. At the Second Great Council, a schism developed regarding how strictly to follow the Vinaya rules. Ten thousand monks were expelled from the Council. They formed a school called the Mahasanghika, which flourished in Northern India. The remaining Buddhists, the Theravadins, or the school of the elders, Buddha's contemporaries—often erroneously known as the *Hinayana*, or the small vehicle—banded together in the south of India. The Theravadins continue to this day in Southeast Asia and parts of India and the United States. The *Mahayana*, or great vehicle, spread to the north and east and was eventually transplanted to Korea, Japan, Nepal, China, Tibet, and the United States.

The Hinayanists, who prefer to characterize their brand of Buddhism as *Theravada*, or the way of the Elders, observed more of the letter of Buddha's teachings. They maintain that spiritual practitioners are "on their own" with progress being based on one's own efforts (Ross, 1966).

Mahayana Buddhism encompasses doctrines ranging from religious faith in the teachings of Buddha to elaborate philosophies and complex cosmologies. For the Mahayanists, unlike the Theravadins, emancipation is contingent on the salvation of others. Grace and love are the *sine qua non* of the path. Theravadin Buddhism remains a unified tradition, whereas Mahayana splintered into five schools stressing such elements as faith, intellectual study, reciting ritual formulas, and intuitive understanding.

Contemporary American Buddhism is largely determined by that divide between Theravada and Mahayana, but the situation is somewhat more complex. American Buddhism can be divided perhaps usually into two large groupings. The first consists of immigrants from Asia who practice Buddhism specific to their culture of origins and usually in the language of that culture. The second consists of the recent, since 1960, emergence of specifically meditative Buddhisms populated generally by middle-class Americans of European descent practicing in English. It is the latter group which has been in most contact with American psychotherapy. This difference is more than cultural. For Asian Buddhists, there is clear difference between the life of the monk and the householder. In some Asian cultures, many young men spend a period of time in monasteries before returning to the world and family. In the United States, many Americans pursuing a meditation practice are in essence trying to follow monastic practices in the context of career and relationships. This struggle is at the center of the psychological life of American Buddhism.

A more specific third group, however, should also be mentioned by virtue of size and unusual demographics. This is the Nicherin Shoshu and the related Soka Gakka (Hurst, 1995). Nicherin was a 13th-century Japanese Buddhist reformer who advocated a form of missionary Buddhism based on devotion and chanting to bring about world peace. The Nicherin went from a relatively minor sect to being a large group only since World War II. Soka Gakka is unique in American Buddhisms because it has been able to attract very significant numbers of Afro-American and Latino members. Soka Gakka has claimed membership as high as 500,000, but presently 50,800 is considered to be more realistic. Soka Gakka is relatively isolated from what is being called here meditative Buddhism. Meditative American Buddhism has its origins in the late 19th century when American and European intellectuals first read Buddhist texts in translation. The mysticism of those texts appealed to many, including such people as Ralph Waldo Emerson and Henry David Thoreau. Contact with Buddhist teachers grew steadily but slowly. Nyogen Senzaki founded a Zen center in San Francisco in 1928, and Shigetsu Sasaki founded a similar center in New

York in 1945. Since then, there has been an exponential explosion in Zen, Tibetan, and Vipassana meditation centers (Fields, 1992).

Within the Mahayana, there exists another form of Buddhism variously termed *tantra*, esoteric, or the Vajrayana. This form of Buddhism was most developed in Tibet but is also found in Mongolia and Japan. Zen students sit facing a bare wall. Vajrayana practitioners employ a panoply of contemplative techniques including elaborate visualizations of personified spiritual ideals, music, body posture, and all manner of ritual. The current popularity of Tibetan Buddhism arises from the richness of meditative techniques, the novelty, and perhaps also a nostalgia for time when an entire culture could be defined by its spirituality rather than by its material excess. However, behind all the color, Tibetan Buddhism is about the direct experience of spiritual life. The goal is personal transformation in this lifetime. On the surface, Vipassana, Zen, and Vajrayana look as different as a Quaker meeting and Easter at a Christian Orthodox cathedral, but at heart, they are at least quite close and there is much community among the three groups in the United States.

SPIRITUAL PRACTICES

More than any other particular belief or practice, meditation practice lies at the heart of Buddhism. The Dalai Lama, the spiritual head of Tibetan Buddhism, often says that one can meditate and be a Christian. For readers not familiar with meditation, we shall briefly describe it.

Buddhist meditation is a generic term for a psychologically cogent and incisive corpus of theories and techniques of mental training, originating 2,500 years ago in India and later developed in China, Japan, and various Far Eastern countries. Devoted to the cultivation of nonexclusionary perception and the ability to observe and listen with nonselective and nonrestrictive awareness, meditation can be of immense value to psychotherapeutic listening, providing systematic and efficacious techniques for cultivating precisely the capacity and state of mind that Freud recommended for optimum listening. Whereas Freud (1912) suggested *what* we need to do, namely to listen with evenly hovering attention, the meditative tradition revealed *how* to do it. Thus, meditation can be used to enrich the psychotherapist's capacity to listen.

The practice of meditation involves relating simply and directly to one's experience. In meditation, one does not try to make something special happen (like quieting the mind), but one relates to whatever is happening in a very different way than we are ordinarily used to, with a spirit of self-friendship. Although meditation is easy to describe and sounds simple to do, it actually involves states of heightened attentiveness and perceptual acuity with which nonmeditators are ordinarily unfamiliar. There are two main types of meditation: concentration and insight.[1] In concentrative meditation, one attends without judgment to a specific object such as the breath. It is an exclusive state of mind by which one is absorbed in the particular phenomena that one is paying attention to. In insight meditation, one is aware of the changing objects of one's experience—sounds, memories, plans, the breath, and so forth.

In Stage 1 of the meditative process, one sits in a comfortable position in a quiet place, closes one's eyes, and attends to one's object, such as the physical sensation of the movement of the stomach. Attention is not thinking about or analyzing what is occurring. It is a simple registering of what is happening. One invariably loses awareness of the abdomen and the mind wanders off and follows thoughts, feelings, fantasies, and associations. When this happens, one simply notices what is happening without further elaboration or criticism. As soon as one is aware that one is wandering, one returns one's attention to the physical movement of the abdomen. When wandering subsequently occurs, the same procedure is followed. When distractedness decreases and attentiveness becomes more sustained and automatic, Stage 2 begins. In Stage 2, one becomes attentive in a nonselective and nonrestrictive way to whatever occurs. Instead of maintaining an exclusively focused awareness (being aware of a specific object such as the abdomen), one has an inclusive attentiveness, fully allowing and remaining aware of whatever occurs. Stages 1 and 2 are not mutually exclusive and do not function in precisely the linear way that our description suggests. Stage 1 provides the foundation for the cultivation of evenly hovering attention in Stage 2 by creating the preconditions for listening with evenly hovering attention, thus decreasing distractions, quieting and focusing the mind, and enhancing the capacity to perceive with nonselective attentiveness. Stage 2 uses this foundation to cultivate and refine sustained evenly hovering attention. Without this foundation, it is much more difficult to listen in this specialized manner.

MORAL AND SOCIAL ISSUES

In general, Buddhist moral and ethical guidelines are consistent with the broad values and rules of the Judeo-Christian tradition. Buddhist ethical directives are usually translated under the rubric of right conduct, but they are not commandments from a supernatural divinity so much as the advice of one person to another on how to have a wholesome life. Wholesome behavior creates a situation wherein it is easier to have a quiet mind, which in turn allows for greater awareness and the emergence of wisdom.

---

[1]We are aware that different schools of Buddhism have different taxonomies of meditation, and the one we have chosen should not be regarded as an absolute last word but rather as an introduction for the inexperienced reader to the varieties of meditative experience.

With wisdom comes the insight of the interconnectedness of all life and with this insight compassion for the situation of other beings. The awareness of interconnectedness or as the Vietnamese Zen Master Thich Nat Hanh terms it, interbeing, show us that all our actions have consequences for ourselves and other beings. A positive feedback loop of right conduct deepening awareness, in turn expanding the boundaries of compassion, which in turn leads to right conduct, is advanced as a real possibility for our daily lives. Good actions produce the consequence of producing wisdom and a more compassionate world of beings and unwholesome actions produce more aggressive, and fearful, and unhappy worlds.

Earlier, we reviewed the Buddha's eightfold path and the five grave precepts. We would now like to share some observations as to how these traditions relate to contemporary social issues that may be of clinical importance. Buddhist ethical rules, it must be remembered, arose to help direct a largely monastic community. Therefore, family and domestic issues are not an area of attention. There are not specific Buddhist teachings directed toward marriage, divorce, or child rearing. The original monastic prescriptions against sexual behavior are often more generally interpreted to mean that one should not cause harm to others by unwholesome sexual acts (i.e., adultery). Attitudes toward homosexuality vary widely. Early Buddhist teachings indicate that homosexuality was forbidden, but in the contemporary American Buddhist communities, gays and lesbians practice and often teach with a generally high degree of support.

Abortion is an area of ethical difficulty for Buddhists as for most religious groups. The prohibition against taking life is usually seen as the first and most important ethical principle of Buddhism. Usually, Buddhism is regarded as an exceptionally nonviolent religious tradition, but there are always exceptions, and Zen Buddhist students fought as combatants in the Japanese army in World War II with the blessings of their teachers.

Robert Aitken, one of America's most senior Zen masters, has tried to address the issue of abortion by creating a special liturgy for terminated pregnancies. The language of that liturgy is not especially sectarian, and one of us has found it helpful to share it with clients struggling with feelings surrounding an incomplete birth including miscarriage (Aitken, 1984).

Vegetarianism is often practiced by Buddhists, but again exceptions abound. The Tibetans are the most frequently mentioned Buddhist carnivores. Given the difficulties of the climate in Tibet, meat was regarded as being essential to a reasonable diet. To avoid violating the precept against killing, Muslims were recruited as butchers.

The Buddha advised against the use of any mind-altering substances and, in much of the Buddhist world, this is interpreted straightforwardly as a complete ban on drugs and alcohol. Huston Smith (1986) recounts that an early Russian czar faced with the choice of a state religion selected Christianity over Buddhism and Islam because the latter two would have required forgoing alcohol. Again, however, exceptions abound. Some American Buddhists cite the more general Buddhist principle of moderation as a rationale for some alcohol use. The Vajrayana or tantric tradition makes use of alcohol in ritual feasts. The notion of rule-defying "crazy wisdom" also supports intoxication as a way of letting go. Unfortunately, such ideas have also led to rationalizing self-destructive behavior. One very influential American Zen master was eventually, after many years, confronted by his students and sought inpatient treatment for alcoholism. A prominent Tibetan teacher created very successful meditation communities in which alcohol played a large part. For some students, this served to mask their addiction. One good result, however, is that the American Buddhist community has adapted the language of Alcoholics Anonymous in a way that does not routinely use the concept of God.

Perhaps the most important contribution of Buddhist ethics has been in the area of ecology. The Buddhist emphasis on the interdependence of all things has been used to help articulate ethical principles which demand that we do no harm in the broadest possible sense. Buddhism is not alone in this, obviously, but one can often detect Buddhist rhetoric in the world of ecological thinking (Macy, 1991).

IMPLICATIONS FOR COUNSELING AND PSYCHOTHERAPY

Issues in the Therapy Relationship

Given the complexity of the emerging Buddhist culture in the United States, one should be prepared for a significant range of expectations from Buddhist clients regarding psychotherapy. Please note our emphasis is on American-born contemplative Buddhists. In the next section, we will consider refugee and immigrant clients. The goal of this section will be to sensitize the clinician to some of the aspects of that range of attitudes. In many Buddhist communities, psychotherapists are overpresented in the membership and the leadership. Probably, the American Vipassana community is the preeminent example. Clients from such a milieu are exceptionally discriminating psychotherapy consumers. They are very likely to have varying degrees of awareness of the complicated relationship between scientific psychology and the spiritual disciplines. The safest generalization is that Buddhist clients will be sensitive to explicit and implicit attitudes of the therapist to spiritual life in general. Obviously, attitudes indicative of disrespect or condescension are likely to be counterproductive.

Some American Buddhists regard psychotherapy as a competing approach to psychological healing, often with their own sense of condescension toward psychotherapy. Such individuals may attempt to engage the therapist in some form of intellectual debate about the relative merits of psychotherapy versus meditation. Such debates are an ancient tradition in Mahayana Buddhism and constitute a fairly typical test of the therapist. No special knowledge is required beyond the usual requirements of honesty, respect, and an appropriate level of openness. Some American Buddhists may feel that seeking psychotherapeutic help constitutes a failure of their spiritual discipline. They may feel a specifically Buddhist shame at having to seek help from a therapist. Sometimes, this stance is actually reinforced by certain attitudes in the Buddhist community, although, in general, such prejudices appear to be softening.

The psychotherapist of Buddhist clients, particularly those from the Mahayana schools of Zen and Tibetan Buddhism, will want to listen for the role of the spiritual teacher in the client's life. Again, the range is large. Some Buddhist teachers play a role in students' lives somewhat like an important music teacher, athletic coach, or psychotherapy supervisor. In such instances, the teacher is a consultant to the meditation practice. American-born meditation teachers tend to be more aware of psychotherapy as part of their students' cultural milieu. Some Asian-born teachers have been more unsure of what psychotherapy is. Sometimes, this unfamiliarity has expressed itself in a central skepticism, which, in turn, has burdened their students with a surge of disloyalty when seeking psychotherapy.

Special mention of the role of the teacher in the Tibetan Vajrayana tradition is appropriate in this context. In traditional Tibetan Buddhism, one's spiritual teacher or guru is at certain advanced levels of practice regarded to be a supreme authority or the Buddha himself. Devotion in a relationship like this also demands obedience. This unconditional devotion has been made even more difficult because of the tradition of "crazy wisdom." Traditional Theravadan and Mahayana Buddhism recommend a caring, disciplined, sober, and nonviolent way of life. However, there also exists the tradition of achieving spiritual progress by violating one's preconceptions of right and wrong. Accounts of wild behavior and extraordinary ordeals in the teacher–student relationship are part of enduring literature of Tibetan Buddhism (Finn & Gartner, 1992). Unfortunately, this nondualistic approach to morality has always been a problem for the Western student of Buddhism. The Beat generation at times used it to justify an "anything goes" approach to living. One hears less of that in contemporary American Buddhism.

The clinical problem has been that this crazy wisdom approach during the 1970s and 1980s was used as a rationalization for an epidemic of boundary violations by spiritual teachers. It is not an exaggeration to report that the majority of Zen and Tibetan Buddhist centers were troubled by teachers taking sexual advantage of students (Boucher, 1993). Even those students not directly involved in these inappropriate relationships felt betrayed. While those communities were in the midst of this exploitation, the organizations inhabited a gray area between a cult, in the pathological sense, and open established learning centers. The result is that Buddhist clients may be victims or victimized by proxy of a spiritual incest. That trauma may cast a shadow on any helping person in authority. It may also further confound the clients' attitudes to therapy. They may feel ashamed of having been involved. They may be struggling to protect what good they derived from their experience from their disappointment and resentment, which, in turn, may be projected onto the therapist. This is a sensitive area, and the entire family of American Buddhists has been touched by it.

The problems with boundary violations by male teachers have coincided with the emergence of significant women teachers in all three families of contemplative Buddhism. Many commentators have remarked that this feminization of Buddhism may be the most important and lasting development of American Buddhism (Boucher, 1993). Women teachers have helped restore a sense of credibility and safety after the excesses of the past. The gender of one's meditation teacher is a matter worth exploring in psychotherapy. The option of choice in the gender of their teacher should be regarded as a resource for students burdened by a traumatic history.

Assessment and Diagnostic Approach and Issues

In diagnosing and assessing spiritual issues in psychotherapy, it is essential to avoid premature judgment or dismissal. Psychotherapy in general has an unconscious bias about religion. Psychotherapy rarely explores its own religious disbelief; it never examines whether agnosticism or atheism has unconscious meanings and serves any unconscious functions. It is useful to heed Freud's (1921) warning to avoid "two sources of [interpretative] error—the Scylla of underestimating the importance of the repressed unconscious, and the Charybdis of judging the normal entirely by the standards of the pathological" (p. 138). The clinician needs to avoid the twin dangers of a priori pathologizing, which would reject Buddhism automatically, or unconstrained idealization, which would accept it uncritically. If psychotherapy has all too often been reductionistic in pathologizing religious phenomena, then challenges to psychotherapeutic reductionism within religion and nonanalytic Western psychotherapies have all too often fallen victim to the reverse pitfall of accepting religious experience too uncritically and simplistically. The complexity and depth of religious phenomena in general and Buddhism in particular are eclipsed in both approaches, and religion and psychotherapy are then both impoverished.

People are attracted to Buddhism, like to any religious or psychological tradition, for a variety of reasons ranging from fulfilling cherished wishes to providing a rationale for self-punishment, to enhancing one's ability to cope with difficulties or crises, to impeding awareness of disturbing thoughts, feelings, or fantasies, to restoring or repairing a fragile sense of self, to feeling a sense of connection with a community and a larger reality. The Buddhists whom we have observed in psychotherapy have struggled with a range of issues, including early emotional losses, disturbing feelings that they were attempting to cope with, perfectionism, powerful feelings of self-contempt and worthlessness, addictions, submissiveness to authority, and pathological selflessness.

The focus of this chapter has been on contemplative Buddhism as presented by American-born students. However, all clinicians need to be aware of the appalling psychiatric consequences of the wars in Vietnam, Cambodia, and Laos. Repeated studies have found staggering rates of post-traumatic stress disorder (PTSD) and severe major depression in nonclinic, general populations (Carlson & Rosser-Hogan, 1991; Kinzie et al., 1990; Kroll et al., 1989). These rates of disorder are so high that any Southeast Asian refugee should be considered at risk. Tibetan refugees should also be included, many of whom have required treatment as victims of torture. The self-centered language of psychotherapy is often anathema to these refugee populations. We recommend Roland's (1988) work as a starting point in considering Western-trained clinicians treating Asian-born patients. Roland argues that the individualism and emphasis on self-expression of Western culture (and psychotherapy) may clash with Asian values of belongingness and connectedness.

Buddhism, like any psychological, spiritual, or religious tradition, has multiple meanings and functions, ranging from defensive to progressive. We have observed the way in which Buddhism can simultaneously perpetuate clients' difficulties in living and aid them in detecting and resolving psychological issues. It is crucial for the client and the therapist to assess the intentions shaping the client's involvement in Buddhism. Here are some questions we find useful in assessing the impact of Buddhism on a client's life: Does Buddhism help the client confront or evade the issues with which he or she is struggling? Is Buddhism used in a way that is compensatory or constructive? Does Buddhism promote enhanced self-care or increased self-neglect? Does Buddhism foster increased capacity for intimacy or greater social isolation? It is important to realize that Buddhism can have simultaneous and divergent effects on the practitioner, by which it is meant that it can enhance self-awareness and decrease self-judgment even as it hides self-aggrandizement and isolation from others.

Buddhism, as indicated earlier, is fundamentally nontheistic. But throughout its varied history its practitioners have taken refuge in what Buddhism terms the three gems: the Buddha, the dharma, and the sangha. Buddha refers to the historical Buddha, the possibility (that Buddha exemplifies) of awakening, and one's teacher. The dharma refers to the teachings and practices of Buddhism. The sangha represents the community of like-spirited spiritual seekers. The three gems are a religious assessment measure that clinicians can use with Buddhist clients to ascertain their relationship to the tradition, their teacher, and the Buddhist community that they are a part of or apart from.

The Tibetan Buddhist tradition of crazy wisdom is a special assessment issue that may arise in only selected cases. Crazy wisdom is a tantric tradition in Tibetan Buddhism in which a practitioner operates outside the strictures of ordinary etiquette and society, engaging in provocative social or ethical behavior, such as excessive drinking or sexuality. Crazy wisdom can be an instance of potential psychopathology that uses tantric notions to justify self-destructive or antisocial behavior. Historically, crazy wisdom has been problematic, although there are signs of increasing sobriety in American Buddhism.

Treatment Issues and Approaches

Of the world's religions, Buddhism is in a unique relationship with modern American psychotherapy. Therapists of every theoretical stripe have participated in Buddhist practice. Psychoanalysts have had a recurrent interest in Buddhism, which has never been stronger than at the present (Epstein, 1995; Finn & Gartner, 1992; Rubin, 1996; Suler, 1993). The discussion between Buddhism and psychoanalysis is large and touches on many points. A course on Buddhism and psychoanalysis is now offered at a major psychoanalytic training center. Buddhism has been part of a reinvigorating of psychoanalysis and particularly in the reopening of a friendlier relationship between psychoanalysis and religion (Finn & Gartner, 1992; Molino, 1998; Rudnick, 1999; Spezzano & Gargiulo, 1997). Buddhism has influenced humanistic psychology most significantly in gestalt therapy. Although the founder of gestalt therapy, Fritz Perls (1969), was critical of the formalities in traditional Zen practice, his emphasis on practicing an open awareness of the present moment derives directly from his exposure to Zen culture. Another influential humanistic therapist, Sheldon Kopp (1976), titled one of his popular books, *If You Meet the Buddha on the Road, Kill Him.* Here again, the experience of the present movement without clinging to judgment or goal is postulated as a basis for the space of psychological healing.

American Buddhism has grown far from its bohemian origins. Hundreds of studies of various forms of meditation, including many Buddhist practices, have now been conducted (see Wilber, Engler, & Brown, 1986). The scientific approach to meditation in general has been transformed from an exotic Asian religious activity to an ordinary healthy habit with a broad set of clinical applications. Cognitive behavioralists have recognized the usefulness of practicing nonjudgmental awareness in psychotherapy. Marsha Linehan's (1993) dialectical behavioral therapy is based on Zen training and is being widely used in the treatment of severely self-destructive patients. Linehan (personal communication, 1988) stated that it is important for therapists to meditate to convey effectively the lessons of her therapy. Clearly, one of the great strengths of Buddhist practices is that they can be used without need to embrace any particular belief system. It may not be too bold to say that meditative practices could both contribute to a great spiritual presence throughout the psychotherapeutic community and perhaps also contribute to a greater ecumenicism among the psychotherapeutic schools.

The entire field of behavioral medicine has been profoundly affected by meditative practice. Medical meditators like Benson, Ornish, and Kabat-Zinn are now firmly part of clinical and popular culture. Although Buddhist teachers are currently in fashion, Buddhism cannot claim this area for its own because of the profound impact of yoga's disciplines derived from Hindu lineages.

Although not always explicit, much of the world's spiritual teachings hold out the possibility for healing at any given instant, at any point in life, no matter how desperate. As has already been mentioned, Buddhism and particularly Tibetan Buddhism have been interested in death as a psychological as well as a physical process. Meditation techniques have been developed both for the dying person and for those providing psychological care for the dying. Stephen Levine (1987) has been a very popular author offering guidance for work with the dying. His work is deeply informed by Buddhism but is presented in a very universal style. Levine's counsel is to work with experience informed by meditation as opposed to doctrine. Buddhist practices again allow one to work with spiritual technique with both religiously committed and noncommitted terminal clients.

Similarities Between Buddhism and Psychotherapy

Psychological interventions may be both congruent and incongruent with Buddhism. The basic psychotherapeutic listening technique is completely in line with the fundamental Buddhist stance in meditation, that is, evenly hovering attention. A therapist, like a meditator, attends to his or her experience without judgment. Listening in this way increases receptivity to the depths of the client's material. This stance fosters a nonjudgmental attitude and an environment of safety and trust. Psychotherapeutic attention to the vicissitudes of the therapeutic relationship also differs from Buddhism. Although some schools of Buddhism pay greater attention to the teacher–student relationship, in general, psychotherapy examines this area with greater comprehensiveness and precision. Another important difference between the two traditions is that psychological interventions are geared toward illuminating the meaning of the client's experience, whereas Buddhism is more focused on altering the practitioner's relationship to that experience. In other words, psychotherapy attempts to cultivate greater insight into internal and interpersonal dynamics, whereas Buddhism is more focused on decreasing pernicious attachment to internal and interpersonal phenomena.

Another central aspect of psychological interventions are interpretations of unconscious dynamics and patterns of relatedness leading to insight. Buddhism is also interested in insight: insight concerning illusory self-conceptions that are said to cause inevitable suffering. The insights arising from such psychological interpretations are of a different sort ranging from the way in which the client's past shapes his or her present to the way in which he or she relates to the therapist in the present moment.

Working With Buddhist Teachers

Buddhist teachers have been in contact with Western psychologists since William James. Although the relationship has had its points of friction, the contact has been long standing. One of the deans of American Buddhism, Robert Aitken Roshi (1982), wrote candidly about his own personal psychotherapy, which he sought long after he was an established Zen master. He also disclosed that he obtained an organizational consultation from a non-Buddhist gestalt-oriented consultant (Aitken, 1982). The distinguished American Zen teacher, Joan Halifax, recruits a marital therapist if she believes that her teaching relationship with a student meditator has become confusing for her (Halifax, personal communication, 1994). John Daido Loori (personal communication, 1990) is another influential American Zen teacher who invited psychotherapists to an active role in his spiritual community. Loori created an oversight committee to monitor the finances and administration of his organization. He included psychotherapists to help screen applicants and assess ongoing mental health. He told a large audience of psychotherapists that, not infrequently, he has to face the anger and disappointment of a student whom he instructs to get more professional help before continuing with full-time spiritual practice.

At least two groups are especially vulnerable during intensive meditation practice. The first are those who already are at significant risk for decompensation because of psychiatric vulnerabilities brought to the setting. Over the past three decades, meditation teachers have become more sensitive to this possibility and have adjusted accordingly. The other group at risk in the early phase are persons with a history of trauma who, in the meditative state with decreased distraction and support, can be flooded. With careful support, the meditation can be to help treat the PTSD (Urbanowski & Miller, 1996). Vanderkooi's (1997) report and much other anecdotal evidence show that American Buddhist teachers have become much more psychotherapeutically sensitive and much more willing to work with professionals, including psychopharmacologists. A small number of more advanced meditators may experience unusual states of mind. Given our limited clinical experience, working with advanced meditators in distress would seem to demand some form of collaborative consultation with a senior meditation teacher. Fortunately, several leading American Theravadan teachers are also practicing clinical psychologists (see the work of Kornfield, 1981; Boorstein, 1997).

Ethical Guidelines

Ethical issues and guidelines for spiritually oriented therapists have been set out by the editors of this volume in an earlier work (Richards & Bergin, 1997). Most important, they insist that psychotherapists are not religious authorities and must avoid becoming such. The spiritual journey lasts at least a lifetime. Any psychotherapy, even a lengthy psychoanalysis, is a time-limited episode in a life. Buddhism presents a special case, however, in the longer issue. Buddhist spiritual practice can be taught as a psychological technique. Is the therapist then just giving a useful behavioral strategy or engaging in spiritual direction? Traditionally, Buddhist teachers could not instruct without formal authorization, but meditation instructions abound in readily available books, and tapes, and centers. In our experience and in reports of others, when the therapist is meditating consistently, whatever means of instruction are employed, he or she will be more effective.

CASE EXAMPLE

Steven, a man in his mid-20s, sought psychotherapeutic treatment because of periodic bouts of mild frustration about his career, self-esteem issues, and as part of a more extensive quest for self-development and perfection. Although judged to be competent and successful by peers and students, he had anxiety about his capacities and often felt flawed and inadequate. He usually became involved with women who were accomplished and "difficult." He generally played the role of caretaker. He often came to resent his role of "healing wounded sparrows." In graduate school, Steven became very interested in Asian thought. He read widely in Asian philosophy and psychology and meditated on a regular basis.

Steven was the oldest of two siblings in a middle-class family. He was 2 years older than his sister. His parents were in their mid-30s when he was born. His parents were atheists. Steven was raised as a secular humanist. He described his parents as intelligent people who related to each other in an affable but superficial manner. As a child, Steven and his mother were close. Initially, he described her as kind and saintly. He remembered her as a sensitive and curious woman who valued him very much. He had fond memories of the time they spent together in his childhood. In the course of therapy, he recovered childhood impressions that she was controlling and infantilizing and used him as though he was an extension of herself. She "wanted me to do what *she* wanted me to do. . . . Everything had to always be her way."

Their relationship changed for the worse when Steven was an adolescent. At that time, family life began to revolve around the plight of his troubled and enigmatic younger sister. She fought with teachers, took various drugs including marijuana and cocaine, and openly defied Steven's parents. Steven felt that family life was dominated by his sister and that he was neglected.

Steven felt he had a distant and emotionally depriving relationship with his father whom he described as a competent, critical, emotionally constrained, and perfectionistic small business owner with a bad temper. Steven feared that any affectively charged situation might ignite his father's temper. He described his father as being susceptible to severe periodic emotional outbursts accompanied by loss of temper, yelling, and screaming. His father tended to become angry or panic when things did not conform to his rigid expectations. Steven remembered making a secret vow to himself that he would never lose his temper and become an "animal" like his father. As the therapy proceeded, material about Buddhism emerged periodically. We gradually came to understand that Buddhism had taken on constructive, defensive, reparative, and restitutive functions for Steven, simultaneously enriching and limiting his life. Steven demonstrated a tremendous ability to access and describe nuances of his thoughts, feelings, and fantasies. Meditation practice seemed to cultivate this unusual degree of self-awareness. It also reduced self-critical tendencies.

This increased awareness facilitated greater access to formerly unconscious material. To cite one example among many: On several occasions while meditating, Steven became aware of the formerly unconscious hurt and rage he felt about the way his parents made him feel responsible for family difficulties, and the extent to which they encouraged him to fulfill their own needs and goals.

His stance toward these feelings also changed. Nonjudgmental attentiveness—the ability to experience thoughts and feelings impartially—replaced his perfectionistic father's criticalness. As his capacity for empathic self-observation increased, self-recriminative tendencies declined. Thoughts and actions that formerly provided ammunition for him to prosecute himself no longer tended to upset him. As he gradually experienced decreased self-criticalness and self-punishment, he came to feel more patience and compassion.

Buddhist ideals were restitutive and restrictive. Buddhist emphasis on self-purification and transformation had a dual unconscious function: It provided a means of attempting to win his perfectionistic father's approval and atone for his unconscious guilt over his imagined crime of not saving and wishing to destroy his damaged sister. Perhaps if he was perfect, then his father would accept him. Buddhism offered an opportunity to offset his sense of badness and repair the damage he felt he had committed. But Buddhism also became an agent of self-condemnation and self-inhibition. The quest for purity of action, like his father's demand for perfection, became one more ideal that he could never attain and thus one more occasion for self-condemnation. He periodically spoke of the guilt he felt when he was not meditating on a regular basis or not living up to Buddhism's ethical ideals.

Buddhism's emphasis on cultivating "cool" rather than "hot" emotions, equanimity rather than passion (Kramer & Alstad, 1993), actually inhibited him in certain ways. For example, it reinforced his defensive passivity. In attempting to develop such qualities as equanimity and compassion, Steven focused on detaching from negative affects rather than experiencing them.

As the treatment progressed, we treated Buddhism more like a dream than a sacred monument, examining Steven's associations to it rather than assigning it a standardized meaning. We attempted to illuminate its unconscious meanings and purposes rather than assume that it was either inherently pathological or unworthy of psychotherapeutic scrutiny. The picture of Buddhism that emerges from such an approach is that of a complex mosaic involving constructive, pathological, restitutive, integrative, and transformative dimensions.

CONCLUSIONS AND FUTURE DIRECTIONS

Buddhism's impact on American culture in general and psychology in particular goes far beyond the relatively small numbers of formal adherents. The Buddhist emphasis on empiricism as opposed to belief and psychological methods for personal change has invited integration, borrowing, and collaboration with Western psychology. The dialogue between the Western psychotherapeutic and Eastern contemplative traditions is very much alive in U.S. culture. The references cited earlier attest to the burgeoning interest in this topic. We hope that our case has illustrated the way in which Buddhism can enrich the experience of psychotherapy, and the way in which psychotherapy can enhance one's experience of Buddhism.

We shall conclude by recommending some productive areas for future investigators as well as highlight unresolved questions. Because meditation cultivates moment-to-moment attentiveness, it could be used as part of psychotherapeutic training. Meditation training could aid student therapists in cultivating greater attentiveness to the therapist's own countertransference as well as increased receptivity to their client's verbal and nonverbal behavior.

The laboratory study of different meditation techniques promises to open new possibilities for clinical strategies. Laboratory study of meditation has already expanded our understanding of body–mind relationships and may go farther in illuminating the biological substrate of religious practices. The usefulness of meditation for specific populations will probably continue to be explored.

At a social level, Buddhism is contributing to an atmosphere of religious pluralism in the United States. Participation and loyalty to several religious traditions is not unusual in Asia but has been less typical in Western monotheistic culture. There are now Roman Catholic priests who are simultaneously ordained by Zen Buddhism. At least two recent books discuss the notion of a combined Jewish–Buddhist identity (Boorstein, 1997; Kamenetz, 1994). An American Jewish Zen master leads periodic Zen retreats at Auschwitz led by an American Jewish Zen master. It remains to be seen how Asian emigrant Buddhism will percolate with American contemplative Buddhism.

Just as indigenous Japanese and Tibetan cultures infused and transformed Indian Buddhism, America has already transformed Buddhism. Buddhism itself has been radically ecumenized. American students can study with Tibetan and Burmese teachers in a single day. Buddhism is being increasingly democratized. The excesses of the guru culture have been tempered by efforts to diffuse authority and build checks and balances into religious organization. This democratization has been associated with the psychologizing of American Buddhism. Psychotherapists have been actively recruited to provide consultation, both ongoing and periodic, by Buddhist organizations. Some Buddhist teachers have even expressed concern that American Buddhism would be diluted by psychotherapy. How the monastic traditions and lay meditation practice will ultimately evolve remains to be seen.

The psychologizing and democratizing of American Buddhism have been both a cause and a consequence of the feminization of American Buddhism. Many commentators within the Buddhist community regard the ascendancy of women teachers and feminist attitudes as the most profound change brought on this ancient religion by American culture. Again, it remains to be seen how this development will interact with Asian immigrant Buddhism, but already American Buddhist women have vigorously and effectively advocated for Tibetan nuns who have been generally less well-treated than their male counterparts. Probably, the safest prediction would be to imagine a continued pluralization within American Buddhism. At the conclusion of Buddhist teachings or periods of meditation, it is often customary to offer any accumulated benefit to the betterment of all beings. With that sentiment in mind, we suppose that the efforts to integrate Buddhism in America are part of a much larger hope that science and most universal religious values of understanding and love can be brought together.

SUGGESTED READINGS

Aitken, R. (1982). *Taking the path to Zen*. San Francisco: North Point Press.

Chodron, P. (1994). *Start from where you are*. Boston: Shambhala.

Goldstein, J. (1994). *Insight meditation: The practice of freedom*. Boston: Shambhala.

Goldstein, J., & Kornfield, J. (1987). *Seeking the heart of wisdom: The path of insight meditation*. Boston: Shambhala.

Harvey, P. (1990). *An introduction to Buddhism*. Cambridge, England: Cambridge University Press.

Molino, A. (1988). *The couch and the tree: Dialogues in psychoanalysis and Buddhism*. New York: North Point Press.

Prebish, C. S., & Tanaka, K. K. (1998). *The faces of Buddhism in America*. Berkeley: University of California Press.

Strand, C. (1998). *The wooden bowl*. New York: Hyperion.

Trungpa, C. (1976). *The myth of freedom and the way of meditation*. Boston: Shambhala.

REFERENCES

Aitken, R. (1982). *Taking the path of Zen*. San Francisco: North Point Press.

Aitken, R. (1984). *The mind of clover*. San Francisco: North Point Press.

Boorstein, S. (1997). *That's funny, you don't look Buddhist*. San Francisco: Harper.

Boucher, S. (1993). *Turning the wheel: American women creating the new Buddhism*. Boston: Beacon Press.

Buddha, G. (1950). *Dhammapada*. London: Oxford University Press.

Burtt, E. (1955). *The teachings of the compassionate Buddha*. New York: New American Library.

Carlson, E. B., & Rosser-Hogan, R. (1991). Trauma experiences, posttraumatic stress, dissociation and depression in Cambodian refugees. *American Journal of Psychiatry, 148,* 1548–1551.

Carrithers, M. (1983). *The Buddha*. New York: Oxford University Press.

Epstein, M. (1995). *Thoughts without a thinker: Psychotherapy from a Buddhist perspective*. New York: Basic Books.

Fields, R. (1992). *How the swans came to the lake: A narrative history of Buddhism in America* (3rd ed.). Boston: Shambhala

Finn, M., & Gartner, J. (Eds.). (1992). *Object relations theory and religion: Clinical applications*. Westport, CT: Praeger Press.

Freud, S. (1921). *Group psychology and the analysis of the ego. S.E.: 18*. London: Hogarth Press.

Freud, S. (1912). *Recommendations to physicians on practicing psycho-analysis. S.E.: 12*. London: Hogarth Press.

Hurst, J. (1995). Buddhism in America: The Dharma in the land of the redman in America's alternate religions. In T. Miller (Ed.), *American's alternate religions* (pp. 161–172). New York: SUNY Press.

Kamenetz, R. (1994). *The Jew and the lotus*. San Francisco: Harper.

Kinzie, J. D., Boehnlem, J. K., Leung, P. K., Moore, L. J., Riley, C., & Smith, D. (1990). The prevalence of posttraumatic stress disorder and its clinical significance among Southeast Asian refugees. *American Journal of Psychiatry, 147*, 913–917.

Kopp, S. (1976). *If you meet the Buddha on the road, kill him*. New York: Bantam.

Kornfield, J. (1981). The seven factors of enlightenment. *The Ten Directions*, 1–4.

Kramer, J., & Alstad, D. (1993). *The Guru papers: Masks of authoritarian power*. Berkeley, CA: North Atlantic Press.

Kroll, J., Habenict, M., MacKenzie, T., Yang, M., Chan, S., Vang, T., Nguyen, T., Ly, M., Dhommasouvanh, B., Nguyen, H., Vang, Y., Souvannasoth, L., & Cabugao, R. (1989). Depression and posttraumatic stress disorder in Southeast Asian refugees. *American Journal of Psychiatry, 146*, 1592–1597.

Levine, S. (1987). *Healing into life and death*. Garden City, NY: Anchor Press/Doubleday.

Linehan, M. (1993). *Cognitive–behavioral treatment of borderline personality disorder*. New York: Guilford Press.

Macy, J. (1991). *Mutual causality in Buddhism and general systems: The Dharma of natural systems*. Albany, NY: State University Press.

Molino, A. (Ed.). (1998). *The couch and the tree: Dialogues in psychoanalysis and Buddhism*. New York: North Point Press.

Perls, F. (1969). *In and out of the garbage pail*. Lafayette, CA: Real People Press.

Prebish, C. S., & Tanaka, K. K. (1998). *The faces of Buddhism in America*. Berkeley: University of California Press.

Richards, S., & Bergin, A. (1997). *Spiritual strategies in counseling*. Washington, DC: American Psychological Association.

Roland, A. (1988). *In search of self in India and Japan: Toward a cross-cultural psychology*. Princeton, NJ: Princeton University Press.

Ross, N. (1966). *Three ways of Asian wisdom*. New York: Simon & Schuster.

Rubin, J. B. (1996). *Psychotherapy and Buddhism: Toward an integration*. New York: Plenum Press.

Rudnick, S. (Ed.). (1999). Buddhism and psychoanalysis [Special issue]. *American Journal of Psychoanalysis, 59*, 1–100.

Smith, H. (1986). *The religions of man.* New York: Harper & Row.

Spezzano, C., & Gargiulo, G. (1997). *Soul on the couch.* Hillsdale, NJ: Analytic Press.

Suler, J. (1993). *Contemporary psychoanalysis and eastern thought.* Albany, NY: State University Press.

Urbanowski, F. B., & Miller, J. J. (1996). Trauma, psychotherapy and meditation. *Journal of Transpersonal Psychology, 28,* 31–49.

Vanderkooi, L. (1997). Buddhist teachers' experience with extreme mental states in Western meditators. *Journal of Transpersonal Psychology, 29,* 31–47.

Warren, H. C. (1977). *Buddhism in translations.* New York: Atheneum.

Wilber, K., Engler, J., & Brown, D. (1986). *Transformations of consciousness: Conventional and contemplative perspectives on development.* Boston: New Science Library.

14

PSYCHOTHERAPY WITH HINDUS

ANU R. SHARMA

If I were asked under what sky the human mind . . . has most deeply
pondered over the greatest problems of life, and has found solutions
of some of them which well deserve the attention even of those who
have studied Plato and Kant—I should point to India. And if I were
to ask myself from what literature we . . . may draw the corrective
which is most wanted in order to make our inner life more perfect,
more comprehensive, more universal, in fact more truly human a life,
not for this life only, but a transfigured and eternal life—again I should
point to India.

—Max Muller

Kundalini, reincarnation, karma, past lives, chakras, multiple gods,
one God, epics, meditation, caste system, myth, Sanskrit, dharma, chants,
pandits, gurus, yoga, animals, fire, ritual, demons, lotus, saffron, arranged
marriages, sacred cows, red dots, cremation, nonviolence, astrology—what
a colorful landscape is Hinduism!

Hinduism recognizes a fundamental truth about humankind: People
are different. From this assumption springs a religion both diverse and
developmental, acknowledging the many paths that humans take to reach
God as well as the many steps required to get there. Multiplicity and numerous stages of growth lead ultimately to oneness, to unity with Brahman,
the undefinable, timeless, one God.

THE FOUR PATHS TO GOD

Hinduism recognizes four fundamental human temperaments. People
are essentially reflective, emotional, active, and empirical or experimental.
For each personality type, a different path to God or self-realization is
appropriate. The path is termed a *yoga*, from the same root as the English
word "yoke," meaning to unite (yoke together) and to place under disci-

pline or training (to bring under the yoke). Thus, yoga, commonly misunderstood in the West as merely a means of exercising the body, is more properly considered to be a spiritual path.

Jnana Yoga, the Path of Knowledge

This path is designed for persons who are philosophical and intellectual in bent. Such persons are encouraged to contemplate, meditate, and consider ideas that will gradually shift their locus of identity from the small personal self (what Western psychology defines as the ego) to the infinite Self or the Divine within. Persons are asked to develop a *Watcher*, a detached aspect of self that watches all actions but remains unattached to them, as an actor dons individual roles but is unattached to these roles. Hindus believe that the self underneath the surface self is perfect in nature but covered with layers of illusion. These layers are solidified as one continues to identify with one's personality, mind, emotions, body, beliefs, and so on. As one ceases to identify with these aspects of the small self, the layers are removed, revealing one's true nature as the infinite Self.

Bhakti Yoga, the Path of Love

This path is best suited to persons whose primary means of receiving input is through their emotions. The path is one of devotion to God through love, that is, ceaseless, unending, single-minded adoration of God as the Beloved. Hindus point to Christianity as the "one great brilliantly lit *bhakti* highway towards God, other paths being not neglected but not as clearly marked" (Smith, 1958, p. 46).

Along this path emerge the multiple forms of God or pantheon of gods for which Hinduism is known. Just as humans love one another differently (love of one's parents is distinguishable from love of children, spouse, or friends), God's many aspects will create in the devotee different experiences of love. Bhakti yoga recognizes that a love object is necessary for lovers, unlike jnana yogis who can meditate easily on an abstract, Infinite Being. Devoting oneself to one image of God, loving that god or goddess will lead to loving all of God's aspects. The aspect chosen is essentially irrelevant, though it is easiest to love God in an incarnate form because humans are already socialized to love other humans. But whether that choice is Krishna, Christ, Buddha, Mohammed, or any other incarnate is an individual choice and immaterial to the ultimate goal.

Mantras are used in bhakti yoga as a means of expressing one's devotion. Mantras are thought forms uttered audibly or silently and mentally. Japa is the technique of repeating a mantrum constantly to bring about the devotee's change in consciousness.

Karma Yoga, the Path of Work

For persons inclined to action, there is karma yoga. The motivation to be active is a significant drive in human nature (any parent faced with a bored child knows this all too well!). God may be found through the mechanics of one's daily activities; it is not necessary to renounce life or enter a contemplative order to achieve self-realization. *What* one does is relatively unimportant; rather, *how* the work is done contains the key to success.

The karma yogi is instructed by the *Bhagavad Gita* (in Smith, 1958, p. 53) to loosen ties of attachment to outcome: "To work you have the right, but not to the fruits thereof." Also required is calm focus and concentration, to do one thing at a time as if it were all that existed and then move on to the next task with equal focus. Finally, there is the dictum to work not for oneself but for God.

Raja Yoga, the Path of Psychological Experimentation

This path is designed for those scientifically inclined; hence, it naturally appeals to Western minds. Although many regard Hinduism as purely a mystical religion, it is nonetheless empirical as well. Its experimentation applies to affairs of the spirit, in the same way in which Western experiments apply to the physical world. The hypothesis to be tested is that a human's true nature is something greater than what is currently experienced through the senses, emotion, and intellect. Raja yoga leads the inquirer through a series of meditations and experiments to discover one's true nature.

FOUR STAGES AND WANTS OF LIFE

Hindus believe that human beings progress through four stages in their lives. The first stage is that of student, in which not only content is imparted but also character. The second stage, beginning with marriage, is that of householder. Here, one's attention is focused outward, on family, work or duty, and community. The third stage occurs with retirement. Up to this point, the individual has lived in the external world; now he or she must turn inward. For those unable to do so, Hinduism warns of a bleak old age. The rewards of physical life wane, and to keep seeking them when their time is up is to pursue a wine that has grown bitter. Instead, persons must ask themselves who they truly are and seek the answer within. The final stage, sannyas, is defined in the *Bhagavad Gita* (in Zimmer, 1951, p. 158) as "one who neither hates nor loves anything." The sannyasin has achieved freedom, is unattached to the world, and has no expectations. He or she has joined the infinite.

As humans move through these stages of life, they pursue four wants. The first is the pursuit of pleasure, primarily sensual pleasure. Although many think Hinduism is renunciatory or ascetic and therefore thumbs its nose at hedonism, this is, in fact, not the case. Hindus believe pleasure is natural and spontaneous and should be pursued; however, its ability to satisfy wanes over time. When sensual pleasures cease to satisfy, persons turn to the pursuit of worldly success, that is, wealth, fame, and power. These, too, are worthy goals and should be pursued with vigor. Nonetheless, they, too, will cease to satisfy the aspirant at some point. He or she then turns to the third want, which is duty or the desire to serve others. This want, to give, to be selfless in the act of helping others is the desire to build the community. These three wants, pleasure, worldly success, and desire to duty, correspond to the first two stages of life, student and householder; their pursuit thus takes up a great portion of a human's life. Hindus believe, though, that these wants are not enough. What humans ultimately want is to be one with God or Brahman, the Supreme Reality. This, Hindus define as *satchitananda* (sat = being, chit = awareness, ananda = bliss). Given enough time, all other wants pale by comparison.

DEVELOPMENT THROUGH LIFETIMES: KARMA AND REINCARNATION

In addition to development within a lifetime (stages), Hinduism explicitly addresses development of a soul. This is done through the concepts of karma and reincarnation (also known as transmigration).

> Worn-out garments
> Are shed by the body:
> Worn-out bodies
> Are shed by the dweller. (*Bhagavad Gita*, in Smith, 1958, p. 77)

Karma is the law of cause and effect: "As a man sows, so shall he reap." Every action has a reaction or consequence. When the body dies, the actions of the body do not die; instead, they travel with the soul, which does not die. In its most literal form, a soul born into bitter conditions in this life is reaping the results of bad actions in past lives; conversely, a soul born into favorable circumstances is benefiting from past good deeds. The soul will continue to reincarnate (be born in physical form) until it has transcended all feelings of pain and pleasure and has released all fears and attachments. Another conception of karma is to understand it as the wheel of time. Every action, thought, intention, feeling, and so on that a human being has is recorded on this wheel. As the wheel turns, these same actions, thoughts, and so on return to the person. Only by transcending time can one escape karma. Hindus believe that even God himself is subject to karma if He takes human form. Thus, all realized or enlightened beings in physical form are subject to karma.

The development of the soul, though it spans many lifetimes, parallels the stages of an individual human's life. An immature soul seeks primarily sensual pleasure. As it matures, the soul seeks worldly success (fame, wealth, power). As it continues its progression toward enlightenment, the soul's many manifestations move toward service and ultimately unity with Brahman—being, awareness, and bliss.

Sin, as it is commonly understood in the West, is not referred to in Hindu scriptures. Hindus believe that humans are inherently divine and that we have only to uncover our perfection by removing the layers of illusion in which we are wrapped. The concept closest to sin, as it exists in Hinduism, is explained by karma, the law of cause and effect. We commit wrong actions or bad karmas (sins) because of ignorance. We do not understand or are unable to see clearly the consequences of our actions. Knowledge or clear understanding eradicates these wrong actions. In general, then, Hinduism stands against the doctrine of sin and the concept that humans are sinners as defined by the West. The Bhagavad Gita also states that union with the Divine is for all. We will all achieve salvation; only the length of time required varies by the individual because of the existence of free will.

FOUR (OR FIVE) STATIONS OF LIFE: THE CASTE SYSTEM

Where do individuals belong? Where do they best fit in the social order? The caste system, for which Hinduism is widely known and condemned, answers this question. This system, said to have evolved in the 2nd millennium BC, divided society initially into four groups on the basis of recognition of individual differences and ways in which people could best contribute. Over time, the four stations grew to include a fifth: the untouchable caste or outcasts. The appearance of this fifth caste and the circumstances of its occurrence have been debated by historians. Perhaps it was due to the influx of Aryans (fair-skinned, blue-eyed peoples) to India and their clashes with the indigenous peoples. Others have speculated differences with regard to immunity to disease, leading to taboos of drinking the same water, eating the same foods, or using the same utensils. Over time, the five-tier caste system grew to prohibit intermarriage across all caste lines; it also defined hereditary boundaries (the caste into which one was born remained so for life) and, ultimately, those in higher castes began to profit at the expense of those in lower castes.

The original four castes were based on natural inclination to occupation:

1. Brahmins or seers;
2. Kshatriyas or administrators;
3. Vaishyas or businesspersons; and
4. Shudras or laborers.

Brahmins, reflective and intellectual, were society's visionaries. In modern-day society, they consist of teachers, philosophers, artists, and religious leaders. Kshatriyas were adept at organizing and executing; in government, they administered affairs of state, and in the military, served as generals and commanders. Vaishyas produced and distributed the commodities of the culture appropriately; they were artisans, craftspeople, farmers, and businesspersons. Shudras were best at following and conforming to the requirements of existing occupations. They were society's unskilled laborers.

The caste system has been the subject of considerable turmoil in India's history and has been deemed to be unconstitutional in recent decades. The individual most responsible for this was Mahatma Gandhi, who lived and worked among the untouchables, making them a part of Indian society instead of its outcasts. As he worked ceaselessly to remove the British from India nonviolently, he did more to raise Western awareness of India and Hinduism than any single man in history.

THE RICHNESS OF THE LANDSCAPE: SPECIFIC BELIEFS AND PRACTICES

The Gods of Hinduism: Unity, Trinity, and Pantheon

Hindus believe that Brahman is the undefinable, timeless, one God. From Brahman emerged Aum (or Om), and Aum is God. (There is a similarity to the Christian belief that creation emanated from the Word, and the Word was God.) From Aum, there came Mother God (Kali) and the Godhead. The Godhead then divided into the Trinity: Brahma, the Creator; Vishnu, the Preserver; and Shiva, the Destroyer (or Completer). Each god has a consort or goddess: Saraswati, goddess of Knowledge (consort of Brahma); Lakshmi, goddess of Prosperity (consort of Vishnu); and Parvati, goddess of Power (consort of Shiva).

The God Shiva bears special explanation because the concept of God as Destroyer often baffles Westerners. In Hinduism, all life is seen as cyclical, that is, as endless cycles of birth and death. Time is not viewed linearly but cyclically, for example, as the wheel of karma, a circular representation of time. Therefore, Hinduism requires a Destroyer God that recognizes the completion of one form of existence and facilitates its transformation from one form to another. Shiva, although powerful, is not considered evil or bad, nor is he feared by Hindus.

When one of these Gods takes human form, that form is called an *avatar*. Best known are the 10 avatars of Vishnu, which include Krishna, Rama, and Buddha. The 10th and final avatar of Vishnu is yet to come and will appear at the end of the current great age, when the world is submerged by floods and deluge.

There are countless lesser gods emerging from these higher beings, representing forces of nature, animals, and qualities of humankind. In fact, Hinduism is said to have $33\frac{3}{4}$ crores (1 crore = 10 million) gods and goddesses. The reason for this is outlined by the path of Bhakti Yoga, that humans worship gods relative to their particular grasp of the Divine.

Kundalini, Chakras, and Tantras

The Tantras are a branch of Hinduism and outline Hindu beliefs regarding enjoyment of material life. The primary deity is Shiva–Shakti, a combination of Shiva and his consort Parvati. Knowledge about the energy of the human body, particularly Kundalini, sexual practices, and chakras are part of the Tantras. The chakras are seven psychic centers or vortexes of energy in the human body. They occur approximately at the base of the spine, base of the genitals, navel, heart, throat, between the eyebrows, and at the crown. Kundalini, also known as serpent power, is an energetic force that lies coiled and inactive at the base of the spine for approximately the first half of one's life. As a person evolves spiritually, this power awakens, traveling through the six chakras, reaching the crown, at which point a person attains cosmic consciousness or self-realization.

Tantric literature also contains erotic and sexual yogic practices that, if misunderstood, have the potential of trapping one in sensual pleasures. If properly practiced, however, they use the duality of the manifest universe (e.g., male and female) to transcend physical form to higher levels of consciousness.

Sacred Texts

Hinduism has a number of holy texts. The *Ramayana* is the story of Lord Rama (an incarnate or avatar of Vishnu) and his wife, Princess Sita, who is kidnapped by Ravana, a 10-headed demon king. The story of the *Ramayana* is the story of Rama's triumph over Ravana. The most famous festival of India, Diwali (Festival of Lights), is a celebration of this victory and Rama's homecoming. The *Mahabharata*, the longest poem in the world, contains 220,000 lines and details the conflict between two families, the Pandavas and the Kauravas. Within it, is contained the *Bhagavad Gita*, often called the Hindu Bible. The Gita is the advice given to the warrior prince Arjuna by his charioteer Lord Krishna at the outset of the Great War between the two families. The Vedas (meaning knowledge) contain the Hindu scriptures. There are four volumes, the most famous being the *Rig Veda*, containing 1,028 hymns. The *Upanishads*, also well known and beloved, consist of 108 books revealing spiritual truths and ways to realize them.

Gurus

In its original usage, the term *guru* means God Himself. Thus, God-realized masters, that is, completely enlightened beings, are called gurus. The appearance of a guru comes through changes in the devotee's consciousness, through desire for God, and by selfless actions. In Hinduism, gurus come in body or physical form and also in spirit.

Sacred Cow

The importance of the cow in Hinduism is baffling to Westerners. (Largely, this is because so many children were taught to finish their meals because "people are starving in India." "If so many people are starving in India, why don't they eat the cows?" replied precocious children.) The significance of the cow is both historical and mythological. Historically, in the Vedic Age, the Aryans had only one domesticated animal, the cow. Cows provided milk, butter, and yogurt, and their hide was used to make clothing and shelter. Over time, the cow was regarded with devotion for its many gifts to human subsistence. The majority of Hindus do not consume beef, and Brahmins, in particular, tend toward strict vegetarianism (no meat, poultry, or fish). Some do not consume eggs as well. Mythologically, the cow is associated with Krishna, one of the avatars of Vishnu. Krishna's playmates were cowherds, and he is depicted as displaying a fondness for dairy products. Hindu children especially love to hear the story in which he stole and ate butter as a boy. Cows also appear in many Hindu religious epics and have been credited with guiding a soul toward heaven.

Rituals

Hinduism is replete with rituals. *Puja* is the most common form of worship; this is the offering of articles (e.g., food, perfumed water, sandalwood paste, incense, flowers, ashes) to a deity. *Aarti* is a common form of Puja in which a butter-soaked cotton wick is lit and moved in a clockwise fashion before the image of a deity. After Puja, food is offered to the worshippers by the host.

Rituals are conducted at nearly every stage of one's life from birth to death. These begin even before one is born, for example, to guarantee conception, protect the fetus, and during the last month of pregnancy. When a child is born, an astrological chart is ritually prepared; additional rituals occur when a child is named, taken out of the house for the first time, fed rice for the first time, has its first haircut, has its ears pierced, learns the alphabet, and so on.

Fire, the symbol of purification which captures the transformation from one state to another, plays a significant role in most Hindu rituals. Marriages take place around fires, funeral pyres are lit by the deceased's eldest son, and many private rituals conducted in homes occur around small fires.

Hindu Marriages

Traditionally, Hindu marriages were arranged by one's parents, and this is still the predominant method of matrimony, even for Indians living in Western society. Even as recently as a generation ago, the bride and groom met for the first time at the marriage ceremony itself. Today, the prospective bride and groom may meet a few times and are permitted to consent or reject one another. However, marriage is still considered to be a social contract between two families and not merely between two people. If two people meet, fall in love, and marry (usually still requiring the consent of their respective families), it is termed a love marriage. Such marriages, due to Western influence, are on the rise, particularly among well-educated Hindus.

What is the significance of the red dot or *bindi* that women wear on their foreheads? Historically, all Hindus, especially Brahmins, wore dots on their foreheads, signifying the importance of the third eye or site of intuition (sixth chakra). Later, the dot was worn by Hindu women to signify marriage. Today both married and unmarried Hindu women wear these dots as an adornment. (They come in all shapes and sizes and are worn to match one's outfit!)

Ages or the Concept of Time

The Hindu concept of time is expansive. "The Himalayas, it is said, are made of solid granite. Once every thousand years a bird flies over them with a scarf in its beak that brushes the ranges as it passes. When by this process the Himalayas have been worn away, one day of a cosmic cycle will have elapsed" (Smith, 1958, p. 81).

What are these cosmic cycles? The universe has no beginning or end but oscillates in endless cycles of birth and destruction called *Kalpas*. One Kalpa is 12,000 years for the gods or 4,320,000 human years. Each Kalpa is divided into four *Yugas* or ages. They are Krita, Treta, Dvapara, and Kali (current age). At the end of the Kali Yuga (427,000 years), the universe will be destroyed by the deluge and cosmic creation will begin anew. Only Brahman (the Absolute) is timeless.

A LIVING RELIGION

"Hinduism was not inspired by one individual but rather evolved organically" (Zysk, 1989, back cover). *Rishis*, men perfected by meditation, heard Eternal Truths in their hearts and taught these truths to their disciples telepathically. These truths were later transmitted orally and, later still, written in Sanskrit in the form of the *Upanishads* and *Vedas*.

Although the Rishis are said to be the first to have heard these eternal truths, they are available to anyone who pursues them. In fact, Hindu scriptures are authored anonymously and tend to be written in third-person format. There has been speculation that the authors of these scriptures deliberately avoided signing their names, perhaps as a clear statement that these truths are eternal and, as such, available freely to all.

Hindus do not claim a monopoly on wisdom but encourage all forms of religious pursuit. There are many paths to the same summit (Smith, 1958). For this reason, there are no Hindu missionaries. Hindus do not preach, proselytize, or attempt to convert others to their religion. Rather, they strive to make a person's faith strong in his or her own religion.

Its organic nature makes Hinduism a living religion. It constantly absorbs new ideas and philosophies, as life itself grows and changes. It is evolving, "recharging itself with modern technology, psychology, parapsychology, modern astronomy, the new physics, and genetics" (Viswanathan, 1986, p. 2). "Hinduism can appear either as an extrovert religion of spectacle, abundant mythology and congregational practices or as a religion which is profoundly interiorized" (Renou, 1963, p. 3). What ultimately attracts one to Hinduism is "utmost freedom of thought" (Viswanathan, 1986, p. 23).

Given these characteristics of Hinduism, what are the implications for therapists and counselors who work with Hindu clients? We turn next to a discussion of these issues. A note of caution, however, is warranted: Because of the paucity of research on psychotherapy with Hindu clients, much of what follows is based on anecdotal evidence and clinical observation by the author.

BUILDING THE RELATIONSHIP WITH A HINDU CLIENT

First, do not assume that an Indian psychotherapy client is Hindu. The Indian subcontinent houses a variety of religions besides Hinduism: Islam, Sikhism, Christianity, Buddhism, Judaism, Zoroastrianism, among others. If one's clients are Indian, they are as likely to be members of one of these religions as they are to be Hindu.

If they are Hindu, spend some time finding out how they practice their religion. Because Hinduism is so diverse and personalized, a client's form of worship or practice is likely unique, even within her or his own family. There is tremendous permission within families to practice Hinduism individually. This personal nature of Hinduism cannot be overstated, and it is important that the therapist understand the client's practices and particular understanding of her or his religion.

Regional differences also play a role. If from Eastern India, people may worship Durga, the Goddess born of Kali, who destroyed evil in the form of the buffalo demon Mahishasura. In northern India, they will likely celebrate Rama's victory over Ravana, signifying the same mythological meaning.

THE INDIAN IMMIGRANT

An assumption is being made that readers of this volume are working with Indian immigrants to the United States and Canada, as opposed to persons living predominantly in India. A few words about characteristics of Indian immigrants may be useful (these apply to Hindus but also to Indians of other faiths). The phenomenon of Indian immigration to the United States and Canada is somewhat unique, in that Indian immigrants did not come here under circumstances of poverty or religious persecution, as did most other immigrant groups. Indian immigrants to the United States and Canada tend to be well educated and of middle or higher socioeconomic class. Moreover, they are relatively recent immigrants, coming to the United States and Canada in the 1950s and later. Many are professionals (doctors, engineers, professors) who came here for education and then decided to stay. Although not necessarily large in census numbers compared with other ethnic minorities, Indians do control a disproportionate amount of resources and wealth, particularly in the United States. In fact, some empirical studies establish Indians as the richest ethnic minority in this country.

Several factors result from this type of immigration, in turn influencing the course of the therapy. First, Indian immigrants value education highly. Indian children tend to be studious, they work hard in school, and high expectations are placed on them with regard to achievement. (Recall the value placed on this by the religion: Student is the first stage of life.) Moreover, certain professions are more highly valued than others, with medical doctor being the occupation of highest status. In fact, Indian adolescents often accuse their parents of steering them solely toward the medical profession, to the exclusion of other occupational choices.

A second result of this immigration is potential guilt over leaving behind family members in India. Indian immigrants to the West were often regarded as the cream of the crop, in that wealthy families in India chose their firstborn son to send abroad for education. When these young people elected to stay abroad, the family at home may have consented with the spoken (or unspoken) expectation that they would eventually transport other family members abroad as well. Or, the young person may have faced family opposition, resulting in guilt over leaving family members behind in India. (This guilt is similar to the survivor guilt experienced by survivors of war, natural disasters, alcoholic family systems, and so on. Partly, this is because conditions in India, except for the extremely wealthy, are far more arduous than in the West.)

In sum, an Indian client is likely to be a recent immigrant, often with extended or nuclear family in India. Thus, circumstances of the client's immigration are relevant to the therapeutic relationship.

DEVALUING OF PSYCHOLOGY: OVERCOMING THIS OBSTACLE

The fact that a Hindu client has gone to see a therapist is a huge step for her or him. The therapist should not take it for granted how difficult it was to walk through the door and ask for help. There is an assumption in Hinduism and among Indians in general that the family should take care of its own. Outsiders are not invited to share in one's problems, particularly not intimate or potentially embarrassing problems. If a Hindu client has sought mental health services, it often means that the problem has escalated to great heights, or the issue is such that he or she is unable or unwilling to discuss it with other family members. But he or she has overcome significant conditioning to seek outside help. The therapist should be gentle with the client regarding this point and acknowledge how difficult it was to seek professional help. Also, one must be patient if the client is unable to talk about the primary problem right away. Also, the client may test the safety of the therapeutic environment for some time. There is a huge taboo against what he or she is doing; it may take time to overcome what may seem like an irrational fear to the therapist. Also, one must be patient if the client discloses a problem that has escalated to heights greater than one would normally see. Hold in check the natural (and human) tendency to be annoyed that this individual waited so long before seeking help.

The family aside, there is general skepticism in Indians regarding the value of psychotherapy. For example, one 16-year-old confided in therapy that she had always wanted to be a psychologist. When she told her father this a few years ago, he said, "Oh, you want to take the easy way out." (Both her parents were medical doctors.) She felt ashamed and never mentioned this desire to anyone again. In therapy, we reframed the issue: Becoming a psychologist does involve fewer years of schooling than medical school, but pioneering a profession in an unsupportive culture is definitely not the easy way out.

MORE ON THE SIGNIFICANCE OF THE FAMILY

If the client is Hindu, never assume that he or she is alone, even in an individual session. Always assume the extended family is there because they are certainly psychologically present in the client's mind. (See Boss & Greenburg's, 1984, research on psychologically present but physically absent persons, e.g., missing in action [MIAs].) A paradigm shift is required —whereas in the West, the unit of analysis is the individual, with Hindus, the unit of analysis is the family. In other words, the basic unit is always the family, even if the client is single or too young to be married (e.g., an adolescent). One must learn to think in terms of family, family, family. (Hinduism itself reflects this value: Every god has a consort. Rama was exiled with his family, i.e., his wife and brother, in the *Ramayana*. The *Mahabharata* is the story of the conflict between two large, extended families.)

One positive side to this aspect of Hinduism is that the therapist can call on family members for support, if the client is willing. It is not at all uncommon for family members to mobilize assistance, to travel long distances (even from India), and to stay for days, weeks, even months at a time if help is needed.

A therapist should take the time to understand the hold that the nuclear and extended family has on a Hindu client, positive and negative; investigate the expectations being placed on them and how they may have met them or disappointed their family through their current predicament. The therapist's respect for the client's place within the family, for the value that Hindus place on family, and her or his understanding of these ties will accomplish much toward establishing trust and a therapeutic alliance. Time must be taken to help the clients articulate any dilemmas they may feel between what is good for them as individuals and how that aligns with family or cultural values.

COMMON CLINICAL ISSUES: WHAT TO EXPECT

The most common issues that emerge with Hindu clients center around relationships. There is tremendous conflict between Hindu and Western concepts and expectations of relationships. Conflicts are arising cross-generationally within Hindu families on this issue as well.

Most Hindu marriages are arranged, and this strikes most Westerners as weird at best and repulsive at worst. "How can you marry someone you don't know? What if you don't like them and you're stuck with them?" From the Hindu perspective, the Western method is equally fraught with peril. "How can two young people know themselves and each other well enough to make a lifetime commitment?" Hindus point to divorce rates in the United States and Canada as ample evidence that this system does not work. Better to leave such an important decision to one's parents, who know best, to arrange this lifetime commitment.

The system of arranged marriage grew out of a Hindu agrarian society and makes sense under those conditions. Families joined through their children, increasing land and assets, and ensuring their futures by combining resources. In industrial society, with the increasing popularity of the nuclear family, conditions have changed. Also, the advent of women in the workforce has changed the rules of marriage. Even in the United States, as recently as a generation ago, marriage was considered to be a social contract, though usually between two people, as opposed to two extended families. Women married for economic security, to have children, a home, and an acknowledged place in society. With the exception of economic security, men married for similar reasons. When women began to achieve financial independence on their own, reasons for marriage became more about relationship, intimacy, and shared goals and dreams. Though increasingly important in Western marriages, these goals are still considered relatively insignificant by Hindus.

In Hindu marriages, a woman marries not a husband but a family, and typically moves in with the extended family (husband's parents, siblings, and their families of procreation). There is virtually no dating in Hindu society. Though this is changing in urban India, the norm is still for marriages to be arranged and for couples to live in extended family settings.

What happens, then, when Hindus move to the United States or Canada without the support of this extended family? The couple, left to their own devices, must look to one another for all the physical, emotional, and spiritual needs that the extended family would normally provide. Their safety net is gone. Moreover, if they do not get along with one another, the option of divorce does not exist. In Hindu society, divorce is the exception, not the rule (again, a huge difference between the two cultures).

Does this mean that Hindu marriages are happy? Not necessarily. In terms of quality of relationship, one cannot definitively state that Hindu marriages have the upper hand. It is simply that divorce is an option in Western society and not so in Hindu families. Divorced women are generally outcasts in Hindu society; at worst, they are looked down upon and at best, are treated awkwardly. One divorced client reported, "My Indian friends don't know what to do with me. It's like they don't know how to treat me, because I don't belong anywhere." Rarely will families in India take a woman back into their fold once she is married. The norm is to send her back to the in-laws no matter what. "Stick it out" is the rule. And most times, there are children involved, and Hindu women are taught never to leave their children.

Thus, relationship issues abound and are likely to be at the forefront of the therapeutic encounter. A Hindu wife may feel trapped but unable to leave. A Hindu husband may wish to make his wife happy but feels powerless and unskilled. Happiness in marriage was not a requirement in India. Why is it one now? Neither husband nor wife grew up with expectations of being happy, but thrown into Western culture, they are faced with cultural clashes that say they deserve more than just economic security and a parent for their children. They deserve fulfillment, and this confounds them.

What of the single Hindu woman or man? Many Hindus come to the West as students and may be thrown into a dating society for the first time. Hindu women are taught that it is immoral to date. For men, there is a double standard: While they may have fun with Western women, they are nonetheless expected to marry a chaste Indian bride, usually one arranged by the family in India. For a strong-minded, independent Hindu woman, a dilemma emerges. If she does not marry, she may have no place in society. But if she does, she may be turning over her independence and power to her husband or in-laws, and she may be genuinely fearful of this possibility.

The strong Hindu value on having children further complicates these issues. Westerners often comment on the delight that Hindus take in their children. They are prized and much beloved. One's status increases in society with the birth of children. In fact, in traditional families, something is gravely wrong if a couple does not procreate. The choice to not have children is as yet a foreign concept in Hinduism, despite the gross overpopulation problem in India.

Again, this is partially explained in historical context. In all agrarian societies, India included, children were considered an asset; this meant more people to work on the farm. In India, a gender preference also emerged, with boys being greater assets than girls. Boys brought brides home with them (meaning more children and more hands), whereas girls removed assets from the home in the form of dowries. Over time, giving birth to boys became a status symbol; conversely, having girl children became a liability. (In extreme cases, this has resulted in selective abortion and female infanticide.)

The complexity continues across generations through the following family dynamics: When a woman marries into a Hindu family, she arrives with little status. Holding the family's status is her mother-in-law, matriarch of the family. She has earned this place through giving birth to and raising her son; now, she is in the period of her life where she can enjoy her position and take charge of the home. The new bride must subsequently gain status by having a son; when she, in turn, becomes a mother-in-law (when her son marries), she will achieve matriarchal status. Power is obtained by having sons and passed down from generation to generation. Loyalty, then, tends to be cross-generational, from mother to son, not from spouse to spouse. This creates tremendous conflict for the husband, who is often torn and finds himself negotiating between wife and mother. Family systems therapists teach that marriages are weakened when one's primary loyalty is cross-generational (parent to child) as opposed to being within-generational (spouse to spouse). When dealing with a Hindu client, the therapist must be aware that the culture has deliberately (and over centuries) set up this very situation.

WHAT OF THE YOUNGER GENERATION?

What of the Hindu adolescent, who may have been born in the United States or Canada, but whose parents were likely born in India? Their issues, too, are most likely relationship based. They are growing up in a society in which dating and exploration between girls and boys is the norm. To whom do they turn for advice on this subject? To whom do they ask about sex? The likelihood is that their parents deny or simply cannot comprehend that their daughter or son is interested in dating. Even if they acknowledge that their child may be experiencing such feelings, what can they tell them? They themselves have probably never dated; hence, they have little practical advice to share. Hindu fathers commonly state that they will not permit their daughters to go to the prom, let alone the movies with any boy, "No group dating, no individual dating—no dating, period."

Some adolescents may obey, the danger being that they may feel left out or somehow "less than" their peers. Bolder or rebellious adolescents may go out anyway but "sneak around," the result being that they feel dishonest and ashamed of exploring their own growing feelings toward the opposite sex. Hindu adolescents also have serious questions about who they will someday marry. Their Hindu parents may magically expect them to marry a Hindu, of the right profession, the right caste, a good family (all the expectations that were placed on them). These adolescents look around and say to themselves, "I don't know many Indians, let alone Hindus, with these 'right' characteristics." Add to that their personal requirement of falling in love, and they may feel their chances diminishing further. Because Hindu children are taught a strong sense of duty and honor toward their parents, these feelings may create significant internal conflict.

The Hindu adolescent girl faces the additional problem of physical attractiveness. In a culture in which blonde and blue-eyed beauty is often the norm, she may feel physically unattractive. To whom does she turn for advice on makeup and fashion, if these interest her? Her mother is unlikely to be of assistance as most Hindu women in India do not wear makeup. Many women adapt to Western dress only after immigration. Physical attractiveness, so important to adolescents, may become an issue for Hindu girls, simply because their mothers may not be able to offer them practical advice and often are unaware that this may be of concern to their daughters.

Issues of academic achievement are less likely to surface because of the high value placed on education. However, for the child who does not achieve academically, the parents may be gravely concerned. Furthermore, a young adult's choice of occupation, particularly occupations perceived as being lower in status (i.e., anything other than secure, prestigious, professional positions) may create conflicts between parent and child.

SPECIAL ISSUES OF CONCERN

There is tremendous denial in Hindu society about certain issues, such as domestic violence and incest. Many women and men, well-educated and professional, say that such issues do not exist in Hindu families. This author disagrees, on the basis of clinical experience and observation of Hindu families. There seems to be a vested interest among Hindus in denying these problems, as if they reflected badly on Hinduism itself. Therefore, clients who report domestic abuse situations must be handled with extreme sensitivity. The therapist needs to know that asking a Hindu woman (assuming the abuse is directed at the woman) to leave such a situation is asking her to do more than leave an abusive husband. She may have to leave her community, source of economic support, children, friends, and home. She may be seriously ostracized by Hindus and may not receive the support of her extended family members. She needs to be prepared for all these very real possibilities. Moreover, unconfronted domestic abuse may be interpreted by children and adolescents in a Hindu family as tacit religious or cultural approval of such behavior, leading to abusive patterns that extend across generations.

The issue of incest is equally problematic and sensitive. Dearth of data makes this difficult to establish, but it is highly likely that incest is rampant in India. The extent to which this translates to Hindus living in the West is unclear. But in a culture that does not permit dating or sexual exploration, in which conditions of overcrowding are present, in which extended family members live together (often entire families in a single room), in which boys and girls share a room and often a bed through their adolescent years (because of overcrowding), conditions are ripe for incest. Yet, incest is vigorously denied by most Hindu families. If Hindu clients (male or female) discuss this, the therapist must proceed with utmost caution and give them permission to talk about this openly. One cannot assume family or religious community support around this issue. As yet, it is not a subject with which Hindus deal comfortably or objectively.

Another issue that may arise, but not in the usual Western form, is aging. Western society is highly youth oriented with a paranoid view of aging as something to be feared and avoided at all costs. Hindus do not subscribe to this belief system. Aging is a venerable and highly respected process. In fact, the persons most beloved in India are children and the elderly. Those in the middle generation are actually least valued; they are the "workhorses," and their function is to support these two age groups. This is the opposite of Western culture in which the valued generation is the middle one, and children and the elderly are marginalized. Hindus in the United States and Canada may expect that they will be cared for in their old age, according to the values of Hindu society, but may grow concerned as their children are exposed to other values. There are no nursing homes in India. There are no child-care centers. The extended family provides these services. How will Hindus in the United States and Canada manage to replicate such care without extended family support?

TREATMENT ISSUES AND APPROACHES

When working with Hindu clients, the natural treatment is a developmental approach. The religion itself is developmental in nature, with stages of progression, within and across lifetimes; therefore, it lends itself readily to this theoretical framework. First, one must determine where the client is in terms of developmental level: What stage of life he or she is in, whether student, householder, or retired. Most clients will come to therapy in the first two stages. Second, one must determine which wants they are pursuing, whether pleasure, worldly success, or duty. The therapist can combine this information with her or his own knowledge of developmental psychology; then, the client and therapist can share a common language. Hindus understand progression through stages; they also understand "the long haul," that is, how long it can take to make progress. The latter stems from their belief in reincarnation and expanded view of cosmic time.

Also critical is a firm grounding in family systems theory, which is needed because of the emphasis in Hinduism on the family. Such knowledge will prove invaluable as the therapist wades through the complex demands of the family on the client's psyche. It must be borne in mind, though, that unlike Western culture in which the nuclear family provides psychological boundaries for the client, the extended family plays this role for Hindu clients. Therefore, the sheer number of persons comprising this larger family system must be taken into account.

358   ANU R. SHARMA

Another approach that lends itself readily to working with Hindu clients is a cognitive–behavioral framework. This suits Hindus not necessarily on the basis of religious values but on the basis of the demographic characteristics of the Indian immigrant population, namely being well-educated and of higher-than-average socioeconomic status. Therefore, an intellectual approach, based on rational thinking, may be appropriate at times. However, this approach alone usually will not be sufficient because Hinduism contains so many contradictions and diverse aspects. Clients can find within the religion justifications for arguing almost any point that is solely rationally based.

One tendency to guard against when working with a Hindu client is that of the client relying on the professional simply because he or she is an authority figure or carries academic credentials. Hindus have been taught to respect and listen to the counsel of authority figures, such as elders or heads of families. They also value education highly and place great faith in persons with advanced degrees. The client may demand answers from the therapist, asking directly, "What should I do?" in a manner that can be disconcerting to Western-trained professionals. Clients may not understand or be willing to explore issues to the extent that Westerners tolerate. Therefore, a strictly Rogerian or phenomenological approach would likely prove to be less effective with Hindus, though certainly such techniques can be used to guide the client toward taking more responsibility for the therapy.

USING KARMA THERAPEUTICALLY

Belief in karma implies a belief in personal responsibility. "The present condition of each individual's interior life—how happy he is, how confused or serene, how much he can see—is an exact product of what he has wanted and gotten in the past; and equally, his present thoughts and decisions are determining his future states" (Smith, 1958, p. 77). The soul chooses all its life circumstances: The family and time in which to be born, as well as all ensuing circumstances most conducive for its evolution. Hindus believe that they choose their parents. This is an empowering aspect and one which often removes the victim mentality, where clients spend hours bemoaning the "unfairness" of life. Hindus do not believe that life is unfair. The therapist can use this belief in karma to help a client assume personal responsibility for his or her life.

An inappropriate use of karma, though, occurs when Hindus use this mode of thinking to be fatalistic, to accept too easily, to not act on their own behalf. "It's my karma (meaning 'it's my fate'), so why do anything about it?" "I was born into these circumstances, and nothing will change in this lifetime." "I must await the next birth for things to be better." In reality, Hinduism does not condone or encourage such thinking. Only by working in *this* lifetime will things improve in the next.

Another implication of karma is the belief that nothing is random, that there is no such thing as accidents. What occurs to a person is his or her due and must be accepted as such. This, too, can help individuals take personal responsibility for themselves. *Why* something occurred is not a useful pursuit of inquiry; *that* it occurred is enough. In this regard, karma can be a practical mechanism to help clients "get on with it."

Finally, clients can realize that not everything has to be experienced in this lifetime. If some life experience is unavailable to them (for example, if they cannot have children), their belief in reincarnation allows for the fact that they were parents in another lifetime and will likely be parents again. In fact, they may well experience every human culture, gender, socioeconomic status, and so on.

If the concept of karma is difficult to understand, it may be helpful to think of it as being equivalent to Western psychology's concept of neurosis. When someone is stuck in a neurotic pattern (e.g., "I'll always be alone, I'll never be happy, my life will always be this way"), he or she is looping endlessly in a repetitive pattern. This is exactly the definition of a karmic pattern—continual repetition of a pattern caught in time (personal communications, Barbara Johnson, September, 1994; and Ronald Mangravite, January, 1995).

USING CONTRADICTIONS

Hindus living in the West are a mass of contradictions. (Hindus living in the East are also!) The religion itself contains all these contradictions, so why would the people be any different? In fact, this is one of the greatest contributions of Hinduism: It is broad, containing all duality, all forms of diversity, all aspects of the manifest universe. The therapist should help clients articulate their conflicts between their individual selves and the family, between Hindu arranged marriages and Western intimacy, between feeling simultaneously part of both cultures and of neither culture. If the therapist can help them name these tensions and hold them in the light for examination, clients can progress. A developmental approach may be especially helpful here, in which the therapist helps the client move from the stage where the conflict exists to a higher stage where it can be resolved (Kegan, 1982).

WORKING WITH LEADERS OF THE COMMUNITY

Leaders in the religious community play a role different in Hinduism than in Western religions. One outgrowth of the caste system has been the allowance and, in fact, encouragement of the Brahmin (priest and scholar) caste to largely withdraw from society. Although they officiate at rituals and ceremonies and are called upon to establish auspicious dates for marriages and other important events, they are typically not used as counselors or persons who give comfort during times of loss, illness, and stress. This differentiates them from Western ministers, priests, and rabbis and, as a result, Hindu religious leaders would likely not be in a position to refer a client to a psychotherapist. Such responsibility falls to leaders of the community at large, usually heads of families, business leaders, professionals, and respected elders. In working with these leaders, one skill especially is paramount. The professional must communicate respect and understanding for the importance of family. What most concerns community leaders is that Western values will infiltrate the Hindu family, leading to divorce, dating, sexual exploration among young people, and so on. The extreme negative stereotype of the Western-trained professional is that he or she counsels adults to leave marriages, encourages young people to make selfish choices over the needs of the family, and so forth. If the professional can establish herself or himself as someone who takes seriously the significance of family relationships, he or she can make strides in gaining credibility with community leaders.

CASE STUDIES

Sharmila

Sharmila, a married woman with three children, had been beaten by her husband for over 20 years. She came to me through the urging of several Caucasian friends. She was torn about whether to leave her husband, even though she was educated, held a professional position, and her children were of late adolescent age, the oldest already in college. Her husband repeatedly told her that if she left him, she would be "nameless and faceless." He said she would have no standing in the Indian community; all their friends would turn against her. Though her parents were long deceased, she talked in session of the disappointment her elder brother (still living in India) would feel were she to leave her husband. She spoke with her siblings often on the phone, and they urged her to stay with her husband, despite her reports of the domestic abuse.

She was moving from the householder stage, relinquishing duty to others (to husband, children, and extended family) toward retirement, when she was beginning to ask, "Who am I truly?" In developmental psychology terms, she was moving from an external to an internal orientation. In therapy, she began to realize that her years of duty were coming to an end; moreover, no interpretation of duty required that she be subjected to domestic violence. She could focus on keeping herself and her children safe. We discussed the reaction of her family in India and her Hindu friends in the United States should she leave her husband, and how to manage their ostracizing, if it occurred. She tested the waters by telling two female friends, both Hindu, and was surprised to find them quite supportive. They offered to let her move in with them should she need temporary shelter. The extended family members in India were less accepting at first. However, Sharmila stuck to her decision and ultimately did leave her husband. At that time, her sister came from India to help her move and reestablish herself independently.

Jaya

Jaya, a 30-year-old graduate student, came to the United States at the age of 25. Her presenting problem centered around marriage: Should she get married, and if so, to whom? Her family in India was pressing her to have an arranged marriage and were preparing to find a suitable match for her. In her 5 years here, Jaya had had two significant relationships, one with an Indian man, the other with a Caucasian man. She felt extremely guilty about both relationships and kept them secret from her parents, fearing their disapproval. She was also confused about her strong, independent nature and how she seemed to flip, that is, become dependent when involved with a man. In fact, both men broke up with her because she became too clingy. "How can I be so competent and independent, and then, as soon as I get into a relationship, act so different?" she asked. In the course of therapy, we identified the conflicts between her values and those of her family, between relationship as defined by the two cultures, and her expectations of marriage. We also named her fears about giving her power away to a man should she get married (the primary picture she had painted of relationships). She began to see clearly her pattern of picking unavailable men (both relationships were with men reluctant to make a commitment), so that she would never be faced with an actual decision about marriage and face her parents' disapproval. We also talked about her age and desire to have children, weighing in on the side of an arranged marriage. She was concerned that she may not meet and fall in love with someone in time to "beat the biological clock." Jaya decided ultimately to explore the possibility of an arranged marriage and to meet several men her parents recommended. She said that "nothing would be lost by keeping an open mind, that maybe I will actually like one of them." After completing graduate school, she returned to India and began that process.

Ramesh

Ramesh was in the householder stage, with a wife and four children. He and his wife had been married for 24 years and had had a "love marriage" in India. Upon immigration to the United States, Ramesh systematically brought his siblings and their families to the United States. His wife's family remained in India. Ramesh came to therapy because he said his wife was unhappy all the time. Despite their 15 years in the United States, she desperately missed her family in India. She became cheerful only on her annual visits there and was depressed the remainder of the time. Ramesh wanted to help her but did not know how. He felt that he was raising the children alone because when depressed, she left household duties and child-care responsibilities to him. Ramesh tended to be domineering and told her repeatedly that she should simply "get over it." During the course of therapy, we identified that his wife was, in fact, clinically depressed and not simply missing her family. She came from an alcoholic family system and depression was part of her family's history as well. After several couples sessions, they decided to seek psychiatric help for her. This was extremely difficult for her because she believed this meant she was inherently weak. It was equally hard for Ramesh, as he thought it showed his inability to properly care for his wife. Her depression did, however, alleviate with appropriate medication. At this stage, they are examining their marriage and working on communication and realistic expectations of each other in their marriage.

Kiran

Kiran, a 16-year-old, was brought to counseling by her mother because her grades were dropping. She was highly intelligent, her mother reported, and there was no reason that she and her husband could identify for this lowered academic achievement. Kiran herself could not say why she was doing more poorly in school. Instead of straight As, she was bringing home Bs and even a C. Her parents decided that perhaps she should be assessed by a psychologist because she may have developed a learning disability. Although learning disabilities are outside my area of expertise, her parents insisted on having me see her initially because of my Hindu background. They said they would trust someone I recommended. In the course of several sessions, it became apparent that Kiran's interests were broadening beyond school. She had always been a pretty and popular girl with a wide range of activities. At this stage, she had never dated but was beginning to feel resentful about not being able to do so (though she had never discussed this with her parents). We talked about the conflicts that she felt over wanting to date. Could she stay popular without dating? How would she feel not being able to go to the junior prom? What would she say if someone asked her out? How could she explain that she was not permitted to go out with boys? Should she broach the subject to her parents? She was also concerned about her physical attractiveness. She wore only lipstick but wanted to try eye makeup. She was also becoming self-conscious about facial hair. A boy in school had made a remark about her having a mous-tache, and she did not know what to do. Though clearly in the student stage, Kiran was developing interests beyond her designated "job" of stu-dent, as defined by Hindu culture. As we explored her concerns, we dis-cussed ways in which she could broach these sensitive topics with her mother. In several sessions with her mother present, Kiran told her mother of her fears of losing her popular status if she could not date, wear makeup, and so on. Her mother understood most of these concerns and talked to Kiran about the family's Hindu values, and why they believed in them. Over the course of therapy, her parents determined that Kiran could wear makeup and go out on group dates. They also said she could go to the prom, if she double dated with a friend they deemed trustworthy. In the future, they will need to tackle the issue of individual dating and the freedoms that Kiran will assume upon leaving home and going to college.

FUTURE DIRECTIONS FOR RESEARCH AND PRACTICE

Future directions for research and practice in working with Hindu clients center around a recent immigration population striving to move from an extended family-based model to a nuclear family model. The Hindu community views with concern the Western fluctuation in relation-ships and yet is baffled as to how to maintain Hindu family values in the face of Western influence. How do Hindu clients living in the United States and Canada maintain extended family values without the physical presence and support of the extended family? How do they cultivate and maintain the strong affection and care given to children and the elderly? How do they accommodate adjustment or developmental problems, as well as critical issues such as domestic abuse and incest? How do they allow these concerns to be seen, heard, and made available for professional sup-port and intervention without feeling as if they had failed? Clearly, both gender and generational roles are in transition as Hindus continue to adjust to Western values and life. Negotiating these conflicts in values, roles, and boundaries, both for individuals and families, will continue to provide im-petus for future research and practice.

SUGGESTED READINGS

Buck, W. (1973). *Mahabharata*. Berkeley: University of California Press.

Divakaruni, C. B. (1995). *Arranged marriage*. New York: Anchor Books.

Easwaran, E. (1987). *Upanishads*. Tomales, CA: Nilgiri Press.

Mascaro, J. (1962). *The Bhagavad Gita*. London: Penguin.

Roy, A. (1997). *The god of small things*. New York: HarperPerennial.

Smith, H. (1994). *The illustrated world's religions*. New York: HarperCollins.

Zimmer, H. (1951). *The philosophies of India*. New York: Pantheon.

REFERENCES

Boss, P., & Greenburg, J. (1984). Family boundary ambiguity: A new variable in family stress theory. *Family Process, 23*, 535–546.

Kegan, R. (1982). *The evolving self: Problem and process in human development*. Cambridge, MA: Harvard University.

Renou, L. (Ed.). (1963). *Hinduism*. New York: Washington Square Press.

Smith, H. (1958). *The religions of man*. New York: New American Library.

Stoddart, W. (1993). *Outline of Hinduism*. Washington, DC: Foundation for Traditional Studies.

Viswanathan, E. D. (1986). *Daddy, am I a Hindu?* Bombay, India: S. Ramakrishnan.

Zimmer, H. (1951). *The philosophies of India*. New York: Panthean.

Zysk, K. G. (1989). *The origins and development of classical Hinduism: A. L. Basham*. Boston: Beacon Press.

VI

ETHNIC-CENTERED
SPIRITUALITY

15

PSYCHOTHERAPY WITH MEMBERS OF AFRICAN AMERICAN CHURCHES AND SPIRITUAL TRADITIONS

DONELDA A. COOK AND CHRISTINE Y. WILEY

He knows, yes, He knows, just how much we can bear.
 Tho' the load gets heavy, your're never left alone to bear it all;
Ask for the strength and keep on toiling, tho' the tear-drops fall.
 You have the joy of this assurance:
The heavenly Father will always answer prayer and He knows,
 Yes, He knows just how much you can bear.

—Roberta Martin

Over 25 years ago, Reginald Jones's (1972) ground-breaking edited book, *Black Psychology*, articulated the need to adapt traditional counseling and psychotherapy practices to the cultural worldviews of African Americans. Wade Nobles (1972) introduced the features of basic African philosophy which form the foundations for Black psychology, that is, philosophical values, customs, attitudes, and behaviors that African Americans share with most West African tribes. Religion or spirituality was a prominent feature of African philosophy which Nobles (1972) proposed as being significant in therapeutic work with African Americans. Although traditional psychology training programs dissuaded discussion of religion and spirituality with clients (Boyd-Franklin, 1989; Helms & Cook, 1999; Richards & Bergin, 1997), African American psychologists recognized that spirituality was integral to the identity of African Americans, thereby necessitating its inclusion in the therapy process.

Spirituality has survived as a core value for African American people, through the legacies of their African heritage and their survival of slavery (Boyd-Franklin, 1989; Wiggins Frame & Braun Williams, 1996). Furthermore, African American churches have been powerbrokers in the fight for African American freedom and justice in the United States, from slavery, through the civil rights movement, to the present day (Moore, 1991).

Whether churched or unchurched, most African Americans are aware of the spiritual influences that have been passed down through generations (Boyd-Franklin, 1989). Regardless of formal church affiliations, most African Americans are cognizant of the role of the church in responding to their psychological, social, cultural, economic, educational, and political needs (Cook, 1993; Wiley, 1991). Both the inner spirit of the individual and the collective spirit of the church are important resources for mental health providers working with African American clients (Cook, 1993).

Before addressing the implications of African American churches and Afrocentric spiritual traditions for counseling and psychotherapy, we provide a historical context for understanding the spiritual worldview of many African Americans as related to African culture and the rise of African American Christian churches from slavery through the present. Because of the rich oral tradition of African American culture, the past is implicitly ingrained in racial identity development and other aspects of mental health of African Americans today (Boyd-Franklin, 1989; Helms & Cook, 1999; Nobles, 1972).

HISTORY OF AFRICAN AMERICAN SPIRITUALITY

In the Beginning: African Culture

As people of African descent, African Americans have inherited a cultural legacy that perceives spirituality as a foundation of personal and communal life. For a detailed discussion of African religion and spirituality, we recommend the original work of John S. Mbiti (1969). According to Mbiti (1969), traditional African culture does not separate spirituality from one's personal identity. Wherever the African is, whatever the African is doing, whether alone or in community, the African is *living* his or her religion. It shapes African cultures, social lives, educational and vocational lives, political organizations, and economic activities (Indowu, 1992). Religion is integrated into one's life and breath, rather than being compartmentalized as religious dogma or regulated beliefs (Boyd-Franklin, 1989; Mbiti, 1969). God is seen in everyone and everything as benevolent, a Supreme Being, and the Creator of all things (Mitchell & Mitchell, 1989).

Indowu (1992) described the internal dynamic of African religion in dominating African people's thinking, sense of security, life adjustment, identity development, code of conduct in different situations, and problem-solving capability. He describes African religious way of life as "essentially ... what healing is about" (Indowu, 1992, p. 193). Mbiti (1969) explained that although African religions change with the times, "in times of crisis they often come to the surface, or people revert to them in secret" (p. 2). Mental health practitioners can explore the potential of this cultural worldview with their African American clients.

African spirituality is communal (Nobles, 1972). An individual ascribes his or her existence to the community, including past generations (Mbiti, 1969). Traditional religions exist foremost for the community, rather than the individual. The traditional African view of self is: "I am because we are; and because we are, therefore, I am" (Mbiti, 1969, p. 108). What traditional analytical psychology would label as enmeshment when an individual ascribes his or her identity to his or her family or social group is recognized as having a healthy collective identity in African culture (Helms & Cook, 1999). African individuals feel responsible for other people such that they are keenly aware of how their behavior impacts on the community, whether contributing positively or negatively to the good of the community. The individual is a reflection of the community, and the community is a reflection of the individual. Africans share in each other's sufferings and joys and recognize the dead as spirits that are still active in their lives (Mbiti, 1969).

Spiritual beliefs and practices are assimilated throughout families and communities and passed down through generations, each generation adapting the traditions in ways suitable to the historical circumstances of the times (Mbiti, 1969). Symbolic imagery and rhythm are rich aspects of religious worship (Phelps, 1990). Religious practices are not confined to sacred buildings or to one sacred day of the week for worship. One acts out of religious meaningfulness and consciousness at any time and in any place (Mbiti, 1969). Religious consciousness is transmitted in African society ubiquitously from heart to heart rather than by written word. According to Mbiti (1969), beliefs concerning God and the spirits represent one way of knowing about African religion. As important is the religious living of the people from "before birth to after physical death" (Mbiti, 1969, p. 4). Religious beliefs and religious actions are intricately intertwined.

For a description of specific African religious beliefs and practices, we recommend John Mbiti's (1991) work, *Introduction to African Religion*. Although religious beliefs and practices vary among African peoples, he attempts to draw upon commonalities. According to Mbiti, Africans believe that God created the universe; as Creator of all things, God also sustains, provides for, and rules over all creation. The Creator is perceived as a just ruler, good, merciful, holy, all-powerful, all-knowing, present everywhere, limitless, never changing, and an invisible everlasting Spirit. God cannot be explained or fully known. For some Africans, God is viewed as their Father, for others, their Mother, and still others see God as their Friend.

The Creator is approached through

- worship,
- prayers,
- sacrificial offerings,
- singing and dancing,
- rituals, and
- human and spiritual intermediaries.

Mbiti (1991) further explains that Africans believe that there are many types of invisible spirits in the universe that were created by God and whose status lies between God and humans. These spirits are of nature or human forms. Nature spirits include those that reside in the sky (e.g., sun, moon, stars, rainbows, rain, wind, thunder, lightning) and those in the earth (e.g., hills, mountains, rocks, trees, metals, water forms). However, all African peoples do not believe in nature and earth spirits, but for those who do believe, these spirits help to explain many of the mysteries surrounding them. Human spirits consist of those who died long ago and who are considered ghosts, and those of people who died recently and are considered to be living dead. The latter matter most to African families as they are believed to lead a personal continuation of life in spirit form. Spirits of the recent dead may live close to family members through four or five generations.

For African American clients rooted in their ethnic culture, African spirituality may represent a holistic approach to living. Spirituality may provide one with (a) a healthy sense of self; (b) a community of belonging and way of relating to others; and (c) spiritual powers to be called upon for direction and protection in all aspects of one's life. Conceptually, spirituality may lie at the heart of a healthy personal existence and collective actualization (contrasted with self-actualization) for African Americans. Although not every African American belongs to organized religions or churches, the religious journey of African Americans as a people dates before birth, from the shores of their homeland in Africa to the shores of their captivity in America. Through the oral tradition, many African Americans know of the strength of their spiritual heritage and the role of African American churches in their survival as an American people.

The Emergence of African American Churches

When Africans were stolen from their tribal communities and transported to America as slaves, attempts were made to destroy their cultural identity. European American slaveholders tried to abolish the spiritual traditions of African slaves; yet, their spirituality was enlisted for survival (Moore, 1991). They found sustenance in the Presence of God, in secret meetings of unity to draw strength from one another, and in covert communication through music and dance (Phelps, 1990). They celebrated God's Presence in the midst of suffering the evils of slavery, "As the drums beat, slaves opened themselves to receive the Spirit, to become united with that spirit which strengthened their lifeforce and restored their wounded bodies" (Phelps, 1990, p. 338).

In the mid-1600s, the European church attempted to Christianize slaves in the interest of saving souls. Slaveholders resisted this for political, social, and economic reasons (Moore, 1991). Christianity was also used for "social control, to produce 'obedient and docile' slaves" (Lincoln & Mamiya, 1990, p. 200). Eventually, African slaves adapted Christian forms of worship to their native spirituality, particularly adopting aspects of Christianity that provided solace in their enslavement (Phelps, 1990). They began organizing their own worship services, creating the "invisible church" (Moore, 1991, p. 152). They met at prearranged times in secret places for singing, preaching, Biblical story telling, and praying. Thus, African American spirituality continued as a practical means of living, promoting a sense of community, providing spiritual expression, catharsis, and developing ideologies of liberation for Africans in America (Moore, 1991). White Americans used Christianity to justify the enslavement of Africans. Nevertheless, Jesus became a liberating figure for enslaved Africans, as they identified with his persecution, were strengthened by his perseverance, and found hope and power in his resurrection (Lincoln & Mamiya, 1990).

In the latter part of the 18th century, congregations and churches for African Americans were formed. Independent African American churches formed in part as a result of their experiences of racism in White congregations (Phelps, 1990). They were conceived and controlled by African Americans, incorporating worship styles and practices compatible with African American spiritual expressions. Other African American churches had limited independence as they were controlled by mainstream White denominations (Moore, 1991). The formation of African American churches allowed African Americans to emphasize aspects of Christianity that spoke to their unique experiences in America. For example, great emphasis was placed on their understanding of themselves as "children of God" rather than their U.S. Constitutional designation as "three-fifths human" (Lincoln & Mamiya, 1990, p. 4).

The "freedom" aspect of Christianity, that is, free "to be all that God intended" (Lincoln & Mamiya, 1990, p. 5) one to be, became the beloved cry of African Americans in the fight for equality in America. The civil rights movement emerged from the outgrowth of the freedom cry in African American churches. African American ministers and lay workers organized the movement; their churches provided financial support and large numbers of dedicated followers. Preachers used their pulpits on Sunday mornings to relay the message of justice and equality. They addressed the negative self-images that many African Americans internalized from oppressive social conditions by affirming the ethnic, physical, cultural, and historical pride of being African people (Lincoln & Mamiya, 1990). Many African Americans converted to the Islamic faith as a result of the historical oppression of White Christianity. The physical images of a White Jesus, accompanied by the hatred espoused in Jesus' name by White extremists, were cause enough for African Americans to follow the teachings of the Honorable Elijah Muhammed of the Black Muslim faith.

However, Black liberation theology later emerged with the notion of a Black God that God or Jesus "should be viewed and interpreted from a people's own experience" (Lincoln & Mamiya, 1990, p. 177). James Cone elaborated on systematic theologies from an African American perspective in his book *Black Theology and Black Power* (1969). Black liberation theology provided answers for racially conscious African Americans who struggled with the blond-hair, blue-eyed images of Jesus that reflected the image of their oppressors rather than their Savior. In addition to providing Biblical descriptions of Jesus that contradicted White images depicted in the pictures and stained glass windows adorning their churches, theologians have educated African Americans regarding the presence of Africans in the Bible (Felder, 1989). Black liberation theology helped to bridge the gap between Black Christians and Black Muslims as they unified in affirming empowering religious images and doctrines for Black people in America.

Along with the racial consciousness movement in African American churches came social consciousness in providing social services to the African American community. Although fighting for an end to racial discrimination for African Americans in the United States, African American churches have also taken responsibility for providing for the social, educational, economic, and psychological welfare of the African American community. Psychologically, African American churches serve as support systems through therapeutic aspects of church services, formal and informal pastoral counseling services, and formal and informal community service programs (Cook, 1993; Wiley, 1991).

Thus, African American churches are solidly embedded within the context of the African American community. They have endured and will continue to sustain themselves as permanent fixtures within American culture. The African American church, as a societal institution, is often characterized as the only institution within American society that is owned and is solely controlled by the African American community (Cook, 1993; Moore, 1991). Although African American churches are recognized as being influential social institutions, they are founded and sustained by the power and presence of an all-sufficient God (Mitchell & Mitchell, 1989).

Knowledge of the history of African spirituality and African American churches is necessary in providing mental health providers with an understanding of how African culture, African slavery in America, and the ongoing fight for African American equality are deeply rooted in the worldview of many African American individuals. Because of the oral tradition and the ancestral importance of African culture, the past is part of the present for many African Americans. Furthermore, the collective consciousness is such that despite individual successes, oppression within the racial group can weigh heavily upon the individual. African American churches have been powerful vessels for retaining as much of traditional African spirituality as possible, under the dehumanizing conditions of slavery and the domination of institutionalized racism. Perhaps the combined African spiritual roots and remarkable survival as an oppressed people contributes to African Americans' strong beliefs in a real and living God (Mitchell & Mitchell, 1989).

CONTEMPORARY AFRICAN AMERICAN CHURCHES

Contemporary African American churches have retained aspects of their historical and cultural roots. Although variability exists among the African American churches of today, we will attempt to keep the focus of our discussion on the question, "What is most important for mental health providers to understand about African American churches when working with individuals from African American church congregations?" We may have presented a rather idealized picture of African American churches because of their pivotal roles in the survival of African Americans throughout the history of the United States. Our discussion now focuses on aspects of contemporary African American churches that for better or for worse may influence the mental health of individuals within church congregations.

Denominational Diversity

Our discussion of church denominations is limited to independent African American-controlled denominations, mainline Protestant denominations consisting of African American churches that belong to White denominations, Roman Catholics, and Holiness and Pentecostals. Independent African American churches include the following Methodist, Pentecostal, and Baptist denominations: African Methodist Episcopal (AME), African Methodist Episcopal Zion (AMEZ), Christian Methodist Episcopal (CME), Church of God in Christ (COGIC), National Baptist Convention of America, Inc. (NBCA), National Baptist Convention, U.S.A., Inc. (NBC), National Missionary Baptist Convention of America (NMDC), and Progressive National Baptist Convention, Inc. (PNBC). Mainline Protestant churches include United Methodist, United Church of Christ, American Baptist, Lutheran, Presbyterian, and Episcopalian. Independent African American Baptist churches and the United Church of Christ function autonomously, whereas individual churches within other denominations typically have an external leadership hierarchy to whom they must report. In the latter cases, Pastors are limited by the organizational structures and doctrines set forth by the denomination.

Perceptions of counseling and psychotherapy vary across denominations. African American churches have in the past been suspicious of counseling, espousing that all one needs is Jesus. However, in recent years, they have become more open to counseling as Pastors have become more educated through seminary training and more women have entered the ministry who have had previous careers in the mental health fields. Furthermore, Pastors have become more inundated with counseling concerns beyond their professional expertise and time constraints. There seems to be less opposition to counseling *if* the Pastor is confident that mental health providers are open to the churches' religious perspective and are attuned to the racial and cultural lives of African Americans. Mainline Protestant and Catholic denominations tend to be most open to counseling because of the influence of the larger White denominations. COGIC and mainline Pentecostal and Holiness churches tend to hold the most conservative attitudes toward counseling.

The meaning of church denomination varies with clients. Many African Americans have remained in the denominations within which they were raised. They may or may not know the doctrines of their denomination. What may be of more importance to them is that they have a community of shared social and spiritual experience. Membership in an independent African American church or in a predominantly African American mainline Protestant, Catholic, or Pentecostal church may be a haven from the bicultural existence with which African Americans must cope in the larger society.

Although denominational differences exist, there are specific Christian beliefs that are important to most African American churches and communities. According to Mitchell and Mitchell (1989), foremost is the belief that the nature of God and His created world is trusting and benevolent. As such, African Americans have a sensitivity of spirit which finds God present in all things and all people, thus, believers are known to "talk to God anywhere" at anytime. African American Christians strongly affirm the "Providence of God. . . . Whatever the cruelty or injustice of an incident, the final outcome will be positive for the child of God" (Mitchell & Mitchell, 1989, p. 104).

Lincoln and Mamiya (1990, pp. 12–15) described six pairs of "dialectically related polar opposites" with which African American churches can be characterized, regardless of denominations. Mental health providers may find such categorizations more meaningful than denominations in understanding differences among African American churches. Exhibit 15.1 presents the dialects and the implications they may have for therapy.

Community Fellowship

The communal foundation of African American churches is most evident. Some individuals become members of their family's church at birth and remain so until they die. The church serves as extended family (Boyd-Franklin, 1989). Values, codes of conduct, and social attitudes of the church and the family are intertwined. In some instances, this can promote healthy lifestyles for individuals, families, and communities. It can also be a source of conflict, particularly as children grow into adolescents and young adults and develop their own standards of behavior (Boyd-Franklin, 1989). The strong communal nature can impinge on church members' privacy, particularly in smaller churches. However, the church's relational aspects of reconciling, healing, sustaining, and guiding remain a positive influence in the African American community (Wimberly, 1991).

African American churches often consist of intricate organizational structures that resemble Western civilizations' governmental systems or African tribal communities. There are numerous leadership and service positions. Most African American churches have developed resources for the basic needs of the community, including food, shelter, financial sustenance, education, child care, health care, communications, political action, safety and security, cultural expression, transportation, emotional support, and recreation. The church exists as a spiritual lifestyle expressing the belief that God is in all of life and that Christians can have a good time serving the Lord.

Resources are available to congregational members and are often extended to individuals in need outside the congregation. Churches have attempted to respond to the social ills and struggles in the community in both spiritual and social services through church-based counseling centers, 12-step programs and support groups, Bible studies, and prayer and healing services (Wimberly, 1991). Wimberly describes how small-group healing meetings may spontaneously occur during evening worship services or choir rehearsals, or planned as ritual healing services. He further explains, "Worship and communal resources are brought to bear on personal needs; and when the emotional, interpersonal, and psychological needs of persons are met in the context of ritual and worship, pastoral care takes place" (Wimberly, 1991, p. 24). Even though most African American churches provide worship and social services 7 days a week, they have not been able to keep up with the growing needs and demands of the community. Consequently,

EXHIBIT 15.1
Church Dialects and Implications for Therapy

Dialects	Emphasis	Therapy Implications
Priestly	Worship and spiritual life	Provides individual attention, healing services, spiritual community, religious restrictions. Skeptical of counseling.
vs.	vs.	
Prophetic	Community service and political issues	Provides social services. Positive racial consciousness may be too involved for individual needs.
Other-worldly	Heaven and eternal life	Encouraged to be patient and wait for rewards in afterlife. Less open to counseling.
vs.	vs.	
This-worldly	State of lives in here and now	Sensitive to individual cares and struggles. Open to counseling.
Universalism	Universalism of Christian gospel	Ignores racial or cultural differences and problems related to racial discrimination. May have strong belief in God solving all problems. If open to counseling, race of counselor would not matter.
vs.	vs.	
Particularism	Confrontation of racial history and oppression	Provides racially liberating messages and advocacy for racial discrimination. Preference for African American counselor.
Communal	Political, economic, educational, social concerns of wider community	Provides social services regardless of church membership.
vs.	vs.	
Privatistic	Services limited to church congregation	Provides services to church members.

Exhibit continues

EXHIBIT 15.1 (*Continued*)

Dialects	Emphasis	Therapy Implications
Charismatic	Charismatic personality of Pastor	Pastor greatly influences church members' lives. Openness to counseling depends on pastors beliefs.
vs.	vs.	
Bureaucratic	Organizational structure, membership, and financial record-keeping	Pastor and church have less influence on church members' lives.
Accommodation	Accommodates to influences of larger society	Follows mainstream religious beliefs and practices. Less focus on African American culture and racial matters.
vs.	vs.	
Resistance	Autonomously affirms African American cultural persective and fosters self-determination	Fosters positive racial consciousness and collective identity development. Creates workshops to fit needs of congregation.

Note. The dialectics and their points of emphasis are based in part on information presented in the 1990 book, *The Black Church in the African-American Experience*, by C. E. Lincoln and L. H. Mamiya.

churches have lost some of their connections with unchurched members of the African American community.

Role of Women

African American churches are composed primarily of women members, who maintain many of the auxiliaries, educational programs, and social services (Lincoln & Mamiya, 1990). Women tend to be faithful followers of their Lord and their Pastor. The leadership structures have been characterized as African American men in the pulpit and African American women in the pew, the men in power and the women following. Many African American Christian clients still hold to the literal Biblical mandate of man as the head of the household. Pastors may become de facto the dominant male in female-headed households. Historically, the church has been the only place in society where African American men consistently hold positions of respect and authority, thus they have been reluctant to share the power with women. Lincoln and Mamiya (1990) provide a historical overview of the role of women in African American churches.

Women have gained increasing influence. There have been breakthroughs in women pastoring and in taking significant leadership positions; however, progress has been gradual. Many women within African American churches prefer the presence of men as head of the church and vehemently stand against women as ministers. The subordinate role of women can foster dynamics of internalized oppression. Women have been nurtured and taken care of within the church but under oppressive conditions. Women who have experienced abuse in their lives often find themselves in churches in which the Pastor is authoritative. The power of a charismatic Pastor has the potential for stirring competition among women for his attention. Therapists should spend time examining the role of women in their clients' churches and the ways in which the nuances of gender in the church relate to clients' social and familial dynamics.

Worship Practices

Worship practices in African American churches are based on belief in the Holy Trinity of God the Father, Jesus Christ the Son, and the Holy Spirit. Faith becomes real to African American Christians by calling upon Jesus as the One who liberates, reconciles, heals, and guides. They hope in the person of Jesus with whom they have a trusting relationship. There is also an "emphasis on God's healing presence in life despite suffering and pain" (Wimberly, 1991, p. 16). "The mainstream of worship is a communal experience of the divine Presence, or the Holy Spirit, manifested often in involuntary acts of praise" (Mitchell & Mitchell, 1989, p. 105).

Many aspects of worship in African American churches can provide cathartic experiences for church members. "The very strength of Black spirituality is in the fact that it is so literally holistic and specifically requires the involvement of the higher emotions and of the senses and limbs as well" (Mitchell & Mitchell, 1989, p. 105). Some researchers have found evidence of therapeutic aspects of African American worship services (Griffith, English, & Mayfield, 1980; Griffith, Young, & Smith, 1984). The music of many African American worship services can be uplifting in providing words of hope and encouragement, rhythms of excitement and anticipation, or words and melodies that speak empathetically to the pain of the downtrodden. In some worship services, clapping, dancing, and shouting further enthralls church members in spiritual expressiveness.

Corporate prayers also encourage members to speak to God freely about their troubles. Testimonials offer hope as the congregation hears what God has done in the lives of others. Scripture readings recall how God is available through the written word, and the stories of God's relationship with the people in the Bible can open new possibilities for believers' relationships with God. The message delivered in the preacher's sermon can be comforting and instructive. Open disclosures by the Pastor and the congregation regarding their life stories extend opportunities for members to feel that they are not alone in their distress. There is an expectation that individuals will be different when they leave the worship experience. They will have received hope, healing, care, and empowerment to negotiate their daily lives. Worship experiences have led many to believe that if they worship, pray, and live their faith, they do not need traditional counseling. Therapists can explore such attitudes with their clients, as well as their responses to aspects of spiritual worship and incorporate appropriate worship activities into the therapy process. Praying, physical movement to inspirational music, and reading inspirational scriptures resemble many of the cognitive and behavioral techniques of psychotherapy (Richards & Bergin, 1997).

Role of Pastor

The role of Pastor is typically one of reverence and great influence in the church, the family, and the community. As in African cultures, knowledgeable religious professionals "act as intermediaries between individuals and God. . . . People go to them for their needs and problems and it is their (the healers') duty to approach God through prayers" (Indowu, 1990, p. 197). Historically, preachers were distinguished during slavery in that they were allowed freedom of movement that others were not afforded (Lincoln & Mamiya, 1990).

The values, morals, and ethics of a Pastor form the foundation of the social conditions of the church. Families call upon Pastors to influence family members during conflicts. Members call upon Pastors to assist them with job disputes, believing the Pastor's influence extends into the larger society. Given their influence, Pastors can be helpful collaborators in the therapeutic process or hindrances. Pastors' attitudes toward counseling and psychotherapy and their religious doctrines and practices can contribute to clients' progress or resistance in therapy (Richards & Bergin, 1997). There are no universal perceptions among African American Pastors regarding counseling and psychotherapy; mental health professionals must assess the influence of each of their clients' relationships with their Pastors.

African Americans have traditionally sought counseling from Pastors, both because of the sacred role of clergy in the African American community and the stigma and mistrust associated with mental health agencies (Boyd-Franklin, 1989; Cook, 1993; Wiley, 1991). Pastors can be important referral resources for mental health providers. Some individuals would not seek counseling without first receiving a referral from their minister. An individual therapist, group practice, or mental health clinic can contribute psychotherapeutic services in collaboration with clergy. In some instances, they can work cojointly with therapists in dealing with spiritual issues, family issues, or providing advocacy for clients beyond the boundaries of a clinician (Boyd-Franklin, 1989; Cook, 1993). Pastors may provide therapists with historical family or social data about clients in their congregations or relevant information about spiritual aspects of clients' lives (Richards & Bergin, 1997).

Seminars and information on psychotherapy can be offered to clergy and church congregations (Cook, 1993). Workshops, retreats, educational programs around issues such as bereavement, forgiveness, depression, and other life issues can be of value in promoting referrals for treatment. Annual depression and anxiety screening days are services that, when offered in the church, appear less threatening.

Grief

Attitudes about life after death are most apparent in African American churches through funeral rituals. In many churches, funerals are conducted as "homegoing" celebrations. The deceased is perceived to have passed from this life into a better life, returning home to join God and previously departed loved ones. Many aspects of a funeral service may celebrate eternal life, including the music, testimonials from friends and family, and the eulogy. Testimonials may speak of the deceased's time spent on earth and may include a projection of what he or she is doing in heaven. The eulogy may provide family members with assurance of the glorious life that the deceased is having in heaven and the reunion that they will share when family members pass on. Given the hardships that African Americans have endured in America, eternal life has always been viewed as a reward for sustaining the struggles of their earthly lives.

Mental health providers need to be mindful of the impact of the celebration service on clients. Depending on clients' grief reactions, the funeral service may prematurely rush clients through stages of sadness and anger. They may feel compelled to rejoice with the church congregation despite their own feelings of mournfulness. African American churches do attend to the mourning process. At the moments of notice of the death of a loved one, church congregations respond immediately through cards, telephone calls, visits, and caring for grieving individuals by managing the routine aspects of life, such as meals and errands. Pastors typically assist in the funeral arrangements and speak to spiritual concerns about the death of a loved one. However, there tends to be less attention given after the funeral to those in mourning. This is a time when therapists can be particularly helpful in working with grieving clients.

Racial Liberation

For some African American churches, racial liberation is at the fore-front of ministry including worship services, social services, political action, and the establishment of Afrocentric Christian schools. Worship services may be very intentional in incorporating African spiritual traditions. Such traditions include

- adorning the church with African paintings and wood carvings,
- dressing in African clothing,
- playing African drums and dancing,
- pouring libations to call upon ancestors, and
- preaching liberating messages proclaiming a proud African heritage and openly confronting racism.

Even churches that do not espouse Afrocentric ideation serve as a liberating force and social equalizer in providing African Americans with opportunities to hold leadership positions that they do not have access to in the larger society (Boyd-Franklin, 1989; Cook, 1993).

Mental health providers must not ignore issues of racial identity with their African American clients. Internalized oppression and the coping methods for dealing with racism influence African American identity development (Helms & Cook, 1999). For instance, biases and discriminations related to skin color among African Americans may be reflected within the church. African American churches can be resources for positive racial identity development of African American clients or for negative influences.

IMPLICATIONS FOR COUNSELING AND PSYCHOTHERAPY

We have integrated relevant therapeutic issues throughout our discussion of contemporary African American churches. This section presents further implications for counseling and psychotherapy with individuals from African American churches and Afrocentric spiritual traditions.

We encourage mental health professionals working with individuals from African American churches to explore with their clients the complex ways that race, spirituality, and their other cultural identities such as gender, social class, sexual orientation, and age influence their everyday lives in general and in the psychotherapy process in particular. We do not offer any generic interventions for all African American Christians; rather, we propose as do Richards and Bergin (1997) and Helms and Cook (1999) that spirituality is another aspect of an individual's identity that is relevant to the individual's experience in therapy. We encourage therapists to explore with African American clients the extent to which they identify with their African heritage, as African spirituality provides a healthy psychological worldview. Furthermore, it is imperative that therapists examine the ways in which aspects of their own cultural identities influence therapeutic interactions (Helms & Cook, 1999). We focus our discussion primarily on the interaction of race and spirituality in considering aspects of the therapy process, including relationship issues, clinical and social issues, assessment issues and approaches, and treatment issues and approaches.

Relationship Issues

Although there has been increased openness to counseling by African American Christians in recent years, mental health professionals must take the time needed in developing a trusting relationship with potentially hesitant clients. Most African American clients may be more trusting of African American therapists; however, for some, a similarity in spiritual traditions is as or more important than race. It is important that therapists validate the spiritual identity of clients and openly address spirituality in developing a therapeutic relationship. The spiritual mechanisms that have been helpful to clients' past functioning can be acknowledged and incorporated into the therapy process as with other personal strengths. Clients for whom spirituality is important may be more receptive to therapy when therapists initiate discussion of their clients' spiritual selves early in the therapy relationship. Furthermore, therapists can build trust in the relationship by acknowledging their own spiritual tradition and assuring clients that they are accepting of their clients' traditions. This does not suggest that therapists must be knowledgeable of all spiritual traditions, rather genuine acknowledgment of their lack of knowledge regarding their clients' spiritual traditions promotes authentic therapy relationships whereby therapists may ask clients for clarification on aspects of their spirituality.

Open discussion of attitudes about counseling and psychotherapy and the messages that clients have received from their religious communities can be helpful. Discussions could include the client's perceptions of therapy, and the family's, church's, and peers' perceptions of therapy. The therapist can provide information about the therapy process and discuss any potential obstacles to the client's involvement in the process on the basis of any of the aforementioned perceptions. Clients should be reassured that their confidentiality will be maintained. If the client has received religious messages that oppose therapy, it may be helpful to identify Biblical scriptures that advocate help seeking, including Biblical characters who sought counsel from others (e.g., Moses) and Jesus' role as an emotional healer.

Clients may have various cultural stereotypes of therapists related to their perceptions of therapists in general and perceptions based on race, gender, socioeconomic background, and religious denomination. African

American clients may assume that White therapists will misunderstand them based on both their race and religious perspectives. Given how segregated churches are in the United States, Whites and African Americans may hold stereotypic images of the other's worship services and religious beliefs. African Americans who live in poverty may feel that therapists cannot comprehend their daily living situations, or they may feel that God has abandoned them in their poverty. Furthermore, African Americans of low socioeconomic backgrounds may have had painful experiences with churches on the basis of their socioeconomic status. In many urban areas, members of middle-class congregations reside in the suburbs to escape urban poverty and return to the inner city only for Sunday services, neglecting responsibility for the surrounding church community.

Many churches have responded to the growing need for counseling by establishing counseling centers within the church. It is not unusual in these cases for the service provider and service recipient to belong to the same congregation. It has been our experience that this is more of an issue for service providers than for service recipients. Service providers trained in traditional mental health programs are taught to adhere to strict ethical guidelines regarding dual relationships with clients, thus, they experience discomfort with the blurred boundaries in worshipping in the same congregation with clients. By contrast, many African Americans prefer seeking help from within their churches and, in many instances, will seek help only under those conditions. They feel that they will be better understood by and can trust professionals from their church communities.

Therapists should spend considerable time discussing boundary issues with clients, including the limits to their interactions outside of therapy sessions and the reciprocal nature of confidentiality in the therapy relationship. Clients may discuss their perceptions of their therapist with others in the congregation, for better or worse. We recommend that therapy relationships between members of the same congregation include continual discussion of relationship dynamics and whether or not the relationship can proceed in a therapeutic manner. We also suggest that the therapist engage in ongoing supervision with a professional outside the church congregation.

Clinical and Social Issues

There are some clinical or social issues that therapists may commonly encounter in working with individuals from African American churches. We are not suggesting that these issues are more prevalent among the African American Christian population than among others; however, we believe that they are worth discussing in light of some issues related to spirituality or the church.

Depression

Often, individuals suffering with depression discontinue the spiritual activities that bring relief. They may have ceased praying, reading the Bible, and even attending church. Because of the sense of hopelessness characteristic of depression, they have difficulty experiencing the hopefulness of their religious faith and isolate themselves. Whereas some individuals are comfortable asking for help from the church, either through prayer or some healing ritual, others may feel shame in admitting that their faith is weak. Some clients may be reluctant to take medication because the church maintains that taking medication reflects doubt in God's ability to heal. Some churches go so far as to view depression as demon possession, which may further discourage a member of the congregation from revealing his or her emotional pain. Some individuals do not recognize their symptoms as depression, rather they describe it as spiritual bankruptcy as they are lacking motivation, focus, direction, or purpose in their spiritual lives.

Clients may need a great deal of support and education regarding depression to engage them in the therapy process. As therapists empathize with their clients' feelings of hopelessness and help them to hold this with the hopefulness of their faith in a healing God, they can gently confront clients on their avoidance of helpful spiritual activities. It can be very helpful to intentionally use clients' spirituality in the therapy session when dealing with depression through prayer, scripture, narratives, and meditative imagery to help clients visualize their spiritual healer (e.g., Jesus, God, Holy Spirit, unconditional love, healing light) joining them in their depressive episodes. However, it is important to process clients' feelings of hopelessness or self-defeat if healing does not occur as miraculously as in Biblical scriptures. Clients may also have to deal with their feelings about God in light of their emotional suffering.

Addictions and Addictive Behaviors

African American churches vary in their stance on supporting individuals with addictions. Some churches admonish members about the use of alcohol and drugs, thereby discouraging individuals from admitting that they have a problem. Other churches recognize the prevalence of addictive behaviors in the community and offer 12-step programs and support groups which draw individuals with problems to the church. Some church members offer frequent testimonies of how God delivered them from their addictions as if they had a higher form of healing than that offered by treatment programs. Such testimonials can be discouraging to other church members, as they cannot understand why God has not healed them and feel that they must wait on God rather than seeking another form of help.

African Americans often engage in addictive behaviors as self-medication for depression. Overeating is a common problem among African American men and women, and the church reinforces eating bountiful meals surrounding various worship services. For some individuals, religion may be an aspect of their addictive process, they may move from one addictive behavior to another in becoming overly involved in church activities, engaging in addictive business within the church or becoming legalistic about spiritual disciplines and doctrines. Therapists must explore clients' positive and negative addictive behaviors and how the church reinforces them. Intentional use of clients' spirituality in therapy can also be helpful for addictive behaviors.

Sexual Abuse and Incest

Both the religious community and the African American community have been slow in responding to issues of sexual abuse and incest (Haskins, 1997). Christians are discouraged from openly discussing sexuality, in general, and that taboo extends to sexual abuse. Thus, incidents of sexual abuse and incest in Christian families tend to be underreported. Mollenkott (1977, cited in Haskins, 1997) has exposed the neglect of evangelical churches in addressing incest. African American churches tend also to neglect sexual abuse. African Americans are reluctant to expose problems that may threaten the family structure. The African American community tends to carry leftover wounds of families torn apart by slavery, particularly of men being killed or sold from the family unit. Racial discrimination in contemporary American society has also had repercussions in dismantling the family unit (Boyd-Franklin, 1989). Furthermore, African American men have not faired well in the justice system (Haskins, 1997). Thus, the African American community and the church are hesitant in exposing problems that jeopardize the family structure or could lead to involvement of the criminal justice system. Although history has validated these concerns, sexual abuse survivors pay the price in remaining unsupported and neglected by the church.

Therapeutic responses to sexual abuse in African American churches must incorporate an education component which provides churches with information on the prevalence of sexual abuse in the African American community and the trauma experienced by victims (Haskins, 1997). Enlisting clergy in prevention and education may encourage their support of survivors within their congregations.

Homosexuality

Homosexuality is an issue that is either admonished or neglected within African American churches. Conservative churches speak out about the evils and sinful nature of homosexuality, some to the extreme of claiming AIDS to be a punishment from God. Churches with more liberal views are accepting of homosexual individuals; however, there is no open discussion of homosexuality as an alternative lifestyle. Most gay and lesbian members of African American churches hide their lifestyles from the church. They endure feelings of invisibility during sermons or programs that only recognize male–female relationships and nuclear families. Few churches are willing to conduct union ceremonies for gays and lesbians. Some individuals feel they must choose between their sexual orientation and their religion.

Gay and lesbian clients may not raise issues of religion in therapy, as some individuals are used to compartmentalizing their sexuality from their religious experience. However, it would be helpful for therapists to discuss with clients how supported they are by their churches. They may need to process discrepancies between their sexual orientation and their religious communities.

Assessment Issues and Approaches

We do not use religious or spiritual assessment instruments in our work with African American clients. Because of the lack of instruments normed on African Americans (Haskins, 1997) and the emotional distance that assessment instruments introduce in the therapeutic relationship, we have found clinical interviews to be the most effective means of assessing clients' spirituality. Relevant assessment information consists of clients' church history, relationship with God, significant religious or spiritual experiences, and spiritual practices. Church history includes the client's (a) current religion, church involvement, and length of time in the current church, (b) family of origin's religion and past church involvement, and (c) if the client has a family or significant other, their religion and church involvement.

Assessment of clients' relationships with God explores (a) who God is in their lives, (b) how they experience God apart from church, (c) how they communicate with God, and (d) ways in which they draw spiritual strength from God. Clients vary as to which persons of the Trinity they most call upon, God, Jesus, or the Holy Spirit. It is helpful to explore what the Person looks like to the client, particularly if meditative imagery will be part of the therapeutic work. Some African Americans have difficulty creating images of Jesus, as the blond hair, blue-eyed images with which they have been exposed do not reflect their racial context.

Significant positive or negative spiritual experiences need to be examined because positive experiences can be used in therapy and negative experiences may need to be worked through. Assessing clients' spiritual practices includes what practices they engage in, as well as when and what happens when they engage in the various practices. During the assessment process, we explore clients' openness and comfort in using any of these practices in therapy. On the basis of this assessment, the therapist is able to determine what spiritual interventions may be helpful to the therapy process. For instance, a client's God image may give a therapist insight into the client's relationships with significant family members and others. A punishing God image may reveal caretakers in a client's life who were punitive and blaming.

Treatment Issues and Approaches

Richards and Bergin (1997) provide a very thorough and practical description of the use of spirituality in psychotherapy. We refer the reader to their work for in-depth presentation, as we provide limited discussion of salient treatment issues and approaches with individuals from African American churches. Our discussion includes:

- the healing potential of African American spiritual beliefs and practices,
- psychological interventions that are congruent and incongruent with the spiritual traditions, and
- a case example.

Healing Potential of Spiritual Beliefs and Practices

In addition to our previous discussion of healing aspects of worship, we highlight the value of prayer, scripture, and certain rituals for their potential in emotional healing. Prayer is prominent in African American spirituality. The act of praying has been passed down through generations, such that many unchurched African Americans continue to pray daily. Many families grow to depend on the elderly to offer intercessory prayers on their behalf. In many churches, members of the congregation are invited to come to the altar during worship services for corporate prayer. There is a belief that as individuals publicly surrender themselves as an annointed minister prays aloud in the pulpit, prayers will be answered. Individuals turn their anxieties and worries over to God through prayer and receive psychological, spiritual, and sometimes physical relief from their pain. If clients are open to prayer, it can be a helpful resource in therapy sessions. A prayer can be recommended also as homework to be incorporated into regular quiet time and journaling.

Scripture also offers comfort and instillation of hope. Common scriptures are passed through generations. Individuals who have never picked up a Bible are likely able to recite some scripture that has been offered repeatedly for comfort throughout their lives. For example, the scriptural reference, "I can do all things through Christ who strengthens me" (Phil. 4:13), helps to affirm and transform individuals' sense of power. Bible stories or narratives offer hope as individuals hear of Biblical people healed and surviving hardships, they believe that God will act similarly in their lives. According to Wimberly (1991, p. 16), the use of Biblical narratives in providing hope and direction for people of today has been a "driving force" of the African American church.

Certain church rituals are also seen as healing. Confirmation and adult baptism draw individuals into membership with the family of God, offering a sense of belonging. It also provides a new beginning and concrete symbol of forgiveness from past mistakes. Communion or celebration of the Eucharist provides continual rededication and remembrance of one's relationship with Jesus and an expression of Jesus' love for each individual. Laying on of hands and annointing with holy oil by ordained ministers are believed to bring forth healing and wholeness for spiritual, psychological, and physical problems.

Psychological Interventions

Some psychological interventions are congruent with African American spirituality. For instance, the very basic psychotherapeutic intervention of empathic understanding is the essence of what African American church members expect to receive from their Pastor and church community. It is heartening to scan the sanctuary as the Pastor is preaching and see the number of heads nodding and hear the resounding "Amen" that signifies that the Pastor has spoken out of the congregation's experiences and emotions. For many, this is what draws them deeper into relationship with the church and with God. They feel connected and supported through shared experiences. The use of Biblical and personal narratives by African American preachers is so powerful because it links the people of the Bible and the people of today's church together as One, through empathic understanding (Wimberly, 1991). Much of the Pastor's power in relationship with the church is derived from the Pastor's ability to speak out of the hearts of the congregation. Thus, the most important psychological intervention provided by mental health professionals is the communication of empathic understanding. Furthermore, the use of Biblical and personal narratives can help in the establishment of the therapeutic relationship (Wimberly, 1991).

Cognitive reframing is also used frequently by preachers in helping the congregation to alter unhealthy life patterns and behaviors. African American preachers take seriously their responsibility to lead the congregation into spiritual, psychological, and social integrity. It is typical for preachers to use examples from the stories that they hear from church members in their sermons to convey self-defeating thoughts and reframe them constructively. Clients are likely to respond to supportive cognitive–behavioral techniques in therapy.

African American Pastors also tend to be very directive in their relationships with church members. They are very instructive in and out of the pulpit. Church members expect the Pastor to know what is best for them and elicit the Pastor's advice. Given that they are used to seeking counseling from Pastors, African American clients may expect professional counselors to reflect a similar helping style as their Pastors. We recommend that therapists discuss their helping style with clients and negotiate a relationship that provides balance between the client's expectations and the therapist's orientation. Therapists may have to be more directive initially as they establish the relationship and openly work with clients toward a less directive relationship.

We have found some aspects of traditional therapy to be incongruent with African American traditions if the relationship has not been established. It is typical for therapists to begin therapy by taking the client's history. History taking could be perceived as rude and intrusive if it is done prematurely or with emotional detachment. For many African American clients, learning about who they and their families are is a right that is earned through the demonstration of genuine caring and mutual sharing.

Referrals for medication evaluations must be negotiated carefully. Historically, African Americans have been used as involuntary subjects for clinical treatment trials (e.g., Tuskeegee syphilis experiment) and negatively labeled within educational, social service, and mental health systems, consequently they may be cautious about seeing psychiatrists and taking medication. Thus, referrals for medication must be done within the context of a very trusting relationship and thorough education. Psychological testing also triggers similar cautions because of the labeling that can follow the individual. Therapists must be cognizant also of the mislabeling that can occur for African Americans given cultural biases in testing (Helms & Cook, 1999). They should carefully consider the necessity of testing and the expertise of the testing professional in cultural psychology and assessment.

CASE STUDY

Setting

The client was seen in a private practice office attached to the home of the therapist. The therapist was an African American, female, licensed clinical social worker. The client was referred to the therapist by the assistant Pastor of her church.

Client Demographic Characteristics

The client, "Mary," was a single African American woman, 38 years of age. She was the youngest of four children, raised in an intact family.

Holding a master's degree in community psychology, she was employed as a community college psychology professor and had worked previously as a part-time therapist in a college counseling center. Mary had been in therapy off and on since her late 20s for depressive episodes.

Presenting Problem

Mary's presenting problem was unresolved grief from the death of her older sister 6 months earlier as the result of a lengthy debilitating illness of lupus. Her sister was unmarried, and Mary helped to care for her during her illness. During the time of caring for her sister, other aspects of her life, romantic involvement, friends, work, and church suffered. At the time that she sought therapy, she was trying to sort through and recover in the aftermath of numerous losses. She reported feeling depressed and unable to deal with the grief of her sister's death.

Assessment

Through clinical interviews, the therapist assessed the client as depressed as the result of significant losses. Mary reported that her spiritual life helped her "survive" her sister's illness and death, and she had recently come to experience Jesus as the spiritual relationship from which she drew strength. From the intake form, it was assessed that Mary was Baptist and participated in several spiritual practices including prayer, scripture and spiritual readings, church worship, and spiritual retreats. Her mother was Baptist, and her father believed in God but did not attend church. She did not currently have a significant romantic partner.

Treatment Process and Outcomes

The therapist provided a supportive relationship for the client, relying heavily on empathic understanding in allowing Mary to tell her story. Mary seemed to have been holding everything inside and avoiding her own feelings as she cared for her sister. She struggled to maintain functioning at work and felt isolated socially. Although Mary spoke freely in disclosing her situation and feelings, she never became tearful. She spoke frequently of her awareness of Jesus in her life and had recently written a letter to God asking him to reveal himself in her depression.

The therapist introduced meditation early in therapy to help Mary relax. Through the use of soft music and visual imagery, the therapist led the client into scenes of unconditional love. Mary responded immediately to the meditative experiences. Whenever the therapist spoke of unconditional love, Mary named it Jesus. She reported that she could not visualize Jesus in clear physical form because the only images she had of Jesus to draw from were Caucasian, and she did not believe that to be true. She also felt that creating an image of an African American Jesus was not authentic, so he remained in her meditations either as a distant figure holding her or as a nonvisual entity touching her.

Through the course of therapy, spiritual meditative imagery was used to help Mary carry a comforting presence with her through the depression. Outside of therapy, Mary maintained a very active prayer life that included meditating with scriptures of Jesus in the Gospels. Mary frequently brought aspects of her prayer into therapy. The therapist began over time to name Jesus as Mary's comforter, particularly as Mary began dealing with painful emotional issues in therapy. Although the therapist would not introduce Jesus or any other religious figure into the therapy process, she realized that, as Mary became increasingly depressed, she needed the concrete image that was most comforting to her. Mary spoke of her appreciation of her therapist's willingness to allow the open expression of her spirituality.

The meditative experiences helped Mary to move into the grief work and experience the feelings that she put on hold throughout her sister's illness. During times of intense feelings of loss and aloneness, Mary had difficulty experiencing the presence of God. Whenever she spoke of this difficulty, the therapist either reminded Mary of the benefits she gained from praying or immediately suggested that they move into meditation. During meditations, the therapist would ask Mary to say aloud what she was experiencing, so that the therapist could adjust the imagery to the client's unique meditative experience.

As Mary allowed her repressed feelings to emerge, she became more depressed. The therapist frequently suggested medication; however, Mary insisted that she wanted to continue to try to make it without medication. The therapist closely monitored Mary's depression and recommended that she extend therapy to two times per week; however, if the depressive symptoms worsened, she would insist that Mary agree to medication. Mary agreed with this recommendation. Mary indicated that part of her desire to delay the use of medication was that she believed that the combination of the therapy and her prayer life could help her, and she would rather develop a psychospiritual process to cope with depression than to have to rely on medication. She also perceived that she needed to feel her emotions to remain motivated to continue the grief work. At one point, she reported that she felt that God had given her emotions to help her to cope authentically with life rather than to avoid the painful parts of life, only to have them accumulate and surface at a later time to overwhelm her.

During the Easter season Mary prayed with scriptures surrounding the crucifixion and resurrection of Christ. During her prayers, she began to recall aspects of her sister's death of which she had previously avoided thinking. She shared these prayerful insights with her therapist. As Mary came to understand the meaning of Christ's death and the eternal life promised through his resurrection, she began to accept her sister's death. Eventually, this cognitive understanding allowed her to experience her feelings of grief during a therapy session that occurred on the anniversary of her sister's death. She cried freely for the first time and spoke out of her feelings of loss, with the support of her therapist and Jesus.

After 1½ years of therapy, Mary was able to work through most of the losses that she had experienced. She and her therapist mutually agreed to termination. Mary had developed new coping strategies to use throughout her life. Her spirituality became more integrated into her Self such that she felt at peace in all areas of her life. She reported being more prepared to face emotional pain because she had Jesus to endure it with her. She also believed that as she had come to know herself better psychologically and spiritually, she could make healthier life decisions.

CONCLUSION

African American psychologists have long understood the importance of spirituality to the mental health of African American clients (Nobles, 1972). African spirituality provides an integrated approach to life that promotes healthy lifestyles and powerful coping strategies. Mental health professionals can help African American clients claim their African spiritual legacy, with or without naming it as such, depending on the racial consciousness of the client. Furthermore, African American churches have been integral to the lives of the African American community, thus the combined natural resources of African American churches and Afrocentric spiritual traditions can be used in very practical ways in the mental health treatment of African American clients. We recommend incorporating spirituality into the therapy process as an aspect of individual identity from intake through termination of therapy.

SUGGESTED READINGS

Cone, J. H. (1984). *For my people: Black theology and the Black church.* Maryknoll, NY: Orbis Books.

Felder, C. H. (1991). *Stony the road we trod: African American Biblical interpretation.* Minneapolis, MN: Fortress Press.

Frazier, E. F., & Frazier, C. E. (1974). *The Negro church in America: The Black church since Frazier.* New York: Schocken Books.

Fulop, T. E., & Raboteau, A. J. (1997). *African-American religion: Interpretive essays in history and culture.* New York: Routledge.

Harris, F. E. (1998). *What does it mean to be Black and Christian? The survival of a whole people: The meaning of the African American church.* Nashville, TN: Townsend Press.

Pinn, A. B. (1998). *Varieties of African American religious experience*. Minneapolis, MN: Fortress Press.

Williams, D. S. (1993). *Sisters in the wilderness: The challenge of womanist God-talk*. Maryknoll, NY: Orbis Books.

REFERENCES

Boyd-Franklin, N. (1989). *Black families in therapy: A multisystems approach*. New York: Guilford Press.

Cook, D. A. (1993). Research in African American churches: A mental health counseling imperative. *Journal of Mental Health Counseling, 15*, 320–333.

Cone, J. (1969). *Black theology and Black power*. New York: Seabury.

Felder, C. H. (1989). *Troubling biblical waters: Race, class, and family*. Maryknoll, NY: Orbis Books.

Griffith, E. E. H., English, T., & Mayfield, V. (1980). Possession, prayer, and testimony: Therapeutic aspects of the Wednesday night meeting in a Black church. *Psychiatry, 43*, 120–127.

Griffith, E. E. H., Young, J. L., & Smith, D. L. (1984). An analysis of the therapeutic elements in a Black church service. *Hospital and Community Psychiatry, 35*, 464–469.

Haskins, D. G. (1997). *African-American attitudes toward incest and child sexual abuse*. Unpublished doctoral dissertation, Loyola College in Maryland, Columbia.

Helms, J. E., & Cook, D. A. (1999). *Using race and culture in counseling and psychotherapy: Theory and process*. Boston: Allyn & Bacon.

Indowu, A. I. (1992). The Oshun Festival: An African traditional religious healing process. *Counseling and Values, 36*, 192–200.

Jones, R. (1972). *Black psychology*. New York: Harper & Row.

Lincoln, C. E., & Mamiya, L. H. (1990). *The Black church in the African-American experience*. Durham, NC: Duke University Press.

Mbiti, J. S. (1969). *African religions and philosophy*. London, England: Heinemann Educational Publishers.

Mbiti, J. S. (1991). *Introduction to African religion* (2nd ed.). Oxford, England: Heinemann Educational Publishers.

Mitchell, E. P., & Mitchell, H. H. (1989). Black spirituality: The values of the "Ol' time religion." *The Journal of the Interdenominational Theological Center, 17*, 102–109.

Moore, T. (1991). The African-American church: A source of empowerment, mutual help, and social change. *Prevention in Human Services, 10*, 147–167.

Nobles, W. W. (1972). African philosophy: Foundations for black psychology. In R. Jones (Ed.), *Black psychology* (1st ed., pp. 47–63). New York: Harper & Row.

Phelps, J. (1990). Black spirituality. In R. Maas & G. O'Donnell (Eds.), *Spiritual traditions for the contemporary church* (pp. 332–350). Nashville, TN: Abingdon Press.

Richards, P. S., & Bergin, A. E. (1997). *A spiritual strategy for counseling and psychotherapy.* Washington, DC: American Psychological Association.

Wiggins Frame, M., & Braun Williams, C. (1996). Counseling African Americans: Integrating spirituality in therapy. *Counseling and Values, 41,* 16–28.

Wiley, C. Y. (1991). A ministry of empowerment: A holistic model for pastoral counseling in the African-American community. *The Journal of Pastoral Care, 45,* 335–364.

Wimberly, E. P. (1991). *African-American pastoral care.* Nashville, TN: Abingdon Press.

16

PSYCHOTHERAPY WITH MEMBERS OF LATINO/LATINA RELIGIONS AND SPIRITUAL TRADITIONS

MARÍA CECILIA ZEA, MICHAEL A. MASON,
AND ALEJANDRO MURGUÍA

First there was the sea. Everything was dark. There was no sun, no moon, no people, no animals, no plants. Only the sea was everywhere. The ocean was the Mother. She was water and water everywhere and she was river, lake, creek, and ocean and she was everywhere. Thus, at the beginning there was only the Mother. Her name was Gaulchovang. The Mother was not people, nor thing, nor anything. She was *Alúna*. She was the spirit of what was about to come and she was thought and memory. The Mother existed only in *Alúna*, in the deepest world, alone.

—Kogi mythology

This Kogi account of the creation of the universe is just one of many accounts that exist within Latino/Latina religions and spiritual traditions. These narratives are complex and rich, and each account deserves years of serious study. No single tradition represents all of Latino culture. Because of its heterogeneity, many traditions in Latino culture range from Indigenous and African-based to Catholic, Jewish, and Protestant religions. Most literature on Latinos/Latinas assumes Catholicism to be the most influential religion for Latinos; however, some important Indigenous and African-based religions also exist in Latino culture, which are fairly unknown yet influential. We discuss only briefly Catholicism and Protestantism because these religions are widely known, and we refer the reader to the chapters on Judaism, Catholicism, and the Evangelical, Episcopalian, Mormon, and Pentecostal churches as all these exist among Latinos/Latinas. The bulk of this chapter is devoted to the Latino spiritual traditions based on Indigenous and African influences because little has been written about these hidden influences, and no extrapolation can be made from the European-based religions. Although these traditions have origin in other countries, many Latinos migrate to the United States and Canada and continue these traditions. Many followers of the Latino/Latina spiritual traditions seek counseling and psychotherapy. However, they are not likely to discuss their religious beliefs with their therapists, and only a well-informed therapist can detect and understand the implications of these traditions on therapy outcomes.

DIVERSITY WITHIN THE LATINO CULTURE

In this chapter, by *Latino* or *Latina* we refer to people of Latin American ancestry born in the United States or to people born in Latin America and who have migrated to the United States. It is impossible to characterize Latino culture as a single culture because Latino culture is vastly heterogeneous. A basic premise in this chapter asserts that although many Latino cultures may share some commonalities, their historical, geographic, socioracial, and linguistic backgrounds differ greatly, along with their religious and spiritual traditions (Zea, Garcia, Belgrave, & Quezada, 1997).

Latinos do not belong to a single racial group. Latinos come from Indigenous, African, European, and Asian ancestry, and every possible combination. Some Latinos are indigenous to the United States, as is the case of Mexican Americans from territories annexed by the United States, such as Texas, Arizona, California, New Mexico, and Colorado. Others are immigrants from Mexico, Central and South America, and the Spanish-speaking Caribbean islands (Cuba, Puerto Rico, Dominican Republic). There is some debate as to whether immigrants from Spain are Latinos, and although many Spaniards self-identify as Latinos, others disassociate themselves from Latin Americans. Similarly, immigrants born in Brazil are Latin American, although they are not Hispanic because Brazil was colonized by Portugal and not by Spain. In this chapter, Brazilian immigrants are considered to be Latinos, and a section is devoted to their multifaceted religious and spiritual traditions.

The diversity within the Latino culture is reflected in many spiritual and religious traditions. Each cultural and racial group contributed with specific traditions to the mosaic of religions and beliefs currently espoused by Latinos. For instance, Spaniards and Portuguese brought Catholicism to the Americas (see chapter 3 for discussion of the Roman Catholic Church). Spanish conquistadors came to the Americas accompanied by Catholic priests on a mission to convert indigenous people. They established missions throughout the Americas and, in some instances, built churches over indigenous temples as is the case with Peru's Inca temples. For many centuries religious freedom did not exist, and being born in a Latin American country was synonymous with being Catholic, with the exception of segments of the population that secretly practiced African and Indigenous religions. Subsequently in many countries, religion constituted a compulsory subject from kindergarten to the senior year in high school. Years of Catholic school have a big impact on individuals. Because for the most part people were Catholic by force and not by choice, many Latinos disagree with the Catholic Church on social matters such as divorce, abortion, homosexuality, and premarital sex, and there are varying degrees of commitment to this religion.

Indigenous people advanced traditions based on the Aztec, Mayan, and Andean worldviews (Ramirez, 1983). Africans brought with them their religions and kept them alive despite the inquisition and the harsh conditions of slavery (Zea, Quezada, & Belgrave, 1997). These worldviews amalgamated into new ones, as is the case of Brazilian Umbanda. Commonalities, as well as fundamental differences, exist among the Indigenous and the Afro-Latino religious perspectives which are discussed later.

During World War II, many Jewish immigrants came to the Americas, established synagogues, and managed to retain Judaism. They did not come with the mission of recruiting new adepts but to survive and, if they were religious, to try to preserve their own tradition. Some of these Jewish Latinos migrated to the United States later on as the result of the waves of antisemitism in some countries, such as in Argentina during the military regime. Jewish Latinos have contributed to religious diversity in the Latino culture. They may disagree with many Latinos in positions regarding social issues, such as divorce and premarital sex.

In the second half of the century, other Christian groups established missions in Latin America despite the opposition from the Catholic Church and recruited many followers to enjoy a wide following, as is the case of the Evangelical Church in Central America. Anglican, Baptist, Mormon, Pentecostal, and Methodist Churches also propagated throughout Latin America (we refer the reader to the pertinent chapters in this book).

During times of political turmoil in Central America, segments of the Catholic Church were aligned with the poor, but others were aligned with those in power. Thus, although the Catholic Theology of Liberation movement proposed changes to the status quo and suggested that religion was an instrument to help the oppressed, other Catholics condemned this movement. Theologians of Liberation endorse women's equality and recognize that women have been oppressed in Latin America and the world throughout the centuries (Tamez, 1988). Contrary to Theology of Liberation, the Evangelical Church is less concerned with equality of women. It also places ultimate responsibility and blame on the individual, disregarding the role of oppressive regimes on poverty in Latin America. Ignacio Martin-Baró (1990), a Jesuit psychologist who was slain by the military in El Salvador because of his ideology, criticized the Evangelical Church in

Central America because this religion was used to force people to "submit to the established order" (p. 96).

AFRICAN-BASED TRADITIONS: THE AFRO-YORUBA TRADITION IN CUBA, PUERTO RICO, AND THE UNITED STATES

With the Spanish colonization of the Americas came the enslavement of millions of Africans to labor in mines and on plantations. Of the 9 to 15 million people enslaved as part of the Atlantic slave trade, close to 1 million were brought to Cuba between 1511 and 1886. Although enslaved people were brought from many parts of Africa, a great plurality were from Yoruba-speaking areas of what are now Nigeria and Benin. They arrived in Cuba during the last 100 years of slavery (Moreno Fraginales, 1977). These people brought with them a dialect from Yoruba called *Lucumí* or *Anagó*, still used in rituals, as well as the symbolically complex and philosophically subtle religious traditions that over time have been transformed into *Santería* or the *Regla de Ocha* (the former is the name more commonly used by outsiders, whereas the latter is more commonly used by followers of the religion). With the exodus of nearly 1 million Cubans after the Cuban Revolution in 1959, Santería has grown dramatically in the United States and Puerto Rico. Once established, most frequently in large urban areas, it has been embraced by other Latinos as well as by an increasing number of African Americans and Anglos.[1]

"The religion," as practitioners often call it, worships a High God who created the universe. The overarching God, called *Olodumare*, *Olofi*, or *Olorun*, is essentially uninvolved in human affairs, but He left the universe in the hands of a vast pantheon of divinities, called *orichas* or *santos* (saints). Along with these deities are ancestors and spirits of the dead, called either *espíritus* or *egun*. These various beings are constantly influencing people in the world, and the religion's many ceremonies focus human worship upon them. Most practitioners interact with the ancestors through Spiritism (see later), whereas *Santería* focuses on the divinities.

The *orichas* are differentiated in lavish detail, and each has distinct areas of influence in nature and human life. Ochún wears yellow, uses gold and brass, and eats honey and hens; she "rules" love, sexuality, sensuality, and the arts, and she "is" the river. Obatalá dresses in pure white, uses

---

[1]At this moment, many voices claim authority to narrate the complex historical process that created this nexus of beliefs and practices. For a simple overview of the historical process that created the religion as it exists today, see Murphy (1981, 1988, 1994). For a detailed account of the history of aesthetic practices within the religion, see Brown (1986). Brandon's (1993) account of the history is by far the most comprehensive and, although the historical material is problematic because it remains too general and schematic, he provides invaluable information about the religion as it is practiced by African Americans.

tools of silver and white metals, and eats meringue and white doves; the father of the orichas, he rules wisdom, purity, creativity, and he lives on mountain tops and hills.[2]

Within the religion, each individual is believed to have a "head" or head ruling oricha and the physical head receives much attention in the complex rituals of the religion. First, the head, called either *orí* or *eledá*, is the spiritual faculty and central being of a human being. Before birth, each *orí* goes before the Creator and receives its essential character. This character, which people closely associate with an individual's destiny, can be either "hot" or "cool" (Cabrera, 1980, p. 121). Practitioners disagree about how mutable the head is as character, in part because the head also idiomatically refers to the *oricha* that rules a person; an individual and the deity also establish this relationship in front of the Creator before birth (Bascom, 1991, p. 115).

This central deity, often called "the owner of the head," represents an important part of the individual's character. For example, a child of the white, calm, and generous oricha Obatalá is often assumed to be slow to anger, relatively intellectual, benevolent, and, others might add, "big-headed."[3] In fact, at times practitioners confuse the "owner of the head" and the individual; "an Obatalá" refers to a child of Obatalá who in ritual may act in the role of oricha.

The *eledá* can be identified through various divination systems, and a growing relationship between an individual and the eledá often leads to initiations, after which the *aché* (power to accomplish, essence) of the oricha literally resides inside the initiate's head. After a priestly initiation, the oricha can "mount" the initiate in trance possession and thus take control of the body that they share.[4]

Wherever this tradition flourishes, practitioners channel *aché*, divine power, by producing elaborate cultural rituals and ceremonies. In possession, the oricha or *egun* uses a human's body to communicate with other members of the community. Through the sacrifice of candles, objects, herbs, food, and animals, people communicate with the spirits. Practitioners of the religion turn to divination to reveal the will and desires of the spirits and to learn their individual destinies. Four pieces of coconut (Lu. [Lucumí] *obí*, Sp. [Spanish] *cocos*), cowrie shells (Lu. [Lucumí] *dilogún*, Sp. [Spanish] *caracoles*), and palm nuts (Lu. *Ifá*) are all used in different but related systems.

Most practitioners follow a predictable trajectory as they enter the

---

[2]These descriptions are not meant to be exhaustive. For an excellent, short description of the religion, see Ramos (1996) and Murphy (1988). The description here is the result of Mason's anthropological fieldwork since 1987.

[3]See Gonzalez-Wippler (1989, p. 229) for an insider's exploration of these psychodietific correspondences. These correspondences are problematic as the ruling deity can compensate for the person's character (see Gleason, 1987, pp. 259–272).

[4]For an extended discussion of the sexual implications of *mounting* in Brazil, see Wafer (1991).

religion. After going for a consultation with a diviner, oricha worshippers often are asked to make sacrifices of various kinds. Working with herbs for physical healing or offerings for spiritual healing, practitioners address a variety of conditions. When indicated, they may also be asked to become initiated at different levels of commitment by "receiving the necklaces" that symbolize their connection to the orichas, or "washing the Warriors," or another oricha that provides them with sacred objects used to create and maintain a shrine, or "making ocha"—becoming a priest or priestess. Each of these rituals channels aché, so that practitioners can experience the blessings of the religion, that is, health, luck, strength, tranquility, and spiritual evolution. These blessings are routinely requested at every ceremony and represent a set of core values to which individuals aspire within the religion.[5] These rituals all transform human experience by putting people into long-lasting relationships with orichas and thus permanently altering their social lives (Mason, 1997).

AFRICAN-BASED TRADITIONS: THE AFRO-YORUBA TRADITION IN BRAZIL AND THE UNITED STATES

The Yoruba and Nago traditions were also exported to Brazil as a byproduct of slavery. Although Umbanda and Candomble are Afro-Brazilian in origin, Candomble has remained a closer expression of African religious beliefs, whereas Umbanda presents an amalgamation of African, Indigenous, and European traditions (Pressel, 1982). These religions are not practiced by Afro-Brazilians only. In fact, substantial numbers of Euro-Brazilians and Brazilians of all racial groups practice Umbanda and Candomble in many cities of Brazil, the United States, and the rest of the world.

As in Santeria, in Umbanda and Candomble there is a main god, Olorum, and there are Orixás,[6] whom according to Verger (1997) are "divinized ancestors" (p. 18) who have control over forces of nature such as water, thunder, and wind. These Orixás have axé, divine power, which also translates as the ability to carry out actions in favor of humans. *Maes de santo* and *paes de santo* (mothers or fathers of saints) are initiates who have a more direct connection with the Orixás and who serve the role of priests and priestesses, usually in *terreiros* (temples) or houses. *Atabaques* (drums) play an important role in the connection with the spirit world. Accounts exist indicating that many drums were confiscated during the colonial pe-

---

[5]It should be noted that these core values unite a tremendous diversity of practices by practitioners who model their actions on traditional lineages called *ramas*.

[6]The Brazilian spelling of Yoruba terms differs from the Cuban. Thus, orixá is the Brazilian equivalent of the Cuban oricha. Differences in the spelling of the names of the deities also occur, but they retain recognizable roots. Yemaya is Iemanja, Changó is Xangó, and so on.

riod, because Afro-Yoruban practitioners were persecuted in Brazil (Murphy, 1994). This persecution led them to keep secret many of their practices and, to this day, noninitiates do not have complete access to these religions' complex body of knowledge. Transmission of tradition is predominantly oral, and the existing written accounts have been produced by anthropologists, historians, or sociologists (e.g., Beniste, 1997; Da Silva, 1995; Herskovits, 1966; Mbiti, 1975; Murphy, 1988, 1994; Pressel, 1982; Verger, 1997; Wafer, 1991).

In Umbanda, aside from the Orixás, there are several major spirit types, who work under the Orixás. These spirits communicate with people through mediums, and they play an important role in helping the community with their physical and mental health problems, as well as issues of spiritual development through *consulta* (consultation). Consultation occurs in the context of ritual, and individuals may receive advice or information about their spiritual development, their issues, or worries, and they may receive treatment with herbs and tobacco.

Two of the major spirit types in Umbanda are *Pretos velhos/velhas* (old wise Black men or women), considered to be the spirits of wise Afro-Brazilian slaves who offer their wisdom in consultation, and *Caboclos* (Indigenous men or women), considered to be helpful in moments in which quick and decisive action is necessary (Pressel, 1982).

In Candomble and Umbanda, there is consultation via cowrie shells (*buzios*), as in Santería. Many times, the outcome of consultation involves making an *ebo* or offering to an orixá, and there are many ways, places, and forms that the *ebo* may take (Da Silva, 1995). For instance, an ebo may consist of offering fruits to Xangó, whereas on another occasion the ebo may consist of offering flowers to Iemanjá (the ocean), depending on the Orixá that is coming to the aid of the individual. The persons offering the ebo experience relief and confidence in solving their problems or in addressing a need through the offering. As such, the ebo plays a therapeutic role in peoples' lives. Thousands of Brazilians go to the beach to welcome in the New Year and to make offerings to Iemanjá. The ebo can take place in public as in the New Year celebrations or occur in more private spaces.

SPIRITISM IN LATINO CULTURE

As the Enlightenment swept Europe in the early 19th century, many people were interested in a "science of spirits" that would make religious and spiritual phenomena explicable within a rational framework. In the United States, Spiritualism was a movement that attempted to make contact with spirits of the dead. In France, Allan Kardec experimented with the principles of Spiritualism and codified his rationalized Spiritism. His ideas then spread throughout Latin America along with other Enlightenment writings, and today Spiritism is widely practiced, especially in Brazil, Cuba, Puerto Rico, and Mexico. In each country, it has taken on its own unique character as it has interacted with other religious traditions and social circumstances (see Goodman, 1988; Macklin, 1974; Pressel, 1973).[7] Perhaps the most striking transformation is the tradition *Santerismo*, a blending of Santería and Spiritism popular among Puerto Ricans in New York City (Pérez y Mena, 1991).

Within Spiritism, a strong hierarchy of spirits exists. God rules a universe in which all spiritual beings are ranked according to their purity or "moral perfection" (Harwood, 1987, p. 40). Angels and saints (including the orichas) are superior to the spirits of heroes and leaders. Regular people's spirits are inferior to these but purer than "intranquil spirits," who are sometimes called low, undeveloped, ignorant, bad, or negative. Human beings can be more or less spiritually developed than these other beings depending on how they live.

All people are believed to come to earth with a specific group of spirits (*espíritus, muertos*) to guide, protect, and heal them. These spirits are called protectors (*protectores*) and are led by a central guide (*guía*) who is in charge of the others. In addition to these spirits, each person attracts spirits similar to his or her level of spiritual and moral development; thus, a contentious person draws difficult spirits, a peaceful person attracts calm and beneficent beings. Spirits often represent ethnic types like Indians (*indios*), different kinds of Africans (*negros, africanos*),[8] Gypsies, Arabs, Hindus, and Haitians. Although spirits sometimes seem stereotyped, often a practitioner will have many spirits of different backgrounds, each with its own distinctive history to account for its abilities and preferences. Similarly, people are often accompanied by their ancestors and other deceased family members and friends.

Practitioners of Spiritism often come to know their spirits because of some kind of difficulty for which they hold a spirit responsible. Fugue states, disassociation, seizures, and "attacks of nerves" are commonly heard examples of the interference attributed to spirits. People also seek consultation from spirits for assistance in problems in their everyday lives. Early consultations with a spiritist (*espiritista, medium*) focus on the nature and cause of the problems as well as the identities of the client's protectors. In turn, spiritist rituals usually involve assisting negative spirits to understand

---

[7]Spiritism is referred to in various ways: *Espiritismo* is the most common name in Cuba and Puerto Rico where practitioners hold spiritual masses (*misas espirituales*). *Mesa Blanca* is another name used in the Caribbean and Brazil; meaning *white table*, this term refers to the altar used in the key ritual of the tradition.

[8]Because of the great diversity of enslaved Africans taken to Brazil, Cuba, and Puerto Rico, Spiritism in these places often differentiates among various African ethnic groups, including *lucumí, congo, calabarí, arará, mina, gangá, mandinga*, and *mocuá* in Cuba and Puerto Rico. Brazilian spiritism often includes *pretos velhos* (old wise Blacks) as a class of spirits, but in some areas, like Bahia, these can be identified by ethnic labels like *nago, mina, gege, kambinda*, and *angola*.

the error in their ways to alleviate the client as well as strengthening the protectors to increase the client's resilience. These consultations also identify any faculties (*facultades*) the client has to see, hear, or sense spirits or to manifest them in possession.

Spiritism's key ceremony is known by various names, such as a meeting (*reunión*), spiritual mass (*misa espiritual*), and white table (*mesa blanca* in Spanish-speaking countries and *mesa branca* in Brazil), a term that refers to the altar used in the key ritual of the tradition. Although different groups elaborate this ceremony in various ways, it always includes a table covered with white cloth to act as an altar, at least one glass of clean water, and one candle. The purity of water draws pure spirits and the candle gives them energy and light so they can have knowledge. After introductory prayers, usually from Allan Kardec's *Selected Prayers*, mediums begin to deliver messages from the spirits. Sometimes mediums will even pass or bring down spirits who possess them. Mediums—possessed or not—can transmit advice, prescribe additional rituals to enhance people's spiritual state or cleanse people of negative spirits in various ways. Perhaps the most dramatic moment comes when a medium works a negative influence by becoming possessed by a low spirit who is afflicting someone at the meeting. These spirits often act out in shockingly antisocial behavior, but they are elevated or educated by others present, so the afflicted person can be liberated from their influence. Obviously, this sort of enactment has profound social and psychological effects that often take some time to be fully appreciated, even by those involved.

In all cases, the work is designed to bring spiritual development to both people and the spirits. As people purify their lives and thoughts, they can draw more elevated spirits. In turn, these spirits can then assist human beings to become more evolved. This relationship of interdependent spiritual growth is sometimes also referred to as charity (*caridad*). This fact has led some researchers to focus on Spiritism as an ongoing moral education (Núñez, 1987), an education that sometimes includes a client's becoming a medium and healing others.

INDIGENOUS-BASED TRADITIONS IN THE AMERICAS

The Spanish colonization also brought dramatic changes to the religious and spiritual beliefs of Indigenous people in the Southwest of the United States and Latin America. The process of colonization involved the destruction of temples and the forced conversion into Catholicism of the Mayans, Aztecs, Incas, and many other Indigenous groups. Despite the organized efforts of the Catholic Church, many Indigenous religious and spiritual beliefs survived and amalgamated with Catholicism. Ramirez (1983) characterized the amalgamation of Latino, Spanish, and Catholic worldviews as the *Mestizo* perspective. The mestizo worldview allowed the development of *Curanderismo*, a spiritual and folk healing system.

Although it is difficult to find the rich descriptions of the religious components of curanderismo to the same extent than in Santería, Umbanda, and Candomblé, most authors agree that Curanderismo's premises are deeply rooted in Indigenous spiritual worldviews (Arenas, Cross, & Willard, 1980) and that Curanderismo combined Indigenous beliefs and practices with Spanish Catholic traditions into a practical folk medicine (Kiev, 1968). Because of geographical isolation, some Indigenous groups (e.g., Kogi, Arhuaco) retained their religious beliefs without synchretizing with Catholicism (Reichel-Dolmatoff, 1991, 1996). In many Indigenous religions, a god or gods rule people's lives, the spiritual and the physical world are connected, divination of the future is possible, and rituals constitute a large component of the religion (Cervantes & Ramirez, 1992; Kiev, 1968; Reichel-Dolmatoff, 1996). The tradition is oral, and priests go through a process of initiation after years of apprenticeship. The Aztecs and the Mayans revered personalized gods in a manner similar to which Curanderismo emphasizes patron saints. Practices used in Curanderismo and by Indigenous populations include the use of religious offerings, the belief in spiritual determination, and disclosure through confession (Kiev, 1968).

Curanderismo emphasizes a harmonious balance among the individual, family, community, and environment (Foster, 1960). Physical health is not viewed as separate from mental or spiritual health. The disruption of the balance among the spiritual, mental, and physical or between the individual and the community causes illness. Treatment entails reharmonizing these systems in a holistic manner. Curanderismo functions as a multidimensional combination of equally influencing physical, spiritual, emotional, social, natural, and supernatural components (Fabrega & Manning, 1973). Forms of treatment include the use of ritual, herbal remedies, prayer, and consultation with the spirit world.

Many illnesses treated by curanderos include those that are not recognized by Western medicine and seem to possess strong psychosomatic and anxious qualities. To effect treatment, the Curandero combines clinical skills, knowledge of the effective traditional remedies, and spiritual considerations.

According to Trotter and Chavira (1983), curanderos use three levels of healing: material, mental, and spiritual. The material level is the most commonly used level of healing. Objects (herbal remedies, candles, religious paraphernalia) and rituals (cleansing, prayer) with healing properties help to provide cures. It is not necessary for the Curandero to be in a trance to carry out the healing. The mental level of healing requires the Curandero to mentally transmit his or her mental energy to the afflicted aspect of the person suffering the illness. The spiritual level is a more sophisticated level of healing which requires the Curandero to enter a trance and become the medium of a spiritual force that will carry out the healing. The ability to enter into a trance is attributed to innate skill (being gifted) or to years of spiritual development.

A therapeutic intervention by a Curandero is exemplified with *mal aire* (evil air), a syndrome that arises when bad or evil air enters the body through cold drafts or spiritual possessions. It may also be caused by bewitchment (Rivera & Wanderer, 1986). Treatment involves ridding the individual of the spiritual possession or canceling the bewitchment.

In sum, Latino/Latina religious and spiritual traditions are diverse, yet they share some commonalities among each other. They have influenced Latino culture and, even when individuals are not religious, some behaviors and attitudes may be traced back to their ancestors' spiritual beliefs. The body of knowledge behind each tradition discussed here is very complex and difficult to access for most therapists. Yet, each tradition has implications for the process of counseling and psychotherapy.

IMPLICATIONS OF RELIGIOUS OR SPIRITUAL TRADITIONS FOR COUNSELING AND PSYCHOTHERAPY

This section includes a discussion of implications of the different religious and spiritual traditions for counseling and psychotherapy. We examine relationship issues between therapist and a Latino/Latina client, assessment and diagnostic issues and approaches, the role of emotions on Latino communities, and treatment issues and approaches.

Relationship Issues

Therapists' Views of Latino Clients

Therapists' views of Latino clients differ depending on their own training and experience with Latino clients. Given the complexity of Latino culture, many non-Latino therapists immediately consider themselves unqualified to work with Latinos. Although language is an objective barrier, many U.S.-born Latinos speak English fluently and many do not speak much Spanish. Many barriers for treatment stem from non-Latino therapists' lack of knowledge about Latino culture and from their unwillingness to be in the apprentice role in the therapeutic session. The debate about whether clients should only work with therapists from their own ethnic group has been addressed extensively elsewhere (see Tyler, Brome, & Williams, 1991), including the advantages and disadvantages of working with clients of similar and different ethnicity. Nevertheless, Anglo therapists may have no choice but to work with Latino clients. To this day, however,

Latino therapists complain of Anglo colleagues not being willing to work with Latino children or youth even when their predominant language is English.

Therapists who realize that their clients practice a religion other than Catholicism or Protestantism may find it difficult to understand their clients' worldviews as they may clash with Western ideas. For instance, a therapist whose Latina client practiced Santeriá expressed frustration toward his client when she let divination through cowrie shells decide what was more appropriate for her, instead of coming to her own conclusions and showing insight about her problems. Agency is a pillar of Western thought and making one's own decisions is important even if one is wrong. In Latino culture, it is important to find the best solution, and orichas such as Eleggua know better than the self, and insight as understood in the West is not essential.

Training of psychologists hardly includes cross-cultural or ethnic psychology (Suarez-Balcazar, Durlak, & Smith, 1994). The existence of other worldviews is ignored or treated as superstition. Ethnocentrism in psychology is so prevalent that even psychologists of color, whose parents or grandparents held non-Western worldviews, have difficulty understanding clients who think like their own grandparents.

Latino/Latina Clients' Views of Therapists

Some Latino groups have extensive experience with therapists (e.g., South Americans of upper-middle-class background), but others have no history of seeking help from a therapist. They are more likely to seek help from a priest, a physician, a family member, a curandero, a *babaloricha* (priest), or a *iyaloricha* (priestess). The authority and power of the iyaloricha or babaloricha is greater than the power of a therapist for many Latinos. Thus, when religious authorities prescribe or suggest an action, few would dare not to follow this suggestion. A therapist's authority is not considered to be important, and an active listening stance is not always seen as beneficial. In the words of a client, "My therapist never told me anything that could help me. She would just listen to me, and that was not enough for me."

Trust and Disclosure Among Latino Clients

For the most part, Latinos do not discuss their religious beliefs with their psychotherapists. Few Latino clients will admit to the therapist believing in or practicing incorporation of spirits because these practices have been kept very secret because of persecution and prejudice against them. It is our experience that it takes some skill to get Latino clients to talk about their religious beliefs. Therapists must demonstrate that they are insiders or, at least, that they have a deep understanding and respect for

Latino religious and spiritual beliefs. Latino clients know that if they talk freely about their religious experiences, most therapists will label them as abnormal. In the words of a man who practiced Umbanda, "When people ask me at work what I did on my weekend, I cannot tell them that I was incorporating spirits."

Assessment and Diagnostic Issues and Approaches

Incorporation of orichas, caboclos, pretos velhos, and spirits of the dead is common for some Latino spiritual and religious perspectives. There is the risk of assuming pathology when the therapist encounters clients who are mediums or *horses* of these entities, or who seek consultation from these entities. Many healthy, productive individuals assume both functions, that of the medium and of the client. Although at times socioeconomic status may be related to these beliefs, there are many instances of highly educated, wealthy individuals, who practice Santeriá in the New York City metropolitan area, Chicago, San Francisco, Los Angeles, Seattle, Austin, Baltimore, Philadelphia, Minneapolis, and South Florida; Umbanda in Maryland and California; and Candomblé in California and the District of Columbia. The practice is not restricted to these places, but the authors have firsthand knowledge of houses and temples in these areas.

New assessment measures to provide insight about Latino clients' worldview are needed. Current measures do not cover the full range of Latino spiritual beliefs. For instance, measures of locus of control do not account for spiritual determination, a concept frequently found among Latinos who share these spiritual worldviews. In addition, many authors rely on acculturation as an indicator of cultural beliefs when, in fact, many nonacculturated immigrant Latinos do not espouse African- or Indigenous-based worldviews. Given the lack of measures to assess these beliefs, semi-structured interviews during intakes or in initial therapy sessions should help the therapist determine the degree of involvement with the Latino spiritual and religious beliefs. How long has the client been involved in the religion? At what level is the client involved? To what extent does the client turn to the tradition for healing in a time of crisis? The therapist then will be able to develop a treatment plan better suited for the needs of the Latino or Latina client.

No systematic body of research exists comparing religious versus non-religious Latinos in terms of mental health. No evidence indicates that Latinos who distanced themselves from African and Indigenous worldviews are psychologically healthier than those who remain anchored to these worldviews. However, there is a lot of prejudice on the part of Latino and non-Latino therapists against clients who endorse these beliefs. This prejudice hinders the ability of the therapist to suspend judgment and listen to the client.

Source and Effects of Emotion in Many Latino Communities:
Envidia, la Lengua, and los Ojos as Obstacles to Personal
Success and Self-Esteem in Caribbean Communities

Because of differing notions about the causes of clinical issues among Latinos/Latinas, Western practitioners will need to consider cultural ideas about the power and effects of emotions and social behavior in many Latino communities from the Caribbean. Common to these cultures is a belief that individuals are affected directly by the emotions held by others. If a person is noticeable in her successes, envy (*envidia*) among those who surround her can lead to losses. Although these losses are sometimes caused directly by human action, within this worldview, envy itself creates entanglements and obstacles. Being watched too frequently by another (*los ojos*) or being the subject of too much gossip (*el chisme, la lengua*) can also create these same difficulties. Although these beliefs inspire behavior that promotes cultural ideals of equality and discretion, some Caribbean Latinos will see their difficulties as the responsibility of other people's emotions and behaviors.

Similarly, illnesses considered physical by Western-oriented practitioners might be considered supernatural by spiritually oriented practitioners. Many of African-based religious traditions share the notion that a curse (*daño* or *maldición* in Spanish) can bring about physical and psychological illness; if left untreated, it can become a *cadena* (chain) that can bring pain and suffering to an entire family for generations. Similarly, some traditions include the belief that certain people are spiritual sponges who collect the negativity of all those they encounter; these individuals often believe that they are cursed and suffer a great deal emotionally. Spiritual traditions like Santería, Espiritismo, Santerismo, Umbanda, and Candomblé all offer spiritual remedies for these difficulties.

Treatment Issues and Approaches

The Healing Potential of the Traditions: A Case Study

Because Indigenous- and African-based traditions and Spiritism all focus on transforming the immediate circumstances of their adherents, each offers healing potential. In most cases, this potential emerges within a working relationship with a spiritual leader from the tradition. During some sort of divination ritual, spiritual leaders usually identify the causes of the individual's suffering and prescribe steps to redress these difficulties. Herein, lie two significant differences from Western forms of therapy: Although some difficulties are conceived to be the result of natural causes, many are thought to be spiritual in origin. Similarly, although most Western therapies emphasize inner processes and their transformation, many of these religious traditions offer ways to externalize the suffering and attribute it to other causes than to the self. To engage these traditions usefully, it may be necessary for Western therapists and counselors to appreciate the symbolic aspects of these externalizations and their effects.

A case study can highlight how these traditions address natural and spiritual aspects of an individual's life, both at social and psychodynamic levels. Jesús, a Mexican man living in Washington, DC, was encouraged by a friend to consult a santero (Santería priest) about his love life. When the santero began to interpret the message from the orichas, he spoke of Jesús's relationship with his ex-boyfriend but focused more on serious health concerns and a lack of self-confidence. According to the orichas, Jesús had experienced the souring of an important emotional relationship which had left him with a complex series of emotions. However, the reading was more concerned with the fact that Jesús had a blood-born disease that had been caused by his own behavior. In addition to this disease, the santero stated clearly that Jesús suffered from a lack of self-confidence that left him unable to put his many skills to good use. As part of this consultation, the santero also identified Jesús's head-ruling oricha as Inle, a divine hunter, fisherman, and healer who at one point had a sexual relationship with another man.[9] In fact, said the santero, Inle was coming to his aid. Children of Inle are thought to be calm, circumspect, creative, wealthy, capable, and flexible in all things.

In fact, Jesús had tested HIV-positive after having unprotected sex despite the fact that he knew about the dangers involved. After a time of being asymptomatic, his T-cell count had plummeted. The grief from losing his relationship was acute, and his emotional instability was exacerbated by the anger he felt toward himself for having exposed himself to HIV. Together, these factors had eroded his self-esteem and had made him less effective at his job as a community health educator.

The santero prescribed a *despojo* (spiritual cleaning) with water in which Inle's sacred objects had sat for some time, as well as an offering of fruit to Ochún, the oricha of love. When performing both these ceremonies, Jesús was to pray for his health and stability. After the rituals, he reported feeling much calmer and more able to deal with the many choices that he needed to make at work and in his personal life. Although he was still mourning his lover, he was able to accept his absence. After the despojo, Jesús's next T-cell count was dramatically higher, and he felt better overall.

Perhaps most important, Jesús had found a new model of his individuality. Before the reading, he had been very identified with Ochún as the embodiment of femininity. Gay men interested in Santería often identify

---

[9]Inle is not one of the orichas whose legends are widely known. Although there are disagreements among practitioners about his history, all agree that he lived with Ochún after having lived with Yemayá, the *oricha* of the sea. All also agree that, at one point, he had a homoerotic relationship.

with Ochún when they perceive themselves as manifesting feminine ideals. After learning that Inle was his head oricha, Jesús began to transfer his loyalty to him. Inle provided him with a divine model upon which to base his identity as a gay man, an identity which had been difficult for him both in Mexico and in the United States. Although the transformation in Jesús came slowly, having a gay divinity to relate to allowed Jesús to value his own choices. Like Inle, he had a series of important relationships. Like Inle, he had gone away from home to gather resources for his home. Like Inle, he loved the company of other men and expressed that love sexually. He began to see his flexibility as an asset rather than a liability. Inle's example provided Jesús with a new way to understand his past and to imagine his future. This case illustrates both the social and emotional components at play in these religious traditions, but it also suggests their similarity to certain aspects of depth psychology. These rituals are parallel to those of Euro-American religions. Appealing to an oricha is similar to appealing to Christian deities and both have similar healing potential.

Psychological Interventions Congruent With Latino Traditions

Latino spiritual and religious traditions (African, Indigenous, or Christian) are collectivistic in nature. This section deals with all of them. Many events and processes or activities for spiritual development take place in the context of a house or temple, and the efforts of the community are involved in an individual's advancement or initiation. Although there may be some moments of solitude and each person's path is unique, Latino spirituality is not a solitary, individualistic path. The curandero, the *mai* or *pai*, and the *padre* or *madre de santo* are important figures as well as other members of the community who play a diversity of roles.

Many times, Latinos do spiritual work on behalf of their families and their communities. Individuals' well-being often depends on the well-being of their family members. Teresa, a Latina mother, described this phenomenon in her relationship with her adult children and grandchildren by saying that so long as all her children and grandchildren were well and happy, she was fine. A major source of stress were her adult children's problems. For Teresa, happiness was not a private, individual matter in that it could not take place in the absence of her family's happiness and well-being.

Psychological interventions that overemphasize individualistic approaches are less congruent with a Latino worldview than those that emphasize collectivist approaches. For instance, telling this Latina mother to take some time for herself because she was entitled to some peace and quiet was not as effective as telling her that, to be a better mother to her children, she needed to relax and take some time off. In the former approach, the individual's needs and rights are emphasized; in the latter, the good of the family is emphasized.

Because of the collectivist nature of Latino culture, and the family being such an important part of people's lives, the degree of closeness among Latino family members can be interpreted by therapists as being enmeshed and pathological. However, for Latinos and Latinas, the opposite is considered to be pathological. Not to care for a family member in need, not to support a relative, is pathological for Latinos. Mauricio, a young Latino immigrant, expressed surprise when he found out that in the United States at a certain age children were expected to move out of the parental home. He thought it was cruel to kick one's children out. Although Latinos, and Latinas in particular, can live with their parents until they marry or die, it is unusual for Anglos to continue to live with their parents beyond a certain age. Similarly, Latinos and Latinas expect to care for their elder parents after a certain point in their lives, a well-respected tradition.

The following case study exemplifies situations in which the client's blind interpretation of religion can be harmful to his health and psychological well-being. A one-session intervention with an HIV-positive, 32-year-old Central-American Evangelical man posed a challenge for the clinician, a nonreligious Latina. This man had enormous difficulty accepting his bisexuality. He felt dirty, undeserving of God's love and, therefore, would not take the antiretroviral medication prescribed for his HIV. He insisted that if God wanted, He could save him even if he did not take his medication. He described feeling worthless, like a worm. The therapist used religious quotes well-known in Latin America, such as, "Help yourself and I will help you," to encourage this client to take his medications. Arguments, such as God had created him the way he was (bisexual), were also used to help restore his shattered self-esteem and help him feel more than a worthless worm. At the end of this one-session intervention, the client was more willing to take his medications and asked for a referral to a service that provided psychotherapy to bisexual men.

Working With Spiritual Leaders

After much work by anthropologists and mental health researchers, there has been increasing interest in including spiritual traditions like Santería, Umbanda, and Spiritism in the treatment options available for Latinos seeking therapy (Brown, 1986; Cros-Sandoval, 1979; Garrison, 1982; Goodman, 1988; Koss-Chioino, 1995; Ruiz & Langrod, 1976). These traditions resemble mainstream psychotherapies in key ways, and they offer forms of treatment that can be more effective than other therapies because they include culturally appropriate values and expectations (Harwood, 1987). Despite their effectiveness and appropriateness, Western therapeutic practitioners often face difficulty determining which spiritual or religious interventions might be productive for their clients and identifying qualified and open-minded spiritual practitioners with whom to collaborate.

The first step in using these traditions in any therapeutic work must always be learning more about them and their place in the lives of their clients. These complex traditions can play a variety of roles in the life of their followers, and so therapists must explore in depth how their clients are engaging with these religions (see Comas-Díaz, 1981). To what extent is this tradition central to the person's sense of self? What role does it play socially? Psychologically? How does this tradition understand or explain the client's current circumstances? These questions should help Western therapists evaluate the usefulness of including the religious tradition as part of a comprehensive treatment. It is important to note that different people from different national groups and socioeconomic levels have various attitudes about their involvement in African- and Indigenous-based traditions, which are still sometimes stigmatized as being primitive, Black, or low-class. For others, their involvement in these traditions is a positive affirmation of Blackness and a tribute to African culture. Similarly, many traditional Central-American Catholics find it difficult to admit their involvement in the Church because of its historical association with the oppressive ruling classes.

After gauging the importance of the religion to the client's situation, Western practitioners may decide that it is necessary to include some aspects of the tradition in treatment. There now exists a considerable anthropological and mental health literature that deals with these traditions, and Western practitioners should avail themselves of these resources (see references at the end of this chapter). Because many of these traditions have no central institution, are based on oral tradition, and include informal training, the practices reported in various accounts often vary greatly.

After studying some of the literature, Western practitioners may find it necessary to consult with Latino practitioners. Within their own communities, these practitioners are usually held in high regard, and therefore it will be necessary to approach them with a certain amount of respect. Simultaneously, because of the history of oppression of Indigenous- and African-based traditions, these practitioners might very well be suspicious of curious Western practitioners. Thus, building rapport will be an essential step in any consultation, and genuine interest, respect, and mutual concern for the client will be the most important ingredients to success. It may be useful to consult more than one practitioner because practitioners differ in levels of training and competency. It is often useful, as part of building rapport, to inquire about the practitioner's history in the tradition and about her or his methods of treating cases similar to the one under consideration. These traditions often include fees for services and rituals performed, but respect and direct communication on the part of the therapist are the most essential components.

Western practitioners should have a sense of how they want to include the traditional practitioners in any given case. Although the nature of the consultation should be clearly stated from the beginning, Western therapists should consider alternatives suggested by their spiritually oriented colleagues. Because different systems of healing imply divergent theories of causation and therefore different treatment plans, Western practitioners may very well encounter situations in which religious practitioners suggest approaching a client's difficulties in ways that the Western therapist had not imagined. Again therapists must decide how to proceed on a case-by-case basis in response to factors like the client's level of involvement, the level of trust among the three parties, and goals of the overall treatment.

Should a Western practitioner work consistently with Latinos and Latinas, it may be fruitful to develop working relationships with a variety of religious practitioners within the community. For example, Western practitioners working with Cuban and Puerto Rican communities in large cities like New York, Chicago, Washington, and Miami might benefit from having ongoing partnerships with santeros and spiritists. There are some joint efforts reported in the literature, such as the therapist–spiritist training project in Puerto Rico (Koss, 1980, 1987). This training project brought together for a period of 10 months spiritist healers and therapists of diverse backgrounds (psychology, nursing, social work, and medicine). They discussed information about each healing system and tried to synthesize the most effective techniques in each system. One outcome of this project was referrals of clients from one system to the other. In addition, on occasions, spiritists and therapists consulted with each other about their own personal problems (Koss, 1980).

Another example of collaboration between religious leaders and psychologists was observed in an Umbanda temple in São Paulo. The babaloricha referred individuals he thought were not psychologically stable to develop their mediumic powers to a psychologist who would screen out people with severe mental illness. Another example was described by a psychologist who is an Umbanda follower. In her psychological practice, she identifies individuals who could benefit from a spiritual consultation and she refers them to their spiritual leaders. Similarly, santeros in Washington, DC, and Miami refer clients to psychologists when divination suggests long-standing emotional traumas that cannot be alleviated in other ways.

As in the Puerto Rico therapist–spiritist training project and in the São Paulo Umbanda examples, it is possible that with time, Western practitioners might discover that certain culturally defined illnesses (like the attack of nerves) might best be treated by a competent spiritist rather than within a Western therapeutic context. If the therapists have already established relationships, they could refer a client, giving a sense of who the traditional practitioners are and how they work as well as feeling confident that the clients would be well treated by the traditional practitioners.

Conclusions and Future Directions

To narrow the gap between Latino/Latina clients and clinicians, it is important that more therapists understand Latino/Latina spiritual beliefs. As this happens, clients will feel that their beliefs have social acceptability similar to other, more mainstream religious beliefs and that their world-views are equally valid. Few clinicians question the religious beliefs of Christianity, Judaism, or Hinduism, yet Latino/Latina Indigenous and African-based beliefs are still ridiculed, stigmatized, and pathologized.

When clients perceive that clinicians respect their worldviews, religion may provide the individual with a stronger sense of empowerment. To a great extent, Latino/Latina spiritual beliefs have been sources of empowerment for individuals and communities because the interplay between humans, spirits, and gods through ritual, sacrifice, and communication provides them with a strong sense of self-determination. In other words, when individuals feel they can negotiate with orichas and spirits, they feel they are in control of their destinies.

Collaboration between clinicians and traditional spiritual leaders may pose difficulties resulting from distrust and incompatible worldviews. Pragmatic issues such as confidentiality and ethical issues on the part of clinicians and the duty to maintain certain secrets only for initiates among religious practitioners may also make collaboration difficult. However, efforts to reach out and learn about the traditions should result in the clinicians' better understanding of their clients, a respectful attitude toward divergent worldviews, and in many instances, a fruitful collaboration between religious and spiritual leaders.

SUGGESTED READINGS

Harwood, A. (1987). *Rx: Spiritist as needed: A study of a Puerto Rican community mental health resource.* Ithaca, NY: Cornell University Press.

Kiev, A. (1968). *Curanderismo: Mexican American folk psychiatry.* New York: Free Press.

Murphy, J. M. (1988). *Santería: An African religion in America.* Boston: Beacon Press.

Murphy, J. M. (1994). *Working the spirit: Ceremonies of the African diaspora.* Boston: Beacon Press.

Pressel, E. (1982). Umbanda trance and possession in São Paulo, Brazil. In F. D. Goodman, J. H. Henney, & E. Pressel (Eds.), *Trance, healing, and hallucination* (pp. 113–225). Malabar, FL: Robert E. Krieger.

Ruiz, P., & Langrod, J. (1976). Psychiatrists and spiritual healers: Partners in community mental health. In J. Westermeyer (Ed.), *Anthropology and mental health* (pp. 77–81). The Hague, The Netherlands: Mouton.

Trotter, R. T., & Chavira, J. A. (1981). *Curanderismo: Mexican American folk healing*. Athens, GA: The University of Georgia Press.

Verger, P. F. (1997). *Orixás: Deuses Iorubás na Africa e no Novo Mundo* [Orishas: Yoruba Gods in Africa and the new world]. Salvador: Corrupio.

Zea, M. C., Quezada, T., & Belgrave, F. Z. (1997). Limitations of an acultural health psychology for Latinos: Reconstructing the African influence on Latino culture and health-related behaviors. In J. G. Garcia & M. C. Zea (Eds.), *Psychological interventions and research with Latino populations* (pp. 255–266). Boston: Allyn & Bacon.

REFERENCES

Arenas, S., Cross, H., & Willard, W. (1980). Curanderos and mental health professionals: A comparative study on perceptions of psychopathology. *Hispanic Journal of Behavioral Sciences, 2,* 407–421.

Bascom, W. (1991). *Ifá Divination: Communication between Gods and men in West Africa*. Bloomington: Indiana University Press.

Beniste, J. (1997). *Òrun, Àiyé: O encontro de dois mundos: O sistema de relacionamiento Nago–Yorubá entre o céu e a terra*. Rio de Janeiro: Bertrand Brasil.

Brandon, G. (1993). *Santería from Africa to the New World: The dead sell memories*. Bloomington: Indiana University Press.

Brown, D. (1986). *Umbanda: Religion and politics in urban Brazil*. Ann Arbor, MI: UMI Research Press.

Cabrera, L. (1980). *Yemayá y ochún*. Miami: Colección del Chicherikú en el exilio.

Cervantes, J. M., & Ramirez, O. (1992). Spirituality and family dynamics in psychotherapy with Latino children. In L. A. Vargas & J. D. Koss-Chioino (Eds.), *Working with culture: Psychotherapeutic interventions with ethnic minority children and adolescents* (pp. 103–128). San Francisco: Jossey-Bass.

Comas-Díaz, L. (1981). Puerto Rican *espiritismo* and psychotherapy. *American Journal of Orthopsychiatry, 51,* 636–645.

Cros Sandoval, M. (1979). Santería as a mental health care system: A historical overview. *Social Science and Medicine, 13,* 137–152.

Da Silva, V. G. (1995). *Orixás da metrópole* [Orishas from the city]. Petrópolis, Brazil: Editora Vozes.

Fabrega, H., & Manning, P. K. (1973). An integrated theory of disease: Latino-Mestizo views of disease in the Chiapas Highlands. *Psychosomatic Medicine, 35,* 223–239.

Foster, G. M. (1960). *Culture and conquest*. Chicago: Quadrangle Books.

Garrison, V. (1982). Folk healing systems as elements in the community. In U. Ruevenir & R. Speck (Eds.), *Therapeutic intervention: Healing strategies for human systems* (pp. 58–95). New York: Human Science Press.

Gleason, J. (1987). *Oyá: In praise of the goddess*. Boston: Shambhala.

González-Wippler, M. (1989). *Santería: The religion*. New York: Harmony Books.

Goodman, F. (1988). *How about demons: Possession and exorcism in the modern world*. Bloomington: Indiana University Press.

Harwood, A. (1987). *Rx: Spiritist as needed: A study of a Puerto Rican community mental health resource*. Ithaca, NY: Cornell University Press.

Herskovits, M. J. (1966). The social organization of the Candomblé. In F. S. Herskovits (Ed.), *The New World Negro* (pp. 226–247). Bloomington: Indiana University Press.

Kiev, A. (1968). *Curanderismo: Mexican–American folk psychiatry*. New York: Free Press.

Koss, J. D. (1980). The therapist–spiritist training project in Puerto Rico: An experiment to relate the traditional healing system to the public health system. *Social Science and Medicine, 14B*, 255–266.

Koss, J. D. (1987). Expectations and outcomes for patients given mental health care or spiritist healing in Puerto Rico. *American Journal of Psychiatry, 144*, 56–61.

Koss-Chioino, J. D. (1995). Traditional and folk approaches among ethnic minorities. In J. F. Aponte, R. Y. Rivers, & J. Wohl (Eds.), *Psychological interventions and cultural diversity* (pp. 145–163). Boston: Allyn & Bacon.

Macklin, B. J. (1974). Belief, ritual, and healing: New England spiritualism and Mexican-American spiritism compared. In I. Zaretsky & M. Leone (Eds.), *Religious movements in contemporary America* (p. 383–417). Princeton, NJ: Princeton University Press.

Martin-Baró, I. (1990). Religion as an instrument of psychological warfare. *Journal of Social Issues, 46*, 93–107.

Mason, M. A. (1997). *Practicing* Santería, *performing the self: The social construction of subjectivity of humans and gods in an Afro-Cuban religion*. Unpublished doctoral dissertation, Indiana University, Bloomington.

Mbiti, J. (1975). *Introduction to African religion*. London: Heinenmann Educational Books.

Moreno Fraginales, M. (1977). Africa in Cuba: A quantitative analysis of the African population in the Island of Cuba. *Annals of the New York Academy of Sciences, 292*, 187–201.

Murphy, J. M. (1981). *Ritual systems in Cuban santería*. Unpublished doctoral dissertation, Temple University, Philadelphia.

Murphy, J. M. (1988). *Santería: An African religion in America*. Boston: Beacon Press.

Murphy, J. M. (1994). *Working the spirit: Ceremonies of the African diaspora*. Boston: Beacon press.

Núñez, M. (1987). Desarollo del Medium: *The process of becoming a healer in Puerto Rican* Espiritismo. Unpublished doctoral dissertation, Harvard University, Cambride, MA.

Pérez y Mena, A. (1991). *Speaking with the dead: Development of Afro-Latin religion among Puerto Ricans in the United States.* New York: AMS Press.

Pressel, E. (1973). Umbanda in São Paulo: Religious innovation in a developing society. In E. Bourguignon (Ed.), *Religion, altered states of consciousness, and social change* (pp. 264–318). Columbus: Ohio State University Press.

Pressel, E. (1982). Umbanda trance and possession in São Paulo, Brazil. In F. D. Goodman, J. H. Henney, & E. Pressel (Eds.), *Trance, healing, and hallucination* (pp. 113–225). Malabar, FL: Robert E. Krieger.

Ramirez, M. (1983). *Psychology of the Americas: Mestizo perspectives on personality and mental health.* New York: Pergamon Press.

Ramos, M. W. (1996). Afro-Cuban orisha worship. In A. Lindsay (Ed.), *Santería aesthetics in contemporary Latin American art* (pp. 51–76). Washington, DC: Smithsonian Institution Press.

Reichel-Dolmatoff, G. (1991). *Indians of Colombia: Experience and cognition.* Bogota, Colombia: Villegas Editores.

Reichel-Dolmatoff, G. (1996). *Los Kogi de Sierra Nevada.* Palma de Mallorca: Bitzoc.

Rivera, G., & Wanderer, J. J. (1986). Curanderismo and childhood illnesses. *The Social Science Journal, 23,* 361–372.

Ruiz, P., & Langrod, J. (1976). Psychiatrists and spiritual healers: Partners in community mental health. In J. Westermeyer (Ed.), *Anthropology and mental health* (pp. 77–81). The Hague, The Netherlands: Mouton.

Suarez-Balcazar, Y., Durlak, J. A., & Smith, C. (1994). Multicultural training practices in community psychology programs. *American Journal of Community Psychology, 22,* 785–798.

Tamez, E. (1988). (Ed.). *Teólogos de la Liberación hablan sobre la mujer* [Liberation theologists speak about women]. San Jose, Costa Rica: Departamento Ecuménico de Investigaciones.

Trotter, R. T., & Chavira, J. A. (1981). *Curanderismo: Mexican American folk healing.* Athens: University of Georgia Press.

Tyler, F. B., Brome, D. R., & Williams, J. (1991). *Ecology, ethnic validity, and psychotherapy: A psychosocial competence approach.* New York: Plenum Press.

Verger, P. F. (1997). *Orixás: Deuses Iorubás na Africa e no Novo Mundo* [Orishas: Yoruba Gods in Africa and the new world]. Salvador: Corrupio.

Wafer, J. (1991). *The taste of blood: Spirit possession in Brazilian candomblé.* Philadelphia: University of Pennsylvania Press.

Zea, M. C., Garcia, J. G., Belgrave, F. Z., & Quezada, T. (1997). Socioeconomic and cultural factors in rehabilitation of Latinos with disabilities. In J. G. Garcia & M. C. Zea (Eds.), *Psychological interventions and research with Latino populations* (pp. 217–234). Boston: Allyn & Bacon.

Zea, M. C., Quezada, T., & Belgrave, F. Z. (1997). Limitations of an acultural health psychology for Latinos: Reconstructing the African influence on Latino culture and health-related behaviors. In J. G. Garcia & M. C. Zea (Eds.), *Psychological interventions and research with Latino populations* (pp. 255–266). Boston: Allyn & Bacon.

17

PSYCHOTHERAPY WITH MEMBERS OF ASIAN AMERICAN CHURCHES AND SPIRITUAL TRADITIONS

SIANG-YANG TAN AND NATALIE J. DONG

Asian Americans often do not know that there are Asian roots to some of the values that they hold—just as many other Americans do not recognize the roots of American values in Puritanism, Calvinism, and the Enlightenment.

—Laura Uba

Asian Americans are a diverse ethnic group that includes people whose origins are Chinese, Japanese, Korean, Filipino, Asian Indian, Southeast Asian, and Pacific Islander. The diversity represented by the term Asian American is reflected in the fact that more than 50 groups speaking any of more than 30 different languages are included in this category (S. Sue, Nakamura, Chung, & Yee-Bradbury, 1994). A fast-growing minority group, Asian Americans differ substantially on the basis of both ethnic origin and rate of acculturation, as well as of religious beliefs and practices. This diversity provided a particular challenge to the task of writing about Asian American religious practices and the implications for counseling and psychotherapy. Although we focus specifically on Christian Asian Americans, the wide range of religious practices and influence of traditional spiritual beliefs and philosophy upon Asian American culture necessitated the inclusion of traditional belief systems (e.g., Taoism, Buddhism, and Confucian philosophy). Furthermore, traditional social values, acculturation, and religious beliefs and practices are closely interwoven, making it difficult to distinguish clearly among them.

Although substantial differences exist between and within Asian American groups, this chapter will focus primarily on the longer term immigrant groups: Chinese, Japanese, and Korean church traditions and the commonalities linking Asian American ethnic groups. Where possible, we include information on issues of particular relevance to specific groups of more recent Asian American immigrants. In this chapter, we will first provide an overview of Asian American religious beliefs and practices, including both Christian spirituality and more culturally traditional spiritual beliefs, practices, and values. We then address cultural considerations for counseling and psychotherapy, including common mental health and assessment issues. We specifically address Christian spiritual interventions in the section on treatment issues and approaches and provide a case example to illustrate typical cultural and spiritual issues when working with Asian American Christian clients.

HISTORICAL CONTEXT

Christian churches and missionaries have a significant historical role in Asian American history. Among Chinese in the United States, early generations of activist Chinese Americans collaborated with Protestant clergy and lawyers to fight discrimination and exclusionary immigration laws (Tseng, 1996). Protestant missionaries were a source of empowerment for Chinese women and children, establishing homes for destitute women and orphans, teaching English, and starting schools for the children, who were barred by law from attending public schools (Yung, 1986).

Among the Japanese in America, the United Methodist Church in particular was crucial to the assimilation of Japanese immigrants and later played a central role in assisting Japanese Americans following their release from relocation camps. The United Methodist Church began the Anglo-Japanese School for the purpose of teaching English to the Japanese in America (Suzuki, 1991). During the war years when Japanese Americans were forcibly interned in relocation camps, churches organized Sunday schools and worship services. Following the war, churches provided shelter to families attempting to find homes and jobs after leaving the camps.

In contrast with other Asian immigrant groups who typically convert to Christianity following their arrival in the United States, Korean Americans bring a strong tradition of Christianity with them from their country of origin. As a result, among Korean Americans churches are a cultural center for a community in which over 70% of individuals identify themselves as being Christian (Kim, 1996).

It is evident that Christian churches have had a significant role in Asian American history and have been integral to the formation and survival of Asian American communities in a country that has often been hostile to their presence. Beginning with the Chinese Exclusion Act of 1882, and later with Executive Order 9066 which forced Americans of Japanese ancestry to abandon homes and businesses to relocate to internment camps, both public policy and public sentiment have often been hostile to Americans of Asian descent. Harassed and attacked, denied the right to own land, denied the rights of citizenship, and barred from testifying in court, Asian Americans have been both lauded as a model minority and attacked as being uncivilized heathens and for unfair workplace competition. This context of discrimination and prejudice is the background against which Americans of Asian descent function and form a self.

RELIGIOUS TRADITIONS

Although reliable demographic information on church membership is not available, it is apparent that Asian Americans subscribe to a variety of religious belief systems. Although over 70% of Korean Americans are Protestant Christians, Pilipinos are heavily Catholic (Kim, 1996; Santa Rita, 1996). Chinese Americans may follow Buddhism, ancestor worship, or Christianity; Japanese Americans may follow Shintoism, Buddhism, or Christianity; and Vietnamese Americans are likely to follow Buddhism or Christianity. Others from Southeast Asia are likely to follow Hinduism, Buddhism, or Animism. As Asian Americans become increasingly acculturated, they are more likely to adopt mainstream religions (e.g., Christianity) which may produce conflicts with more traditional family members (E. Lee, 1996a).

In 1991, the *New York Times* reported (as cited in Busto, 1996) that among Asian Americans, 33.6% affiliated with Protestant denominations, 27.1% with Roman Catholic, 19.1% with no religion, and only 7.8% affiliated with Hindu or Buddhist religions. Among college students, large numbers of Asian Americans have turned to evangelical Christianity. This has been due, in large part, to the activities of parachurch organizations such as Campus Crusade for Christ, the Navigators, InterVarsity Christian Fellowship, and the Asian American Christian Fellowship ministry of the Japanese Evangelical Missionary Society (Busto, 1996). In addition, the activities of other Bible study groups, such as those sponsored by churches or established independently by students, have also had an influence. Asian American Christians are predominantly Protestant and have a tendency to come from pietistic, conservative, evangelical churches. Asian American parachurch groups focus on traditional tenets of evangelical Christianity while seeking to make the gospel ethnically relevant. Busto writes that Asian American students appear to be disproportionately involved in campus parachurch organizations compared with other ethnic minority groups.

This may be simply a reflection of the large number of Asian American college students compared with other ethnic minority college students.

The Asian American Christian community tends to be divided into congregations that are primarily older or Asian language speaking, and congregations that are younger and English speaking. Older, Asian-language-speaking churches tend to be more theologically conservative and emphasize a traditional order of worship, including the singing of hymns. Among the younger English-speaking congregations, there is a greater likelihood of the church demonstrating the influence of the widespread non-denominational, charismatic, evangelical influence. In these churches, the order of worship typically emphasizes the use of contemporary praise songs and worshippers are more likely to stand or lift their hands in prayer and praise during the worship service. These churches are also likely to emphasize more heavily the importance of "seeker sensitive" church services that are designed specifically to reach those who do not yet believe in Christianity but are exploring it.

TRADITIONAL CULTURE, VALUES, AND RELIGIOUS BELIEFS

Traditional beliefs, values, and philosophy have strongly influenced Asian culture in many ways, both subtle and overt. Many of these cultural factors have a defining role in Asian Christian beliefs, families, personality, communication styles, and identity. Although the majority of converts to Christianity seek to maintain religious integrity and relinquish other belief systems, cultural values and practices rooted in traditional philosophies or religious beliefs may continue to influence individuals. These influences produce varying degrees of conflict, to a large extent depending on the degree to which the individual is aware of the influences as well as by the ties they maintain with their ethnic community and how much pressure is exerted by more traditional family members. Many Asian Americans have found it necessary to become bicultural, practicing more Western values and communication styles in the workplace while maintaining a more traditional orientation at home and in their community. To begin to understand Asian American Christians, it is therefore essential that mental health professionals have some knowledge of traditional cultural beliefs and values.

Belief in the Supernatural

Among traditional Asian ethnic groups, there is often a belief in the existence of the spirit world and a recognition of multiple gods that rule the universe (Hopfe, 1983). Asians may hold belief systems that include superstitions involving the supernatural realm (Tan, 1991a), and deceased ancestors are often seen as links to the spirit world. Families may seek to cultivate the assistance of their ancestors by maintaining a small shrine or altar in the home where ancestors are remembered and offerings may be made.

Confucian Influences

Confucian beliefs, which originated in China, have had a widespread influence throughout Asia. At its core, Confucianism is a system of ethics focusing on proper or harmonious social order (Hopfe, 1983). Confucian principles form the basis for the heritage of androcentrism, patriarchy, and emphasis on filial piety in Asian cultures. These principles are frequently demonstrated in the submission of the self to the family, maintenance of proper relations between youth and elders, and obedience by the wife to the husband.

Filial piety is a strong value which refers to the respect, obligations, duty, and obedience that a person holds toward his or her parents. Love for the family is defined in terms of obedience by the children to the parents. This obligation continues even after the children are married and have begun their own nuclear families (D. Sue & Sue, 1993).

Confucian principles also emphasize the authority of the eldest male in the family. Thus, obedience of children to the father, siblings to the eldest son, and wife to husband are central to maintaining an orderly family. In traditional Asian families, fathers are generally authoritative, remote, aloof, strict, and dignified, and sons are highly valued with the eldest son considered to be the most important child (D. Sue & Sue, 1993; Uba, 1994).

Taoist Influences

One of the major principles of Taoism focuses on the importance of living in harmony with nature and with others (Hopfe, 1983). These influences may be seen in the emphasis on harmonious interpersonal relationships and the avoidance of direct confrontation (Tomine, 1991). Among Asian American families, communication is often indirect and disapproval is communicated through the use of shame, guilt, and loss of face. Harmony and cohesion within the family and the broader community are valued above individual achievement (Matsui, 1996).

Buddhist Influences

The Buddhist perspective on fate and suffering has influenced traditional Asian responses (such as passive acceptance) to perceived injustice or personal suffering. For example, the Japanese term *shikata ga nai*, "it can not be helped," expresses an approach to suffering as being something that must be endured quietly. Some schools of Buddhism assert that all existence is suffering, life is full of pain, and a spiritual release from suffering is possible through achieving a state of nondesire (Wenhao, Salomon, & Chay, 1993).

Group Orientation

Among Asians, the needs and wishes of the family group and the collective community are given a higher priority than individual desires and goals (Ho, 1985; Moy, 1992). Maintaining the honor and reputation of the family is a primary concern, as is compliance with parental expectations regardless of the age of the child.

Duty and Obligation

The priority given to actions that benefit the family translates into an emphasis on fulfilling one's duty and obligations to others, especially for children to fulfill their obligations to family and parents (Moy, 1992) and to refrain from behavior that may have negative effects upon others (Morrow, 1989). Failure to fulfill one's duty and obligations to others can produce feelings of shame, guilt, and alienation (D. Sue & Sue, 1993; Uba, 1994).

Hierarchy and Status

Asian culture emphasizes hierarchy and status in social relationships, with communication patterns flowing down from those of higher status (Moy, 1992). Negotiation and open discussion are foreign in a cultural tradition that prescribes deference and obedience to those of higher status with confrontation and expression of strong feelings viewed as being inappropriate and unacceptable.

Deference

Traditional Asian values place a high value on deference and indirect, restrained communication to achieve or maintain harmony and peace in the social group (Moy, 1992; D. Sue & Sue, 1993; Uba, 1994). A high value is placed on anticipating the needs of others so that it is unnecessary to express one's own needs verbally, thus preventing the other person from appearing rude, demanding, or selfish (Uba, 1994). This insight and sensitivity to subtle cues is cultivated in children, who learn to be ashamed of themselves when they are not insightful into the needs of others (Toupine, 1980).

Self-Control

Asian culture values self-restraint in verbal communication and control over strong emotions (Moy, 1992; Uba, 1994). Indirect and nonverbal communication is emphasized in Asian families, with physical demonstrations of affection occurring rarely if at all. In the context of marital and family therapy, open expression of emotions, especially negative feelings, may produce significant disruption in family functioning.

THE CHALLENGE TO INTEGRATE MULTIPLE VALUE SYSTEMS

Many Asian Americans struggle with generational, cultural, and religious conflicts. To varying degrees, they may simultaneously maintain both Asian and Western traditions, and both Christian and traditional belief systems (Chao, 1992; Hopfe, 1983; Tan, 1991a). Awareness of these potential conflicts is important for effective psychotherapy with many Asian Christians. It should be noted that although most Asian Christians seek to embrace Biblical teachings and Christian values, they may be subtly influenced by traditional cultural values and beliefs. This is especially true of those cultural values and beliefs that are present in their family of origin.

Although traditional Asian beliefs in the existence of multiple gods, goddesses, and spirits is theologically incompatible with the monotheism of Christianity, these traditional beliefs do translate readily into a Christian worldview that incorporates the existence of the supernatural realm, including a belief in demonic and in spiritual warfare (Tan, 1991a). Many Asian Christians, particularly in the evangelical and charismatic traditions, rely on intercessory prayer and on the power of the Holy Spirit in day-to-day coping. In addition, they may readily interpret difficulties as the work of demonic forces or spiritual warfare.

In both family and church life, Asian Americans tend toward patriarchal, androcentric, authoritarian leadership. Within the church, the established power structures typically exclude women from leadership and religious authority. Controversies over women's ordination and authority to preach from the pulpit and the use of noninclusive language to define and describe religious life and experience exemplify the exclusion of women from leadership in the church. An emphasis on biblical passages that call for the submission of women combined with a cultural tradition which relegates women to secondary status produces a tendency toward patriarchal authority structures in Asian American churches. There are, however, some Asian churches that have become more progressive in the area of gender roles and that support the ordination of women or the more complete inclusion of women in church leadership positions. In addition, there is a growing number of Asian churches that are moving away from the traditional clergy-centered authoritarian structures and affirm the use of lay leaders and nonordained staff in specific ministries within the church.

In general, Asian Americans tend to take more conservative positions on social and moral issues (e.g., gender roles, divorce, politics) both within the church and society at large. This may have arisen as a survival tactic in a racist and hostile society, as Asian Americans attempted to avoid drawing negative attention to themselves that would have further hindered their ability to succeed and prosper.

CULTURAL CONSIDERATIONS FOR COUNSELING AND PSYCHOTHERAPY

Numerous authors have consistently reported in the literature that Asian Americans underuse mental health services (Bradshaw, 1994; Moy, 1992, S. Sue, Nakamura, Chung, & Yee-Bradbury, 1994). With prevalence rates of mental health problems equal to or surpassing those of other ethnic groups, it has been suggested that, when Asian Americans finally seek mental health treatment, it is after attempting all other means of assistance, resulting in a greater severity of problems seen (S. Sue & Morishima, 1982).

Mental illness is highly stigmatized, often viewed as a sign of personal weakness or punishment by spirits and as reflecting poorly on one's family (E. Lee, 1996b; Moy, 1992). Misfortune, including mental illness, may be seen as a punishment for family sins, past or present. The Japanese term *bachi*, "what goes around comes around," reflects the perception that people are fated to suffer for their wrong doing or that of their family. Asian American clients may be reluctant to seek help from outsiders because of a sense of shame surrounding this perceived punishment.

Western approaches to mental health emphasize the distinct separation of the mind and body, whereas traditional Asian approaches make no distinction between physiological and psychological problems (Wenhao, Salomon, & Chay, 1993). This difference can result in Asian American clients being labeled as somatizing (Lin, 1996). In general, Asian clients believe that mental disturbance is associated with physical causes, and that the emotional disturbance will disappear once the physical illness is appropriately treated. Depression and other psychological problems are likely to be expressed primarily through somatic symptoms, such as headaches, weakness or fatigue, and insomnia (D. W. Sue & Sue, 1990). Traditional approaches to healing may include acupuncture, herbal medicine, religious rituals, or dermabrasive practices such as coin rubbing and are likely to be used simultaneously with Western medical treatment (Mollica & Lavelle, 1988).

In general, when problems do arise, family members are the first and primary resource from which assistance is sought. It is unheard of in traditional Asian cultures to seek help for personal problems from a stranger. When family members are unable to resolve the problem, they may turn to trusted leaders within the community, such as community elders, spiritual leaders, traditional healers, and physicians (Solberg, Choi, Ritsma, & Jolly, 1994).

Factors Influencing Therapy

Asian Americans may be reluctant to seek help from mental health professionals if culturally sensitive providers are not available. Individuals are likely to be discouraged from seeking help from mental health providers when they sense that the therapist does not understand or recognize Asian American values and styles of interacting, or when the therapist misinterprets their culturally influenced behavior (Uba, 1994). Thus, Asian American clients may tend to prefer therapists who are also Asian American, regardless of the number of generations for which they are removed from their country of origin.

A common set of beliefs and values between the therapist and the Asian American client is an important factor in the success of therapy and the prevention of premature termination. The values of psychotherapy as they have traditionally been conceptualized may be in conflict with many values held by traditional Asian clients. D. W. Sue and Sue (1990) provide an extensive discussion of potential sources of value-based conflict in counseling. Among Christian Asian American clients, similarity of religious beliefs is crucial. When this population does seek the services of professionals, they indicate a preference for Christian professionals over non-Christian professionals (Misumi, 1993). For Christian clients, sharing the same religious beliefs with their therapist facilitates the establishment of adequate credibility and status on the part of the therapist (see S. Sue & Zane, 1987).

The credibility and status of the therapist may influence the readiness of Asian American clients to seek out and stay in treatment. S. Sue and Zane (1987) describe credibility as referring to the client's perception of the therapist as an effective and trustworthy helper. The status of the therapist is of importance in a culture that traditionally respects those in authority. It should also be noted that among Asian American clients, age and marital status may be relevant to establishing therapist credibility and status, with a tendency to prefer older and married therapists.

Building Trust and Credibility

S. Sue and Zane (1987) describe the concept of gift giving as a means for building credibility with clients and preventing early termination. Gift giving refers to the client's perception that something was received or some benefit acquired from the therapeutic encounter and may be essential early in the therapy process to prevent early termination. Some of the gifts that the therapist can offer include depression relief, anxiety reduction, reassurance, skills acquisition, hope, a coping perspective, and goal setting. J. Lee and Cynn (1991) suggest that the normalization of family problems as a typical acculturation process may be the most valuable gift possible. Credibility is enhanced by academic training, credentials, and experience. Thus, clinicians need to convey confidence and should not hesitate to reveal their educational background and work experience, especially with clients who may be skeptical or apprehensive about seeking treatment (E. Lee, 1996b).

S. Sue (1988) has pointed out that ethnic matches of client and therapist may not be as meaningful or helpful as cultural matches. Although one of the most salient aspects of therapist match for Asian American clients is an ethnic and language match (S. Sue, Zane, & Young, 1994), differences in acculturation, values, attitudes, and religious beliefs may supersede similarity of ethnic background as factors influencing therapy outcome. Reliance on ethnic matches can result in cultural mismatches if a therapist and a client from the same ethnic group have markedly different values. At the same time, a therapist and a client from different ethnic backgrounds may be culturally matched on the basis of similar values, lifestyles, and experiences (S. Sue, 1988). For female Asian American clients, in particular, the availability of therapists who are of the same ethnic and gender background may be crucial to staying in therapy (Fujino, Okazaki, & Young, 1994).

When therapist and client are culturally mismatched, problems can occur because of differences in communication styles. The therapist who is unaware of these cultural distinctives may be perceived as rude or disrespectful for engaging in direct, assertive communications or for asking deeply personal questions. Conversely, therapists may interpret their client's communications as being indicative of low self-esteem, shyness, repression, inhibition, or resistance (Uba, 1994).

Among more traditional, less acculturated Asian Americans, it may be especially useful to incorporate the family and the extended family network into treatment or to use them as treatment resources. When family therapy is used, it is important for the therapist to be sensitive to maintaining the family's honor and preserving the hierarchy of authority. In spite of potential difficulties, the loyalties and support extended by family members are cultural strengths that can be used creatively to facilitate the therapeutic process (E. Lee, 1996b).

In general, Asian Americans tend to prefer a less reflective, more structured approach to therapy. A nondirective, reflective therapist is likely to increase the anxiety of the Asian American client and undermine the therapist's credibility. Structured therapy focused on concrete methods will help therapy to make sense and increase the likelihood of a client returning to therapy (Root, 1985).

Special Considerations Among Southeast Asians

Individuals from Southeast Asian countries are among the newest and most traumatized Asian Americans. Unlike early Chinese and Japanese immigrants who were drawn to the United States by the lure of opportunity, Southeast Asian immigrants, such as those from Vietnam (Leung & Boehnlein, 1996) and Cambodia (McKenzie-Pollock, 1996), are typically refugees who escaped war and violence in their homelands. As newer arrivals to the United States, they are likely to be struggling with language barriers, financial difficulties, under- or unemployment, trauma related to the refugee experience, cultural difficulties with children raised in the United States, and disruption of the family hierarchy.

ASSESSMENT AND DIAGNOSTIC ISSUES AND APPROACHES

In a population as diverse as the Asian American community, there are numerous considerations to be taken into account when working with Asian American clients. In the following section, we discuss some of the issues that we felt to be most salient across Asian American ethnic groups.

Cultural Bias in Therapist Perceptions

Ethnically mismatched therapists may perceive their Asian American clients through biased perceptions. White Americans may perceive Chinese clients as being more depressed and inhibited, and less socially poised than would Chinese American therapists (S. Sue, Nakamura, Chung, & Yee-Bradbury, 1994). Uba (1994) summarizes the literature examining differences in personality patterns among various Asian American groups and European Americans. Failure to take these cultural differences into account can lead to significant errors in intervention and assessment.

Common Mental Health Issues

Acculturation Issues

Problems relating to acculturation difficulties may frequently arise in therapy with Asian American clients. New immigrants have to contend with adapting to a new environment, including learning the American culture, learning a new language, and struggling to find adequate employment, transportation, child care, and housing (E. Lee, 1996b). Many new immigrants have numerous losses, separations, and traumas to resolve. As children adapt to the majority culture, parents may adjust more slowly and problems can arise when traditionally oriented parents expect their children to retain old world values and reject American culture.

Conflicts between traditional roles and those adopted in a new country may be a significant source of disruption in families. These role conflicts can emerge when English-speaking children are relied upon as interpreters by parents and grandparents. Role conflicts may also occur when Asian women find that they are earning more income than their husbands or find themselves to be the sole wage earner in the family. This disrupts the authority of the husband and displaces him as the financial support of the family.

Individuals also experience a loss of status and identity after leaving their country of origin. Language barriers and other factors may trap many immigrants in restaurant and garment industry work with no alternatives (E. Lee, 1996b). Underemployment of former professionals and executives, displacement of husbands as sole wage earners, and financial difficulties produce a loss of status that can be devastating to families.

Asian American Christians have a tricultural adaptation to negotiate. These individuals must find a way to function within the heritage culture typically maintained most strongly by parents and grandparents. They need to adapt to the dominant Western culture, with its different values and styles of relating. Additionally, these individuals need to adapt to the Christian subculture, which has its own set of values, customs, language, and behaviors. These individuals may experience difficulty moving between and within these various cultures, particularly when values clash between them.

Filial Piety and Religious Conflicts

Family harmony can be significantly disrupted when children adopt religious beliefs that differ from those of their parents. Many traditional parents perceive the child's adoption of a differing religious system as being disrespectful and disobedient. Parents may expect their Christian children to participate in Buddhist ceremonies or to engage in worship rituals to honor ancestors. Failure to comply with these parental expectations is perceived as being disrespectful and as bringing shame upon the family. In addition, many families may believe that defiance of traditional religious practices (e.g., Buddhist or ancestor worship) will risk bad luck or misfortune.

Somatization

In general, Asian Americans frequently somatize their mental health problems (Uba, 1994). Somatization may be a socially acceptable means of gaining attention and support, as well as of avoiding shame and maintaining the honor of the family (E. Lee, 1996b; Uba, 1994). It is essential to attend to the client's somatic complaints and avoid the appearance of discounting physical symptoms, prior to addressing personal conflicts. It may also be useful to encourage the simultaneous use of alternative methods of healing, including religious and traditional interventions.

Women's Roles and Identity

Traditional Asian culture, based on the Confucian patriarchal and hierarchical structure, tends to relegate women to a secondary status lacking self-determination, leadership, or authority. Asian American women who seek greater freedom and opportunity for achievement, particularly within church leadership, may not find acceptance within their culture of origin or within their church. The alternatives then are to repress or relinquish their desire for achievement, assimilate with the majority culture, attempt to change their own culture, or attempt to transcend both cultures (Bradshaw, 1994). It can be useful to explore the conflicts that Asian American Christian women experience and to normalize this conflict as part of the cultural conflict that they experience negotiating the three distinct cultures of their heritage, the majority environment, and their Christian faith.

Filial Piety and Vocational–Educational Dilemmas

The traditional expectation that children will be obedient and respectful toward parents can produce difficulty as children are exposed to Western ideas of independence and self-determination. Individuals may experience significant distress as they contemplate college majors and make vocational decisions, trying to balance their individual interests with sometimes differing parental expectations. Exploration and education around these conflicts, focused on helping clients to understand that many Asian Americans are struggling with similar problems and that these are symptomatic of larger cultural differences, can help (Moy, 1992).

Intergenerational Conflicts

Asian American families in which the parents immigrated and the children were either born or raised in the United States are the most likely to experience serious intergenerational conflicts, although these conflicts may also arise in more acculturated families who have been in the United States for many generations. Parents may fear that their children will lose traditional values and behavior, and may impose strict rules governing their behavior. Children may be expected to place their highest value on the family with their parents interpreting extracurricular activities or church fellowship groups as indicating an uncaring and disrespectful attitude. Independent action (contrary to the wishes of the parents) on the part of a child, no matter what his or her age, may be interpreted as rude, selfish, and inconsiderate behavior (D. Sue & Sue, 1993).

Posttraumatic Stress Disorder (PTSD) in Southeast Asian Clients

PTSD is a significant clinical issue among Southeast Asian refugees. Many of these refugees experienced serious multiple traumas, including torture (Mollica & Lavelle, 1988). Among Cambodian families, the most common treatment issues are trauma and loss (McKenzie-Pollock, 1996), with Southeast Asian refugees being in general at high risk for developing PTSD (Abe, Zane, & Chun, 1994). Refugees may experience a large number of physical complaints and are likely to interpret their difficulties as having somatic or supernatural causes (Nishio & Bilmes, 1993). A treatment plan may involve using a traditional healer, couple or family therapy, and use of medications (McKenzie-Pollock, 1996).

Assessment Measures and Issues

Psychological assessment tools, such as personality inventories and other measures of psychopathology, must be interpreted with caution when used with Asian American clients. Limited or inadequate standardization on Asian American populations can produce misinterpretation of testing results if cultural factors are not taken into account. A number of rating scales developed for Western patients have been found by Westermeyer and his colleagues (e.g., Westermeyer, 1986; Westermeyer, Vang, & Neider, 1983) to be reliable and valid for Asian patients as well. However, other investigators have not consistently found such results. Asian Americans, particularly Southeast Asians, tend to somatize depressive reactions and are likely to describe their psychiatric problems in terms of somatic complaints (Marsella, Kinzie, & Gordon, 1973; see also D. Sue & Sue, 1987), which may render frequently used measures of depression invalid among Asian American clients.

In addition to limitations based on inadequate standardization, assessment tools may be inappropriate as measures of well-being, adjustment, or pathology caused by value conflicts with the dominant culture. Traditional Asian values that place emphasis on interdependence, emotional restraint, and deference, as well as spiritual emphases on submission and experiencing the presence of God, may be interpreted as pathological by psychological assessment measures.

Assessing the degree of acculturation can be an important part of formulating an appropriate plan for intervention with clients. One measure that can be useful for assessing acculturation is the Suinn-Lew Asian Self-Identity Acculturation Scale (SL-ASIA). The SL-ASIA (Suinn, Rickard-

Figueroa, Lew, & Virgil, 1987) is a 21-item multiple-choice questionnaire that assesses both actual behaviors and ideals related to acculturation among Asians. Items are rated on a 5-point scale, with higher scores indicating greater acculturation.

Religious and Spiritual Measures

It may be helpful for therapists to assess the religious and spiritual well-being of Christian clients. Clinical interviewing is often the most useful method for assessing what role and significance religion has in clients' lives. The Religious Status Inventory and the Spiritual Well-Being Scale are two objective measures that may also be useful for this purpose with Christian Asian Americans.

Religious Status Inventory (RSI)

The RSI (Malony, 1988) is a 160-item questionnaire designed to measure religious functioning along eight dimensions assessing Christian maturity. The RSI has scores on eight major subscales:

- awareness of God,
- acceptance of God's grace and steadfast love,
- being repentant and responsible,
- knowing God's leadership and direction,
- involvement in organized religion,
- experiencing fellowship,
- being ethical, and
- affirming openness in faith.

Although this measure has had limited use with Asian Americans, it appears to be a promising measure of religious functioning and Christian maturity.

Spiritual Well-Being Scale (SWBS)

The SWBS (Ellison, 1983) was developed to provide a quality-of-life measure that includes both religious and existential well-being (Ellison & Smith, 1991). The scale consists of 20 items divided into two subscales of religious well-being and existential well-being. Although the SWBS has been found to have ceiling effects that may limit its usefulness with conservative Christians (Ledbetter, Smith, Vosler-Hunter, & Fischer, 1991), research has found positive correlations with physical health, adjustment to physical illness, and psychological and relational well-being (Ellison & Smith, 1991). Ellison and Smith suggest that this measure may be useful as an inexpensive tool for general assessment of well-being. Although it has had limited use among Asian Americans, this measure appears to be promising.

Treatment Issues and Approaches

Using Cultural Strengths

During difficult times, Asian American clients can usually rely on a supportive network of family, friends, and community organizations, which can be explored and used as a resource in therapy. Asian American churches are an important source of support and assistance that can also be used to assist clients. Church communities can provide supportive networks to individuals in crisis or distress, are an important link to resources within the ethnic Christian community, and may be able to assist with financial, housing, or employment needs in addition to helping care for the mental health needs of individuals.

Psychological Interventions

In general, Asian American clients are thought to prefer a more directive, situationally oriented, and problem-solving focused therapeutic orientation (see E. Lee, 1996a; D. Sue & Sue, 1990) that is time limited and focused on concrete resolution of problems (e.g., cognitive–behavioral therapy or systemic approaches to marital and family therapy). The therapist who takes an active and directive role is likely to be more successful because the client will rely on the counselor to furnish direction. Among more traditional Asian Americans, an early emphasis on nondirective approaches or emotional expressiveness is likely to be unsuccessful and may result in premature termination from therapy. Asian American clients may find emotionally oriented goals incomprehensible or impractical in a cultural tradition that values the restraint of strong emotions. The therapist who challenges the client to discuss his or her negative feelings and experiences in detail may inadvertently provoke feelings of shame or improper disclosure of private matters. Admission of emotional problems and receiving help from outside of the family may be interpreted as weakness or loss of face (E. Lee, 1996a). To minimize the client's embarrassment, it is suggested that therapists be sensitive to the need for the client to save face, using restraint when gathering information (D. W. Sue & Sue, 1990) and avoiding direct confrontation too early in the counseling process (Tan, 1991a).

Spiritual Interventions

This section will primarily address counseling with Christian Asian Americans, who usually believe in the reality of evil and the demonic, and in spiritual warfare (Tan, 1991a). Therefore, these individuals may be more open to Christian counseling that uses the explicit and appropriate use of prayer, the scriptures, and the power of the Holy Spirit.

When working with Asian American Christian clients, mental health professionals who do not share their clients' religious beliefs should avoid challenging such beliefs early in therapy. Clients may perceive such challenges as shaming, embarrassment, or a lack of understanding. If the therapist sees ways in which the clients' belief structure is a part of the problem (e.g., believing it is sinful to ever get angry), these should be approached gradually and only after a strong therapeutic rapport has been established. The therapist should address the client from within his or her belief system and encourage the use of spiritual resources such as prayer, meditation, and Bible study. Christian mental health professionals may, when appropriate, use prayer for inner healing or healing of memories (Seamands, 1985; Tan & Ortberg, 1995).

The use of scriptures in therapy can be an effective way to guide and teach clients who hold inaccurate beliefs about themselves, others, or their situations. Therapists who hold different religious beliefs can encourage their clients to seek scriptural models of faith and action to guide clients to their true value and image in the eyes of God. Scripture can also be used to demonstrate a model of emotional expressiveness in Jesus, teaching clients that emotions such as anger, sadness, or grief do not need to be repressed or ignored.

Asian Christian clients who are affiliated with a church can be encouraged to seek the support of their pastor. Such support can be a significant resource, providing prayer, encouragement, and Biblical teaching. With client consent, and when appropriate, therapists may find it helpful to consult with a client's pastor and enlist his or her perspective and involvement in the client's healing. Asian Christian clients who do not have a church that they regularly attend can be encouraged to find a congregation where they can receive the benefits of prayer, worship, Biblical teaching, and fellowship with other Christians. Therapists may find it helpful to become familiar with local Asian American churches to facilitate their ability to refer clients to appropriate congregations. Additionally, therapists can use the resources of parachurch groups, such as healing and recovery ministries, or Bible studies and fellowship groups for prayer, teaching, and social support.

Working With Religious Leaders and the Religious Community

Appropriate status and credibility are crucial for therapists working with religious leaders and the religious community. Mental health professionals should not hesitate to disclose their academic training, professional credentials, experience, and religious affiliation. Such information will help to provide credibility and establish the therapist as being a person with expertise.

When working with the Asian American religious community, mental health professionals need to be sensitive to the patriarchal structure existing in both the culture and the church. In general, male professionals command a higher status than female professionals. Regardless of gender, professionals who work with religious leaders in the community should be sensitive to the need to maintain proper respect and avoid inadvertently shaming or appearing rude.

Mental health professionals can build cooperative relationships with church communities by offering their expertise to pastors, lay leaders, and church groups (see Tan, 1997). By educating and equipping churches to address the mental health needs of their congregation more effectively, therapists help to demystify and destigmatize mental health services. Therapists should maintain a respectful attitude toward the biblical values and teaching of the church, especially when working with churches and Christian leaders who may be skeptical of psychology and resistant to the use of such psychoeducational interventions.

Guidelines for Implementing Spiritual Interventions

Spiritual interventions should always be implemented with clinical sensitivity, ethical wisdom, and biblical balance to avoid under- or over-using spiritual resources and interpretations (see Tan, 1996). The therapist must use discernment in assessing whether the client is ready to use spiritual resources, especially if he or she is not a Christian or is a Christian struggling with his or her faith and has doubts about God.

Once the therapist has carefully determined that the client is ready to use spiritual resources, this should be implemented only after the client has given informed consent to do so. Particularly in the use of prayer for inner healing and release, it is important to explain the procedure to the client clearly and thoroughly prior to obtaining consent. Spiritual interventions that are implemented must be relevant to clients and to their problems. Therapists should avoid using scripted or routine prayers and teaching, tailoring instead spiritual interventions to the clients' particular needs and problems.

Prior to implementing spiritual interventions, therapists should have explored the client's faith and beliefs, to ensure that there is a foundation of shared beliefs. Therapists or clients may mistakenly assume that their religious beliefs and values are the same, simply because they are both Christians. When therapists differ from their clients on some topic of faith, they should be careful to maintain a respectful attitude and refrain from imposing their opinion on the client. Therapist competence with spiritual interventions is crucial to their effective implementation (Tan, 1991a; 1999; also see Tan & Gregg, 1997).

Case Example

The following hypothetical case example will help to illustrate some of the principles mentioned for effective psychotherapy and counseling with Christian Asian American clients. James is a 19-year-old Chinese American Christian in his first year of college, majoring in biology at Stanford University. He was the top student in his high school with a straight A record and a total SAT score of 1500. He grew up in a typical Chinese family, originally from Taiwan, and lived in the Los Angeles area after emigrating to the United States with his family when he was 3 years old. His father is a physician and his mother an accountant. He has a younger sister who is 16 years old and in high school. Academic excellence is highly valued in his family, especially by his father.

Therefore, James has applied himself diligently to his academic studies and has excelled thus far. He became a Christian while in high school when he was 15 years old. Since then, he has been very active in a local Chinese church, as a leader in the church youth group and as an elementary Sunday school teacher. His parents are from a Buddhist background, and although they are not actively practicing, they do not share the Christian faith and beliefs of James. They allowed him to be active in church and high school Christian activities so long as these did not interfere with his academic performance.

In his first year at Stanford University, James has had significant struggles trying to balance his academic studies with activities at a local Christian church near the campus and with the university's chapter of Inter-Varsity Christian Fellowship. The academic work has been very demanding, and he has had to stay up late many nights to study and prepare for exams. Recently, James has been feeling fatigued, depressed, and stressed. He has felt a strong obligation to his parents to excel academically and gain admission to medical school because his father has always wanted him to be a physician. He also desires to stay active at church and in the university fellowship. However, he has been finding it nearly impossible to keep up with this schedule. He decided to see a Chinese psychologist at the university counseling center because of symptoms of fatigue, stress, and depression. Additionally, he has recently received B grades on his tests.

James did not inform his parents about seeking professional help from the Chinese psychologist for fear of shaming them. Although the psychologist was not a Christian, he was a spiritually sensitive therapist with some knowledge of Christianity and Chinese churches. James therefore felt comfortable discussing both Chinese culture and Christian faith issues openly with him. A primarily cognitive–behavioral approach was used to provide greater structure and direction in the therapy.

James learned stress management strategies and was able to restructure his rigid and perfectionistic ways of thinking. James realized that doing his best with God's help is good enough, even if he could not get As in everything. He also learned to take better care of his body as the temple of the Holy Spirit. He revised his schedule so that it was less hectic, reducing his activities at church and in the campus fellowship, realizing that he needed time to adjust to the demanding academic workload. He was also able to see that this did not mean that he was being a bad Christian.

After 2 months of weekly counseling sessions, James began to feel significantly better although he kept the therapy a secret. When he told his parents that he had reduced his activities to focus on his academic studies, they were pleased. His parents were able to accept the B grades he had received on tests but told him to try to get A grades. James promised to do his best, motivated to excel academically to glorify God and to please his parents. Through the counseling, James was able to realize he had a desire to become a physician to serve God, rather than just to please his father.

Summary and Future Directions

Asian Americans comprise a rapidly growing, diverse segment of the population with substantial between- and within-group differences. The Asian American population consists of numerous subgroups and, as such, generalizations about culture and psychopathology should be made only with the greatest caution. As with other ethnic minority groups, Asian Americans must become fluent in both their heritage culture and the dominant culture of the society in which they live. Christian Asian Americans must also negotiate the culture of their religious faith and contend with potential conflicts with family elders who do not share the same beliefs. Knowledge of a client's heritage culture and potential problems that may arise out of religious faith can equip the mental health professional to meet the needs of Christian Asian American clients sensitively and competently.

There remains an ongoing need for greater research investigating the mental health needs of Asian American Christians, as well as a need for more available, accessible, and affordable mental health services for this distinct community. Research directions may focus on examining the prevalence and severity of mental health problems, help-seeking patterns, and strengths and barriers resulting from religious faith. Additionally, research on women's mental health within the Asian American Christian culture of patriarchy and submission may be useful in designing interventions to address the conflict and abuse suffered by many women.

The use of lay counseling ministries within the church conducted by Christian nonprofessionals or paraprofessionals (see Tan, 1991b) is an approach that can be used to meet the needs of a population among which formal counseling is stigmatized. Similarly, it has been suggested that Chinese immigrants who have been living in the United States for 6 years or more may be effective as paraprofessional or lay helpers for more recent Chinese immigrants who are struggling with adaptation or adjustment problems (S. Sue & Zane, 1985).

Although there are many Asian American therapists in private practice, affordability of services remains a barrier for many individuals. The nonprofit Asian American Christian Counseling Service in Southern California, which operates on a sliding-fee scale, receives nearly half of its referrals from churches and pastors (Asian American Christian Counseling Service, 1998). It is suggested that such clinic settings that are distinctively both Asian American and Christian can provide greater affordability and flexibility in scheduling as well as meet the longer term needs of clients whose problems are beyond the scope of lay counselors or pastoral care.

SUGGESTED READINGS

Lee, L. C., & Zane, N. W. (1998). *Handbook of Asian American psychology.* Thousand Oaks, CA: Sage.

Takaki, R. (1989). *Strangers from a different shore: A history of Asian Americans.* New York: Penguin Books.

Uba, L. (1994). *Asian Americans: Personality patterns, identity, and mental health.* New York: Guilford Press.

REFERENCES

Abe, J., Zane, N., & Chun, K. (1994). Differential responses to trauma: Migration-related discriminants of posttraumatic stress disorder among Southeast Asian refugees. *Journal of Community Psychology, 22,* 121–135.

Asian American Christian Counseling Service. (1998). *AACCS clinical accounting report: 1996–1997.* Alhambra, CA: Author.

Bradshaw, C. K. (1994). Asian and Asian American women: Historical and political considerations in psychotherapy. In L. Comas-Díaz & B. Greene (Eds.), *Women of color: Integrating ethnic and gender identities in psychotherapy* (pp. 72–113). New York: Guilford Press.

Busto, R. V. (1996). The gospel according to the model minority?: Hazarding an interpretation of Asian American Evangelical college students. *Amerasia Journal, 22,* 133–147.

Chao, C. (1992). The inner heart: Therapy with Southeast Asian families. In L. Vargas & J. Koss-Chioino (Eds.), *Working with culture: Psychotherapeutic interventions with ethnic minority children and adolescents* (pp. 157–181). San Francisco: Jossey-Bass.

Ellison, C. W. (1983). Spiritual well-being: Conceptualization and measurement. *Journal of Psychology and Theology, 11,* 330–340.

Ellison, C. W., & Smith, J. (1991). Toward an integrative measure of health and well-being. *Journal of Psychology and Theology, 19,* 35–48.

Fujino, D. C., Okazaki, S., & Young, K. (1994). Asian-American women in the mental health system: An examination of ethnic and gender match between therapist and client. *Journal of Community Psychology, 22,* 164–176.

Ho, D. Y. F. (1985). Cultural values and professional issues in clinical psychology: Implications from the Hong Kong experience. *American Psychologist, 40,* 1212–1218.

Hopfe, L. M. (1983). *Religions of the world.* New York: Macmillan.

Kim, B.-L. C. (1996). Korean families. In M. McGoldrick, J. Giordano, & J. Pearce (Eds.), *Ethnicity and family therapy* (2nd ed., pp. 281–294). New York: Guilford Press.

Ledbetter, M., Smith, L., Vosler-Hunter, W., & Fischer, J. (1991). An evaluation of the research and clinical usefulness of the Spiritual Well-Being Scale. *Journal of Psychology and Theology, 19,* 49–55.

Lee, E. (1996a). Asian American families: An overview. In M. McGoldrick, J. Giordano, & J. Pearce (Eds.), *Ethnicity and family therapy* (2nd ed., pp. 227–248). New York: Guilford Press.

Lee, E. (1996b). Chinese families. In M. McGoldrick, J. Giordano, & J. Pearce (Eds.), *Ethnicity and family therapy* (2nd ed., pp. 249–267). New York: Guilford Press.

Lee, J., & Cynn, V. (1991). Issues in counseling 1.5 generation Korean Americans. In C. Lee & B. Richardson (Eds.), *Multicultural issues in counseling: New approaches to diversity* (pp. 127–140). Alexandria, VA: American Association for Counseling and Development.

Leung, P. K., & Boehnlein, J. (1996). Vietnamese families. In M. McGoldrick, J. Giordano, & J. Pearce (Eds.), *Ethnicity and family therapy* (2nd ed., pp. 295–306). New York: Guildford Press.

Lin, K.-M. (1996). Asian-American perspectives. In J. Mezzich, A. Kleinman, H. Fabrega, & D. Parron (Eds.), *Culture and psychiatric diagnosis: A DSM-IV perspective* (pp. 35–38). Washington, DC: American Psychiatric Press.

Malony, H. N. (1988). The clinical assessment of optimal religious functioning. *Review of Religious Research, 30,* 3–17.

Marsella, A. J., Kinzie, D., & Gordon, P. (1973). Ethnic variations in the expression of depression. *Journal of Cross-Cultural Psychology, 4,* 435–458.

Matsui, W. T. (1996). Japanese families. In M. McGoldrick, J. Giordano, & J. Pearce (Eds.), *Ethnicity and family therapy* (2nd ed., pp. 268–280). New York: Guilford Press.

McKenzie-Pollock, L. (1996). Cambodian families. In M. McGoldrick, J. Giordano, & J. Pearce (Eds.), *Ethnicity and family therapy* (2nd ed., pp. 307–315). New York: Guilford Press.

Misumi, D. (1993). Asian-American Christian attitudes towards counseling. *Journal of Psychology and Christianity, 12,* 214–224.

Mollica, R., & Lavelle, J. (1988). Southeast Asian refugees. In L. Comas-Diaz &

E. Griffith (Eds.), *Clinical guidelines in cross-cultural mental health* (pp. 262–293). New York: Wiley.

Morrow, R. (1989). Southeast Asian child rearing practices: Implications for child and youth care workers. *Child and Youth Care Quarterly, 18,* 273–287.

Moy, S. (1992). A culturally sensitive, psychoeducational model for understanding and treating Asian-American clients. *Journal of Psychology and Christianity, 11,* 358–367.

Nishio, K., & Bilmes, M. (1993). Psychotherapy with Southeast Asian-American clients. In D. Atkinson, G. Morten, & D. W. Sue (Eds.), *Counseling American minorities: A cross-cultural perspective* (4th ed., pp. 225–234). Dubuque, IA: Brown & Benchmark.

Root, M. P. P. (1985). Guidelines for facilitating therapy with Asian American clients. *Psychotherapy, 22,* 349–356.

Santa Rita, E. (1996). Pilipino families. In M. McGoldrick, J. Giordano, & J. Pearce (Eds.), *Ethnicity and family therapy* (2nd ed., pp. 324–330). New York: Guilford Press.

Seamands, D. (1985). *Healing of memories.* Wheaton, IL: Victor Books.

Solberg, V. S., Choi, K.-H., Ritsma, S., & Jolly, A. (1994). Asian-American college students: It is time to reach out. *Journal of College Student Development, 35,* 296–301.

Sue, D., & Sue, D. W. (1993). Ethnic identity: Cultural factors in the psychological development of Asians in America. In D. Atkinson, G. Morten, & D. W. Sue (Eds.), *Counseling American minorities: A cross-cultural perspective* (pp. 199–210). Dubuque, IA: Brown & Benchmark.

Sue, D., & Sue, S. (1987). Cultural factors in the clinical assessment of Asian Americans. *Journal of Consulting and Clinical Psychology, 55,* 479–487.

Sue, D. W., & Sue, D. (1990). *Counseling the culturally different: Theory and practice* (2nd ed.). New York: Wiley.

Sue, S. (1988). Psychotherapeutic services for ethnic minorities: Two decades of research findings. *American Psychologist, 43,* 301–308.

Sue, S., & Morishima, J. (1982). *The mental health of Asian Americans: Contemporary issues in identifying and treating mental health problems.* San Francisco: Jossey-Bass.

Sue, S., Nakamura, C. Y., Chung, R. C., & Yee-Bradbury, C. (1994). Mental health research on Asian Americans. *Journal of Community Psychology, 22,* 61–67.

Sue, S., & Zane, N. (1985). Academic achievement and socioemotional adjustment among Chinese university students. *Journal of Counseling Psychology, 32,* 570–579.

Sue, S., & Zane, N. (1987). The role of culture and cultural techniques in psychotherapy: A critique and reformulation. *American Psychologist, 42,* 37–45.

Sue, S., Zane, N., & Young, K. (1994). Research on psychotherapy with culturally diverse populations. In A. E. Bergin & S. L. Garfield (Eds.), *Handbook of psychotherapy and behavior change* (4th ed., pp. 783–817). New York: Wiley.

Suinn, R. M., Rickard-Figueroa, K., Lew, S., & Vigil, P. (1987). The Suinn-Lew Asian Self-Identity Acculturation Scale: An initial report. *Educational and Psychological Measurement, 47,* 401–407.

Suzuki, L. E. (1991). Persecution, alienation, and resurrection: History of Japanese Methodist churches. In A. R. Guillermo (Ed.), *Churches aflame: Asian Americans and United Methodism* (pp. 113–134). Nashville: Abingdon Press.

Tan, S.-Y. (1991a). Counseling Asians. *Urban Mission, 9,* 42–50.

Tan, S.-Y. (1991b). *Lay counseling: Equipping Christians for a helping ministry.* Grand Rapids, MI: Zondervan.

Tan, S. Y. (1996). Religion in clinical practice: Implicit and explicit integration. In E. P. Shafranske (Ed.), *Religion and the clinical practice of psychology* (pp. 365–387). Washington, DC: American Psychological Association.

Tan, S. Y. (1997). The role of the psychologist in paraprofessional helping. *Professional Psychology: Research and Practice, 28,* 368–372.

Tan, S. Y. (1999). Cultural issues in Spirit-filled psychotherapy. *Journal of Psychology and Christianity, 18,* 164–176.

Tan, S. Y., & Gregg, D. (1997). *Disciplines of the Holy Spirit.* Grand Rapids, MI: Zondervan.

Tan, S.-Y., & Ortberg, J., Jr. (1995). *Understanding depression.* Grand Rapids, MI: Baker.

Tomine, S. I. (1991). Counseling Japanese Americans: From internment to reparation. In C. Lee & B. Richardson (Eds.), *Multicultural issues in counseling: New approaches to diversity* (pp. 91–105). Alexandria, VA: American Association for Counseling and Development.

Toupine, E. A. (1980). Counseling Asians: Psychotherapy in the context of racism and Asian-American history. *American Journal of Orthopsychiatry, 50,* 76–86.

Tseng, T. (1996). Chinese Protestant nationalism in the United States, 1880–1927. *Amerasia Journal, 22,* 31–56.

Uba, L. (1994). *Asian Americans: Personality patterns, identity, and mental health.* New York: Guilford Press.

Wenhao, J., Salomon, H. B., & Chay, D. M. (1993). Transcultural counseling and people of Asian origin: A developmental and therapeutic perspective. In J. McFadden (Ed.), *Transcultural counseling: Bilateral and international perspectives* (pp. 239–259). Alexandria, VA: American Association for Counseling and Development.

Westermeyer, J. (1986). Two self-rating scales for depression among Hmong refugees: Assessment in clinical and nonclinical samples. *Journal of Psychiatric Research, 20,* 103–113.

Westermeyer, J., Vang, T. F., & Neider, J. (1983). A comparison of refugees using and not using a psychiatric service: An analysis of *DSM-III* criteria and self-rating scales in cross-cultural context. *Journal of Operational Psychiatry, 14,* 36–41.

Yung, J. (1986). *Chinese women of America: A pictorial history.* San Francisco: Chinese Culture Foundation.

18

PSYCHOTHERAPY WITH NATIVE AMERICANS: A VIEW INTO THE ROLE OF RELIGION AND SPIRITUALITY

ALEX TRUJILLO

Life Song

This is my heart as I travel all over; my spirit, my life, and living.

—Flathead

The purpose of this chapter is to provide clinically relevant information to mental health professionals regarding the religion and spirituality of the Native American. The terms *religion* and *spirituality* are used as a reference for the purpose of conceptual organization to assist Western science identify the Native American's concept of the Sacred. The Sacred knowledge, ways, and practices encompass the notion of what may be considered to be the religion and spirituality of the Native American. Maintaining cultural respect and dignity for the Sacred is important in seeking ways in which the life of the Native American may possibly gain and improve. Thus, it is with delicate understanding and sensitive awareness of the historical and present-day life experience of the Native American that this discussion is undertaken.

The religion and spirituality of the Native American is a very complex topic, as all the different tribes, approximately 2 million people representing 542 tribal groups and 150 languages (U.S. Bureau of the Census, 1991), have religion and spirituality as a cultural value and belief. Each individual tribal expression of religion and spirituality is unique, which

445

adds to the difficulty in addressing the topic. Native Americans have a special concern with what and how information about their religion and spirituality is disseminated. Many have attempted to reveal information about the Sacred, which should be available only to a select group of individuals in each tribe and needs to remain in the domain of the tribal membership, whereas others have misrepresented the Native American's religion and spirituality. Even in aboriginal times, the Sacred was protected and remained a secret. Thus, an honorable balance of respect and integrity for the Native Americans is necessary in presenting information about their religion and spirituality.

In this chapter, religion and spirituality will be related to their application and implications for mental health services so that the mental health professional may benefit from this information and provide effective treatment for Native American clients and so that religion and spirituality may be integrated into the clinical process to address such areas as interviewing, assessment, diagnosis, treatment, and follow-up. Native Americans will thus benefit from the clinical experience, resulting in a positive attitude and understanding about mental health services and mental health professionals.

The information in this chapter is intended to serve as an overall guide and not to convey information about any specific tribe or information that may be disrespectful or misleading concerning the religion and spirituality of the Native American. This work is presented to honor Native Americans by protecting the Sacred in ways that are culturally meaningful.

HISTORICAL AND CULTURAL BACKGROUND

Religious Conflict and the Native American

From aboriginal times, religion and spirituality have played a powerful role in the life and survival of the Native American. Yet, many aspects of the Native American way of life have been strongly challenged. Historically, these challenges include attempts to

1. exterminate the Native American people,
2. relocate the Native Americans from their native land,
3. use boarding schools to change the lives of Native Americans,
4. destroy the Native American peoples' culture, and
5. destroy the Native Americans' religion and spirituality. (Beck & Walters, 1977; Choney, Berryhill-Paake, & Robbins, 1995)

These historical events continue to have an impact on their present-day lives and culture, contributing to their problems, conflicts, and stress of coexisting.

Efforts to destroy the Native American culture have been consistent with the federal policy of assimilation including, at worst, the outlawing of traditional religion and spirituality in the late 1800s (Swinomish Tribal Mental Health Program, 1991). Legislation focused toward the conversion of the Native American through an increased number of missionary schools and religious outposts. Then in 1978, the American Religious Freedom Act made it legal to practice native religions. But, at one point, the conflict between Native Americans and non-Native Americans over the issue of religion and spirituality was so intense that the Native Americans moved their religion and spirituality underground (Swaney, 1994).

The Christianization of Native Americans proved to be the most effective means of assimilation as it did accomplish, with some of them, the change in attitude and behavior not present in other acculturation efforts (Choney, Berryhill-Paake, & Robbins, 1995). It is important to recognize that the religion and spirituality of Native Americans have undergone a history of persecution through legislation that lasted from the late 1800s to 1978. Nevertheless, religion and spirituality have survived and remain viable today. They also provide the means and substance for Native Americans' lives and histories.

Most Native Americans have not abandoned the values, beliefs, and practices of their cultural heritage. Religion and spirituality are recognized extensively among the Native Americans who maintain their tribal traditions, which have endured the test of time with each passing generation. The strength, power, truth, and meaning to life that religion and spirituality provide must be properly understood. Much time has been required for the Sacred of Native Americans to be recognized as a true religion. The foreign imposition of non-Native American religions has contributed to minimizing the religion and spirituality of Native Americans. As the population of the United States has grown, non-Native Americans, along with their entourage of philosophy, science, technology, way of life, religion, and government, have come into contact with Native Americans. Efforts to convert them to the ways of non-Native Americans are an aspect of history that continues to the present day (Beck & Walters, 1977; Ponterrotto, Casas, Suzuki, & Alexander, 1995).

Unfortunately, these efforts concerning religious and spiritual issues seemed to suggest that Native Americans did not have a religion or, if there was a religion, that the religion and spirituality of non-Native Americans was better. This is an important historical and present-day consideration. If the religion and spirituality of Native Americans are not regarded with respect, the people themselves are not regarded with respect. The effects of oppression and racism that have occurred through colonization must be recognized as a major concern because Native Americans have endured the conflict between two cultures and continue to experience difficulties from these relationships and interactions.

Tribal Traditions and the Sacred

Religion and spirituality began with tribal traditions based on aboriginal practices that remain relatively unchanged to the present. Oral tradition continually conveys Sacred knowledge, ways, and practices perpetuating the religion and spirituality that are fundamental for Native Americans to live and survive. Despite the intrusion of Western thought, science, technology, and politics, Native Americans have remained true to their way of life and are very much dedicated to their religion and spirituality. These roots are resilient, as they are woven into the fabric of the culture and extend through a remarkable history. Sacred knowledge, ways, and practices generate the necessary rituals, ceremonies, and prayers for each tribe to maintain its religion and spirituality. The ongoing use of tribal traditions renews and strengthens Native Americans' distinct way of life through the practice of religion and spirituality.

Tribal traditions use religious and spiritual events to express the invisible (i.e., the mystical and experiences beyond the ordinary) aspects of the Sacred with manifestations that are visible (i.e., rituals expressed through dance). Pointing to the Native American life experience that is characterized with a distinct view of the world and a unique perception of reality, in which everyday life is integrated into religion as an expression of spirituality (Beck & Walters, 1977; Gill, 1976), the tribal tradition of the Sacred continues to provide a viable system of values, beliefs, and way of life that gives meaning, dignity, and wholeness to the Native American existence (Brown, 1976). Religion and spirituality provide the basis for how Native Americans function in everyday living (Toelken, 1976). This brings into perspective the magnitude of the unseen powers and mysteries of life in the Native Americans' way of life. The pathway to the source of life involves bringing the Sacred into practice. This concept is fundamentally simple and logical, except to the person whose thinking, understanding, and perception of reality and world do not recognize the Sacred. Equally important are the differences in what is known to be meaningful in the cultural education of Native Americans and how religion and spirituality guide their life experience.

Unity Among Native American Diversity

Each tribe is distinct and diverse, providing richness to the Native American cultural heritage. Each tribe remains independent in language, traditions, identity, and lifestyle, reflecting a unique identity that is fundamental to the people. Each member contributes to maintaining the tribe's historical roots by participating in the traditional values and beliefs of their religion and spirituality, individually and collectively. Yet, with all the diversity of the tribal groups across the United States and the other countries in which Native Americans live, respect prevails among the different tribes. The basis for this respect includes a number of factors common to all the tribes: their common bond as Native Americans, their cultural heritage, similarities in history and life experiences, and the critical factor of religion and spirituality (Beck & Walters, 1977).

Religion and spirituality serve as the gathering point about and toward the Native Americans' view of life. It is this regard for life that generates a foundation in each tribe that moves the people onward and across time. Religion and spirituality are fundamental, and respect is the quality that bridges the different tribal groups to gather and communicate about common issues affecting their people, guided by the clarity of their common view on life and their mutual regard for religion and spirituality. Respect is given to those who protect the Sacred knowledge, ways, and practices by which religion and spirituality continue in the lives of Native Americans, a common pursuit for all tribes (Beck & Walters, 1977).

Although the different tribes maintain their respective traditional values, beliefs, and practices about religion and spirituality, there are a number of shared views that most tribes have in common:

1. A belief or knowledge exists about the unseen powers, and reference is to deities, mystery, and great powers.
2. Knowledge that all things in the universe are dependent on each other, and reference is to the notion of balance and harmony.
3. Personal worship creates the bond among the individual, tribal members, and the great powers; worship is a personal commitment to the source of life.
4. Responsibility of persons knowledgeable in the Sacred is to teaching and guiding in the Native American way of life.
5. For most tribes, a shaman is responsible for specialized, even secret Sacred knowledge; oral tradition is used by the shaman to pass Sacred knowledge, ways, and practices from generation to generation.
6. A belief exists that to be human is a necessary part of the Sacred and an acknowledgment that human beings make mistakes. (Beck & Walters, 1977)

Native American Way of Life

Religion and spirituality have been and continue to be an important and integrated part of the Native American way of life (Ruthledge &

Robinson, 1992). This time-honored tribal tradition of religion and spirituality entails Sacred knowledge, ways, and practices and has remained constant, dating from aboriginal times, as Native Americans have pressed forward over time and as their life experiences have continued to their present existence. Everyday living includes the cognitions and behaviors necessary to maintain a lifestyle guided by the Sacred, as a means to provide direction, continuity, and design to the quality of life. This life experience with the Sacred reflects the Native American cultural heritage, honoring the past generations for preserving a way of life that is fundamental for the future generations to live and survive, thus allowing the Native Americans to live well and long, individually and collectively. Religion and spirituality are their cultural expression (i.e., way of life) and are the essence of the means (i.e., practice of the Sacred) to pursue the source of life.

The importance of recognizing and accepting the role of religion and spirituality in life is a basic step toward understanding Native Americans individually and as a people. The Native Americans' lifestyle is directly related to their religion and spirituality, which is about the Sacred, providing a means to express their cultural values and beliefs. Thus, it is important to understand that organized religion, as it is known in Western thought, ideology, and philosophy, is not a concept that fits into the Native American's traditional view of the Sacred. To know about the religion and spirituality of Native Americans requires learning a whole new set of cognitions, behaviors, orientation, and interpretation about life (Toelken, 1976). It is with such a distinct view of the world and reality that the Sacred knowledge, ways, and practices are put to use by the Native American people. The use of the Sacred is guided and conducted by the tribal shaman (Beck & Walters, 1977), for it is this individual who has historically been the source of knowledge of the Sacred traditions of the Native American culture (Beck & Walters, 1977; Halifax, 1982).

Religion and spirituality are regarded as a relationship between the Native American people and the Sacred processes of the world (Toelken, 1976). The world of Native Americans has various possible descriptions, but for the purpose of this chapter, three worlds will be identified: underworld, middle world, and celestial world (Halifax, 1982). The context of these worlds encompasses (generally) the universe, earth, life, and death. More specific to life and death is the notion of the path of life, which relates to the changing worlds, as the Sacred has no beginning and no end (Beck & Walters, 1977). To address these three intricate, elaborate, and extensive worlds is beyond the scope of this chapter. The information serves as a brief background on the religion and spirituality of Native Americans and how it fits into their way of life.

450   ALEX TRUJILLO

The Sacred

The Shaman

The complexity of the religion and spirituality of Native Americans is addressed by the shaman (Beck & Walters, 1977). To access such a vast source of Sacred knowledge, ways, and practices is the means to experience the source of life. The Sacred is an entity of infinite design, but of such simplicity that it guides how the Native American lives and survives. The ability of the shaman to have a special and particular relationship with the natural elements, the creatures of nature, the unseen powers, and ultimately, the source of life, makes this person an invaluable member of the tribe (Beck & Walters, 1977). The wisdom and work of the shaman allow him or her to intervene in social and environmental crises, thus increasing the possibility for the tribe to live and survive. Sacred rituals, ceremonies, and prayers are used by the shaman to help the people of the tribe address their needs. The knowledge and wisdom of the shaman is generally not accessible to the ordinary human being. The shaman provides a social rather than a personal role in serving the needs of the Native American people, being concerned with the tribe and its well-being (Beck & Walters, 1977; Halifax, 1982). He or she also acquires the knowledge and skills necessary to access the Sacred, for this will give the shaman strength to help members of the tribe to seek life (Beck & Walters, 1977; Halifax, 1982). Thus, the shaman is critical to tribal life and survival.

Not all Native Americans are qualified to partake in the Sacred as is the shaman. This explains the very special regard and respect that the shaman has been given. To acquire the knowledge, understanding, and skills necessary to practice the Sacred involves a specific and unique life experience and training that is individually personalized. The life experience that enables the shaman to access the Sacred is beyond the scope of this chapter. However, some examples of the shaman's knowledge and understanding about the Sacred encompass the ability to experience (a) the continuity between life and death, (b) a relationship to ancestral spirits, and (c) the mediation between the spirits and humans (Halifax, 1982). The shaman conveys various types of knowledge and wisdom to the tribe. This task is not simple or singular in nature. The shaman's life training has evolved to such a level that he or she can use the elements in their proper order and structure, resulting in balance and harmony.

To address the order and structure of things requires knowledge and understanding about using the proper and appropriate Sacred actions. The end product of these Sacred actions is that the life and survival of the Native American people continues. It is a monumental accomplishment to perpetuate the lives of these people on the basis of Sacred knowledge, understanding, ways, and practices. The religion and spirituality of Native

Americans is indeed the means to the source of life (Beck & Walters, 1977).

A fundamental tenet in the Native Americans' way of life is "knowing the order and structure of things" (Beck & Walters, 1977). The tenet provides the means to seek life through the practice of the Sacred. This source of Sacred knowledge and understanding is unique in the Native American's perception of the world and interpretation of reality. It guides the Native Americans' orientation toward life and relationships with life. This tenet is about life and all manifestations of life. This complex premise of the order and structure of things involves the Sacred knowledge and understanding that allows access to the underworld, middle world, and celestial world as a means to experience the universe, earth, life, and death. The order and structure of things involves some of the following knowledge and understanding:

1. the world is made of four elements: earth, water, air, and light;
2. things remain together by a balance of these four elements and the order of these elements in each type of life is different;
3. a select type of life may be used to keep balance via Sacred actions that allows the shaman to give life to help another life. (Beck & Walters, 1977)

The Sacred knowledge and understanding of these notions lead to the use of rituals, ceremonies, and prayers for the purpose of maintaining harmony that results in the balance of life (Beck & Walters, 1977). In addition, placing religion and spirituality in this context allows access to those aspects of the Native Americans' life experience that are mystical and beyond the ordinary. These Sacred actions require qualified knowledge and understanding of the Sacred (Halifax, 1982; Beck & Walters, 1977).

An important aspect in the religion and spirituality of the Native American involves the regard for life. An example is hunting. The death of the wild animal is accompanied with the appropriate ritual, ceremony, and prayer that brings balance between the animal's death and the life given to the people who are able to continue living, resulting in harmony. Thus, demonstrating the application of the Sacred in a real-life situation. The religion and spirituality of Native Americans involve all life and emphasize the importance of maintaining balance and harmony in the order and structure of things. This balance and harmony are basic for the Native Americans' well-being and existence. This life orientation maintains that all that is on the earth has a viable life force. Respect and regard for the order and structure of things apply to the interactions that the Native Americans have with any life force, relationships that are necessary to their life and survival (Brown, 1976). It is this type of Sacred information that the shaman and the Native American people protect.

Sacred Moments

Native Americans historically have embraced spirituality as an expression of their humanity (Beck & Walters, 1977). This sense of humanity is a principle in their religion that encompasses the Native American's way of life. Religion and spirituality guide them to experience the Sacred. The Native Americans' sense of humanity demonstrates an immense reverence for their way of life, including manifestations of the mystical and experiences beyond the ordinary as a journey into the Sacred. To the individual Native American, the religious and spiritual experiences are an expression about life.

For Native Americans to have a good and long life, it is important to experience Sacred moments. To be able to understand any particular relationship encompassed by the order and structure of things brings forth a Sacred moment. To actually experience hidden meaning in the guiding vision is a Sacred moment (Beck & Walters, 1977). Thus, Sacred moments provide clarity and meaning for reaching the source of life. Then too, the pathway is illuminated. Given the Native American way of life, Sacred moments may contribute to Sacred knowledge and understanding that preserve the balance and harmony of the different aspects of the Native American way of life.

Access to the mysterious powers requires Sacred knowledge that must be properly understood and expressed in the appropriate Sacred ways and practices. The practice of the Sacred is a life-long experience that integrates the guiding vision, which adds to the meaning and understanding of why rituals, ceremonies, and prayers are undertaken and conducted. The Sacred allows Native Americans to encounter the mysteries of the source of life. Specifically, elements exist that are Sacred and mysterious in their religious and spiritual worlds. To most Native Americans, the Sacred involves elements beyond the ordinary, as experienced by how the soul is shown in dreams and visions. It is this hold on their humanity that allows access to their more intense, extensive, and different religious and spiritual experiences and views of reality.

Worship

For the Native American people, their religious and spiritual experiences are life events that surround them all the time (Toelken, 1976). They may be in personal worship from the time they rise in the morning until they go to sleep at night. They commemorate every aspect of life: birth through life and death, and the seasons, for example. Personal worship helps keep the Native Americans in contact with themselves, family, tribe, and all other important religious and spiritual needs (Ruthledge & Robinson, 1992). Their way of life brings into focus the Sacred, and their worship reflects their way of life. Religion and spirituality manifest how Native Americans practice the Sacred for the purpose of living well and long.

IMPLICATIONS FOR COUNSELING AND PSYCHOTHERAPY

Therapeutic Relationship Issues

Native Americans and the Mental Health Profession

Native Americans remain an enigma in the field of mental health services. It is difficult to establish a clear understanding of their mental health problems because of their distribution throughout the United States (U.S. Bureau of Census, 1990). This dispersion has led to difficulties in obtaining adequate and meaningful information to address this matter in a systematic way. Thus, information about Native Americans' mental health status is limited, generally, to service outlets that they frequently use (i.e., Indian Health Service facilities), usually located in reasonable proximity to the reservation. However, such data are limited and do not constitute a representative sample of the total Native American population. Thus, knowledge on research and treatment about Native Americans are years behind the majority of the American culture (Neligh, 1988). In spite of the limited status of the existing research and treatment data on the Native American, several problem areas have been identified.

Problems exist in areas that include Native American attitudes toward mental health services, such as lack of awareness of mental health services (Dinges, Trimble, Manson, & Pasquale, 1981), fear and mistrust of mental health services (Dukepoo, 1980), and a negative attitude toward the mental health professional (Manson & Trimble, 1982). Native Americans are almost twice as likely not to return after the first session than non-Native American clients (Sue, Allen, & Conaway, 1981). Native Americans who participate in therapy are opposed to the imposition of Western biases on their behaviors and beliefs. Some well-intentioned mental health professionals believe that to be helpful they should encourage Native Americans to change their value system to the Western value system. Mental health professionals may not be aware that Western psychological techniques and approaches to well-being may undermine traditional values and beliefs that some Native Americans hold and practice (La-Fromboise, 1988).

However, the willingness of Native Americans to provide information about themselves has been gradually evolving and improving to the point to which some Native Americans are willing to offer information about medical complaints and alcohol problems, but not about mental health matters. Unfortunately, the health care sites that the Native Americans frequent have a high turnover rate of personnel. Thus, Native Americans are not able to establish a long-term meaningful and trusting relationship for which they need time and stable providers. In the absence of such relationships, a Native American is not likely or willing to reveal problems of a mental health nature (Guilmet & Whited, 1987). Thus, an important consideration for effective clinical treatment that may lead to developing, maintaining, and implementing mental health services for Native Americans is that a level of stability in the personnel be present over time.

Building Trust

It is important for mental health professionals to remember that Native Americans' perception of the world and understanding of reality are markedly different from that of non-Native Americans. At times, their view of reality is likely to be misinterpreted or misunderstood by non-Native Americans, who may possibly infer aspects of superstition or other qualities related to their adaptive functioning and stability, and also may suggest an absence of a meaningful religion and spirituality. Mental health professionals need to be careful not to be influenced by uninformed views on the Native American way of life. They must accept the Native American's religion and spirituality as equal to and as valued as their own religious and spiritual views. Mental health professionals must also be able to recognize the importance of using treatment strategies compatible with cultural pluralism and an ecumenical therapeutic stance (Richards & Bergin, 1997). Cultural competence is essential in establishing a meaningful relationship and is basic to clinically interacting with the Native American.

Clinically, this translates into a therapeutic relationship characterized by trust. The presence of trust for the Native American leads to confidence in the mental health professional's clinical knowledge and skills as supported by cultural competence. The trust is developed as the mental health professional accepts the Native American's cultural, religious, and spiritual values and beliefs. Trust also comes from the mental health professional being reliable and dependable as a service provider, and this trust promotes the sharing of a worldview by the Native American with the mental health professional. In the presence of trust, confidence in the mental health professional creates the clinical opportunity for treatment to be implemented in a manner that is plausible in the Native American's worldview.

ASSESSMENT AND CLINICAL ISSUES

General Considerations

The existing standards for determining acceptable adaptive functioning (i.e., *Diagnostic and Statistical Manual of Mental Disorders* [4th ed.]) may not extend to encompass the Native American's reality, as precisely as they do with the non-Native American. This status brings into focus the Native American's limited documented standing and understanding in the mental health field (Neligh, 1988). For example, the notions of beyond the ordinary and the mystical that are held and practiced by Native Americans and the supporting cognitions, behaviors, and view of reality are clinical issues worthy of proper and thorough analysis. Does the Native American's life orientation, perception of reality, and worldview fit into a ready-made diagnostic classification? Or do the cultural differences between Native Americans and non-Native Americans increase the risk of improper clinical judgment by the mental health professionals?

Another assessment issue for the mental health professional to consider is the perception about life. For example, the Native American holds important the relationships with the land, wild life, and nature, or, more comprehensively, for the Native American all things on the earth have life and must be respected. It is when these relationships are broken or altered that problems may arise. To the Native American, the role of religion and spirituality, as practiced in the Sacred, serves to keep all these relationships and interactions in accordance with the Native American way of life. This is but one more reason why it becomes important for the mental health professional to recognize the Native American's regard for religion and spirituality. The relationship between religion and spirituality and treatment is a clinical matter that must be examined properly to avoid placing the Native American at risk for clinical error (e.g., inappropriate services, clinical practice injustice, and, for the mental health professional, ethical issues about professional practice). This involves paying clinical attention to the complex personal situation the Native American may have. In light of the fact that the number of Native American mental health professionals is small and that the Native American client is likely to be treated by a non-Native American (Choney, Berryhill-Paake, & Robbins, 1995), such cultural considerations are crucial.

The process of the intervention needs to acknowledge, at minimum, the Native Americans' life experience involving religion and spirituality. The mental health professional may provide the wrong service by failing to recognize the multiple cultural influences in the Native Americans' life experience. The realization of how important these influences are is basic to understanding who the Native American is as an individual and as a people. To some degree, these cultural influences will have an impact on each tribe and its membership. Because each of the tribes is distinct and different in its own accord, the complex relationships and interactions of the cultural influences become unique in their development and final composition.

Demographics

At the end of the 19th century, it was believed that the Native American culture would vanish. Instead, the number of Native Americans has increased. Specifically, from 1980 to 1990, the percentage of increase for Native Americans was higher than for any other racial group. Even if the growth rate is small, the Native Americans may eventually regain the population (approximately 5 million) that was estimated to have been present when the first European explorers made contact (Snipp, 1989). It is important to consider the demographics pertaining to the Native American. The distribution of the total Native American population includes approximately 37% who live on some designation of tribal land. The remaining 63% are spread throughout rural and urban areas in the United States. In all likelihood, some of the 63% do travel to their tribal land periodically. The major concentration of Native Americans by state is 15.6% in Alaska; 8.9% in Oklahoma; 8.9% in New Mexico; and 5.9% in Arizona. The distribution of Native Americans in cities in the United States is as follows: Los Angeles, 87,487; Tulsa, 48,196; New York City, 46,191; Oklahoma City, 45,720; and San Francisco, 40,847 (Paisano, 1991). The Native American median age reflects a relatively young population, with age ranges from 18.8 to 26.3 years among those living on the reservations (U.S. Bureau of the Census, 1991). Even though their population is small, Native Americans live just about anywhere in the United States.

Problem Areas and Clinical Issues

Native American Adolescent

Native American adolescents may have more serious mental health problems than are reported for other racial minority populations in the United States (U.S. Office of Technology Assessment, 1990). Priority problems for this population include developmental disabilities, depression, suicide, anxiety, alcohol and substance abuse, self-esteem problems, alienation, running away, and dropping out of school. Sadly, it may be said that Native American adolescents have lives filled with stressors not shared by non-Native American adolescents. They seem to be extremely susceptible to high stress levels related to problems and developmental tasks of identity formation. They feel particularly caught between two cultures. The developmental implications from the problem areas of Native American adolescents, if not remedied, seem to indicate that the problems will continue into the next developmental stage of adulthood, thus exacerbating the problems they will face as adults, making adulthood a greater task to master.

Native American Adult

The problems in Native American adults include alcoholism, suicide, murder, accidental death and injury, assault, theft, social discord, unemployment, and divorce (Price, 1975). Furthermore, the use of alcohol has been the primary and most destructive coping strategy used to remedy their sense of hopelessness and loss of identity created by intergeneration post-traumatic stress disorder, acculturative stress, and other problems (Berlin, 1987; Yates, 1987). The problems vary in type and severity as a result of the differences among the tribes, which include such factors as life on the reservation, rural or urban living, in addition to the age and sex of the individuals (Neligh, 1988).

To explore the causes of all the problems that impact the Native American is beyond the scope of this work. What is important is for the mental health professional to recognize that Native Americans do have mental health problems, which are reasons for seeking mental health services. For example, depression is the most frequently reported mood disorder present (A National Plan for Native American Mental Health Services, 1995). The causes for depression are related to a complex interaction of different factors in their lives such as problems related to poverty, lack of employment, racial discrimination, geographical isolation, inadequate educational opportunities, and cultural identity issues created by the presence of a dominant western and technological society (i.e., multiple cultural influences). This complex interaction of different factors causing depression also includes the historical problems in the Native American's life experience. Furthermore, the presence of mental illness, dysfunction, or self-destructive behaviors impacts approximately 480,000 or 21% of the total Native American population (U.S. Department of Health and Human Services, 1990). Thus, treatment implications are not simple. Depression and anxiety problems seem to exist with comorbid conditions (LaFromboise, 1988; Nelson, McCoy, Stetter, & Vanderwagon, 1992).

Usually alcohol is one of the contributing problems (Shore, Manson, Bloom, & Keepers, 1987). Certainly an obvious impact is the family, particularly, the parent–child relationship. Mental health services must consider and implement a clinical treatment regime commensurate with the complexity of the problems the Native American is presenting and experiencing.

Acculturation

Acculturation becomes an issue when the Native American first considers the possible use of mental health services. However, this is not necessarily the only problem that may be present. To rule out the role of religion and spirituality as part of the mental health problem is a major accomplishment or error, depending on the clinical knowledge, skills, and cultural competence of the mental health professional in understanding the life experience of the Native American. That is, the role of acculturation and the related problems in this process become clear, and a clinical focus is facilitated. It is important to recognize that the Native American who seeks mental health services is aware of the two cultures, the Native American and the non-Native American. To what extent this awareness has been reached may be indicative of the degree of the Native American's participation in the non-Native American culture. Some indicators for acculturation include the extent of formal education, industrialization pressures, and urbanization (Sinha, 1988).

Yet, this does not conclusively equal acculturation. Certain aspects of the individual may be affected by acculturation, whereas others may not (Berry, Poortinga, Segall, & Dasen, 1992). The mental health professional needs to distinguish and separate accurately the effects of acculturation (i.e., clinical and cultural competence) for the individual. Religion and spirituality may be present in some but not all areas of the individual's life, given the presence of two cultures. The assessment process addressing the effects of acculturation needs to consider the difference between the tribal group (e.g., social structure, economic base, and political organization) and the individual (e.g., identity, values, and attitude) in terms of acculturation stress and attitude. The critical element that the mental health professional must recognize fully and properly is not his or her understanding of acculturation but the Native American's view of acculturation needs and changes (Berry, Poortinga, Segall, & Dasen, 1992).

Having an existing knowledge base about religion and spirituality of the Native American will greatly assist the mental health professional in reaching a determination about the issue of acculturation in the therapeutic process. Awareness about the religion and spirituality of the Native American will more likely minimize clinical errors and allow the mental health professional to focus properly on the real problem, given the proper clinical examination of the client's life experience.

Identity

To the Native American, ethnic identity is very important and it usually relates to a specific tribal group. Ethnic identity is a process in which the individual is constantly assessing the "fit" between self and the social system in the environment (Spencer & Markstrom-Adams, 1990). This fit is essential to the Native American's well-being because identification with one's ethnic group is important for positive mental health. Acceptance leads to positive self-esteem, and rejection leads to self-estrangement and maladaptive psychological functioning.

The person whose ethnic identity is anchored to group membership is more likely to be psychologically healthy than the person whose identity is marginal in relationship to group membership (Smith, 1991). The important concern about ethnic identification is that the person has an ethnic sense of belonging to a specific ethnic group, thus preventing social alienation and self-estrangement (Sodowsky, Kwan, & Pannu, 1995). The role of the following factors about ethnic identity needs to be considered:

(a) how an individual selects to label his or her membership;
(b) a sense of belonging, specific to the degree to which an individual gives importance to and is emotionally attached to his or her ethnic group;
(c) positive or negative attitudes about one's own group;
(d) participation in ethnic activities and cultural practices. (Phinney, 1990)

Religion and spirituality provide a critical link for Native Americans to establish, maintain, and continue ethnic identification with their tribe. Native Americans experience a life-long involvement with religion and spirituality, which then leads to the practice of religion and spirituality in the Native American's life, simultaneously engaging in traditional tribal activities that reinforce the individual's identity and tribal membership. Even to those who live off the reservation, religion and spirituality are the reasons why they return to their tribal land. This participation is a means to perpetuate values, beliefs, and ethnic identification. The return to their tribal roots and renewal of their way of life through religious and spiritual rituals, prayers, and ceremonies continue their bond with and honor for their Native American identity. Religion and spirituality are fundamental cornerstones reflecting a process of how each individual is integrated into the tribe. This integration serves to solidify firmly the person's identity at the individual and group level.

An important consideration about the religion and spirituality of the Native American and its limited access by the non-Native American may be explained in the context of the visible and invisible elements of ethnic identity; that is, the core of the invisible elements about ethnic identification (e.g., cultural values, beliefs) may be more resistant to change and may show less tendency to acculturation over time. The visible elements of ethnic identification may show participation effects from the dominant society's way of life (e.g., attire, language, education, employment; Rosenthall & Feldman, 1992). The important points for the mental health professional to consider are clearly the invisible elements of ethnic identity. This is specifically where the Native American client will show a difference that needs to be properly understood and carefully examined. The visible elements of ethnic identity are readily recognized but are not the true indicators for ethnic identity. The mental health professional should be aware of this important distinction about ethnic identity. The means for the mental health professional to effectively separate and understand the visible and invisible elements of ethnic identity for the Native American require cultural competence.

Treatment Issues and Recommendations

General Considerations

Cultural competence is essential to establishing a meaningful relationship basic to clinically interacting with the Native American. The clinical relationship will develop from the mental health professional being reliable and dependable as a service provider. The combination of the mental health professionals showing cultural competence and being reliable and dependable will, in turn, lead to the Native American having confidence in them and, more important, in trusting their clinical knowledge and skills.

Cultural competence will be manifested in how the mental health professionals are able to practice their knowledge and skills effectively in cultural matters, specifically, about their way of life, religion, spirituality, and life experiences. The Native American will need a clear sense that the mental health professional is culturally competent and that the risk is low for any violation of cultural values and beliefs.

Cultural competence allows for the mental health professional to select the proper treatment methodology that fits into the Native American's worldview of what is acceptable. The Native American will recognize the mental health professional's cultural competence and will be willing to participate in the treatment process. The treatment process that the mental health professional selects then becomes a cultural fit for the Native American. Thus, the issue of what is the best treatment methodology is answered on the basis of the mental health professional's integration of cultural competence and clinical knowledge and skills.

The Importance of Religion and Spirituality in Treatment

The consideration of religion and spirituality as a clinical matter in mental health services is an important topic. To Native Americans, the role and presence of religion and spirituality are an accepted part of their life. Mental health services, on the other hand, are a relatively new concept for them as a treatment alternative. The use, participation, and treatment benefits they have gained from mental health services are at best minimal. Native Americans have yet to accept mental health services fully as a true alternative for help with their mental health problems. Although some Native Americans have been involved with mental health services, this effort may be described as conservative within the context of the total Native American population. The need to improve their standing and understanding of mental health services is an important goal.

To address clinically the multiple cultural influences of the Native American's life experience is an important clinical matter. Clinical progress in cultural competence and benefits from mental health services are not yet fully realized for Native Americans. Adding religion and spirituality as other elements in their life experience, although it is a needed and important clinical step, is a substantial concern. To address religion and spirituality specifically involves the fine line of cultural competence, exemplified with respect and an awareness of the Sacred boundaries.

If the reader has invested an effort to gather information about Native Americans, adding religion and spirituality will expand the knowledge base. The presence of cultural competence establishes a reasonable framework, fundamental to reaching a level in which clinical knowledge and skills may be modified differentially to fit more adequately the Native American client. To the Native American, if the mental health professionals demonstrate a sincere interest in being culturally aware, sensitive, competent, personally and professionally responsible and recognize their own limits, the clinical interface has the prospect of success.

Native Americans are not seeking to make major or substantial changes in their way of life or in religious and spiritual values and beliefs. They are seeking help for their mental health problems, given the existing multiple cultural influence in their life experience. If the mental health professional is able to keep a clear perspective of the relevant cultural matters to include religion and spirituality, clinical access is readily open for mental health services. But the critical factor for integrating religion and spirituality and mental health services for Native Americans is trust! That is, the mental health problems should be specifically targeted without disrupting or altering their way of life. To promote this way of life and religion and spirituality within the context of their experience is clinically and therapeutically fundamental to the success of mental health services.

Considering religion and spirituality as areas of clinical attention is a venture into the life experience of the Native American. Religion and spirituality are highly protected domains. The Native American people have serious regard and respect for assuring that the Sacred remains properly cared for. It is important to acknowledge on their behalf that their religion and spirituality will remain intact. Information on their religion and spirituality is available, but it is important to maintain the respect necessary to perpetuate the integrity of the Sacred. The availability of information about the religion and spirituality does not mean that it is acceptable to reveal the Sacred. It is not an academic exercise to address the religion and spirituality, as the Native American's way of life integrates the Sacred.

To provide a clinical approach, procedure, technique, or other treatment methodology to address the Native American's religion and spirituality is a moot point. The Western orientation for mental health services obscures the obvious, which is the person-to-person relationship. The relationship with the Native American is built through the mental health professional demonstrating and using cultural competence effectively. The person-to-person relational process is critical in initiating, establishing, and maintaining a viable interaction with the client. It is the trust of the person-to-person contact, connection, and relationship that opens the door to the clinical treatment methodology that may be applied. How flexible or restricted the treatment approach is depends on how effective the mental health professional has been in successfully establishing this relationship with the Native American client. The treatment approach involving individual, couple, family, or group that may be used for therapy depends on the quality of this relationship. Cultural competence will set the cultural and clinical stage for

- the person-to-person relationship,
- the participation of the Native American client in mental health services,
- the opportunity for the mental health professional to designate the proper treatment, and
- the opportunity for the mental health professional to provide a treatment setting compatible with the Native American.

The mental health professional should be able to properly use information about the Native American's way of life, religion, and spirituality for the appropriate treatment and to bring into focus the Native American's mental health problems. Access to religion and spirituality requires a treatment process (i.e., cultural competence) in which trust is established and this type of sensitive information is available within reasonable limits. It is at the level of establishing a quality-based person-to-person relationship with trust that actually allows access to almost any area of their life experience that the Native American is willing to reveal.

The Native American should come into focus as one clear picture, as a human being. The life experience of this human being is unique to the culture. The culture exists in the context of the Sacred and of the Native American's way of life, and Native American religion and spirituality as a life manifestation of the Sacred. The Sacred knowledge, ways, and practices are a means to experience the unseen powers, the mystical, and events beyond the ordinary. Religion and spirituality guide the Native American through the developmental life span to pursue the source of life. The use and expression of rituals, ceremonies, and prayers maintains the Native American on the pathway for living long and well. Religion and spirituality are the fundamental cornerstones to a way of life that has existed since aboriginal times, generation after generation, that perpetuates the eternal source of life for the Native American to live and survive! Is the mental health professional clinically prepared and culturally competent to match this task, to sustain the well-being of the Native American with this cultural heritage for life?

REFERENCES

Beck, V., & Walters, A. L. (1977). *The sacred ways of knowledge: Sources of life.* Tsaile (Navajo Nation), AZ: Navajo Community College Press.

Berlin, I. N. (1987). Effects of changing Native American cultures on child development. *Journal of Community Psychology, 13,* 299–306.

Berry, J. W., Poortinga, Y. H., Segall, M. H., & Dasen, P. R. (1992). *Cross-cultural psychology: Research and applications.* New York: Cambridge University Press.

Brown, J. E. (1976). The roots of renewal. In W. H. Capps (Ed.), *Seeing with a native eye* (p. 27). New York: Harper & Row.

Choney, S. K., Berryhill-Paake, E., & Robbins, R. R. (1995). The acculturation of American Indians: Developing frameworks for research and practice. In J. G. Ponterotto, J. M. Casas, L. A. Suzuki, & C. M. Alexander (Eds.), *Handbook of multicultural counseling* (p. 73). Newbury Park, CA: Sage.

Dinges, N. G., Trimble, J. E., Manson, S. M., & Pasquale, F. L. (1981). Counseling and psychotherapy with American Indians and Alaska Natives. In A. J. Marsella & P. B. Pedersen (Eds.), *Cross-cultural counseling and psychotherapy* (pp. 243–276). New York: Pergamon.

Dukepoo, P. C. (1980). *The elder American Indian.* San Diego, CA: Campanile.

Gill, S. D. (1976). The shadow of a vision yonder. In W. H. Capps (Ed.), *Seeing with a native eye* (p. 57). New York: Harper & Row.

Guilmet, G. M., & Whited, D. L. (1987). Cultural lessons for clinical mental health practice: The Puyallup tribe community. *American Indian and Alaska Native mental Health Research, 1*(2), 32–49.

Halifax, J. (1982). *Shaman: The wounded healer.* London: Thames & Hudson.

LaFromboise, T. D. (1988). American Indian mental health policy. *American Psychologist, 43,* 388–397.

Manson, S. M., & Trimble, J. E. (1982). American Indian and Alaska Native communities: Past efforts, future inquiries. In L. R. Snowden (Ed.), *Researching the underserved: Mental health needs of neglected populations* (pp. 143–163). Beverly Hills, CA: Sage.

Neligh, G. (1988). Major mental disorders and behavior among American Indians and Alaska Natives [Monograph 1]. *American Indian and Alaska Native Mental Health Research, 1,* 116–159.

Nelson, S. H., McCoy, G. G., Stetter, M., & Vanderwagen, W. C. (1992). An overview of mental health services for American Indians and Alaska Natives in the 1990s. *Hospital and Community Psychiatry, 43,* 257–261.

Paisano, E. L. (1991). *Major findings on American Indian and Alaska Native populations from the 1990 census.* Washington, DC: U.S. Bureau of the Census.

Phinney, J. S. (1990). Ethnic identity in adolescence and adulthood: A review of research. *Psychological Bulletin, 108,* 499–514.

Ponterotto, J. G., Casas, J. M., Suzuki, L. A., & Alexander, C. M. (Eds.). (1995). *Handbook of multicultural counseling.* Newbury Park, CA: Sage.

Price, J. A. (1975). An applied analysis of North American Indian drinking patterns. *Human Organization, 34,* 17–26.

Richards, P. S., & Bergin, A. E. (1997). *A spiritual strategy for counseling and psychotherapy.* Washington, DC: American Psychological Association.

Rosenthal, D. A., & Feldman, S. S. (1992). The nature and stability of ethnic identity in Chinese youth: Effects of length of residence in two cultural contexts. *Journal of Cross-Cultural Psychology, 23,* 214–227.

Ruthledge, D., & Robinson, R. (1992). *Center of the world Native American spirituality.* North Hollywood, CA: Newcastle.

Shore, J. H., Manson, S. M., Bloom, J. D., & Keepers, G. (1987). A pilot study of depression among American Indian patients with research diagnostic criteria. *American Indian and Alaska Native Mental Health Research, 1*(2), 4–15.

Sinha, G. (1988). Exposure to industrial and urban environments and formal schooling as factors in psychological differentiation. *International Journal of Psychology, 23,* 707–719.

Smith, E. J. (1991). Ethnic identity development: Toward the development of theory within the context of majority/minority status. *Journal of Counseling and Development, 70,* 181–188.

Snipp, C. M. (1989). *American Indians: The first of this land.* New York: Sage.

Sodowsky, G. R., Kwan, K. K., & Pannu, R. (1995). Ethnic identity of Asians in the United States. In J. G. Ponterotto, J. M. Casas, L. A. Suzuki, & C. M. Alexander (Eds.), *Handbook of multicultural counseling* (p. 137). Newbury Park, CA: Sage.

Spencer, M. B., & Markstrom-Adams, C. (1990). Identity processes among racial and ethnic minority children in America. *Child Development, 61,* 290–310.

Sue, S., Allen, D. B., & Conaway, L. (1981). The responsiveness and equality of mental health care to Chicanos and Native Americans. *American Journal of Community Psychology, 6,* 137–146.

Swaney, G. (1994, August). American Indian issues in therapy. In S. K. Bennett (Chair), *Psychological issues in the treatment of American Indian families.* Symposium conducted at the annual meeting of the American Psychological Association, Toronto, Ontario, Canada.

Swinomish Tribal Mental Health Program. (1991). *A gathering of wisdom.* Tacoma, WA: Author.

Toelken, B. (1976). How many sheep will it hold? In W. H. Capps (Ed.), *Seeing with a Native eye* (p. 23). New York: Harper & Row.

U.S. Bureau of the Census. (1990). *Census of population: Social and economic characteristics, American Indian and Alaska Native areas* (Publication No. CP-2-1 A). Washington, DC: U.S. Government Printing Office.

U.S. Bureau of the Census. (1991). *1990 census count of American Indians, Eskimos, or Aleuts, and American Indian and Alaska Native areas*. Washington, DC: U.S. Government Printing Office.

U.S. Department of Health and Human Services. (1990). *A national health plan for Native American mental health services* (amended 1995). Washington, DC: Author.

U.S. Office of Technology Assessment. (1990, January). *Indian adolescent mental health: OTA special report* (Report NO. OTA-H-446). Washington, DC: Author. (ERIC Document Report Service No. ED 324 177 RC 0 17 777)

Yates, A. (1987). Current status and future directions of research on the American Indian child. *American Journal of Psychiatry, 144*, 1135–1142.

VII

AFTERWORD

19

RELIGIOUS DIVERSITY AND PSYCHOTHERAPY: CONCLUSIONS, RECOMMENDATIONS, AND FUTURE DIRECTIONS

P. SCOTT RICHARDS AND ALLEN E. BERGIN

We feel we can differ theologically with people without being disagreeable in any sense. We hope they feel the same way toward us. We have many friends and many associations with people who are not of our faith, with whom we deal constantly, and we have a wonderful relationship. It disturbs me when I hear about any antagonisms.... I don't think they are necessary. I hope that we can overcome them....

Be friendly. Be understanding. Be tolerant. Be considerate. Be respectful of the opinions and feelings of other people. Recognize their virtues; don't look for their faults. Look for their strengths and their virtues, and you will find strength and virtues that will be helpful in your own life.

—Gordon B. Hinckley

After reading the chapters in this book, we are again led to exclaim, "The religious landscape of North America is breathtaking in its diversity and vibrancy!" By now, you as a reader undoubtedly have much more insight into the rich tapestry of religious customs, beliefs, doctrines, rituals, sacred writings, spiritual practices, and healing traditions. We hope that this increased insight will help you understand and empathize more fully with your religious and spiritually oriented clients and work more effectively with them. We hope that it also leads you to undertake additional study in religious and spiritual issues as they pertain to mental health and psychotherapy.

There is some danger that the many differences that you have learned about in this book could leave you feeling overwhelmed or even confused. Perhaps, this is a normal reaction when a person is first exposed to such diversity. Yet, there are some patterns or themes amidst the diversity. For example, we have discerned some commonalities among these spiritual traditions with regard to their worldviews, moral values, and attitudes toward psychotherapy and mental health professionals. We now briefly discuss some of these themes and then offer a few recommendations and speculations about future directions for theory, research, and practice in this domain.

SIMILARITIES AND DIFFERENCES IN WORLDVIEWS AND VALUES

Table 19.1 summarizes some of the similarities and differences in the worldviews of Western and Eastern spiritual religious traditions (Richards & Bergin, 1997). Despite much diversity between and within the various Western (theistic) religious traditions about specifics, there is considerable similarity among them regarding their general views about deity, human nature, purpose of life, spirituality, morality, and life after death. For example, they all teach that there is a God, a Supreme Being, who created the world and that human beings were placed on the earth by the Creator for a divine purpose. They also teach that human beings can receive spiritual guidance and strength from God, and that God has revealed moral and ethical truths or commandments to guide human behavior and social relations.

It is more difficult to find commonalties among the Eastern religions, although some similarities exist. First, some of the Eastern religions teach that there are many gods or deities who, along with all of nature and humanity, are all ultimately One. But they do not necessarily believe in a Supreme Being or God. Some of them (e.g., Confucianism) do not concern themselves with gods or deities at all. All of the Eastern religious traditions affirm that human beings have moral agency. They all reject hedonistic philosophies and instead teach that there are moral paths that are ethical, moral, and honorable that lead to enlightenment, peace, honor, and ideal relationships.

The Western and Eastern spiritual worldviews have some similarities,

> including the general notions that (1) some sort of harmony with an eternal principle or essence (with God or an impersonal One) is possible; (2) human beings have free will; (3) there are moral or ethical principles or laws human beings should seek to live in harmony with; and (4) there are paths or ways which lead to personal and social harmony, enlightenment, growth, peace, and happiness. (Richards & Bergin, 1997, p. 67)

In addition to agreeing that there are ethical and moral values that need to be taught and transmitted from one generation to the next, there is also considerable agreement among the major spiritual traditions of the world about what general principles and moral values should be transmitted.

TABLE 19.1
Comparison of the Western and Eastern Spiritual Worldviews

Worldview	View of diety	View of human nature	Purpose of life	View of spirituality	View of morality	View of life after death
Western (monotheistic)	There is a God, a Supreme Being, who created the universe, the earth, and human beings. God is eternal, omnipotent, and all-knowing. God loves and assists human beings.	Human beings are creations of God. Human beings have an eternal soul or spirit. Human beings have free will and the capacity to choose good over evil and to obey God's commandments.	There is a transcendent, divine purpose to life. Human beings are here upon the earth to learn to be obedient to God's will, to choose good over evil, and to prepare to live in a joyful and peaceful afterlife.	Human beings can communicate with God through prayer and meditation. People can grow spiritually as they obey God's will, worship him, and love and serve their fellow human beings.	God has revealed laws and commandments to guide human behavior. Obedience to God's laws promotes spiritual growth, harmonious social relations, personal happiness and prepares people for rewards in the afterlife.	The spirit or soul of human beings continues to exist after mortal death. There is an afterlife of peace and joy for those who live righteously in mortal life. The wicked are punished or suffer for their sins in the afterlife.
Eastern	There is no Supreme Being or God. There may be nature deities or helping beings, but they are not all-powerful and all-knowing. There may be an eternal, impersonal, universal essence or One.	Human beings may or may not have an eternal soul. Individual identity eventually ends either in extinction or in mystical unity with the eternal, universal One. Human beings do have free will and the capacity to choose a path that leads to enlightenment and harmonious relationships.	The purpose of life is to learn to follow a path to enlightenment and harmony. To live an ethical and moral life so that one can obtain release from endless rounds of rebirth, or at least so that one can enjoy honor, peace, and ideal relationships in this life.	Spiritual enlightenment comes from living in harmony with the ethical path and through meditation and self-denial. Enlightenment leads to insight into the true nature of the universe and of reality.	A variety of notions exist about what is moral and desirable behavior. There tends to be agreement that a moral path or way does exist and that following it leads to enlightenment and personal and social harmony.	Considerable variety regarding beliefs about the afterlife, ranging from a belief that we cease to exist at death to the belief that we are immortal but no longer have individual identity and are part of the universal One and to the belief that some type of individual soul persists after death.

Note. From *A Spiritual Strategy for Counseling and Psychotherapy,* by P. S. Richards and A. E. Bergin, 1997. Copyright 1997 by the American Psychological Association. Adapted with permission.

According to Ninian Smart (1983), a respected world religion scholar, "the major faiths have much in common as far as moral conduct goes. Not to steal, not to lie, not to kill, not to have certain kinds of sexual relations —such prescriptions are found across the world" (p. 117). There is, of course, much variation in the specific interpretations of these general principles and values. Nevertheless, as Table 19.2 makes apparent, there is considerable agreement among the religious traditions and denominations[1] included in this book regarding contemporary moral issues, such as abortion, birth control, sexuality, marriage and divorce, alcohol and drugs, and euthanasia. Most religions take rather conservative official positions on most of these issues, although there is often controversy among members about their interpretation and application. An awareness of such worldview and value themes should be useful for psychotherapists as they work with clients from these various backgrounds, although they should of course not make assumptions about a specific client's values on the basis of religious affiliation alone.

SIMILARITIES AND DIFFERENCES IN ATTITUDES TOWARD PSYCHOTHERAPY

Table 19.3 summarizes some of the similarities and differences among the spiritual traditions included in this volume with regard to their views of psychotherapy and healing. Perhaps the most striking theme in this table is that many members in most of these traditions tend to have negative perceptions of the mental health professions, distrust therapists and the process of psychotherapy, and underuse mental health services. We discussed this religiosity or credibility gap at the beginning of the book and identified it as a serious problem for the mental health professions (Bergin & Jensen, 1990). The chapter authors have provided additional insight into the reasons for this credibility gap, and they have also offered suggestions that could help psychotherapists begin to overcome it. We will return to this topic a bit later in this chapter.

Another striking theme is that all of the religious and spiritual traditions encourage their members to engage in a variety of spiritual practices and traditions that presume to have mental health benefits. Research evidence appears to support this notion of a healing potential in religious and spiritual communities (Benson, 1996; Pargament, 1997; Richards & Bergin, 1997), but unfortunately most psychotherapists have not yet tapped it. We feel optimistic that the insights provided in these chapters will help

[1]African American, Latino/Latina, Asian American, and Native American spiritual traditions are not included in this table because there is such religious diversity in each of these racial–ethnic groups that it was not possible to summarize their views concisely on these social–moral issues.

TABLE 19.2
Official Positions of Religious Traditions and Denominations on Contemporary Moral Issues[a]

Tradition	Abortion and birth control	Sexuality[b]	Marriage and divorce	Alcohol and drugs	Suicide and euthanasia
Roman Catholic	Abortion and artificial contraception are considered wrong and sinful.	Premarital, homosexual, and extramarital sexual behavior are considered sinful.	Marriage is considered a holy union. Civil divorce does not affect the sacramental status of marriage; separation is permitted and annulments are sometimes granted.	Temperance is encouraged in the use of alcohol, tobacco, and medicine. Using illegal drugs is considered a grave offense.	Suicide and direct euthanasia are considered morally unacceptable, although discontinuing overzealous treatment can be legitimate.
Eastern Orthodox	Abortion is forbidden. Contraception is officially condemned, but in practice the church leaves it between husband and wife.	Premarital, homosexual, and extramarital sex are considered sinful.	Marriage is sacred. Divorce and remarriage are forbidden, but divorce is granted on grounds of abandonment, incompatibility, and abuse.	Use of alcohol in moderation is accepted, but drunkenness and use of illegal drugs are condemned.	Suicide and direct euthanasia are considered morally wrong, although withdrawing life support may be appropriate.
Mainline Protestant	Abortion is generally discouraged except in cases of rape, extreme fetus abnormalities, or danger to mother's life, although there is some variability among denominations about when it is acceptable. Contraception is accepted among all denominations.	Sex has typically been discouraged outside of marriage, and homosexual behavior was considered immoral. Emphasis has shifted slightly toward mutual understanding and tolerance and slightly away from normative prescriptions about sexuality.	Marriage is considered a blessing or vocation. Divorce was traditionally considered wrong, but is now viewed more tolerantly, as are single-parent families and remarriage.	Lutherans, Presbyterians, and Episcopalians discourage excessive use of alcohol, tobacco, and other drugs. Moderate use of alcohol is tolerated, although Methodists disapprove of even moderate use of alcohol.	Suicide is considered wrong. Physician-assisted suicide is opposed, although there is some acceptance of passive euthanasia (withdrawal of life support and the forgoing of heroic measures to sustain life).

Table continues

TABLE 19.2 (Continued)

Tradition	Abortion and birth control	Sexuality[b]	Marriage and divorce	Alcohol and drugs	Suicide and euthanasia
Evangelical and Fundamentalist Protestant	Abortion is strongly opposed, except in an ectopic pregnancy and danger to mother's life. Contraception is accepted.	Oppose premarital, homosexual, and extramarital sexual activity.	Oppose divorce and remarriage (except due to spouse's infidelity).	Oppose alcohol and drug use.	Suicide and euthanasia are wrong.
Pentecostal	Abortion is vigorously opposed, except for ectopic pregnancies or danger to mother's life. Contraception for married couples is accepted.	Sexuality is a sacred gift from God and should be celebrated only in marriage. Homosexual behavior is seen as unnatural and contrary to scripture.	Marriage is valued and divorce and remarriage is strongly discouraged, although differing opinions exist about when divorce or remarriage is acceptable.	Drunkenness and drug abuse in any form are opposed. Classical Pentecostals encourage total abstinence from alcohol, but some Charismatic churches accept moderate use.	Suicide and euthanasia are opposed.
Latter-day Saint	Abortion is vigorously condemned, except in cases of rape, incest, and danger to mother's life. Contraception is accepted but child bearing is encouraged.	Sexual relations between husbands and wives are considered beautiful and sacred. Premarital, homosexual, and extramarital sex are considered sinful.	Marriage is a holy union, intended to last for time and eternity. Divorce is strongly discouraged, although the church grants divorces for infidelity, abuse, and severe incompatibility. Remarriage is accepted.	Any use of alcohol, illegal drugs, tobacco, coffee, and tea is considered sinful. Complete abstinence from these substances is the norm.	Suicide is considered against God's will. Active euthanasia is considered morally unacceptable, although passive euthanasia may be acceptable.

	Abortion and Contraception	Sexuality	Marriage and Divorce	Alcohol and Drugs	Suicide and Euthanasia
Seventh-day Adventist	Abortion is condemned except in cases of rape, incest, or danger to the health of the woman. Contraception is accepted.	Premarital, homosexual, and extramarital sex are considered wrong.	Marriage is regarded as a divinely established institution. Divorce and remarriage are discouraged, except in cases of adultery.	Abstinence from alcohol and drug use is required, as is any form of smoking. Drinking caffeinated coffee or tea is greatly discouraged.	Suicide and euthanasia are considered morally wrong, although passive euthanasia may be acceptable.
Orthodox Judaism	Abortion is a grave sin except when mother's life is in danger and during the first 40 days of pregnancy when a rabbi may sanction it. Contraception is discouraged, but permitted for medical reasons.	Premarital, homosexual, and extramarital sex are considered sinful. Male homosexual behavior is considered a much graver offense than female homosexual behavior.	Marriage and having children is considered a "mitzvah" (commandment or good deed). Divorce is permitted but not considered lightly. Remarriage is encouraged.	Using alcohol (in moderation) is permissible. Illegal drug use is considered reprehensible. Smoking tobacco is discouraged. A variety of dietary laws are adhered to.	Suicide is forbidden. Euthanasia is also forbidden, although passive euthanasia may be acceptable.
Conservative and Reform Judaism	Abortion to preserve the life or health of the mother is permissible. Abortion for frivolous purposes is not acceptable, but this may not be interpreted with rigor. Contraception is acceptable.	Lawful sexuality is a gift and joy. Pre-marital sex is largely a matter of personal choice. Adultery and incest are forbidden. Male homosexual behavior is prohibited, but the law is silent about female homosexual behavior.	Marriage and children are highly valued, but divorce is accepted and easy to arrange. Remarriage is encouraged.	Alcohol, in moderation, is viewed as a gift from God, but drunkenness is not acceptable. A variety of dietary laws may or may not be observed.	Suicide and euthanasia are not acceptable, although passive euthanasia may be.

Table continues

TABLE 19.2 (Continued)

Tradition	Abortion and birth control	Sexuality[b]	Marriage and divorce	Alcohol and drugs	Suicide and euthanasia
Islam	Abortion is discouraged but permitted within the first 4 months of pregnancy, except if mother's life is at risk or in cases of rape or incest. Contraception is permitted.	All sexual relations outside of marriage are forbidden. Homosexual behavior is forbidden.	Marriage and children are encouraged. Dating, courtship, and "romantic love" are not seen as prerequisites to marriage. Polygamy is permitted, but rarely practiced and is illegal in the U.S. Divorce is discouraged but permitted, and is easier to obtain for men.	Drinking alcohol and using illegal drugs are forbidden. Some dietary guidelines are also prescribed.	Suicide and direct euthanasia are forbidden, although passive forms of euthanasia may be accepted.
Buddhism	Respect for life is the most important ethical principle, and so abortion is viewed as unethical. Contraception is accepted.	One should not cause harm to others by unwholesome sexual acts (e.g., adultery). Homosexual behavior was forbidden in early Buddhist teaching, but in contemporary American Buddhist communities, it is accepted.	No specific Buddhist teachings about marriage, divorce, or child rearing.	Use of mind-altering substances is discouraged. Many Buddhists totally abstain from alcohol and drugs, but some American Buddhists advocate moderation in the use of alcohol. Vegetarianism is often practiced, but exceptions abound.	Suicide and active euthanasia are discouraged, although passive forms of euthanasia may be acceptable.

	Birth control/abortion	Sexual behavior	Marriage	Alcohol and drugs	Suicide and euthanasia
Hinduism	Birth control is an acceptable practice. Abortion is accepted as a method of ending unwanted pregnancy.	Sexual chastity is valued. Premarital and extramarital sex are discouraged. Hinduism is tolerant of homosexuality.	Marriage and child rearing are highly valued. Most marriages are arranged. Divorce is strongly discouraged, though allowed under certain conditions.	Alcohol use in small amounts is acceptable. Use of hard drugs not permitted. Tradition within some groups of using hallucinogens to enhance spiritual awareness.	Though not considered wrong per se, suicide is not approved of as an act to escape suffering but is viewed as an act of religious merit (the ultimate austerity) for aged and venerated holy men. Euthanasia not permitted. Killing anyone or anything is considered wrong.

[a]We recognize that without the context of the information provided in the entire chapters, there is some danger that the information in this table could be misleading and perhaps even convey stereotypes. Despite this risk, we believe that these brief comparative summaries are helpful in highlighting similarities and differences among the various spiritual traditions. We encourage readers to keep in mind the risks associated with such brief, simplified summaries and to interpret the table within the context of the additional information provided in the book chapters.

[b]It is clear that the major religious traditions regard sexuality as having sacred functions and boundaries and that they are generally conservative, especially with regard to incest, adultery, homosexuality, and so on. However, there is a trend toward increased acceptance of gay and lesbian persons in several denominations, particularly for those willing to remain celibate. In addition, there are those, such as the Metropolitan Community Churches, which support openly gay and lesbian lifestyles.

TABLE 19.3

Psychotherapy, Healing Practices, and Clinical Issues and Guidelines for the Religious and Spiritual Traditions[a]

Tradition	View of therapy	Spiritual practices and healing traditions	Religious–clinical issues	Assessment recommendations	Treatment recommendations
Roman Catholic	Some conservative Roman Catholics may prefer a therapist whose faith perspective is consonant with their own, but there is probably a wide range of opinions among Roman Catholics about the importance of this issue. Open to the use of psychotropic medications.	Sacraments (e.g., baptism, confirmation, eucharist, penance [confession], anointing of the sick, holy orders, matrimony), prayer, and devotions.	Authority conflicts, sexuality, interreligious marriage, divorce, abortion, suicide, artificial insemination, genetic engineering, and euthanasia.	Inquire about past and present religious experience and affiliation, including religious training, sacraments received, salience of church teaching and authority, use of religious resources, God image, and normative status of religious beliefs and behaviors.	Be aware of motifs for healing within the Church (e.g., teachings about suffering, death, resurrection, confession, and reconciliation). Assess and work through internalized unconscious God representations. Be sensitive to countertransference issues. Explicitly integrate religious resources and interventions when appropriate. Consult with clergy.
Eastern Orthodox	Orthodox immigrants will probably be unfamiliar with therapy and unlikely to seek it or to self-disclose; 2nd- and 3rd-generation Orthodox and converts may be more open to therapy. Open to use of medications.	Worship (which includes prayers, hymns, burning incense, eucharist), baptism, chrismation, repentance or confession, holy orders, marriage, Jesus Prayer, and anointing of the sick.	Language and cultural assimilation and barriers. Sexuality, abortion, divorce.	Assess the level of client's involvement in the Orthodox faith.	Support clients in their spiritual growth and development.

Group					
Mainline Protestant	Tend to have positive views of mental health professions. Open to psychological, biological, and medical understandings of illness. Some clients might fear therapists will undermine their religious beliefs and values.	Attending worship services, prayer, spiritual meditation, reading Bible and other spiritual writings, and teachings about grace and forgiveness.	Sexuality, divorce, excessive alcohol or drug use, abortion, and euthanasia.	Assess clients' religious and spiritual functioning and how it might be relevant to their psychological issues and treatment planning.	Likely to be comfortable with most secular approaches to therapy. Use interventions that help clients grant forgiveness, seek forgiveness, and feel forgiven. Collaborate with pastoral care centers. Some spiritual interventions may be appropriate.
Evangelical and Fundamentalist Protestant	Evangelicals tend to have positive views of mental health profession; Fundamentalists do not. Both prefer therapists of their own faith.	Participation in church services and activities. Social support from the religious community. Healthy lifestyle practices (e.g., abstaining from drug use). Prayer and Bible study.	Authority figure fears and conflict, unhealthy group dependency, perfectionism, excessive guilt and shame, low self-esteem, and rigidity and dogmatism.	Fundamentalists may not be open to psychological or religious assessments, although Evangelicals are likely to be. A number of psychospiritual measures may be useful for assessment purposes.	Many secular theories of therapy have some value. A variety of spiritual interventions may be helpful, including forgiveness, prayer, challenging distorted religious beliefs, consulting with religious leaders.
Pentecostal	Tend to view behavioral sciences with suspicion and oppose any kind of therapy that is not strictly biblical.	Participation in church services and activities. Social support from the religious community. Healthy lifestyle practices (e.g., abstaining from drug use). Prayer and Bible study.	Overly harsh, punitive images of God. Religiously based guilt, anger, and anxiety. Poor self-image or self-esteem. Inhibited sexuality and sexual guilt. Difficulties with forgiveness. Divorce and remarriage.	Explore the role and importance of the client's religious faith. Inquire about client's religious background and current beliefs about their church and God.	Do not use psychological interventions that are contrary to Pentecostal scriptural understandings. Prayer, scriptural teachings and stories, and consulting with clergy may be helpful interventions.

Table continues

TABLE 19.3 (Continued)

Tradition	View of therapy	Spiritual practices and healing traditions	Religious–clinical issues	Assessment recommendations	Treatment recommendations
Latter-day Saint	Tend to have fairly positive views of the mental health professions, although considerable distrust of "secular" psychotherapy exists. Most members tend to prefer working with LDS therapists.	Worship services, temple ordinances and services, prayer, scripture study, family home evenings, blessings (laying on of hands), fasting, church and humanitarian service, hymns, partaking of sacraments, baptism, family history work.	Perfectionism and shame, authority conflicts and abuses, sexual guilt and inhibition, denial of anger and conflict, gender role conflict and sexism, and social conformity and pressure.	Assess clients' degree of involvement with the religious community and to what degree religious beliefs and involvement are a positive or negative influence. Other religious dimensions may also be relevant to assess.	Variety of psychological and spiritual interventions could be appropriate, including teaching spiritual concepts, spiritual self-disclosure, and prayer. Consulting with clients' religious leaders can often be helpful.
Seventh-day Adventist	Many SDA members, especially conservative ones, may distrust mental health professionals and prefer therapy from Christian therapists.	Sabbath-day observance, worshipping, social support, prayer, scripture study, baptism and laying on of hands, healthy lifestyle behaviors (e.g., "clean" meats or vegetarian food; abstinence from alcohol and drug use).	Perfectionism, authority issues, sexual inhibitions and guilt, fear of dependency on the therapist, guilt and shame, depression, and sexism in some gender roles.	Do not use psychological assessments that may appear unsympathetic toward religious persons. Several projective tools, and some objective spiritual assessment measures may be helpful.	Relaxation training, rational–emotive therapy, transactional analysis, and Rogerian therapy can be helpful. Child, marriage, and family counseling are accepted.

Tradition	View of therapy	Religious practices	Common problems	Assessment considerations	Therapy approach
Orthodox Judaism	Some Orthodox Jews are reluctant to seek therapy because they fear it will conflict with their values. Most Orthodox Jews see no problem with taking psychotropic medication.	Study of the Torah, Mishna, and Talmud. Prayer and worship, observing biblical holidays and associated ceremonies (e.g., Rosh Hashanah, Yom Kippur, Passover, Sukkot), and observing mitzvot (commandments).	Marital discord, sexual problems, fears of homosexuality, masturbation, feelings of spiritual inadequacy, interfaith marriage, and spiritual identity crises.	Assessing the degree of clients' religious commitment and observance may be helpful, and whether it is authentic or neurotic. Intrinsic–extrinsic scale not suitable for Orthodox Jews.	Psychodynamic therapy may be viewed with distrust by some, but valued by others. Some spiritual interventions may be helpful (e.g., discussing religious concepts). Consulting with rabbis may be helpful.
Conservative and Reform Judaism	Most Conservative and Reform Jews are familiar and comfortable with therapy. They may be especially drawn to psychoanalysis. They may be quicker to trust a Jewish therapist but are open to therapy with non-Jews.	Study of the Torah, Mishna, and Talmud. Prayer and worship, observing biblical holidays and associated ceremonies (e.g., Rosh Hashanah, Yom Kippur, Passover, Sukkot), and observing mitzvot (commandments).	Identity conflicts, depression, paranoia, intellectual identification, guilt and inappropriate feelings of responsibility, intermarriage, and family enmeshment.	Debate and argument should not necessarily be interpreted as resistance. May be helpful to ask clients to explain cultural aspects of their lives. Assess clients' religious identity. Separate traditional religious behaviors from neuroses.	Psychodynamic and other cognitively oriented approaches may be most accepted. Debate, discussion, and argument may be appropriate. Consulting rabbis and other knowledgeable people can be helpful.
Islam	Most Muslims view the mental health professions with suspicion and few seek therapy.	Ritual prayers, zakat (alms giving), fasting, pilgrimage, visiting a mosque, reading or listening to recitations of the Koran, and participating in Islamic holidays and festivals (e.g., Ramadan).	Cultural and value conflicts, depression and somatization, family problems, psychosis, and suicide ideation.	Assess what it means for the client to be a Muslim in North America. Assess client's level of acculturation, level of social and family support, and degree of religious affiliation, especially affiliation with a mosque.	Educate oneself about religious and cultural values of Muslim clients. Family may need to be involved in treatment. Consulting with members of the Muslim community may be helpful.

Table continues

TABLE 19.3 (Continued)

Tradition	View of therapy	Spiritual practices and healing traditions	Religious–clinical issues	Assessment recommendations	Treatment recommendations
Buddhism	A range of attitudes about therapy, including acceptance, reluctance to seek it, and active distrust of it. There is a significant number of Buddhist psychotherapists.	Meditation, working with one's spiritual teacher or guru, studying Buddhist teachings, daily worship and rituals, participating in holy days and festivals, and participating in rites and passages.	Early emotional losses, disturbed feelings, perfectionism, self-contempt, addictions, submissiveness to authority, pathological selflessness, and posttraumatic stress disorder.	Avoid premature judgment or dismissal. Avoid a priori pathologizing. Assess the intentions shaping the client's involvement in Buddhism. Is the client's spiritual faith compensatory or destructive?	Supportive and encouraging meditative practices may be helpful. Consulting and working with Buddhist teachers may be helpful. Insight-oriented approaches may be consistent with Buddhist clients' values.
Hinduism	In general, Hindus are skeptical about the value of therapy. Many Hindus feel the family should take care of its own. It can be a major taboo to seek outside help.	Meditation, yoga, religious devotions and prayers, rituals, festivals, and pilgrimages.	Acculturation and value conflicts, family and marital problems, dating and marriage concerns, domestic violence, and incest.	Assess level of acculturation and nature of the family system. Do not pathologize cultural differences. Assess where clients are in terms of developmental level (or stage of life).	A development therapy approach may be most natural. Use karma therapeutically to help clients take responsibility for their lives. Help clients explore the contradictions they feel. Learn more about the Hindu religion.

African American	Perceptions of therapy vary across denominations. In past, African American churches have been suspicious of counseling, but in recent years have become more open to it. May be very cautious about using psychotropic medications.	Community fellowship, worship (including sermons, prayer, scriptural readings, music, dancing, clapping), rituals (e.g., baptism, communion, laying on of hands and anointing with oil), and seeking spiritual direction from pastors.	Relationship issues, depression, grief, racial identity development, and potential for negative responses to addictions, sexual abuse and incest, and homosexuality.	Clinical interviews are recommended for assessing clients' spirituality because of lack of assessment instruments. Assess clients' church history, relationship with God, and spiritual experiences and practices.	Empathic understanding is essential. Biblical and personal narratives, and supportive cognitive–behavioral techniques, may be helpful. History-taking may be perceived as intrusive if done prematurely. Testing may be viewed with suspicion.
Latino/Latina	Those from higher SES are more likely to seek therapy, as are Argentinian immigrants (compared with Central American immigrants). Some Latino/Latina people will not seek help from therapists, but prefer a priest, physician, or family member.	Community support, seeking direction from spiritual leaders, rituals, prayer, consultation with the spirit world.	Acculturation and value conflicts, racial–ethnic identity issues, sexuality, anger and stress, depression, occupational stress, and family problems.	Do not assume pathology when clients are mediums or seek consultation from them. Use clinical interview to assess clients' spiritual beliefs. No objective measures available.	Individualistic intervention approaches are less congruent with Latino worldview than collectivist approaches. Consulting with spiritual leaders and practitioners may be helpful.

Table continues

TABLE 19.3 (Continued)

Tradition	View of therapy	Spiritual practices and healing traditions	Religious–clinical issues	Assessment recommendations	Treatment recommendations
Asian American	Asian Americans underuse therapy services. Prefer to seek help from family, trusted community and spiritual leaders, traditional healers, and physicians.	Prayer, church attendance, reading Bible, worship and rituals, participation in fellowship and Bible study groups, and seeking support from pastors. Traditional practices such as acupuncture, herbal medicine, and dermabrasion (e.g., coin rubbing) may also be used simultaneously with Western medicine.	Acculturation issues, filial piety and religious conflicts, somatization, women's roles and identity, vocational and educational dilemmas, intergenerational conflicts, and posttraumatic stress disorder.	Avoid cultural biases in assessing functioning. Interpret assessment tools with caution in light of possible cultural biases. Religious Status Inventory and Spiritual Well-Being Scale may be helpful with Christian Asian Americans.	Use the support network of family, friends, church, and community to help clients. Be directive, but use restraint in gathering information. Avoid direct confrontations and undue emphasis on emotions. Spiritual interventions may be helpful. Consulting with pastors may be helpful.
Native American	Native Americans will seek help from the shaman first. Most are willing to seek medical assistance, but many will not seek help for mental health problems unless the provider has built a trusting relationship by demonstrating cultural competence over time.	Rituals (e.g., vision quest), prayers, healing ceremonies, songs and dances, experiencing sacred moments (e.g., dreams and visions), seeking to live in harmony and balance with nature, seeking knowledge and wisdom from the shaman.	Alcoholism and drug abuse, acculturation conflicts, ethnic identity, depression, suicide, social discord, family and parent–child problems, low self-esteem, and unemployment and poverty.	Cultural competence is needed to conduct a valid assessment. Assess level of acculturation, ethnic identity, and spirituality in the context of the Native Americans' life experience. Be cautious not to impose cultural biases in assessing functioning and pathology.	Important to establish a trusting, person-to-person relationship. Be sensitive to cultural and spiritual beliefs and values. Do not violate the sacred. Use interventions that respect clients' spiritual worldview and belief in the importance of relationships (with the land, wildlife, water, community, and so on).

[a]We recognize that without the context of the information provided in the entire chapters, there is some danger that the information in this table could be misleading and perhaps even convey stereotypes. Despite this risk, we believe that these brief comparative summaries are helpful in highlighting similarities and differences among the various spiritual traditions. We encourage readers to keep in mind the risks associated with such brief, simplified summaries and to interpret the table within the context of the additional information provided in the book chapters.

therapists understand better how they can use religious and spiritual healing resources to benefit their clients.

Table 19.3 also makes clear that there are a wide variety of clinical issues that may be intertwined or connected in some way with clients' religious and spiritual beliefs. We wish to emphasize again, as did many of the authors, that the identification of these clinical issues with members of specific religious communities does not necessarily mean that they struggle with these issues more frequently than do other people. Until comparative research studies are conducted, such conclusions would be premature, but we are saying that these particular clinical issues may have religious overtones or implications for clients from these groups. To help religious clients work through such issues most effectively, considerable acumen in the clients' religious beliefs and cultures may be needed. Hence, we again emphasize the necessity for training in religious diversity if one wishes to be fully effective with clients from diverse religions.

Concerning assessment and treatment recommendations, we discerned several themes. Many of the authors recommended that therapists assess the degree of clients' identification and involvement with the religious tradition, and whether clients' religious beliefs and practices are normative for that faith and are being used in healthy or unhealthy ways. Several authors pointed out the importance of not pathologizing cultural–religious differences and avoiding psychological or spiritual assessment measures that do so. Specific treatment recommendations vary from faith to faith, but there was agreement that it is essential to avoid interventions that conflict with normative religious beliefs. There was also widespread agreement that a variety of psychological and spiritual interventions may be appropriate, depending on the client, the nature of the problem, and the therapist's religious affiliation. There was also widespread endorsement of the notion that consulting with religious leaders can be beneficial in many cases if it is done appropriately, and that not doing so can prove detrimental to client welfare.

RECOMMENDATIONS, FUTURE DIRECTIONS, AND CONCLUSIONS

We think that psychotherapists and the leaders of mainstream mental health professional organizations should make efforts to engage in more constructive relationships with members and leaders of traditional religious communities (Bergin, 1991; Jones, 1994; Shafranske & Malony, 1996). Building trust and bridges of mutual respect and understanding with people from diverse backgrounds could have many benefits for the mental health professions. For psychotherapists, it could lead to increased referrals from religious communities and to more respect from the general public. It could also lead to increased credibility, influence, and stature in society. For clients, it could increase the likelihood that they will receive the mental health services they need from "someone who understands their perspective and who does not automatically interpret their beliefs in pathological terms" (Bergin & Jensen, 1990, p. 7).

How can psychotherapists, and the mental health professions as a whole, build trust and develop more sensitive and effective helping relationships with religious clients, leaders, and communities? This is not an easy question because the alienation that exists between the behavioral sciences and religious traditions has been a century in the making (Bergin, 1980; Campbell, 1975; Jones, 1994; Richards & Bergin, 1997). In all likelihood, it is going to take considerable time and effort for this to change significantly. Just because mental health professionals decide they would like to close the religiosity gap does not mean that they know how to do so (Weaver et al., 1997), nor does it mean that all religious leaders and communities will want to.

We agree with Jones (1994), who suggested that if a constructive relationship between psychology and religion is to be achieved, a "dialogical and not unilateral" relationship is needed. Historically, secular mental health professionals have tended to interact with religious tradition and communities in a unilateral manner in which they studied religious experience scientifically (objectified it), supplied psychological information to guide pastoral care, or used "psychological findings or theories to revise, reinterpret, redefine, supplant, or dismiss established religious traditions" (Jones, 1994, p. 185). A dialogical relationship suggests mental health professionals and religious leaders will come together in mutual respect and with a desire to help each other achieve their common goal of promoting healing and growth. Such a relationship also presumes "the willingness of scientists and professionals to become theologically and philosophically literate and for theologians and philosophers to become scientifically and professionally literate" (Jones, 1994, p. 195). Such attitudes and understandings will not occur overnight, but we think they are achievable if people of goodwill from diverse religious and professional backgrounds are willing to make the effort.

Increased education in religious and spiritual diversity in mental health training programs is essential if the religiosity gap is going to be closed (Shafranske & Malony, 1996). Currently, very few professionals receive any training in religion or spirituality during graduate school and few seek postgraduate training in it (Kelly, 1994; Shafranske, in press; Shafranske & Malony, 1990; Sheridan, Bullis, Adcock, Berlin, & Miller, 1992). For the sake of clients and for the sake of the mental health disciplines, it is time for this to change. Mental health professionals can individually, or in groups, organize workshops or seek out readings and other training opportunities in religious and spiritual diversity.

We join with others in urging directors of graduate education programs to include training in religious diversity in their multicultural course work and practica offerings (Shafranske & Malony, 1996). We note and applaud the fact that the American Medical Association now requires all psychiatric residency programs in the United States to address spiritual and religious issues in their formal training (American Medical Association, 1995). We hope that leaders of other helping professions will do likewise, and we call upon members of professional licensing boards to make training in religious diversity a condition for licensure as a mental health professional.

In addition to training, there is also a need for increased research on how mental health professionals can work more effectively with religious leaders and communities. It would also be helpful to gain additional insight into the professional needs and challenges of religious leaders, and how mental health professionals might be of support and service to them and to members of their communities. Although substantial efforts along these lines have been made over the years within some denominations and in some professional organizations (e.g., American Association of Pastoral Counselors), relatively little has been published about these topics in mainstream psychology journals (Weaver et al., 1997). Pargament's and his colleagues' *Congregation Development Program* (1991) provides a helpful example of such possibilities. Rayburn and her colleagues have also done some pioneering research and writing about these concerns (Rayburn, 1991a, 1991b; Rayburn, Richmond, & Rogers, 1986, 1994). We hope that more will be published about such issues in mainstream mental health and psychotherapy journals in the years to come.

Gaining additional insight into how religious leaders and communities can assist mental health professionals with their work would also be valuable. There is reason to believe that their support and assistance can significantly enhance and maintain the outcomes of psychotherapy if used appropriately (Richards & Bergin, 1997).

Finally, there is a need for much more research about the mental health issues and needs of members of various religious traditions, and for research into which psychotherapy approaches are most appropriate and effective for them. The lack of behavioral science research about members of specific religious and spiritual traditions is a glaring deficiency in the field. We hope that this deficiency will be corrected in the coming decade, and that this research will contribute to the development of more spiritually sensitive and effective strategies for healing and change with members of diverse religious and spiritual traditions. Such a prospect is exciting to contemplate because it would represent a major step forward in the quest to promote healing and mental health for all sectors of the human family.

REFERENCES

American Medical Association. (1995). *Graduate medical education directory, 1995– 1996: Program requirements for residency education in psychiatry.* Chicago: Author.

Benson, H. (1996). *Timeless healing: The power and biology of belief.* New York: Scribner.

Bergin, A. E. (1980). Psychotherapy and religious values. *Journal of Consulting and Clinical Psychology, 48,* 75–105.

Bergin, A. E. (1991). Values and religious issues in psychotherapy and mental health. *American Psychologist, 46,* 394–403.

Bergin, A. E., & Jensen, J. P. (1990). Religiosity of psychotherapists: A national survey. *Psychotherapy, 27,* 3–7.

Campbell, D. T. (1975). On the conflicts between biological and social evolution and between psychology and moral tradition. *American Psychologist, 30,* 1103–1126.

Jones, S. L. (1994). A constructive relationship for religion with the science and profession of psychology: Perhaps the boldest model yet. *American Psychologist, 49,* 184–199.

Kelly, E. W. (1994). The role of religion and spirituality in counselor education: A national survey. *Counselor Education and Supervision, 33,* 227–236.

Pargament, K. I. (1997). *The psychology of religion and coping: Theory, research, and practice.* New York: Guilford Press.

Pargament, K. L., Falgout, K., Ensing, D. S., Reilly, B., Silverman, M., Van Haitsma, K., & Warren, R. (1991). The congregation development program: Data-based consultation with churches and synagogues. *Professional Psychology: Research and Practice, 22,* 393–404.

Rayburn, C. A. (1991a). Clergy couples and stress: Clergy married to clergy. *Psychotherapy in Private Practice, 8,* 127–130.

Rayburn, C. A. (1991b). Counseling depressed female religious professionals: Nuns and clergywomen. *Counseling and Values, 35,* 136–148.

Rayburn, C. A., Richmond, L. J., & Rogers, L. (1986). Men, women, and religion: Stress within leadership roles. *Journal of Clinical Psychology, 42,* 540–546.

Rayburn, C. A., Richmond, L. J., & Rogers, L. (1994). Women religious professionals and stress. In L. B. Brown (Ed.), *Religion, personality, and mental health* (pp. 167–173). New York: Springer-Verlag.

Richards, P. S., & Bergin, A. E. (1997). *A spiritual strategy for counseling and psychotherapy.* Washington, DC: American Psychological Association.

Shafranske, E. P. (in press). Spiritual beliefs and practices of psychiatrists and other mental health professionals. *Psychiatric Annals.*

Shafranske, E. P., & Malony, H. N. (1990). Clinical psychologists' religious and spiritual orientations and their practice of psychotherapy. *Psychotherapy, 27,* 72–78.

Shafranske, E. P., & Malony, H. N. (1996). Religion and the clinical practice of psychology: A case for inclusion. In E. P. Shafranske (Ed.), *Religion and the clinical practice of psychology* (pp. 561–586). Washington, DC: American Psychological Association.

Sheridan, M. J., Bullis, R. K., Adcock, C. R., Berlin, S. D., & Miller, P. C. (1982). Practitioner's personal and professional attitudes and behaviors toward religion and spirituality: Issues for education and practice. *Journal of Social Work Education, 28*, 190–203.

Smart, N. (1983). *Worldviews: Crosscultural explorations of human beliefs*. New York: Scribner.

Weaver, A. J., Samford, J. A., Kline, A. E., Lucas, L. A., Larson, D. B., & Koenig, H. G. (1997). What do psychologists know about working with the clergy? An analysis of eight APA journals: 1991–1994. *Professional Psychology: Research and Practice, 28*, 471–474.

AUTHOR INDEX

Numbers in italics refer to listings in reference sections.

491

Pérez y Mena, A., 404, *419*
Price, J. A., 458, *465*
Proctor, R., 221, *233*
Propst, L. R., 16, *25*, 84, *87*

Quezada, T., 398, 399, *419*

Rabinowitz, A., 245, *257*
Rachal, K. C., 122, 123, *128*
Racy, J., 299, 306, *314*
Rahman, F., 298, *314*
Ramirez, M., 399, 405, *419*
Ramirez, O., 406, *417*
Ramos, M. W., 401, *419*
Rayburn, C. A., 137, 138, 146, *153*, 216,
    217, 222, 225, 231, *233*, 487,
    488
Redlich, F. C., 277, *285*
Reichel-Dolmatoff, G., 406, *419*
Reile, D. H., 213, 214, 221, 227, *233*
Reilly, B., *488*
Renik, O., 84, *88*
Renou, L., 350, *365*
Resnick, J., *127*
Rice, R. R., 132, 136, *153*
Richards, P. S., 3, 5, 10, 12–15, 17–20,
    23, 25, 75, 76, 83, 86, *87*, 122,
    123, *128*, 196, 197, 204, 205,
    208, 247, *257*, 334, *339*, 369,
    381–383, 389, 396, 455, *465*,
    470–472, 486, 487, 488
Richmond, L. J., 222, 231, *233*, 487, 488
Rickard-Figueroa, K., 434, 435, *444*
Riley, C., *339*
Ritsma, S., 429, *443*
Ritter, K., 78, *87*
Rivera, G., 407, *419*
Rizzuto, A. M., 82, *87*, 255, *257*
Robbins, R. R., 447, 456, *464*
Robinson, L. H., 250, *257*
Robinson, R., 450, 454, *465*
Rochester, C. S., 212, 219, *233*
Rogers, L., 487, *488*
Rokeach, M., 141, *153*
Roland, A., 330, *339*
Romero, C. G., 69, *87*
Roof, W. C., 59, *87*
Root, M. P. P., 431, *443*
Rosenheim, E., 243, *257*

Rosenthal, D. A., 460, *465*
Ross, N., 323, *339*
Rosser-Hogan, R., 330, *338*
Rothbaum, S., 142, *153*
Rourke, M., 134, 139, *153*
Rubin, J. B., 331, *339*
Rudnick, S., 331, *339*
Ruiz, P., 413, *419*
Ruthledge, D., 449, 454, *465*

Salomon, H. B., 426, 428, *444*
Samford, J. A., *489*
Sandage, S. J., 121, 122, *128, 129*, 145,
    152
Sanders, S. J., 10, *26*
Sanford, J. A., 124, *129*
Santa Rita, E., 423, *443*
Sanua, V. D., 248, *257*
Sarna, N. M., 259, 266, 267, *286*
Sartorius, N., 306, *314*
Saur, M., 143, *153*
Saur, W., 143, *153*
Scharman, J. S., 202, *208*
Schmidt, J. M., 116, 117, *128*
Schmidt, M., 113, *129*
Schwarz, K. A., 74, *87*
Seamands, D., 437, *443*
Segall, M. H., 459, *464*
Sell, K. L., 10, *25*
Shafranske, E. P., 3–5, 9, *25*, 205, 209,
    485–487, 486, 488, 489
Sheridan, M. J., 486, *489*
Sherrard, P., *104*
Shore, J. H., 458, *465*
Shrock, D. A., 20, *25*
Silverman, M., *488*
Singer, I. B., 261, *286*
Singh, N., 52, *55*
Sinha, G., 459, *465*
Sloat, D., 140, 141, *153*
Smart, N., 9, 21, *25*, 472, *489*
Smith, C., 408, *419*
Smith, D., *339*
Smith, D. L., 380, *395*
Smith, E., *25*
Smith, E. J., 460, *465*
Smith, H., 320, 321, 326, *340*, 342, 343,
    344, 349, 350, 359, *365*
Smith, J., 435, *442*
Smith, L., 435, *442*

Weintraub, W., 277, 286
Wenhao, J., 426, 428, *444*
Westermeyer, J., 434, *444*
Whalen, W. J., 87
Whaling, F., 114, *129*
Wheat, E., 177, *184*
Wheat, G., 177, *184*
White, E. G., 216, 219, 220, *233, 234*
Whited, D. L., 455, *464*
Whiteford, J., 94, *104*
Wiesenthal, S., 267, 286
Wiggins Fame, M., 369, 396
Wilber, K., 331, *340*
Wilcox, G., 123, *129*
Wiley, C. Y., 370, 374, 381, *396*
Willard, W., 406, *417*
Williams, A. S., 87
Williams, J., 407, *419*
Williams, P., Sr., *104*
Williams, P. W., 62, 87
Williams, T. M., *104*
Wimberly, E. P., 377, 380, 390, *396*
Wittberg, P., 87
Woods, J., *127*
Wormser, R., 289, 291, 293, *314*
Worthington, E. L., Jr., 10, 13, 26,

121–124, *128, 129*, 137, 145,
152, 209
Wright, J. W., 30, 33, *55*, 59, 87, 112,
129, 134, *153*
Wright, P. G., 124, *129*
Wulff, D. M., 3, 26
Wyatt, S. C., 121, *129*

Yancey, P., *153*
Yang, M., *339*
Yao, R., 141, 142, *153*
Yates, A., 458, *466*
Yee-Bradbury, C., 421, 428, 431, *443*
Yeung, P. P., 279, 286
Young, A., *104*
Young, J. L., 71, 87, 380, *395*
Young, K., 10, *25*, 430, *442, 443*
Yung, J., 422, *444*
Yusuf Ali, 296, *314*

Zane, N., 10, *25*, 429, 434, 441, *441,
443*
Zea, M. C., 398, 399, *419*
Zimmer, H., 343, *365*
Zysk, K. G., 350, *365*

SUBJECT INDEX

American–born Buddhists and, 323, 327–330

Asian Americans and, 423, 425–426

beliefs in, 50–51, 320–322

case study and, 334–336

diversity within, 322–324

ecumenization of, 337

Hinduism and, 319–320

historical perspective on, 317–319

history in North America, 49–50

moral issues and, 325–327, 476

psychotherapeutic considerations and, 327–334, 482

similarities between psychotherapy and, 332–334

spiritual practices in, 324–325

worldwide distribution of, 28

Calvert, George, 30

Calvin, John, 30, 110–111

Cambodian Americans. *See* Southeast Asians

Canada

See also North America

Christian denominational rankings in, 5, 8–9, 30

history of Christianity in, 29–33

religiosity in, 29

Candomble, 402–403

Caribbean traditions. *See* Latino–Latina spiritual traditions

Case studies

Asian American Christian client and, 439–440

Buddhist client and, 334–336

collaboration with religious authorities, 250–251

effects of religious knowledge and, 15–16

Fundamentalist patient and, 149–151

Hindu clients and, 361–364

Jewish patients, 250–251, 252, 253, 273, 276, 281, 282

Latter–Day Saints patient and, 205–207

meditation practice and, 334–336

Muslim patient, 310–312

Pentecostal patient and, 181

Protestant patient and, 124–126

religiosity gap and, 10–11

religious insensitivity and, 12–13

Seventh–Day Adventist patient and, 228–231

Catholicism. *See* Eastern Orthodox Christianity; Roman Catholicism

Chance events, and Pentecostals, 175

Charismatic movement, 40, 76, 158–159, 164–165, 165–167

See also Pentecostalism

Charity

See also Tithing

in Islam, 294

Judaism and, 267

Spiritism and, 405

Childrearing practices

See also Family relationships

Islam and, 298–299

Judaism and, 244, 269–270, 283

Pentecostals and, 167

Seventh–Day Adventists and, 219

Chinese Americans, 423

See also Asian American Christians

Chmielnitzki, Bogdan, 262

Christian Association for Psychological Studies, 138, 148

Christianity

See also Eastern Orthodox Christianity; Mainline Protestantism; Roman Catholicism; Upstart Protestantism; *entries for specific protestant denominations*

emergence of African American churches and, 372–375

history in North America, 29–33

spiritual assessment measures and, 435–436

uniqueness of Catholicism within, 64

U.S. and Canadian rankings of denominations, 5, 8–9

worldwide distribution of, 28, 90–91

Christian Library (Wesley), 113–114

Christian Missionary Alliance, 134

See also Evangelical Protestantism

Churches of Christ, 134

See also Evangelical Protestantism

Church–based counseling, 122–123, 385, 440–441

Church of Canada, 32

Church of England. *See* Episcopalians

Church of God (Anderson, IN), 163

Church of God (Cleveland, TN), 163

See also Pentecostalism

Church of God in Christ, 163

Church of God in Christ (*continued*)
  See also Pentecostalism
Church of Jesus Christ of Latter–day
    Saints. *See* Latter–Day Saints
    (LDS)
Church of the Nazarene, 134
  See also Evangelical Protestantism
Clergy. *See* Spiritual leaders
Clinical issues
  in compared religious traditions, 478–
    484
  Hinduism and, 353–356
  Islam and, 305–308
  Judaism and, 279–284
  Latter–Day Saints and, 196–203
  Orthodox Judaism and, 246–249, 252–
    256
  Pentecostalism and, 169–173
  Roman Catholicism and, 77–80
  Seventh–Day Adventists and, 222–227
Clinical practice. *See* Treatment
Closed systems, and fundamentalist
    mindset, 141–142
Cognitive–behavioral framework
  African American clients and, 390
  Asian American clients and, 436,
    439–440
  Hindu clients and, 358
Cognitive restructuring. *See* "Praying
    through"
College students. *See* Generational differ-
    ences
Communion
  Eastern Orthodoxy and, 99
  Latter–Day Saints and, 193
Community
  See also Religious communities
  African American culture and, 370–
    371, 374
  Asian Americans and, 426
  Latino culture and, 412–413
Compulsive behaviors, 178–180
Confession
  in Eastern Orthodoxy, 96–97, 99, 100
  psychotherapy with Roman Catholic
    clients and, 82
Confucianism, 425
Congregationalism, 31, 134
  See also Mainline Protestantism
Conscience
  Catholic moral teaching and, 69–70
  Protestant moral teaching and, 117

Conservative Judaism, 42, 259–261, 263,
    475
  See also Judaism
Consultation with religious authorities,
    84–85, 103, 124, 203, 205, 413–
    415
Contraception
  Eastern Orthodoxy and, 97
  Islam and, 298
  Judaism and, 244, 270
  mainline Protestantism and, 117
  Pentecostals and, 167
  Roman Catholicism and, 71
  Seventh–Day Adventists and, 218
  views of compared religious traditions
    on, 473–477
Corporal punishment. *See* Childrearing
    practices
Counseling. *See* psychotherapy
Countertransference
  See also Therapeutic relationship
  beliefs of therapist and, 150, 251
  Catholic clients and, 83–84
  orthodox Jews and, 251
Crazy wisdom, Buddhist tradition of, 328,
    331
Credibility
  See also Trust building
  Asian Americans and, 429–430, 437–
    438
  Latter–Day Saints and, 200, 202
  strategies for building, 120–121, 138–
    139
  training in religious diversity and, 10–
    12, 200, 202
Cuba, Afro–Yoruba tradition in, 400–402
Curanderismo tradition, 406–407

Dancing, 214–215
Death, beliefs about
  See also Euthanasia; Life, purpose of
  in African American churches, 382
  Buddhism and, 319, 332
  in Eastern *vs.* Western traditions, 471
  Hinduism and, 346–347
  Islam and, 297, 299–300
  Judaism and, 248–249, 268
  Pentecostals and, 175
  Seventh–Day Adventists and, 213
Decision processes
  Latino traditions and, 408

Latter–Day Saints and, 189
Pentecostals and, 174–175
Deference, and Asian Americans, 426
Deity, representations of
in African spirituality, 371–372
in Afro–Yoruba tradition, 400–402
Asian Americans and, 424–425, 427
conservative Protestants and, 145–146
Eastern Orthodox beliefs and, 93–94
in Eastern vs. Western traditions, 471
in Hinduism, 342, 346–347
Judaism and, 265, 268n
in Latino traditions, 404–405, 411–412
Latter–Day Saints and, 191
Pentecostals and, 163, 169–170, 174–175, 176
Roman Catholic beliefs and, 82–83
Seventh–Day Adventists and, 216
similarities among traditions and, 470, 471
Demographics
Islam and, 291–292
Latter–Day Saints and, 188, 190
Native Americans and, 457
Pentecostalism and, 161–162
Protestant shift in, 132
Roman Catholicism and, 71–73
Seventh–Day Adventists and, 211–212
statistics on religious affiliation, 5–9, 30
Denominational therapeutic stance, 17, 19
Denominations with American roots, 40–41
See also Jehovah's Witnesses; Latter–Day Saints; Seventh–Day Adventists
Depression
African Americans and, 386, 390–394
Asian Americans and, 428
Evangelicals and, 15
Hinduism and, 363
Islam and, 305–307
Judaism and, 254, 268, 276, 279–280
Latter–Day Saints and, 205–207
Native Americans and, 458
Pentecostals and, 171
Seventh–Day Adventists and, 225–227, 228–231
Developmental approach, 358
Diagnostic assessment. See Assessment

Dietary practices
Buddhism and, 326
fasting by Muslims and, 294–295
Hinduism and, 348
Judaism and, 271
Diocese, in Catholic church organization, 73
Dionysius the Areopagite, 93
Disciples of Christ. See Mainline Protestantism
Diversity issues
Fundamentalism and, 139
Pentecostals and, 169
Seventh–Day Adventists and, 222
Divorce
Eastern Orthodoxy and, 97
Hinduism and, 354–355
Islam and, 298
Judaism and, 244, 251, 269
Latter–Day Saints and, 195, 201–202
mainline Protestantism and, 116
Pentecostals and, 167, 173
Roman Catholicism and, 79
Seventh–Day Adventists and, 218
views of compared religious traditions on, 473–477
Dobson, James, 136
Domestic abuse, 357, 361–362
Dominion theology, 165, 166
Dream analysis, 176–177
Dreyfus, Alfred, 263–264
Drug use
African Americans and, 386–387
Buddhism and, 326
Judaism and, 244, 271
mainline Protestantism and, 118
Pentecostals and, 167, 178–180
Roman Catholicism and, 71
Seventh–Day Adventists and, 214
views of compared religious traditions on, 473–477
Duty. See Responsibility

Eastern Europe, Judaism in, 262–263, 265
Eastern Orthodox Christianity, 89–104
beliefs in, 35–36, 92–93
church organization and, 91
distinctive characteristics of, 93–96
history in North America, 29, 30, 90–99

Eastern Orthodox Christianity (*continued*)
  moral issues and, 97–98, 473
  perspectives on healing in, 100–102
  psychotherapeutic considerations and,
    99–100, 478
  spiritual practice in, 98–99
Eastern religious traditions
  See also entries for specific traditions
  Buddhism, 49–51
  Hinduism, 47–49
  Sikhism, 51–53
Ecumenical movement, 32, 63
Ecumenical therapeutic stance, 17, 18,
  455
Education
  Fundamentalism and, 136, 155–156
  Hinduism and, 351–352, 357, 359
  Judaism and, 243
  of Pentecostal preachers, 160
  Roman Catholicism, 62
  Seventh–Day Adventists and, 212, 217
Eightfold Path, 50
Elder care
  in Hinduism, 358
  in Islam, 299
Eliezer, Israel ben (Baal Shem Tov),
    262–263
Elizabeth I (queen of England), 112
Encyclopedia of American Religions (Mel-
    ton), 5
Environmental issues
  Buddhism and, 327
  Judaism and, 244
  Native Americans and, 452, 456
Episcopalians, 31
  See also Mainline Protestantism
  beliefs of, 36
  historical perspectives on, 111–112
  subgroups within, 107
Eternal life, concept of, 175
Ethical issues
  See also Moral issues
  Buddhist practice and, 334
  implementation of spiritual interven-
    tions and, 148
  need for training in religious diversity
    and, 12–16
Euthanasia
  See also Death, beliefs about; Elder care
  Judaism and, 270
  mainline Protestantism and, 118
  Roman Catholicism and, 71, 79–80

views of compared religious traditions
    on, 473–477
Evangelical Congregationalism, 134
Evangelical Covenant Church, 134
Evangelical Free Church. *See* Evangelical
    Protestantism
Evangelical Lutheran Church, 36
  See also Lutherans
Evangelical Protestantism, 131–153
  See also Charismatic movement; Pente-
    costalism
  Asian Americans and, 423
  beliefs in, 39–40, 134–135, 140–141
  distinguished from Fundamentalism,
    133, 135
  diversity issues and, 139
  historical perspectives on, 132–133
  Latinos and, 399–400
  moral issues and, 136, 172, 474
  positive therapeutic outcomes and, 15
  practices within, 135–136
  psychological interventions and, 144–
    145
  psycho–spiritual assessment measures
    and, 142–143
  psycho–spiritual issues common to,
    140–141
  psychotherapeutic considerations and,
    137–151, 479
  spiritual interventions and, 145–151
Evil, Jewish understanding of, 252–253,
    266–267
  See also Sin, concept of

Family relationships
  See also Childrearing practices; Elder
    care; Generational differences
  African American churches and, 387
  Asian Americans and, 425, 426, 428–
    429, 430, 433–434
  boundary issues and, 283–284
  Hinduism and, 352, 353–356, 358
  Islam and, 297–298, 302, 307–309
  Judaism and, 269–270, 280–281, 283–
    284
  Latter–Day Saints and, 194–195, 201–
    202, 204
  as treatment resource, 430
Family systems approach
  Asian Americans and, 430, 436
  Hindu clients and, 358

Muslims and, 308–309
Fard Muhammad, 293
Fasting, in Islam, 294–295
Filial piety, 425, 432, 433
Foot washing, 216
Forgiveness
    conservative Protestants and, 145
    Judaism and, 267
    mainline Protestants and, 122
    Pentecostals and, 171–172
    Seventh–Day Adventists and, 227
Freud, Sigmund, 276
Fugue states, 404
"Full Gospel message," 157
Fundamentalism, 32, 40, 131–153
    See also Upstart Protestantism
    beliefs in, 134–135, 141–142
    distinguished from Evangelical Protestantism, 133, 135
    diversity issues and, 139
    moral issues and, 136, 474
    origins of, 132–133, 155–156
    practices within, 135–136
    psychological interventions and, 144–145
    psycho–spiritual assessment measures, 142–143
    psycho–spiritual issues common in, 141–412
    psychotherapeutic considerations and, 137–151, 479
    social support and, 143–144
    spiritual interventions and, 145–151
"Fundamentalist mindset," 141–142
The Fundamentals (Bible Institute of Los Angeles), 132

Gandhi, Mahatma, 346
Gender issues
    See also Women, role of
    Asian Americans and, 427
    conservative Protestants and, 136, 139, 147
    Hinduism and, 136, 139, 147353–357
    Islam and, 297–298, 307
    Judaism and, 43, 270
    Latter–Day Saints and, 12–13, 187–188, 189–190, 201
    Roman Catholicism and, 73–74
    Seventh–Day Adventists and, 216–217, 226

Sikhism and, 53
General Council of the Assemblies of God, 163
Generational differences
    See also Family relationships
    Asian Americans and, 423–424, 432, 433–434, 439–440
    Catholic belief and practice and, 71–73
    Hinduism and, 356–357, 362, 363–364
    Native Americans and, 457–458
Genetic engineering, 79–80
Geneva, Switzerland, 110–111
Gift giving, concept of, 429–430
Glossolalia, 161, 163, 165, 176
God, representations of. See Deity, representations of
Graham, Billy, 133
Gratitude, state of, 294
Guilt
    Indian clients and, 351–352
    Judaism and, 255, 277–278
    Latter–Day Saints and, 199–200, 229
    Pentecostals and, 168–169, 171–172
    Seventh–Day Adventists and, 225
Gurus, 348

Hajji Ali ("Hi Jolly"), 44
Halakhah, 242, 250, 253
Hare Krishna movement. See Hinduism
Hasidic Jews, 43, 236, 240, 262–263
Healing potential of traditions
    African American churches and, 389–390
    for compared religious traditions, 478–484
    conservative Protestantism and, 143–144
    Curanderismo and, 406–407
    Eastern Orthodoxy and, 100–102
    empirical findings on, 13–14
    Judaism and, 273–276
    Latino traditions and, 410–412
    Latter–Day Saints and, 203–205, 227, 231
    mainline Protestantism and, 122–123
    Pentecostalism and, 157, 165, 173–177
"Health–wealth" gospel, 165
Herzl, Theodore, 264

five pillars of, 293–295
historical perspective on, 290–291
moral issues and, 297–300, 476
in North America, 44–45, 289–290,
    303–304
psychotherapeutic considerations and,
    300–312, 481
stereotypes and, 303–304
sub–traditions in, 292–293
worldwide distribution of, 28

Japanese Americans, 423
    See also Asian American Christians
Jehovah's Witnesses, 41
Jesus Prayer (Prayer of the Heart), 99,
    100–101
Jewelry, 214, 215
Jnana yoga, 342
John XXIII (pope), 63–64
Judaism
    See also Conservative Judaism; Ortho-
        dox Judaism; Reform Judaism
    action and, 277–278
    anti–Semitism and, 263, 264, 272, 277
    Ashkenazic and Sephardic branches of,
        239, 261–262, 265
    atrocities and, 248, 262, 264
    beliefs in, 42–44, 238, 242–243, 265–
        269, 277–278
    common clinical issues with, 279–284
    the Diaspora and, 261–265
    dietary laws and, 271
    historical perspectives on, 41–42, 237–
        241, 259–265
    holidays and traditions in, 43–44, 243,
        265, 268
    Holocaust and, 248, 264, 271–272,
        280
    Jewish law and, 238–239, 242, 250,
        253, 260–261, 276
    Jewish philosophy and, 239–240
    Latinos and, 399
    moral issues and, 243–244, 269–272,
        475
    psychotherapeutic considerations and,
        245–256, 272–278, 481
    religious movements in, 42, 240–241,
        262
    treatment issues and, 278–284
    worldwide distribution of, 28
Justice, Judaism and, 267

Kabbalah, 240
Kardec, Allen, 403–404, 405
Karma, 48–49, 52, 53–54, 344–345
    therapeutic use of, 359–360
Keller, R. R., 21
Kennedy, John F., 62
Keswick Conference, 160
Koran, 291
Korean Americans, 422, 423
    See also Asian American Christians

Language
    patient idioms and, 138
    of psychotherapy, and Asians, 330
    religious assessment and, 304
Latino–Latina spiritual traditions, 397–
    419
    Afro–Yoruba traditions, 400–403
    beliefs in, 400–404
    case study and, 410–412
    consultation with leaders in, 413–415
    curses and, 410
    heterogeneity of, 397, 398–400
    indigenous–based traditions in Ameri-
        cas and, 405–407
    Latino cultural diversity and, 398–400
    power of emotions in, 410
    psychological interventions congruent
        with, 412–415
    psychotherapeutic considerations and,
        407–416, 483
    social issues and, 399
    spiritism and, 403–405
    treatment approaches and, 410–415
    trust building and, 408–409, 416
Latter–Day Saints (LDS), 185–209
    beliefs of, 41, 190–195, 204–205
    case studies involving, 12–13
    case vignette and, 205–207
    characteristics of members of, 185–186
    church organization and, 191–192
    common clinical issues with, 196–203
    demographics and, 188, 190
    diversity within, 188–190
    gender issues and, 12–13, 187–188,
        189–190
    historical perspective on, 185–188
    interventions congruent with, 203–205
    lifestyle practices and, 193–194
    moral issues and, 194–195, 474

Latter–Day Saints (LDS) (*continued*)
  psychotherapeutic considerations and,
    195–205, 480
  religious practices and, 192–193, 204
  Reorganized Church and, 188–189
  spiritual interventions and, 205
LDS. *See* Latter–Day Saints
Life, purpose of
  See also Death, beliefs about
  in African traditions, 371, 372
  in Eastern *vs.* Western traditions, 471
  Islam and, 297
  Judaism and, 265–266, 267, 268
  Native American traditions and, 448,
    449–450, 451–454, 456
Loss of faith, 81–82
Love, and Hinduism, 342
Luther, Martin, 108–109
Lutherans
  See also Mainline Protestantism
  beliefs of, 36–37
  historical perspectives on, 29–30, 108–
    109
  subgroups within, 107

Mahan, Asa, 159
Mahayana Buddhism, 50, 322, 323, 328
Maimonides, 239–240, 261
Mainline Protestantism, 36–38, 105–129
  See also Charismatic movement; Epis-
    copalians; Lutherans; Methodists;
    Presbyterians
  African American denominations and,
    376
  beliefs in, 114–115
  case study in, 124–126
  mainline as term and, 106
  moral issues and, 115–118, 473
  origins of traditions within, 108–114
  practices in, 114–115
  psychotherapeutic considerations and,
    118–124, 479
  similarities within, 106–107, 114–115
  social issues and, 115–118
  traditions included in, 105–106
Mamout, Yarrow, 44
Marital counseling
  Asian Americans and, 436
  Fundamentalists and, 149–151
  Hinduism and, 362–363
  idealized expectations and, 252
  Islam and, 307

Latter–Day Saints and, 205–207
  orthodox Jews and, 251, 252
  Pentecostals and, 177, 181
  Seventh–Day Adventists and, 228–231
Marriage
  conservative Protestants and, 136
  domestic abuse and, 357, 361–362
  Eastern Orthodoxy and, 97
  Hinduism and, 349, 354–356, 362
  Islam and, 297–298
  Judaism and, 243–244, 247–248, 251,
    269, 281–282
  Latter–Day Saints and, 193, 194–195,
    201–202
  mainline Protestantism and, 116
  Pentecostals and, 166
  polygamy in LDS culture and, 188
  Roman Catholicism and, 70–71, 79
  Seventh–Day Adventists and, 218
  views of compared religious traditions
    on, 473–477
Masturbation
  Latter–Day Saints and, 12–13
  orthodox Jews and, 254–255
  Pentecostals and, 172
  Seventh–Day Adventists and, 215, 224
Mayans. *See* Indigenous–based traditions
    in Americas
Measures of Religiosity (Hill & Hood),
    143
Mecca, pilgrimage to, 295
Meditation
  African American clients and, 392–
    393
  Buddhism and, 323, 324–325, 328,
    331–332
  meditative process and, 325
  psychotherapeutic practice and, 331–
    332, 336–337, 437
  vulnerability during, 333–334
Mennonites, 134
Mental health
  conservative Protestant faith and, 143–
    144
  findings on religion and, 13–14
  Islamic views of, 295–296, 300–301
Mental health profession, view of
  See also Psychotherapy, discipline of;
    Therapeutic relationship
  African American churches and, 376,
    381–382, 384–385
  among Buddhists, 327–328

among compared religious traditions, 478–484

among conservative Protestants, 137

among Hindus, 352–353

among Latter–Day Saints, 195–196

among mainline Protestants, 118–119

among Muslims, 301–303

among Pentecostals, 168–169

Asian Americans and, 429–431

Judaism and, 249–250, 276–277

Latino clients and, 408

Native Americans and, 454–455

status of therapist and, 429

Messiah, in Judaism, 267–268

Mestizo worldview, 406

Methodists

    See also Mainline Protestantism

    Asian Americans and, 422

    beliefs of, 38

    historical perspectives on, 112–114

    subgroups within, 107

Miller, William, 212

Mind, Character, and Personality: Guidelines to Mental and Spiritual Health (White), 219–221

Missions, 194

    See also Evangelical Protestantism

Missouri Synod Lutheran Church, 36

    See also Lutherans

Mitnagdim, 43

Mitzvot, 242–243

Modern Orthodox Judaism, 43

Modesty

    Judaism and, 246

    Seventh–Day Adventists and, 214, 228

Moral issues

    See also Clinical issues; *entries for specific issues*

    Asian Americans and, 428

    Buddhism and, 325–327

    in compared religious traditions, 473–477

    conservative Protestants and, 136

    Eastern Orthodoxy and, 97–98

    in Eastern *vs.* Western traditions, 471

    Islam and, 297–300

    Judaism and, 243–244, 269–272, 475

    Latter–Day Saints and, 194–195

    mainline Protestantism and, 115–118

    Roman Catholicism and, 69–71, 72, 75–76

Seventh–Day Adventists and, 214–215, 218–219, 475

similarities among traditions and, 470, 472, 473–477

Mormons. *See* Latter-Day Saints (LDS)

Motovilov, N., 98–99

Movies, 215

Muhammad, 290–291

Multicultural counseling

    See also African American spiritual traditions; Asian American Christians; Latino–Latina spiritual traditions; Native American spirituality

    acculturation issues and, 431–432, 458–459

    Asian–born patients and, 330

    cultural bias and, 431

    interactions between religious and cultural diversity and, 19–20

    mainline Protestantism and, 121

    Muslims and, 312–313

    Seventh–Day Adventists and, 222

    specialized religious knowledge and, 12–13

Multidimensionality, 147–148

Napoleon, 263

National Baptist Convention of America, 133

National Baptist Convention of the U.S.A., Inc., 133

Native American spirituality, 46–47, 445–466

    See also Latino-Latina spiritual traditions

    assessment issues and, 455–456

    beliefs in, 451–454

    common clinical issues and, 457–461

    continuity of tribal traditions and, 448, 449–450

    demographics and, 457

    diversity within, 445, 448–449

    federal assimilation policies and, 446–448

    historical perspective on, 446–454

    organized religion and, 450

    psychotherapeutic considerations and, 454–456, 457–464, 484

    revelation of the Sacred and, 446, 462

Native American spirituality (*continued*)
  unity among traditions within, 448–449
Nelson–Malony Religious Status Interview, 143
Newsweek, 289–290
Nicene Creed, 66, 67, 90, 92
Nicherin Shoshu, 323
Nondenominational megachurches, 134
Non–Wesleyan Pentecostal groups, 163
North America
  See also Canada; Native American spirituality; United States
  demographic statistics on religious affiliation in, 5–9, 30
  history of Buddhism in, 49–50
  history of Christianity in, 29–33
  history of Hinduism in, 47–48
  history of Islam in, 44–45
  history of Judaism in, 41–42
  history of Sikhism in, 51–52
  religiosity in, 29
Nuns. *See* Religious orders

Obedient person, role as, 141
Obligation. *See* Responsibility
Ockenga, Harold, 132
Oglethorpe, John, 113
Ordained clients. *See* Spiritual leaders
Orichas, 400–401, 411–412
Orthodox Christianity. *See* Eastern Orthodox Christianity
Orthodox Judaism, 42
  See also Judaism
  beliefs in, 242–243
  common clinical issues with, 246–249, 252–256
  historical perspectives and, 237–245, 262–263
  moral issues and, 243–244, 475
  psychotherapeutic considerations and, 245–256, 481
  social issues and, 243–244
  spiritual interventions and, 252–256
  treatment issues and, 249–251
Overeating, and African Americans, 386–387

Palmer, Phoebe, 159
Panic attack case study, 15

Paranoia, 280
Parent, idealization of, 284
Parham, Charles, 33
Parish
  American Catholicism and, 60–63
  Church organization and, 73
Patient idioms, 138
PC (USA). *See* Presbyterians
Penn, William, 31
Pentecostal Holiness Church, 163
Pentecostalism, 155–184
  beliefs in, 40, 157–158, 163, 165–167, 173–177
  common clinical issues with, 169–173
  demographics of, 161–162
  heterogeneity within, 162–165
  historical perspective on, 33, 134, 155–158
  interventions incongruent with, 176
  moral issues and, 166–167, 474
  Non–Wesleyan groups, 163
  Pentecost, as term, 158
  psychotherapeutic considerations and, 168–182, 479
  religious assessment and, 169
  social issues and, 166
  spiritual interventions and, 177, 181
  subgroups within, 158–161
Perfectionism
  Holiness movement and, 159
  Latter–Day Saints and, 197–198, 202
  orthodox Jews and, 253–254
  Seventh–Day Adventists and, 222–223
Physical health, findings on religion and, 13–14
Physician–assisted suicide. *See* Euthanasia
Polygamy
  Islam and, 297–298
  Judaism and, 244
  Latter–Day Saints and, 188
Postpartum psychosis case study, 181
Posttraumatic stress disorder (PTSD)
  Asian–born patients and, 330, 434
  meditation and, 333
  Protestant case study and, 124–126
Prayer
  African American churches and, 380–381, 389
  conservative Protestants and, 147
  in Eastern Orthodoxy, 98–99
  in Islam, 294
  Judaism and, 273–275

Pentecostals and, 157, 161, 166, 169, 175–176
Roman Catholicism and, 69
in therapeutic practice, 169, 205, 273–275, 437
"Praying through," 177–178
Predestination
doctrine of, 110
Islamic beliefs and, 296
Presbyterian Church—U.S.A. [PC (USA)]. *See* Presbyterians
Presbyterians
See also Mainline Protestantism
beliefs of, 37–38
evangelical, 134
historical perspectives on, 107
subgroups within, 107
Preston, Rachel Oakes, 213
Professional societies, promotion of religious and therapeutic interface by, 138
Prophecy
Islam and, 296
Seventh–Day Adventists and, 213
Protestant Episcopal Church. *See* Episcopalians
Protestantism. *See* Mainline Protestantism; Upstart Protestantism; *entries for specific denominations*
Protestant Reformation, 108, 111
Protestant work ethic, 146–147
Psychosis, 307–308
Psychotherapeutic implications
See also Assessment; Clinical issues; Spiritual interventions; Therapeutic relationship; Treatment
Asian Americans and, 428–431, 484
Buddhist patients and, 327–331
conservative Protestantism and, 137–151
Eastern Orthodoxy and, 99–102
Islam and, 300–312
Judaism and, 245–256, 272–278
Latter–Day Saints and, 195–205
mainline Protestantism and, 118–124
orthodox Judaism and, 245–256
Pentecostalism and, 168–182
Protestant concerns about, 120, 137
Roman Catholicism and, 74–85
Roman Catholics and, 74–85
Seventh–Day Adventists and, 219–222
Psychotherapy, discipline of

See also Mental health profession, view of; Religious diversity competency
bias about religion in, 329
as Jewish science, 276–277
relationship with Buddhism, 331–332
research and, 487
training programs and, 415, 486–487
PTSD. *See* Posttraumatic stress disorder
Puerto Rico, Latina traditions in, 400–402, 404, 415
Puritanism, 31, 165

Quakers, 31, 134

Ramayana, 347–348
Rationalist Enlightenment theology, 157
Rebel, role as, 140
Reform Judaism, 42, 240, 259–261, 263, 475
See also Judaism
Religious, as term, 5n
Religious Beliefs and Health Care Decisions (Park Ridge Center for the Study of Health, Faith, and Ethics), 115
Religious beliefs *vs.* internalized God representations, 82–83
Religious communities
African American churches and, 377–379
Asian Americans and, 436
Hinduism and, 360–361
Islam and, 300, 309–310
Judaism and, 254, 275
therapist relationship with, 12n, 148, 182, 205, 228
Religious diversity competency
attitudes characteristic of, 16–20
caveats concerning, 20–21
credibility and, 10–12
cultural diversity and, 19–20
diversity as fact and, 5–10
ethical obligations and, 12–13
need for, 5–16, 485–487
recommendations for, 17–18, 485–487
resources of religious communities and, 13–16
Religious leaders. *See* Spiritual leaders

Sanctification, 159
Santería, 400, 408, 409
Santerismo tradition, 404
Saund, Dalip Singh, 52
Schleiermacher, Friedrich, 157
Science
   See also Education; Intellectual activity
   evolution and, 132, 162
   Hinduism and, 343
   Seventh–Day Adventists and, 219
   split among Protestants and, 32, 115
Scopes Monkey Trial, 132, 162
SDAs. See Seventh–Day Adventists
Seixas, Gershom Mendes, 41
Self control, and Asian Americans, 426
Self–image, 170–171
Self–worth, 252–253, 254, 276
Separatism, and Fundamentalists, 135–
   136, 142
Seraphim of Sarov (saint), 98–99
Seventh–Day Adventists (SDAs), 211–
   234
   beliefs of, 40–41, 213–217
   common clinical issues with, 222–227
   demographics and, 211–212
   historical perspective on, 211–213
   intervention issues and, 227–228
   moral issues and, 214–215, 218–219,
      475
   psychotherapeutic considerations and,
      219–222, 480
   research recommendations with, 231–
      232
   social issues and, 218–219
   White's Guidelines to Mental and Spiri-
      tual Health and, 219–221
Sexual abuse, 387
Sexuality
   See also Homosexuality; Masturbation
   African American churches and, 387
   Buddhism and, 326
   conservative Protestants and, 136
   Eastern Orthodoxy and, 97–98
   Hinduism and, 347
   Judaism and, 243–244, 247, 269
   Latter–Day Saints and, 194–195, 199–
      200
   mainline Protestantism and, 116–117
   Pentecostals and, 166, 172
   Roman Catholicism and, 70–71, 78–
      79

Seventh–Day Adventists and, 215–
   216, 223–224
unintegrated 223
views of compared religious traditions
   on, 473–477
Seymour, William, 160
Shaman, 451–453
Shame
   Asian Americans and, 428
   Islam and, 306
   Latter–Day Saints and, 197–198, 229
   Seventh–Day Adventists and, 225
Shattered Faith Syndrome, 142
Shi'ism, 292
Siddhartha Gautama (the Buddha), 317–
   318
Sikhism, 51–53
Sin, concept of
   See also Evil, Jewish understanding of
   Hinduism and, 345
   Judaism and, 266
   Pentecostals and, 174–175
Singh, Gobind, 53
Singlehood
   Hinduism and, 355, 362
   Latter–Day Saints and, 201–202
Slavery
   African American churches and, 372–
      373, 381
   Latter–Day Saints and, 187
   Methodists and, 114
SL–ASIA. See Suinn–Lew Asian Self–
   Identity Acculturation Scale
Smith, Joseph, 186–187, 188
Social issues
   African American churches and, 374
   Asian Americans and, 425, 428
   Buddhism and, 325–327
   conservative Protestants and, 136
   Hindu caste system and, 345–346
   Hinduism and, 357–358
   Islam and, 297–300
   Judaism and, 243–244, 269–272
   Latter–Day Saints and, 194–195
   mainline Protestantism and, 115–118
   Pentecostals and, 165–167
Social status, and Asian Americans, 426–
   427, 429, 432, 438
Social support
   See also Family relationships; Religious
      communities

ABOUT THE EDITORS

P. Scott Richards received his PhD in counseling psychology in 1988 from the University of Minnesota. He was a faculty member at Central Washington University (1988–1990). He has been a faculty member at Brigham Young University since 1990 and is currently an associate professor in the Department of Counseling Psychology and Special Education. Dr. Richards is coauthor of *A Spiritual Strategy for Counseling and Psychotherapy*, which was published in 1997 by the American Psychological Association (APA). He was given the Dissertation of the Year Award in 1990 from Division 5 (Evaluation, Statistics, and Measurement) of the APA for his psychometric investigation of religious bias in moral development research. In 1999, he was awarded the William C. Bier Award from Division 36 (Psychology of Religion) of the APA for an outstanding contribution to findings on religious issues. He is a licensed psychologist and maintains a private psychotherapy practice at the Center for Change in Orem, Utah.

Allen E. Bergin received his PhD in clinical psychology in 1960 from Stanford University. He was a faculty member at Teachers College, Columbia University (1961–1972) and is professor emeritus of psychology at Brigham Young University (1972–1999) since 1972 where he has served as the director of the Values Institute (1976–1978) and director of the PhD program in clinical psychology (1989–1993). Dr. Bergin is past-president of the Society for Psychotherapy Research and coeditor of the classic *Handbook of Psychotherapy and Behavior Change*. He is coauthor of *A Spiritual Strategy for Counseling and Psychotherapy* (1997). In 1989 he received an Award for Distinguished Professional Contributions to Knowledge from the American Psychological Association (APA). In 1990, Division 36 (Psychology of Religion) of the APA presented him with the William James Award for Psychology of Religion Research. He has also received the Society for Psychotherapy Research's Distinguished Career Award (1998) and the American Psychiatric Association's Oskar Pfister Award in Psychiatry and Religion (1998). Dr. Bergin is a licensed psychologist and maintains a small consultation practice.